Growth and Development
of Children

GROWTH AND DEVELOPMENT OF CHILDREN

EIGHTH EDITION

George H. Lowrey, M.D.
Professor Emeritus of Pediatrics
University of California, Davis, School of Medicine
Davis, California

YEAR BOOK MEDICAL PUBLISHERS, INC.
Chicago • London

Library of Congress Cataloging-in-Publication Data
Lowrey, George H. (George Harrison), 1917–
  Growth and development of children.

  Includes bibliographies and index.
  1. Children—Growth.   2.   Child development.
I. Title. [DNLM: 1.   Child Development.   2.   Growth.
WS 103 L921g]
RJ131.L687   1986   612'.65   85-29623
ISBN 0-8151-5645-6

Sponsoring Editor: Stephany S. Scott
Manager, Copyediting Services: Frances M. Perveiler
Production Project Manager: Carol Ennis Coghlan
Proofroom Supervisor: Shirley E. Taylor

1 2 3 4 5 6 7 8 9 0   ML   90, 89, 88, 87, 86

To my wife
PATRICIA
and
To my children
PATRICIA GAIL, THOMAS, and GEOFFREY

Preface

Children are our most enduring and vulnerable legacy. For nations as well as for individual families, they represent the link between past and future, between experience and promise. The nurturing of future generations is a basic, and most important, human activity.

—From the preamble of the Constitution of the American Academy of Pediatrics

Study of the characteristics of normal growth and development of children has become a large and important part of the practice and teaching of pediatrics and of research in all fields related to child health. Included in such studies are not only physical measurements but also observation of all of the dynamic physiologic and psychologic changes taking place from conception to maturity. In preparing the present volume the author, as in previous editions, was faced with the problem of determining a logical limit to the material to be presented. The book was designed to be of practical size for greatest usefulness and yet to be inclusive enough to be of value to a broad range of workers involved in the care of children. Helpful criticisms from those who have read previous editions were carefully considered in preparing the present one. It is hoped this has resulted in few important omissions and improved clarity of the text.

Many more articles were examined than appear as references at the end of each chapter. The selection of the references was made to include, wherever possible, those of a review nature and recent origin and from sources generally available so that they may be used to augment material given in the text.

I must acknowledge my very sincere appreciation to Dr. Hilda Knobloch and Dr. Ralph Gibson who made important contributions to chapter 6 in previous editions, and much of their material remains as originally presented.

Major changes or additions since the seventh edition include new material on maternal-fetal endocrinology, physiology of the low birth weight infant, the controversy concerning maternal-infant bonding, development of the central nervous system in the fetus and infant, and environmental influences affecting that development. Many additions and a few deletions as well as attempts to improve the presentation of material have been made throughout the book.

Year Book Medical Publishers has continued to be most cooperative and supportive in the preparation of this edition. Finally, it is the author's sincere hope that this and previous editions have made at least a modest contribution to the improvement of child health in all of its aspects.

GEORGE H. LOWREY, M.D.

Contents

1 / History and Introduction

> Know then thyself, presume God to scan,
> The proper study of mankind is man.
> —Alexander Pope

Historical Background

The earliest records concerning the science of child health were primarily concerned with the preservation of life and therefore describe in some detail the proper methods of infant rearing and the diseases common to each age. From the time of ancient Egypt through the classical Greek and Roman periods, there was obvious interest and there were many descriptions of the various stages of human development. Both Hippocrates (ca., 460 to 370 B.C.) and Aristotle (384 to 322 B.C.) wrote rather elaborate accounts of the age changes in form and function. An interesting excerpt from Aristotle's *Historia Animalium* describes adolescent changes: "When twice seven years old, in most of the cases, the male begins to engender seed, and at the same time hair appears on the pubis. . . .About the same time, the voice begins to alter, getting harsher and more uneven, neither shrill as formerly nor deep as afterward, nor yet of any even tone, but like an instrument whose strings are frayed and out of tune, and it is called, by way of by-word, the bleat of the billy goat."[37] Unfortunately, there is very little in the way of quantitative information available, e.g., height, weight, or other measurements. Nutrition, education, and discipline were discussed in some detail, but little of this literature could be considered based on any kind of sound observation. Superstition and religious dogma played a major part in the rules laid down for bringing up children. Often the old texts would give an account of the preparation for birth, care of the newborn, nursing, and the introduction of other foods and then deal with specific diseases. Standards for normal growth and development did not exist. It was a situation in which the only measurement of good health was survival.

The first publication to treat the differences between the anatomy of the

1

infant, child, and adult was by Gabriele Zerbi, a professor at Padua, in 1502.[1] Leonardo da Vinci (1452 to 1519), the greatest artist and scientist of the Italian Renaissance, made drawings of the fetus in utero that were the first to be accurate.[37] The Flemish physician and anatomist Andreas Vesalius (1514 to 1564), while at the University of Padua, published results of his dissections of the fetus correcting many errors, particularly of the circulation, that had been handed down from Galen's time (c.a. 130 to 200 A.D.). Considerable knowledge of the normal and abnormal is apparent from the art of this period. Albrecht Durer (1471 to 1528) and Titian (1477 to 1576) depicted infants and children in proper anatomical proportions. Durer's careful analysis of infant proportions was strikingly accurate. Several of the paintings by Diego Velazquez (1599 to 1660) are beautiful examples of normal children as well as several types of dwarfism, including achondroplasia. *The Anatomy Lesson of Doctor Frederick Ruysch* by Jan van Meck, painted in 1683, displays the famous anatomist dissecting a newborn baby with the cord and placenta attached. In another corner of this masterpiece is the articulated skeleton of an infant. Ruysch (1638 to 1731) is best remembered for his studies of the vascular system, including the relationship of the fetal and maternal vessels in the placenta. He was a professor at the University of Leiden.

In 1651 William Harvey, better known for his work on the circulation, published his *Exercitationes de Generatione Animalium*, which, although not entirely accurate, helped to dispel the concept that the human embryo was completely preformed from the time of conception and helped to launch embryology as a science. François Mauriceau[2] was the first to give accurate descriptions and illustrations of the proportions of the fetus and newborn. His book, which included some information concerning the physical measurements of infants, was printed in 1694. Although Mauriceau was the greatest French obstetrician of his time, his observations were not free from error. The average weight of the newborn was given as between 14 and 15 lb (based on our present standards). This error was perpetuated in many translations and was not properly challenged until the German J. C. Roederer read a paper in 1753 before the Royal Society of Göttingen. This work may be considered the first to record normal birth weight and length accurately.[2]

Albrecht von Haller (1708–1777), the great Swiss physiologist, had published a similarly correct indication of birth weight a year prior to Roederer, but his observation was an isolated one and his method of arriving at the figure was not given. In England Joseph Clarke had the distinction of being the first to report correct figures for weight at birth and also normal head circumferences at this age. His paper was presented at a scientific meeting in 1786 and was based, for the first time, on what we would consider to be adequate data.[3]

The oldest, and still one of the best, longitudinal studies of the growth of a child was that by Count Philibert Gueneau de Montbeillard, which was completed in 1777 but was published by his friend, Buffon, in 1837. This was a curve of the body length of his son from birth to 18 years, recorded every six months. This study is often quoted as a classic accomplishment, and justifiably so.[4] Buffon was the first to postulate the seasonal changes in growth, based on the figures that were then available to him. He also reported on the smallest adult dwarf so far recorded, a man 36 years of age who was only 16 in. (39 cm) tall.

John Hunter (1728 to 1793) was a very colorful figure in the history of English medicine, and his fame is based upon his discoveries relative to surgical procedures and investigations of infections. However, his interests were broad and included records of measurements of the human body. His museum in London contained a number of skeletons of dwarfs and giants. The most renowned was that of the Irish giant O'Brien. The story of Hunter's acquisition of the body against O'Brien's last wishes and carefully laid plans makes fascinating, though macabre, reading. An apt pupil of Hunter was Samuel von Soemmerring (1775 to 1830) from Poland. He first described in detail the condition of achondroplasia with measurements and drawings, which were published in an atlas of congenital anomalies in 1791.

Certainly we owe the credit for the first complete study of the physical growth of children to the Belgian astronomer and statistician Lambert Adolphe Jacques Quetelet (1796 to 1874). He was director of the Royal Observatory in Brussels for many years and contributed a large number of articles on many scientific subjects during his life. Possibly because of his failure to find satisfactory material on growth in his search of the literature up to that time, he carried out extensive studies of heights and weights of male and female subjects of all ages. These findings were published in 1835.[6] His figures of body dimensions have been used for comparative purposes in growth studies until recent times. The term *anthropometry* was also originated by Quetelet.

A very complete statistical study of the growth of children from the Boston, Massachusetts area was made by H. P. Bowditch[7] in 1875. Bowditch was the grandson of Nathaniel who was a famous mathematician and navigator. His graduation from Harvard Medical School in 1868 was delayed for four years because of his participation in the Civil War as a member of the Massachusetts Cavalry. After a brief period of study in Europe, he returned to Harvard to become a member of the faculty and established the first physiology laboratory for students in the United States. Later, as dean of the school, he became an influential leader in medical education. Bowditch's observations on growth were made on several thousand individuals classified according to age. In a number of subsequent publications, he presented numerous tables and analyses pertaining to height and weight, nationality, economic backgrounds, and the patterns followed by each sex. We can be thankful that a man of his caliber carried out these studies because he set a sterling example for those who followed him in similar endeavors. His published material served as the usual guide for comparison in most of the standard pediatric texts until well into the 20th century.

William Camerer[25] in Germany collected important data relating to various aspects of metabolism and energy requirements for growth from birth to adult size. These studies were published over a period from 1880 to 1896. Camerer's material included physical measurements for infants and children younger than those included by Bowditch. Together, the work of these two constituted the standards used for measuring physical growth for nearly half a century.

In 1921 and 1922, respectively, R. M. Woodbury and B. T. Baldwin[8] published new charts depicting the growth of children in the United States from birth through adolescence. The former's material consisted of a widespread population of children under six, while the latter's consisted of the entire age range, but of a more homogeneous socioeconomic group. A large number of growth charts have been published in this country and abroad in the past 50 years. A few of these are described in some detail in chapter 4.

The great increase in interest in physical growth and development that was taking place at this period was evident from the appearance between 1900 and 1925 of nearly 3,000 published titles on the subject.[1] Krogman[9] collected over 2,000 references published between 1914 and 1940. The bulk of work following World War I began to shift from Europe to the United States and has continued so until very recent times. Part of this undoubtedly was a result of the aftermath of the war, but much of it resulted from the change in the character of the approach to children's health and the rapid growth of American medicine. More and more emphasis was being placed on a sound knowledge of the subject in the fields of pediatrics, preventive medicine, and education. The very essence of preventive medicine in children has as its goal normal growth and development.

Purely anatomical studies of the infant and child began in the 14th and 15th centuries. Modern anatomy in this field was largely confined to the European literature, mainly German, until after World War I. Among such works may be mentioned Henke's *Anatomie des Kindesalters* (1873), Ribemont's *Recherches sur l'anatomie topographique de fétus* (1878), Symington's *The Topographic Anatomy of the Child* (1887), and Stratz's *Der Körper des Kindes* (1904). R. E. Scammon's summary of anatomy in Abt's *Pediatrics* is a rich and valuable compilation printed in 1923.

A number of research centers for the study of growth and development were established as early as the 1920s, including the Iowa Child Welfare Research Station, the Brush Foundation at Western Reserve University, the Yale Clinic of Child Development, the Child Health Division of the Harvard School of Public Health, the Child Research Council of the University of Colorado, and the Fels Research Institute for the Study of Human Development, Antioch College. One of the important reasons for the creation of such centers was the longitudinal study of the child. Although cross-sectional studies have value, more detailed knowledge can be obtained by following individual children throughout part or all of their growing period. In 1923 the National Research Council sponsored a Committee on Child Development to foster and coordinate the rapidly growing research in this field. The White House Conference of 1930, and the resulting publications, may still be considered one of the finest sources for material on growth and development of children.[13] Although all of the pediatric journals carry articles on the subject, special publications now came into existence. *Growth: A Journal for Studies of Development and Increase* appeared in 1937 and *Child Development* a few years prior to that.

In 1895 the discovery of x-rays and their properties by Roentgen offered a means of studying the growth of the bony structure of the body in the living. Since then great advance has been made in standardization of techniques of roentgenology and in the appraisal of bone growth. Preston Hickey of Detroit in 1904 reported on his studies of the skeletal maturation of the fetus, infant, child, and adolescent. Pryor (1905)[10] and Thomas Rotch (1907)[5] were the first to show the usefulness of this method in estimating maturation by the examination of the number of bones and their size and shape in the hand. Rotch, who was the first professor of pediatrics at Harvard University, also made other researchers on the "physiologic" age of children. Although T. Wingate Todd published his well-known *Atlas of Skeletal Maturation* in 1937 as a result of his studies carried on at the Brush Foundation, similar but less complete outlines were available previously, based on the work of Baldwin and his co-workers (1928), P. C. Hodges (1933), and C. D. Flory (1936). It is interesting to note that at the same time Pryor and Rotch were discussing physiologic age in terms of skeletal development, an educator, C. W. Crampton,[11] was discussing the same subject in terms of body development, especially the appearance of secondary sexual characteristics. The latter author is credited with being the initiator of the term *physiologic age* (1908).

The first paper to describe the roentgenologic appearance of the fetus was printed the year following the discovery of the x-ray and was written by E. P. Davis of New York. Escherich of Graz, Austria, presented the initial lengthy report on x-ray examination in infants and young children and discussed its potentials as a diagnostic tool (1898).[12] Reyher's monograph of 1908 was the first review of the literature in German, and Rotch's *The Roentgen Rays in Pediatrics* appeared two years later in the United States. Subsequently a number of fine texts have been published, of which Caffey's *Pediatric X-Ray Diagnosis* is outstanding (first edition, 1945).[12]

The concept of types of structure of the body and their possible relationship to specific growth patterns, personality, and predisposition to disease is an ancient one. Hippocrates[23] described the tall thin type as *habitus phthisicus* with an increased incidence of tuberculosis; the short obese person was designated *habitus apoplecticus* with susceptibility to vascular accidents. Shakespeare alludes to the personality of different types in *Julius Caesar*:

> Let me have men about me that are fat
> Sleek-headed men, and such as sleep o'nights.
> Yond Cassius has a lean and hungry look;
> He thinks too much: such men are dangerous.

Leo Rostan of France in 1828[14] proposed that people be classified in terms of body build under one of four categories: *digestif* (short and obese), *musculaire* (solid and muscular), *respiratoire* (combination of *musculaire* and *cerebral*), and *cerebral* (tall and thin). Nearly one hundred years later, Ernst Kretschmer.[15] in Germany described three body types and related them to personality traits and mental diseases. The round-faced, well-nourished person was called *pyknic* and characterized as an extrovert. Manic-depressive psychosis was more commonly found in this group according to Kretschmer. *Asthenic* was the term applied to the tall and thin person who was introverted and the type in which the schizoid person was identified. Between these two in temperament and physique was the *athletic* type. Although little credence is given today to the association of somatotype with specific personalities or diseases, its rough clinical evaluation may have some value in predicting growth patterns.

A few comments may be given to the history of growth studies of special age groups. Although a number of treatises had been written on fetal growth prior to Von Baer's important work of 1829 describing the germ layers and their formation in the embryo, these earlier works broke no new ground not explored by Mauriceau in the late 17th century. It was not until after the formulation of the cell theory by Schleiden and Schwann (1839) that the significance of Von Baer's work was appreciated. A classic summary of anatomy of human embryos *(Anatomie menschlicher Embryonen)* was brought out by His of Germany in 1880. After the turn of the century Dafner of Germany and Mall in the United States supplied accurate figures on the age, growth, and external form of the human embryo.[26] From here to the premature infant would seem but a short step. However, growth and development of these "problem children" resisted concentrated attention until late in the 19th century, when Camerer brought attention to them in his studies, already mentioned. Ylppö[17] of Finland published in 1919 the first comprehensive report of the physical growth of the premature infant through childhood with many tables of measurements. Hess et al.[18] of Chicago wrote about their experiences with a group of premature babies followed for several years; this was in 1934. Although recent work has thrown some doubt upon certain conclusions of these men, their studies are of more than historical interest.

Charles-Michel Billard, who died at the age of 32, published in Paris in 1828 the first monograph on the newborn infant, which began with a careful consideration of the expected height and weight and color of skin, attitudes, and pulse rate. This text, *Traité des maladies des enfants nouveaunés et à la mamelle*, long remained the standard and was translated into several languages. Another milestone in pediatric literature was August von Reuss's *Krankheiten des Neugebornen*, printed in Vienna in 1914. Like Billard's book, it was primarily concerned with disease but outlined normal growth and development and the meager knowledge then available of physiology of the neonatal period. Unique in this field was the first edition of Clement A. Smith's *The Physiology of the Newborn Infant*, which immediately became a classic upon publication in 1945.

Intensive study of the growth and development of the adolescent is of relatively recent origin. Wilhelm Kotelmann (1839 to 1908) studied the physical development of students in private and public schools in Hamburg and noted the individual differences in the adolescence growth spurt and that children of the upper socioeconomic class at all ages were superior in mean height and weight to those of the public schools. His observations were first published in 1879.[42] Karl Vierordt (1818 to 1884)[19] of Tubingen along with Bowditch made important contributions at about the same time in the late 1870s. They divided periods of growth according to age and to other aspects of maturation recognizing the adolescent spurt and also that girls enter this period sooner than boys. Franz Boas (1858 to 1942),[43] born and educated in Germany, came to the United States where he served on the faculty of Clark University and later Columbia University as well as holding important positions as an editor and museum curator. He wrote extensively on growth throughout his life. He recognized the individuality of the adolescent growth spurt and stressed the importance of the longitudinal studies to show that individuality. The two volumes on adolescence by Stanley Hall (1846 to 1924),[22] published in 1904, were especially complete for their time recognizing the secular trend in growth and the effects that socioeconomic factors had upon it and menarchial age. In 1923 the

Scandinavian Carl Schiotz (1877 to 1938)[46] published his findings based on Oslo children indicating the effects of social class on body dimensions and secular changes in height, weight, and age at menarche in comparison with previous populations. In the United States, Shuttleworth[44] and Stuart[45] and, in England, Tanner[16] have made particularly large contributions on the subject of the adolescent.

Physiologic and biochemical differences among infants, children, and adults were relatively recent subjects of interest. It should be recalled that physiology passed beyond metaphysics and speculation as recently as the first half of the 19th century. This change was due mainly to the efforts of the Frenchmen François Magendie (1783 to 1855) and Claude Bernard (1813 to 1878). Both insisted upon proof of facts by the experimental technique. Special study of the body functions of the pediatric age group became well established in Germany in the last half of the 19th century. At first this was primarily concentrated upon nutrition and related aspects of physiology. In 1878 Friedrich Ahlfeld emphasized the relationship of an infant's weight to adequate nutrition. At the same time, Joseph Forster studied the respiratory gases in the newborn and showed that they produced more carbon dioxide per unit of weight than the adult. Shortly after this, Camerer introduced the scientific investigation of infantile metabolism with special reference to energy requirements. Max Rubner and Otto Heubner in 1898 published *Die natürliche Ernährung eines Saüglings*, which is often considered the starting point of all modern work on infant metabolism. Rubner also was among the first to relate rate of energy metabolism to surface area. Heubner later became the director of the Pediatric Clinic in Berlin and was given the first full professorship in Germany in 1894. Adalberg Czerny of Prague made many contributions in regard to infant feeding and was among those first interested in the products of intermediate metabolism. He also anticipated the modern behaviorists in his teachings on child rearing. In 1913 he assumed the chair of pediatrics in Berlin, following Heubner. In his time Czerny was undoubtedly the European leader in pediatrics, and his influence was felt throughout the world.[20]

In the United States John Murlin, Fritz Talbot, and Francis Benedict made particularly significant contributions to the understanding of energy metabolism in the early years of the present century. It is beyond the scope of this review to mention all of the important work in this and related biochemical fields, and new developments of today are changing previously held concepts at a rapid rate. It would be an unpardonable omission, however, not to acknowledge the work in chemistry of John Howland (1873 to 1926) of Johns Hopkins University and William McKim Marriott (1885 to 1936) of Washington University in St. Louis. These two men were directly responsible for emphasizing the importance of laboratory methods in studying clinical problems, a concept that is largely taken for granted now.

The behavior and psychologic development of the child was first approached on an educational basis. The general attitude until quite recent times was that children were inferior objects and did not warrant any special study. Education was important only because it aided the child in assuming the tasks of the adult and becoming a dependable parent. Johann Amos Comenius (1592 to 1670), a Moravian bishop, published several works on education and first emphasized the individuality of children and that education should be directed according to ability rather than to a desire to mold into a socially acceptable pattern. The philosophical implications of Jean Jacques Rousseau (1712 to 1778) have carried considerable weight upon ideas of children's behavior and methods of teaching. He extolled natural methods as opposed to the disciplinary ones practiced in teaching at that time: "Nature never deceives us; it is always we who deceive ourselves." He wrote that the child has ways of observing, thinking, and feeling that are peculiar to him or her. In Germany Friedrich Froebel (1782 to 1852), the father of the kindergarten, preached much the same concept in his attempt to reform contemporary education, basing his ideas upon careful observations of children in the school and the home.

Although records were incomplete, it is estimated that only one of every two children born in America 200 years ago would live to reach the age of 21 years. Infectious diseases were the major reason for this mortality, of which diarrhea and enteritis were the leading causes.[30] As recently as 1910, 30% of all infant deaths were caused by diarrhea and enteritis. Most mothers breast-fed their infants but this was often supplemented with milk or water from contaminated sources. Wet-nursing was common since women did not hesitate to suckle each other's children. The superstition that the milk might be responsible for passing on the characteristics of the woman supplying it was so strong that it imposed considerable limitations to a practice that might have saved more lives. The time of weaning was one of worry since many ills had their onset then.[31]

Substitutes for breast milk included the milk from cows, goats or asses, and occasionally other animals. These animals often were easier to obtain and cheaper than human wet nurses. One of the first texts on child care, published in this country in 1825, called attention to the value of various animal milks in infant feeding.[32] Some authorities in America and Europe considered the use of a specific animal's milk, added to the diet, as having remedial qualities. Well into the present century, a major portion of time in pediatric training was devoted to the preparation of infant formulas.

Reduced infant morbidity and mortality from contaminated formulas was the result of a number of important developments beginning at the end of the 19th century. The recognition of bacterial origins of disease resulted in improved public health measures including milk and water inspection. The advent of nearly universal pasteurization and, shortly after, the availability of refrigeration further improved the situation for the infant and child.

Child rearing in America from colonial times to the beginning of the present century was often influenced by superstition and religious dogma.[31, 34] Relatively minor mishaps or events occurring during pregnancy were blamed for hemangiomas or congenital malformations in the infant. The exact (astrological) time of birth could account for future personality traits or mental or physical illness. To many parents, the infant was born in sin and was in urgent need of being saved from hell. Many children were, some few still are, raised in the strict observance of religious taboos and received severe punishment for often trivial misbehaviors. Play of any kind on the Sabbath was forbidden. The content of children's books was more often moralizing in character than educational or for pleasure. Educators and education for children were given very low priorities except among the wealthy who could afford to hire tutors or send their offspring to private schools. Until the early 1920s school health programs were virtually nonexistent.

In the latter part of the 18th century, interest in studying the child turned from a purely educational approach to biographic methods. Johann Heinrich Pestalozzi (1746 to 1827) from Switzerland was noted for his ideas concerning education and greatly influenced Froebel. In addition, he wrote the first well-documented developmental biography of a child, his own son, which may be considered the initial scientific record of this kind. In 1787 the German physician Tiedemann published similar but more complete observations on the development of his children. However, his work was long neglected and required republishing more than a hundred years later to attract attention. In 1877 Charles Darwin wrote his delightful and instructive A Biographical Sketch of an Infant. Wilhelm Preyer's Die Seele des Kindes first appeared in 1882 and reached eight editions.

The limitations of the biographic approach to the study of behavior were recognized and have been largely replaced by longitudinal and experimental methods. Reflex behavior, or the response to specific stimuli, was the subject of a monograph by Adolf Kussmaul in 1859. Kussmaul, who became professor of medicine at four German medical schools, made numerous important contributions including the first use of thoracentesis and esophagoscopy and wrote the description of the respiratory pattern seen in diabetic acidosis that bears his name. In 1918 Ernst Moro, a German pediatrician, noted the reflex now known by his eponym. The sensorimotor responses in infants were described by the Shermans[21] in 1925. A very productive period of study of infant and child behavior occurred in the

1930s and 1940s resulting in publications by Nancy Bayley, Arnold Gessell, M. B. McGraw, and M. M. Shirley. Each of these Americans, working independently, was largely responsible for cataloging the expected norms of behavior at various stages of development that are now in common use.

Jean Lamarck (1744 to 1829), the famous French naturalist, attributed the maturation of behavior to the inheritance of acquired traits. Although subsequent studies threw considerable doubt upon the validity of these concepts, it was not until the late 1800s and early 1900s that new theories concerning child behavior were formulated. Sigmund Freud (1856 to 1939) reported his controversial ideas about infantile sexuality and its influence upon behavior in 1908. Even though modified or entirely unaccepted by some psychologists and psychiatrists, these theories have had great influence in stimulating thought and methods of investigation. Not so startling were the concepts of the school of "behaviorism" led by John Watson. He introduced many new experimental technics. In 1914 he began publishing a series of works on child behavior that largely denied the existence of instinct and consciousness and therefore were antagonistic to Freud. Among other contributions to a discussion of personality development was the monograph by Stanley Hall on the psychology of adolescence (1904).[22] This was a truly monumental work, and it maintains a place of eminence in the field. Although this was not the first material to call attention to the relationships of physical to mental development, it had the greatest influence on those interested in the study of the growth of the whole child. Hall was largely responsible for the formation of the National Association for the Study of Children, the first child study society in America (1893). The first International Child Study Congress was held in Berlin in 1906.

Of very great influence during the last several decades has been the work of the Swiss psychologist Jean Piaget (1896 to 1980). He described a theory of cognitive and intellectual development according to which development proceeds in genetically determined stages that always follow the same sequential order. He demonstrated that children reason differently than adults and do not use logical reasoning until approaching adolescence. His conclusions resulted largely from observations of his own three children.

Until the early part of the 20th century the measurement of mental growth occupied almost no place in the scientific literature. To the American James Cattell must go much of the honor for the concept of mental testing, which he outlined in 1890.[24] Binet and Simon, in Paris, were carrying out similar experiments about the same time, and in 1908 they published what must be considered the first adequate test scale. Goddard, in this country, was an important figure in making these experiments available and promoting their use. Lewis M. Terman was instrumental in introducing mental tests into the schools and in developing further refinements of the methods (1916 to 1937). The "developmental" tests of Gesell are now well known and nearly universal in their use. Several test methods are now available for specific age groups and are also used to aid in attempting more definitive diagnostic criteria.

As a final note in this review, attention should be called to an international foundation for the study of the growth and development of children, the Centre International de l'Enfance, which was opened in Paris in 1953. The center has sponsored studies in a number of countries, holding regular meetings to promote knowledge, understanding, and cooperation and has released a number of important publications.

Some Principles of Growth and Development

The terms *growth* and *development* are often used interchangeably, and it is certainly true that each depends on the other for fruition. In the normal child each parallels the other and any separation would be an artificial one. For convenience, however, we may distinguish between them. We restrict, when possible, the term *growth* to mean an increase in physical size of the whole or any of its parts. Growth, therefore, may be measured in terms of inches or centimeters and pounds or kilograms. It can be measured also in terms of metabolic balance, i.e., retention of calcium and nitrogen by the body. *Development* is used to indicate an increase in skill and complexity of function. The individual develops neuromuscular control, dexterity, and character. Maturation and differentiation are frequently used as synonyms for development. Used in this sense, it is evident that development is related to growth but is not the same.

Comparative aspects of growth and development are of special interest. Some of the lower forms of life, particularly certain species of insects, emerge from the egg in a fully mature state, capable of carrying on all of the activities of the adult, including reproduction. Even among some higher forms a considerable degree of maturity is rapidly attained. The newly born guinea pig can shift for itself three days after birth. Humans are set apart from other animals by the protracted period of infancy and childhood. Nearly one third of a human's life span is spent in preparation for living the latter two thirds. It is as though nature, cognizant of the human's unique cerebral attributes, provides a long training period. The human is essentially a learning animal and biologically speaking develops so slowly that his or her mental processes are enabled to use and absorb the cumulative experiences of all who have gone before. In some animals, the potential for growth never ceases. In the cold-blooded or poikilothermic species, growth slows with age but is never-ending during life. In the rat the epiphyses never close, which makes this animal unique and, incidentally, somewhat of a problem for the interpretation of growth studies. Only the primates appear to have the second period of accelerated growth that we associate with early adolescence in humans. Other animals follow a relatively smooth decelerating curve with advancing age until adulthood.

The basic process of protein synthesis is shared by two dissociable bits of ribonucleoprotein that form the workshop of protein manufacture. All cells have transfer RNA and messenger RNA (see chapter 2), and their function in transmitting the genetic code is a universal one. In fact, experiments have been carried out in which transfer RNA from bacteria was used with messenger RNA from reticulocytes of a rabbit to make hemoglobin.[29]

At fertilization two very important events occur. The egg is provided with a paternal genome and metabolic processes are initiated that are required for renewed cell division and cell differentiation. Until the multicelled blastocyst becomes implanted in the uterine wall, cell division is accomplished with little or no protein synthesis and each new cell is smaller than its parent cell. This is the only time in human development when cell division is not proceeded by growth in size and protein synthesis. Differentiation must depend upon changes in the protein content of developing cell populations. An important aspect of messenger RNA is that it is unstable, with a relatively short half-life. Thus, a continuing supply of it is necessary to maintain protein synthesis. This permits alterations in the programs for ribosomes to produce a variety of proteins according to cellular need or function. It also permits changes in the rate of production of a specific protein, since rate depends upon the concentration of messenger RNA. In differentiation an important aspect of the development of specialized cells is the production of proteins that permit realization of their unique role. For example, stem cells that are precursors of those blood cells that will become erythrocytes during maturation convert to cells in which most of the messenger RNA codes for hemoglobin. The number of identifiably different proteins increases rapidly with the length of gestation in the early embryonic period.

It has been demonstrated that the production rate, and therefore quantity, of ribosome RNA varies with the course of development regardless of chronologic age. Embryonic cells disturbed from forming the gastrulation stage will not synthesize ribosome RNA at the same rate as chronologically equal cells that have been permitted to reach gastrulation.[29]

Chemical controls of growth mechanisms also play an important role early in development. Once an enzyme molecule has been formed by the ribosome, its metabolic activity will modify the substrate. This in turn will increase or decrese the activity of the indicated enzyme, as well as possibly modify other enzymes. There is some evidence that induction or activation of an enzyme is dependent upon a critical concentration of a specific substrate. In this way the checks and balances of growth become established.

Little is known about how growth and physiologic activity are mediated in various tissues. Muscle, bone, nerve, and skin are types of tissue that may be stimulated by local influences, or inhibited by them. In the case of muscle, stimuli could result from nerve impulses. Blood pressure changes in the heart and larger vessels and stress upon bones might represent important influences upon growth. Physical features such as temperature, total mass, and surface area may affect the ultimate rate or direction of growth.

Immediately following fertilization, all cells of the organism divide at an equal rate. Differential and nonrandom proliferation very quickly replace the former pattern. Renewing cell populations consist of stem cells that divide to yield new stem cells and also differentiating cells. In turn, some of these cells eventually become senile cells that have lost the ability to divide and are removed from the population. It is likely that much of the growth control is exerted by *chalones*. These substances, which inhibit cell proliferation, have been reportedly isolated from a number of tissues. The implication is that cells of a specific organ would multiply indefinitely unless prevented by the chalone. It is postulated that this substance is produced by many, perhaps all, cells but it remains inactive as long as it is within the cell. In the course of growth, as the number of cells increases, the amount of chalone released from dying cells also increases. Once in the circulation in sufficient quantity, it inhibits further increase in cell population by influencing receptors on the cell surface. These polypeptides are stated to be organ specific.[35]

The important role played by the pituitary, thyroid, gonadal, and pancreatic hormones in growth has long been recognized. Now we realize that there are a number of so-called growth factors that act to increase cell size and proliferation and prolong cell survival in specific tissues independent of the systemic hormones.[39] These are polypeptides that exhibit growth-promoting activity in vivo and in vitro. These factors are believed to initiate activity by attaching to specific receptor sites on the plasma membrane of cells, which sets off a series of reactions within the cell of an anabolic nature. Most of the growth factors have specific receptor sites except for the somatomedins and insulin, which may share sites (see chapter 9). The somatomedins, possibly three different types, are derived from a number of different tissues but mainly liver. Their presence in serum appears to be necessary for the pituitary growth hormone to be effective in linear bone growth. The growth factors stimulate DNA synthesis and generally can be classified according to source as fibroblast growth factor, epidermal growth factor, nerve growth factor, platelet-derived growth factor, bone morphogenic protein, and bone-derived growth factor. Using the last two as examples, bone morphogenic protein induces differentiation of perivascular mesenchymal cells into osteoprogenitor cells and bone-derived growth factor stimulates mitosis and DNA synthesis. It is postulated that these two factors are necessary to sustain bone mass since bone is a tissue constantly undergoing remodeling and regeneration.[40]

An example of a highly specific growth-promoting factor is found in erythropoietin. This substance is produced by the kidneys and stimulates both the production of erythrocytes and their release from the marrow to the circulation. The stimulus for release of this protein hormone is renal hypoxia, either by reduced blood flow or decreased oxygen saturation of the blood. Erythropoietin is present in the circulation from the time of late fetal development.

Some students of growth have defined three basic patterns of cellular proliferation in tissue: *renewing, expanding,* and *static.* Some tissues of the body are in a lifelong renewal at the cellular level, a balance of loss and replacement, e.g., epidermis and blood cells. An important attribute of this type of tissue is that the differentiated cells have limited life spans and are incapable of proliferation. Expanding tissues are made up of cells with indefinite longevity and their differentiation is compatible with mitosis; they retain their potential for proliferation, which may be elicited by injury or heightened work loads. The kidneys and many endocrine and exocrine organs are examples. Mitotically static tissues are mainly the nerves and muscles. The fully differentiated cell is so specialized that its ability for division is lost in early developmental stages. In mitotically static tissue, growth can occur only by cellular hypertrophy. However, even though the cells of the kidneys can multiply, the number of nephrons is fixed early in development. Similarly, pulmonary alveoli, seminiferous tubules, and heart muscle have limited capacity to multiply functional units early in development. Osseous tissue, blood cells, and endocrine cells remain capable of hyperplasia until death.[41]

Among other interesting theories proposed to explain growth regulation are those based upon functional demand and total body mass, each with their specific feedback mechanisms.[35] (See also chapter 9.)

The inherent urge to grow and develop is very strong in children. It can be blighted by many factors, e.g., malnutrition, acute and chronic infections, endocrine disturbances, congenital malformations, and genetic defects. Prenatal influences determine to no small extent the size, viability, and general health of the newborn infant. Whether complete recovery and normal development will occur following an insult depends upon several factors. The nature, severity, and duration of the incident are of obvious importance. In most animals the timing is important; the earlier the insult, the more likely it is to cause permanent harm. The term *critical period* is often used to describe the time of greatest sensitivity of an organ or system to a specific action. Absence of fetal testicular hormone at the critical period of differentiation and development of the wolffian duct system will result in its degeneration and permit predominance of the müllerian ducts. This situation can be accomplished by castration in animals. A delay of a few days in the operative procedure will not interfere with full male ductal system development. Artificially supplying the hormone after the critical period is passed will not cause a reversal of the degenerative process.

If an insult occurs at a less crucial time and it does not persist, recovery is possible. Temporary deprivation of adequate nutrition in an older child may markedly retard growth in height and weight. When normal food intake is resumed, there usually follows a period of rapid recovery until former levels of height and weight are attained. The accelerated growth period is referred to as *catch-up growth* and is a common phenomenon experienced by most children following major illnesses.

In subsequent pages an attempt is made to emphasize the individuality of growth and development. No single schedule can be anticipated for any one child. When this is properly understood and given due consideration, many errors can be avoided in evaluating a child. For instance, we would not expect comparable accretions of height and weight for two children, one of whom was born of Japanese parentage and the other of English parentage, even though both were reared in a similar environment. Likewise, we cannot establish a common calendar for the events of maturation that characterize adolescent development. First, there is a difference between the sexes; second, in the same sex there can be considerable variation within normal limits; finally, various organ systems and functions within the individual reach maturity at different times. This concept of individuality has gained great impetus resulting in the use of graphs and charts on which each child establishes his or her own pattern of development. However, the concept of the usual range or distribution of physical, mental, or physiologic attributes is important and it is desirable to compare each measurement of the child under observation with this distribution rather than with any single norm. Obtaining and interpreting such measurements improve clinical judgment and may bring to one's attention characteristics that might otherwise be overlooked. The first indication of disease may be failure to gain or actual loss of weight or failure to increase in stature. Some phases of development do not lend themselves to easy or simple methods of measurement, for example, personality and emotional behavior. This does not decrease their importance in considering the child as a whole individual. In some fields of behavior we do have fairly well-defined or expected patterns of behavior and, as with physical or biochemical measurements, these are useful as guiding principles, especially in the counseling of parents.

Every child has the privilege and the right to develop to the limits of his or her capacity. It is the great responsibility of physicians, parents, educators, and public health and social service workers to see that the child is given the best opportunity to carry this privilege and this right through to completion. It is hoped that the information presented in the following pages may serve as a guide to the accomplishment of these ideals. It is only through the continued study of children that optimal levels may eventually be defined and attained.

Although there is great variation, it may be helpful for purposes of discussion to divide the periods of growth. Several different lists have been given by various writers; the following grouping seems satisfactory. Such a division of periods will also acquaint the reader with the terms used hereafter.

GROWTH PERIOD	APPROXIMATE AGE
Prenatal	From 0 to 280 days
Ovum	From 0 to 14 days
Embryo	From 14 days to 9 weeks
Fetus	From 9 weeks to birth
Premature infant	From 27 to 37 weeks
Birth	Average 280 days
Neonate	First 4 weeks after birth
Infancy	First year
Early childhood (preschool)	From 1 to 6 years
Later childhood (prepubertal)	From 6 to 10 years
Adolescence	
Girls	8 or 10 to 18 years
Boys	10 or 12 to 20 years
Puberty (average)	
Girls	13 years
Boys	15 years

Each of the periods has one or more characteristics relative to growth and development that set it apart from the others, aside from the chronologic differences. There is no sharp line dividing the periods; they blend imperceptibly from one into another. Prenatal and postnatal growth are one continuous process, but the incident of birth and the beginning of extrauterine existence is an important dividing point. The period of the ovum is characterized by increase in complexity and cell multiplication with little increase in total size. For a part of this time the new organism is self-sufficient, living on its own food stored in the yolk sac. The embryo is parasitic and derives its nutrition from the maternal organism, as does the fetus. It is during the embryonic period that rapid differentiation takes place and all of the organ systems are established. During fetal life there is further development, and early functional activities are apparent. Most pronounced is the rapid increase in body mass.

At birth the parasitic existence is terminated, and as a result there are the initiation of respiration; changes in the circulatory system largely related to the onset of pulmonary function; dependence on an external source of nutrition and upon the digestive system for assimilation of the offered food; dependence upon the organism's own resources to maintain proper body heat; and finally, the excretion of unwanted metabolic substances. It is during this time that the greatest risk to life is experienced, and this fact has stimulated an intense amount of research. Infant mortality rate is regarded as a sensitive index of a country's or community's concern with its health. It is also this period and that of early infancy that many investigators consider to be the most critical relative to the lasting effects of serious injury or disease. Rapid growth and continued maturation proceed during infancy, especially by increase in the functions of the nervous system. It is important to note that very little cell division occurs in the human brain after five months of age and further growth results from increase in cell size. Another interesting fact is the noisiness of the human infant as compared with infants of nearly all other species. At no other time is the velocity of growth so great. Throughout both early and late childhood growth is relatively slow but steady. Only the lymphoid tissue continues to accelerate. There is increasing coordination of functions with the development of skills and intellectual processes. Emotional development is undergoing constant fluctuations and perhaps represents the least stable factor in the entire period.

The period of adolescence has had many definitions. By general use, however, the term is associated with accelerated growth in height and weight, appearance of sexual characteristics, and the decelerating growth curve that follows and is terminated in the union of the epiphyses. The ability to reproduce is the culmination of sexual development. More briefly, but less exactly stated, adolescence represents the period of "growing up" or the change from child to adult. There are no sharp lines of demarcation at the start or end of this time interval, and for each subject the chronologic ages may vary. Puberty refers to the time of appearance of dark, pigmented pubic hair in both sexes and includes the age of menarche in girls. Ovulation and the ability to reproduce follow some time after the first menstrual period in most girls. On the average puberty is assumed to take place about two years later in boys than in girls. The "adolescent spurt" of growth is steroid (sex hormone) mediated and is more pronounced in boys, who also grow for a longer total period than girls.

Boys have a larger muscle and skeletal mass at all ages and a larger energy requirement for both maintenance and growth. These sex differences are increased during adolescence. Girls constantly have a more advanced skeletal maturity (bone age) and are ahead of boys in most psychomotor skills in the earlier years. Contrary to the usually accepted ideas of growth, increase in stature may continue through age 25. The median age for American children at which statural growth ceases is 21.2 years for boys and 17.3 years for girls.[36] Increase in muscle mass usually continues into the 20s and increase in skeletal mass into the 30s in both sexes.

Each growth period produces some behavioral characteristics; however, these are not necessarily the same for each child. Along with increasing motor skills and gain in self-confidence, the 3-year-old becomes more sociable and is able to share and take turns. Physical size and function have important influences on status with peers and on the individual's approach to people and situations. For the adolescent there is the combination of "threat" of separation and the "joy" of independence from parents. Facing the world as an individual rather than as a member of the family is a step usually accomplished comfortably by virtue of adequate preparation. Sexual development, with its implications of assuming the responsibilities of partner and parent, normally produces some anxieties that in turn have been and will be influenced by society and the world as it is.

REFERENCES

1. Scammon R.E.: The literature on the growth and physical development of the fetus, infant, and child: A quantitative summary. *Anat. Rec.* 35:241, 1927.
2. Cone T.E.: The history of weighing the newborn infant. *Pediatrics* 28:490, 1961.
3. Clarke J.: Observations on some causes of the excess of mortality of males above that of females. *Trans. R. Soc.* (London) 76:358, 1786.
4. Scammon R.E.: The first seriation study of human growth. *Am. J. Phys. Anthropol.* 10:329, 1927.
5. Garrison F.H.: History of pediatrics, in Abt I.A. (ed.): *Pediatrics*, vol. I. Philadelphia, W.B. Saunders Co., 1923.
6. Quetelet L.A.J.: *Sur l'homme et le développement de ses facultés, un essai de physique sociale*, ed. 2. Brussels, 1869.
7. Bowditch H.P.: *Eighth Annual Report, State Board of Health, Mass.* 1875.
8. Baldwin B.T.: *The Physical Growth of Children from Birth to Maturity.* Iowa City, State University of Iowa Press, 1922.
9. Krogman W.M.: *Bibliography of Human Morphology*, 1914–1939. Chicago, University of Chicago Press, 1941.
10. Pryor J.W.: Development of the bones of the hand as shown by the x-ray method. *Bull. State Coll. Ky.*, 1905.
11. Crampton C.W.: Physiological age, a fundamental principle. *Am. Phys. Educ. Rev.* vol. 13, nos. 3–6, 1908.
12. Caffey J.: *Pediatric X-Ray Diagnosis*, ed. 6. Chicago, Year Book Medical Publishers, Inc., 1972.
13. *White House Conference on Child Health and Protection.* Section I: Part I,

Growth and Development; Part II, Anatomy and Physiology. New York, Century, 1933.
14. Rostan L.: *Cours élémentaire d'hygiène*. Paris, 1828.
15. Kretschmer E.: *Körperbau und Charakter*. Berlin, A. Springer, 1921.
16. Tanner J.M.: *Growth at Adolescence*. Springfield, Ill., Charles C Thomas, Publisher, 1955.
17. Ylppö A.: Das Wachstum der Frühgeborenen von der Geburt bis zum Schulalter. *Z. Kinderheilkd.* 24:111, 1919.
18. Hess J.H., Mohr G.J., Bartelme P.F.: *The Physical and Mental Growth of Prematurely Born Children*. Chicago, University of Chicago Press, 1934.
19. Vierordt K.: Physiologie des Kindesalters und Wachstum, in Gerhard C. (ed.): *Handbuch der Kinderkrankheit*. Tübingen, 1877.
20. Veeder B.S. (ed.): *Pediatric Profiles*. St. Louis, C.V. Mosby Co., 1957.
21. Sherman M., Sherman I.C.: Sensori-motor responses in infants. *J. Comp. Psychol.* 5:53, 1925.
22. Hall G.S.: *Adolescence: Its Psychology and Its Relations to Physiology, Anthropology, Sociology, Sex, Crime, Religion and Education*. New York, Appleton-Century Crofts, Inc., 1904.
23. Hoefnagel, D., Lüders D.: Ernst Moro (1874–1951). *Pediatrics* 29:643, 1962.
24. Cattell J.M.: Mental tests and measurements. *Mind* 15:373, 1890.
25. Camerer W.: Bermerkungen über Wachstum. *Z. Biol.* 36:24, 1880.
26. Mall F.P.: On measuring human embryos. *Anat. Rec.* 1:129, 1907.
27. Caffey J.: The first sixty years of pediatric roentgenology in the United States: 1896 to 1956. *Am. J. Roentgenol.* 76:437, 1956.
28. Smith R.M.: Fifty years of medical progress: Medicine as a science: Pediatrics. *N. Engl. J. Med.* 244:176, 1951.
29. Malt R.A. (ed.): *Macromolecular Synthesis and Growth*. Boston, Little, Brown & Co., 1967.
30. *Child Health in America*. U.S. Dept. of Health, Education and Welfare, Public Health Service, 1976.
31. Radbill S.K.: Colonial pediatrics. *J. Pediatr.* 89:3, 1976.
32. Radbill S.K.: The role of animals in infant feeding, in Hand W.D. (ed.): *American Folk Medicine*. Berkeley, University of California Press, 1976, p. 21.
33. Hippocrates: *The Genuine Works of Hippocrates*, trans. by F. Adams. New York, William Wood, 1886.
34. Black H.: Childhood in the early colonial period. *Pediatrics* 54:71, 1974.
35. Goss R.E. (ed.): *Regulation of Organ and Tissue Growth*. New York, Academic Press, 1972.
36. Roche A.F., Davila G.H.: Late adolescent growth in stature. *Pediatrics* 50:874, 1972.
37. Boyd E.: *Origins of the Study of Human Growth*. Portland, University of Oregon Health Sciences Center Foundation, 1980.
38. Tanner J.M.: *A History of the Study of Human Growth*. Cambridge, England, Cambridge University Press, 1983.
39. Nevo Z., Laron Z.: Growth factors. *Am. J. Dis. Child.* 133:419, 1979.
40. Urist M.R., De Lange R.J., Finerman G.A.M.: Bone cell differentiation and growth factors. *Science* 220:680, 1983.
41. Goss R.J.: *The Physiology of Growth*. New York, Academic Press, 1978.
42. Kotelmann L.: *Die Körperverhaltnisse der Gelehrtenschuler des Johanneums in Hamburg: Ein statisticher Beitrag zur Schulhygiene*. Berlin, Koniglichen Statischen Bureau, 1879.

43. Boas F.: The growth of children. *Science* 19:256, 281, 351, 1892.
44. Shuttleworth F.K.: *The Adolescent Period: A Graphic and Pictorial Atlas.* Monogram, Society for Research in Child Development. Washington, D.C., National Research Council, 1938.
45. Stuart H.C.: Normal growth and development during adolescence. *N. Engl. J. Med.* 234:666, 1946.
46. Schiotz C.: Physical development of children and young people during the age of 7 to 18–20 years. *Skr. norske Videns Akad,* 1923.

2 / Heredity and Environmental Factors

> Heredity sets limits, environment decides
> the exact position within these limits.
> —E.C. MacDowell

Heredity

The materials with which embryonic life is begun consist of the cytoplasm and the nucleus of the fertilized egg, received from the two parents. The nucleus contains the genes, which differ much in each individual, and these differences affect all of the characteristics of the organism. The manifestations of the results of differences among the genes are known as *heredity*. Obviously one cannot hope to cover this broad field in a few paragraphs, and the purpose of this discussion is to point out the more important known factors and to attempt to evaluate them in relation to growth and development.

One of the fundamental properties of life is the ability to reproduce. Reproduction is always of the organism's own kind, so there is a very close resemblance between parent and progeny. This is also true of individual cells in the replacement of loss due to ordinary "wear and tear." Rarely, as in some nervous tissues, with complete maturity reproductive abilities may be lost. There is, therefore, continuity of the total organism as well as its separate parts. The material in cells responsible for the continuity is DNA, which makes up the chromosomes and the genes.

The molecular model of DNA consists of two helical chains of alternate sugar (deoxyribose) and phosphate. These chains are linked, similarly to rungs in a ladder, by pairs of nitrogen bases that are bonded to the sugar molecules. The nitrogen bases have been identified as purines, adenine and guanine, and pyrimidines, cytosine and thymine. The pairs of bases are joined by hydrogen bonds (Fig 2–1). The DNA molecules are extremely large, with a molecular weight probably in the millions.

23

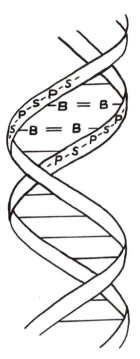

Fig 2–1.—A schematic diagram of the double helix of deoxyribonucleic acid (DNA). The outside chains consist of alternating sugar *(S)* and phosphate *(P)* molecules. On the inside of the cylinder are the bases *(B)*, of which thymine and adenine are examples. The *double bars* indicate hydrogen bonds between the bases.

The pairing of the bases is always the same, adenine with thymine and cytosine with guanine. Consequently, if the order in one helix is known, the order in its matched pair can easily be deduced. This sequence is the basis of the *genetic code*. At the time of the reduction division *(meiosis)* of the sperm and egg, the DNA splits into single chains. These single chains then attract from the environment the appropriate bases to build two copies that are spatially the exact duplicates of the original double helix. Fertilization of the germ cell is at least one of the stimuli for the initiation of this replication.

The chemical identity of human genes has not been ascertained, but probably they consist of several nucleotides (a base plus a sugar and phosphate molecule). There are potentially thousands of genes to each DNA molecule, and the total number of genes in humans has been estimated to be not less than 100,000.[6, 21]

All of life's functions are dependent upon protein synthesis. Proteins are composed of several or many units of polypeptides. The polypeptides are made up of amino acids linked in chains. There are 20 amino acids, but since one polypeptide may contain more than 200 amino acids in a number of different sequences, the possible variations for protein structure are nearly unlimited. The structure and function of a protein depend upon the amino acid sequence. The arrangement of the bases in the chain of the ribose phosphate of the DNA acts as a template for protein synthesis and the order of the amino acid sequence. The genetic information is carried from the gene, found in the nucleus, to the cytoplasm by a specific type of ribonucleic acid called *messenger* RNA. This is a much smaller chain than DNA, very labile and with a half-life measured in minutes or hours. The messenger RNA is synthesized by the DNA strand with a complementary pairing of the bases, except that uracil replaces thyamine. The messenger RNA passes from the nucleus to the cytoplasm in which are located the ribosomes, which appear to be the main site of synthesis of the final protein. From the cytoplasm are drawn the amino acids used as building materials. It is believed that the free amino acids are attached to, and some orderly arrangement is made by, another ribonucleic acid referred to as *transfer* RNA. These are very short chains. In order, then, the DNA makes messenger RNA, which gives the code to transfer RNA, which conveys the selected amino acids to the ribosomes where they "line up" according to the template and linkage occurs. Still another ribonucleic acid, *ribosome* RNA, is responsible for the product produced.

We can now go one step further in our understanding of the action of the genes. All biologic reactions are catalyzed by enzymes. An enzyme is a protein that may be specific to one reaction and one substrate or may catalyze a group reaction, such as the oxidation of all aldehydes by aldehyde oxidase. Each enzyme has a specific structure and, as noted, a specific function. All biochemical processes are resolvable into a series of individual reactions, each dependent on the proceeding reaction. Each reaction is, in turn, under the influence of a different enzyme. Since the enzyme is an individual protein, it will be modified in its structure by the genes. Finally, it seems well established that a change (mutation) of a single gene results only in an alteration in the ability of a cell to carry out a single chemical reaction. This postulate of one gene for one enzyme appears to be valid under all circumstances so far tested.[35]

An example is the difference between normal hemoglobin and the abnormal hemoglobin of sickle cell disease in humans. The sequence of amino acids in the abnormal hemoglobin varies from that in normal hemoglobin only in the substitution of a single valine for a glutamic acid in each half molecule. This apparently slight change produces a difference in certain properties, including solubility, leading to morbid consequences in the individual who is homozygous for the abnormal hemoglobin.

The nuclear substance of the zygote and of all the somatic cells derived therefrom contains 46 chromosomes. The germ cells (spermatocyte and ovum) contain half as much chromatin material, due to the reduction division, or meiosis. The union of the two gametes (germ cells) re-establishes in the fertilized cell the number of chromosomes characteristic of the somatic cells of the species. Of the 46 chromosomes, 23 are of paternal origin and the other half are of maternal origin. Each series of chromosomes contains a complete assortment of genes and therefore a complete set of developmental potentialities. The paternal and maternal chromosomes can be grouped into 22 homologous pairs containing 22 sets of genes. These chromosomes are termed *autosomes*. In addition, there are two *sex chromosomes*, homologous in the female (XX) and nonhomologous in the male (XY). Every hereditary trait is under the influence of a pair of genes, but other influences, possibly including other gene pairs, may modify their action. In general, the two members of a pair have a similar principal function. However, they may or may not differ in their qualitative or quantitative potentialities. An individual who carries a pair of genes that tend to produce very similar or identical results is said to be *homozygous* with regard to genes and the trait. On the other hand, if the members of the pair tend to produce different results, the individual is *heterozygous*. If one of the genes has a more potent influence than the other, it is said to be *dominant*, and the relatively weaker gene is called *recessive*. A recessive gene can express its characteristic fully only when paired with a similar gene or in a homozygous person.

To express the difference in appearance as determined by genes, the term *phenotype* is used. This incidates the morphologic or perhaps physiologic characteristic of an individual. *Genotype* on the other hand, expresses the genetic make-up of the individual, or the combination of genes present. When the pair of genes influences a certain physiologic or anatomical characteristic in different ways, i.e., tallness or shortness, they are referred to as *alleles*. These genes are believed to occupy the same relative positions in the paired chromosomes.

The formation of germ cells is preceded by a so-called reduction division in which the members of each chromosome pair separate and pass into two different mature germ cells. Each germ cell in humans, therefore, contains 23 chromosomes. There are free intermingling and segregation of what were originally maternal and paternal chromosomes, and the variant germ cells may contain all possible combinations in accord with the laws of chance. With a human's 46 chromosomes it has been estimated that some 17,000,000 different combinations are possible at the time of the reduction division.[1]

When one gene has a greater capability in producing its own effect than another, the former is dominant over the latter. In different pairs of alleles there will be found a wide spectrum of such dominance relationships. A completely dominant gene, by definition, will achieve the type effect regardless of the nature of its allele. An incompletely dominant gene acts in the direction of the type effect, but requires support from its allele to produce the full type. These are sometimes referred to as genes of *intermediate dominance*. A person who has a strongly dominant abnormal trait is usually heterozygous. The abnormal person has one dominant, abnormal gene (A) and one recessive, normal gene (n) for the trait under discussion. The individual shows the pathologic trait because the normal gene is suppressed. Such an individual has the genotype (An). If this individual has children by a person without the abnormal trait, the following offspring result:

Parents		(An)	×	(nn)	
Germ cells	A	n		n	n
Offspring	(An)	(An)		(nn)	(nn)

One half of the offpsring will be heterozygous and show the abnormal trait. The other half will be homozygous and normal.

There are some situations in which heterozygous individuals show the phenotype of both, and true dominance is not apparently manifested by either gene. The person with blood type AB is such an example. There are also genes that appear to have an intermediate dominance in their effect. The sickle cell hemoglobinopathies serve as a good example. The substitution of a single valine molecule for glutamic acid has already been noted as the cause for change in properties of the abnormal hemoglobin. The basic defect arises from a mutation in an autosomal gene. The heterozygous occurrence of the sickle gene is associated with a clinically benign course, even though 30% to 45% of the red cell hemoglobin is of the sickle type. Such a person is said to have "sickle cell trait." The homozygous individual with 100% abnormal hemoglobin suffers from a severe, chronic hemolytic anemia and has "sickle cell disease."

It may be of value to outline some characteristics of conditions inherited in a dominant manner. The dominant pathologic traits and diseases outnumber those due to recessive genes, and in contrast to these they have a tendency to a later age of onset and are less severe. They would naturally appear in more than one generation, but unless one percent has the disease they are seldom found in a subship, only one of the brothers and sisters usually have the condition. There is likely to be considerable variety among the affected members of a family with regard to degree or severity.[19] Marfan's syndrome and osteogenesis imperfecta are typical examples of dominant genes in heterozygotes.

A heterozygous individual with an abnormal recessive gene may appear normal owing to dominance of the normal gene. However, if that person has offspring by another heterozygous individual, one fourth of the progeny will display the abnormality and three fourths will carry the abnormal genotype. Assuming N to be the normal dominant and p the abnormal recessive gene, the pattern of heredity will be the following:

Parents	(Np)		×	(Np)	
Germ cells	N	p		N	p
Offspring	(NN)	(Np)		(Np)	(pp)

Only the genotype (pp) will show the abnormality. It is much more likely for such a pairing of abnormal recessive genes to take place in consanguineous marriages than in normal marriages

When a person who is homozygous for a pathologic trait marries a person with normal phenotype but heterozygous genotype for the same trait, one half of the children will be abnormal, and the other half will appear normal but will be carriers of the recessive pathologic trait. Such an example follows:

Parents	(Np)		×	(pp)	
Germ cells	N	p		p	p
Offspring	(Np)	(Np)		(pp)	(pp)

Superficially such a family (two generations only) may appear to represent a pattern of a dominant pathologic trait such as the first diagram showed. Only a careful and complete study of more than two generations will reveal the true state of affairs.

If a homozygous normal (NN) marries a homozygous individual with abnormal recessive genotype (pp), all the offspring will appear normal but will carry the abnormal trait.

Most of the so-called inborn errors of metabolism are due to recessive genes. In contrast to the characteristics of the dominant traits, these diseases are more severe and usually have an early age of onset, and the distribution within a family is such that several siblings are often affected. The victims of such diseases are often sterile or less fertile than the normal population. Phenylketonuria is such a condition. The child has a block in the synthesis of tyrosine from phenylalanine owing to the loss of activity of the enzyme system involved. There is an accumulation of phenylalanine and other precursors, apparently resulting in neurologic damage and some loss in pigment formation. If untreated, these children early in life manifest mental retardation and light hair and pale blue eyes. It is interesting to note that some heterozygotes, although showing no evidence of disease, when given a large intake of phenylalanine cannot convert it as completely or as rapidly to tyrosine as a normal individual. Here again we are probably dealing with a gene that is not completely recessive, just as some dominant genes are not completely dominant.

The mode of inheritance may be a guide in the analysis of the basic defect in genetic disorders. A gene-determined enzyme deficiency is likely to be reflected in the phenotype only when homozygogenicity exists. When the mutation concerns a nonenzyme protein, e.g., a structural protein like collagen, that change in the protein will very probably alter physical properties to such an extent as to produce a typical phenotype even though only half the protein is of the mutual type. This implies, as previously suggested, that all inborn errors of metabolism will be recessive and most purely anatomical errors will be dominant. There are some exceptions for the anatomical errors, but none for the biochemical or metabolic.[6]

Hereditary factors may depend on their expression upon a number of variables in addition to a gene. Diabetes mellitus is a good example of this. It is certainly a familial-oriented disease, yet the time of clinical onset, even in identical twins, will vary considerably. The environment in the form of infection, nutrition, or emotional stress may individually, or in combination, play a role in the final results of heredity.

Still another phenomenon is the quality of *pleiotropy*, that condition wherein a single gene has a number of different effects on different organ systems. Marfan's syndrome, previously mentioned, is such an example. Here a single mutant gene causes alterations in several organ systems. The tubular bones are elongated, the musculature is hypotonic, the subcutaneous fat is decreased, the lens of the eye is dislocated, retinal detachment is often found, and malformations of the aorta and aortic valves are frequently present.

It was previously mentioned that only 22 pairs of the human chromosomes are homologous. The remaining pair are the sex chromosomes. In the male these are unequal in size; the larger is designated X and the smaller Y. In the female they are equal, and both are termed X chromosomes. In reduction division in the male, one germ cell receives the X chromosome and one the Y chromosome. Fertilization may result in combination of X and Y and the production of a male, or the combination may be (XX), resulting in a female. Since the genes of the X chromosome in the male are not matched by an equal number of homologous genes in the smaller Y chromosomes, the genes in the former are in a unique position to exert influence on the developing organisms. Thus, recessive traits in the X chromosome of the male are not dominated by a corresponding gene in the Y chromosome. In the female such a recessive gene is usually overbalanced by its partner in the second X chromosome. Certain hereditary traits may therefore appear only in the male. Hemophilia and color blindness are well known examples of this pattern of sex-linked inheritance.

Mutation is defined as a permanent transmissable change in the character of an offspring from either of its parents that is brought about by a change in the gene through modification of DNA structure. Mutations have classically been attributed to DNA damage or misprocessing. Recent findings indicate that an additional cause is the presence of mobile genetic elements often present in large numbers in each cell.[20] Mutations result from changes in the sequence of the four bases that provide the informational content of DNA and also from deletion or addition of one of more base pairs. Such changes disrupt gene function and alter the encoding of protein synthesis. An example is the invasion of a chromosome by a virus, which may leave some of its own DNA or may destroy or delete some of the host's DNA. This popping in and out of chromosomes by DNA can have profound effects both in terms of the physical well-being of the individual (birth defects, cancer, etc.) and evolution of the species. Mutations of even greater extent affecting many, hundreds to thousands, of base pairs are termed chromosome mutations or abnormalities and will be described subsequently.

The complete set of hereditary factors (genes) as contained in the haploid assortment of chromosomes is the human *genome*. At present approximately 400 genes have been assigned to specific autosomes, another 115 to the X chromosome, and one to the Y chromosome. Assuming there are 100,000 genes in the human genome, it is evident that less than 1% have been mapped.[22] It must also be realized that there are large quantities of "genetic material" that do not code for specific proteins but may have other functions such as regulating the rate of activity of DNA and RNA, especially messenger RNA.

By special techniques the number and morphology of each of the 46 chromosomes can be ascertained in cells from many kinds of tissue. The term *karyotype* designates this mapping of the chromosomes. Deviations from the normal number, or the addition or subtraction of a portion of a chromosome, have been associated with clinical syndromes. In 1959 it was first reported that an individual with Down's syndrome had an extra autosomal chromosome, or a total of 47. Subsequently this was identified as trisomy 21 (the presence of three number 21 chromosomes). This is the most common autosomal abnormality in humans, with a frequency of 1 in 668 live births. Other examples of chromosomal polymorphism have been described, and in nearly every instance, this has resulted in gross abnormality. Retardation of both physical growth and mental development is quite characteristic, and all three germinal layers are usually involved. The severity of the involvement usually helps to distinguish these abnormalities from gene mutations.[15, 49, 50]

The sex chromosomes may similarly be involved in abnormalities.[51] Indications of such abnormalities were first appreciated from a study of cells in subjects with intersex problems. A deeply staining intranuclear body resting against the wall of the nucleus was seen in a large percentage of the cells from tissue of a normal female, whereas this structure was very rarely observed in male cells.[38] This heavily staining material has been designated *sex-chromatin body*. When this is absent, the individual has been termed *chromatin-negative*—a characteristic of the normal male's cells. It should be emphasized that this term is to be preferred to *sex-negative* or *male-somatotype* when referring to the chromatin body. The presence of two X chromosomes is necessary for the formation of chromatin-positive cells. The incidence of chromatin-positive cells from the buccal mucosa, the most frequently used source for these studies, may be significantly lower for the first three or four days of life in normal female infants. The reason for such a peculiarity is not known, but it indicates caution in the interpretation of such cells obtained before 5 days of age.

Klinefelter's syndrome is displayed by chromatin-positive phenotypic males. The external genitalia appear to be those of a normal male, but during adolescence gynecomastia appears and female distribution of pubic hair occurs. These individuals are sterile due to aspermatogenesis secondary to atrophic and sclerotic changes in the small testes. The urine contains an increased amount of gonadotropins (follicle-stimulating hormone). Studies have revealed that 47 chromosomes are present, with the extra one being a sex chromosome (XXY).

Turner's syndrome is characterized by moderate dwarfism, lack of sexual development at the expected time of puberty, and often other abnormalities such as congenital webbing of the neck, cubitus valgus, and mental retardation. The appearance of the external genitalia is female. These individuals have chromatin-negative cells and a karyotype with 45 chromosomes, the single sex chromosome being X (usually designated XO). The ovaries are rudimentary and do not contain normal follicular structures. (See also chapter 13).

As another example of syndromes displayed by persons with abnormal karyotypes, we can mention the clinical picture of combined Klinefelter's syndrome and Down's syndrome. As could be predicted, these persons have an extra autosome, and the sex formula is XXY, with a total of 48 chromosomes present.

Most geneticists explain the variations in chromosome number as being a result of a mechanism known as *nondisjunction*. In preparation for division of the cell, duplicate chromosomes align on the equatorial plate. Then they separate, and members of each pair go to opposite poles. If nondisjunction occurs, both chromosomes of the pair go to the same pole, resulting in an extra chromosome in one of the daughter cells and a deficiency in the other daughter cell. If this unequal division takes place during the formation of gametes, either in mitosis of ancestral cells or during meiosis, the abnormality is passed on to the next generation.

In some patients with chromosomal abnormalities, the abnormality will be demonstrable in only one type of cell. Cultures of white blood cells might demonstrate an abnormal number, while cultures from skin or mucosa would be normal in the same individual. Such a phenomenon is known as *mosaicism*. Most often, all cells are similar in their chromosome content.

The following outline may be helpful in describing some of the presently known chromosomal abnormalities and examples of the associated syndromes.[13, 54]

Aneuploidy—abnormal number of chromosomes

    Monosomes—absence of one pair of chromosomes (Turner's syndrome XO; most autosomal deletions are lethal)

    Trisomy—triplicate chromosomes (Down's syndrome and Klinefelter's syndrome; trisomies 13 and 18 are severe and usually fatal within a year.

    Polyploidy—more than one added chromosome (few live born with autosomal excess; some live with excess sex chromosomes as in XXXY Klinefelter's syndrome)

Structural—abnormal morphology

    Deletion—absence of part of chromosome 5 in cri-du-chat syndrome; absence of part of chromosome 18 in syndrome associated with microcephaly, mental retardation, and abnormal facial features

    Translocation—portion of one chromosome attached to another (Down's syndrome)

    Inversion—following two breaks a new alignment of the segments (rare and difficult to prove, but possible)

    Isochromosomes—horizontal instead of vertical division with fusion of the two long and the two short arms (mostly sex chromosome anomalies)

It has been estimated that the frequency of the most common chromosomal abnormalities in a live newborn population is as follows[2]:

Aneuploidy	2.0 per 1,000
Translocation	2.5 per 1,000
Trisomy	1.0 per 1,000

From the experience of one clinic, the causes of major congenital anomalies consisted of 50% chromosomal, 30% unknown, 14% dominant autosomal gene, 3% drug induced and 1% recessive autosomal gene.[34] Due to the difficulty of obtaining an accurate history, it is emphasized that the anomalies due to drugs may actually be considerably larger. By far the most common malformation was Down's syndrome, which made up 43% of the 768-patient total.

Of 100 fertilized eggs, only approximately 31 will end in a live-born baby. Most of the 69 lost are abnormal and one quarter to one half have chromosomal abnormalities. The earlier in the pregnancy the abortion occurs, the more likely the association with an abnormal chromosome. Gross malformations have been reported in up to 30% of abortuses and stillborn infants. Of viable newborn infants, approximately 4% will have structural malformations, e.g., cleft palate or meningocele. The minimal expected frequency of chromosomal errors in a newborn population will be between 5% to 8% of which 10% will be phenotypically normal and not identifiable at birth, e.g., trisomies XYY and XXX.[4, 5, 40, 53, 54]

Another approach to this confusion of numbers and an aid in understanding the nomenclature is the following table[42]:

BIRTH DEFECT CATEGORY	INCIDENCE IN LIVE-BORN
Structural malformation	1 per 20
Mental retardation	1 per 30
Genetic disorders	1 per 100
Chromosomal errors	1 per 200
Congenital deafness	1 per 1,000
Congenital blindness	1 per 7,000

The fact that slightly different figures are given by different authors probably reflects the particular population studied. Of the children with major structural malformations, nearly half will have significant degrees of mental retardation.

Although we have used as examples mainly pathologic traits, the same rules hold for variations of normal traits. Through the processes of blending and the additive effects of genes, each individual has a great tendency to follow a predestined pattern of growth and development that is very similar for all children. Although considerable variation does occur, the more or less common design that is inherited by the vast majority of persons is extremely important to realize. In studying the abnormal subject, one is apt to forget the equally fascinating normal subject. The inheritance of the urge to grow normally and the overall similarity of development among children have received little attention from a hereditary standpoint. The problem is indeed complex, but the implications are great.

The physical resemblance of family members is too well known to merit extended comment. There exists a fairly high correlation with regard to stature and weight of siblings, and there is evidence that rates of growth are more alike among siblings than among nonrelated individuals. In certain families accelerated growth and early maturation are the rule, while in others growth is slow and maturation is delayed. For stature, sitting height, and head length and breadth, the correlation between monozygotic twins is higher than between fraternal twins and between siblings. These dimensions tend to hold true even when the twins are reared apart. Such a relation does not hold for weight.[11]

The search for size factors in mammals has shown that various genes are pleiotropic in their effects, affecting size as well as some other characteristic. There are some types of dwarfism and giantism in which inheritance is perfectly marked and definite.[49] (These are described in some detail in chapter 13.) Most important for the physician to remember is that some children are small because of their genetic constitutions and not because they have endocrine or nutritional disturbances and that other children may be of above average size or development because of heredity. In some cases only a careful study of the child and family will reveal that heredity can offer the only explanation for seeming abnormalities.

From studies of sex chromosome abnormalities, it appears that the Y chromosome confers extra stature. Children and adults with Turner's syndrome are abnormally short. The XYY male is often in excess of 6 ft tall, and the addition of further Y chromosomes has further similar influence. Along with the height increase, there is often an associated aggressive personality with antisocial behavior.[11]

Since different populations, even within a single geographic or national area, are subject to much variability in their environment, it is difficult to determine the degree of the effect of the genotype upon growth. American white and black children ultimately reach the same height and weight as adults. Their rates of growth and body proportions will differ slightly. The Japanese child will never have the relatively long legs of the white child, let alone the even longer legs of the native African. Thus, we must conclude that there are indeed subtle but definite racial differences in the pattern of growth.[10]

The role of genetics in the development of mental characteristics, especially intelligence, is a hotly debated subject. A recent review of familial studies of intelligence included 111 valid reports accumulated from the world's literature. That the data support the inference of genetic determination of IQ is indisputable. The correlations are consistent with a polygenic mode of inheritance, but in addition, there is a marked degree of heterogeneity of the correlations within family groupings.[91] The effects of severe malnutrition, illness, and socioeconomic disadvantage on both intellectual and physical development have been and will be referred to many times. Delinquent behavior, mental retardation, and tall stature in phenotypic males with XYY chromosomes is an example of a rare but well recognized entity. In two studies of American children of superior intelligence, favorable parental, social, and educational backgrounds were found to be the best correlates.[72, 73] Personality characteristics, such as timidity, self-esteem, and aggressiveness, are probably more strongly influenced by environment than heredity.

Prenatal Environment

It has been estimated that in the normal prenatal period 44 successive cell divisions take place and that an equivalent of only four additional divisions is necessary to change the newborn to adult size. The velocity of cell multiplication is particularly rapid in the first eight weeks, during which time the zygote is converted into the fetus, an organism possessing all of the essential features of an adult human being. Although the genes may be said to contain the plan of the future organism, this plan can be variously modified by environment. Differentiation, for instance, does not depend on genes alone. The type of cell developing in a certain part is determined by the close interaction of the nuclear material (containing the genes) with the internal (nucleus plus cytoplasm) and the external environments. Development consists of countless physiochemical processes. Whether the genes act as enzymes or catalysts, their normal mode of behavior depends on the presence of a normal cytoplasm and a normal external environment. So integrally related are inherent and environmental influences that it is impossible, except under controlled experimental conditions, to differentiate their respective contributions to the development of an organism.

Anomalies of the environment or of the genes may lead to faulty development or to malformations. Certain genetic as well as environmental changes may, therefore, result in a very similar congenital defect. It should be emphasized that it is not a simple matter to classify a given congenital anomaly as "hereditary" or "nonhereditary." Between conception and birth the growing organism may be injured by many external factors. If injury occurs during the embryonic period, the result is arrest of development and often irreparable malformation. During the fetal period (ninth week to birth), injuries result in changes more closely resembling those of postnatal damage, such as mutilations and scars. Apparently the various organs are more sensitive to noxious agents at the time of rapid differentiation or maturation that occurs during the embryonic period than they are later. The following prenatal environment factors include most of those either established or suspected of having important influences during pregnancy: (1) nutritional, (2) mechanical, (3) chemical, (4) endocrine, (5) actinic, (6) infection, (7) immune reactions, (8) anoxia, and (9) thermal.

The epidemiology of spina bifida (including myelomeningocele and anencephalus) is an excellent example of some of the difficulties in determining the cause of the malformation. The occurrence of this condition is four to five times more frequent in Wales and some other areas of the British Isles than in the United States. One study indicated the mothers of children with this abnormality grew up under less favorable conditions than a control group of similar age and gestational history.[76] Another study noted that these less favorable conditions included poor nutrition with particular emphasis on folic acid deficiency.[77] The expected recurrence of the malformation appeared to be reduced in women who supplemented their diet with folic acid. Recurrence of the malformation also appeared to be reduced if the mother migrated from the specified areas in the British Isles to the United States. Such a migration may have resulted in improved diet and other environmental factors. There appears to be no genetic cause. It is concluded that "the multifactorial model involving environmental agents interacting with a polygenic predisposition . . . seems the most reasonable model," but the main factor is environmental.[78]

Warkany has been able to produce congenital anomalies in animals by feeding the pregnant mothers diets severely deficient in certain vitamins.[16] The types of malformation could be predicted by the omission of a specific vitamin. Poor diet during pregnancy can result in a high incidence of stillbirths and neonatal deaths. When malnutrition becomes sufficiently severe, conception is prevented altogether. In this regard one might quote Joseph Warkany, who said; "The most serious congenital malformation is never to be conceived at all."

In the discussion of the low birth weight infant (see chapter 5), it will be pointed out that small infants are born to small mothers who come from lower socioeconomic groups. It may well be that the mother's growth during childhood might have a very great influence on her offspring, regardless of the social stratum she occupies at the time of her pregnancy.

Mechanical factors, particularly abnormalities of fetal position, have been associated with congenital malformations as clubfoot, sirenomelia, anencephaly, limb reduction, renal angenesis, and anal atresia. Such conditions as twinning, bicornuate uterus, short umbilical cord, septate uterus, early loss of amniotic fluid, and oligohydramnios may cause constraint malformations.[3] The frequency of aberrations in morphogenesis is increased in twins as compared with singletons, especially so in monozygotic twins.[25] Occasionally in twins, placental positioning and umbilical cord development will result in a much richer supply of essential nutrients to one of the twins at the expense of the other. This may result in great dissimilarity of size at the time of birth. Death of one twin may permit thromboplastin to enter the circulation and cause disseminated intravascular coagulation in the living twin resulting in such conditions as intestinal atresia, microcephaly, hydrocephalus, and restricted growth of various parts of the body.

When there is considerable difference in the sizes of twins the smaller one may follow a growth pattern in which he or she remains relatively small all of his or her life and, in addition, may suffer some degree of mental retardation.[58]

At the time the first edition of this book was published in 1951, there was little solid evidence that chemical agents might act as teratogenic factors in humans, although this was a well-established fact in experimental animals. Now a long list of chemical agents has been shown to cause some degree of intrauterine abnormality, from severe malformation to mild growth retardation.[16, 66, 67] In some instances, the exposure in utero may become manifested years later, as in the occurrence of adenocarcinoma of the vagina in young women exposed to stilbestrol administered to their mothers during the pregnancy. The most notorious of these agents is thalidomide, which may cause a number of severe defects in the fetus if taken early in pregnancy. Among the malformations reported are phocomelia, heart defects, and anomalies of the brain and special sensory organs. Harelip, cleft palate, hydrocephalus, and cranial dysostosis have followed the use of a number of cancer chemotherapeutic drugs, such as aminopterin and the nitrogen mustards.[39] Tetracycline causes less severe changes including mildly retarded skeletal growth and staining of primary teeth with varying degrees of poor enamel formation. Many other drugs and chemicals could be added. The factors involved in the manner and degree of response include dosage, the developmental stage of the embryo or fetus, and the duration of exposure to the potential teratogen.[52]

Exposure of the fetus to the commonly used narcotics, e.g., heroin and morphine, is often associated with intrauterine growth retardation, prematurity, and postdelivery withdrawal symptoms in the infant. Congenital anomalies do not appear to be increased in frequency. A very interesting observation is that mothers who had used heroin only prior to pregnancy also had babies of low birth weight. Infants born to mothers on methadone maintenance during pregnancy also were of lower than average weight, but were significantly less severely affected than infants whose mothers abused heroin.[69]

Children of heroin-addicted mothers and of methadone-maintained mothers have a significant incidence of head circumferences below the third percentile at birth. By age 3 years the size returns to normal. Poor fine motor coordination, poor social adjustment abilities, but near normal psychometric test scores were present in these children observed as preschoolers (ages 3 to 6). The prenatal condition of the mother, prenatal care, and home environment were more predictive of neurobehavioral problems than the degree of narcotic use by the mother in recent evaluations of the children.[79, 80]

Low birth weight and brain malformations associated with varying degrees of mental retardation and physical abnormalities (e.g., microcephaly, small palpebral fissures, strabismus, upturned nose, absent or reduced philtrum, nail hypoplasia, and hirsutism) have been described as frequent consequences of alcoholism during pregnancy. Even moderate alcohol consumption resulted in smaller newborns but without the more serious developmental problems. Furthermore, a history of maternal alcoholism poses a risk to fetal growth independent of alcohol use during pregnancy. Ethanol is the most common teratogen causing mental retardation in the United States and Europe.[62, 81] Immune deficiency is another problem found in children suffering from the fetal alcohol syndrome.[82]

Smoking during pregnancy increases the risks of premature delivery, decreased birth weight, increased perinatal mortality, and increased chance of spontaneous abortion. The exact cause of these risks is not known but has been postulated as due to nicotine-caused vasoconstriction resulting in relative placental insufficiency or the resultant carbon monoxide increase in maternal blood causing relative hypoxia in the fetus, or a combination of the two. All of the listed risks are proportionate to the amount of smoking measured in the number of cigarettes consumed per day. There is some difference of opinion as to the long-term effect of smoking on future growth, some studies finding little residual effect as soon as eight months and others contending retarded growth lasts at least for eight years.[62, 83] No congenital malformations have been attributed to the use of tobacco.

Women who worked during the third trimester gave birth to newborns who weighed 150 to 400 gm less than the control group who remained at home. The growth retardation was greatest when women were underweight pregravid and had a low pregnancy weight gain and when the work required standing. The frequency of placental infarcts increased when women continued standing work into late gestation.[84]

Hyperthermia, a well-known teratogenic factor in animals, has recently been described in humans. The causes of hyperthermia in the cases studied ranged from febrile illnesses to prolonged hot tub or sauna bathing. The temperatures recorded exceeded 40 C and occurred from 4 to 14 weeks after conception. All of the subjects showed signs of mental deficiency, hypotonicity, or other evidence of central nervous system damage and many had structural abnormalities, especially of the head and face.[85]

Pregnancies maintained at high altitudes are known to lead to newborn infants of a lower mean size than the average population.

In many instances where a specific environmental influence has been cited as giving rise to a cause-and-effect phenomenon, it is often difficult, if not impossible, to eliminate important socioeconomic factors with their additional influence upon the fetus. To illustrate the complexity of the problem with a single example: a pregnant narcotic addict is often the recipient of poor prenatal care, is subject to many infections, and suffers from malnutrition.

Although endocrine factors may harmfully affect the fetus, few well-substantiated reports of such cases can be found in the literature. Endemic cretinism is more probably the result of an iodine deficiency in the maternal diet than the result of endocrine influence. Mothers suffering from hypothyroidism and Addison's disease have borne apparently normal children when under proper therapy. The adrenogenital syndrome is caused by excessive androgenic hormone production from the adrenal cortex. In the female the effect of this hormone leads to anomalies of the external genitalia with hypertrophy of the clitoris and often the formation of a common urogenital tract into which both the vagina and urethra open. The term "pseudohermaphrodite" has been used for this condition but should more properly be applied to a purely anatomical variant unassociated with the adrenogenital syndrome. Virilizing tumors of the adrenals or ovary and administration of androgenic hormones as well as the synthetic progestins have resulted in masculinizing the genitalia of female infants.

Infants of diabetic mothers have greater morbidity than infants of nondiabetics. Both insulin-dependent and gestational (chemically) diabetic women's infants may experience an increased risk of macrosomnia (birth weight often in excess of 4 kg, or 9 lb), hypoglycemia, respiratory distress, heart failure, and hyperbilirubinemia. The incidence of serious congenital anomalies is four times higher for the newborns of diabetic mothers compared with the nondiabetic. The most frequent anomalies involve the neural tube and cardiovascular system. The better the metabolic control of the diabetes the less the chance of morbidity. If the diabetes is in an advanced stage (according to White's classification) the potential of complications increases.[8, 24]

The average age of mothers at the birth of infants with Down's syndrome, Klinefelter's syndrome, and some other congenital anomalies is significantly greater than that of mothers at the birth of normal children. It will be recalled that in both of those syndromes there is an extra chromosome (trisomy), an autosome in Down's syndrome and typically XXY in Klinefelter's syndrome. In the karyotypes of adults' blood there is an increasing frequency of abnormalities with age beginning in the mid-thirties, most often aneuploid cells involving the sex chromosome. These changes are very prominent by the fifth and sixth decades. These findings parallel the occurrence of Down's syndrome in the general population where the incidence is 1 in 700 live births to women in their twenties, 1 in 365 in their mid-thirties, and 1 in 30 in their mid-forties.[24, 54]

Older paternal age is a major factor relative to the frequency of fresh gene mutation in humans. As with Down's syndrome related to female aging, there is a ten-fold increase in the occurrence of certain specific anomalies (e.g., achondroplasia, hemophilia A, Apert's syndrome, Marfan's syndrome, and other craniofacial malformations) in families as the father passes from the third to the sixth decade.[68] There are over 600,000 infants born to adolescent mothers each year in the United States, accounting for just under 20% of the total live births. In 1978, 32% of these births were out of wedlock in the 15- to 19-year-old age group and 87% out of wedlock at the 15-year-old level. Many studies have indicated that young teenaged mothers are at greater risk of having preterm deliveries, low birth weight infants, stillbirths, and neonatal deaths than postadolescent mothers.[87, 88] The younger the mother the greater the risks. Careful evaluation of these pregnancies indicates that with the exception of mothers 15 years old and less the poor outcomes are not related to the age of the mother but to other factors. Among these are poor nutritional status of the mother throughout pregnancy with competition from growth needs of young mothers and the developing fetus. Adverse social conditions, low income, and low social class often result in poor prenatal care, often none until term. The unmarried status of many may augment the self-neglect. Smoking and narcotic use are commonly found among these adolescent girls predisposing to prematurity and small infant size. Iron deficiency anemia is one of the most common nutritional deficiencies seen in this age group. Preeclampsia (pregnancy-induced hypertension) is particularly prevalent among socioeconomically depressed teenage pregnancies regardless of ethnic background. The adolescent is at a slightly greater risk of having a baby with a birth defect than is a woman 20 to 30 years of age. Most frequent among the defects are those involving the neural tube.[86–88]

The growth retardation evident in the newborns of very young mothers disappears during childhood, usually by seven years, if there are no further complications. Although the data on the psychosocial outcome of these children are sparse, it would appear the intellectual, developmental, and educational expectations have been lower than those born to older mothers. Some evidence indicates that test scores at seven years increase with increasing maternal age.[87, 88]

Injudicious use of radium or roentgen ray therapy during pregnancy has resulted in malformation of the fetus. Microcephaly, spina bifida, mental retardation, and deformities of the extremities have been described in such instances.[16, 36, 46]

A tragic lesson concerning the effects of atomic radiation on the fetus was learned at Hiroshima, Japan.[18] If exposure to the atomic blast took place within the first 20 weeks of gestation and the mother was within 1,200 meters of the hypocenter, the chances of delivering a normal baby were indeed small. Seven of 11 mothers so exposed delivered children with diagnoses of microcephaly and mental retardation. Other anomalies in other fetuses less severely exposed because of greater distance from the hypocenter included congenital dislocation of the hip, congenital malformations of the eyes, congenital heart disease, and Down's syndrome. Children who were exposed in utero and who did not show immediate evidence of anomalies at birth have often shown subsequent slower physical growth than controls, as indicated by a low value for height, weight, and head circumference.[57] A study of children exposed to heavy fallout on the Marshall Islands revealed that nine years later growth was retarded, as well as skeletal maturation, if they had been under age 5 years at the time of exposure.[56] It is of considerable interest, and also curious to note, that in both of these observations boys were more affected than girls.

Although the fetus is susceptible to a number of viral infections, relatively few of the hundreds to which humans are constantly exposed are transmitted to the fetus. Bacterial infections rarely, if ever, cross the placental barrier, though they may infect the uterine contents as an ascending process through the lower reproductive tract. Viral agents that have been associated with abortion, stillbirth, intrauterine infection, or congenital malformation are given in the following table with their most frequent effect.[14, 17, 64, 65]

VIRAL AGENT	DISEASE
Influenza	Abortion
Mumps	Abortion
Rubella	Abortion
Vaccinia	Congenital infection
	Congenital malformations of heart, eyes, ears, brain
	Abortion
	Congenital vaccinia
Varicella-zoster	
Poliovirus	
Echovirus	Congenital infections
Coxsackievirus	
Equine encephalitis	
Cytomegalovirus	Congenital infection
	Microcephaly
	Deafness
	Mental retardation

Cytomegalovirus is the leading cause of congenital viral infection with an incidence of about 1% in all live births. Clinically this may be inapparent in the neonatal period. Some 5% to 10% have the more virulent form with hepatitis, petechiae, jaundice, and death. Late complications develop among those who survive. Among 10% with subclinical infections will subsequently develop varying degrees of central nervous system disorders and deafness. The reason for the wide variability in symptoms and severity of sequelae is unknown. When rubella is not epidemic, the cytomegalovirus is the most common infectious cause of mental retardation and deafness as congenital lesions. Infection resulting from primary maternal infection during pregnancy is more likely to be serious than from a recurrent infection. Like individuals infected by other members of the herpesvirus family, a large percentage of adult population have experienced a symptomless infection and this may occur during pregnancy.[17]

There is some question of the association of the herpesviruses and coxsackieviruses with true congenital anomalies. Only those infections during the first trimester are apt to cause morphologic abnormalities, but later periods of infection may result in low birth weight and delayed physical and mental development.

Toxoplasmosis, as a prenatal infection during the first months of pregnancy, may cause the classic triad of chorioretinitis, cerebral calcification, and hydrocephaly. It has been estimated that approximately 2% of severe mental retardation in the United States is the result of congenital toxoplasmosis. Congenital syphilis, which had nearly disappeared following World War II, has recently increased in incidence along with other venereal diseases. The spirochete is transmitted by hematogenous spread across the placenta. If promptly recognized and adequately treated, no sequelae result.

The ability of the fetus to respond to these infections with the production of specific immunoglobulins, such as IgM and others, is of utmost importance diagnostically and will be given further consideration in chapter 7.

The conditions of erythroblastosis and kernicterus due to red blood cell incompatibility between fetus and mother are so well known that they need be discussed but briefly. In barest outline, the fetus inherits a blood type (Rh, A, B, AB, etc.) that differs from the mother's type. If cells from the fetus enter the mother's bloodstream, or if she has been previously sensitized by transfusion, antibodies to the fetal red cells are produced, which then cross the placental barrier and cause hemolysis. Hyperbilirubinemia and some anemia as well as other pathologic changes result. If these changes are of sufficient degree, especially the hyperbilirubinemia, permanent damage may result, with the brain being especially susceptible (kernicterus).

Regional and seasonal variations in the occurrence of some congenital anomalies have been reported, as well as a suggested increase in their incidence in the lower socioeconomic classes. It must be admitted that no single major cause of developmental defects has been found.

Parity, or order of birth of the child, may affect size at time of delivery as well as some aspects of intellectual functioning later in life. The average birth weight increases with increasing order, i.e., the birth weight and linear dimensions of the firstborn are less than those of subsequent infants. The weight of infants of parity order 5 averages about 100 gm more than that of infants of parity 2 to 4.

A study of the relation of birth order and family size to intellectual competence was made of the total population of 19-year-old men of the Netherlands.[63] For both mean family size and birth order, there was a consistent gradient in the level of performance: as the test scores became poorer, mean family size and birth order became progressively larger. These results were obtained in all of three social groups into which the subjects were divided.

The effects of racial differences upon birth weight are often difficult to assess because of additional factors that may be involved. These include nutritional habits of the mothers, adequacy of perinatal care, and geographic differences. The frequency of low birth weight (less than 2,500 gm) in various areas of the world is briefly discussed in chapter 5. Within the boundaries of the United States, the incidence of low birth weight babies is approximately twice as great in blacks as in whites. Among primiparous mothers, the mean birth weight is roughly 250 gm greater for white compared with black infants. A gestational period that averages eight days less in the black mother is an important contributing factor to this difference.[75]

The relationship between size at birth and size at a later age, including the adult, has received considerable attention. Illingworth,[41] in a study of English children, found a fairly high correlation between birth height and weight and height and weight at subsequent ages through the 14th year. The children with the smallest birth weight tended to remain the smallest, and this was especially true in early childhood. Many investigators have found that the smallest of the low birth weight infants (whether premature or not) remain small throughout all of their childhood. Falkner concluded that the size of the newborn and infant, excluding low birth weight infants, is not strongly related to size in the future. However, after any prenatal influences have largely been eliminated, there is a good correlation between height at age 2 or 3 years and adult height.[44] Such factors as socioeconomic environment or frequency and severity of illness have seldom been studied for their possible effects upon final size. In one study[45] of low birth weight infants, it was found that the mothers were significantly shorter than the control group of mothers who delivered babies of normal size. It was also found that the low weight infant is more frequently born into a low socioeconomic group, further jeopardizing his or her changes of optimal growth and development. In summary, birth length relates predominantly to maternal height, and by 2 years of age and thereafter, the length or height correlates best to the mean parental height (see chapter 4).[71]

In chapter 3, on fetal growth and development, other important points not discussed here receive consideration. We have attempted to show in the foregoing paragraphs that nothing is produced by the genes without intracellular and intercellular factors playing an important role. Anyone desiring to understand completely the growth and development of chidlren must be aware of this interesting field in which new observations are constantly modifying old concepts and perhaps pointing to new potentialities in the realm of practical therapeutics.

Postnatal Environment

Environment after birth may be varied in so many ways that well-controlled studies are exceedingly difficult to make. Most of our knowledge is based on very gross differences that are easily apparent. Children vary in their potentialities for modification. These remain used or unused to the extent that the environment offers opportunity for their realization. As mentioned in chapter 1, the human organism has a long period of immaturity that gives time for the development of many qualities, good and bad, necessary or detrimental to survival.

Children are not all alike, and consequently we cannot expect exactly similar responses to similar changes in environment either in single individuals or in groups of individuals. Further, we know that the continuity of growth implies a resistance to displacement (both mental and physical) and a tendency to restoration of the normal pattern of development for a given child. An excellent example of this is shown by the premature infant. Early in life its measurements of physical growth are below those of the term infant, but in a relatively short time there is little difference between them, and thereafter the growth of one parallels that of the other for all practical purposes. Differences in nutrition or environment may either speed up or slow down the period before equality is reached, but the tendency to convergence toward average trends will always hold.

Some of the more clearly understood environmental factors are discussed here; others are considered in the chapters that follow.

Geographic variations appear to be of little importance within the boundaries of the United States. Mills[9] has stated that children living in tropical regions show retarded growth and inferior adult size. However, since such children frequently suffer from poor diets and other poor socioeconomic factors, one can doubt that climate alone is responsible for the differences noted. Mills also found that full sexual maturity is reached later in the tropical and frigid zones than in the temperate zones. We feel that this statement needs further clarification. Among Filipino girls born and raised in tropical conditions and receiving good nutrition and medical care the average age of menarche was just over 13 years, which compares very favorably with average American girls. The observations of Ellis[26] and Tanner[27] support the fact that climate has little effect on adolescent development.

There is considerable evidence to show that the growth rates of weight and height are influenced by the seasons of the year and that these differences are particularly striking in older children. Growth rates in weight are at a minimum in the spring and early summer and are maximal during late summer and autumn. Conversely, growth in height is greatest in the spring in this country.[74]

Measurements of infants born in a poor socioeconomic group are in general inferior to similar measurements of infants born in a high socioeconomic group. In many countries throughout Europe and in this country it has been shown that the stature of adult laborers is inferior to that of students, who presumably represent a more prosperous group. The rate of growth of children both of whose parents were unemployed was found to be inferior to that of children with one employed parent. Thus, socioeconomic factors are of great importance in determining the physical status of children.[7, 10] In the 1940s the growth and development of American-born Japanese children in California were compared with those of children of the same sex and age in Japan. There was a striking superiority in regard to weight, height, and skeletal age for the California-born children. Inferior diet and other unfavorable environmental conditions found in Japan at that time undoubtedly were responsible.[47] A contemporary study indicates no differences between American-born and Japanese-born Japanese children.[10]

Although ill health is generally acknowledged to be more common in poor adults than their more fortunate peers, the relationship between poverty and health in childhood is poorly documented. A recent study in the state of Maryland showed that the prevalence and severity of illness, both acute and chronic, are greater in the poor children than in the nonpoor. Even more pronounced was the evidence for consistently greater severity of problems or likelihood of sequelae among poor children.[89]

There is also an increasing accumulation of evidence that mental development is related to socioeconomic factors. The concept that some children are functioning at substandard levels because of faulty nutrition and other adverse environmental conditions is relatively new. Whether actual intelligence is influenced or whether it is the ability to use the inherited potentialities that is affected remains to be proved. Another point to be considered is the possibility that genetic potentialities are such that the child born in the lowest socioeconomic group has less chance to raise himself or herself above this level than the child born in a better environment. The important point introduced by several studies is that children's behavior should be interpreted with a knowledge of the interrelation of growth and organic development. As we will repeat again and again, significant advances in the study of child development can be made only with a careful correlation of all of the apparently isolated facts.

Over the past century or more, there has been a general trend toward increases in height and weight with each succeeding generation in the more developed nations.[27, 28, 30] This trend has been noted within the first few months of life and persists throughout the entire growing period. For example, selecting boys aged 14 with similar ethnic backgrounds and living in the United States, in 1877 the average height was 145 cm and weight 39 kg; by 1920 they were 155 cm and 45 kg and in 1970 they were 163 cm and 51 kg, respectively. The average height and weight of the United States Army recruit was 4 cm and 4.5 kg greater in World War II than in World War I.

The secular trend in physical growth has been paralleled by a similar trend of the age of menarche. Tanner[27, 90] gathered statistics from several northern European countries and found considerable similarity in all. In the period from 1850 to 1950 there was an average decrease in age of the first menses from around 16 to 13.5 years. In the United States one study indicated the average age at menarche in 1900 was 14.5 years and at present is 13 years in the same geographic area.[29] In the second half of the 19th century in England the difference in age at menarche between the well off and the poor was about one year and in Germany was 18 months. In the United States the difference in ages between the well off and the poor was about one year in 1890. The adolescent spurt in growth occurs sooner and final stature is attained at an earlier age than was true 100 years ago. As menarche occurs at an earlier age, so menopause occurs at a later one.[59, 60]

These changes in growth have been noted over a period of at least 100 years. The beginning may be marked by the emergence from the lowest levels of the Industrial Revolution. For the countries that are more fortunate in terms of good health care, there is some evidence that the trend is slowing and perhaps near-optimal levels have been reached. There appears to be little difference in the average figures for height in children in the United States today as compared with a generation ago.

In both humans and lower animals the capacity for growth is very great. If the rate of growth in a child is retarded temporarily, as by illness from infection, starvation, or hypothyroidism, and this is corrected, an accelerated rate of growth then takes place. This rate may exceed normal for height and skeletal maturation by three- or four-fold. Once the child's normal levels have been attained, the velocity decreases to that which had been present before the illness.[55] If interference with statural growth takes place over a long period of time, this is usually accompanied by a similar delay in bone maturation, resulting in an actual lengthening of the growing period. If a child is held at a constant weight by underfeeding, he or she will again gain weight if no further decrease in food intake occurs. Such studies portray the tremendous impetus to grow and develop despite adverse environmental conditions. They re-emphasize the resistance to displacement from an average trend.[12]

Exercise may also be an important factor in the complete picture of development and growth. Growth processes are inseparable from dynamic processes, and physiologic activity of protoplasm favors its further development. The disuse atrophy and weakness of an immobilized limb are examples of this important principle. The development of "skills" through practice might serve as still another illustration.

Practical Applications

It is no longer believed that the child has inherited certain traits as finished products. What the child does inherit is a large assortment of genes that determine his or her make-up. Each of the many genes influences some particular part of the developing embryo and child. From the time of conception until death each phase of development is influenced by the interplay of the inherited genes and the many environmental factors whose roles begin at fertilization. Growth, both mental and physical, is constantly creating its own new conditions as it proceeds. In appraising development we must consider all factors: family tree, cultural milieu, siblings, sickness, nutrition, sunshine, education, and all other possible influences.

Since a new combination of genes is formed with every child, there may be great diversity among siblings or between parents and the child. However, in general it may be stated that the child will show genetic characteristics similar to those of relatives if he or she comes from a distinctly superior or inferior family. But there is no such thing as certainty in predicting the characteristics of children from knowledge of the family, with the possible exceptions of some of the congenital anomalies previously mentioned in which the mode of inheritance is known.[6]

If a child is born with a deficient genetic constitution, a change in environment will not go far toward improving him or her. On the other hand, individuals with superior gene combinations are precisely those who may take advantage of the opportunities that environment presents to them. Still other individuals seem to have inherited strong tendencies in particular directions. Here environment may have a good effect by assisting in the further development of the beneficial tendencies and/or repressing undesirable ones.

With increasing knowledge and improvements in technics more and more congenital anomalies are subject to remedy or improvement. However, therapeutic measures and environmental correction cannot cure defectiveness of genes. Nature's frequent remedy for this situation is to "neutralize" the defective genes by pairing them with normal genes from the other parent. The fact remains, however, that they are carried to future generations. The only method of preventing this is to prevent propagation by the individuals who carry the defect. It can be seen that the problem becomes extremely complex when the physician is confronted with a request for advice regarding adoption or advisability of parenthood. The interested reader should consult the references at the end of this chapter for further discussion of these very real problems.

The human may be considered the most successful product of biologic evolution so far. From an obscure beginning as a rare animal in an isolated area, most probably Africa, humans multiplied to become one of the most numerous of mammals. Although numbers may not be an unaltered blessing, they are an important measure of biologic success. In humans alone, adaptation can occur through alteration of culture as well as by natural selection. Technology not only has improved environment (e.g., heat and clothing) but has permitted persistence and increase of abnormal genes (e.g., diabetes mellitus), neither of which was in the realm of any creature before humans. Regulation of population size cannot be postponed much longer, and the genetic problem will have to be met. As Dobzhansky[48] has written, "The question how many people and what kind of people will be solved together, if they are solved at all."

Summary of the Factors That Influence Growth

Genetics	This may influence the response of end organs to all sorts of stimuli, e.g., hormones, nutrients, and external environment. In addition it may influence growth profoundly through congenital malformations of the end organ, as in achondroplasia.
Nutrition	This may include quantitative and qualitative amounts of the building materials, i.e., protein, carbohydrate, fats, minerals, and vitamins. Nutrition may also be influenced by diseases of the gastrointestinal tract, e.g., diarrhea and celiac disease. Finally, local or general nutritional failure may result from circulatory changes such as congenital heart disease.
Internal milieu	Optimal growth presupposes normal function of all organs and normal metabolism. Severe liver or kidney insufficiencies are examples of conditions that preclude normal growth due to impairment of tissue metabolism of all parts of the body.
Hormones	Secretions of the endocrine glands act as catalysts to the normal growth

potentials of the body. Some are growth-promoting, as the pituitary growth-stimulating hormone and androgens. Others cause maturation: thyroid hormone, androgens, and estrogens. Some may be antagonistic to growth but useful in other ways when in proper balance—the adrenal glucocorticoids, for example.

Environment   Severe disease may influence ultimate growth. There are definite seasonal variations in increments of weight and height. Emotional disturbances may affect growth, e.g., anorexia. Socioeconomic aspects may be important in relation to nutrition, clothing, disease, etc. Such factors as fetal position, faulty implantation of the ovum, rubella during pregnancy, etc., are among the earliest adverse environmental influences on the growing organism.

REFERENCES

1. Fraser F.C., Nora J.J.: *Genetics of Man*. Philadelphia, Lea & Febiger, 1975.
2. Jacobs P.A.: Epidemiology of chromosome abnormalities in man. *Am. J. Epidemiol.* 105:180, 1977.
3. Miller M.E., Dunn P.M., Smith D.W.: Uterine malformation and fetal deformation. *J. Pediatr.* 94:387, 1979.
4. Court Brown W.M.: *Human Population Cytogenetics*. Amsterdam, North Holland Publishing Co., 1967.
5. Reid D.E., Ryan K.L., Benirschke K.: *Principles and Management of Human Reproduction*. Philadelphia, W.B. Saunders Co., 1972.
6. Erbe R.W.: Current concepts in genetics, principles of medical genetics. *N. Engl. J. Med.* 294:381, 1976.
7. Meredith H.V.: Stature and weight of children of United States, with reference to influence of racial, regional, socioeconomic and secular factors. *Am. J. Dis. Child.* 62:909, 1941.
8. Cowett R.M., Schwartz R.: The infant of the diabetic mother. *Pediatr. Clin. N. Am.* 29:1213, 1982.
9. Mills C.A.: Climatic factors in health and disease, in Glasser O. (ed.): *Medical Physics*, vol. I. Chicago, Year Book Medical Publishers, Inc., 1944, p. 232.
10. Eveleth P., Tanner J.M.: *Worldwide Variations in Human Growth*. London, Cambridge University Press, 1976.
11. Gall J.C.: Genetic factors in physical growth and development. *Mich. Med.* 67:1209, 1968.
12. Robbins W.J., Brody S., Hogan A.G., et al.: *Growth*. New Haven, Conn., Yale University Press, 1928.
13. Summitt R.L.: Abnormalities of the autosomes and their resultant syndromes. *Pediatr. Ann.* 2:40, 1973.
14. Swan C., Tostevin A.L., Mayo H., et al.: Further observations on congenital defects following infectious diseases during pregnancy with special reference to rubella. *Med. J. Aust.* 1:409, 1944.
15. Oakley G.P.: Incidence and epidemiology of birth defects, in Kaback M.M. (ed.): *Genetic Issues in Pediatric and Obstetric Practice*. Chicago, Year Book Medical Publishers, Inc., 1981, p. 25.
16. Warkany J.: *Congenital Malformations*. Chicago, Year Book Medical Publishers, Inc., 1971.
17. Stagno S., Pass R.F., Dworsky M.E., et al.: Congenital cytomegalovirus infections. *N. Engl. J. Med.* 306:945, 1982.

18. Plummer G.: Anomalies occurring in children exposed in utero to the atomic bomb in Hiroshima. *Pediatrics* 10:687, 1952.
19. Ford C.E., Hamerston J.L.: The chromosomes of man. *Nature* 178:1020, 1956.
20. Drake J.W., Glickman B.W., Ripley L.S.: Updating the theory of mutation. *Am. Sci.* 71:621, 1983.
21. McKusick V.A.: *Mendelian Inheritance in Man*, ed. 5. Baltimore, The John Hopkins Press, 1978.
22. McKusic V.A.: The anatomy of the human genome. *Hosp. Prac.*, April 1981, p. 82.
23. Reed S.C.: *Counseling in Medical Genetics*, ed. 2. Philadelphia, W.B. Saunders Co., 1965.
24. Kalter H., Warkany J.: Congenital malformations, etiologic factors, and their role in prevention. *N. Engl. J. Med.* 308:424, 1983.
25. Schinzel A.A.G.L., Smith D.W., Miller J.R.: Monozygotic twinning and structural defects. *J. Pediatr.* 95:921, 1979.
26. Ellis R.W.B.: Age of puberty in the tropics. *Br. Med. J.* 1:85, 1950.
27. Tanner J.M.: *Growth at Adolescence*, ed. 2. Springfield, Ill., Charles C Thomas, Publisher, 1962.
28. Meredith H.V.: Measurements of Oregon school boys. *Hum. Biol.* 23:24, 1950.
29. *Age at Menarche: United States.* U.S. Dept. of Health, Education and Welfare, Public Health Service, 1973.
30. Meyers E.S.A.: Height-weight survey of New South Wales school children. *Med. J. Aust.* 1:435, 1956.
31. McKusick V.A.: Approaches and methods in human genetics. *Am. J. Obstet. Gynecol.* 90:1014, 1964.
32. Hewitt D., Stewart A.: A study of the influence of social and genetic factors on birthweight. *Hum. Biol.* 24:309, 1952.
33. Warkany J. (ed.): Congenital malformations (a series of papers by various authors on various aspects). *Pediatrics* 19:719, 1957.
34. Hall B.D.: The twenty-five most common multiple congenital anomaly syndromes, in Kaback M.M. (ed.): *Genetic Issues in Pediatric and Obstetric Practice.* Chicago, Year Book Medical Publishers, Inc., 1981, p. 141.
35. Jukes T.H.: The genetic code. *Am. Sci.* 53:477, 1965.
36. Puck T.T.: Radiation and the human cell. *Sci. Am.* 202:142, 1960.
37. Norris A.S.: Prenatal factors in intellectual and emotional development. *J.A.M.A.* 172:413, 1960.
38. Barr M.L.: Sex chromatin and phenotype in man. *Science* 130:679, 1959.
39. Warkany J., Beandry P.H., Hornstein S.: Attempted abortion with aminopterin (4-aminopteroylglutamic acid): Malformations of the child. *A.M.A. J. Dis. Child.* 97:274, 1959.
40. Carr D.H.: Genetic basis of abortion. *Ann. Rev. Genet.* 6:65, 1971.
41. Illingworth R.S.: Birth weight and subsequent weight. *Br. Med. J.* 1:96, 1950.
42. Flynt J.W.: Extent of the birth defects problem. *Pediatr. Ann.* 2:10, 1973.
43. Hook E.B.: Behavioral implications of the human XYY genotype. *Science* 179:139, 1973.
44. Falkner F.: Some physical measurements in the first three years of life. *Arch. Dis. Child.* 33:1, 1958.
45. Drillien C.M.: A longitudinal study of the growth and development of prematurely and maturely born children. *Arch. Dis. Child.* 33:423, 1958.
46. Ruch R.: X-irradiation effects on the human fetus. *J. Pediatr.* 52:531, 1958.

47. Greulich W.W.: Growth of children of the same race under different environmental conditions. *Science* 127:515, 1958.
48. Dobzhansky T.: Man and natural selection. *Am. Sci.* 49:285, 1961.
49. Smith D.: *Recognizable Patterns of Human Malformation*, ed. 2. Philadelphia, W.B. Saunders Co., 1976.
50. Holmes L.B.: Inborn errors of morphogenesis, a review of localized hereditary malformations. *N. Engl. J. Med.* 291:763, 1974.
51. Gerald P.S.: Current concepts in genetics, sex chromosome disorders. *N. Engl. J. Med.* 294:706, 1976.
52. Sutherland J.M., Light I.J.: The effect of drugs upon the developing fetus. *Pediatr. Clin. N. Am.* 12:781, 1965.
53. Bauld R., Sutherland G.R., Bain A.D.: Chromosome studies in investigation of stillbirths and neonatal deaths. *Arch. Dis. Child.* 49:782, 1974.
54. Kaback M.M.: Medical genetics: An overview. *Pediatr. Clin. N. Am.* 25:395, 1978.
55. Prader A., Tanner J.M., von Harnack G.A.: Catch-up growth following illness or starvation. *Pediatrics* 62:646, 1963.
56. Sutow W.W., Conrad R.A., Griffith K.M.: Growth status of children exposed to fallout radiation on Marshall Islands. *Pediatrics* 36:721, 1965.
57. Burrow G.N., Hamilton H.B., Hrubec Z.: Study of adolescents exposed in utero to the atomic bomb, Nagasaki, Japan. *J.A.M.A.* 192:357, 1965.
58. Babson S.G., Kangas J., Young N., et al.: Growth and development of twins of dissimilar size at birth. *Pediatrics* 33:327, 1964.
59. Bakwin H.: The secular change in growth and development. *Acta Paediatr. Scand.* 53:79, 1964.
60. Frommer D.J.: The changing age of the menopause. *Br. Med. J.* 2:349, 1964.
61. Day R.L.: Factors influencing offspring. *Am. J. Dis. Child.* 113:179, 1967.
62. Barr H.M., Streissguth A.P., Martin D.C., et al.: Infant size at 8 months of age: Relationship to maternal use of alcohol, nicotine and caffeine during pregnancy. *Pediatrics* 74:336, 1984.
63. Belmont L., Marolla F.A.: Birth order, family size and intelligence. *Science* 182:1096, 1973.
64. Overall J.C., Glasgow L.A.: Virus infections of the fetus and newborn infant. *J. Pediatr.* 77:315, 1970.
65. Hanshaw J.B., Scheiner A.P., Moxley A.W., et al.: School failure and deafness after silent congenital cytomegalovirus infection. *N. Engl. J. Med.* 295:468, 1976.
66. Wilson J.G.: Present status of drugs as teratogens in man. *Teratology* 7:3, 1973.
67. Herbst A.L., Poskanser D.C., Robby S.J., et al.: Prenatal exposure to stilbestrol. *N. Engl. J. Med.* 222:334, 1975.
68. Jones K.L., Smith D.W., Harvey M.A.S., et al.: Older paternal age and fresh gene mutation: Data on additional disorders. *J. Pediatr.* 86:84, 1975.
69. Kandall S.R., Albin S., Lowinson J., et al.: Differential effects of maternal heroin and methadone use on birthweight. *Pediatrics* 58:681, 1976.
70. Evans H.E., Glass L.: *Perinatal Medicine*. New York, Harper & Row, 1976.
71. Smith D.W., Truog W., Rogers J.E., et al.: Shifting linear growth during infancy: Illustration of genetic factors in growth from fetal life through infancy. *J. Pediatr.* 89:225, 1976.
72. Fisch R.O., Bilek M.K., Harrobin J.M., et al.: Children with superior intelligence at 7 years of age. *Am. J. Dis. Child.* 130:481, 1976.
73. Terman L.M., Oden M.H.: *The Gifted Child Grows Up*. Stanford, Calif., Stanford University Press, 1947.

74. Marshall W.A.: The relationship of variations in children's growth rates to seasonal climate variations. *Ann. Hum. Biol.* 2:243, 1975.
75. Niswander K.R., Gordon M.: *The Collaborative Perinatal Study of the National Institute of Neurological Disease and Stroke: The Women and Their Pregnancies.* U.S. Dept. of Health, Education and Welfare, 1972.
76. Sever L.E., Emanuel I.: Intergenerational factors in the etiology of anencephalus and spina bifida. *Develop. Med. Child Neural.* 23:151, 1981.
77. Laurence K.M.: Neural tube defects: A two-pronged approach to primary prevention. *Pediatrics* 70:648, 1982.
78. Elwood J.M., Elwood J.H.: *Epidemiology of Anencephalus and Spina Bifida.* New York, Oxford University Press, 1980.
79. Rosen T.S., Johnson H.L.: Children of methadone-maintained mothers: Follow up to 18 months of age. *J. Pediatr.* 101:192, 1982.
80. Lifschitz M.H., Wilson G.S., Smith E.O., et al.: Factors affecting head growth and intellectual function in children of drug addicts. *Pediatrics* 75:269, 1985.
81. Golden N.L., Sokol R.J., Kuknest B.R., et al.: Maternal alcohol use and infant development. *Pediatrics* 70:931, 1982.
82. Johnson S., Knight R., Marmer D.J., et al.: Immune deficiency in fetal alcohol syndrome. *Pediatr. Res.* 15:908, 1981.
83. Fielding J.E.: Smoking and pregnancy. *N. Engl. J. Med.* 298:337, 1978.
84. Naeye R.L., Peters E.C.: Working during pregnancy: Effects on the fetus. *Pediatrics* 69:724, 1982.
85. Pleet H., Graham J.M., Smith D.W.: Central nervous system and facial defects associated with maternal hyperthermia at 4 to 14 weeks gestation. *Pediatrics* 67:785, 1981.
86. Zuckerman B., Alpert J.J., Dooling E., et al.: Neonatal outcome: Is adolescent pregnancy a risk factor. *Pediatrics* 71:489, 1983.
87. Naeye R.L.: Teenaged and pre-teenaged pregnancies: Consequence of the fetal-maternal competition for nutrients. *Pediatrics* 67:146, 1981.
88. Lawrence R.A., Merrit A.: Infants of adolescent mothers: Perinatal, neonatal and infancy outcome. *Sem. Perinatol.* 5:19, 1981.
89. Egbuonu L., Starfield B.: Child health and social status. *Pediatrics* 69:550, 1982.
90. Tanner J.M.: Menarcheal age, letter to editor. *Science* 214:604, 1981.
91. Bouchard T.J., McGue M.: Familial studies in intelligence: A review. *Science* 212:1055, 1981.

3 / The Placenta and Fetal Development

> This child was prisoner of the womb, and is
> By law and process of great nature thence
> Freed and enfranchised.
> —William Shakespeare, *Winter's Tale*

The Placenta

The placenta is an organ of exceptional accomplishments. It can perform some of the functions of the liver, intestinal mucosa, lung, kidney, and several endocrine glands. In addition it has some characteristics that are unique. Because of its profound influence on the earliest stages of growth and development with respect to nutrition, excretion, hormonal relationships, and immunity, the placenta merits some discussion before proceeding to the subject of the fetus.[1, 3]

The fetal portion of the placenta develops from a combination of the two primary fetal membranes, the allantois and the serosa. These fuse to form the chorion, which in turn fuses with the lining of the uterus. The serosa is made up of an outer cell layer termed the trophoblast and can be recognized at a very early stage as cells extending outward from the earliest cell mass. Shortly thereafter a second layer of mesodermal cells reinforces the trophoblast, and the two layers form the trophoderm. Almost as soon as the hindgut of the embryo is formed, a diverticulum, the allantois, arises. The human allantois exhibits only a rudimentary lumen confined to the belly stalk region, but its mesoderm, or supporting tissues and blood vessels, grows out beyond the lumen and spreads over the inner surface of the trophoderm. The fusion of the allantois and serosa brings to the latter a highly vascular layer that is connected to the vascular supply of the embryo. Later this connection is maintained through the umbilical arteries and vein. Once the embryo is implanted, there follow rapid changes in both chorion and endometrium. As early as the second week after implantation, villi have formed from the trophoderm. The villi are fingerlike pro-

53

jections with a vascular core. Through continuous branching and invasion of the endometrium by the villi, growth and complexity of the placenta increase. Erosion of maternal vessels produces small pools of blood that form the intravillous spaces. It is estimated that at term the fetal surface of the placenta is approximately 10 sq m, with only a very thin tissue layer separating fetal and maternal circulation. The trophoblast undergoes considerable modification and toward term largely disappears, and only the syncytium remains of the chorion.

Certain aspects of the structure of the placenta are not yet defined. Furthermore, as the placenta ages, its structure changes. These details are beyond the scope of this book. One important factor, however, should be brought out. The structure of the human placenta is sufficiently unique that experiments carried out with other species must be applied or interpreted with great caution in terms of the human organism.

The placenta functions as the main organ of homeostasis for the fetus. It serves as the organ of respiratory exchange. In some aspects it is an immunologic barrier between mother and fetus, yet there is evidence that some fetal portions of the placenta may enter the maternal circulation during normal pregnancy and, possibly by this method, establish tolerance to the fetus. It is an alimentary organ supplying proteins, lipids, carbohydrates, minerals, and water required for growth and development. As an excretory organ it functions as a kidney for the fetus. As an endocrine gland it synthesizes gonadotropins, progesterone, estrogens, and other steroids whose actions are still not certain. With increasing age several of these functions undergo distinct changes that are not necessarily related to changes in vascularity or permeability of the membranes.

Simple diffusion from maternal to fetal circulation is exemplified by oxygen, carbon dioxide, water, electrolytes, urea, and bilirubin. There is active transport of calcium, phosphorous, and magnesium across the placenta to the fetus; in each instance the accumulation by the fetus is greatest during the third trimester. The total amount of calcium in the fetus at term is about 30 gm, 20 gm of which is deposited in the last trimester. At birth, serum phosphate levels in the infant are about twice those of the mother. (See also chapter 9 concerning neonatal calcium and phosphorus metabolism and their controlling hormones.) Whether fetal parathyroid glands are involved in intrauterine mineral homeostasis is not known. In the newborn period there is a brief period of relative hypoparathyroidism resulting in a transient rise of serum phosphorus. Concentrations of calcitonin in human cord blood are significantly higher than in maternal blood. All of these findings would appear to be ideal for rapid bone formation. Presently it appears that vitamin D and its metabolites play very little role in maternal-fetal exchange.[2]

It appears that carbohydrate metabolism during the first two thirds of pregnancy is independent of insulin or glucagon action. During this time, glucose is actively transferred from the mother to the fetus as are the amino acids. In the third trimester, insulin assumes the dominant role in directing the disposition of nutrients, including glucose and amino acids, for anabolic storage in the form of glycogen (principally in the liver), fat, and protein in anticipation of their utilization immediately after delivery. Fetal cells at this time demonstrate an increase in absolute numbers of insulin receptors. The insulin is all fetal as there is no transfer of insulin across the placenta in either direction. Glucagon has no functional role in utero and development of its receptors on target cells is delayed until after delivery. At birth there is a surge of glucagon probably mediated by an increase in catecholamine release, and together they prepare for the transition to extrauterine life, activating glycogenolysis, gluconeogenesis, and ketogenesis.

Glucose is the principal source of energy for the fetus. Throughout pregnancy the fetal blood level of glucose is lower than in the mother (Table 3–1). This is not a result of fetal consumption alone, but because the placenta maintains a gradient in that direction. Placental content of glycogen stores increases during the early stages of pregnancy and then rapidly falls. It has been postulated that this source of carbohydrate, although small in comparison with the total quantity required, is made available to the fetus during its period of rapid growth. The net transfer is in the direction of the fetus, and near term the placenta must transfer more than 20 mg of glucose per minute. The placenta is stereospecific and otherwise selective in its transport mechanism. For instance, D-xylose passes much more rapidly than L-xylose, and glucose more rapidly than fructose.[3, 21, 28]

Very early in gestation there is a dependence on maternal sources for lipids. The placenta can metabolize and transport fatty acids. However, the fatty acid concentration in fetal blood is much lower than in the mother and fluctuations in maternal fatty acid content are not reflected in the blood

TABLE 3–1.—RELATIVE CONCENTRATIONS OF SOME
SUBSTANCES IN MATERNAL AND CORD BLOOD
INDICATING CERTAIN ASPECTS OF PLACENTAL AND
FETAL FUNCTIONS

HIGHER IN FETUS	EQUAL	LOWER IN FETUS
Phosphorus	Urea	Total lipids
Calcium	Uric acid	Cholesterol
Potassium	Creatine	Glucose
Lactic acid	Magnesium	Albumin
Amino acids	Chloride	
Water soluble vitamins	Sodium	
	γ-globulin	

of the fetus. Triglycerides do not cross the placenta. The fat content of fetal tissues increases nearly 300-fold from the second to the ninth month of pregnancy, by far the greatest increase occurring during the final trimester. The lipid concentration and the fatty acid composition do not vary significantly throughout that period.[40, 48] Lipid synthesis by the fetus, primarily from glucose, is well established early in gestation and the rate of production parallels the rate of growth of the fetal organs.

Amino acids easily and quickly pass from the mother to the fetus, and their concentration is usually higher on the fetal side. They can readily be incorporated into protein. The placenta transfers intact proteins in a highly selective manner. The only source of γ-globulin until well after birth is the maternal organism. At birth the fetal and maternal levels are equal. Small but significant amounts of albumin cross the placenta from the mother, even though the fetus is very capable of manufacturing its own. There is some evidence that the placenta can synthesize proteins, but the value of this to the fetus remains obscure. (See also discussion on development of immunity, chapter 7.)

Proof of the existence of any mechanism other than simple diffusion for the exchange of oxygen and carbon dioxide has not been established. All indications are that the fetus exists in utero under conditions that are hypoxemic by postpartum standards. Oxygen saturation near term is considerably below that found shortly after birth, but provided there is a large enough systemic blood flow to fetal tissue and the oxygen-carrying capacity of the blood is great enough, this saturation of the fetal blood is clearly sufficient to supply tissue needs with some margin of safety. Maternal arterial blood at term has a PO_2 of 95 mm Hg while umbilical venous blood has a PO_2 of 28 mm Hg. Two factors contribute to the adequacy of fetal tissue oxygenation. The oxyhemoglobin dissociation curve for fetal blood is shifted to the left in comparison with adult blood. Thus, oxygen saturation of fetal hemoglobin can be accomplished at a much lower PO_2 level. The actual hemoglobin concentration is considerably higher in the fetus than in the adult, a hematocrit of 53 at term for the fetus compared with an average of 44 for an adult female. In addition, the metabolic rate of the fetus is relatively low since there is no thermal loss and little physical activity.

The placenta has a high rate of metabolism, being comparable to active adult organs such as the liver and the kidney. It can carry on a wide spectrum of anabolic and catabolic reactions, including a glycolytic cycle, the Krebs tricarboxylic acid cycle, and the synthesis of fatty acids and proteins from small precursors. Approximately 60 enzymes have been identified in the placenta.[38] Active transport involves enzymatic action against a gradient. In the case of large molecules, e.g., γ-globulins, pinocytosis is the mechanism of transfer.

The placenta is a major endocrine organ that is known to produce at least three protein hormones de novo, analogues of pituitary hormones and, from chemical precursors of fetal and maternal origin, the steroids progesterone and estrogens.[25, 27, 60] Human chorionic gonadotropin (HCG) is produced in very large quantities in early gestation and then drops off to maintain a slightly fluctuating, but still much higher than normal maternal serum level for the remainder of gestation. HCG closely resembles luteinizing hormone produced by the pituitary. Although its physiologic functions are not completely understood, especially in view of the early very high levels, HCG appears to maintain the action of the corpus luteum during the transition from the menstrual cycle to pregnancy. It has also been noted that HCG may play a role in blocking maternal immunologic responses directed against the fetus, thus preventing a reaction similar to graft rejection.

A second protein hormone produced by the placenta has both growth hormone and prolactin-like activities. Previously identified as chorionic somatomammotropin, it is now identified as human placental lactogen. Maternal serum levels of human placental lactogen rise at a steady rate throughout gestation, fairly accurately paralleling placental weight.[18]

Other polypeptide hormones produced by the placenta include a chorionic thyrotropin, a chorionic follicle-stimulating hormone, a uterotropic placental hormone (promotes cell proliferation in uterus and mammary glands in animals), luteinizing and thyrotropin-releasing factors, and a nerve growth factor. The precise function of these hormones is still under investigation.[18]

Of the estrogens synthesized by the placenta, one of great importance is estriol. Despite considerable ignorance of its physiologic role, maternal urine or serum levels of estriol are a valuable index of the status of the fetus. An essential precursor for the production of this steroidal hormone comes from the fetal adrenal gland. In normal pregnancy, during the final trimester, there is a slow but steady increase in its production. In anencephaly, associated with lack of development of a functional adrenal cortex, levels remain low. In threatened abortions with a poor prognosis for fetal survival, the levels are below normal, but if survival occurs and pregnancy proceeds, the levels will be normal and a steady increase will ensue.[25, 39]

The level of maternal serum estriol correlates accurately with placental and fetal weight as follows:

WEEK OF GESTATION	ESTRIOL (μG/L)
25	3.5–10.0
30	4.5–14.0
35	7.0–25.0
38	9.0–32.0
40	10.5–34.0

Progesterone, another steroid hormone produced by the placenta, is important in maintaining the endometrium for the continuation of gestation. Maternal cholesterol is the basic building block for the synthesis. There is a steady rise in the maternal serum and urine as pregnancy progresses. It has been postulated that progesterone, crossing to the fetus, serves as the precursor for the male fetus to manufacture testosterone and therefore plays an important role in sexual differentiation and development.

The relationship of changes of structure and function in the placenta to the growth and development of the fetus, infant, or child is difficult to define in many circumstances. The study of the placental changes in morphology throughout pregnancy and the establishment of adequate normal standards are of recent origin. Most of the studies so far published describe rather gross changes in the placenta associated with fetal abnormality. As our ability to measure more subtle changes improves, the list of insults to the fetus resulting from placental insufficiency will undoubtedly expand.

Using weight versus time as the criterion, the placenta grows most rapidly during the first trimester of pregnancy, and then the rate drops off rather quickly. In contrast, the fetus grows slowly initially and then rapidly in the final trimester. The fetus and placenta are equal in weight at 3.5 months, but at term the placenta is about 12% to 15% of the infant's weight. Although there is a direct relationship between placental and fetal size, there is a surprising frequency of exceptions to the rule.

Low birth weight, when associated with low socioeconomic status and maternal malnutrition, does appear to correlate with a low functional placental mass. Morphologically, this is accompanied by a diminution in the vascular area available for exchange. By necessity, human studies of placental size and presumed function have been limited in number, and control groups used for comparison have often been poorly selected. If indeed there is such an entity as placental insufficiency, then questions must be asked as to the etiology. Is the major cause maternal malnutrition, a genetic or chromosomal abnormality in the fetus, chronic illness in the mother, the long-term effect of many generations of deprivation including small size of the mother, or an actual anatomical and physiologic defect in the placenta?[24, 33, 34, 36]

Recent studies have established that placentas from infants with "intrauterine growth failure" have fewer cells when compared with controls. These findings were true whether the cause of the infant's smallness was malnutrition, intrauterine infection, or a chromosomal disorder. In many of the organs of these infants there was a significant reduction in cell numbers. Data from laboratory animals have shown similar results and also indicate that even with optimum conditions following birth there remains a deficit in cell number. These findings suggest that early programming of ultimate cell numbers of various organs, including the brain, takes place in utero and may be unchangeable despite subsequent events.[42, 43]

Normal human pregnancy lasts 290 days on the average, seven to eight days less for the average black. Approximately 11% of all term pregnancies exceed the estimated time of confinement by more than five days. Most of these babies appear and develop in a normal manner. Although statistics vary slightly, 8% to 10% (or 1% of all deliveries) of the prolonged gestation babies will manifest recognizable abnormalities that have been termed *postmaturity* or *dysmaturity* syndrome and by some as *placental dysfunction*. Since the same findings rarely exist in a normal term or even slightly preterm infant, the term "dysmature" seems more appropriate. Also, because the pathologic findings in the placenta are minimal or absent the use of "placental dysfunction" would be inappropriate. The findings in the infant vary in degree and generally are more severe the longer the pregnancy. The skin is parchment-like in feel and appearance with peeling and meconium staining. The face appears alert and awake. There is decreased subcutaneous fat giving the limbs and body a very thin and dystrophic appearance. Aspiration and respiratory difficulty are frequently encountered as well as hypoglycemia, which probably results from poor glycogen and fat storage. This condition occurs more frequently in older (over 29) primiparous mothers and in blacks as compared with whites. Oligohydramnios is often associated with dysmaturity. Although neonatal morbidity and mortality is increased, if the infant survives, the long-range prognosis for growth and development seems unimpaired.[3, 24, 33, 62, 63]

In mothers who develop hypertension and toxemia of pregnancy, placental size is reduced and the vascularity of the villi is curtailed.[33] Similar changes with thrombotic lesions have been described in pregnancy associated with the diabetic who has developed degenerative vascular complications.[31] Abnormalities in the fetuses of such pregnancies are frequent. Nodularity of the placental surface and oligohydramnios in the condition termed *amnion nodosum* are frequently seen with renal agenesis or polycystic kidney in the fetus.[35] The small size of both placenta and newborn has been repeatedly noted when a chromosomal abnormality existed.

The occurrence of a single umbilical artery is about 1% in all pregnancies. The incidence is slightly higher in whites than in blacks and is more frequent in low birth weight infants. Although originally thought to be more common in twin pregnancies, this now seems doubtful. Statistics vary in different studies, but from 30% to 40% will be associated with recognizable congenital anomalies, of which a quarter will die in early infancy.[29, 59] The organ systems most frequently involved are the cardiovascular and the genitourinary. It is interesting, and fortunate, to note that follow-ups of surviving children indicate they have essentially normal growth and development, even though they will have a higher incidence of some malformations than the general population.[58, 59]

Vascular anastomoses in monochorionic twin pregnancies may lead to plethora in one twin and anemia in the other. The donor twin is always considerably smaller and may remain so for many years.[35]

Fetal Monitoring

The growing fetus is surrounded by amniotic fluid that aids in maintaining a steady body temperature, protects from physical injury, and serves as a media for fluid exchange. In early pregnancy the amniotic fluid contains little protein and is probably a dialysate of maternal serum. Later the fluid becomes hypotonic as it becomes diluted with fetal urine. Maximum volume of approximately 1,400 ml is reached at the seventh month and then decreases to about 800 ml in uncomplicated term pregnancies. The turnover rate of amniotic fluid is around 600 ml per hour, at least 75% of this exchange being through the fetus and placenta by swallowing and excreting a urine that is essentially a glomerular filtrate. These facts explain the frequent complication of polyhydramnios with congenital obstructive lesions of the gut. In contrast, oligohydramnios is seen with renal aplasia or urethral obstruction. Average values for some components of the fluid near term are protein, 100 to 500 mg/100 ml; nonprotein nitrogen, 25 mg/100 ml; uric acid, 4.5 mg/100 ml, and glucose, 20 to 60 mg/100 ml.[3]

Within the last two decades, great advances have been made in the ability to study the developing fetus in both normal and abnormal circumstances. The new techniques used to accomplish this are amniocentesis, chorionic biopsy, fetoscopy, and ultrasound imaging or sonography. These methods have been of considerable value in the diagnosis and/or prognosis (and possibly eventually in therapy) of the fetal condition. More than 70 different inborn errors of metabolism are identified by specific enzyme measurements of amniotic fluid or of cultured desquamated skin fibroblasts obtained by amniocentesis. Examples are Tay-Sachs disease, Gaucher's disease, thalassemia, glycogen storage diseases, cystinosis, mucopolysaccharidoses, cystic fibrosis, and galactosemia. Cytogenetic studies of fetal fibroblasts may be indicated in high-risk mothers for Down's syndrome or for other potential genetic abnormalities (previous infant or parent with aneuploidy, etc.). Chorionic villus biopsy is done through the cervical os and the villi can be analyzed for biochemical and chromosomal abnormalities. A major advantage of this method is that it can be carried out much earlier than amniocentesis, 8 to 10 weeks versus 16 to 20 weeks, and the results of the test can be completed in hours versus weeks. Fetoscopy carries greater risks to both fetus and mother than amniocentesis but does permit direct visualization of the fetus. In some of the hemoglobinopathies, fetal blood is required to make the diagnosis and this can be obtained through fetoscopy. The increasing improvements in sonography have made it a valuable and noninvasive method to study the fetus. It is useful in determining malformations such as neural tube defects, congenital heart disease, and limb reductions. It has great value in determining fetal measurements and thus aids in determining fetal maturity and presence of intrauterine growth retardation. Finally, through observation of heart rate and other movements, sonography can be used in monitoring movements and screening for fetal distress. In conjunction with amniocentesis and fetoscopy it is an aid in visualizing and avoiding dangerous placements of those instruments.[14, 19, 20, 23, 64–66]

Direct fetal heart monitoring, through application of electrodes to the scalp after rupture of the membranes, has proved to be a valuable means of determining such conditions as cord compression, uteroplacental insufficiency, and simple head compression with uterine contractions.[12]

Throughout pregnancy, as increasing amounts of fetal urine are excreted, the creatinine concentration rises in the amniotic fluid. A level above 2 mg/100 ml is taken as an indication of at least 36 weeks of gestation. As the fetal lung matures, surfactant phospholipids are found in increasing amounts in tracheal fluid. Since there is continuity between the fetal lung and the amniotic fluid, concentration of the phospholipids in that fluid can be a measure of the degree of maturation. Determinations are usually made of the lecithin/sphingomyelin ratio since the change in that ratio is an accurate reflection of physiologic maturity. Ratios of less than 1 persist until about 30 weeks of gestation after which the ratio increases to 2 by 35 weeks. The method has been of great value in predicting the possible occurrence of the respiratory distress syndrome (see chapter 5).[17]

Not related to the amniotic fluid but of use in evaluating fetal progress and development is recognition of the presence of significant amounts of α-fetoprotein in maternal serum when the fetus has a neural tube defect such as myelomeningocele. Testing between the 16th and 18th weeks can detect most affected pregnancies and indicates the need for further diagnostic studies such as sonography.[37]

Fetal Growth

That growth and development do not begin at the time of birth is quite obvious, but for the pediatrician, birth marks the onset of growth and development from a clinical standpoint. To provide a clear understanding of these phenomenon after birth, the changes that occur before birth and continue to take place in the postnatal period are reviewed here.

Life as a new individual commences at the moment of fertilization. Growth becomes an inherent force in that individual and continues, in stature at least, until the average postnatal age of about 20 years unless disease, accident, or death interferes. During this time there are also marked changes in differentiation or maturation of specific organs as well as in the body as a whole.

Figure 3–1 shows the curves for length, surface area, and weight for a normally developing fetus. The steepness of the curves is better appreciated when it is realized that growth is plotted by monthly increments, rather than by yearly increments as is commonly done for the postnatal period. During the second month the embryo tends to grow about 1 mm a day in "sitting height" and thereafter averages 1.5 mm per day.[9] In comparison, a 10-year-old child who had continued to grow at the rate of 1.5 mm a day would be 20 ft tall.

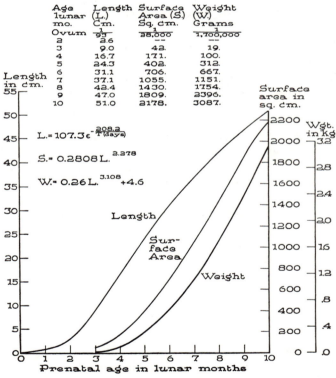

Age lunar mo.	Length (L.) Cm.	Surface Area (S.) Sq. cm.	Weight (W.) Grams
Ovum	$\frac{1}{93}$	$\frac{1}{38,000}$	$\frac{1}{1,700,000}$
2	2.6	--	--
3	9.0	42.	19.
4	16.7	171.	100.
5	24.3	402.	312.
6	31.1	706.	667.
7	37.1	1055.	1151.
8	42.4	1430.	1754.
9	47.0	1809.	2396.
10	51.0	2178.	3087.

$$L. = 107.3\epsilon^{-\frac{208.2}{T(days)}}$$

$$S. = 0.2808 L.^{2.278}$$

$$W. = 0.26 L.^{3.108} + 4.6$$

Fig 3–1.—Curves of prenatal growth: length (crown-heel), surface area of the body and weight from time of conception to birth. (From Patten[9], after Edith Boyd.)

The increase in weight is even more surprising. From birth to maturity the weight is increased 20-fold. From the time of fertilization to birth the increase in weight is approximately 6 billion times.

The rate of growth of total body mass constantly increases during intra-uterine life, and for several years after birth the curve of growth shows a steady decline. Maximal linear growth during gestation occurs in the sixth and seventh months and decelerates during the last two months of the fetal period.[10]

Figure 3–2 shows the relative proportions of different parts of the body during fetal and postnatal life and portrays the changes taking place with growth better than any written discussion. It is not until the third month that the fetus definitely resembles a human being. The head is dispropor-tionately large, and the umbilical herniation is reduced due to the return of the intestine into the abdominal cavity. The nails are forming, and sex can be determined. At 5 months, hair is present on the head and body, and shortly thereafter eyebrows and eyelashes form. At 7 months the fetus looks like a dried-up old man with red and wrinkled skin. The eyelids are no longer fused. By the eighth lunar month, subcutaneous fat begins to accumulate, and the nails are completely formed. The major changes from this time until birth are due to progressive accumulation of fat, and the downy hair coat is shed.[1, 9, 10]

In the following chapters will be found brief references to fetal organ development, and they will not be repeated here. By the end of the second fetal month, definition of the permanent organs is so far advanced that the subsequent growth of the fetus is devoted to the development of parts already formed. In general, the growth of organs during prenatal life fol-

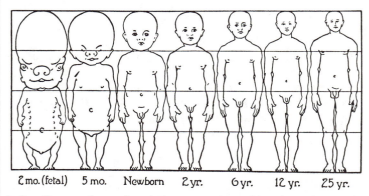

2 mo. (fetal)   5 mo.   Newborn   2 yr.   6 yr.   12 yr.   25 yr.

Fig 3–2.—Stages of growth: relative proportions of head, trunk and extremities for different ages. (From Robbins W.J., et al.: *Growth*. New Haven, Conn., Yale University Press, 1928.

lows an accelerating smooth curve that is in marked contrast to the divergent growth curves following birth (see Fig 7–7).

Some aspects of human fetal development are outlined in the following tabulation. The figures in parentheses refer to fetal age in months of gestation.[1, 9]

Integument	Three-layered epidermis (3)
	Body hair begins (4)
	Skin glands form, sweat and sebaceous (4)
Mouth	Lip fusion complete (2)
	Palate fused completely (3)
	Enamel and dentin depositing (5)
	Primordia of permanent teeth (6 to 8)
Gastrointestinal	Bile secreted (3)
	Rectum patent (3)
	Pancreatic islands appear (3)
	Fixation of duodenum and colon (4)
Respiratory	Definitive shape of lungs (3)
	Accessory nasal sinuses developing (4)
	Elastic fibers appear in lung (4)
Urogenital	Kidney able to secrete (2.5)
	Vagina regains lumen (5)
	Testes descend into scrotum (7 to 9)
Vascular	Definitive shape of heart (1.5)
	Heart becomes four-chambered (3.5)
	Blood formation in marrow begins (3)
	Spleen acquires typical structure (7)
Nervous	Commissures of brain complete (5)
	Myelinization of cord begins (5)
	Typical layers of cortex (6)
Special senses	Nasal septum complete (3)
	Retinal layers complete, light-perceptive (7)
	Vascular tunic of lens pronounced (7)
	Eyelids open (7 to 8)

Fetal Behavior

Behavior depends to a great extent on morphology and structure, and one cannot discuss behavior without also discussing developmental anatomy. There are regulating growth mechanisms that govern the order in which successive patterns of behavior emerge. Most fundamental are the structures of the muscle and nerve cells and the manner in which these structures come into functional relationship.

Fetus at 8 Weeks

The major components of both trunk and limb musculature are evident in the embryo at the end of the second fetal month.[6] The nerves as yet have no anatomical or physiologic connections with either smooth or striated muscle. During this time the embryo has floated quiescently in the amniotic fluid. However, movement has already taken place in this new individual. Since 4 weeks of age the heart has been beating at a fairly regular rate.[16] Skeletal muscle may have developed an intrinsic tonus by this time also. The available evidence indicates that the fetus becomes capable of responding to tactile stimulation at 8.5 weeks. The trunk flexes and the head extends. Anatomically, by this time, there are found all of the necessary components of the reflex arc.[6]

Fetus at 12 to 14 Weeks

With increasing age and maturation of the neuromuscular system the movements spread caudally and become more pronounced in the lower trunk. Then discrete reflexes appear, accompanying spread of the skin areas sensitive to stimulation. By 14 weeks the human fetus has largely ceased to exhibit the earlier, more generalized responses and activity becomes less stereotyped.[6]

Windle[68] has stated that behavior, in general, goes through five stages: (1) myogenic responses, (2) neuromotor responses, (3) reflex responses, (4) integration of simple reflexes, and (5) integration and control from higher centers. From this it can be seen that behavior follows closely the differentiation of structures in the fetal nervous system. Evidence concerning the functions of the central nervous system during prenatal life indicates that behavior, until about the beginning of the sixth month, is largely controlled by spinal mechanisms.[8] At a slightly later period there are indications that the medulla and lower brain centers participate in the control of specific reflex activities. (It is possible that a strong stimulus may affect the medulla before this, however, as indicated by the respiration-like movements that occur at 20 weeks). There is no evidence that the cerebral cortex exerts any specific influence on behavior until some time after birth.[8]

By the end of the first trimester the fetus makes brief jerky movements without artificial stimulation. By the twentieth week the sucking reflex is present and the first patterns of respiratory movements manifest themselves.[5, 16]

Fetus at 28 Weeks (Viable)

The fetal age at 28 weeks approximately demarcates the zone between viability and nonviability. The following outlines of behavior are based on the observations of Gesell[5] in premature infants from fetal ages of 28 to 40 weeks. He states that this behavior probably varies only slightly from that which would take place in utero. To support this contention he was able to demonstrate: (1) that all infants of the same fetal age follow a very similar pattern of behavior, (2) that, in general, the week-old neonate exhibits a behavior picture remarkably like that of the mature "fetal-infants," and (3) from previous studies, that in older premature infants the fundamental rates and patterns of development are little disturbed by displacements of birth.

Fetus at 28 to 32 Weeks

Movements meager, fleeting, poorly sustained
Lack of muscular tone
Mild avoidance responses to bright light and sound
In prone position turns head to side
Palmar stimulation elicits barely perceptible grasp
Breathing shallow and irregular
Sucking and swallowing present but lack endurance
No definite waking and sleeping pattern
Cry may be absent or very weak
Inconstant tonic neck reflex

Fetus at 32 to 36 Weeks

Movements sustained and positive
Muscle tone fair under stimulation
Moro's reflex present
Strong but inadequate response to light and sound
In prone position turns head, elevates rump
Definite periods of being awake
Palmar stimulation causes good grasp
Good hunger cry
Fairly well-established tonic neck reflex

Fetus at 36 to 40 Weeks

Movements active and sustained
Muscle tone good
Brief erratic following of objects with eyes
Moro's reflex strong
In prone position attempts to lift head
Active resistance to head rotation
Definite periods of alertness
Cries well when hungry and disturbed
Appears pleased when caressed
Hands held as fists much of time, good grasp
Tonic neck reflex more pronounced to one side (usually right) than to
    the other

Good, strong sucking reflex

Each infant in Gesell's series showed individuality as well as a general sameness of overall behavior pattern. It can be seen that the development of fetal behavior lays a necessary foundation for the later development of postnatal behavior, the latter not merely being imposed on the former but arising from it by a process of maturation of existing activities.

Metabolism of the Fetus

In utero the fetal temperature is about 0.5 C above the maternal temperature. Environmental temperature for the fetus is unfluctuating, and ambient temperature control puts little metabolic demand upon the organism. Little physical activity, depressed muscle tone, and insulation against heat loss all contribute to a relatively low metabolic rate. During normal gestation the oxygen consumption of the fetus, based upon weight, remains relatively constant and at a level of approximately one third that of the newborn. A large proportion of the caloric intake of the fetus is used to satisfy growth requirements, about 50% of the total in contrast to 15% to 20% in a 10-year-old child.[16, 22]

Newborn babies with fetal growth retardation, regardless of cause, have relatively low rates of oxygen consumption for gestational age, but high rates for body weight. It has been suggested that this reflects recovery from fetal malnutrition and rapid increase in tissue (cell) growth.[61]

Nutrition of the Fetus

The physiologic processes of the body are considerably altered during pregnancy, and additional demands are imposed upon the maternal organism during this period. Although it seems well established that the state of maternal nutrition influences the nutrition and subsequent well-being of the child, precise definition of the relationship is beset with considerable difficulties primarily because nutrition seldom, if ever, exists as an independent variable. It is part of a cluster of social, economic, medical, and genetic characteristics making it very difficult to estimate its effect per se. There is a clearly demonstrable positive correlation between maternal weight, both preconceptional and gain during gestation, and weight of the infant at birth.[3, 41, 48] If the need arises, the fetus is to a certain extent provided for at the expense of the mother. Growth of the placenta is closely tied into that of the fetus and shares a similar preferential position. When the maternal intake of iron, calcium, or phosphorus, as examples, is inadequate, the fetus draws on her stores to supply its own requirements. Iron deficiency anemia is, therefore, rare in early infancy. Of the total weight gain during pregnancy, slightly more than half is maternal in the form of increased blood volume, uterine and breast growth, and increased fat storage. However, during the third trimester, the gain reflects largely the fetal component. On this basis, it could be predicted that the correlation between maternal weight gain and birth weight, alluded to previously, would be stronger in the third trimester than earlier. These observations will also have considerable importance in the consideration of fetal growth retardation when we discuss the low birth weight infant in chapter 5. A severe reduction in protein intake, as in famine or starvation, will lead to a lower than average weight, length, and head circumference in the newborn.[13, 51, 52] When starvation is sufficiently severe, amenorrhea and sterility may result. Although spontaneous abortion may be slightly more frequent in pregnancies associated with extreme dietary insufficiency, malformations do not appear to increase. Although stillbirths, prematurity, congenital anomalies, and early neonatal death have been attributed to maternal malnutrition, the evidence supporting such claims is very poor.

Although many reports indicate the harmful results of a poor or marginal maternal diet on fetal growth and development, the differences between such infants and those exposed to an adequate diet are often minimal. The striking results that can be produced in the experimental animal are almost never seen in the human. Total, or nearly total, withholding of essential nutrients is seldom obtained in pregnant women. In the human, fetal growth is very slow. In the mouse, by comparison, the weight of a litter is 30% of the mother's weight and is reached in three weeks. In the human, the weight of the newborn is 5% of the mother's, and this is reached in 40 weeks. The rate of metabolic changes in one as compared with the other is obviously great. The relatively gradual development may serve to protect the human fetus and limit the deleterious effects of a poor diet. In fact, most studies indicate, the major effect of maternal malnutrition occurs during the rapid growth period of the final trimester, long after the critical period of organogenesis.[50, 52] Toward the end of gestation, the fetus lays down 500 mg of nitrogen, 300 mg of calcium, and about 200 mg of phosphorus each day. It has been estimated that the fetus requires 5% of the total calcium in the plasma of the mother every hour during the last three months. The whole body of the fetus has about 9 gm of carbohydrate at 33 weeks of gestation and 34 gm at term.

The critical issues relate to the long-term effect of maternal undernutrition. There is general agreement that small physical size of the newborn is a result. Some continued relatively slow growth and delayed maturation may occur, but normal, or near normal, adult size can be expected unless there is continued poor food intake.[44-49] Subsequent development of the central nervous system and intellectual performance is a subject upon which there is some disagreement. Unfortunately, the elimination of continued exposure of the infant and young child to a poor socioeconomic climate is not always possible in evaluation studies. The selection of properly matching control subjects for comparison is not an easily accomplished task. The conditions under which such studies must be carried out is far from ideal in most instances. Therefore, we must state opinions with reservations. The effects suffered by a fetus from a single maternal episode of undernutrition, as in the Netherlands in 1944 to 1945, may not be properly equated with multiple generations of malnutrition as experienced in some of the developing countries. In the former, i.e., a single episode of maternal undernutrition, the fetus would appear to suffer only temporary slowing of physical development.[54, 56, 57] In the situation where multiple factors may be involved, and where poor nutrition is essentially chronic, the results of maternal malnutrition may be an important factor contributing to premature delivery, small size at birth, slowed physical development, compromised intellectual development, and possibly decreased immunologic protection.[44–49, 53]

In the newborn infant small for the time of gestation, the possible role of the placenta is still somewhat of a riddle. We are often at a loss as to the cause, although we use such terms as "placental dysfunction" and "placental dysmaturity." The reason the small and apparently poorly functioning placenta became that way is far from clear. One can ask whether the placenta is small because of the small fetus and reduced requirements, or whether the fetus is small because the placenta is inadequate.[24]

Teenage pregnancies are often associated with socioeconomic deprivation and neglected health care and generally poor or marginal nutrition. The combination of these factors plus biologic immaturity has been blamed for low birth weight and increased perinatal morbidity. (Further discussion of teenage pregnancies is in chapter 2.)

The effect of specific vitamin deficiencies is not so well known. There have been isolated reports of infants born with beriberi,[15] rickets,[3] and scurvy.[7] As mentioned previously, Warkany produced congenital malformations of the eyes and other tissues in animals by depriving the mother of vitamin A. He has also shown a relationship between riboflavin deficiency in the rat and certain congenital skeletal defects.

It may be concluded that the pregnant woman requires more calories, minerals, vitamins, and protein than the nonpregnant woman to ensure proper or optimal growth of the fetus.

At the 15th week the placenta and fetus are equal in weight and contain similar amounts of glycogen, fat, phosphorous and potassium. As the end of gestation is approached, the fetus weighs six to seven times as much as the placenta, and the concentrations of glycogen, fat, calcium, and phosphorous in the fetus exceed those of the placenta. The concentrations of sodium and potassium remain the same. Table 3–2 indicates the changes occurring in fetal growth relative to concentrations of some substances.[34]

The human fetus begins to lay down fat at a weight of 800 to 1,000 gm or around the six lunar month of pregnancy. At a weight of 3,000 gm the body contains an equal amount of fat and protein, but from this point on the fat exceeds the protein.[34] Fat deposition, especially in the subcutaneous tissues, as an insulating material to conserve body heat is very important. The fat of the fetus and newborn differs from that found later in life in having a higher melting point, greater saturation, and a higher content of palmitic but less stearic and oleic acids. By midfetal life, deposits of brown fat are evident, and these increase quantitatively until birth. Brown fat is an important thermogenic source in response to cold and thus differs considerably in its function in contrast to the more metabolically stable white fat. (See also chapter 10).

Internal Environment

As growth progresses, the relative content of the total body water decreases. The 6-week-old fetus contains about 97% water, the newborn about 72%, and the adult about 60%. While the loss of water there results a proportionate loss of sodium and chloride (Fig 3–3). The reduction of fluid content of the body is due almost entirely to a reduction of extracellular fluids. Since the concentration of sodium and chloride in the extracellular fluid is the same for the fetus, the newborn infant, and the adult, the total body content of these minerals changes with growth in order to maintain this even concentration. The percentage of total body content of chloride is fetus, 0.27; newborn, 0.25; and adult, 0.21.[11]

With the increase in tissue mass that occurs with growth there is an

TABLE 3–2.—Concentration of Substances in the Fetus During Late Pregnancy and in the Newborn*

SUBSTANCE	FETUS 1,500 GM	FETUS 2,500 GM	TERM INFANT 3,500 GM
Protein	11.6	12.4	12.0
Fat	3.5	7.6	16.2
Water	82.5	77.3	68.8
Sodium	0.23	0.21	0.19
Calcium	0.68	0.76	0.81
Iron	7.10	7.40	7.52

*Values are expressed as gm per 100 gm body weight except for iron, which is mg.

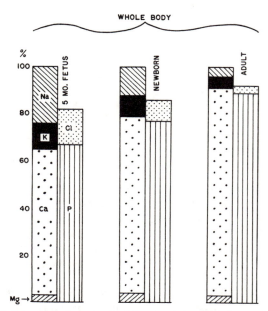

Fig 3–3.—Total mineral content of the body at different periods of development; trace elements are not represented. The apparent excess of positive ions is compensated for by organic acids and protein. (From Shohl.[11])

increase in the total amount of intracellular fluid. To maintain ionic and osmotic equilibrium, the increase in potassium content of the body parallels the increase in intracellular fluid. Table 3–3 shows these changes. The sodium and potassium ion concentrations are given for the whole body. The percentages of extracellular and intracellular water are computed on the basis that the sodium is entirely extracellular and the potassium intracellular.[11] The sum of the two cations of the total body fluids equals approximately 162 mEq/kg of water throughout life. These figures show that as growth continues and the number of cells increases, an ever-increasing amount of water becomes intracellular.[67]

Practical Applications

Recently the role of the placenta in embryonal and fetal growth and development has received considerable interest. It is recognized that this organ of chemical exchange between mother and fetus displays a remarkable degree of selectivity that bears little resemblance to a passive semipermeable membrane. During its brief existence it acts as an important depot for

TABLE 3–3.—CHANGES IN DISTRIBUTION OF WATER AND POSITIVE IONS
THROUGHOUT LIFE

| | TOTAL BODY WATER | | TOTAL BODY FLUID | |
	NA$^+$ MEQ/KG	K$^+$ MEQ/KG	EXTRACELLULAR, %	INTRACELLULAR, %
Fetus	125	52	71	29
Newborn	97	63	63	37
Adult	67	95	42	58
Adult (correct for intracellular sodium)	. . .	. . .	30	70

glycogen and synthesizes hormones that are important in maintaining the pregnancy and may have other important metabolic functions relative to fetal development. As a means of gaseous exchange it compares favorably with the lung. Careful study of structure and physiology of this long-neglected organ, upon which fetal survival is absolutely dependent, has led and will continue to lead to an approved understanding and prognosis for intrauterine life.

Growth and development have progressed to a considerable degree before birth. All the organ systems are well established by the second fetal month, and at no time after birth is growth as rapid as during the prenatal period. Through an understanding of fundamental embryology a better concept of congenital anomalies is obtained, as well as an appreciation of future trends in growth and development. We have seen that most of the vital reflexes are well established and prepared for the initial shock of extrauterine existence. Behavior depends on functional and morphologic development and is influenced by regulating growth mechanisms that determine the pattern of behavior both prenatally and postnatally. Behavior may well be a better criterion of the degree of maturity than physical measurements during the neonatal period.

The availability of techniques to make antenatal diagnosis of congenital malformations and heritable metabolic diseases may alert the physician to prepare for a therapeutic abortion or for special and energetic methods of treatment. The counseling of families in such situations involves the complex interplay of ethics, genetics, and knowledge of the extent of medical abilities to influence end results in the infant, child, and adult.

The importance of maternal nutrition during pregnancy has been stressed because there is little doubt that this factor influences the development of the fetus and the well-being of the organism for some time after birth. A better knowledge of the physicochemical changes that take place just before and after birth will aid us in further reducing neonatal mortality.

REFERENCES
1. Moore K.L.: *The Developing Human, Clinically Oriented Embryology.* Philadelphia, W.B. Saunders Co., 1973.
2. Schedewie H.K., Fisher D.A.: Perinatal mineral homeostasis, in Tulchinsky D., Ryan K.J. (eds.): *Maternal Fetal Endocrinology.* Philadelphia, W.B. Saunders Co., 1980.
3. Reid D.E., Ryan K.J., Benirschke K.: *Principles and Management of Human Reproduction.* Philadelphia, W.B. Saunders Co., 1972.
4. Warshaw J.B.: Factors affecting fetal growth, in Gluck L. (ed.): *Modern Perinatal Medicine.* Chicago, Year Book Medical Publishers, Inc., 1974.
5. Gesell A.: *The Embryology of Behavior.* New York, Harper & Brothers, 1945.
6. Hooker D.: Reflex activities in human fetus, in Barker R.G., et al. (eds.): *Child Behavior and Development.* New York, McGraw-Hill Book Co., 1943, p. 17.
7. Jackson D., Park E.A.: Congenital scurvy: Case report. *J. Pediatr.* 7:741, 1935.
8. Munn N.L.: *Psychological Development.* Boston, Houghton Mifflin Co., 1938.
9. Patten B.M.: *Human Embryology,* ed. 3. New York, McGraw-Hill Book Co., 1968.
10. Scammon R.E., Calkins L.A.: *The Development of Growth of the External Dimensions of the Human Body in the Fetal Period.* Minneapolis, University of Minnesota Press, 1929.
11. Shohl A.T.: *Mineral Metabolism.* American Chemical Society Monograph Series. New York, Reinhold Publiching Corp. 1939.
12. Evans H.E., Glass L.: *Perinatal Medicine.* New York, Harper & Row, 1976.
13. Smith C.A.: Effects of maternal undernutrition upon the newborn infant in Holland (1944–1945). *J. Pediatr.* 30:229, 1947.
14. Burton B.K.: Intrauterine diagnosis of biochemical disorders. *Sem. Perinatol.* 4:179, 1980.
15. Van Gelder D.W., Darby F.V.: Congenital and infantile beriberi. *J. Pediatr.* 25:226, 1944.
16. Dawes G.S.: *Foetal and Neonatal Physiology.* Chicago, Year Book Medical Publishers, 1968.
17. Gluck L., Kulovich M.V.: The evaluation of functional maturity in the human fetus, in Gluck L. (ed.): *Modern Perinatal Medicine.* Chicago, Year Book Medical Publishers, 1974.
18. Osathanondh R., Tulchinsky D.: Placental polypeptide hormones, in Tulchinsky D., Ryan K.J. (eds.): *Maternal-Fetal Endocrinology.* Philadelphia, W.B. Saunders Co., 1980.
19. Simpson J.L.: Antenatal diagnosis of cytogenetic abnormalities. *Sem. Perinatol.* 4:165, 1980.
20. Thompson J.N.: Antenatal detection of heritable disorders in man. *Pediatr. Ann.* 2:83, 1973.
21. Sperling M.A.: Carbohydrate metabolism: Glucagon, insulin, and somatostatin, in Tulchinsky D., Ryan K.J. (eds.): *Maternal-Fetal Endocrinology.* Philadelphia, W.B. Saunders Co., 1980.
22. Villee C.A.: *The Placenta and Fetal Membranes.* Baltimore, Williams & Wilkins Co., 1960, pp. 131–244.
23. Rowley P.T.: Genetic screening: Marvel or menace. *Science* 225:138, 1984.
24. Gruenwald P.: Placental insufficiency: A questionable concept. *Arch. Dis. Child.* 49:915, 1974.
25. Gluckman P.D., Grumback M.M., Kaplan S.L.: The human fetal hypothala-

mus and pituitary gland, in Tulchinsky D., Ryan K.J. (eds.): *Maternal-Fetal Endocrinology*. Philadelphia, W.B. Saunders Co., 1980.

26. Hendricks C.H.: Discussion, in *Physiology of Prematurity, Transactions of the Fifth Conference*. New York, Josiah Macy, Jr., Foundation, 1961, p. 217.

27. Goebelsmann V., Freeman R.K., Mestman J.H., et al.: Estriol in pregnancy. *Am. J. Obstet. Gynecol.* 115:795, 1972.

28. Dancis J.: The role of the placenta in fetal survival. *Pediatr. Clin. N. Am.* 12:477, 1965.

29. Bourne G.L., Benirschke K.: Absent umbilical artery: Review of 113 cases. *Arch. Dis. Child.* 35:534, 1960.

30. Gruenwald P., Minh H.N.: Evaluation of body and organ weights in perinatal pathology. *Am. J. Obstet. Gynecol.* 82:312, 1961.

31. Driscoll S.G.: Pathology and the developing fetus. *Pediatr. Clin. N. Am.* 12:493, 1965.

32. Wigglesworth J.S.: Foetal growth retardation. *Br. Med. Bull.* 22:13, 1966.

33. Aherne W., Dunnill M.S.: Morphometry of the human placenta. *Br. Med. Bull.* 22:5, 1966.

34. Behrman R.E.: Placental function and malnutrition. *Am. J. Dis. Child.* 129:425, 1975.

35. Wilson M.G.: Placental abnormalities and fetal disease. *Am. J. Dis. Child.* 108:154, 1964.

36. Laga E.M., Driscoll S.G., Munro H.N.: Comparison of placentas from two socioeconomic groups. *Pediatrics* 50:24, 33, 1972.

37. Holtzman N.A.: Prenatal screening for neural tube defects. *Pediatrics* 71:658, 1983.

38. Barnes A.C.: *Intrauterine Development*. Philadelphia, Lea & Febiger, 1968.

39. Ryan K.J.: Placental synthesis of steroid hormones, in Tulchinsky D., Ryan K.J. (eds.): *Maternal-Fetal Endocrinology*. Philadelphia, W.B. Saunders Co., 1980.

40. Robertson A.F., Sprecher H.: A review of human placental lipid metabolism and transport. *Acta Paediatr. Scand.* (suppl.) 183:3, 1968.

41. Singer J.E., Westphal M., Niswander K.: Relationship of weight gain during pregnancy to birth weight and infant growth and development in the first year of life: Report from collaborative study of cerebral palsy. *Obstet. Gynecol.* 31:417, 1968.

42. Naeye R.L.: Prenatal organ and cellular growth with various chromosomal disorders. *Biol. Neonate* 11:248, 1967.

43. Winick M., Rosso P.: The effects of severe early malnutrition on cellular growth of human brain. *Pediatr. Res.* 3:181, 1969.

44. Lechtig A., Delgado H., Lasky R., et al.: Maternal nutrition and fetal growth in developing countries. *Am. J. Dis. Child.* 129:553, 1975.

45. Sinclair J.C., Saigal S.: Nutritional influence in industrial societies. *Am. J. Dis. Child.* 129:549, 1975.

46. Rush D.: Maternal nutrition during pregnancy in industrial societies. *Am. J. Dis. Child.* 129:430, 1975.

47. Naeye R.L., Diener M.M., Harcke H.T., et al.: Relation of poverty and race to birth weight and organ and cell structure in the newborn. *Pediatr. Res.* 5:17, 1971.

48. Miller H.C., Merritt T.A.: *Fetal Growth in Humans*. Chicago, Year Book Medical Publishers, 1979.

49. Simpson J.W., Lawless R.W., Mitchell A.C.: Responsibility of the obstetrician to the fetus: II. Influence of prepregnancy weight and pregnancy weight gain on birthweight. *Obstet. Gynecol.* 45:481, 1975.
50. Naeye R.L., Blanc W., Paul C.: Effects of maternal nutrition on the human fetus, *Pediatrics* 52:494, 1973.
51. Stein H.: Maternal protein depletion and small-for-gestational-age babies. *Arch. Dis. Child.* 50:146, 1975.
52. Stein Z., Susser M.: The Dutch famine, 1944–45, and the reproductive process: Effect on six indices at birth. *Pediatr. Res.* 9:70, 76, 1975.
53. Birth H.G.: Functional effects of fetal malnutrition. *Hosp. Pract.* 3:134, 1971.
54. Stein Z., Susser M., Saenger G., et al.: Nutrition and mental performance. *Science* 178:708, 1972.
55. Chase H.P., Welch N.N., Dabiere C.S., et al.: Alterations in human brain biochemistry following intrauterine growth retardation. *Pediatrics* 50:403, 1972.
56. Babson G.S., Henderson N.B.: Fetal undergrowth: Relation of head growth to later intellectual performance. *Pediatrics* 53:890, 1974.
57. Fujikura T., Froehlich L.A.: Mental and motor development in monozygotic co-twins with dissimilar birth weights. *Pediatrics* 53:884, 1974.
58. Froehlich L.A., Fujikura T.: Follow-up of infants with single umbilical artery. *Pediatrics* 52:6, 1973.
59. Bryan E.M., Kohler H.G.: The missing umbilical artery: II. Paediatric follow-up. *Arch. Dis. Child.* 50:714, 1975.
60. Friesen H.G.: Placental protein hormones and tissue receptors for Hormones, in Gluck L. (ed.): *Modern Perinatal Medicine.* (Chicago, Year Book Medical Publishers, 1974.
61. Sinclair J.C.: *Energy Metabolism and Fetal Development.* New York, McGraw-Hill Book Co., 1970.
62. Clifford S.H.: Postmaturity with placental dysfunction. *J. Pediatr.* 44:1, 1954.
63. Ting R.Y., Wang M.H., McNair Scott T.F.: The dysmature infant. *J. Pediatr.* 90:943, 1977.
64. Kolata G.: First trimester prenatal diagnosis. *Science* 221:1031, 1983.
65. Birnholz J.C., Farrell E.E.: Ultrasound images of human fetal development. *Am. Sci.* 72:608, 1984.
66. Depp R.: Present status of the assessment of fetal maturity. *Semin. Perinatol.* 4:229, 1980.
67. Frus-Hansen B.: Body water compartments in children: Changes during growth and related changes in body composition. *Pediatrics* 28:169, 1961.
68. Windle W.F.: *Physiology of the Fetus.* Philadelphia, W.B. Saunders Co., 1940.

4 / Physical Measurements

Eat no green apples or you'll droop
Be careful not to get the croup
Avoid the chicken pox and such
And don't fall out of windows much.
—Edward Anthony, *Advice to
Young Children*

The relationship of the rate of growth and adequacy of body development to physical fitness is generally recognized. By comparison of the physical measurements of a given child over a period of time with those of other healthy children it is possible to determine, within limitations, whether he or she is doing as well as should be expected. The purpose of this discussion is to present normal body measurements and charts illustrating their use in the evaluation of progress of normal growth. It should be kept in mind that such measurements are made to reinforce and improve clinical judgment and not to displace it. The methods or technics used in obtaining measurements of physical growth must be followed closely to ensure adequate comparison with the standards established. When a child is being evaluated in the usual clinic setting, by far the most common reason for an unexpected deviation in weight, height, head circumference, etc., is due to an error in obtaining the measurement. Several excellent monographs on methodology are available.[15, 16, 20, 43]

In the recent literature on measurements of children it has become common practice to use one of two different standards as a means of assigning a given individual some point of reference relative to the group of his age. One method uses a mean value and one or more standard deviations. Such a system of presenting figures gives a good indication of just where a given child is in relation to the so-called normal group. One standard deviation includes 66.6% of the total number, two standard deviations include 95%, and three include 99.7%. Many of the tables presented here are given in this form. The other method of presenting such data is in percentiles. The number of the percentile indicates the position that a measurement would

77

hold in a typical series of 100 (100%). Thus, the 10th percentile gives the value for the 10th child of a group of 100. Nine children will be smaller in the measurement under consideration, and 90 will be larger. At the 50th percentile an equal number of children will be smaller or larger than the measurement. Tables 4–5 and 4–6, for height and weight, were constructed according to this method. Both the percentile and the standard deviation method are of value in estimating where a given child stands relative to a large group of the same age and sex. In some of the material presented in this chapter neither method has been used because the group studied was too small to give reliable trends or it was believed that these technics would add little of value to simple averages from a purely practical standpoint.

It is difficult to select truly representative figures of measurements in children. Many of the tables commonly used as acceptable standards are out of date so far as today's children in this country are concerned. Some figures are of doubtful value because of the selection of subjects used for the study, e.g., children from a special socioeconomic group or from a limited geographic area. Furthermore, there are few studies pertaining to racial groups or to one race in different environments. The use of standards such as those outlined in the foregoing paragraph does not rule out the objection that such tables are usually compiled from a more or less heterogeneous population in which many of the individuals are below optimal development. The tables used here are from relatively recent sources and represent measurements of children reared under relatively satisfactory conditions. Within the boundaries of the United States they can probably be considered adequate for clinical purposes.

Differences between populations in the size and shape of adults depend upon the variations in their gene pools and the influence of their environments. Differences in size and shape of children have a similar basis, plus the added effect arising from variations in the rate of maturation. Two populations may reach nearly identical adult size, but the children of one may be larger because they have a more rapid growth, enter puberty earlier, and stop growing earlier. Such differences are present, to a mild degree, in the black and white populations in the United States. Physical measurements and assessments of development of all countries and of ethnic groups within a country are highly desirable. The accumulation of this kind of material in a convenient form is just beginning to be realized.[24, 25] Tanner[54] has emphasized the need of such studies and has also pointed out some of the difficulties in the interpretation of results. The response of the individual and of the population have separate counterparts in the study of growth. An example is the superiority in height and weight of Japanese children born and raised in California as compared with those born and raised in Japan a generation ago. Differences in tempos and patterns of development would become better known and it is hoped that their significance would be understood. Another example to illustrate the point relates to the time of onset of menarche among different racial groups. Among European girls, menarche occurs just after the peak of the adolescent growth spurt, while in Nigerians it appears near the end of growth in height. Still another observation indicates that throughout childhood Chinese girls (Hong Kong) have skeletal maturation behind that of American girls until the age of 12 years when the Chinese forge ahead. This results in earlier completion of growth and a mean adult height that is shorter.[37, 38]

The recently completed studies of American youth have revealed some most interesting data as well as making available, for the first time, adequate figures for the black population.[3, 5, 7, 26] There was a marked diminution and near cessation of the trend to constantly increasing size of successive generations of American children. In this population, the so-called secular trend has come to an end. Only a small portion of children at the lower ends of the height and weight charts moved up the scale in the past couple of decades. When socioeconomic standards are analyzed and applied to this data, Hamill et al.[3] make the following comment, "When the stragglers will finally achieve their genetic potential to full stature can probably be better predicted by economic and social factors than by biologic ones."

Individual Growth Patterns

When the growth and development status or level of a given child is being appraised, the physician must keep in mind that this child, like others, has an individual growth pattern. The child's growth will resemble that of other children, but will have a timetable that is strictly his or her own. For this reason, mean or average values for height and weight should not be considered more than points of reference. When sequential measurements can be made, the percentile method of recording height and weight is much more useful than tables stating means and standard deviations. It is more important to know that a child is consistently maintaining a given relationship (in height and weight) to other children of his or her sex and age than it is to know that the child is tall or short. The progress of growth (height and weight) is predictable for a given child once his or her approximate percentile position or channel is established.

General Body Configuration

Alteration of body configuration or proportions results from selective regional rates of growth at different stages during the developmental period. In infancy the head grows at a relatively rapid rate so that during the first year the head circumference is greater than that of the chest. Thereafter the chest circumference becomes increasingly larger in proportion since growth of the head is relatively slow after the first year. The extremities are shorter than the trunk at birth but grow more rapidly later. At birth the infant's hands cannot reach to touch over the top of the head due to the shortness of the arms. During adolescence the major gain in height results from growth of the trunk. The ratio of mean sitting height/standing height changes from 0.51 to 0.52 in white males between the ages of 12 to 18 years. Although the exact figures vary, similar changes occur in white females and in both sexes in American blacks. This is a reversal of the ratio changes during the first 12 years. At birth the ratio is 0.85 and at six years is 0.55 indicating a greater contribution to stature of the lower extremities during early and middle childhood.[5, 7] The ratio of distance of crown to symphysis/symphysis to sole of the foot changes from 1.7 at birth to 1.0 by 11 years. In boys, span exceeds height after the 10th birthday and in girls after the 14th birthday (Fig 4–1).

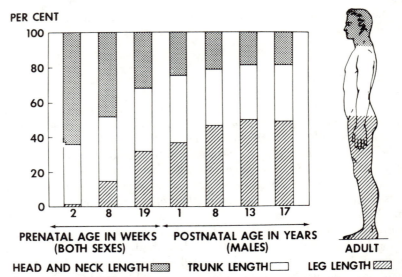

Fig 4–1.—Body proportions at different ages. The portion of head and neck length, trunk, and leg length that make up the total stature at different stages of development.

During most of childhood, growth appears to be primarily linear. In the adolescent, growth also assumes a process of "filling out" that is largely under the influence of the sex hormones (see chapter 9). Linear growth does not cease entirely until maturity is reached, at about 17 or 18 in girls and 20 to 21 in boys. However, after a rather short period of rapid statural increase associated with puberty, linear growth diminishes abruptly and tapers off to an insignificant amount after age 16 in girls and 18 for the majority of boys. Growth in height averages about 3 in. (7.6 cm) after menarche (see discussion in chapter 9 and Fig 9–4). During adolescence, girls have an increase in hip width that is not present in boys.[22] These changes are easily demonstrated by use of the width-length index, obtained by dividing the pelvic bicristal diameter (pelvic breadth) by standing height (Table 4–1).[9] Shoulder breadth, on the other hand, is found to expand more rapidly at this time in boys.

Longitudinal studies have demonstrated that children pass through the phase of accelerated growth associated with adolescence at widely different chronologic ages, but that they follow the same pattern or sequence for any particular measurement. In general, the sooner the phase is entered, the sooner growth (in height and weight) is completed. Children who enter the period early are apt to be slightly shorter as adults than are those who enter the period later. The stimulus to advanced or retarded growth is a general one and affects all dimensions.

The apparent smooth and gradual adolescent growth curves seen on most charts can be very deceiving. Each percentile line represents an average for a large number of children who may have entered the growth spurt at many different ages covering at least a six-year span of time. Plotting this

TABLE 4–1.—WIDTH-
LENGTH INDEX FOR BOYS
AND GIRLS AT DIFFERENT
AGES*

AGE	BOYS	GIRLS
Under 1 yr	0.173	0.175
1 yr	0.168	0.172
3 yr	0.166	0.168
5 yr	0.161	0.161
7 yr	0.159	0.159
9 yr	0.157	0.159
11 yr	0.157	0.161
13 yr	0.156	0.163
15 yr	0.155	0.164

*From Lucas and Pryor.[9] The
figures express the mean for normal subjects.

phenomena for a single individual may indicate a much more abrupt change, which appears to be more rapid and of shorter duration than a cross-sectional representation.

Some of the many different measurements suggested for proper evaluation of growth in children have considerable importance to the research worker. A volume that purports to be brief and practical is of necessity selective, and the measurements included in this chapter are believed to represent the most significant ones because experience has shown them to be more reliable. They are based on easily accessible bony landmarks and therefore are least subject to errors of interpretation or to variation of muscle tonus. In addition to linear or weight measurements alone, various authors have used indexes in an attempt to demonstrate body proportions better. Two examples have been given: the trunk-extremity proportion and the width-length index. Both may be useful in determining certain factors in the maturation of children. As a single example, it is known that the trunk-extremity index remains high in untreated children with hypothyroidism, i.e., infantile proportions are maintained. Other useful indexes are referred to at various points in the discussion that follows.

Constitutional (Somatic) Types

Since ancient times, attempts have been made to associate distinctive body types with personality traits or with predilection to specific diseases. At times these efforts have been pushed to extremes. However, some of these correlations have stood up better than others. In the study of the epidemiology of obesity, it appears that one has a good chance of predicting the obese adult from the body habitus of the infant and child (see chapter 13).

In this country, Sheldon[36] has suggested the classification of endomorphy, mesomorphy, and ectomorphy. In the first of these, the person is stocky with abundant subcutaneous fat. Sheldon felt such individuals had a predominance of structures derived from the endodermal embryonic layer. Mesomorphy shows a predominance of muscle, bone, and connective tissue. "Athletic" is a word commonly applied to this habitus. Ectomorphy, corresponding to the habitus phthisicus of Hippocrates, is characterized as thin, linear, and poorly muscled.

Sheldon has popularized the use of several techniques for somatotyping; principal among these is the use of photography of the nude subject standing before a calibrated grid. Certain technical details are necessary to avoid errors of parallax. In addition careful anthropometric observations are made, including widths of the head (bitemporal), of the shoulders (biacromial), and of the hips (bi-iliac and bitrochanteric). With these are included circumference measurements of neck, biceps, midthigh, calf, and ankle and estimation of thickness of the fat layer made with special tension calipers. Complete somatotyping according to the 20-odd measurements made by Sheldon is quite an undertaking and probably should be reserved for the serious student of anthropology.

Sheldon devised a numerical scale by means of which measurements could be made to yield a somatotype for any given individual. The somatotype is usually expressed by a series of three numerals, each of which expresses the relative strength or preponderance of one of the primary components—endomorphy, mesomorphy, or ectomorphy. The numerals are either 1, 4, or 7 and are always written one after another from left to right, the first numeral indicating the degree of endormorphy present, the second, mesomorphy, and the third, ectomorphy. Number 1 indicates less preponderance, number 4, medium, and number 7, maximum preponderance. It can thus be seen that the endomorphic type could be expressed by the numeral 7 followed by the numerals 1 or 4, depending upon the examiner's estimate of those structures derived from the mesodermal layer, and that this numeral would, in turn, be followed by a 1 or 4, depending upon the degree of development of structure derived from ectoderm. Thus, the extreme endomorph is 7 1 1. The extreme athletic type is 1 7 1 and the extreme ectomorph is 1 1 7 (Fig 4–2). The pediatrician and general practitioner are more likely to depend on such simple measurements or estimations as height, weight, and head and chest circumferences and a rough estimate of the thickness of the subcutaneous fat layer.

Photography

Good photographs may be of considerable aid as an accessory in growth studies. The graphic record of change afforded by photographs of a subject often portrays points difficult to show by figures, description, or curves. Such photographs should be made with the subject nude, in anterior and lateral views, with a measured grid as a background that will show up well in the print (see Fig 4–2). The child should stand as close as possible to the grid to avoid large errors from parallax. If the camera is high, near the eye level of the subject, the error due to parallax is minimized for those attempting to read actual height directly from the background grid.

Head Measurements

One of the most important measurements in the evaluation of children is the circumference of the head because this is related to intracranial volume and permits an estimation of the rate of brain growth. It is a measure-

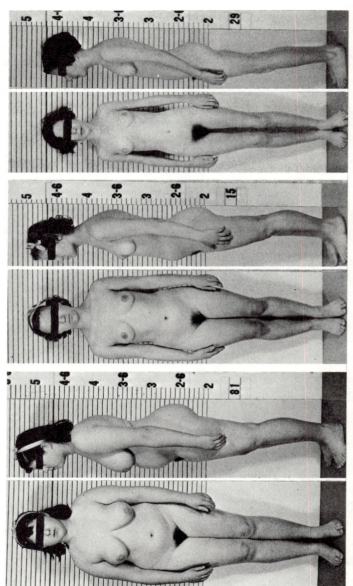

Fig 4-2.—Somatotyping. In a general way the photographs above illustrate the different body builds which have been described as somatotypes. All are 16-year-old girls. **Left,** this girl conforms roughly to the endomorphic type and may be designated 7 1 1. **Center,** this girl is a mesomorphic or athletic type and can be designated 1 7 1. **Right,** this girl is a linear type, though she should be taller to be the typical 1 1 7 type of Sheldon.

ment having a relatively narrow range for any age group, with a standard deviation that remains small and nearly constant for the entire growing period. There is almost no variation based on racial, national, or geographic factors.[47] Although there is a slight difference between the sexes, the circumference of males being greater, the difference does not exceed 1 cm for the mean at any age. Table 4–2 is constructed using a mean of both sexes and is adequate for any clinical appraisal. Sequential measurements of the head circumference plotted on a graph may reveal significant abnormal trends not apparent in an isolated value. A rapid increase, although remaining within the limits of two standard deviations, may be the first indication of hydrocephalus. This is especially true during infancy, when normal growth is relatively fast (Figs 4–3 and 4–4).

Any disturbance in the growth of the brain or injury to it may result in such varied conditions as microcephaly and hydrocephaly. During the early months of life, when maturation and growth of the brain proceed at a rapid rate, it may be easier to detect such anomalies or abnormalities from excessive variations in head circumference than from other means of evaluation, including a neurologic examination or observation of performance level. It should be pointed out, however, that visual inspection alone may be misleading, and it is not uncommon to suspect hydrocephalus in the

TABLE 4–2.—AVERAGE HEAD CIRCUMFERENCE
OF AMERICAN CHILDREN

AGE	MEAN IN.	MEAN CM	STANDARD DEVIATION IN.	STANDARD DEVIATION CM
Birth	13.8	35	0.5	1.2
1 mo.	14.9	37.6	0.5	1.2
2 mo.	15.5	39.7	0.5	1.2
3 mo.	15.9	40.4	0.5	1.2
6 mo.	17.0	43.4	0.4	1.1
9 mo.	17.8	45.0	0.5	1.2
12 mo.	18.3	46.5	0.5	1.2
18 mo.	19.0	48.4	0.5	1.2
2 yr	19.2	49.0	0.5	1.2
3 yr	19.6	50.0	0.5	1.2
4 yr	19.8	50.5	0.5	1.2
5 yr	20.0	50.8	0.6	1.4
6 yr	20.2	51.2	0.6	1.4
7 yr	20.5	51.6	0.6	1.4
8 yr	20.6	52.0	0.8	1.8
10 yr	20.9	53.0	0.6	1.4
12 yr	21.0	53.2	0.8	1.8
14 yr	21.5	54.0	0.8	1.8
16 yr	21.9	55.0	0.8	1.8
18 yr	22.1	55.4	0.8	1.8
20 yr	22.2	55.6	0.8	1.8

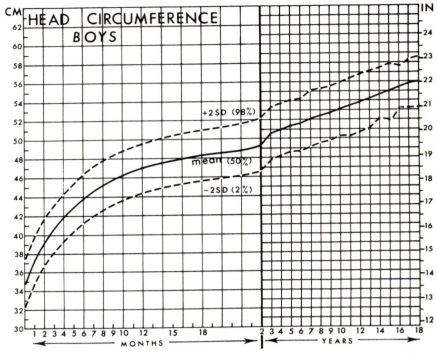

Fig 4–3.—Head circumference for boys from birth to 18 years. (From Nellhaus.[47])

low birth weight infant when accurate measurements will dissipate such errors. It is in such subjects that the proportions of head to chest or trunk may cause ungrounded fears (see also chapter 5).

Head circumference is measured by passing a tape measure over the most prominent part of the occiput and just above the supraorbital ridges. This is not necessarily the "maximum head circumference" that has been incorrectly used by some for evaluation. Growth is very rapid during the early months of life, and then there is deceleration. There is a 5-cm increase in the first four months, or about 0.5 in. a month. A second increase of 5 cm is not completed until the end of the first year. From then until age 18 there is only another 10-cm increase. The slight but definite increase that occurs during adolescence and early adult life reflects a greater thickness of cranium and cutaneous tissues rather than any change in brain size.

A number of studies have been published indicating that a large percentage, as high as 80%, of children whose head circumferences fall below

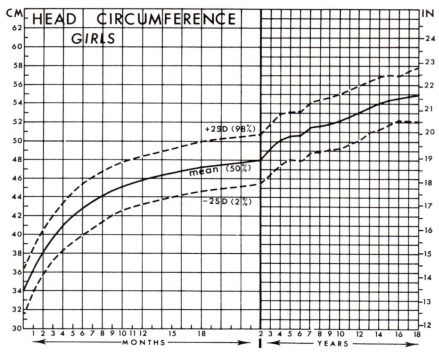

Fig 4–4.—Head circumference for girls from birth to 18 years. (From Nellhaus.[47])

the 2 percentile measurement will have mental retardation.[2, 29, 39, 51] Studies by the author indicate that there are some interesting and important exceptions. A relatively large number of children with severe congenital heart disease, and resultant retarded growth, maintained head circumferences well below that expected for their chronologic ages, but only rarely did they manifest any neurologic deficit. A small number of children with moderate to severe degrees of malabsorption syndrome, stunted growth, and head circumference below two standard deviations had normal psychometric testing. Similar findings have been reported by others.[28] Approximately 2% of children in a normal school population were found to have head circumferences two or more standard deviations below the mean at ages 5 to 18 years. Although there was minimal difference in IQ compared with the control group (99.5 versus 105), the microcephalics had a significantly lower performance in academic achievement scores (49 versus 70; $P = .001$).[42] Nevertheless, it must be recognized that a small head circumference, regardless of cause, is often associated with other evidence of neurologic impairment.

A special group of infants with small head measurements constitutes the premature and low birth weight babies (see chapter 5). For the neonate and early infancy, it is important to use appropriate standards of measurements such as those established by Lubchenco et al. (see Fig 5–1) in the evaluation. Microcephaly at birth (head circumference below the 10th percentile for gestational age) or found later was frequently associated with poor neurobehavioral outcome. In fact, head circumference at birth may be the single most important variable for subsequent development. Major neurologic deficits at 4 to 5 years were more frequently associated with microcephaly at birth than any other finding (Table 4–3).[16, 18, 21]

Children with large heads, above two standard deviations, often fall into a group where there is a familial incidence of large heads. These children are characterized by above normal rate of growth of head circumferences during infancy and a preponderance of males to females of 4:1. The majority of these children are quite normal neurologically. Obviously, such conditions as spina bifida, achondroplasia, subdural effusion, neurofibromatosis, etc., as possible causes of macrocephaly have been eliminated.[27, 40] Children with superior intelligence often have head circumferences well above the mean, but within two standard deviations beginning in late infancy.

The shape of the adult head differs conspicuously from that of the infant, the cranium being much more prominent in the latter (Fig 4–5). Separation of the cranial bones during the neonatal period is not uncommon, not is a slight degree of overlapping (see also chapter 12). If these changes are severe or if some other abnormality of the shape of the skull exists, e.g.,

TABLE 4–3.—PATHOLOGIC CONDITIONS
ASSOCIATED WITH MICROCEPHALY*

Genetic
    Seckel's bird-headed dwarfs
    Inborn errors (e.g., phenylketonuria)
Chromosome abnormalities
    Trisomies (Down's syndrome)
    Deletions (cat cry syndrome)
    Translocations (Down's syndrome)
Environmental
    Intrauterine infection (rubella, cytomegalovirus)
    Irradiation in utero
    Birth asphyxia
    Kernicterus
    Hydrocephaly
    Meningitis
    Subdural hematoma
Dysmorphic syndromes
    de Lange's syndrome

*From Lemire RJ.[61]

oxycephaly, scaphocephaly, or brachycephaly, then measurements will not indicate the true volume of the cranial vault. During the first week after birth, there may actually be a very slight decrease in head circumference possibly related to fluid loss or redistribution.[8] Such "shrinkage" may be fairly pronounced in "small for date" or low birth weight infants and is associated with generalized sodium and fluid loss.[22]

A measurement commonly used for obstetric purposes and to estimate the degree of maturity at birth is the occipitofrontal diameter. The range for full-term infants is 10.5 to 13 cm (4 to 5 in.) Owing to molding during labor, much variation can result that tends to invalidate the use of this method in the early neonatal period. At age 1 year the mean diameter is 16 cm (6.5 in.), at age 2, 17 cm (7 in.), and at age 18, approximately 19 cm (8 in.).

Attempts have been made to establish some reliable measurement standards for size of the fontanelles, especially the anterior one. For a number of reasons this has not been found practical. Definitive points to use for the measurements have not been uniformly agreed upon. There is great variation in the size and shape of the fontanelles within the limits of normal. Other methods are availabe and more reliable than estimating the significance and/or cause for a large or small fontanelle. Since the fontanelle is covered by a soft and pliable tissue, it can be used as a kind of manometer to judge intracranial pressure. If there is abnormally increasing pressure the fontanelle becomes tense, palpable arterial pulse is obliterated, and, finally, bulging occurs. Normally the anterior fontanelle is closed to palpation by 12 to 18 months, though a slight depression may still be evident. Sutures cannot be felt after the first few months, but they are not anatomically obliterated until 12 to 15 years (Figs 4–5 and 4–6).

Chest Measurements

Measurements of the chest should be taken with the subject recumbent at the level of the nipples midway between inspiration and expiration. Mean values are given in Table 4–4. At birth the transverse and anteroposterior diameters are nearly equal. The thoracic index, which is the ratio of the former to the latter, at this time is 1.0. The transverse diameter increases more rapidly than the anteroposterior, so that at age 1 year the index is 1.25 and at 6 years, 1.35. The ratio changes little thereafter.

Abdominal and Pelvic Measurements

During infancy and early childhood the abdomen is more prominent than at subsequent ages. The circumferences of the abdomen and thorax are about equal until age 2 years; after this time the abdominal circumfer-

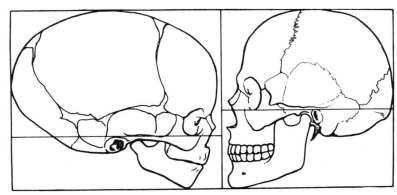

Fig 4–5.—The skull of a newborn infant **(left)** and an adult **(right)** drawn to the same scale. The changes due to the differences in growth are apparent in the relatively large cranial vault of the infant and the greater increase in size of the facial bones in the adult. The *horizontal lines* cross the same bony landmarks in each illustration.

ence is considerably less than the thoracic. Because the abdominal circumference is influenced by the phase of respiration, the degree of voluntary and involuntary muscle tone, and possible gaseous distention, it is a variable and relatively unreliable measurement.

A measurement less subject to variations in posture or tone of the mus-

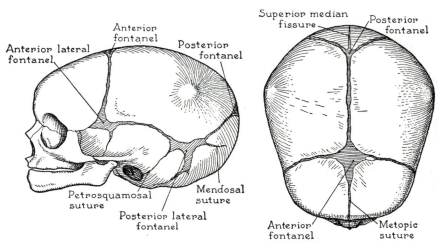

Fig 4–6.—The cranium at birth, showing major sutures and fontanelles. No attempt is made to show molding or overlapping of bones, which sometimes occurs at birth. (From Caffey.[58])

TABLE 4–4.—AVERAGE CHEST CIRCUMFERENCE AND
INTERCRISTAL WIDTH OF AMERICAN CHILDREN

| AGE | CHEST CIRCUMFERENCE | | PELVIC BICRISTAL DIAMETER | |
	IN.	CM	IN.	CM
Birth	13.7	35	3.2	8
3 mo	16.2	40	4.3	11
6 mo.	17.3	44	4.8	12
1 yr	18.3	47	5.1	13
18 mo.	18.9	48	5.5	14
2 yr	19.5	50	6.0	15
3 yr	20.4	52	6.2	16
4 yr	21.1	53	. . .	. . .
5 yr	22.0	55	7.2	18
6 yr	22.5	56	. . .	. . .
7 yr	23.0	57	8.2	20
8 yr	24.0	59	. . .	. . .
9 yr	24.5	60	8.5	21
10 yr	25.1	61	. . .	. . .
12 yr	27.0	66	9.0	22
14 yr	29.0	72	11.0	28
16 yr*	31.0	77	. . .	. . .
18 yr*	33.0	82	12.2	31
20 yr*	34.5	86	12.6	32

*Males only.

culature is the pelvic bicristal diameter. This represents the maximal distance between the external margins of the iliac crests, measured by calipers with the child in a recumbent position. Older children may be measured in erect position. The breadth of the pelvis usually reflects quiete well the general stockiness of the child. Average values for different ages are recorded in Table 4–4.

Weight and Height

In any group of measurements that of the body weight, because it sums up all the increments in size, is probably the best index of nutrition and growth. This is particularly true in infancy. In any period of life there are wide variations within normal limits. Careful clinical evaluation of the subject is necessary to avoid errors. The obese infant, although he or she weighs more than a healthy one wisely fed, is certainly not in a better state of nutrition. Infants in whom edema is developing will show a gain that is quite misleading in the absence of frank edema. Such factors, and more could be listed, must be recognized to evaluate properly the meaning of an individual's weight.

During the first few days of the neonatal period some loss of weight is normal, usually less than 10% of birth weight. This is accounted for by the initial loss of meconium and urine and by the inadequacy of the milk supply from the breast at this time. In some infants, particularly prematures, some of this loss may be due to disappearance of a "physiologic" edema during the first week. Birth weight is generally regained by the 10th day. Thereafter, in healthy infants, a steady gain ensues. The mean birth weight is usually given as 7.0 to 7.5 lb (3.4 kg). During the first three months, the average baby gains close to 1 kg (2.2 lb) a month, or nearly 30 gm (1 oz) a day. More than half of healthy infants will have doubled their birth weight within 3 to 4 months. Generally, weight gain is slightly greater in the formula-fed as compared with the breast-fed baby. By six months the average gain per month is down to 0.5 kg (1 lb). Birth weight is usually tripled by the end of the first year and quadrupled by the end of the second year. During the second year, the average monthly increment is about 0.25 kg, the rate of gain steadily decreasing. The older the child, the less regular is the increase in weight, and it may remain stationary for weeks at a time in perfectly healthy subjects. After age 2, the approximate annual increment in weight will be 2.3 kg (5 lb) until the individual begins his or her adolescent growth spurt.

The time of onset of rapid gain in weight during adolescence corresponds closely in both sexes with the gain in height. The duration of the gain in weight, however, covers a longer span.[22] The adolescent acceleration occurs earlier in girls than in boys, the most rapid spurt beginning in girls at 10 to 12 years and in boys two years later. This rapid growth is greatest the year before menarche.

All weight measurements should be obtained with the subject undressed and upon scales that are checked for accuracy periodically. Although these statements seem axiomatic, it must be emphasized that failure to observe both constitutes a common source of error.

Unlike those in weight, the annual increments in height continually diminish from birth to maturity, except for a short period referred to as the adolescent spurt of growth. The average birth length is about 50 cm (20 in.). By the end of the first year the infant has increased his or her birth length by about 50%. He or she has doubled it by age 4 years. During the early school years the curve of height increments is nearly flat, and the average annual gain is 5 cm (2 in.) or a little better. By the 13th year the birth length has trebled.

In girls the adolescent acceleration of growth in length occurs from approximately age 10 to 12 years, whereas for boys the acceleration is usually from age 12 to 14. From age 13 years in girls and 15 years in boys the rate of growth in stature rapidly decelerates. Growth ceases in girls at age 17 to 19 years but may continue in boys at a very slow rate beyond the 20th birthday.[10] In each individual child the rapid spurt of growth is most pronounced during the earliest period of the acceleration. It is only when a cross section of many children is considered that the curve is broadened.[22] Thus, the individuals grows at a much more rapid rate and for a relatively shorter time than a composite curve would indicate. The menarchial relationships to the time of attainment of terminal height are the same as those described for weight. Of course, there is variation in the annual increments of stature among children of the same age. For any given year a child's gain in height may be very small and still be normal for him or her, even though others of the child's age are becoming taller. Apparent growth retardation is most significant at the stages when growth should be accelerated. For instance, during infancy failure to grow in stature should be regarded with suspicion even in the absence of obvious disease.

The United States Public Health Service recently reported a survey of height and weight and other measurements of children in the United States.[3-5, 26] This consisted of examinations of over 7,000 children in the age range 6 to 18. The project covered the entire geographic area of the United States and, for statistical purposes, divided the groups into white and black. Though other races were included, their numbers were too small to be significant. This material was supplemented by other studies of equally recent origin to adequately cover the entire age span of childhood. All measurements were done between 1962 and 1974. In comparison of mean height and weight, or 50th percentiles, it is surprising how similar the USPHS figures are to the material of the Stuart and Meredith statistics published in 1946.[30] In height there is virtually no difference at any age for boys in the three studies. For girls, the differences are never greater than 2.5 cm. There is considerably greater variability in weight, but even here the differences probably have little or no clinical significance in their use as a means for comparison in the evaluation of a single child. The most recent study does indicate some increase in stature in the lower percentiles. Essentially no differences are present between the white and black races relative to height. Black girls do begin the pubertal acceleration of growth at a slightly earlier age than white girls and for a brief period are slightly taller. Both black boys and girls weigh slightly less than their white peers between the ages of 6 and 12. It does not appear necessary to publish separate standards for black and white children based upon the differences cited.[27, 35, 53, 56]

The changes in body proportions that follow the growth in height are important. At birth the sitting height represents 70% of the total length, but decreases to only 57% by age three, and roughly 50% by adulthood. Black children have slightly shorter sitting height but have longer lower extremities than white children at all ages.[5, 34]

Some boys and girls may be taller and heavier than the average from early childhood for genetic reasons. They also will mature more rapidly and complete their linear growth sooner. Conversely, genetically slow children will follow another pattern of growth at a lower level on the growth chart. The fact that other members of the family have experienced similar patterns of growth is helpful in arriving at the correct diagnosis in such situations. The child born small for gestational age is prone to grow more slowly than his or her peers and even remain small as an adult.[32, 45]

Common sources of error or confusion in comparing measurements obtained at different times result from poor technique. It is highly desirable to use reclining length for the first three years and thereafter standing height. The table or stand must be solid and firm, and the equipment used must not contribute to the problem, as is true of most measuring devices attached to weight scales found in many physicians' offices.

By the correlation of the height-age and weight-age data, a number of tables have been constructed that present mean weight for sex-age-height groups. Given the age, sex, and height of a child, the expected weight may be ascertained. This expected weight is the average for a large group of children. Several objections have been raised to the use of such tables in the appraisal of physical status: (1) There is a difference of opinion concerning the amount a given child may deviate from the mean figures before he or she should be considered abnormally overweight or underweight for his or her age, sex, etc. (2) Unless deviations from the usual physique are excessive, they are apt to be overlooked. (3) Furthermore, such tables fail to present a graphic picture of the mean against which the individuals' progress may be compared. The mean itself may be criticized as an undesirable standard because it is based on a child population that includes different levels, many of which are not optimal. Such tables do provide, nevertheless, a convenient standard and are frequently used.

Tables 4–5 and 4–6 give data for weight and height in percentiles, based on anthropometric charts, against which a child's development may be observed. Weight measurements for a child usually fall in the same percentile group at succeeding ages or change only gradually from period to period. Height and weight often differ in their actual percentile positions, but tend to maintain the same general relationships from period to period. Eighty percent of the weight measurements of children at a given age would be expected to fall between the 10th and 90th percentiles. Allowance must, of course, be made for the adolescent spurt in girls between ages 10 and 14 and in boys between 11 and 16. Children with weight and height measurements that (1) fall in different percentile groups, (2) shift percentile groups, or (3) fall near to or outside the 5th and 95th percentile should be reviewed for growth abnormalities.

TABLE 4–5.—Weight and Height Percentile Table: Boys
(Birth to Age 18)

WEIGHT IN LB			WEIGHT IN KG				HEIGHT IN IN.			HEIGHT IN CM		
10%	50%	90%	10%	50%	90%	AGE	10%	50%	90%	10%	50%	90%
6.3	7.5	9.1	2.86	3.4	4.13	Birth	18.9	19.9	21.0	48.1	50.6	53.3
8.5	10.0	11.5	3.8	4.6	5.2	1 mo	20.2	21.2	22.2	50.4	53.0	55.5
10.0	11.5	13.2	4.6	5.2	6.0	2 mo	21.5	22.5	23.5	53.7	56.0	60.0
11.1	12.6	14.5	5.03	5.72	6.58	3 mo	22.8	23.8	24.7	57.8	60.4	62.8
12.5	14.0	16.2	5.6	6.3	7.3	4 mo	23.7	24.7	25.7	60.5	62.0	65.2
13.7	15.0	17.7	6.2	7.0	8.0	5 mo	24.5	25.5	26.5	61.8	65.0	67.3
14.8	16.7	19.2	6.71	7.58	8.7	6 mo	25.2	26.1	27.3	63.9	66.4	69.3
17.8	20.0	22.9	8.07	9.07	10.39	9 mo	27.0	28.0	29.2	68.6	71.2	74.2
19.6	22.2	25.4	8.89	10.7	11.52	12 mo	28.5	29.6	30.7	72.4	75.2	78.1
22.3	25.2	29.0	10.12	11.43	13.15	18 mo	31.0	32.2	33.5	78.8	81.8	85.0
24.7	27.7	31.9	11.2	12.56	14.47	2 yr	33.1	34.4	35.9	84.2	87.5	91.1
26.6	30.0	34.5	12.07	13.61	15.65	2½ yr	34.8	36.3	37.9	88.5	92.1	96.2
28.7	32.2	36.8	13.02	14.61	16.69	3 yr	36.3	37.9	39.6	92.3	96.2	100.5
30.4	34.3	39.1	13.79	15.56	17.74	3½ yr	37.8	39.3	41.1	96.0	99.8	104.5
32.1	36.4	41.4	14.56	16.51	18.78	4 yr	39.1	40.7	42.7	99.3	103.4	108.5
33.8	38.4	43.9	15.33	17.42	19.91	4½ yr	40.3	42.0	44.2	102.4	106.7	112.3
35.5	40.5	46.7	16.1	18.37	21.18	5 yr	40.8	42.8	45.2	103.7	108.7	114.7
38.8	45.6	53.1	17.6	20.68	24.09	5½ yr	42.6	45.0	47.3	108.3	114.4	120.1
40.9	48.3	56.4	18.55	21.91	25.58	6 yr	43.8	46.3	48.6	111.2	117.5	123.5
43.4	51.2	60.4	19.69	23.22	27.4	6½ yr	44.9	47.6	50.0	114.1	120.8	127.0
45.8	54.1	64.4	20.77	24.54	29.21	7 yr	46.0	48.9	51.4	116.9	124.1	130.5
48.5	57.1	68.7	22.0	25.9	31.16	7½ yr	47.2	50.0	52.7	120.0	127.1	133.9
51.2	60.1	73.0	23.22	27.26	33.11	8 yr	48.5	51.2	54.0	123.1	130.0	137.3
53.8	63.1	77.0	24.4	28.62	34.93	8½ yr	49.5	52.3	55.1	125.7	132.8	140.0
56.3	66.0	81.0	25.54	29.94	36.74	9 yr	50.5	53.3	56.1	128.3	135.5	142.6
58.7	69.0	85.5	26.63	31.3	38.78	9½ yr	51.4	54.3	57.1	130.6	137.9	145.1
61.1	71.9	89.9	27.71	32.61	40.78	10 yr	52.3	55.2	58.1	132.8	140.3	147.5
63.7	74.8	94.6	28.89	33.93	42.91	10½ yr	53.2	56.0	58.9	135.1	142.3	149.7
66.3	77.6	99.3	30.07	35.2	45.04	11 yr	54.0	56.8	59.8	137.3	144.2	151.8
69.2	81.0	104.5	31.39	36.74	47.4	11½ yr	55.0	57.8	60.9	139.8	146.9	154.8
72.0	84.4	108.6	32.66	38.28	49.71	12 yr	56.1	58.9	62.2	142.4	149.6	157.9
74.6	88.7	116.4	33.84	40.23	52.8	12½ yr	56.9	60.0	63.6	144.5	152.3	161.6
77.1	93.0	123.2	34.97	42.18	55.88	13 yr	57.7	61.0	65.1	146.6	155.0	165.3
82.2	100.3	130.1	37.29	45.5	59.01	13½ yr	58.8	62.6	66.5	149.4	158.9	168.9
87.2	107.6	136.9	39.55	48.81	62.1	14 yr	59.9	64.0	67.9	152.1	162.7	172.4
93.3	113.9	142.4	42.32	51.66	64.59	14½ yr	61.0	65.1	68.7	155.0	165.3	174.6
99.4	120.1	147.8	45.09	54.48	67.04	15 yr	62.1	66.1	69.6	157.8	167.8	176.7
105.2	124.9	152.6	47.72	56.65	69.22	15½ yr	63.1	66.8	70.2	160.3	169.7	178.2
111.0	129.7	157.3	50.35	58.83	71.35	16 yr	64.1	67.8	70.7	162.8	171.6	179.7
114.3	133.0	161.0	51.85	60.33	73.03	16½ yr	64.6	68.0	71.1	164.2	172.7	180.7
117.5	136.2	164.6	53.3	61.78	74.66	17 yr	65.2	68.4	71.5	165.5	173.7	181.6
118.8	137.6	166.8	53.89	62.41	75.66	17½ yr	65.3	68.5	71.6	165.9	174.1	182.0
120.0	139.0	169.0	54.43	63.05	76.66	18 yr	65.5	68.7	71.8	166.3	174.5	182.4

TABLE 4–6.—Weight and Height Percentile Table: Girls (Birth to Age 18)

WEIGHT IN LB			WEIGHT IN KG			AGE	HEIGHT IN IN.			HEIGHT IN CM		
10%	50%	90%	10%	50%	90%		10%	50%	90%	10%	50%	90%
6.2	7.4	8.6	2.81	3.36	3.9	Birth	18.8	19.8	20.4	47.8	50.2	51.0
8.0	9.7	11.0	3.3	4.2	5.0	1 mo	20.2	21.0	22.0	50.4	52.8	55.0
9.5	11.0	12.5	4.1	5.0	5.8	2 mo	21.5	22.2	23.2	53.7	55.5	59.6
10.7	12.4	14.0	4.85	5.62	6.35	3 mo	22.4	23.4	24.3	56.9	59.5	61.7
12.0	13.7	15.5	5.3	6.2	7.2	4 mo	23.2	24.2	25.2	59.6	61.0	64.8
13.0	14.7	17.0	5.9	6.8	7.7	5 mo	24.0	25.0	26.0	60.7	64.2	67.0
14.1	16.0	18.6	6.4	7.26	8.44	6 mo	24.6	25.7	26.7	62.5	65.2	67.8
16.6	19.2	22.4	7.53	8.71	10.16	9 mo	26.4	27.6	28.7	67.0	70.1	72.9
18.4	21.5	24.8	8.35	9.75	11.25	12 mo	27.8	29.2	30.3	70.6	74.2	77.1
21.2	24.5	28.3	9.62	11.11	12.84	18 mo	30.2	31.8	33.3	76.8	80.9	84.5
23.5	27.1	31.7	10.66	12.29	14.38	2 yr	32.3	34.1	35.8	82.0	86.6	91.0
25.5	29.6	34.6	11.57	13.43	15.69	2½ yr	34.0	36.0	37.9	86.3	91.4	96.4
27.6	31.8	37.4	12.52	14.42	16.96	3 yr	35.6	37.7	39.8	90.5	95.7	101.1
29.5	33.9	40.4	13.38	15.38	18.33	3½ yr	37.1	39.2	41.5	94.2	99.5	105.4
31.2	36.2	43.5	14.15	16.42	19.73	4 yr	38.4	40.6	43.1	97.6	103.2	109.6
32.9	38.5	46.7	14.92	17.46	21.18	4½ yr	39.7	42.0	44.7	100.9	106.8	113.5
34.8	40.5	49.2	15.79	18.37	22.32	5 yr	40.5	42.9	45.4	103.0	109.1	115.4
38.0	44.0	51.2	17.24	19.96	23.22	5½ yr	42.4	44.4	46.8	107.8	112.8	118.9
39.6	46.5	54.2	17.96	21.09	24.58	6 yr	43.5	45.6	48.1	110.6	115.9	122.3
42.2	49.4	57.7	19.14	22.41	26.17	6½ yr	44.8	46.9	49.4	113.7	119.1	125.6
44.5	52.2	61.2	20.19	23.68	27.76	7 yr	46.0	48.1	50.7	116.8	122.3	128.9
46.6	55.2	65.6	21.14	25.04	29.76	7½ yr	47.0	49.3	51.9	119.5	125.2	131.8
48.6	58.1	69.9	22.04	26.35	31.71	8 yr	48.1	50.4	53.0	122.1	128.0	134.6
50.6	61.0	74.5	22.95	27.67	33.79	8½ yr	49.0	51.4	54.1	124.6	130.5	137.5
52.6	63.8	79.1	23.86	28.94	35.88	9 yr	50.0	52.3	55.3	127.0	132.9	140.4
54.9	67.1	84.4	24.9	30.44	38.28	9½ yr	50.9	53.5	56.4	129.4	135.8	143.2
57.1	70.3	89.7	25.9	31.89	40.69	10 yr	51.8	54.6	57.5	131.7	138.6	146.0
59.9	74.6	95.1	27.17	33.79	43.14	10½ yr	52.9	55.8	58.9	134.4	141.7	149.7
62.6	78.8	100.4	28.4	35.74	45.54	11 yr	53.9	57.0	60.4	137.0	144.7	153.4
66.1	83.2	106.0	29.98	37.74	48.08	11½ yr	55.0	58.3	61.8	139.8	148.1	157.0
69.5	87.6	111.5	31.52	39.74	50.58	12 yr	56.1	59.8	63.2	142.6	151.9	160.6
74.7	93.4	118.0	33.88	42.37	53.52	12½ yr	57.4	60.7	64.0	145.9	154.3	162.7
79.9	99.1	124.5	36.24	44.95	56.47	13 yr	58.7	61.8	64.9	149.1	157.1	164.8
85.5	103.7	128.9	38.78	47.04	58.47	13½ yr	59.5	62.4	65.3	151.1	158.4	165.9
91.0	108.4	133.3	41.28	49.17	60.46	14 yr	60.2	62.8	65.7	153.0	159.6	167.0
94.2	111.0	135.7	42.73	50.35	61.55	14½ yr	60.7	63.1	66.0	154.1	160.4	167.6
97.4	113.5	138.1	44.18	51.48	62.64	15 yr	61.1	63.4	66.2	155.2	161.1	168.1
99.2	115.3	139.6	45.0	52.3	63.32	15½ yr	61.3	63.7	66.4	155.7	161.7	168.6
100.9	117.0	141.1	45.77	53.07	64.0	16 yr	61.5	63.9	66.5	156.1	162.2	169.0
101.9	118.1	142.2	46.22	53.57	64.5	16½ yr	61.5	63.9	66.6	156.2	162.4	169.2
102.8	119.1	143.3	46.63	54.02	65.0	17 yr	61.5	64.0	66.7	156.3	162.5	169.4
103.2	119.5	143.9	46.81	54.2	65.27	17½ yr	61.5	64.0	66.7	156.3	162.5	169.4
103.5	119.9	144.5	46.95	54.39	65.54	18 yr	61.5	64.0	66.7	156.3	162.5	169.4

Height-Weight Curves

The presentation of norms in terms of curves has a decided advantage, providing a running account of the individual's measurements plotted against the pattern of growth of a large group of his or her own age. A child growing normally tends to maintain his or her relative position (percentile level) with respect to his or her age group. The child's growth trend as compared with the growth trend of other children is represented in such a way that deviations from the norm may become apparent earlier than otherwise.

Once the measurements are plotted, one looks at a picture of growth with the intermediate numerical steps dispensed with once and for all. Patterns of growth of the individual are compared with curves of the chart: levels of growth attained by the individual are examined in relation to the levels of the different percentiles of the chart. The weight-age curve is compared with the height-age curve to determine the subject's build and nutritional status. Any marked deviation from the curves of the chart must be interpreted in the light of the medical and social history of the child and the results of physical examination (Figs 4–7 and 4–8).

Velocity of Growth

The rate or velocity of growth is an extremely important aspect of the evaluation of any child. This is especially so if information on the longitudinal growth is meager or absent for a particular subject. Growth is not constant and is characterized by periods of acceleration occurring at different times but in similar sequences for healthy children. The velocity of growth is most rapid immediately after birth and then falls off rapidly (Table 4–7). From age 2 until about 11 in girls and 13 in boys the rate or velocity continues slowly decelerating, and then the adolescent increase begins. For girls this peaks at approximately age 12 and for boys at 14. Except for infancy, the usual time interval used in measuring either height or weight velocity is one year. It should be pointed out that the adolescent peak for weight in girls follows height by about one year, or at age 13, while the peaks occur nearly simultaneously in boys.

In velocity standards a child does not have the same tendency to stay in the same percentile position from one age to another as in the usual height or weight versus age graphs. The child may occupy a relatively high or low position at one stage of his or her development, but if the child enjoys good health, he or she will tend to move toward a more central or average rate of increment in the following stage.

When considering height velocity, two important facts must be remem-

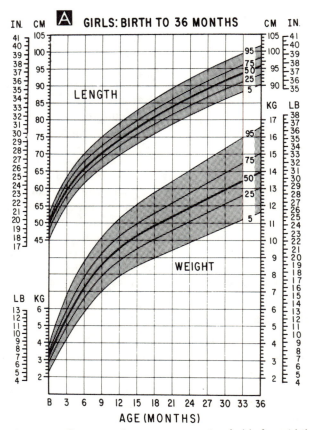

Fig 4–7.—A, percentile curves for measurements of girls from birth to 3 years. Length was obtained in a recumbent position during the first 3 years, thereafter as standing height. Where the length and height measurements overlap, the results have been modified to result in a smooth uninterrupted curve. (The growth charts are reproduced by permission of the National Center for Health Statistics.[3] *(Continued.)*

bered as they apply to the individual child. The adolescent peak (time of most rapid increase in height growth) will occur at different ages for each subject, depending upon his or her rate of sexual maturation. The relative velocity for boys is greater than for girls; an increase of 9.2 cm as compared with 8.3 cm in the maximal year are mean figures, based on Tanner's work[55] (Fig 4–9).

Comparisons of percentile positions held by measurements at repeated periodic examinations indicate adherence to or possibly significant deviation from previous percentile positions. In normal circumstances one ex-

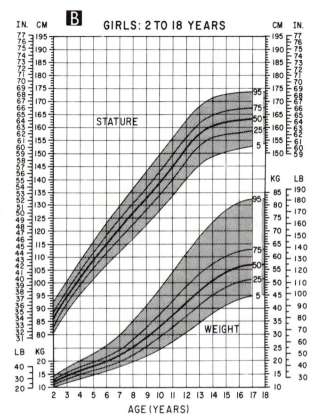

Fig 4–7 (cont.).—B, percentile curves for measurements of girls from 2 to 18 years.

pects a child to maintain a similar position from age to age, i.e., on or near one percentile line or between the same lines. Occasional sharp deviations or gradual but continuing shifts from one percentile position to another call for further investigation as to their causes.

Predicting Growth

Anyone who has occasion to appraise growth and development of children appreciates the need for systems of remembering approximate heights and weights at various ages. Common aides in general use include the following:

Height at 2 years is one-half adult height

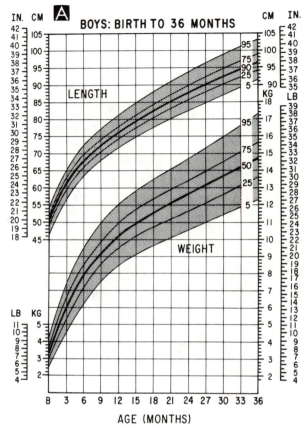

Fig 4–8.—A, percentile curves for measurements of boys from birth to 3 years. See legend for Figure 4–7, A. *(Continued.)*

At 3 years the child is 3 ft tall
At 4 years the child is 40 in.
At 3.5 years, weight is 35 lb
At 7 years, weight is seven times birth weight (lb)
Weight equals age + 11 (lb)
Height equals 2.5 × age + 30 (in.)
Tanner[41] has devised the following formulas using the height reached at age 3 years (H_3):
Adult height (cm) = 1.27 × H_3 + 54.9 (males)
Adult height (cm) = 1.29 × H_3 + 42.3 (females)

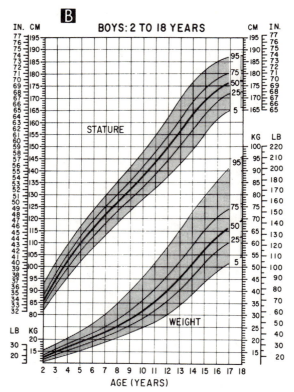

Fig 4–8 (cont.).—B, percentile curves for measurements of boys from 2 to 18 years.

Tanner found that height at age 3 years showed better correlation with height at maturity than at any other early age.

Recognizing the influence of the degree of maturity present at the time the estimation is made, Bayer and Bayley[43] compiled tables of adult height based upon present measurements of height and bone age (Fig 4–10). Other students in the field of prediction have emphasized the role of genetics and used parental height in their calculations.[49, 59] Commonly, "parental midpoint" is used; the height of both parents is added and divided by 2 (Figs 4–10 and 4–11).

Garn and Rohmann[49] have emphasized the interaction of nutrition and genetics as determinants of growth and as factors influencing the timing of growth. They use midparent stature (the average of father's and mother's

TABLE 4–7.—Expected Increments
in Weight and Height*

AGE	WEIGHT, KG		HEIGHT, CM	
0–1 mo	0.64		3.8	
1–3 mo	1.54		6.1	
3–6 mo	1.77		6.4	
6–9 mo	1.36		4.6	
9–12 mo	1.00		4.1	
12–18 mo	1.40		6.6	
18–24 mo	1.22		5.6	
24–30 mo	1.04		4.8	
30–36 mo	0.95		4.3	
36–42 mo	1.04		3.8	
42–48 mo	0.95		3.6	
48–54 mo	1.09		3.6	
54–60 mo	1.00		3.3	
60–66 mo	1.14		3.6	
66–72 mo	1.18		3.3	
	BOYS	GIRLS	BOYS	GIRLS
6–7 yr	2.2	2.1	6.1	6.1
7–8 yr	2.4	2.4	5.6	5.8
8–9 yr	2.5	2.5	5.6	5.6
9–10 yr	2.7	2.8	5.1	5.8
10–11 yr	2.5	3.5	5.1	6.7
11–12 yr	3.0	4.5	5.1	8.3
12–13 yr	4.1	7.8	6.6	5.8
13–14 yr	5.5	4.3	9.2	3.0
14–15 yr	9.0	2.3	6.5	0.8
15–16 yr	4.5	1.8	3.1	0.1
16–17 yr	3.2	1.2	1.5	0.1

*Data represent averages from several sources.

statures in the fourth decade) in preparing parent-related age-size standards for children. They used the Fels longitudinal studies data to compile
tables that should be more helpful in predicting probable age-height and
final height values for individual children. Figure 4–12 clearly shows the
effect of parental size on the stature of children. Tables 4–8 and 4–9 provide a more precise reference than do conventional age-size standards long
in general use. For example, the 10-year-old boy of parents whose average
(midparent) stature is 163 cm would be expected to be near 132.5 cm tall,
whereas a boy of the same age whose parents averaged 178 cm would be
expected to be more than 10 cm taller. Within the first years of life the
children who were offspring of tall parents were taller than those of shorter
parents. With increasing age these differences become more apparent.

It seems fair to say that the final word on formulas to predict final height
from early measurements has not yet been spoken. Certainly three variables appear to be important enough to include in such calculations. These

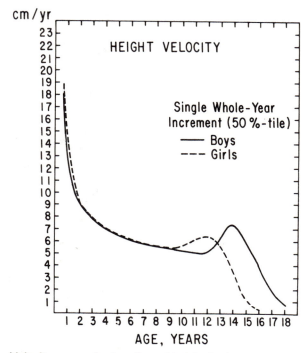

Fig 4–9.—Velocity curves for length and height for boys and girls based upon intervals of one year. They indicate the rapid deceleration following birth and the relatively short duration of the adolescent acceleration. Each curve represents the mean of the sex and the mean for age and height increase. Normal variations from these are to be expected, but the relative shape of the curve will be followed by each child. The shape of the curve for the adolescent growth "spurt" for an individual child will usually be narrower (less time) and higher (more accumulated height) than the mean illustrated.

are the height of the parents, the bone age of the child at varying ages, and the age of the mother at menarche (especially related to time of onset of maturational changes in boys).

Individual differences in growth become accentuated with the onset of adolescence. The variations of heights and weights and degree of maturation seen in schoolchildren, sixth through tenth grade, are enormous. The girl who matures early is much larger than average at age 11 but will usually be shorter than the average at maturity, whereas the girl who matures later will, in most physical measurements, be smaller than average until age 14 or 15 years but will continue to grow for a longer time and is likely to be taller than average when growth is completed. This tendency for

Skeletal Age

% of Mature Height

Ht. (inches)	6-0	6-3	6-6	6-9	7-0	7-3	7-6	7-9	8-0	8-3	8-6	8-9	9-0	9-3	9-6	9-9	10-0	10-3	10-6	10-9	11-0	11-3	11-6	11-9	12-0	12-3	12-6	12-9	13-0
% of Mature Height	68.0	69.0	70.0	70.9	71.8	72.8	73.8	74.7	75.6	76.5	77.3	77.9	78.6	79.4	80.0	80.7	81.2	81.6	81.9	82.1	82.3	82.7	83.2	83.9	84.5	85.2	86.0	86.9	88.0
41	60.3																												
42	61.8	60.9	60.0																										
43	63.2	62.3	61.4	60.6																									
44	64.7	63.8	62.9	62.1	61.3	60.4																							
45	66.2	65.2	64.3	63.5	62.7	61.8	61.0	60.2																					
46	67.6	66.7	65.7	64.9	64.1	63.2	62.3	61.6	60.8	60.1																			
47	69.1	68.1	67.1	66.3	65.5	64.6	63.7	62.9	62.2	61.4	60.8	60.3																	
48	70.6	69.6	68.6	67.7	66.9	65.9	65.0	64.3	63.5	62.7	62.1	61.6	61.1	60.5	60.0														
49	72.1	71.0	70.0	69.1	68.3	67.3	66.4	65.6	64.8	64.1	63.4	62.9	62.3	61.7	61.3	60.7	60.3	60.0											
50	73.5	72.5	71.4	70.5	69.6	68.7	67.8	66.9	66.1	65.4	64.7	64.2	63.6	63.0	62.5	62.0	61.6	61.3	61.1	60.9	60.8	60.5	60.1						
51	75.0	73.9	72.9	71.9	71.0	70.1	69.1	68.3	67.5	66.7	66.0	65.5	64.9	64.2	63.8	63.2	62.8	62.5	62.3	62.1	62.0	61.7	61.3	60.8	60.4				
52	76.5	75.4	74.3	73.3	72.4	71.4	70.5	69.6	68.8	68.0	67.3	66.8	66.2	65.5	65.0	64.4	64.0	63.7	63.5	63.3	63.2	62.9	62.5	62.0	61.5	61.0	60.5		
53	77.9	76.8	75.7	74.8	73.8	72.8	71.8	71.0	70.1	69.3	68.6	68.0	67.4	66.8	66.3	65.7	65.3	65.0	64.7	64.6	64.4	64.1	63.7	63.2	62.7	62.2	61.6	61.0	60.2
54	79.4	78.3	77.1	76.2	75.2	74.2	73.2	72.3	71.4	70.6	69.9	69.3	68.7	68.0	67.5	66.9	66.5	66.2	65.9	65.8	65.6	65.3	64.9	64.4	63.9	63.4	62.8	62.1	61.4
55	80.9	79.7	78.6	77.6	76.6	75.5	74.5	73.6	72.8	71.9	71.2	70.6	70.0	69.3	68.8	68.2	67.7	67.4	67.2	67.0	66.8	66.5	66.1	65.6	65.1	64.6	64.0	63.3	62.5
56			80.0	79.0	78.0	76.9	75.9	75.0	74.1	73.2	72.4	71.9	71.2	70.5	70.0	69.4	69.0	68.6	68.4	68.2	68.0	67.7	67.3	66.8	66.3	65.7	65.1	64.4	63.6
57				80.4	79.4	78.3	77.2	76.3	75.4	74.5	73.7	73.2	72.5	71.8	71.3	70.6	70.2	69.9	69.6	69.4	69.3	68.9	68.5	67.9	67.5	66.9	66.3	65.6	64.8
58					80.8	79.7	78.6	77.6	76.7	75.8	75.0	74.5	73.8	73.0	72.5	71.9	71.4	71.1	70.8	70.6	70.5	70.1	69.7	69.1	68.6	68.1	67.4	66.7	65.9
59							80.0	79.0	78.0	77.1	76.3	75.7	75.1	74.3	73.8	73.1	72.7	72.3	72.0	71.9	71.7	71.3	70.9	70.3	69.8	69.2	68.6	67.9	67.0
60								80.3	79.4	78.4	77.6	77.0	76.3	75.6	75.0	74.3	73.9	73.5	73.3	73.1	72.9	72.6	72.1	71.5	71.0	70.4	69.8	69.0	68.2
61									80.7	79.7	78.9	78.3	77.6	76.8	76.3	75.6	75.1	74.8	74.5	74.3	74.1	73.8	73.3	72.7	72.2	71.6	70.9	70.2	69.3
62											80.2	79.6	78.9	78.1	77.5	76.8	76.4	76.0	75.7	75.5	75.3	75.0	74.5	73.9	73.4	72.8	72.1	71.3	70.5
63												80.9	80.2	79.3	78.8	78.1	77.6	77.2	76.9	76.7	76.6	76.2	75.7	75.1	74.6	73.9	73.3	72.5	71.6
64														80.6	80.0	79.3	78.8	78.4	78.1	78.0	77.8	77.4	76.9	76.3	75.7	75.1	74.4	73.6	72.7
65																80.5	80.0	79.7	79.4	79.2	79.0	78.6	78.1	77.5	76.9	76.3	75.6	74.8	73.9
66																		80.9	80.6	80.4	80.2	79.8	79.3	78.7	78.1	77.5	76.7	75.9	75.0
67																							80.5	79.9	79.3	78.6	77.9	77.1	76.1

Fig 4-10.—Percentages and estimated mature heights for boys with skeletal ages one year or more retarded for their chronologic ages. This is one of several tables published by Bayley and Pinneau, by means of which an estimate of the height at maturity is made from present height and skeletal age. Skeletal age is determined from an x-ray wrist plate (Fig 4-11) and use of the Greulich-Pyle Atlas. Using this table, we see that the patient shown in Figure 4-11, who is now 58 in. tall and who has a skeletal age of 12 years, 3 months, has achieved only 85.2% of his expected growth, and should eventually be approximately 68.1 in. tall. Bayley and Pinneau found an error of less than 1 in. in prediction of final height in boys 14½ years of age. (From Bayer and Bayley.)[43]

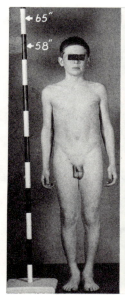
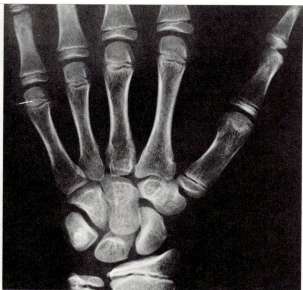

Fig 4–11.—Boy, age 14¼. Complaint: smallest boy in his class. Height: 58 inches, weight 91 pounds, bone age 12–3 (by Greulich-Pyle Atlas). Height at 2 years was 34½ inches, at 3 years 37½ inches. Height of father 72 inches, mother 63½ inches. The problem is one of predicting final height. It is obvious that reassurance can be given the patient and his family if it appears that final height will be satisfactory and that present shortness is one of delayed velocity rather than dwarfism. The following calculations illustrate different methods of estimating the boy's final height. In the formulas below H_m is height at maturity, H_2, height at 2 years and H_3, at 3 years. As can be seen, all methods indicate satisfactory eventual height.

Tanner, H_m (cm) $= 1.27 \times H_3 + 54.9$ cm
$H_m = 175$ cm or 68.8 in
Garn and Rohmann, Table 4–12 $= 173$ cm or 68.1 in
Traditional, Hm $= 2 \times H_2$ or 68.5 in
Bayer and Bayley, Fig 4–9 $= 68.1$ in

early maturation to bring about early curtailment of growth is much more marked in girls than in boys. It is generally accepted that female sex hormones (estrogens) will cause epiphysial closure and cessation of statural growth once they reach the levels seen with onset of menses. The presence or absence of secondary sexual characteristics, such as pubic and axillary hair, size of the male genitalia, and degree of breast development, are valuable adjuncts in the clinical estimation of future growth potentials. Using a grading system based upon the stages of development, some authorities contend that quite accurate predictions can be made.[52]

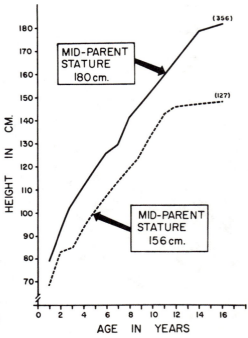

Fig 4–12.—Effect of parental size on the statural growth of children. Child no. *356,* whose midparental (average of both) stature was 180 cm, was considerably taller than subject no. *127,* whose midparental stature was 156 cm. (From Garn and Rohmann.[49])

Growth as a Whole

Olson and Hughes,[12, 13] of the University of Michigan Laboratory School, have devised a table to show the longitudinal development of the child as a whole. On one table are plotted measurements of various mental and physical attributes. These workers feel that by using such a method they have the "life history of any given child over a significant age span" and also a table that takes into consideration the interrelationship of many factors of development. The unit of description is age, and each measure is converted into an age value. Using this principle, one can plot height, weight, number of erupted teeth, strength of grip, carpal age, mental age (Kuhlmann-Binet), educational age (Stanford), social age (Doll), and many others against a common scale. A manual has been compiled to assist in the translation of the various measurements into age units (reprinted from Olson and Hughes[13]).

Data so far acquired by the use of this table have shown a remarkable correlation of all of the measures used, i.e., in most instances there is a

TABLE 4–8.—Fels Parent-Specific Standards for Height: Girls' Stature by Age and Midparent States*

AGE	PARENTAL MIDPOINT, CM									
	161	163	165	167	169	171	173	175	177	178
Birth	47.3	48.9	49.0	49.2	49.2	48.8	49.7	49.1	49.0	47.5
0–1	53.0	53.4	54.2	52.0	53.3	53.1	53.5	53.2	55.8	52.8
0–3	57.4	58.4	59.6	57.4	59.4	59.6	59.4	58.0	61.5	57.6
0–6	64.4	64.7	65.6	65.7	64.6	66.5	66.6	67.4	67.3	65.8
0–9	68.2	69.0	70.2	70.1	69.8	71.5	71.5	71.0	72.2	69.8
1–0	72.3	73.0	73.8	74.0	74.0	75.2	75.5	74.6	77.3	73.2
1–6	78.8	79.5	80.6	81.4	80.2	81.7	82.6	81.6	84.0	81.0
2–0	84.6	84.0	86.5	87.4	85.5	88.8	88.7	88.2	89.5	87.6
2–6	89.1	87.2	91.0	91.6	89.9	93.2	92.9	92.6	93.9	92.0
3–0	93.2	90.4	94.5	95.8	93.8	97.1	96.5	96.5	98.5	96.2
3–6	96.7	93.5	98.3	99.6	97.8	101.4	100.3	102.0	102.4	103.0
4–0	100.1	96.8	102.4	103.5	103.9	104.9	104.0	103.8	105.8	104.3
4–6	103.5	100.2	106.0	106.7	105.8	108.6	107.5	107.4	109.4	108.0
5–0	106.8	103.5	108.9	109.9	109.1	111.6	110.9	111.0	112.6	111.7
5–6	110.0	107.0	112.2	113.2	112.0	114.8	114.4	114.2	115.8	115.4
6–0	113.2	110.2	115.0	116.2	115.0	118.2	117.8	117.3	119.1	118.8
6–6	116.1	113.4	117.8	119.4	117.6	121.6	121.2	120.8	122.6	122.3
7–0	118.8	116.5	120.6	122.4	120.2	124.4	124.4	124.0	125.0	125.5
7–6	121.7	119.4	123.5	125.7	122.9	127.6	127.6	127.3	127.8	128.7
8–0	124.6	122.4	126.3	128.8	125.8	130.7	130.8	130.2	130.8	132.0
8–6	127.3	125.5	129.4	131.8	128.5	133.8	133.8	133.4	133.9	135.0
9–0	130.1	128.6	132.2	134.7	131.4	137.1	136.7	136.6	137.0	138.2
9–6	132.7	131.6	135.6	137.5	134.2	140.2	139.8	139.8	139.9	140.9
10–0	136.0	135.1	139.0	140.3	136.9	143.8	142.9	143.1	143.8	143.6
10–6	139.1	138.5	142.3	143.2	140.0	147.4	146.0	146.6	147.4	146.4
11–0	141.9	141.6	145.9	146.0	143.4	150.3	149.0	149.6	151.3	149.4
11–6	145.0	144.8	149.4	148.9	146.6	153.2	152.1	152.8	155.3	152.2
12–0	148.0	147.8	152.8	151.8	150.3	156.4	155.2	155.8	159.0	154.9
12–6	150.8	151.1	155.8	154.4	154.0	159.0	158.2	158.8	161.1	158.0
13–0	152.9	154.2	158.8	157.0	157.0	161.0	161.1	161.7	162.3	160.5
13–6	154.5	157.2	161.0	159.1	159.0	163.0	163.3	164.0	163.0	162.5
14–0	155.4	158.8	161.7	160.9	160.4	163.7	165.0	165.9	163.9	164.1
14–6	155.7	159.4	162.2	162.5	161.5	164.0	166.2	167.4	164.5	165.5
15–0	155.9	159.8	162.6	163.7	162.2	164.0	167.1	168.4	165.0	166.5
15–6	156.1	160.1	162.7	164.7	162.9	164.0	167.5	169.2	165.3	167.8
16–0	156.0	160.5	162.8	165.5	163.4	164.1	167.8	169.7	165.5	168.7
16–6	156.1	160.7	162.9	166.1	163.8	164.2	167.8	170.3	165.6	169.4
17–0	156.2	160.8	163.0	166.5	164.0	164.3	167.9	170.9	165.7	170.0
17–6	156.2	160.9	163.0	166.9	164.2	164.4	167.9	171.4	165.7	170.4
18–0	156.2	161.0	165.0	167.2	164.3	164.4	167.9	171.8	165.7	170.8

*From Garn and Rohmann.[49] No attempt has been made to eliminate sampling fluctuations.

TABLE 4–9.—Fels Parent-Specific Standards for Height:
Boys' Stature by Age and Midparent States*

AGE		161	163	165	167	PARENTAL MIDPOINT, CM 169	171	173	175	177	178
Birth	. . .	47.1	49.7	50.3	50.0	48.3	50.7	50.0	51.5	51.4
0–1	. . .	52.7	54.6	54.7	57.6	53.2	53.6	52.2	55.6	55.9
0–3	. . .	58.9	60.8	60.0	62.2	57.4	60.8	61.2	61.4	62.6
0–6	. . .	65.1	66.2	66.8	67.4	65.8	70.2	69.0	70.2	70.3
0–9	. . .	70.7	72.9	73.8	73.2	71.0	74.8	75.2	77.1	75.7
1–0	. . .	73.1	75.6	75.7	75.1	73.4	76.6	77.1	79.6	77.8
1–6	. . .	79.9	82.4	81.7	82.0	81.2	82.6	83.4	86.8	85.2
2–0	. . .	85.4	87.2	87.0	87.4	87.8	88.0	88.9	92.0	91.3
2–6	. . .	88.8	91.3	92.0	92.1	93.2	93.5	94.0	96.7	96.0
3–0	. . .	93.2	94.9	96.1	96.0	97.2	98.1	98.3	100.7	99.9
3–6	. . .	96.3	98.4	100.0	99.5	101.0	102.3	102.6	104.5	103.5
4–0	. . .	99.5	102.2	103.5	103.1	104.6	106.0	106.3	108.0	107.0
4–6	. . .	102.7	105.4	107.1	106.6	108.0	109.6	109.6	111.4	110.4
5–0	. . .	105.6	108.5	110.6	110.0	111.5	113.2	112.7	114.6	113.8
5–6	. . .	108.3	111.3	113.4	112.7	114.5	116.3	115.8	117.4	116.8
6–0	. . .	110.9	114.1	116.4	115.4	117.4	119.4	118.7	120.4	119.8
6–6	. . .	113.6	116.9	119.3	118.4	120.3	122.4	121.7	123.4	122.8
7–0	. . .	116.2	119.7	122.3	121.3	123.2	125.6	124.6	126.4	125.6
7–6	. . .	118.9	122.5	125.1	124.3	126.1	128.8	127.6	129.5	128.4
8–0	. . .	121.6	125.0	127.8	126.8	128.8	131.6	130.4	132.8	131.6
8–6	. . .	124.2	127.6	130.7	129.3	131.5	134.9	133.2	135.9	134.6
9–0	. . .	126.9	130.4	133.3	131.9	134.1	138.0	136.0	138.8	137.5
9–6	. . .	129.9	132.9	136.1	134.6	136.9	141.0	138.8	142.0	140.5
10–0	. . .	132.5	135.8	138.8	137.4	139.8	143.8	141.5	145.3	143.2
10–6	. . .	135.6	138.8	141.5	140.3	142.6	146.8	144.3	148.6	146.0
11–0	. . .	138.5	141.8	144.1	143.0	145.4	149.9	146.8	151.9	148.9
11–6	. . .	141.6	144.9	146.9	145.6	148.3	152.8	149.6	155.4	151.6
12–0	. . .	144.7	148.0	149.7	148.4	151.4	155.7	152.4	158.8	154.5
12–6	. . .	147.7	151.1	152.6	151.6	154.6	158.3	155.8	162.6	157.5
13–0	. . .	151.0	154.2	155.7	154.9	158.0	161.7	159.6	166.3	160.5
13–6	. . .	154.5	157.7	158.9	158.1	161.6	164.6	163.6	170.1	163.8
14–0	. . .	158.8	161.7	162.3	161.6	165.7	167.6	167.8	173.4	166.9
14–6	. . .	162.6	164.9	165.9	164.8	169.6	170.3	172.0	175.2	171.3
15–0	. . .	165.8	168.1	169.1	167.9	172.9	173.0	174.7	176.4	175.2
15–6	. . .	168.0	171.3	172.0	170.6	174.5	175.6	175.8	177.0	178.6
16–0	. . .	169.4	173.3	174.3	172.8	177.3	177.5	176.6	177.4	181.0
16–6	. . .	170.3	174.2	175.8	174.4	178.4	178.7	177.3	177.4	182.8
17–0	. . .	170.9	174.7	176.8	175.4	179.2	179.4	177.8	177.5	184.3
17–6	. . .	171.2	174.9	174.4	176.0	180.0	179.9	178.2	177.6	185.4
18–0	. . .	171.5	175.0	177.9	176.2	180.5	180.2	178.6	177.6	186.3

*From Garn and Rohmann.[49]

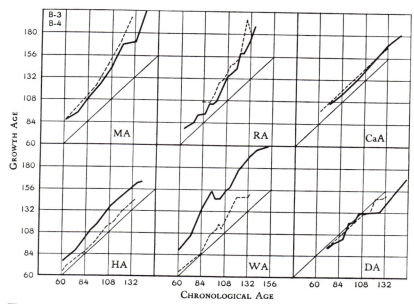

Fig 4–13.—Curves showing similarity of growth patterns of brothers born 33 months apart. Course of growth is shown for mental age, *MA;* reading age, *RA;* carpal ossification, *CaA;* height, *HA;* weight, *WA;* and dental development, *DA.* (From Olson and Hughes.[13])

marked homogeneity of all measures of physical and mental growth.* Studies of siblings have shown a high degree of similarity in the pattern of growth (Fig 4–13). Finally, the diverse data for each subject are averaged from all of the age levels, and this is plotted against chronologic age. This average for the individual has been termed the "organismic age" by Olson and Hughes. They state that the liberty taken in averaging these diverse data is based on the hypothesis that all data are samples of structures and functions of the organism and that individuals having different patterns may be "organismically" equal. "Organismic age" divided by chronologic age equals the "organismic quotient" that can be used to determine, in general, the status of any child. Figure 4–14 shows the data and the table of one subject studied who exhibited an accelerated total growth and of another subject with slow growth.

---

*In a study of gifted children (those with an IQ of 140 and over) Terman and Oden[23] found that both physical and mental development were above the average and that this superiority continued into adult life. They believe that favorable environment alone cannot explain these observations.

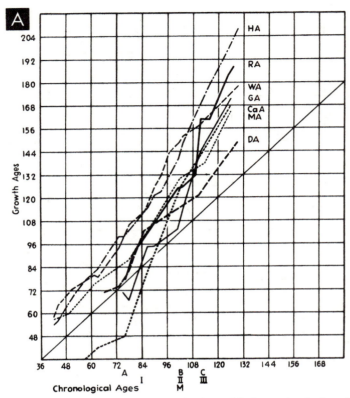

Fig 4–14.—The Olson-Hughes growth chart. Various physical and mental measurements plotted, **A,** for a girl above average, and **B,** for a boy slightly below average. On the abscissa *A, B,* and *C* represent advancing degrees of breast development; pubic hair development is indicated as *I* present, *II* pigmented, and *III* pigmented and curly; *M* indicates menarche. The straight, unbroken diagonal line represents average course for all measurements. For both children the homogeneity of all the factors measured is clearly apparent. The functions measured are abbreviated as in Figure 4–13, plus *GA,* which is strength of grip. The values indicated on the ordinate are obtained from a manual designed by the authors giving age equivalents. (From Olson and Hughes.[13]) *(Continued.)*

In general, when a wide scattering of the several elements which are measured is maintained throughout several successively plotted points, it can be postulated that the inherited characteristics have been variable. For example, when the parents of a child are of widely different physical builds, there may be a wide range in the different physical measurements of the child. The lines of height, weight, and carpal age may fall far apart

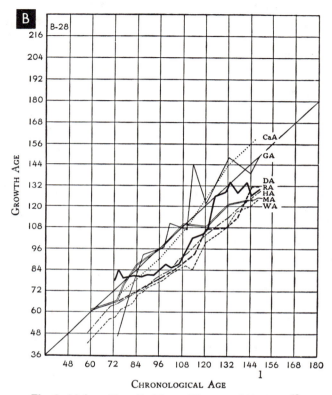

Fig 4–14 (cont.).—B. (From Olson and Hughes.[13])

on the table. Disease and emotional stress are quickly reflected by a lowering of all or some of the elements measured. The authors cite one example in which death of the mother resulted in a drop in weight and "reading age" over a period of six months until a suitable adjustment was accomplished.

Olson and Hughes have applied statistical tests to many similar systems of curves for individual children and have concluded that in all growth there is an underlying unity. They also believe that achievement in school is a function of the total growth of the child, and they doubt that school achievement is primarily a matter of curriculum and method, provided environment is suitable. When the "organismic age" for a child is calculated for successive life ages and the points are plotted and connected, much stability and predictability of trend are revealed. As a matter of fact, each child tends to grow in a more steady and orderly manner when the average values for "organismic age" are used than when a single attribute is plotted. This type of evidence suggests some "central maturational tempo or release of energy at a steady rate, with a tendency toward a balancing of the various aspects of the whole."[12]

The Fels Composite Sheet

The Fels method makes use of variability units to describe growth in many factors relative to time.[19] The mean and standard deviations of each measure (height, weight, ossification, dietary adequacy, biochemical values, performance tests, etc.) are first calculated by age and sex. Thereafter any measurement obtained can be described or plotted in terms of variability rather than in terms of the absolute value of the units used in orig-

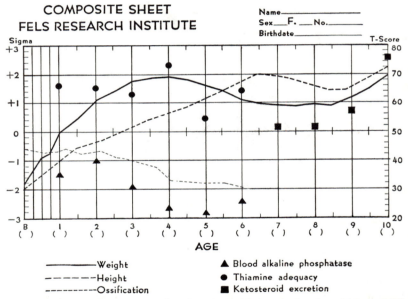

Fig 4–15.—The Fels composite sheet, showing growth of a girl from birth to age 10. The abscissa is in units of chronologic age. The left ordinate is expressed in units of 1 or more standard deviations *(sigma)* of expected values for a specific age on the abscissa; the right ordinate, in units of the T-score in which 50 represents the expected mean. At birth the child was 2 sigmas below the mean for height and weight, but by 4 years was above the mean in weight and near the mean in height. From this record one can conclude that at birth she was small but well proportioned and at 4 was of stocky body build. Various other factors are indicated according to the key below the chart. (From Sontag and Reynolds.[19])

inally collecting the data. With this method the average is always arbitrarily placed at 50 and the scale is then laid out in terms of variability units. One standard deviation above the average or mean is always 60; two standard deviations above are 70, etc. A single standard deviation below would then be 40. The score for any measure is called the T-score, average T-score being 50. In the plotting of this material, the abscissa represents age in years (or months) and the ordinates are in units of T-score and sigma (units of standard deviation). The advantage of the standard deviation method is that many measures that do not show an age trend but which do reveal individual differences can be plotted to show relative status in the group. By plotting a series of determinations, profiles at various ages on a vertical axis will be obtained (Fig 4–15).

Examples of many other tables and curves could be presented, many of which have considerable merit. However, those described seem to represent fairly the basic principles that have been used in an effort to answer that most important question, "Is this child growing normally?" Again it should be emphasized that an adequate clinical history is vital for an understanding and proper interpretation of somatic and mental growth. Deviations from the expected average are without meaning unless such factors as illness, emotional trauma, nutrition, and genetics are all properly evaluated.

Practical Applications

Measurements of physical growth may give a very general indication of a subject's health when other more detailed methods are not available, as in schools where the medical personnel is limited. This monitoring function of periodic measuring as a screening process is common, but its yield in identifying previously unidentified abnormality is not readily available. It must be admitted that growth deviations from normal often accompany or follow, rather than herald, diseases. The development of the methods and the accumulation of data have added immeasurably to our understanding of the growth and development of children. Though given tables or graphs do not indicate or define the optimum, they have revealed such interesting trends as the so-called secular changes during the past decades.

Cross-sectional tables and curves are inferior to longitudinal studies of the individual child. The former do not indicate the variability of rates of maturation, which may be earlier or later than the average, nor do they portray the individual variations in rate of growth. They may even give a false sense of security when a single measurement of a child falls within the "normal" range.

Considerable value may be realized from their use as a graphic means of presentation to parents. Showing a mother that her child is following or deviating from the expected curve is often more convincing than a purely verbal explanation. Also, in evaluating the effect of treatment on growth, the availability of standard curves is most helpful.

Posture

Man is the only animal that walks erect. Although some of the higher primates can walk erect, they do so only for short spans of time and are unable to completely extend their legs as can humans. The rigid shape of the pelvis is similar in humans and primates but the unique structure of the spine in humans permits an erect posture, and bipedal locomotion adapted to free the arms and hands for manipulation. Our arms, legs, and spine are the human heritage of millions of years of evolution. The various curves of the spine that develop with growth and locomotion are beautifully adapted to the muscle stresses of our method of ambulation.

Posture changes with age.[1, 12] There are many factors involved, but at least two important ones are the variations in the curves of the vertebral column and the shifting center of gravity. At birth the entire presacral vertebral column is extremely flexible, and no particular curve may be described as truly characteristic since the curve depends entirely on the position of the infant. At age 3 or 4 months, when the infant begins to hold up his or her head, an anterior convexity of the cervical portion appears. Nevertheless, the cervical vertebrae remain freely movable and at no time become fixed in any one position. By the time an upright posture is assumed the forward lumbar convexity develops, but it is not far advanced for several years. An important contribution to this curve is the fact that the anterior portion of the last three lumbar vertebrae become increasingly thicker than the posterior portions. Even the intervertebral disks in this region develop similar inequalities. The tilting of the pelvis and the pull of the psoas muscles in an erect position tend to maintain the lumbar curvature. In the thoracic region, growth of the vertebral bodies is the reverse of that of the lumbar area, i.e., the posterior portions of the bodies are thicker than the anterior portions, resulting in a forward concavity. The sacral curve is present from birth but contributes little to posture except in maintaining the position and relationship of the pelvis. The only two relatively fixed curves of the vertebral column involved in the posture of the child are the lumbar and the thoracic, and even these can be said to show great flexibility throughout the entire growing period.

Since the proportions of head, trunk, and extremities vary so greatly with growth, it is natural that the center of gravity of the body changes

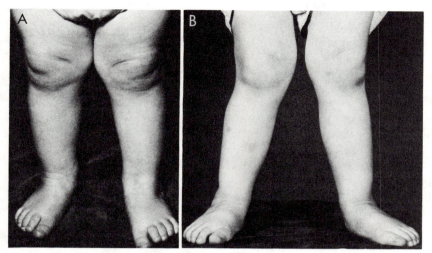

Fig 4–16.—A, normal feet and legs of 13-month-old child just beginning to walk, the stance giving the appearance of genu valgum and some pronation. Observation of the child in action indicated good sturdy legs and feet. **B,** simple flatfoot with resulting genu valgum. Whole foot rotates outward, the longitudinal arch disappears, heads of the astragali thrust medially and the heel is everted.

with age.* The location of this point is relative not only to posture but to all functions in which balance is involved. In the newborn in an erect position the center is near the level of the xiphoid, and throughout early childhood it remains above the umbilicus. At 5 to 6 years it is just below the umbilicus and is below the crest of the ilium by 13 years. With increasing age there is also an increasing ability to maintain balance because of muscle coordination and strength. Although posture may be said to have some basis in nutrition and exercise, it is strongly influenced by the unfolding design of growth of skeletal, muscular, and neuromuscular mechanisms.

During the first 2 to 3 years after an erect posture is assumed, the feet are relatively flat; there is a tendency to inward bowing of the legs from knee to ankle; some lordosis is apparent, which varies a great deal from child to child; and the abdomen is prominent. In the early school period the shoulders are "rounded," and this is little influenced by exercise. A

---

*Center of gravity may be determined by the formula $y = 0.557 \times X + 1.4$ cm, where y equals distance of the center above the soles and X equals height in centimeters.[14]

"military" posture of head high, shoulders back, and chest equal with the plane of the abdomen comes with adolescence. In general, a satisfactory posture may be said to exist at this time if a straight line passes from in front of the ear through the shoulder and the greater trochanter to the anterior part of the longitudinal arch of the foot. Such a posture distributes the weight equally to the balls of the feet and permits an erect yet comfortable standing position. Forcing such an attitude on a child, however, is hardly to be advised. Posture, to a degree, reflects strength and health, and these factors are the more basic conditions that should receive our consideration.

To the clinician a peculiarity of posture may be viewed as a sign of simple fatigue or of some more definite organic or mental disturbance. It must be emphasized that both the general and the detailed forms of the body are highly variable. We cannot assume that there is a single correct posture any more than we can assume that there is a single correct height or weight. The old idea of admonishing school children to "stand straight" or "sit straight" in the interest of better posture often confuses cause and effect. A child typically adopts that posture that keeps the parts of his or her body in proper balance. Frequent action and change of activity in school are excellent preventives of faulty posture.

Growth and Development of Legs and Feet

The legs and feet grow more rapidly than the trunk during childhood. Both legs and feet respond to some degree to external factors that may be

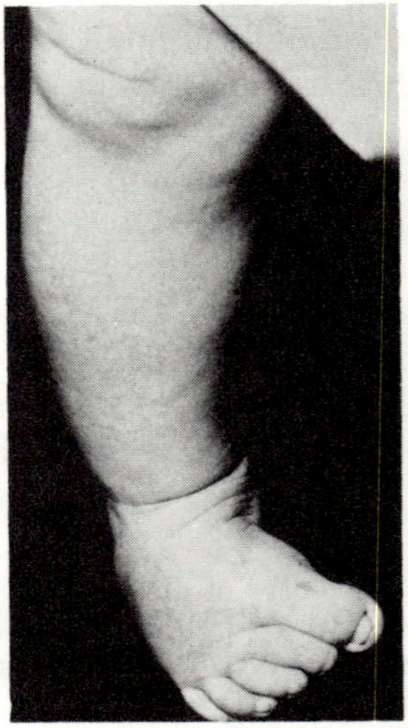

Fig 4–17.—Pigeon-toed foot. Ankle and knee of a boy of 13 months are in normal relationship, but forefoot deviated medially and is rotated. This foot seems far worse than it really is, and the boy could walk with support.

operative before or after birth. Bowed tibiae have been attributed to abnormal and restricted positioning in utero. Many varieties of clubfoot are seen at birth, some of which seem rather clearly to be due to abnormal positioning or pressures in utero. Imbalance of muscle groups and muscle pull will produce grotesque anomalies of foot or leg, as in arthrogryposis.

The normal foot of the newborn infant is proportionately fatter and wider than that of the adult. Fat pads obliterate the longitudinal arch, giving the appearance of "flatfoot," and this is accentuated by normally pliant muscles. Fetal positioning, dorsiflexion of the foot on the tibia, stretches the Achilles tendon thus making it impossible to elicit that tendon reflex for several months. As the infant learns to walk, the apparent pronation is further exaggerated by abduction of the foot and eversion of the heel (Fig 4–16). A well-formed arch is not visually obvious until most children are 3 to 4 years of age.[31]

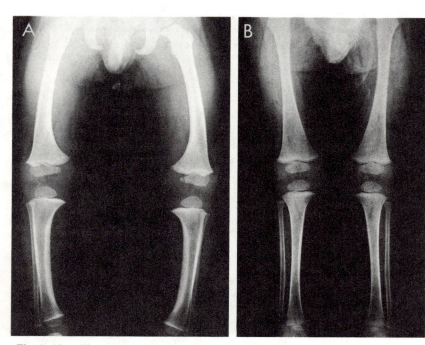

Fig 4–18.—Physiologic bowing of the legs. **A,** film of legs of healthy 18-month-old boy. By inspection the legs appeared to be bowed. X-rays show thickening of medial tibial cortex, flaring and exaggerated recurving of medial lips of femoral and tibial metaphyses at the knees. The distal femoral epiphyses are wedged. **B,** the same child 3 years later. Clinical and roentgenologic appearance is entirely normal; recovery was spontaneous. (From Holt and Watson.[48])

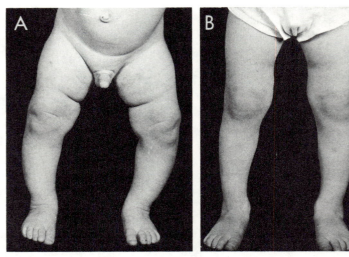

Fig 4–19.—Brother of boy whose x-rays appear in Figure 4–18. **A,** legs at 10 months and **B,** at 3 years. This change was spontaneous and accompanied by x-ray findings like those shown in Figure 4–18.

Toeing in or "pigeon-toe" is not uncommon in the early stages of walking, and is seldom a serious problem (Fig 4–17). It is often associated with tibial torsion, itself a benign condition that corrects with normal growth. True adduction of the forefoot, metatarsus adductus, is due to a boney deformity and requires specific treatment of plaster casting.[33]

Physiologic bowing of the legs is a normal variant and is self-correcting (Figs 4–18 and 4–19). It is present at birth but may become evident only as the infant stands and begins to walk. Radiologic examination indicates thickening of the medial tibial cortex as well as the bowing (see Fig 4–18, A). None of the typical findings of rickets is present, the abnormal condition with which it is most often confused.[48]

REFERENCES
1. Appleton A.B.: Posture. *Practitioner* 156:48, 1946.
2. Winick M., Rosso P.: Head circumference and cellular growth of the brain in normal and marasmic children. *J. Pediatr.* 74:774, 1969.
3. Hamill P.V.V., Drizd T.A., Johnson C.L., et al.: *NCHS Growth Charts, 1976,* Monthly Vital Statistics Report. U.S. Dept. of Health, Education and Welfare, 1976.
4. *Height and Weight of Children: Socioeconomic Status, United States.* U.S. Dept. of Health, Education and Welfare, Public Health Service, 1972.
5. *Body Weight, Stature, and Sitting Height: White and Negro Youths 12–17 Years, United States.* U.S. Dept. of Health, Education and Welfare, Public Health Service, 1973.

6. Harris J.A., Jackson C.M., Paterson D.G., et al.: *The Measurement of Man.* Minneapolis, University of Minnesota Press, 1930.
7. *Body Dimensions and Proportions, White and Negro Children 6–11 Years, United States.* U.S. Dept. of Health, Education and Welfare, Public Health Service, 1974.
8. De Souza S.W., Ross J., Milner R.D.G.: Alterations in head shape of newborn infants after caesarean section or vaginal delivery. *Arch. Dis. Child.* 51:624, 1975.
9. Lucas W.P., Pryor H.B.: Range and standard deviations of certain physical measurements in healthy children. *J. Pediatr.* 6:533, 1935.
10. Meredith H.V.: *The Rhythm of Physical Growth,* State Univ. of Iowa Studies in Child Welfare, vol. 11, no. 3, 1935; Boynton B.: State Univ. of Iowa Studies in Child Welfare, vol. 12, no. 4.
11. Meredith H.V.: A "physical growth record" for use in elementary and high schools. *Am. J. Public Health* 39:878, 1949.
12. Olson W.C.: *Child Development.* Boston, D.C. Heath & Co., 1949.
13. Olson W.C., Hughes B.O.: Growth of the child as a whole, in Barker R.G., et al. (eds.): *Child Behavior and Development.* New York, McGraw-Hill Book Co., 1943.
14. Palmer C.E.: Study of the center of gravity in the human body. *Child Dev.* 15:99, 1944.
15. Shuttleworth F.K.: *The Adolescent Period: A Graphic and Pictorial Atlas,* monograph, Social Research in Child Development, vol. III, no. 3. Washington, D.C., National Research Council, 1938.
16. Gross S.J., Oehler J.M., Eckerman C.O.: Head growth and developmental outcome in very low-birth-weight infants. *Pediatrics* 71:70, 1983.
17. Simmons K., Greulich W.W.: Menarcheal age and height, weight and skeletal age of girls age 7 to 17 years. *J. Pediatr.* 22:518, 1943.
18. Lipper E., Lee K., Gartner L.M., et al.: Determinants of neurobehavioral outcome in low-birth-weight infants. *Pediatrics* 67:502, 1981.
19. Sontag L.W., Reynolds E.L.: The Fels composite sheet: I. A practical method for analyzing growth progress; II. Variations in growth patterns in health and disease. *J. Pediatr.* 26:317, 1945.
20. Owen G.M.: The assessment and recording of measurements of growth of children: Report of a small conference. *Pediatrics* 51:461, 1973.
21. Gross S.J., Kosmetatos N., Grimes C.T., et al.: Newborn head size and neurological status. *Am. J. Dis. Child.* 132:753, 1978.
22. Williams J., Hirsch N.J., Corbet A.J.S., et al.: Postnatal head shrinkage in small infants. *Pediatrics* 59:619, 1977.
23. Terman L.M., Oden M.H., et al.: *The Gifted Child Grows Up.* Stanford, Calif., Stanford University Press, 1947.
24. Eveleth P., Tanner J.M.: *Worldwide Variations in Human Growth.* London, Cambridge University Press, 1976.
25. Snyder R.G., Spencer M., Owings C., et al.: *Source Data of Infant and Child Measurements.* Bethesda, Md., Children's Hazard Division, Food and Drug Administration, 1973.
26. *Height and Weight of Children, United States.* U.S. Dept. of Health, Education and Welfare, Public Health Service, 1970.
27. Lorber J., Priestley B.L.: Children with large heads: A practical approach to diagnosis in 557 children, with special reference to 109 children with megalencephaly. *Devel. Med. Child Neurol.* 23:494, 1981.

28. Martin H.P.: Microcephaly and mental retardation. *Am. J. Dis. Child.* 119:128, 1970.
29. Pryor H.B., Thelander H.: Abnormally small head size and intellect in children. *J. Pediatr.* 73:593, 1968.
30. Stuart H.C., Meredith H.V.: Use of body measurements in the school health program. *Am. J. Public Health* 36:1365, 1946.
31. Miller W.R.: Observations on the examination of children's feet. *J. Pediatr.* 51:527, 1957.
32. Lacey K.A., Parkin J.M.: The normal short child: Community study of children in Newcastle upon Tyne. *Arch. Dis. Child.* 49:417, 1974.
33. Compere E.I.: Foot problems in the young child. *Rocky Mt. Med. J.* 47:747–751, October, 1950.
34. *Selected Body Measurements of Children 6–11 Years, United States.* U.S. Dept. of Health, Education and Welfare, Public Health Service, 1973.
35. Garn S.M., Owen G.M.: Growth standards for American Negro (black) boys and girls. *J. Pediatr.* 84:160, 1974.
36. Sheldon W.H.: *The Varieties of Human Physique.* New York, Harper & Brothers, 1940.
37. Meredith H.V.: Findings from Asia, Australia, Europe and North America on secular change in mean height of children, youths and young adults. *Am. J. Phys. Anthropol.* 44:315, 1976.
38. Meredith H.V.: Body size of contemporary groups of eight-year-old children studied in different parts of the world. Monogr. Soc. Res. Child Dev. 1:34, 1969.
39. Nelson K.B., Deutschberger J.: Head size at one year as predictor of 4-year I.Q. *Dev. Med. Child Neurol.* 12:487, 1970.
40. Day R.E., Shutt W.H.: Normal children with large heads: Benign familial megalencephaly. *Arch. Dis. Child.* 54:512, 1979.
41. Tanner J.M., Healy M.J.R., Lockhart R.D., et al.: Aberdeen growth study I. *Arch. Dis. Child.* 31:372, 1956.
42. Sells C.J.: Microcephaly in a normal school population. *Pediatrics* 59:262, 1977.
43. Bayer L.M., Bayley N.: *Growth Diagnosis.* Chicago, University of Chicago Press, 1959.
44. Garn S.M.: Physical growth and development. *Am. J. Phys. Anthropol. N.S.* 10:1969, 1952.
45. Falkner F.: Velocity growth. *Pediatrics* 51:746, 1973.
46. Tuddenham R.D., Snyder M.M.: *Physical Growth of California Boys and Girls from Birth to Eighteen Years.* Berkeley, Calif., University of California Press, 1954.
47. Nellhaus G.: Head circumference from birth to eighteen years. *Pediatrics* 41:106, 1968.
48. Holt J.F., Watson E.H.: Physiologic bowing of the legs in young children. *J.A.M.A.* 154:390, 1954.
49. Garn S.M., Rohmann C.G.: Interaction of nutrition and genetics in timing of growth. *Pediatr. Clin. N. Am.* 13:353, 1966.
50. Heimer C.B., Freedman A.M.: The physical development of prematurely born Negro infants. *Am. J. Dis. Child.* 109:500, 1965.
51. O'Connell E.J., Feldt R.H., Stickler G.B.: Head circumference, mental retardation and growth failure. *Pediatrics* 36:62, 1965.
52. Wainer H., Roche A.F., Bell S.: Predicting adult stature without skeletal age and without paternal data. *Pediatrics* 61:569, 1978.

53. Scott R.B., Hiatt H.H., Clark B.G., et al.: Growth and development of Negro infants. *Pediatrics* 29:65, 1962.
54. Tanner J.M.: Growth and physique in different populations of mankind, in Baker, P.T., Weiner J.S. (eds.): *The Biology of Human Adaptability*. Oxford, Clarendon Press, 1966.
55. Tanner J.M., Whitehouse R.H.: Longitudinal standards for height, weight, height velocity, weight velocity and stages of puberty. *Arch. Dis. Child.* 51:170, 1976.
56. Malina R.M.: Growth and physical performance of American Negro and white children. *Clin. Pediatr.* 8:476, 1969.
57. Fisch R.O., Bilek M.K., Horrobin J.M., et al.: Children with superior intelligence at 7 years of age. *Am. J. Dis. Child.* 130:481, 1976.
58. Caffey J.: *Pediatric X-Ray Diagnosis*, ed. 6. Chicago, Year Book Medical Publishers, 1972.
59. Roche A.F., Wainer H., Thissen D.: The RWT method for the prediction of adult stature. *Pediatrics* 56:1026, 1975.
60. Smith D.W.: *Growth and Its Disorders*. Philadelphia, W.B. Saunders Co., 1977.
61. Lemire R.J., Loeses J.D., Leech R.W., et al.: *Normal and Abnormal Development of the Human Nervous System*. New York, Harper & Row, 1975.

5 / Low Birth Weight and Premature Infants

Here we have a baby. It is composed of a bald head and a pair of lungs.

—Eugene Field

From the standpoint of morbidity and mortality, low birth weight represents the most important problem of the neonatal period. A birth weight of less than 2,500 gm is a direct cause, or is associated with other conditions as a cause, of approximately 80% to 90% of infant deaths in the United States. It is estimated that as many as one third of the survivors have significant mental or motor handicaps.[1, 6] Although many different factors are involved, it is recognized that the smaller the infant, the less are his or her chances for survival. The problems of low birth weight must be approached from two aspects: prevention and extension of our knowledge of these infants so improvement in care will be possible. An obvious part of this necessary knowledge pertains to growth and development. In the following paragraphs the physical growth and development of low birth weight infants are summarized, and some of the more important physiologic differences between them and the normal term infants are outlined.

Definition and Incidence

As a term of general use, *low birth weight infant* has replaced the term *premature infant*, since the former includes all infants with a birth weight of less than 2,500 gm regardless of the duration of gestation. Premature should be used to indicate a period of gestation of 37 weeks or less. (The weeks of gestation are counted from the first day of the last menstrual period.)

Because estimations of the duration of pregnancy, based upon history, are often inexact, more objective measures of prematurity are commonly sought. In chapter 2 some discussion was given to the use of amniocentesis,

123

sonography, and amounts of estriol excreted during pregnancy as means of estimating fetal age. The ratio of lecithin to sphingomyelin in amniotic fluid was pointed out to be a particularly valuable guide to fetal lung maturity. A gradually increasing number of lipid-containing cells and an increase in the creatinine content in amniotic fluid correlate well with gestational age. Exposure of the fetus to radiation, as well as the great variability in interpretation, has discouraged roentgen examination of the fetus for size or bone maturation. Once delivered, the criteria given in Tables 5–1 and 5–2 have proved to be of considerable aid in estimating gestational age.[2, 5, 8]

Neurologic development and the changes in the electroencephalogram are among the most reliable indicators of maturational age. This assumes, of course, that no major anomalies or diseases are present. Before 28 weeks of gestation the EEG is polymorphic with long silent periods. The waves that appear are slow and diffuse. After 28 weeks the pattern becomes simpler and the voltage of activity bursts is lower than before. They are regular rhythmic theta waves lasting 1 or 2 seconds.[38] Between 30 and 34 weeks there emerges a new pattern of slow activity superimposed on rapid rhythms, and the bursts last 3 to 10 seconds. The right and left electrodes for the first time are isopotential. After 32 weeks the pattern becomes more continuous with delta waves added, and the occipital area no longer predominates. Between 37 and 40 weeks of conceptional age the most dramatic change is the appearance of a difference between the waking and sleeping tracings. The response of the EEG to an auditory stimulus also changes with maturation and may prove of value in judging gestational age.[3, 39]

Another method of value in assessing the degree of maturity is the measurement of motor nerve conduction velocity.[41, 42] The conduction velocity of nerve depends on the thickness of the myelin sheath. The degree of myelination of peripheral nerve increases with age, but the changes are most pronounced during the end of gestation and throughout the early years of life. The slower conduction time seen in the less mature newborn will persist for as long as a year and affords an objective measurement of maturity of the infant and his or her nervous system.

Although charts showing intrauterine growth in length, weight, and head circumference for each geographic area and socioeconomic class of population would be highly desirable in the proper evaluation of the low birth weight infant, the records prepared by Lubchenco et al. seem adequate for almost all clinical situations (Fig 5–1).[21, 22]

With the improvements in sonography it is now possible to make very accurate measurements of the fetus, which is a great aid in determining gestational length and fetal development. One of the most reliable measurements is that of the biparietal diameter (Table 5–3).[9]

Table 5–1.—Representative Physical Signs at Different Gestational Times

	28 weeks	32 weeks	36 weeks	40 weeks
Skin	Transparent, veins numerous, dark red, edema of hands and feet, no subcutaneous fat	Transparent, veins numerous, pink, no edema, no subcutaneous fat, lanugo abundant	Few vessels seen, pale pink, lanugo thinning, some subcutaneous fat	Few vessels indistinct, pale, pink palms, soles, lips and ears, lanugo patchy, abundant subcutaneous fat
Plantar creases	None	Single anterior crease	1/2–2/3 of anterior covered with creases	All of sole covered with creases
Eyes	Lids just separating, pupillary membrane complete	Lids open, central clearing of pupillary membrane	Pupillary membrane absent	
Ears	Pinna soft, flat, no recoil to folding	Soft, easily folded, slow recoil	Cartilage to edge but soft, moderate recoil	Pinna firm, outer edge folded along upper portion, prompt recoil to folding
Breasts	Nipple present, no areola, no nodule	Areola smooth and flat, breast nodule < 0.5 cm diameter	Areola stippled, < 0.75 cm diameter, breast nodule 0.5–1.0 cm diameter	Areola raised, > 0.75 cm diameter, breast nodules > 1.0 cm diameter
Genitalia				
Female (hips abducted)	Labia majora separate, libia minora exposed		Labia majora cover labia minora	
Male	Testes undescended	Testes may descend, scrotum smooth	At least one testis in scrotum	Scrotum wrinkled, testes descended

TABLE 5–2.—Representative Neurologic Signs or Reflexes at Different Gestational Times

	28 WEEKS	32 WEEKS	36 WEEKS	40 WEEKS
Posture and tone	Hypotonic	Thighs begin flexion	Flexion of 4 limbs, tone moderate	Flexion of 4 limbs, tone strong
Moro's reflex	Weak or absent	Present, may not repeat promptly	Present and repeat elicited easily	Present and repeat elicited easily
Popliteal angle*	Reaches 150 degrees	Reaches 110 degrees	Reaches 100 degrees	Less than 100 degrees
Scarf sign†	Lack of tone permits full scarf position	Tone limits arm extension	Extension limited so elbow just past midline	Elbow just short of midline
Neck position on lifting from supine	No tone, head drops	Neck muscles contract but head drops	Head lags, comes forward abruptly	Head may follow trunk and briefly holds position
Rooting reflex	Response slow and incomplete	Response prompt	Response prompt and sustained	Response prompt and sustained
Glabella tap reflex (blinks)	Absent	Inconstant	Present	Present
Palmar grasp reflex	Rarely present	Present but weak	Present	Present
Stepping movements	Absent	Inconstant	Usually present	Present
Head rising prone	Absent	Absent	Weak or absent	Present

*Position assumed while in supine position and with maximum flexion of the hips.
†Scarf sign is elicited by throwing arm across chest with full extension and elbow below the chin, similar to the position of a scarf.

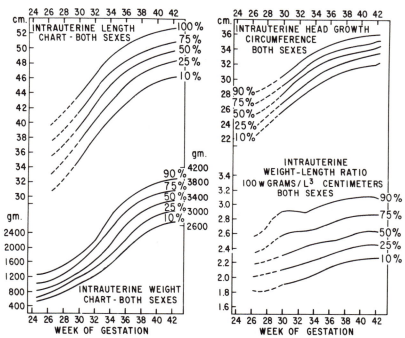

Fig 5–1.—Curves of intrauterine growth in length, weight, and head circumference. The subjects were all live-born, white, and mainly from middleclass society in the United States. The estimated week of gestation was obtained by careful history. The weight-length ratio is indicative of adequacy of intrauterine nutrition when high and of insufficiency when of a low value. (Modified from Lubchenco et al.[21])

The neurologic examination may be of little value during the first few hours after birth for determining gestational age, due to the "shock of birth." Since the very small infant may subsequently suffer problems that influence neurologic responses, the interpretation may be difficult. Nevertheless, the evaluation of muscular tone and reflexes may be helpful in arriving at an estimate of the duration of pregnancy. At 28 weeks the angle measured at the popliteal fossa with the leg extended and the pelvis fixed in supine position is 180 degrees, but by 37 weeks this narrows to about 100 degrees. By 34 weeks the heel-to-ear maneuver, which previously was easily accomplished, becomes increasingly difficult. General muscular tone and recoil to extremity extension increase with gestational age and are minimal at 24 to 26 weeks but pronounced by 37 to 38 weeks. Moro's reflex is first elicited at 28 to 29 weeks. The walking reflex is not present before 34 weeks but is usually well established by 37 to 38 weeks. The grasp reflex

TABLE 5–3.—Mean Biparietal
Diameter[9]

WEEK OF GESTATION	DIAMETER (CM) +/− 2 SD
18	4.0 +/− 0.5
20	4.5 +/− 0.5
22	5.1 +/− 0.6
24	5.7 +/− 0.7
26	6.1 +/− 0.7
28	6.7 +/− 0.7
30	7.4 +/− 0.8
32	8.0 +/− 0.6
34	8.4 +/− 0.6
36	8.9 +/− 0.6
38	9.2 +/− 0.5
40	9.3 +/− 0.5
42	9.4 +/− 0.5

is feeble before 28 weeks, present and strong by 34 weeks, and sufficiently powerful by 37 weeks to lift the infant partially or totally from the bed surface.[3, 37, 40]

The incidence of prematurity is extremely difficult to determine. Until fairly recently all low birth weight babies were lumped together as being premature. Estimates for the United States are about 75% of all low birth weight infants. The incidence of hospital births below 2,500 gm is approximately 7.6% in the United States, 6.5% in Great Britain, 5.5% in Sweden, 7% in France, and 10% in Japan. On the basis of weight alone, the incidence in parts of India exceeds 35%, but the mean birth weight was 2,700 gm in that area making the evaluation of such figures difficult.[7] The incidence of premature births versus low birth weight caused by fetal malnutrition in developing countries is virtually impossible to assess. Socioeconomic and racial (genetic) factors undoubtedly play a role. The frequency of low birth weight infants among blacks in the United States is twice that in whites.[4, 5, 7, 9]

Synonyms that have been used to designate the condition of the low birth weight infant include small for date, intrauterine growth retardation, fetal malnutrition, and fetal growth retardation. Part of the reason for the confusion in terms is that this is a heterogeneous group of infants as the following paragraphs will explain.[24]

The causes of low birth weight have been discussed by numerous investigators. The incidence is higher in low socioeconomic levels. Poor maternal nutrition, before and during pregnancy, is frequent. Low newborn infant weight is common if the mother is short or underweight at conception and if weight gain is poor during her pregnancy. Some have suggested the small size of the mother may be multigenerational.[16, 17] There is a definite correlation with an increasing frequency of congenital malformations as the weight for gestational age decreases. At least in some instances, these anomalies are genetic or chromosomal in origin. There is a tendency for recurrence of small newborns in some women. Twins and other multiple births are almost always small for their gestational age compared with singletons, and frequently one infant is considerably smaller than the other or others. Extremes of age in the mother, under 16 and over 35, are definite contributing factors. Hypertension and preeclampsia are often associated with small neonates. Chronic disease in the mother, especially renal failure, has been cited as a cause as well as metabolic conditions, e.g., diabetes mellitus. Intrauterine viral infections, e.g., rubella and cytomegalovirus, are well recognized as being responsible for retarded growth and development of the fetus. Intrauterine bacterial infections, amnionitis, may play a major role in the initiation of premature labor. This type of infection occurs most often during the last trimester of pregnancy and results from sexual intercourse.[4, 5, 7, 11–13]

The incidence of placental lesions associated with small neonates is quite high, as much as 50% in some studies. Placental vasculitis is one of the most frequently encountered in association with prematurity and amnionitis. Other findings are anomalous insertion of the umbilical cord, infarction, abruptio placentae, and circumvallate placenta with a weight more than two standard deviations below normal for the gestational age. The paucity of abnormal findings, except for reduction in size, in the placentas of newborns with fetal growth retardation has been noted in chapter 3.[4, 14]

Maternal behavioral conditions frequently found with low weight newborns include lack of prenatal care, drug and alcohol abuse, and excessive cigarette smoking.[19]

The interrelationship of these various factors is difficult to evaluate. No clearly established critical period for the fetus, so far as determinant of size, has been established, and many safeguards are provided. Placental lesions, vascular incompetence (hypertension and preeclampsia), and maternal undernutrition may all interfere with fetal nutrition and growth. There are abundant animal studies supporting these concepts. It is important to recognize that the timing as well as the length of the insult will influence the outcome. In the United States about 25% of low birth weight babies fall into the category of fetal growth retardation. The incidence must be considerably higher in areas of the world where adequate nutrition and prenatal care are minimal or nonexistent. It is interesting to note that where therapeutic abortion is permitted and widely practiced, the incidence of both prematurity and fetal growth retardation is declining.[8, 18–20, 24]

Physiologic Handicaps

Immaturity renders the premature infant's physiologic functions less well equipped to cope with external hazards encountered at birth, with the result that capacity for adaptation is low. The small but gestationally older infant appears to have fewer handicaps, and his or her initial survival and development are less precarious.[43]

The following outline is far from complete but hopefully will serve the purpose of identifying the more important problems facing the clinician.

RESPIRATION.—The respiratory pattern of the premature infant is irregular, rapid, and often shallow with periods of apnea. The shorter the gestational period, the more irregular is the pattern. Cyanosis is common and easily precipitated by slight changes in environment. Among the recognizable causes of respiratory difficulty are (1) high threshold of the respiratory center in the brain, requiring stronger afferent stimuli for response; (2) reduced number of capillaries in the lung, impeding gas exchange and possibly other chemical factors responsible for activating enzymes; (3) sparsity of pulmonary elastic tissue and decreased "surfactant," leading to slower and often incomplete expansion of the lungs; (4) feeble muscle strength and tone of thoracic cage and diaphragm, together with (5) a soft cartilaginous cage, resulting in reduced intrathoracic pressure changes with respiratory efforts; (6) the fact that fetal hemoglobin releases oxygen less readily; and (7) deficiency of some enzymes, such as carbonic anhydrase, was once considered to interfere with gaseous exchange, but there is almost total lack of evidence to support this.[45, 46]

The respiratory distress syndrome (hyaline membrane disease) is certainly one of the most common causes of death in prematurely born infants. The incidence varies, but in the smaller subjects may exceed 50%. The basic defect is inadequate pulmonary exchange of oxygen and carbon dioxide. Metabolic acidosis eventually develops. During fetal life, blood bypasses the lungs. With the first breath the pulmonary circulation increases and vascular resistance decreases normally. In the respiratory distress syndrome, pulmonary vascular resistance is higher than normal, probably secondary to arteriolar constriction. Consequently, blood shunts from the pulmonary circulation and the foramen ovale remains fully functional. Hypoxia, cyanosis, and respiratory distress follow. Since hypoxia causes an increased secretion of epinephrine and norepinephrine and these agents further constrict the pulmonary arterioles, a vicious cycle results. Atelectasis and alveolar coating with transudate increase the difficulty of gas exchange between the blood and alveoli. Fibrin and other protein products from the transudate are responsible for the formation of the hyaline membrane, which does not form unless the infant lives for at least a few hours. The lungs have a developmental sequence during the fetal period. If this is shortened or interrupted, the immaturity may be life-threatening to extrauterine existence. On expiration, after the first breath, the lungs retain considerable air in the normal-term infant. This lessens the required effort to fill the lungs with any subsequent breathing. Present in the airway, and especially in the alveoli, is pulmonary surfactant, which, by virtue of its effect on surface tension, stabilizes these fine air spaces and prevents their collapse. As pointed out in chapter 3, pulmonary surfactant appears late in fetal life and usually does not attain adequate functional levels until about the 34th or 35th week of gestation. Without it, the alveoli tend to collapse following each inspiration. The hyaline membrane is of secondary importance though it may add further impediment to respiratory efforts. It is interesting to note that fetal surfactant maturation can be accelerated by stress, such as premature rupture of the membranes, or administering large doses of glucocorticoids to the mother or fetus.[45, 47, 56] The condition of respiratory distress syndrome is more common in male than in female neonates.[57]

Recurrent apnea occurs most frequently in those with the lowest weight and gestational age at delivery. A number of studies support the hypothesis that apnea in the preterm infant is correlated with a disturbance or immaturity in the brain stem.[33, 50] Some 75% of babies weighing less than 2,000 gm will have apnea of 15 seconds or longer duration that is usually accompanied by bradycardia. It seems highly probable that sudden infant death syndrome (SIDS) is related to or initiated by recurrent apnea. SIDS has been defined as sudden unexpected death in an infant where careful examination fails to reveal an adequate cause. Postmortem findings are minimal and only indicate some degree of hypoxemia.[53] SIDS occurs most often during sleep or rarely during feeding (which are also associated with the times apnea is most prevalent). It is infrequent in the first few weeks of life and unusual after 6 months. It occurs in 2 to 3 infants per 1,000 live births, which makes it the single largest cause of postneonatal infant mortality in the United States.[33, 67]

TEMPERATURE CONTROL.—Inability to maintain a steady and normal body temperature is characteristic of the small premature infant. Much of this disability is based on anatomical differences in comparison with the normal newborn. Their large surface area relative to weight affords greater opportunity for heat loss. Very little subcutaneous fat is present to act as an insulation. The smallest of the premature infants do not have the ability to shiver, which is an important element in heat production under stress. Even without stress the premature infant, in terms of calories produced, may produce only half that of the normal-term newborn. Failure to maintain an ideal body temperature leads to metabolic disturbances that may play a role in morbidity and mortality. Among the changes are a slower rate of recovery from asphyxia, rapid exhaustion of lipid and glycogen stores, and an increased risk of hypoglycemia. Temperature control of small-for-date infants (fetal growth retardation) is less of a problem than for the premature of comparable weight. (See chapter 10 for further discussion and references.)

IMMUNITY.—Both the premature and small-for-date baby have decreased resistance to infection when compared with the normal newborn.[26, 50] There does not appear to be a greater liability dependent upon longer or shorter gestation. This observation does not correlate well with the concentrations of gamma G and gamma M immunoglobulins. The initial levels of G do correlate with the gestational age; the longer the time, the higher the concentration. Infants of very short gestational age have a relatively poor capacity to synthesize gamma M.[48] Phagocytosis has also been demonstrated to be reduced in the circulating cells of premature infants.[49] Thin and fragile skin increases the liability of the short-gestation baby to superficial infections.

NUTRITIONAL METABOLISM.—Of the main foodstuffs, the premature infant seems to be intolerant only of large amounts of fat, which is adequately split but is largely excreted in that form in the stool.

Hypoglycemia is a common finding in small-for-date infants.[51] At least two factors are important: rapid exhaustion of hepatic and muscle stores of glycogen and glucose, and rapid utilization by the relatively large brain, which is almost totally dependent upon glucose. Inadequate exogenous sources can be partially corrected by early feeding or parenteral glucose administration.[52] Observations by a number of investigators have indicated that early feeding of carbohydrate may not only enhance glucose homeostasis but benefit acidosis and hyperbilirubinemia.[53, 54] Hypoglycemia, as does asphyxia, appears to add an important additional threat to the prognosis of the low birth weight baby. Central nervous system damage is found more often in subsequent years in these children than those who escaped the low blood sugar.[5, 58]

Neither human milk nor commercial formulas contain sufficient amounts of calcium to allow calcium acquisition at the rate that existed in utero. The otherwise normal premature infant will have a relative hypocalcemia for several days to weeks that usually is asymptomatic but may have some influence on related metabolic functions.

Hyperbilirubinemia and jaundice are common in the premature infant, less so in the small-for-date infant. In the breakdown of the excess of he-moglobin present at birth, large amounts of unconjugated (indirect) biliru-bin are formed that normally are bound to albumin. This is lipid soluble and can cross the blood-brain barrier and produce kernicterus. The binding capacity increases with gestational age. Hypoxia, hypocalcemia, acidosis, hypoglycemia, and hypothermia all act to reduce the albumin-binding ca-pacity and thus increase the risk of kernicterus.[63] (See chapter 11 for dis-cussion of other topics concerned with nutrition of the low birth weight infant.)

BLOOD-VASCULAR SYSTEM.—Owing to the reduced antenatal storage of iron, anemia is common in nearly all prematures at some time during the early months of life. Marrow studies of normal compared with low birth weight infants reveal no essential differences. The life span of the red cell that contains fetal (F) hemoglobin is much shorter than the one containing adult (A) hemoglobin. The shorter the period of gestation, the greater the amount of F hemoglobin, which may exceed 90% at birth. This rapid turn-over of red cells does not appear to be a factor in the anemia.

Hemorrhagic manifestations may be slightly more frequent in the pre-mature infant as compared with the small-for-date infant due to increased capillary fragility. A rare form of true hemorrhage disease that occurs ex-clusively in prematures is characterized by prolonged bleeding time and diminished factor V. It is not prevented by use of vitamin K.

The normal hypercoagulable state found in the neonate is exaggerated in the preterm infant. Babies who die within the first few weeks of birth have a high incidence of hemorrhagic lesions, such as intraventricular bleeding associated with subependymal infarction. Renal thrombosis and thrombotic complications of indwelling venous or arterial catheters are not uncommon. A low level of the naturally occurring anticoagulant, antithrombin III, is closely related to gestational age and may contribute to these complica-tions.

RENAL FUNCTION.—The kidneys in the premature are less efficient ex-cretory organs than in the mature newborn or small-for-date baby. Avail-able evidence suggests this deficiency is due to a decreased glomerular filtration rate. Under stress this may lead to water and electrolyte imbal-ances and edema or dehydration.

Even though the majority of premature infants are unable to concentrate the urine beyond 700 mOsm/kg this limit is seldom reached, let alone ex-ceeded. Since half of the renal solute load resulting from breast or cow's milk is usually diverted into forming new tissue, as long as growth occurs there is little danger of surpassing renal ability.[59]

Prognosis: Physical and Neurologic

The prognosis for the smallest of the surviving low birth weight infants relative to physical and mental development is less favorable than for those of normal weight. There may be a birth weight below which normal development is not possible. In a number of animal species, perinatal undernutrition will retard growth in both cell numbers and cell size.[20] If the insult is either prenatal or postnatal, the reduction is nearly the same, but if both periods are combined, the resulting retardation is more severe than the sum of the two independently. Some organs are more vulnerable than others. Thymus, spleen, and liver are most influenced, while the heart and brain are less so. Decrease in placental size in these animals is clearly evident. Experimental vascular deficiency to the pregnant uterus results in similar findings, except that the brain is completely spared. Though exact comparisons to the human fetus and neonate cannot be drawn, there is evidence that the differences may not be great. Study of human placentas has revealed similar diminution in size (cell number and cell size) with severe malnutrition. Infants who have died as a result of undernourishment during the first year have a decrease of 15% to 20% in total brain cell number, as well as a reduction in body size. In prematurely born infants (by weight) who then suffered malnutrition and death, the reduction in brain cell number was 60%. As in the experimental animal, doubling the insult may more than double the effect.

It is difficult to select truly representative statistics for survival of low birth weight infants. All such figures indicate that the percentage of deaths is inversely proportional to the weight at birth. In the United States there has been a steady upward trend of survival over the past 20 years. As shown in Table 5–4, the improvement has been most pronounced among the smaller infants. With the increase in number of intensive care units for newborn infants and the improvement in available therapeutic procedures, there are indications that the number of handicapped children associated with low birth weight is decreasing.[26]

Because low birth weight babies are such a heterogeneous group it is

TABLE 5–4.—Survival of Low Birth Weight Infants

BIRTH WEIGHT (GM)	SURVIVAL (%)	
	1945	1980
2,001–2,500	94	99
1,501–2,000	84	94
1,000–1,500	53	82
Under 1,000	10	47

difficult to categorize them in terms of prognosis, both physical and neurologic. Factors that need to be taken into account, but unfortunately are often neglected in many studies, include the following:
Inborn or transported to nursery
Socioeconomic level of mother before delivery and during care of infant/child
Age and size of mother
Nutritional history of mother before and during pregnancy
The delivery, labor, complications, etc.
Length of hospitalization
Use of mechanical ventilation
Single or multiple births
The length of the follow-up (age of the child) is another important factor since it has been observed that some intellectual problems do not become apparent until school age.

There are two fairly distinct patterns of growth followed by low birth weight infants. If the baby is premature, but appropriate weight for gestational age, after a period of adjustment following birth, he or she will exhibit some "catch-up" growth followed by a rate that parallels that of full-term infants. The lower the weight at birth and the shorter the gestational age the lower the percentile curve followed in subsequent growth (Fig 5–2). The infants who are small for gestational age (intrauterine growth retardation) do not have much potential for "catch-up" growth. If the intrauterine retardation was of recent origin, manifested by low weight but normal length for the period of gestation, then there may be some early acceleration of growth.[16] In general, for height, weight, and head circumference, the measurements of children who were born small for gestational age remain farther behind those who were born prematurely and who were within the normal range for length of pregnancy.[5, 16, 17, 61] Even very low birth weight (1,000 to 1,500 gm) children, if they did not experience intrauterine retardation, will often attain normal physical size by late childhood.[66]

Evidence continues to accumulate that two factors are of utmost importance in improving both the physical as well as the neurologic prognosis in these infants. One is a favorable environment in the home. A good socioeconomic level in the family, both before and after delivery, greatly enhances the outcome. A prompt supply of adequate calories and carbohydrates helps to minimize the adjustment to extrauterine existence and prevent hypoglycemia.[13, 62, 63] By 18 to 24 months both the premature as well as the small-for-date infant are usually well established in their growth patterns.

Damage to the central nervous system by severe malnutrition of the fe-

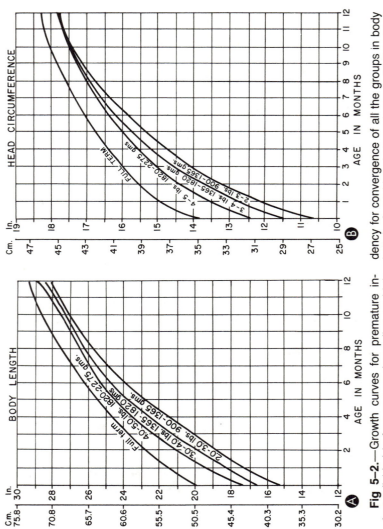

Fig 5–2.—Growth curves for premature infants divided in four groups depending on birth weight. It will be noted that as the end of the first year of life is reached there is a definite tendency for convergence of all the groups in body length, **A**, and head circumference, **B**. (Modified by smoothing the curves from Woolley and Valdecanas.[28])

tus or in the perinatal period is of primary importance in causing neonatal mortality, mental retardation, and cerebral palsy.[18, 44, 48] In autopsy material, 75% of low birth weight infants will have evidence of central nervous system lesions. In order of frequency, the most common are intraventricular and subdural hemorrhages, cortical infarctions, and spinal cord and brain stem lesions due to trauma. The long duration of some of these findings would indicate they existed prior to delivery. Intrauterine hypoxia and "placental insufficiency" have been described as causing such lesions. Severe neonatal hypoglycemia has been associated with intracranial bleeding. In modern neonatal intensive care units, the incidence of periventricular-intraventricular hemorrhage in infants born weighing less than 1,500 gm or after less than 35 weeks of gestation is between 40% and 50%.[68–72] It occurs within the first 72 hours, often in the first six hours after delivery. Although the possible causes are multiple, important related factors are that it occurs most frequently in infants under 34 weeks' gestation when vessels and supporting structure are immature and vulnerable to rupture, there is a disproportionate amount of cerebral blood flow in the periventricular area, and any stress can increase intracranial arterial and venous pressures. Periventricular-intraventricular hemorrhage is the most important adverse neurologic event in the newborn period.

Hypoxia, hypoglycemia, and hyperbilirubinemia, all of which occur with increasing frequency as the length of gestation decreases, as mentioned previously, can have deleterious effects upon the brain of the low birth weight infant. Falling neonatal mortality among low birth weight infants in Western Australia coincided with an increased incidence of spastic cerebral palsy.[49] "Prematurity" is the single most common etiologic factor for cerebral palsy in the United States.

Retrolental fibroplasia of sufficient degree to cause visual problems occurs in approximately 30% of infants with a birth weight of 1,500 gm or less. It is more frequent and severe in those receiving mechanical ventilation. Although exposure to oxygen as a part of therapy is carefully monitored in all intensive care units, the estimated incidence is 2% to 4% of blindness in the very low weight survivors.[71]

The incidence of significant hearing loss matches that of blindness with about 2% of low weight infants requiring hearing aids.

A number of studies have indicated that a low birth weight is a liability to intellectual development, the smaller the weight and briefer the gestation the greater the chance of handicap. A disturbing feature in comparing those studies completed 20 or 30 years ago with those of very recent vintage is that while the survival rate has increased, the incidence of sequelae, especially among those weighing 1,500 gm or less, has remained essentially unchanged.[26, 35, 36, 43, 65, 66] Admittedly there are difficulties in analyzing or comparing studies where the source of the population is quite different. Among those weighing 1,500 gm or less, up to 50% have demonstrable abnormalities of neurologic or intellectual abilities. In another study of infants born weighing less than 1,250 gm the incidence of moderate-to-severe neurologic abnormalities was 72% in those ventilated compared with only 20% in those not requiring ventilation.[65] By contrast, a study of similar nature from a different intensive care unit found 54% of ventilated very low birth weight infants developed neurologic sequelae of which half were major handicaps. Statistics of infants inborn and not requiring transportation to an intensive care unit fared better than those who were outborn. In summary, Lubchenco[5] and Rubin et al.[31] (1976) indicate that a gestational age less than 28 weeks and a birth weight less than 1,200 gm each carry at least a 70% risk of moderate-to-severe handicap. A gestational age between 28 and 31 weeks or a birth weight between 1,200 and 1,500 gm has a risk of about 50% of either neurologic or intellectual problems.

There does not appear to be a clear-cut difference in the prognosis of intellectual performance between the premature and small-for-date infant of equal birth weight. Both types of infants experience an increased incidence of learning and reading difficulties in the usual school situation.[44, 55] Approximately 20% of low birth weight children may appear to have normal development until they reach 4 to 6 years at which time mild diplegia or ataxia, with or without hypotonia, becomes evident. A number of investigators have reported an increased incidence of behavioral problems in children of low birth weight.[16, 64] Anxiety and long separation from the mother may play a role in these manifestations. It has already been stated that a good steady home environment is an important adjunct to a favorable prognosis. Very relevant to this point is the fact that the occurrence of the "battered child syndrome" is considerably higher among low birth weight children than in the general population.[64]

Of very great concern is the relatively high incidence of permanent neurologic complications in those who survive. A question that is difficult to face is whether the improved methods of care to reduce mortality are worth the price to increase the number of children who may be incompetent in our social milieu. This question particularly pertains to the very low birth weight and/or very premature infant. Both cell size and number may be so compromised in these individuals that future growth and development cannot rectify the consequences nor permit recovery to a normal status.

REFERENCES
1. Quilligan E.J., Paul R.H., Sacks D.A.: Results of fetal and neonatal intensive care, in Gluck L. (ed.): *Modern Perinatal Medicine*. (Chicago, Year Book Medical Publishers, 1974.)

2. Usher R., McLean F., Scott K.E.: Judgment of fetal age: II. Clinical significance of gestational age and an objective method for its assessment. *Pediatr. Clin. N. Am.* 13:835, 1966.
3. Koenigsberger M.R.: Judgment of fetal age: I. Neurologic evaluation. *Pediatr. Clin. N. Am.* 13:823, 1966.
4. Naeye R.L., Tafari N.: *Risk Factors in Pregnancy and Diseases of The Fetus and Newborn.* Baltimore, Williams & Wilkins Co., 1983.
5. Lubchenco L.O.: *The High Risk Infant.* Philadelphia, W.B. Saunders Co., 1976.
6. *Vital Statistics Report: Summary Report, 1971.* U.S. Dept. of Health, Education and Welfare, Public Health Service, 1974.
7. Corner B.: *Prematurity: The Diagnosis, Care and Disorders of the Premature Infant.* (Springfield, Ill., Charles C Thomas, Publisher, 1960.
8. Evans H.E., Glass L.: *Perinatal Medicine.* New York, Harper & Row, 1976.
9. Cook L.N.: Intrauterine and extrauterine recognition and management of deviant fetal growth. *Ped. Clin. N. Am.* 24:431, 1977.
10. Freeman M.G., Graves W.L., Thompson R.L.: Indigent Negro and Caucasian birth weight: Gestational age tables. *Pediatrics* 46:9, 1970.
11. Fischer-Rasmussen W.: Causes of low birth weight in infants. *Dan. Med. Bull.* 13:1, 1966.
12. Naeye R.L.: Malnutrition, probable cause of fetal growth retardation. *Arch. Pathol. Lab. Med.* 79:284, 1965.
13. Drillien C.M.: The small-for-date infant: Etiology and prognosis. *Pediatr. Clin. N. Am.* 17:9, 1970.
14. Shanklin D.R.: The influence of placental lesions on the newborn infant. *Pediatr. Clin. N. Am.* 17:25, 1970.
15. Battoglia F.C., Frazier T.M., Hellegers A.E.: Birth weight, gestational age, and pregnancy outcome, with special reference to high birth weight–low gestational age infant. *Pediatrics* 37:417, 1966.
16. Villar J., Smeriglio V., Martorell R., et al.: Heterogeneous growth and mental development of intrauterine growth-retarded infants during the first 3 years of life. *Pediatrics* 74:783, 1984.
17. Drillien C.M.: Later development and follow-up of low birth weight babies. *Pediatr. Ann.* 1:44, 1972.
18. Scott K.E., Usher R.: Fetal malnutrition: Its incidence, causes and effects. *Am. Obstet. Gynecol.* 94:951, 1966.
19. Miller H.C., Merritt T.A.: *Fetal Growth in Humans.* Chicago, Year Book Medical Publishers, 1979.
20. Winick M.: Cellular growth in intrauterine malnutrition. *Pediatr. Clin. N. Am.* 17:69, 1970.
21. Lubchenco L.O., Hansman C., Dressler M., et al.: Intrauterine growth as estimated from liveborn birth weight data at 24 to 42 weeks' gestation. *Pediatrics* 32:793, 1963.
22. Lubchenco L.O., Hansman C., Boyd E.: Intrauterine growth in length and head circumference as estimated from live births at gestational ages from 26 to 42 weeks. *Pediatrics* 37:403, 1966.
23. Lubchenco L.O.: Assessment of gestational age and development at birth. *Pediatr. Clin. N. Am.* 17:125, 1970.
24. Graham G.G.: Poverty, hunger, malnutrition, prematurity, and infant mortality in the United States. *Pediatrics* 75:117, 1985.

25. Gordon H.H., Levine S.Z., McNamara H.: Feeding of premature infants: A comparison of human and cow's milk. *Am. J. Dis. Child.* 73:442, 1947.
26. Vohr B.R., Hack M.: Developmental follow-up of low-birth-weight infants. *Ped. Clin. N. Am.* 29:1441, 1982.
27. Speirs A.L.: An anthropometric study of prematurely born children at the age of 5 years. *Arch. Dis. Child.* 31:395, 1956.
28. Woolley P.V., Valdecanas L.Q.: Growth of premature infants. *Am. J. Dis. Child.* 99:642, 1960.
29. Harper P.A.: Discussion, in *Physiology of Prematurity, Transactions of the Fifth Conference.* New York, Josiah Macy, Jr., Foundation, 1961, pp. 218–221.
30. Yu V.Y.H., Hollingsworth E.: Improving prognosis for infants weighing 1,000 gm or less at birth. *Arch. Dis. Child.* 55:422, 1980.
31. Rubin R.A., Rosenblatt C., Below B.: Psychological and educational sequelae of prematurity. *Pediatrics* 52:352, 1973.
32. Benton A.L.: Mental development of prematurely born children: A critical review of the literature. *Am. J. Orthopsychiatry* 10:719, 1940.
33. Spitzer A.R., Fox W.W.: Overview of infant apnea and approach to medical management, monograph series, vol. 1. Port Washington, N.Y., DSA Communications, 1984.
34. Knobloch H., Rider R., Harper P., et al.: Neuropsychiatric sequelae of prematurity. *J.A.M.A.* 161:581, 1956.
35. Knobloch H., Pasamanick B.: Environmental factors affecting human development, before and after birth. *Pediatrics* 26:210–218, 1960.
36. Dann M., Levine S.Z., New E.V.: The development of prematurely born children with birth weights or minimal postnatal weights 1,000 grams or less. *Pediatrics* 22:1037, 1958.
37. Amiel-Tison C.: Neurologic problems in perinatology. *Clin. Perinatol.* 1:33, 1974.
38. Dreyfus-Brisac C.: The bioelectric development of the central nervous system during early life, in Falkner F. (ed.): *Human Development.* Philadelphia, W.B. Saunders Co., 1966, p. 286.
39. Graziani L.J., Weitzman E.D., Velasco M.S.A.: Neurologic maturation and auditory evoked responses in low birth weight infants. *Pediatrics* 41:483, 1968.
40. Thomas A., Chesni Y., St. Anne Dargassies A.: *Examen neurologique du nourrison.* Paris, La Vie Médicale, 1955.
41. Ruppert E.S., Johnson E.W.: Motor nerve conduction velocities in low-birth-weight infants. *Pediatrics* 42:255, 1968.
42. Blom S., Finnstrom O.: Motor conduction velocities in newborn infants of various gestational ages. *Acta Paediatr. Scand.* 57:377, 1968.
43. Westwood M., Kramer M.S., Munz D., et al.: Growth and development of full term nonasphyxiated small-for-gestational-age newborns: Follow-up through adolescence. *Pediatrics* 71:376, 1983.
44. Towbin A.: Central nervous system damage in the human fetus and newborn infant. *Am. J. Dis. Child.* 119:529, 1970.
45. Avery M.E.: *The Lung and Its Disorders in the Newborn Infant,* ed. 3. Philadelphia, W.B. Saunders Co., 1974.
46. Dawes G.S.: *Foetal and Neonatal Physiology.* Chicago, Year Book Medical Publishers, 1968.
47. Gluck L.: The evaluation of functional maturity in the human fetus, in Gluck

L. (ed.): *Modern Perinatal Medicine*. Chicago, Year Book Medical Publishers, 1974.
48. Berg T.: Immunoglobulin levels in infants with low birth weights. *Acta Paediatr. Scand.* 57:369, 1968.
49. Dale A., Stanley F.J.: An epidemiological study of cerebral palsy in Western Australia, 1956–1975: Spastic cerebral palsy and perinatal factors. *Develop. Med. Child Neurol.* 22:13, 1980.
50. Brooks J.G.: Apnea of infancy and sudden infant death syndrome. *Am. J. Dis. Child.* 126:1012, 1982.
51. Shelley H., Neligan G.A.: Neonatal hypoglycemia. *Br. Med. Bull.* 22:34, 1966.
52. Avery M.E., Hodson W.A.: The first drink reconsidered. *J. Pediatr.* 68:1008, 1966.
53. Naeye R.L.: Hypoxemia and the sudden infant death syndrome. *Science* 186:837, 1974.
54. Rabor I.F., Oh W., Wu P.Y., et al.: The effects of early and late feeding of intra-uterine fetally malnourished infants. *Pediatrics* 42:261, 1968.
55. Wiener G.: The relationship of birth weight and length of gestation to intellectual development at ages 8 to 10 years. *J. Pediatr.* 76:694, 1970.
56. Fencl M. de M., Tulchinsky D.: Total cortisol in amniotic fluid and fetal lung maturation. *N. Engl. J. Med.* 292:133, 1975.
57. Lee K., Eidelman A.I., Tseng P., et al.: Respiratory distress syndrome of the newborn and complications of pregnancy. *Pediatrics* 58:675, 1976.
58. Pildes R.S., Cornblath M., Warren I., et al.: A prospective controlled study of neonatal hypoglycemia. *Pediatrics* 54:5, 1974.
59. Ziegler E.E., Ryer J.E.: Renal solute load and diet in growing premature infants. *J. Pediatr.* 89:609, 1976.
60. Francis-Williams J., Davies P.A.: Later intelligence in low-birth-weight infants. *Dev. Med. Child. Neurol.* 16:709, 1974.
61. Cruise M.O.: A longitudinal study of the growth of low-birth-weight infants: I. Velocity and distance growth, birth to 3 years. *Pediatrics* 51:620, 1973.
62. Miller H.C., Hassanein K., Chin T.O.Y., et al.: Socioeconomic factors in relation to fetal growth in white infants. *J. Pediatr.* 89:638, 1976.
63. Schaffer A.J., Avery M.E.: *Diseases of the Newborn*. Philadelphia, W.B. Saunders Co., 1971.
64. Klein M., Stern L.: Low birth weight and the battered child syndrome. *Am. J. Dis. Child.* 122:15, 1971.
65. Rothberg A.D., Maisels M.J., Bagnato S., et al.: Outcome for survivors of mechanical ventilation weighing less than 1,250 gm at birth. *J. Pediatr.* 98:106, 1981.
66. Kitchen W.H., Ryan M.M., Rickards A., et al.: A longitudinal study of very low-birth-weight infants: An overview of performance at eight years of age. *Develop. Med. Child Neurol.* 22:172, 1980.
67. Gerhardt T.G., Bancalari E.: Apnea of prematurity: Lung function and regulation of breathing. *Pediatrics* 74:58, 1984.
68. Volpe J.J., Herscovitch P., Perlman J.M., et al.: Positron emission tomography in the newborn: Extensive impairment of regional blood flow with intraventricular hemorrhage and hemorrhagic intracerebral involvement. *Pediatrics* 72:589, 1983.
69. Dolfin T., Skidmore M.B., Fong K.W., et al.: Incidence, severity, and timing

of subependymal and intraventricular hemorrhages in preterm infants as detected by serial real-time ultrasound. *Pediatrics* 71:541, 1983.
70. Volpe J.J.: Neonatal intraventricular hemorrhage. *N. Engl. J. Med.* 304:886, 1981.
71. Lucey J.F., Dangman B.: A reexamination of the role of oxygen in retrolental fibroplasia. *Pediatrics* 73:82, 1984.
72. Tarby T.J., Volpe J.: Intraventricular hemorrhage in the premature infant. *Ped. Clin. N. Am.* 29:1077, 1982.

6 / Behavior and Personality

When children are little they make our heads ache;
when grown our hearts.
—Italian proverb

No field related to growth and development of children is in a greater state of flux than that of behavior, including personality and intelligence. There are several reasons for this. In contrast to the physical aspects of child development, our methods of measurement are inexact, controversial, and greatly influenced by personal prejudices. There are nearly as many theories on cognitive development as there are authors who choose to write about it. The same may be said about the subject of personality. For most of the present century arguments have been very heated as to whether genetic or environmental influences, nature versus nurture, are most important in shaping the minds of our children.

Behavioral development obviously is dependent upon the growth and functional maturation of the central nervous system. In the evaluation of the infant or child there is considerable overlapping of the neurologic with the behavioral aspects. The behavioral or developmental assessment is used to measure a person's achievements or accomplishments in functional areas. This involves a steady, largely predictable, increase of abilities with increasing age as a result of interaction between the nervous system and environmental experiences. The neurologic assessment measures the integrity of neural mechanisms appropriate to the age of the subject. Although these two different assessments will usually parallel or complement each other, exceptions can exist. A child with cerebral palsy might have some neurologic abnormalities but the developmental evaluation could be entirely normal.

Some aspects of the development of the central nervous system and of the special senses are discussed in chapter 7.

CHAPTER 6

The Child's Family

For better or worse the American family is undergoing a transition that can not help but have important influences on child development. Presently 75% of families live in urban areas of which 70% are in large metropolitan areas. Since 1900 our nation has become greatly diversified in population in terms of national origin, ethnicity, religion, and race. Structurally, the contemporary family is predominantly nuclear, i.e., the typical family includes only parents and children—only two generations. It is separated in space from relatives and thus from their interaction and social contact. Today's family is smaller than the traditional family at the beginning of this century when the average household had five persons. Now the number is less than three. In 1900 women bore an average of five children; today the predictions are that women born in the 1950s and 1960s will average two children. An important trend is the increasing role assumed by mothers in the economy of the family, which takes them outside the home. In 1940, 25% of married women were employed outside the home. Presently 53% are working or looking for work.[97] This trend plus more effective birth control has resulted in a delay in childbearing and greater maturity in mothers. In 1982, of women aged 25 to 29, over 36% were childless. While in 1950 only 3% of people never married, it appears that at least 10% of young people will never marry in the present population.[98]

In the last three decades the divorce rate has risen steadily. Among couples married in 1952, within 25 years 29% were divorced. Of those married in 1967 the same percentage were divorced within ten years. If current rates continue, almost half of recent marriages will end in divorce. Since four out of five divorced people remarry, this indicates that interpersonal relations were at fault. The average duration of marriage prior to divorce was 6.7 years; therefore, the children involved would be young. In the year 1979 to 1980 approximately 1.2 million children in the United States were added to the 17 million who were already living in homes headed by a single parent, usually the mother. These children live in a fatherless home an average of 5 years. One out of five households with minor children was headed by a single mother in 1982. Despite the relative availability of birth control measures, 18% of all births occur in unmarried women, about one third in teenage girls.[97, 100] The high rate of divorce and the numbers of children born out of wedlock have altered the traditional portrait of the family.

Some aspects of maternal-infant bonding and cross-cultural studies of the families' attitudes' influence on child development will be discussed in following sections. The role of parents in childrearing constitutes a very important element in the theories of Freud and Piaget as described later. The manner in which children view their parents has a strong effect upon the children. Until fairly recently the father's role in care was minimal compared with that of the mother. Traditionally, the child, beyond infancy, sees the father as more punitive and more dominating in the family milieu. In early adolescence children usually consider their same-sex parent as the more punitive. Children from different social classes view their parents differently depending upon the handling of discipline. Middle class parents are fairly tolerant of children's needs, consider motives, are egalitarian, and correct by reasoning or appeal to conscience. Lower class parents, especially fathers, are envisioned as being rigid and authoritarian and less accessible. The middle class father is seen by teenage boys as being more supportive of their scholastic and other endeavors than is true of the lower class father. It does appear that parents, fathers included, are becoming more aware of children's needs regardless of the socioeconomic level.[95]

In view of the statistics quoted regarding divorce and separation, it is important to evaluate the effect these have on the children involved. A child living within an unhappy or bitter marriage is at risk. The preschool or young school-aged child is particularly vulnerable because the child's frame of reference includes the entire family. If there is a separation the child faces an extended period of emotional and social readjustments. To him or her this represents a personal, familial, and social loss and this is often associated with a feeling of guilt because the child thinks he or she may somehow be responsible. Hostility is often directed toward the mother, who is usually the caretaker, for failing to keep the family together. Rutter[95] felt that family discord and disharmony are the damaging factors and separation is largely incidental. In support of this concept is the fact that delinquency rates are higher in homes broken by divorce than in homes in which a parent has died. Considerable damage to the child may result if the child is used by one parent to harm the other or if a depressed parent becomes overdependent on the child for companionship and support. Very significant is the fact that five years after divorce 30% of involved children were intensely unhappy and dissatisfied with their lives.[99, 100]

On the average, children of working mothers develop just as well as those whose mothers remain at home. It is more important to have a satisfied, happy mother than to have an unhappy mother at home all day. Obviously, day care benefits or liabilities depend upon the quality of care provided. Not only should physical needs be met, but there also must be opportunities for play and verbal interaction, and very important is consistency in caretaker personnel.[95]

Neonatal Development

The use of representative reflexes and neurologic signs in determining gestational age is outlined in chapter 5. It is important to reiterate that in the evaluation of the neonate it is assumed that the infant has not suffered unusual trauma from the delivery nor experienced the effects of drugs that could influence his or her responses to stimuli. The environment for any testing situation, infant or child, must be such as not to distract nor interfere with accurate observation. The infant should be awake. Reflex response is greatly modified by the state of sleep or wakefulness of the baby and failure to recognize this has resulted in inconsistent and unpredictable behavior standards.

The fetus exhibits reflex movement of a very crude order as early as eight or nine weeks. These consist of flexion of the trunk, retraction of the head, and retraction or backward movement of the arms. By 14 to 16 weeks the fetus is quite active, showing elementary movements of short excursion involving extremities, trunk, and neck. The motor and most of the reflex behavior in late fetal life is mainly under control of the medulla and spinal cord. Many of the so-called primitive reflexes, especially those involving the extremities, depend upon the tonic and myotactic reflex, i.e., recoil from stretch. These appear by or after 32 gestational weeks (see chapter 5, Table 5–2). At birth, tonicity and activity are equal bilaterally, and the resting position assumed is one in which there is a tendency for all extremities to be flexed in an attitude of the fetal position. Most of the time the hands are tightly fisted. Spontaneous rotation of the head in supine and prone positions occurs and assures the ability of the newborn infant to free his or her nose of obstruction and maintain the airway. There is usually good tone throughout the body, and this is partly exemplified by the resistance to extension of all the extremities. The presence or lack of this tone is a useful method in evaluating gestational age. An object placed in the hand of the mature newborn infant stimulates a strong grasp, sometimes of such magnitude that the baby can be lifted free of the surface of the table.[2, 23] This grasp reflex is present by 32 weeks of gestation, but is less sustained and weaker then.

The tonic neck reflex of Magnus and de Kleijn is inconstant in the newborn but assumes a predictable reaction in the normal month-old infant. When the head is turned forcibly to one side while the infant is in the supine position, the arm, and less consistently the leg, of the side to which the head is turned will extend, and the opposite arm and leg will be flexed. This is often described as the "fencing position" and will persist until four to six months.[7]

Both premature and term infants respond to a sudden change in position, jarring or a loud noise by a startle response consisting of increased muscle tone and some extension of the extremities. Of much greater significance is the Moro's reflex, which is elicited by abrupt removal of support of the infant's head when held in a supine position. Infants of less than 35 weeks of gestation extend and abduct the upper extremities only. After 35 weeks the extension is followed in one continuous movement by adduction and flexion. This has been described as an embracing action. Normal infants lose this reflex by 5 months.[24]

When the newborn is supported vertically and the plantar surfaces of the feet are placed on a flat surface, the legs become extended and partially support the infant. If the infant is then lightly propelled, he or she makes walking movements with good coordination and relatively steady positioning of the feet in a "stepping movement." This reaction persists for about six weeks.

One of the earliest reflex patterns to crystallize is that of sucking. By 14 to 16 weeks the fetus will protrude his or her lips in unmistakable preparation for sucking. Tongue and pharynx can adequately adapt to swallowing by this time. The full-term newborn and all but the smallest premature infant suck vigorously upon a fingertip introduced into the mouth. When the cheek is lightly touched, the infant turns his or her head toward the stimulus and purses the lips. This reaction has been termed the rooting reflex.

Shortly before term, reflex blinking to strong light is present, and a similar response is elicited by a loud noise. Light reflex action of the pupil is present as early as 32 weeks of gestation. Sneezing in response to nasal irritation as well as bright light is found in the newborn. Both coughing and the gag reflex are elicited by appropriate stimuli by 32 weeks of gestational age.

Repeated pricking of the skin between the costal margin and the iliac crest causes a concave curving in of the trunk on the stimulated side. This persists from birth through the second month and then reappears much later.[2]

The Babinski reflex is variable, and the response is subject to different interpretations. If plantar flexion of the great toe in response to a stroking of the lateral plantar surface from heel to toe is termed "positive," then more than 90% of infants in the late fetal and newborn period have a positive Babinski. Wakefulness, supine position, and neutral attitude of the extremities are important prerequisites in evaluating the response. Fanning of the toes is not often present. This type of response often lasts throughout the first year.[10]

The deep tendon reflexes are usually easily elicited at birth. These may be more brisk than in the adult throughout early childhood. If the baby is born with a positional marked dorsiflexion of the feet, the resulting stretching of the Achilles tendon may obviate the ankle jerk. Some ankle clonus, less than ten contractions, may be found in normal infants for a year or more. Sustained clonus is abnormal.

Rhythmic or clonic movements, elicited by stimuli or spontaneous, occur in many infants. They are often associated with crying and are stronger and more sustained in term than in preterm infants. The parts involved include all of the extremities and the chin. Though the reaction is usually symmetrical, not all parts are always participating. With increasing age there is decreasing frequency and disappearance by six to seven months.

Most of the superficial, cutaneous reflexes are present at birth or before. These include the abdominal, sphincter, cremasteric, as well as the rooting and sucking responses already described. (Table 6–1).

In the behavioral examination, the baby's state of consciousness and reaction to specific stimuli are evaluated. In the Brazelton[13] examination there are graded series of producers e.g., sounds, pulling to sitting position, restraint, and the response is recorded on a point system. The reaction to a small bell ring may be used as an example of the scoring system.

1. No reaction
2. Either respiratory change or blink
3. Quieting plus item 2
4. Stills, brightens
5. Shifts eyes, turns toward sound plus item 4
6. Alert, eyes and head turn
7. Alert, head turns, eyes search
8. Prolongation of item 7
9. Turning and alerting on both sides with every presentation of stimulus

It is sometimes difficult to break down the response to such a fine distinction as 9 points in some of the suggested procedures. Brazelton points

TABLE 6–1.—EVOLUTION OF
NEONATAL REFLEXES

REFLEX	APPEARS	DISAPPEARS
Tonic-neck	20 fetal wk	7–8 mo.
Moro's	28 fetal wk	2–3 mo.
Palmar grasp	28 fetal wk	3–4 mo.
Trunk in-curve	28 fetal wk	4–5 mo.
Doll's eyes*	32 fetal wk	10 days
Babinski	38 fetal wk	12–16 mo.

*Eyes open, head is rotated from side to side. Positive response is contraversive conjugate deviation of eyes.

out that repeated tests over several days on a baby enhance the value of the examination and that results are reproducible among trained examiners.[13]

Typical procedures in the assessment scale include the following: response to bright light, response to pin prick, response to inanimate visual object, response to human voice, pull-to-sit position, and covering face with cloth.

In addition to the specified items listed in the assessment scale, the examiner notes other aspects of behavior and records these in a similar manner. Among these are consolability, irritability (to aversive stimuli), tremulousness, amount of startle response, and hand-to-mouth facility.

In all, there are a total of 27 major items to be scored. The author claims no attempt was made to create a summary score that would indicate optimal development. An average score would be 5 for each item.

The ultimate value of the Brazelton scale or other methods in predicting the future intellectual competence of neonates or older infants has yet to be determined. Some discussion of this point will be considered later in this chapter. There does seem to be general agreement that reflex behavior, sensorimotor development in early life, the changing patterns of sleep (to be discussed), and the EEG are strongly dependent upon gestational age.

For a considerable period of time in this century the environmentalists dominated attitudes in child psychology, indicating that a child's relations to family and society were most influential in shaping behavioral development. There is increasing awareness that infant and child temperament are to a considerable degree independent of parent-child interaction. The term *temperament* designates the behavioral style, conduct, and thinking, irrespective of content, level of ability, or motivation of a particular activity. Thomas and Chess[11] identified three constellations of temperament but also emphasized that children vary widely in the degree and sharpness with which they exhibit these categories. The "easy child" is characterized by regularity, a positive mood in approach to new situations, and easy adaptability. The "difficult child" demonstrates considerable irregularity, a preponderance of withdrawal reactions to new situations, many negative mood expressions, and slow adaptability. The third type is designated "slow to warm up child." Such a child has many withdrawal responses and negative moods, mild reactions, and slow, but eventual, adaptability.[11, 14]

The child's temperament influences the behavior and attitudes of peers, older children, siblings, parents, and teachers. It is important for parents to recognize that all children do not react to the same stimulus in the same manner. The easy child may require so little attention as an infant that the child is actually neglected by grateful parents and reacts with feelings of rejection. Parents of the difficult child may feel threatened and inept in their role as caretakers. They may use pressures, appeasements, and finally punishment to accomplish toilet training, avoidance of accident-prone situations, and good eating habits, as examples. Parents, like their offspring, have different temperaments and respond in varying ways to their children's behavior.

Behavior and Environment

The human organism is remarkably plastic in its adaptability and is extremely dependent on social interaction for its specifically human qualities. From birth onward it needs a close interrelationship with protective and responsive adults to gain the type of maturity of personality for which we all strive. All personality is both genetically and environmentally influenced. The former influence is responsible for the limitations of the central nervous system typical of the individual, even though these restrictions are quite broad and allow great latitude in the response to environment.

Environmental influences begin before birth. Impaired development, for example, can result from a large number of factors occurring during pregnancy including infections (especially rubella, herpes, and cytomegalovirus), drugs, alcohol, and irradiation. Smoking, malnutrition, and maternal infections not transmitted to the fetus may have deleterious consequences on the developing organism. Attitudes of parents toward the unborn child are of great importance in the initial acceptance and care of pregnancy and of the newborn infant. Desire for pregnancy or lack of it, economic status of the home, marriage status, reactions of the father, number of siblings, interval from last pregnancy, the course of previous pregnancies, and present problems such as the degree of nausea or other discomforts are some of the factors having psychologic influences that may carry over and modify childrearing.

Often a mother's acceptance of her child will not come immediately. Doubts and actual fear of her ability to assume the new role may present themselves to the mother after delivery. There is strong evidence that early and repeated physical contact with her baby is an important element in allaying such fears and doubts.[16] How closely the infant matches or differs from her fantasy of him or her becomes a factor in how the mother handles and stimulates the infant. Many of her original attitudes will change, but the original feelings will continue to influence her throughout her entire association. The very fact that the child changes through growth and development causes a constant reevaluation among all members of the family.

Affectional ties can be disturbed, perhaps permanently, by illness in the perinatal period. A major problem, e.g., extreme prematurity or major congenital anomalies, often causes prolonged separation and anxiety and feelings of guilt. Even minor problems, such as feeding difficulties, may cause residual worries that will influence maternal, as well as paternal, attitudes for years unless a satisfactory resolution is achieved before baby and mother leave the hospital. The high percentage of behavioral problems in high-risk infants may not be totally dependent on the child's deficiencies, but in part, are related to the ability of parents to deal with the situation. The interruption or impairment of the reciprocal interactions that establish and refine the infant's communication with his or her mother early in life may be at fault.[16, 19]

The development of attachment between infant and mother has been described in four phases.[9] During the first two to three months the infant has the range of sensorimotor mechanisms to orient herself to her social environment but is essentially *undiscriminating* in social responsiveness. Any person that will satisfy hunger, comfort, and furnish tactual-kinesthetic stimulation will do. The second phase is *discriminating* as the baby begins to differentiate her mother from others and manifests this by rather specific types of smiling, vocalization, and crying in response to her presence or voice or lack of it. The third phase begins after six months with more explicit proximity-seeking and contact-maintaining behavior. All of the earlier attachment activities are still present but added to them is ambulation that facilitates proximity and contact. The infant's signals, vocal as well as body movements, are more effective and often used to evoke a response from the mother or other caretaker. Ainsworth calls this the phase of *active initiative in seeking proximity and contact*. As the child grows older and her thinking encompasses more complex ideas, she becomes able to anticipate her mother's goals and actions. This may well correlate with Piaget's developmental stage when internalization of thought becomes apparent at around 2 to 3 years of age.[52] Now the child begins to attempt to alter the mother's goals and plans to improve her own position in regard to contact, proximity, and interaction. This phase has been described as that of *goal-corrected partnership*. It has been postulated that there may be a critical period for the interaction between baby and mother to form attachment, and that if it does not occur by 18 to 24 months it will never occur.[9] Very important for this development is the sensitivity and responsiveness by the mother to the infant's signals and communication. Routine care is not sufficient though it is important as a means to provide for the interaction.

Two important points need to be made at this time. It is not necessary or even optimal for mother and child to form an exclusive partnership. A spreading of secondary attachments over other figures is probably healthy and beneficial for complete development. Brief separations from the mother are eventually well tolerated if the maternal bond is a secure one. Where the relationship is tentative, separation becomes very stressful to the child. The second point is that fostering maternal-infant attachment does not "spoil" the child. A sure way to cause overdependent reactions and increase the amount of crying is to ignore the crying and/or react in a perfunctory manner.

One result of secure bonding is the earlier and more aggressive exploratory behavior of the infant and young child. In an older individual we would probably refer to this as self-confidence. It is certainly suggestive, though perhaps more difficult to prove, that a good mother-child attachment is a necessary preliminary to a satisfactory adjustment to society. Nonacceptance by the parent, especially the mother, during the first two to three years is said to be associated with increased frequency of both withdrawn-neurotic behavior and antisocial aggressiveness later in life.[19]

In recent years there has been considerable controversy concerning the effects of early physical contact between the newborn infant and his or her mother. Klaus and Kennell indicated that there was a "sensitive period" in the first minutes or hours after birth during which close contact with the mother was essential for optimal development.[16] These authors as well as others have contended that this bonding of mother-newborn has resulted in more sustained breast feeding, improved maternal attitudes toward the child, and even a reduction in the frequency of child abuse. Subsequent reviews and further well-controlled studies have cast doubt on any benefits other than a modest but beneficial short-term effect.[93, 94]

Many investigators have emphasized the beneficial results of good child-rearing in the first few years of life relative to intellectual attainment and social adjustments.[27, 64] A satisfactory parental environment has the potential to minimize the effects of prematurity, of low birth weight and other perinatal complications and to maximize the reservoir of intellectual abilities.

Kagan[28] has suggested that maternal deprivation or lack of stimulation need not be devastating to the future development of the infant. He cites a number of studies that indicate neither intellect nor behavior are impaired if remedial efforts are made to correct past deficits. Such efforts can accomplish good results even if delayed for some time after infancy or early childhood. Can we then improve the state of the disadvantaged child by such programs as the preschool *Head Start,* and will they have a lasting effect on the children involved? The facts are at best only slightly encouraging.[92] Preschool participation versus nonparticipation produces an immediate seven-point IQ score benefit, but this is reduced to four points in another two years and disappears by the fifth or sixth grade. Participants had slightly superior reading and mathematic achievement at grade 3 level that disappeared by grade 6. At ages 15 and 20 the participants had no higher educational or occupational aspirations than the controls. One of the most important differences in the two groups was that preschool attendance decreased the percentage of placements in special-education classes. It is important to recognize that once enrolled in special education, children seldom work their way back to the mainstream and escape from the onus that is associated with an isolated, small, special group.

Extensive and carefully designed cross-cultural studies to evaluate the relationship between cognition, schooling, and literacy have been carried out. Conclusions indicate exposure to components of reading and writing skills may result in improved test scores measuring language processing and some cognitive skills, but literacy alone does not inevitably lead to improved results in memory, classification, and logical inference. More difficult to evaluate in such studies is the effect of cultural socialization on test results. In all groups there was continued improvement in problem-solving ability; however, it may be delayed as much as 4 years in children raised in a poor community in a nonindustrialized condition as compared with children from a middle class society in an industrialized nation.[86, 91, 95]

Kagan[28, 44] and others[96] have stressed that development is fluid and it is never too late for changes to take place. The child has great resilience and he or she can benefit from programs designed for cognitive stimulation. Some of the difficulties in evaluating qualitative and quantitative effects relate to the intensity and duration of corrective programs and the cultural and socioeconomic environment from which the children come and to which they return. Nevertheless, there may be potential error in assuming family influences and social experiences mold the child's development to the exclusion of the effects of maturation and the temperamental qualities of infants. One need not deny the influences of the environment to recognize that the maturation of the central nervous system alters the child's receptivity to the experiences presented by the environment.

If there is no other depriving condition, Rabin[61] found that mother sharing in the kibbutz resulted in no marked differences of personality or intelligence as compared with a conventionally raised control group of children. Similar findings have been emphasized for adopted children.[28] Provided there is sufficient contact (no author has offered to define "adequate" or "optimal" in this relationship) between parent and child, the effects of maternal employment,[65] communal childrearing,[66] or day care[67] have not been demonstrated to endanger the well-being of the child. Lacking in most of these studies are long-term follow-ups and adequate evaluations of critical ages of the children, parental attitudes, and the influence of the socioeconomic status of the families.

It has been pointed out that the low language skills of the underprivileged are not due to a quantitative lack of exposure, but rather to the chaotic and undisciplined nature of the stimuli.[60] If Piaget and other investigators are correct in the emphasis they put upon the role played by language in cognitive development, then indeed these children are at a great disadvantage. By the age of 3 years the specific information and ideas furnished and fostered by the parents or caretakers become increasingly important to mental growth. The more extensive the education (not necessarily formal), the richer the reservoir of ideas and information that can come from the parents. There is a large and still growing literature supporting the concept that family social differences and language have enormous influence upon intellectual performance of the child.[28, 68–71] Whether the measurement of social class is by occupation, income, or educational background, the higher the rating of the parents the stronger will be the child's school performance, the higher will be his or her IQ scores, the greater his or her language skills. Regardless of birth history or early (first two years) developmental history, the intelligence of the teenager is more clearly related to his or her social class than to any other factor.[28, 70] For the mother, the incidence of poor prenatal care, undetected infections, and poor nutrition during childhood, as well as during pregnancy, is greater in the economically disadvantaged. For the child, these factors contribute to a lowered potential even before the exposure to an impoverished environment. Such conditions seriously impair the opportunity for the quantity and quality of stimulus needed for normal development. Delay or poor timing of the stimulus may be partly correctable.[28]

Size of family is also related to intellectual ability. A recent study indicates that the larger the family and the higher the birth order the lower will be the score on standardized intelligence testing. The authors of the study postulate, but do not conclude, that dilution of parental attention or economic factors may play a part.[72]

Cross-cultural study is interesting as a means of comparing some aspects of environmental influence upon behavior.[70, 73] Traditionally reared rural infants accomplished motor milestones of development more rapidly than "westernized" urban infants in Africa. This persisted throughout the first year. ("Traditional" refers to a relaxed and leisurely attitude by parents with few expectations. Breast feeding on demand, nearly constant body contact with an adult caretaker, no toilet training, lack of clothing, and membership in a large stable family are typical features.) On the average, all native African children achieved motor milestones at an earlier age than Caucasian children. During the second year, progress in language and adaptive behavior (Gesell and Bayley items) were slower in the African children as compared with the Caucasian. Since weaning usually takes place for the black infants at about 12 to 18 months, Werner[73] attributes some of the relative decline to the onset of poor nutrition and infections, especially parasitic. In those cultures characterized by isolation of infants and absence of any type of stimulation, motor and language development were considerably delayed. In the Kauai study,[70] a 10-year follow-up of several ethnic groups was possible. The incidence of serious school problems was quite high, but 90% of school failures were unrelated to any deleterious perinatal condition. Children with poorly educated parents and unstable homes at age 10 had lower IQ scores, had a high percentage of disturbed social and emotional development, and lacked communication skills. These findings were more common in children from Filipino, Hawaiian, and Portuguese descent than those from an Anglo-Saxon or Japanese family. An analysis of early family environment showed that parental language styles, attitude about achievement and concern for the young child have a very significant impact upon its future. The pattern of development during the first two years seems interrelated to ethnicity, caretaker attitudes, nutritional status, and socioeconomic position. The Kauai study further supports the concept that to be productive, enrichment programs must begin early.

The sexual role assimilated by the child appears to become deeply imbedded by the third or fourth year. Recent studies now give great force to the idea that sexual orientation almost exclusively is determined by the mode of rearing. The child assumes the assigned sex and all of its psychologic attitudes regardless of the hormonal, genital, or gonadal sex. These findings were made possible by the study of children of varying ages in which true or gonadal and chromosomal sex was opposite to that assigned them because of congenital anomalies of the external genitalia or hormonal aberrations, as in the adrenogenital syndrome in girls. Their parents had regarded them as normal boys or girls and treated them accordingly. The children responded by establishing a pattern of psychosexual behavior conforming to the demands of their culture. When attempts were made to change their gender after the third year, in almost every case there was great psychologic difficulty. This gender orientation is certainly a strong example of the fact that psychic influences are durable and extremely potent.[74]

Fetal hormonal sex exercises some influence on sexual pathways in the hypothalamus and related limbic structures of the brain (see chapter / 9). Girls who become virilized in utero as a result of exposure to androgens (iatrogenic or the adrenogenital syndrome) will definitely show a tendency in their behavior to "tomboyism." In view of their medical history, parents often become disturbed. With adequate counseling, child and parents can make satisfactory adjustments. Such girls can adequately assume the female role in lovemaking and marriage, though they may persist in preferring competitive sports and choosing less feminine dress, hobbies, etc. Money[74] points out that there is no corresponding term for "tomboy" to apply to boys who may be artistic and sensitive and dislike athletic pursuits. In our present society it is more difficult for the unmasculine man to gain acceptance than it is for the unfeminine woman.

The sex roles of parents and other members of society are important in conditioning the child in his or her own sex role. Children demonstrate in their play and conversation at an early age recognition that the male is expected to be physically stronger, more aggressive, and more punitive while the female is more dependent and passive. This image is still dominant today, although perhaps the degree of contrast in America is less than it was a decade or two ago. Parents set the pattern throughout childhood by assigned dress, toys, and duties, and physical differences are recognized by children as early as three years. Sex role behavior is largely determined throughout early childhood by parent models. The effect of a fatherless family upon boys is variable and seems to reflect the results of loneliness, anxiety, and social adjustment in the mother as well as the absence of a father figure. If the fatherless child is sufficiently exposed to other males, of all ages, his sex identity is usually undisturbed.[75]

Sibling Rivalry

The manifestations of sibling rivalry may be fairly severe in about half of first-born children and is rarely a major problem in later-born children. It is usually more pronounced in same-sex siblings and in children between 1.5 and 3.5 years of age. As might be anticipated, children in the temperament group of the "difficult child" have greater difficulty in accepting the new baby. Sibling relationships are characterized by a "love-hate" feeling with a mixture of affection and jealousy in being displaced as the center of attention. The latter feeling often produces a reaction of guilt and a sense of loss.[11, 14]

Mothers react differently to the first child after the birth of the second child in several ways. Less playful attention is offered by the mother and they are not as sensitive to the child's interests and desires or demands. The mothers become more authoritative, giving more orders with the result of an increase in confrontations.

The first child characteristically reacts by regression to a pattern of earlier behavior: thumb sucking, enuresis, requesting to nurse from the breast or bottle, and using "baby talk." Some children withdraw and become relatively quiet, refusing to talk or play. Some suggest taking the baby back to the hospital, flushing it down the toilet, or giving it away. Rarely there may be an attempt to injure or physically dispose of the baby. The more secure the older child feels, an important role for fathers to play at this time, the less likely he or she will resort to extremes of behavior.

Later, as the new sibling grows older and acquires toys and other "belongings," the older sibling may attempt to gain possession of these objects, hide them, or actually destroy them. He or she will compete for attention and, especially at the 2-year level, attempt to displace the newcomer on the mother's or father's lap. Such behavior is usually only an attention seeking mechanism and of brief duration.

Cognitive Development

Cognition is the means by which an individual accumulates organized knowledge of the world and the use of that knowledge to solve problems and modify behavior. There are numerous theories about how a child thinks and about his or her cognitive development. The author will attempt to make an outline of ideas common to most of these theories and discuss one of them in some detail.

In the neonate there is little evidence from behavior of anything that could be termed cognitive, yet there is evidence that some perceptual (visual) choices are made when confronted with different patterns. Later in infancy, selective attention is given to familiar objects and anticipatory behavior is apparent as demonstrated by quieting upon the approach of the mother. Another early indication of cognitive development is curiosity and exploration of surroundings and perceived objects. By the second to third year the intellectual progress is dominated by language. This is communicative in reporting with some accuracy internal requirements such as hunger and the need to eliminate. The language is also referential as the names for objects and activities begin to be cataloged. Not until after five is language used as a conceptual tool for reasoning and thinking and problemsolving. Standards for behavior are established in the preschool years. The child begins to understand the viewpoint of others and to take his or her turn. Discrimination of some abstract ideas now appears, e.g., fair-unfair, near-far, fast-slow, and masculine-feminine. Language gains are in grammar, vocabulary, and pronunciation.

A very significant change occurs in the increased capacity for thought and reasoning between the ages of 6 and 11. Learning becomes systematic and selective and is applied with increasing ease to a variety of contexts. Thought becomes more inductive and insightful with increasing abilities to deal with abstractions. Increasingly refined use of language is an important element of these developments leading to improved verbal reasoning and the use of symbolic and graphic representations. There is an understanding of the relevance of new information and improved discrimination of levels of abstraction and generalities.

Most investigators agree upon the units involved and the basic process of cognition although there may be some disagreement in the use of terms. The units or media are usually designated *images, symbols* (which include language), and *concepts.* Images are mental representations of objects and happenings. The use of symbols or language in thinking is a way of managing the vast amount of coded information that has accumulated in the mind. Concepts are the characterizations of an action or a thing. A concept stands for a set of common attributes. Justice may be conceptualized as the defeat of evil and the victory of good.

Cognitive processes begin with the *perception,* or comprehension, of a question or problem. The next step involves *memory*—whether the problem resembles a past experience. The third process is the *generation of ideas* to bring about a possible solution. To produce good ideas the child must have accurate perception and possess the right set of images, symbols, and concepts. The child wishes to resolve uncertainties and to understand. To find an answer the child reaches into his or her store of knowledge for information that will aid in explaining a new event. Finally there is *evaluation* as the child measures the accuracy of his or her conclusions. The application of the two processes, generation of ideas and their evaluation, toward the solution of a given problem is the very essence of thinking.[28, 76]

Piaget[52, 53, 78] has theorized that cognitive development occurs in three stages throughout infancy and childhood. In each stage there is a period of genesis resulting in specific attainments. The order of the stages is constant, since the development of a new attainment depends upon the completion of past ones. The reader may also wish to follow the same stages as related to Piaget's ideas about personality development outlined later in this chapter.

STAGE ONE, SENSORIMOTOR.—Stage one occupies the first two years. The infant changes from an organism that responds primarily through reflexes to purposeful movement and organized activity in relation to the environment. Characteristic of this stage is the appearance of repetitive activity that eventually becomes planned indicating thinking before acting. Two major abilities of this period are object permanence, knowledge that objects continue to exist though not being perceived, and object recognition, use of information acquired to identify an object. One of the last developments is the initiation of manipulating the environment and imitation of people.

STAGE TWO, PREOPERATIONAL.—Stage two extends from 2 to approximately 7 years. The most distinguishing characteristic of this period is the development of symbolic functioning, e.g., words used to describe activities of the past and to give some references to the future.

STAGE THREE, CONCRETE OPERATIONS.—Stage three lasts from 7 to 11 years and is distinguished by the development of "symbolic functioning." Symbolic functioning is the ability to make one thing represent a different thing that is not present. As implied by the term "concrete" the child applies his or her mental operations solely to real (concrete) objects and events. He or she cannot divorce themselves from the objective world and think about hypothetical propositions. The child begins to perform logical operations that can be described as a system for logical notation. It is a time of refinement of concepts and their use in thinking.

STAGE FOUR, FORMAL OPERATIONS.—Stage four begins at about 11 or 12 years and extends through adulthood. Having reached this stage, the individual can now think in abstract terms and deal with hypothetical situations. Due consideration is now given to the *possible* and *what might be.* The child is capable of making extrapolations to reach conclusions. One property of formal operations is that they are reflective; the adolescent cannot only apply a set of solutions to a specific problem but can consider the effects of all possible variables.

Two major criticisms of Piaget's theories have been expressed. One is that he ignores the cumulative effect of experience in cognitive development with excessive emphasis upon maturation as outlined in his stages. The second points out the lack of experimental evidence and too great a reliance upon speculation. It should be mentioned that none of the experimental data so far available have disproven any of the proposed concepts.

Control processes of the memory system that direct strategies for encoding, rehearsal, and retrieval have become an important topic in understanding memory and cognitive development in children. How does the infant and child spontaneously discover techniques and integrate them into his or her cognitive repertoire? Unfortunately, work in this field is as yet very scanty. Some observations imply that the major development is in the maturation of the control processes and that there is little change in memory function with age. These changes appear to be based upon the child's awareness of his own memory and its limitations. The young child may lack control processes not only because he has had little opportunity to practice them, but because it does not occur to him to attempt retrieval or to prepare for future retrieval. With experience, the child learns that certain cues can be effective aids to remembering and that rehearsal and self-testing improve retention. It is suggested that not until he has some awareness of his mnemonic abilities and limitations will he begin to develop the control processes that characterize memorization in the adult.[76]

Early Social Behavior

Social behavior has been discussed in several sections of this chapter as related to parents, sex, personality, adolescence, and other age groups. A few important points not covered elsewhere will be considered here.

Voice and physical contact can elicit responses in the neonate including visual, auditory, and consoling or quieting activity. Between 2 and 3 months, parents are recognized by sight and voice with appropriate reactions such as smiling, cessation of crying, or reaching. Social laughing is present by this time also. By 7 or 8 months, fear of strangers is manifested by visual avoidance, frowning, crying, reducing physical activity, and clinging to a parent. This apparent fear seems to reach a peak between 9 and 12 months and usually subsides by 18 to 24 months. Some children will find separation from a parent or parents, e.g., baby-sitter or day-care center, a very distressing experience until after 3 years.

At 1 year, simple tricks or games such as peak-a-boo are enjoyed. The 18-month infant is fairly self-contained and, if the caretaker is in close proximity, can spend long periods alone with toys. By 2 years there is usually considerable emotional equilibrium and decreasing number of tantrums, which reached a peak at 18 months. The 2-year-old uses tone and loudness of voice symbolically. She likes to show off and can be coy.

At 3 years, cooperative and group play are possible. The child is ritualistic in many activities that include dress, arranging toys, and the pattern of going to bed. There is increasing evidence of the desire to please parents and one manifestation of egocentricity is jealousy of siblings. To an increasing extent, a child's conception of herself is related to her skills. She has an opportunity to test her skills against those of her peers and she adds to the conception of herself as her peers react to her skills. It is through continuing ego development that socialization becomes a prominent part of the child's life. Recognition of self as a complete entity permits this phase of development.

The psychoanalyst emphasizes that the ritualistic and repetitive play that is so characteristic of the 3- and 4-year-old is simply a method of gaining confidence and self-assurance. The strongest fears at this time are those of separation from parents and self-injury. These fears are usually satisfactorily resolved by the well-adjusted 6- to 7-year-old. It seems reasonable to delay elective hospitalization and surgery until such resolution takes place.

Although the 4-year-old may appear argumentative, this ploy is often used in a desire to experience new actions and new words and as a test of parental reaction. Boasting, exhibitionism, exaggeration of humor, physical aggressiveness, verbal profanity, and excessive pride in accomplishments are some of the difficulties parents must expect at this age. There is a strong feeling of "me," "mine," and "I" but a continuing recognition of other people as social entities. There is even the first glimmer of self-criticism.

Play and Discipline

Until fairly recent times no serious thought was given to the significance of play in the child's development. In fact, it was often looked upon as a pleasant but unnecessary or superfluous part of early life and was to be discouraged so that the more serious role of learning and work could be attended to. It is now recognized that play is an extremely important activity beginning in infancy and progressing through a series of overlapping stages that can be readily documented and that appear to be essential for normal developmental maturation.[19, 30, 53]

Many of the important contacts between the child and the environment take place through the medium of play. The pleasure this activity provides, in the presence or absence of adults and peers, serves to discharge tension and permits him or her to exercise imagination. Social play, sometimes with imaginary people, is essential for the development of the personality by modifying egocentric concepts with exposure to the feelings and behavior of others. The child assumes many different roles in his or her play, which is an important preparation for entering adult life. Early in life play is a useful means of decreasing dependence upon parents and serves as a way for the catharsis of strong emotional reactions.

The earliest manifestations of play can be observed between 3 to 4 months when the infant first laughs aloud. Some authors consider the earlier appearance of the smile as a social reaction to be differentiated from the kind of response resulting in the laugh. Next he discovers and manipulates his hands and fingers and then his feet. By 7 months he vocalizes to his toys, which includes squealing, laughing, and imitative sounds. By 9 months his repertory includes the nursery games of pat-a-cake and waving bye-bye, and he can accomplish a broad spectrum of facial expressions both as a means of stimulus as well as a response to stimuli. At 14 to 15 months, play includes activity with a favorite doll or stuffed toy with much conversation and the beginning of role-taking. This is further elaborated by the child's assuming the role of the parent at around 2 years of age. The previous undirected play of the baby merges into practice play with evident objectives. He repeats because he enjoys the pleasantly familiar and because he is becoming goal-oriented. The child watches, listens, and imitates. Repetition and imitation constitute important aspects of play throughout life.

Learning what he must do and how he must act to obtain a pleasant sensation is also the beginning of discipline. The child's relation to parents involves his need for acceptance by them. He wants to learn how to control his actions so that life is happy. As he becomes ambulatory he also becomes exploratory, inspecting his environment with all of his senses. This inevitably leads to some conflicts with parents and siblings and the increasing application of discipline.

By 2 years the child plays for relatively long periods independently of mother. The sensory pleasures of play and consistent discipline condition the child to an appreciation of the joys of learning. But he now experiences some anxieties in the conflicts between his sensory pleasures and that discipline. In a normal setting the child can cope with these disturbing emotions and they do not destroy his desire to continue to explore the world. One method for coping with moderate degrees of anxiety is through symbolic play. He will relieve his frustrations and anger by acting out or dramatizing his feelings. He may spank his "mother" doll or scold another one for behaving badly. In the fantasy of play he does many of the things he does not dare to do in real life. In much of this type of symbolic play the child is not always aware of what or why he is acting out. This is in contrast to the imaginative play where he pretends to be an airplane but knows that he is not.

Not until 3 years of age is the average child sufficiently mature to enter into cooperative play that involves sharing and taking turns. From this age on few normal children will actively avoid social contact with their peers, though there are wide ranges of how aggressively he or she will pursue such contacts.

The type of play entered into by the early school years is characterized by the need for conformity and tends to follow a ritualistic pattern. This is especially true of games that have fixed and unvarying rules. Play by this time, and for the remainder of childhood, often leads to the acquiring of many skills. This leads to self-confidence as he gains stature with his peers. Not all play is directed toward games. As children grow older they become interested in many other pursuits which may include music, art, sewing, cooking, etc. This is also the time of collecting. At first the collections may be an odd assortment of objects and are not well organized, but later in the school years more meaningful objects are accumulated and often carefully cataloged, such as stamps, books, or records.

Parents' understanding, usually an intuitive one, of the importance of play is essential for a satisfactory child-parent relationship. The child learns by experimenting and from that gains competence. He constructs new abilities from past experiences and enjoys each new achievement. Parents should be supportive without fostering excessive dependence or inhibiting the development of skills. Completing a task for a child without allowing adequate experimentation or time to find his own solution, if done repeatedly, could lead to lack of development of autonomous abilities. At the other extreme are parents who constantly set difficult goals for their children and then deride them for their failures. Both types of parents are found fairly often among the children with learning difficulties in school.

No grand plan for childrearing exists. Parents who are aware of the developmental continuum experienced by all children are better able to cope with behavior problems as they arise. Mothers and fathers should be encouraged to manage their children in terms of their present capabilities, their cultural heritage, and anticipation of developing requirements. The ultimate aim is to achieve security and independence that is commensurate with the child's level of development.

The child, to become an accepted member of the community, must acquire a set of socially desirable traits. Such traits can usually be obtained by systematic reward without resorting to punishment. Reward in this connotation means the showing of approval and affection. Firm, but reasonable, expectations of behavior are effective means of guiding children. Without guidelines, without limits established by parents and consistently followed, the infant and child feel helpless and unloved. When discipline must be enforced, the child must understand the reason for it. Its administration should not be unduly delayed beyond the time of the event that necessitated it. Discipline that is consistent, firm, and friendly and that does not ask the impossible is seldom unsuccessful. Discipline that is administered in an unpredictable (at least to the child) fit of anger and threatens the withdrawal of parental love is poorly accepted and creates unnecessary fear and anxiety. An explanation to the child that one can understand his feeling of anger or frustration but that his behavior was unacceptable is an important measure to assure the child of continued affection by the parent.

Measuring Behavior

Intelligence (associative memory) of a high order and quality characterizes humans. Growth of this attribute in the child is eagerly anticipated by the parents and looked for by the physician. Considerable variation in intelligence is noted, but the limits of normal are generally accepted. Understandably, intelligence above the normal range is welcomed, while a failure of growth of intelligence to keep pace with chronologic age causes alarm.

Sooner or later the child with subnormal intelligence will be recognized as being retarded, the time of recognition depending on the degree of retardation and on the ability of parents or physician to recognize abnormal behavior.

When slowness of neuropsychologic development is suspected, the physician is usually consulted, and he or she sets about making a diagnosis much as he or she does when looking for diseases in other organ systems. A careful history with emphasis on pregnancy, delivery, neonatal period, and course of development is obtained. The status of hearing, sight, and motor control must be established, as serious impairment in any may distort the manifestation of normal developmental potential. A check for evidence of metabolic diseases known to be associated with slowed mental development should be routine. Hypothyroidism, phenylketonuria, and galactosemia are examples of conditions that should be diagnosed at the earliest possible moment, since treatment is available that may prevent or minimize their deleterious effects on mental development. Hurler's syndrome (gargoylism) and Down's syndrome are representative of conditions associated with mental deficiency, and although corrective measures are not available, it is important to the family that these conditions be recognized early enough to permit suitable counseling and advice.

Because of the rapidity of development and the wealth of complex integrations about which data are available, infancy is the period in which deviations from normal are most easily detected. This is particularly true of these relatively minor deviations from which compensations occur but which may have lasting effects on the later organization of learning and behavior.

The developmental examination and/or screening inventory is a standardized clinical procedure that can be adapted to the needs of the child. The examination situations and test objects are so designed that characteristic responses are expected at each developmental stage (Gesell) or the expected percentile at a given chronologic age range (Thorpe and Frankenberg). Systematic observations of large numbers of normal and abnormal infants have demonstrated that development proceeds in an orderly and predictable fashion. Although there are some differences in the age norms given by different authors, the spread is seldom very large.[7] Explanations for the differences may be due to variations in methods of standardization, recording, and in the definition of test items or techniques. In some items, but not all, cultural differences have substantial influence. Especially in motor development and language, acceleration may result from environmental stimulation.

Neurologic and developmental assessment are inseparably related and should be evaluated together. Some of the screening examinations combine the two, e.g., reflexes plus functional items, but there may be a dilution of each as a result. The material that is included in this text is a combination of a number of tests which the author has found of greatest value in his own practice. The largest percentage of items comes from Gesell and Amatruda[6] but also include some from Thorpe,[79] Frankenburg,[80] Bayley,[81] and Illingworth.[82] Since growth is a complex process and behavior an expression of complex interactions, diagnosis depends upon the total picture presented. A complete knowledge of normal growth and development is the basis for the detection of abnormality. The discussion that follows is restricted to a consideration of a small number of selected behavior patterns which can be used as reference points in *screening* children. This is not intended to represent a diagnostic examination but a method to alert the examiner to the need for further evaluation.

Epidemiologic investigations indicate the narrow range of variability in behavior in infancy.[38] During the first year the effects of racial and socioeconomic factors are minimal. Only 1.8% of the usual infant population has a developmental quotient (discussed later) under 85, compared with 14% in a group of white children of school age. In the small percentage with below-average intellectual functioning there was a high incidence of organic disease including low birth weight, bleeding, and toxemia during pregnancy, and both physical and neurologic abnormality in early infancy. In later childhood, by age 3, a sharp division along socioeconomic lines is present. The changes predominate in the fields of adaptive behavior and language.[40] Except for a relatively small number of hereditary diseases giving rise to mental deficiency, the genetic factors that are present cannot be considered as primarily responsible for significant differences in behavioral functioning, according to Knobloch and Pasamanick.[6, 40] The structure and basic functions of humans are genetically determined; it is the individual's sociocultural milieu that modifies his or her behavior and makes one individual significantly different from another.

Most investigators feel that the predictive value of early developmental screening, or even more thorough examination, is not very high. Not only are tests carried out during the first 2 years unreliable in predicting scores at school age, but individual infants may have high scores in one category at one time and low results in the same category 6, 12, or 18 months later.[68, 83, 84] It should be emphasized that infant tests are most useful in identifying defective development resulting from organic pathology. The child's development after the first 2 years is determined largely by his or her environment and no test can be expected to predict that variable.

Behavior, for testing purposes, is usually divided into four major categories: motor, adaptive, personal-social, and language. Gesell divides motor into fine and gross, while Frankenburg combines fine motor and adaptive. Thorpe enlarges the language category to include all communication skills. Bayley uses two separate scales, one motor, one mental development. All authors emphasize the importance of observing such factors as emotional stability, span of attention and the nature of the attentional pattern, muscle tone and control, perceptual abilities (these include vision and hearing), fatigue, and general appraisal of health status.

Gross motor behavior includes the control of the head, trunk, and extremities, and fine motor behavior pertains to the achievement of the control of fine movements of the fingers. Although it is true that there is no evidence that any thinking has taken place unless there is some observable motor reaction, it is important to avoid the mistake of using acquisition of motor control as the criterion of intellectual ability. Motor behavior is most important in the evaluation of neurologic integrity and may sometimes be so disordered that the evaluation of intellectual potential is extremely difficult. Acceleration in motor development does not contribute to intellectual abilities, nor does motor defect necessarily mean that there is a concomitant defect in intelligence.

Language behavior includes the production of sounds, single words and combinations of words, facial and gestural expressions, and understanding of the communications of others. Just as motor behavior in infancy is incorrectly used as an important criterion of intelligence, language behavior is somewhat similarly misused later in the preschool period as a sole index. A child who can neither talk nor understand the language he or she hears is not necessarily mentally defective. There is considerable variation in the time of the appearance of the "talking" aspects of language, and they may be delayed in otherwise entirely normal children with good developmental potential. Normal speech production will occur if a child hears, understands the language of others (is not aphasic), and has no intellectual or neurologic defect.

Personal-social behavior has the widest variation of all of the fields and depends to a larger extent on culture and environment, but its expression is also a function of neuromotor maturity. It includes such things as feeding and sleep habits, bladder and bowel function, identification of objects and persons, and the ability to work and play with others and to adapt to the regulations imposed by society.

Adaptive behavior includes manipulation and exploitation of objects, the use of motor capacities in the execution of practical situations, as well as the utilization of past experience in the solution of new problems.

Adaptive behavior is the most important field; judgment of intellectual potential is based largely on the adaptive maturational status. However, intellectual potential takes into account not only the developmental level but also the quality of behavior. The concept of intellectual potential is concerned with prognosis and implies that if nothing happens to damage the infant organically, socially or psychologically, his or her future development will be at an essentially constant rate in terms of an overall level of adaptive functioning. This level is related to, but not equated with, school age or adult tests of intelligence. Intelligence tests as now constituted tend to measure limited functions, and the downward trend in test results between infancy and childhood that occurs largely in the lower socioeconomic groups would indicate that these children have less exposure to the kinds of experience that later tests are designed to evaluate. The upward spreading in the curve can be explained adequately only on the basis of learning; but even learned behavior, though it is greatly modified by environmental factors, must be dependent on the basic integrity of the central nervous system.

The developmental quotient (DQ) is a clinical estimate of maturity based on the overall picture and is a guide to the rate of developmental progress, which can be different for each of the fields of behavior.

$$DQ = \frac{\text{maturity age}}{\text{chronologic age}} \times 100$$

A diagnosis does not result from a DQ score. An adequate history and physical examination are necessary as well as evaluation of emotional aspects of development for a final diagnosis.

Development progresses in a cephalocaudal and proximodistal direction. Control of the eyes and the head is achieved in the first quarter of the first year, that of the upper trunk and arms in the second quarter, that of the lower trunk and the use of the fingers for fine prehension in the third quarter, and integration of the legs in the erect position begins in the last quarter of the first year of life. Figure 6–1 illustrates the general trend and the major achievements, primarily in motor behavior, at the various age levels. The differences that can be found in the literature on the age of attaining various developmental milestones can usually be explained by differences in defining the behavior that is meant. Sitting may be accomplished with support by leaning forward on the hands for brief periods, which occurs at 28 weeks, or indefinitely and steadily without the use of hands for support, which occurs at 40 weeks. Thus, definition of terms is essential.

In the first year of life, development is estimated in terms of weeks rather than months because it progresses so rapidly that the use of monthly intervals may be misleading. "Four months" may mean just over 17 weeks or almost 22 weeks of age, and the developmental change in this period of time is tremendous. Further, the chronologic age must be corrected for the amount of prematurity, since development must really be measured

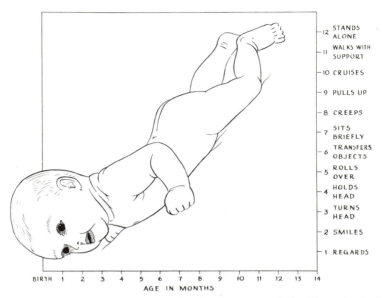

Fig 6–1.—Developmental diagram for the first year of life. The infant's figure represents a diagonal line on which is plotted the progress of behavior (right of the diagram) against chronologic age. The cephalocaudal pattern of behavior is diagrammatically illustrated by position of the figure. (After Aldrich.[3])

from the time of conception and premature birth does not confer any advantage to the maturing nervous system. The "key ages," which are at 12-week intervals in the first year, represent turning points and major integrative periods in the developmental paths and correspond roughly to the quarters of the year previously mentioned.

It should be understood that the behavior patterns given below represent the average performances for a large group of healthy subjects. An individual pattern might deviate 20% to 25% from these standards and still be within normal limits. Nevertheless, it is important to emphasize that norms for neuropsychologic behavior are as essential as are norms for any of the other aspects of development discussed in this book.

It is important to understand just what it is an infant evaluation predicts. It is not meant to assign a precise quotient, a number that will not change with time. What happens to the infant and the influences to which the infant is exposed before reaching school age will affect his or her ability to perform on an intelligence test at that time. Unless qualitative changes in the central nervous system are caused by noxious agents or gross changes in milieu alter major variables of function, the infant's Stanford-Binet IQ will be above 85, provided it can be stated in infancy that he or she has no neuromotor impairment and has an intellectual potential within the normal range. In actuality the predictions are much more precise than this clinically acceptable statement, and the Gesell developmental examination performs as reasonably in predicting in infancy as other examinations do at later ages. Its usefulness goes beyond what one expects of a clinical neurologic method: namely, identification of the abnormal infant with a below-average potential, usually on an organic basis, and definition of the nature of his or her abnormality.[50]

The screening should be done in a quiet, comfortable, and isolated environment. If the mother is present she should be told not to correct answers or persuade the child in any manner. The infant or child should be awake and not fatigued, nor should the examination displace nap time. The examiner should permit the child a brief examination of the room, but items used in the tests should be introduced only as needed, and then removed before progressing to the next part. Verbal or other instructions should be given slowly, deliberately, and in terms the child is sure to understand. In presenting tasks in any category, the initial level should be one easily accomplished to prevent discouragement or boredom. The examiner should be completely familiar with the method of presenting the test items. Some may be introduced first with an opportunity for spontaneous response, failing which, verbal instructions or demonstration may be used. Both by facial expression as well as tone of voice, the examiner should acknowledge the response as being acceptable, whether or not it is correct. An achievement observed should carry greater significance than one obtained by history from a parent or caretaker.

Developmental Screening Inventory*

4 WEEKS

Motor: Gross	1. Asymmetrical tonic neck reflex positions predominate
	2. Head sags forward in sitting
Fine	1. Hands fisted
	2. Hands clench on contact
Adaptive	1. Regards object in line of vision only
	2. Follows to midline
	3. Drops toy immediately
Language	1. Vague indirect regard
	2. Small throaty noises

---

*Much more detailed inventories are available and should be consulted by anyone who plans to participate in screening technics. A number of teaching films have also been prepared.[13, 51, 79, 81] The age placement of an item is that at which roughly 50% of infants and children achieve success.

| Personal-social | 1. Stares indefinitely at surroundings |
| | 2. Regards observer's face and diminishes activity |

16 weeks

Motor: Gross	1. Symmetrical postures predominate
	2. Head steady in sitting
	3. Head lifted 90 degrees when prone on forearms
Fine	1. Hands engage
	2. Reaches, grasps objects, brings to mouth
Adaptive	1. Eyes follow slowly moving object well
	2. Arms activate on sight of dangling toy
	3. Regards toy in hand and takes to mouth
	4. Regard goes from hand to object when sitting
Language	1. Laughs aloud
	2. Excites and breathes heavily
Personal-social	1. Spontaneous social smile
	2. Hand play with mutual fingering
	3. Pulls dress over face
	4. Anticipates food on sight

28 weeks

Motor: Gross	1. Sits briefly leaning forward on hands
	2. Supports large fraction of weight in standing
	3. Bounces actively in supported standing
	4. Rolls over
Fine	1. Has radial palmar grasp of toy
	2. Rakes at small pellet with whole hand
Adaptive	1. One-hand approach and grasp of toy
	2. Bangs and shakes rattle
	3. Transfers toy from one hand to the other
Language	1. Vocalizes "m-m-m" when crying
	2. Talks to toys
Personal-social	1. Takes feet to mouth
	2. Reaches for and pats mirror image

40 weeks

Motor: Gross	1. Sits indefinitely steady
	2. Creeps and pulls self to feet at rail
Fine	1. Crude release of toy
	2. Plucks pellet easily with thumb and index finger
	3. Exploring poke with forefinger
Adaptive	1. Matches two objects in hands
	2. Index finger approach
	3. Spontaneously rings bell
Language	1. Says "mama" and "dada" with meaning
	2. One other "word"
Personal-social	1. Waves "bye-bye" and pat-a-cakes (or other nursery trick)
	2. Feeds self cracker and holds own bottle

52 weeks

Motor: Gross	1. Walks with one hand held
	2. Stands momentarily alone
	3. Cruises

Fine	1. Neat pincer grasp of pellet
Adaptive	1. Tries to build tower of two cubes
	2. Releases cube in cup (after demonstration)
	3. Serial play with objects
Language	1. Two words besides "mama" and "dada"
	2. Gives toy on request or gesture
Personal-social	1. Offers toy to image in mirror
	2. Cooperates in dressing

15 MONTHS

Motor: Gross	1. Toddles independently
	2. Creeps upstairs
Fine	1. Puts pellet into bottle
Adaptive	1. Builds tower of two cubes
	2. Puts six cubes in and out of cup
	3. Incipient imitation of stroke
Language	1. Jargons
	2. Four to six words, including names
	3. Follows simple commands
Personal-social	1. Says "thank you" or equivalent
	2. Points or vocalizes wants
	3. Indicates wet pants
	4. Casts objects in play or refusal

18 MONTHS

Motor: Gross	1. Walks, seldom falling
	2. Seats self in small chair and climbs into adult chair
	3. Hurls ball in standing position
Fine	1. Turns two to three pages of book at once
Adaptive	1. Builds tower of three to four cubes
	2. Imitates stroke with a crayon and scribbles spontaneously
	3. Dumps pellet from bottle
Language	1. Has ten words
	2. Looks selectively at pictures and identifies one
	3. Names ball and carries out two directions ("on the table," "to mother")
Personal-social	1. Pulls toy on string
	2. Carries and hugs doll
	3. Feeds self in part with spilling

24 MONTHS

Motor: Gross	1. Runs well, no falling
	2. Walks up and down stairs alone
	3. Kicks large ball on request
Fine	1. Turns pages of book singly
Adaptive	1. Builds tower of six to seven cubes
	2. Aligns cubes for train
	3. Imitates vertical and circular strokes
Language	1. Uses pronouns
	2. Three-word sentences; jargon discarded
	3. Carries out four directions with ball ("on the table," "on the chair," "to mother," "to me")
Personal-social	1. Verbalizes toilet needs consistently
	2. Pulls on simple garment
	3. Inhibits turning of spoon in feeding
	4. Plays with domestic mimicry

30 MONTHS

Motor: Gross	1. Jumps up and down
	2. Walks backward
Fine	1. Holds crayon in fist
Adaptive	1. Copies crude circle, closed figure
	2. Names some drawings: house, shoe, ball, dog
	3. Formboard: places three blocks on presentation, errors corrected on reversal
Language	1. Refers to self as "I"
	2. Knows full name
Personal-social	1. Helps put things away
	2. Unbuttons large buttons

3 YEARS

Motor: Gross	1. Alternates feet going upstairs
	2. Jumps from bottom step
	3. Rides tricycle, using pedals
Fine	1. Holds crayon with fingers
Adaptive	1. Builds tower of nine to ten cubes
	2. Imitates three-cube bridge
	3. Names own drawing
	4. Copies circle and imitates cross
	5. Formboard: adapts without error to reversal of initial presentation
Language	1. Uses plurals
	2. Gives action in picture book
	3. Gives sex and full name
	4. Obeys two prepositional commands ("on," "under")
Personal-social	1. Feeds self well
	2. Puts on shoes

4 YEARS

Motor	1. Walks downstairs alternating feet
	2. Does broad jump
	3. Throws ball overhand
	4. Hops on one foot
Adaptive	1. Draws man with two parts
	2. Copies cross
	3. Counts three objects with correct pointing
	4. Imitates five-cube gate
	5. Picks longer of two lines
Language	1. Names one or more colors correctly
	2. Obeys five prepositional commands ("on," "under," "in back," "in front," "beside")
Personal-social	1. Washes and dries face and hands; brushes teeth
	2. Distinguishes front from back of clothes
	3. Laces shoes
	4. Goes on errands outside of home

5 YEARS

Motor	1. Skips, alternating feet
	2. Stands on one foot more than 8 seconds
	3. Catches bounced ball

Adaptive	1. Builds two steps with cubes
	2. Draws unmistakable man with body, head, etc.
	3. Copies triangle
	4. Counts ten objects correctly
Language	1. Knows four colors
	2. Names penny, nickel, dime
	3. Descriptive comment on pictures
	4. Carries out three commissions
Personal-social	1. Dresses and undresses without assistance
	2. Asks meaning of words
	3. Prints few letters

6 YEARS

Motor	1. Advanced throwing
	2. Stands on each foot alternately, eyes closed
	3. Walks line backward, heel-toe
Adaptive	1. Builds three steps with blocks
	2. Draws man with neck, hands, and clothes
	3. Adds and subtracts within 5
	4. Copies diamond
Language	1. Uses Stanford-Binet items (vocabulary)
	2. Defines words by function or composition, e.g., "house is to live in"
Personal-social	1. Ties shoelaces
	2. Differentiates A.M. and P.M.
	3. Knows right from left
	4. Counts to 30

Structure of Behavior

The development of cube behavior is presented here in some detail to illustrate how behavior grows, the complex neuromotor mechanisms involved, the interrelationships between patterns, and the importance of accessory supporting behavior in the emergence of specific patterns during the course of the developmental process. It shows also how many details of development are known; such a fine dissection has been done not only in the field of cube behavior but in many of the other aspects of growth as well.[6]

Not until age 12 weeks does the infant sit supported with his head bobbingly erect and fix his eyes more than momentarily on so small an object as a 1-in. cube; this involves both control of the eye muscles and some control of the neck muscles. At 16 weeks, in the supine position, he is able to rotate his head freely a full 180 degrees, but without this accessory support in the sitting position, he holds his head steady only so long as it is set forward, and he does not turn it to one side. Macular vision has developed, and he regards the cube promptly and for prolonged periods. The eyes still have the lead, but the beginnings of eye-hand coordination are seen as he looks from hand to cube and back again. When he is supine and able to move his arms more freely because his head is supported by the crib platform, he activates his arms at the sight of a dangling object; but he is unable to do this in a sitting position until age 20 weeks. By then his head is held in the axis of his body, and he can turn it to the side without losing control of it. Consequently, he has more freedom of movement of his arms, and there is even the very beginning of finger movements in conjunction with the gross movements of the arms. He scratches at the tabletop as he regards the cube, and as he moves his arms under the influence of the symmetrotonic reflex, they come together toward the midline and approach the cube. But only if his hand comes in contact with the cube does he close on it and grasp it. When it is placed in his hand, he holds it precariously with an ulnar-palmar grasp. Simultaneously with the achievement of control of the arms, grasp is moving across the palm toward the eventual specialization of the radial digits. At 24 weeks approach and grasp occur as one movement—on sight of the cube the arms go out and pick it up. It is still a crude bilateral coralling motion, although the grasp itself is now palmar. With the emergence of vertical movements in addition to the symmetrical in-and-out activity in a horizontal plane characteristic of the earlier ages, he takes the cube to his mouth and retrieves it if he drops it.

At 28 weeks the symmetrotonic reflex has disappeared, and the asymmetry necessary for more complex movements is present. Eye-hand coordination is very well developed, and the infant makes an immediate one-hand approach and grasp on sight of the cube, with further specialization, since grasp, although still palmar, is now at the radial side of the palm. The beginning of handedness now appears, but in a very rudimentary stage, and the 28-week-old infant shows his bilaterality in his transfer of the cube from one hand to the other. Just prior to this stage one hand pulls an object out of the other in a very crude transfer. But at 28 weeks simultaneous grasp and release are still reflex, as shown by transfer and the dropping of a cube held in one hand as the other hand goes out to pick up a second cube being presented. The combination of perception and manipulation is very active, and the infant regards the cube intently as he takes the cube from mouth to tabletop with each hand alternately.

At 32 weeks there is the first inhibition of the simultaneous grasp and release reflex as the infant picks up and holds the first and then the second cube presented. But the inhibitory aspects are so strong that he is unable to drop one of these cubes to pick up a third. Not until 36 weeks is there the first voluntary release as the infant drops one of the cubes he is holding to pick up the third cube. This release is extremely crude, for it is indeed only an opening of the hand and dropping the cube from it.

Concomitantly there is differentiation in the stimulus value of objects, particularly in relation to size, and the ability to encompass more than one object at a time. At the earliest age (12 weeks), the infant can contact only the large cup, then the massed cubes (20 weeks), and finally (24 weeks) a single cube. The larger objects have the greater stimulus value, and not until 32 weeks does the infant retain a cube when the cup is presented. At 28 weeks only if the massed cubes are presented does he grasp and hold a cube with each hand more than momentarily. As already indicated, not until 36 weeks is there enough inhibition of reflex activity so that the infant can exploit more than two objects in succession. At 36 weeks, also, his horizon is widening, and he combines an object in his hand with another on the tabletop, hitting cube against cube or cube against cup. Until greater control is achieved, the concept of "more than one" is restricted to one object only in his hands, so long as very active manipulation such as banging is prominent.

There are two other diverse threads to be picked up that are also being incorporated into the behavior picture simultaneously. So far as cube behavior is concerned, radial specialization has been achieved, and the radial digits, not the palm, are used in manipulation. Further specialization of the radial digits is concerned with precise manipulation of small objects, which lags behind the facile use of the fingers for larger objects. The other thread concerns the relation of the arms to trunk control. The arms are free for such complex manipulations only if the trunk is supported, either by fastening the child into a specially constructed infant Morris chair or by holding him on someone's lap. Otherwise, both hands at first, and then one hand, must be used to support the body in the sitting position.

At 40 weeks he has new achievements, but they are limited by new restrictions. He now combines two objects more definitely, holding a cube in each hand and matching both together. Crude release, independent of grasp, is present; he no longer merely opens his hand to let the cube drop, but puts it down on the tabletop and removes his hand from it. A dim awareness of dimension is developing—he first notices the cube that the examiner has dropped into the cup, and he reaches in and fingers it. It is less mature to grasp than to release, as development up to now has indicated, and at 44 weeks he removes the cube from the cup; but within its confines he is unable to release, and he merely thrusts hand and cube together into the cup. By 52 weeks release has developed to the point where he puts a cube into the cup after demonstration; but fine motor control is still too imprecise to enable him to release one cube on top of another, and his attempts to build a tower fail. At 56 weeks he has coordinated his understanding and his ability to release well enough so that he puts one cube into the cup on request.

By 15 months release has come sufficiently under voluntary control to allow him to build a tower of two cubes. He exhibits his new-found power by casting cubes to the floor and putting five or six cubes into the cup.

Here again the integration of more than one simultaneously developing pattern appears. At the earlier age of 48 weeks he also begins to encompass a series of objects; his horizons are widening. Rudiments of sequential behavior appear as he takes the cubes in succession from the table to the crib platform. Further elaboration of the sequential cube behavior results from an increasing attention span and greater fine motor skill in release. At 15 months his attention is easily distracted by new stimuli, and his drive is not sustained, so that he begins to take the cubes out of the cup again after the fifth or sixth one. Not until 18 months does he have the prolonged attention for and sense of completing a task so that he fills the cup with the cubes. He now builds a tower of three or four cubes before it falls; but this fine motor control grows slowly, and it takes him another six months to add three more cubes to his tower, making a tower of six or seven cubes at 24 months. Not until 36 months is he precise enough to add the final three cubes for a tower of nine or ten.

Human Figure Drawings

Young children use drawings to express their ideas. In addition, there is a progressive improvement with age in both detail and complexity. Using the human figure as the subject, Goodenough and Harris[41] developed a point system for scoring in which a single point is awarded for each of a series of body parts or features. A total score is achieved by summing the individual parts and this total score can then be translated into mental age. This is based upon the accumulated experience of the authors and comparing results with other intelligence tests. This method of testing has several advantages. Instructions are simple, brief, and readily understood. The child usually enjoys drawing and does not feel the stress usually associated with an examination. It is a performance test that enhances its value for the subject with hearing or speech difficulties. Between the ages of 5 and 11 years there is good correlation with other measures of intellectual development.[85] As described here, the test should be considered only as screening procedure in a manner similar to the developmental inventory.

Instructions given to the child should be straightforward and simple, e.g., "On this paper I want you to draw a picture of a person. Make the very best picture you can and take your time." When the picture is completed the child is asked to tell the examiner about the drawing.

The 30 items listed in Table 6–2 are not all-inclusive but should give some indication as a guide to scoring. Each item in the list is worth a single point. See Figures 6–2 and 6–3 for examples of scoring.

TABLE 6–2.—SCORING ITEMS FOR FIGURE DRAWING

1. Head present (outline and some features)
2. Arms present
3. Legs present
4. Trunk present
5. Trunk length greater than width
6. Shoulders indicated
7. Attachment of arms and legs to trunk
8. Feet present
9. Neck present
10. Eyes present
11. Nose present
12. Mouth present
13. Nostrils indicated
14. Hair present
15. Hair more than on crown
16. Nose two-dimensional
17. Mouth two-dimensional
18. Clothing indicated (buttons, belt, tie, etc.)
19. At least two articles of clothing (hat, dress, coat)
20. Costume complete (at least four articles)
21. Fingers present (add point for correct number)
22. Hand distinct from arm and fingers
23. Limb joints indicated (point for upper, point for lower)
24. Proper proportion of head to body
25. Proper proportions of all parts of body
26. Hip indicated
27. Heel indicated
28. Ears present
29. Eye details (one point each: pupils, lashes, brows)
30. Points added for increased detail and avoiding irregularities such as transparencies or overlaps

Point score	= Mental age in years
2	3
6	4
10	5
14	6
18	7
22	8
26	9
30	10

Evaluation of Intelligence Testing*

The intelligence test has two functions: diagnosis and prediction. Prediction requires knowledge of what a particular test score means. For example, if a test has proved reliable in predicting school performance and a

---

*This section was prepared by Ralph Gibson, Ph.D.

Fig 6–2.—Drawing by girl aged 4 years 9 months. Point score of 12 for the items credited as numbered in Table 6–2. Credit for 1, 2, 3, 4, 5, 8, 10, 11, 12, 14, 21, and 28. This would indicate a mental age of 5 years and 6 months.

child obtains a low score, we need know nothing about the reason for the low score to predict low school performance. However, if diagnosis is the goal of testing, it is important to know what characteristics of the child caused the low score. The intelligence test is a procedure for comparing the behavior of two or more persons and for standardizing clinical observation of behavior. It can be evaluated quantitatively and qualitatively.

The quantitative evaluation subserves the function of prediction. Once the score, or IQ, is obtained, it is necessary to relate it to the norm group. It is assumed that in a random population the distribution of scores can be plotted on a normal curve, as are measurements of biologic characteristics such as height and weight. Following this basic assumption it becomes imperative that certain facts about the particular test be known: the variability of IQ scores around the mean, the reliability of the scores, and the validity of the scores.

When the standard deviation is known, a particular IQ score can be assessed in comparison with the norm group. Thus, on the 1960 revision of the Stanford-Binet Intelligence Scale the standard deviation is 16 IQ points.

Fig 6–3.—Drawing by boy aged 7 years. Point score of 21 for the items credited as numbered in Table 6–2. Credit for 1, 2, 3, 4, 5, 7, 8, 10, 11, 12, 14, 16, 17, 18, 21 (2 points), 22, 24, 25, 28, and 29. This would indicate a mental age of 7 years 9 months.

On the Wechsler Intelligence Scale for Children—Revised[43] the standard deviation is 15 IQ points. Therefore, an IQ score of 90 obtained on either test would fall within one standard deviation below the mean of an IQ of 100.

When, in addition to the standard deviation, the reliability coefficient or the accuracy of the measure is known, the error of the IQ score can be determined. The score on the test is determined principally by the ability or knowledge of the child who takes it, but the score is also affected by the inaccuracy of the test itself. The reliability coefficient shows the extent to which errors of measurement influence scores on the test. The complexity of factors that may influence scores on a test is indicated in the following list prepared by R. L. Thorndike.[42]

Possible Sources of Differences in Performance on a Test

I. Lasting and general characteristics of the individual
   A. General skills and techniques of taking tests
   B. General ability to comprehend instructions

    C. Level of ability on one or more general traits that operate in a number of tests

II. Lasting but specific characteristics of the individual

    A. Specific to the test as a whole (and to parallel forms of it)

        1. Individual level of ability on traits required in this test but not in others

        2. Knowledge and skills specific to particular form of test items

    B. Specific to particular test items

        1. The "chance" element determining whether the individual does or does not know a particular fact

III. Temporary but general characteristics of the individual (factors affecting performance on many or all tests at a particular time)

    A. Health

    B. Fatigue

    C. Motivation

    D. Emotional strain

    E. General test-wiseness (partly lasting)

    F. External conditions of heat, light, ventilation, etc.

IV. Temporary and specific characteristics of the individual

    A. Specific to the test as a whole

        1. Comprehension of the specific test task (insofar as this is distinct from I–B)

        2. Specific tricks or techniques of dealing with the particular test materials (insofar as distinct from II–A–2)

        3. Level of practice on the specific skills involved, especially in psychomotor tests

        4. Momentary "set" for a particular test

    B. Specific to particular test items

        1. Fluctuation and idiosyncrasies of human memory

        2. Unpredictable fluctuations in attention or accuracy

V. Variance not otherwise accounted for (chance)

    A. Luck in the selection of answers by "guessing"

Another very important source of differences in performance resides in the relationship between the child and the examiner. The test is basically a standardized interview in which the psychologist serves in the role of a participant observer. This implies that he or she is not only observing the child's behavior, including the test responses, but is also contributing something of a negative or positive value to the child's willingness to exhibit a representative sample of his or her behavior. To obtain a valid test, the psychologist must endeavor in various ways to meet the child's immediate emotional needs. The psychologist can begin with a nonverbal test for a child who is anxious about talking to a stranger, can begin with easier items with a child who is greatly concerned about failure and needs to experience immediate success, or can begin by responding to and possibly interpreting feelings expressed by the child's behavior or conversation. It is apparent that to obtain a valid result, the psychologist must be well grounded, not only in testing procedures but in the psychodynamic aspects of the emotional development of children.

Reliability coefficients estimate the extent to which some or all of the factors cause random changes in the score. The reliability coefficient, how-ever, has two drawbacks: (1) its numerical value depends, to a large extent, on the spread of the scores, and (2) it does not help directly in evaluating the obtained score. Unfortunately, there is no practical method to deter-mine the precise amount of error in an individual case. Statistical methods have been developed, however, for estimating the margin of error that should be allowed in test scores. One of the most useful of these is the standard error of measurement. If we know the exact obtained score and the standard error of measurement of the particular test, we can define the limits around the obtained score within which we would be reasonably sure to find the true score. For two thirds of all children tested the observed score will lie within one standard error of measurement of the true score, and for 19 out of 20 children the observed score will not be more than two standard errors away from the true score.

When the precision of the Binet IQ is determined by comparing Form L and Form M IQs obtained a few days apart, a correlation of about .91 is obtained. Thus the Stanford-Binet test is established as one of the most reliable intelligence tests. However, the average shift of IQs from form to form is substantial: 5.9 for IQ 130, 5.1 for IQ 100, and 2.5 for IQs below 70. Thus, the test is more precise for low IQs. However, for a child with an IQ of 130 on Form L, the quotient on Form M a few days later may range from 124 to 136 if we accept one standard error as a reasonable limit.

On the Wechsler Intelligence Scale for Children—Revised, the average reliability coefficients and standard error of measurements for the verbal IQs, performance IQs, and full scale IQs are reported by Wechsler[43] as follows:

	VERBAL IQ	PERFORMANCE IQ	FULL SCALE IQ
Reliability coefficient	0.94	0.90	0.96
Standard error of measurement	3.60	4.60	3.19

Thus, if we were to accept one standard error as a reasonable limit, we could state if a child obtains a verbal IQ of 89, the true score lies between 85 and 93, a performance IQ of 89, the true score lies between 84 and 94, and a full scale IQ of 89, the true score lies between 86 and 92.

From our discussion it should be clear that the smaller the standard error of measurement, the more confident one can be that the obtained score approximates the true score and that a prediction based on the obtained score is warranted.

Knowledge of the validity of the intelligence test is the final and pivotal information necessary to carry out the predictive function. A test is valid to the degree that we know what it measures or predicts. A vast body of literature clearly shows that mental ability is significantly related to school performance, vocational success, etc. Thus both the Stanford-Binet test and the Wechsler Intelligence Scale for Children—Revised are positively related to school achievement. However, intelligence is only one facet of individuality to be considered in a practical decision about a child.

A special problem of prediction is encountered in the assessment of the intelligence of infants. There has been no clear evidence in the literature that test results in infancy correlate significantly with intelligence test scores in later childhood, adolescence and adulthood. However, infant intelligence scales are widely used in clinical situations to assess the current developmental status of babies. In the author's experience, these scales can provide pertinent information regarding deviations in development that necessitate further medical evaluation, educative counseling of parents, and frequent medical evaluation of the infant's development. However, one must be constantly aware of the caveat suggested by Lewis and McGurk,[84] who state, "This use of infant intelligence scales is justified only if, in interpreting the result scores, the scores are regarded solely as measures of present performance and not as indices of future potential." The author is in complete accord with the view enounced by Schwartz and Elonen[90] based on their longitudinal study of adopted and nonadopted children. At the time of each psychological examination, records were made of such pertinent facts concerning the child's life and family as accidents, deaths, moves, adoption, birth or adoption of a sibling, and the child's reactions to these events. The reports were obtained in interviews with family members as well as with the child. The children were evaluated first when they were under twelve months of age and the final evaluation done when they were over sixteen years of age. The IQ test scores varied over time and in some instances quite dramatically. However, the investigators were able to associate the variance with developmental transitions in cognitive, emotional, and social function and with unevenness in cognitive development and significant life events and experiences. Thus, the assessment of the child did not stress IQ scores per se but rather fitted intelligence into the process of adaptation, and the issue of the predictive validity of infant intelligence tests was not the primary concern.

The classification of intelligence by IQ score is very misleading and tends to give a picture of rigidity of score and ability. However, since the classification is so widely used in the reporting of intelligence testing, it is given with the hope that its operational limitations will be kept in mind.

The clinical usefulness of the intelligence test is particularly outstanding when its second function, diagnosis, is explored. It is at the level of diagnosis that the need for remedial measures can be seen. It is the qualitative evaluation of the test performance that is particularly helpful in total clinical evaluation of behavior. The emphasis in the diagnostic function is to describe how the child arrived at the obtained IQ score. Consideration is given not only to the various aspects of the test performance but also to the behavior exhibited by the child during the course of the examination.

IQ	CLASSIFICATION
120 and above	Superior
110–119	Upper average or bright normal
90–109	Average
80–89	Dull average or dull normal
70–79	Borderline
69 and below	Mental defective or retarded

The need for complete evaluation of all clinical and laboratory data in addition to the intelligence test score is highlighted by taking as illustrations eight children aged 7 years who obtain an IQ of 92 on a given test of intelligence. They are functioning toward the lower end of the average range of intelligence. Their true scores fall somewhat below or above the obtained scores, depending on the standard error of measurement of the test used. One can predict a lowered degree of school achievement on the basis of the known relationship between obtained scores on the test and school achievement.

When we analyze the test performance of child A, it is immediately apparent that she was unable to demonstrate any abilities or pass any items commensurate with her age level. She shows relative lag in all abilities underlying the test items. Her range of successes, whether in terms of age levels on the Stanford-Binet or in terms of scaled scores on the Wechsler Intelligence Scale for Children, is relatively narrow. This qualitative analysis suggests that the reason that child A is having school difficulty is basically because her ability level is low average and she might well be competing with children who are better than average. By noting her reactions to failure during the course of the examination, one might ascertain whether or not any reported distractibility or inattention is secondary to her lowered ability to compete with good average children.

In the case of child B an analysis of the test performance might reveal consistent difficulty on all the test items related to perceptual abilities. On the other hand, items related to other abilities might be passed at or above the level of expectancy for the child. In addition, the child may manifest considerable distractibility and/or hyperactivity during the testing session. The behavior may appear on close observation to be unrelated to interpersonal problems. In fact, the parents often report that the behavior has been characteristic of the child since birth. In general, this is the type of child identified as the "brain-injured child." It should be quickly pointed out that in many cases the medical history and neurologic examination will be entirely negative for organic brain pathology. However, operationally the child does have a rather specific deficit in intellectual functioning, which can be further demonstrated by specific tests designed to measure perceptual abilities.

In the case of child C an analysis of the test performance might reveal consistent difficulty in abstract reasoning ability, i.e., the ability to generalize and to conceptualize relationships. On the other hand, items related to language skills, general comprehension, memory, and perceptual abilities may be near or beyond the expectancy level of the child. The deficit can be further demonstrated by specific tests designed to measure abstract reasoning ability. This child may exhibit distractibility, hyperactivity and negativism, which should be evaluated in terms of their relationship to his deficit and the parental reactions and attitudes toward the child.

In the case of child D the analysis of his test performance might indicate significant difficulty on items related to memory, in contrast to average or above-average performance on items related to other abilities. This, then, is another type of deficit pattern. At the present time it is not possible in the case of children to turn to a specific test of memory to confirm the impression gained from the intelligence test.

Another type of deficit pattern might be exhibited by child E. The analysis of the test performance might indicate significant difficulty on all items involving language. The problem could range from that of having difficulty in naming pictures to being unable to communicate information and comprehension verbally in a meaningful way. In such a case it would be necessary to administer a nonverbal test of intelligence to obtain a valid picture of the child's intellectual abilities.

In the case of child F a basic reading deficit might be revealed and reading retardation would be suspected. Three major diagnostic groups of children exhibiting reading retardation have been identified. One group consists of those children in whom the capacity to read is impaired by frank brain dysfunctioning manifested by clear-cut neurologic deficits. The second group consists of those children in whom the capacity to read is impaired with no definite brain dysfunctioning being suggested either in the medical history or on the neurologic examination. The defect lies in the inability to deal with letters and words as symbols, with decreased ability to integrate the meaningfulness of written material. The reading problem appears to reflect a basic disturbed pattern of neurologic organization. Because the case is endogenous, these children are diagnosed as exhibiting *primary reading retardation.* These children also exhibit language and conceptual difficulties and in this sense are like child C and child E. The third group consists of children whose capacity to learn to read is intact but is utilized insufficiently for the child to achieve a reading level appropriate to his or her basic intellectual ability. The causative factor is exogenous, as represented by interpersonal difficulties like those of child G or limited opportunities for schooling. The children who exhibit the deficit patterns described are often diagnosed as exhibiting minimal brain dysfunction or learning disability. However, these diagnostic terms are used interchangeably to describe a child who is not grossly impaired but does exhibit cognitive and behavioral deviations. While an underlying central nervous system dysfunction is implied, in most cases it cannot be proven. Unfortunately, it is the author's opinion that these diagnoses are made too often without a careful evaluation of the child's total home and school adjustment.

In the case of child G an analysis of the test performance might reveal no single area of consistent difficulty but marked inconsistency. This would be the situation in which relatively easy items are failed and relatively difficult items are passed. Attention difficulties might be characteristic of the child's behavior. The intrusion of personalized material might characterize the test responses. This pattern we characterize by the term "variability." In general, it is observed in children with various degrees of interpersonal difficulties and resultant emotional disturbance.

Finally, in the case of child H an analysis of the test performance might suggest a pattern of emerging abilities. On all intelligence tests the child is required to pass a specified number of subparts of an item to get credit for it, to perform the item correctly within a specific time limit, or to respond in such a way that the answer is similar to the ones given by the standardization population. However, sometimes a child passes fewer of the subparts on items than expected, gives the correct answers beyond the time limit, or answers so that the response is not quite comparable to the expected one. In each instance it is apparent that the child exhibits some basic comprehension of the items, and it might be expected that the qualitative understanding would approach the qualitative criteria in the course of subsequent development. This is the typical pattern exhibited by the average normal child.

While tests[45, 46] have been devised to measure a specific deficit in perceptual motor integration, no adequate measure of abstracting ability in children has been forthcoming. However, the author would propose the Leiter International Performance Scale as such a test. In studies of children with hydrocephalus with and without meningocele,[47] postencephalitis syndrome, posttraumatic head injuries, and poorly controlled convulsive disorders,[48] the Leiter score has been found to be consistently significantly below the score on the Stanford-Binet[49] and the Wechsler Intelligence Scale for Children. However, a deficit in abstract reasoning is suggested by both of the last-mentioned tests. In contrast, children diagnosed as hebephrenic, prepsychotic, or neurotic tend to do significantly better on the Leiter test. At least part of the difference seems to be due to the fact that the Leiter test involves no verbal directions by the examiner and no verbal responses by the child. Furthermore, the items minimize interpersonal material. Thus, the child whose disturbance is based upon interpersonal experiences is better able to demonstrate his or her ability on this test, which places a minimum emphasis on the interpersonal factor.

The foregoing qualitative analysis of the test performances of eight children with an IQ of 92 points up the "kind" of intelligence the children possess. An understanding of the qualitative differences between children with the same score is a prerequisite for counseling parents and helping educators to provide the best possible educational setting for the child.

Psychoanalytic Theories of Personality Development

There are a number of reasons for considering the theories of personality development as advanced by psychoanalysts. Although they have not been universally accepted, these concepts have become very useful tools in terms of reference and in approach to therapy. Criticisms of the theories have emphasized that they are narrowly bound from a cultural standpoint and that they are based on suppositions that cannot be proved. A further weakness is that the theories are direct statements about, or personifications of, attributes of personality rather than an explanation of raison d'être. However, nowhere else in the psychologic literature does there appear a complete set of hypotheses on how personality is formed.

One of the basic principles of living organisms is the constant adjustment to environmental changes, with achievement of a satisfactory state of existence. As a result of these adjustments, conflicts may develop between the outside forces and inner forces, or instincts. Instincts are somatically based urges arising in the body and seeking gratification. (The term *instinct* as used by Freud[34] refers to such things as hunger and erotic urges and does not, as often in biology, indicate a stereotyped behavior.) Much of personality development arises through such conflicts and the resolution of them.

The structure of personality consists of three parts. At the time of birth personality is made up primarily of the *id*. The id is the reservoir of the instincts, or their mental representative. The newborn infant has only the barest nucleus of an *ego*.[31] From this nucleus the ego grows and expands and gains ever greater mastery over the id. The ego is the seat of consciousness and serves as the mediator between the inner instinctual desires and the outer world. It is that part of the personality we refer to as "I" or "me." Furthermore, it is the receiving center for the five special senses. It controls voluntary movements and is concerned with memory and judgment. One of the major functions of the ego is the formation of the mechanisms of defense.[30, 31] These mechanisms are the means by which the ego wards off unconscious and unwelcome instinctual impulses. As the development of the personality is described, we will note these mechanisms of defense in relation to the stage of development at which they appear and their changes with age.

According to Freud, a large area of mental functioning always remains beneath conscious awareness. Between the ego and the id are formed the boundaries of the conscious and unconscious. The division between these two in the infant is very indistinct, but as growth progresses and the ego grows, the division becomes ever more clear. The outer world has little influence on the unconscious, and time and logic do not affect it. These are important aspects, as they account for the apparent emergence of long-repressed and illogical memories in their original strength.

The third division of the personality is the *superego*, which acts as a censor concerning the acceptability of thoughts, feelings, and behavior. This portion of the personality develops last, with the child's parents serving as an external superego in the early years. The permanent structure of the superego does not begin to form until after age 3 or 4 years and then becomes increasingly important as the judge over actions, thoughts, and feelings. Clear separation of ego and superego is not always possible. However, only a portion of the latter is conscious. The superego is built up of all types of experiences and exposures—teaching, reading, etc.—and is responsible for that very uncomfortable feeling of guilt.

One common misunderstanding should be avoided before progressing further. The term *sexual* indicates anything pleasurable and includes "love" in a limitless sense or any positive creative force. The infant who enjoys sucking his or her thumb is experiencing sexual pleasure in the psychoanalytic sense.

Children are said to pass through five stages of psychosexual development, but it is emphasized that each phase blends into the next without clear separation.[31] Also, children vary in regard to the relative prominence of each stage and in the way a particular one is manifested. The *oral phase* covers the first year of life and is so termed because the mouth is the primary erotic (pleasure) zone. The infant associates the pleasure of hunger satisfaction with oral stimulation, and he soon learns to stimulate his mouth for pleasure even though no nutrition is accomplished, as in thumbsucking. Less often in the oral phase physical stimulation of the other anatomical parts, e.g., ear or nose, may replace or accompany oral stimulation. During the first six months the infant is relatively parasitic in his adjustments and emotionally is very dependent. In the second half of the first year, especially with the eruption of teeth and increasing muscular control, there begins a more aggressive approach to his environment. To some extent adults perpetuate this oral phase, the best example being smoking. The psychoanalysts refer to this as "oral dependency."

Previously we stated that the establishment of defense mechanisms of different kinds is characteristic of the maturation of the personality. *Projection* is one of the earliest and most primitive of defense mechanisms. The infant's immature ego conceives of everything pleasurable belonging to him and that which is unpleasant being outside of him. In the older child this same mechanism is often seen but is more clearly understood because it is given verbal reference. As an example, the boy working with a piece of wood has such difficulty that he makes an error and calls the wood "stupid" or "no good." He is projecting his feeling of inadequacy to feel more comfortable.

The *anal phase* follows the oral phase and remains through the next two to three years. The child now becomes ambulatory. His interests widen, his pleasures are not so closely associated with oral stimulation, and the primary erotic zone changes to the anal region. The functions of elimination take on new importance. Pleasure is found not only in defecation but in the retention of feces, and this leads to some of the difficulties experienced in toilet training.

There is a diminishing dependency on parents, and obstinacy becomes quite apparent. The 2-year-old is extremely selfish. He manifests a certain amount of sadism, which arises from two sources.[34] The first is the feeling of mastery or superiority engendered by cruelty to dolls, animals, or even playmates. Freud feels that this is justly suspected of emanating from the erogenous zones and must be considered as a kind of sexual activity. (Once again it should be pointed out that Freud's use of the term "sexual" is related to any feeling of pleasure or satisfaction.) Second, the sadism arises from curiosity and the resultant investigative activity which becomes so evident at this time.

Identification is one of the mechanisms of defense that assumes prominence at this phase of personality development. It refers to the assumption of the qualities of someone else. The toddler, for example, recognizing the power of the adult, attaches himself to the adult, but in such a way that the latter is the all-powerful person and the child is only a dependent. A child may also act out an unpleasant experience in reverse, using a doll, sibling, or smaller playmate as the focus of his aggression. An example would be the girl who assumes the role of the mother who recently punished her and in turn punishes her doll. This is an attempt to relieve the emotion of the original traumatic situation. In later childhood the boy or girl identifies with the parent of the same sex and attempts to copy him or her.

A common occurrence during the anal phase is a relapse in behavior to a more infantile manner. Confronted by a new baby in the home and the threat this makes to his security, the child reverts to enuresis, encopresis, demands for bottle feeding, and "baby talk." Such a defense mechanism is termed *regression* and can occur when any anxiety-producing situation arises, such as moving to a new neighborhood, starting school or the birth of a sibling.

In the third phase the primary erotic zone shifts to the genital area, and it will remain there. This period, covering from approximately 3 or 4 to 6 years of age, is termed the *phallic,* or *genital, phase.* The child begins to attribute greater importance to the anatomical difference between the sexes. The beginning inquisitiveness, described in the preceding anal phase, continues, and especially turns to the genitalia. This may be combined with some exhibitionism, as though the child hopes that this will lead to a sharing of exposure and therefore of knowledge. During this time the Oedipus complex develops, and genital masturbation increases over that previously apparent.

The *Oedipus complex* is the feeling in the child of possessiveness toward the parent of the opposite sex and rivalry toward the parent of the same sex. The boy observes that his father has many privileges with his mother from which he is excluded. He is envious of his father, not only because of these liberties but because the father has a larger penis. The boy develops some anxiety about his own genitalia in this relationship. He fears any paternal retaliation may involve this most prized anatomical part. This anxiety has apparent foundation, by his own reasoning, in the fact that some people do not have such parts, namely girls. This fear is termed the *castration complex* and, according to the psychoanalytic school, is manifested not only in relation to the genitalia but also in the child's preoccupation with any bodily injury that is so evident during these years. The boy finally resolves the Oedipus dilemma by renouncing his erotic feelings toward his mother and identifying himself with the father. He will be like his father and marry someone like his mother.

The young girl at this time feels that she has been cheated and is inferior to boys because she has no penis. The girl assumes castration has taken place and holds her mother responsible. This resentment causes her to turn favorably toward her father, first in the hope that he will give her a penis and later that he will give her a baby. The girl's Oedipus complex does not come to such a sharp end point as the boy's, for the resolution of the penis envy is more difficult than the resolution of the castration complex. The normal girl goes through a considerable period of being a "tomboy" and is said to completely accept her femininity only when her first child is born.[31, 34]

In addition to the defense mechanisms previously described, *reaction formation* is especially characteristic of this age. This is the development of behavior which is the opposite of that dictated by the unconscious impulses. The perfectionistic child is often used as an example. His unconscious anality includes impulses toward messiness, sadism, and selfishness, but on the surface his character appears to be the opposite, and he is overly clean and thoughtful.

Repression is another mechanism of defense first apparent at this age, but it is common to all phases that follow. Repression is purposeful, unconscious, forgetting. It involves the consigning of ideas and emotions to the unconscious and, according to Freud, the use of energy to keep this material out of consciousness. The relatively complete inability to recall memories from early childhood, especially the Oedipus years and before, is due to repression. This concept forms a major part of the whole psychoanalytic movement.

The next phase is called *latency* because the previous libidinal and aggressive drives become latent. Anna Freud[33] describes this period as one of a truce in the battle between the id and the ego; and puberty sees the end of that truce once again. At the beginning of the latency phase the superego becomes more firmly internalized. Children's intellectual thinking at this time is apt to be concrete, useful, earthbound, and rather closely associated with the everyday events of their lives. Normally, social adjustment is more homosexual than heterosexual. Increasing accumulation of knowledge increases the child's independence from his parents and broadens his outlook. He can compete and lose more gracefully than before. In general, he accepts his parents and their authority with little question.

By the time of the latency phase the mechanisms of defense used by each individual are well developed and characteristic. Some of these, for any one individual, may have been used but later discarded as inadequate. Two mechanisms that have not been previously considered require our attention. *Rationalization* is the mechanism closest to the conscious level and is used by everyone to some degree. This is the endeavor to provide an acceptable reason for doing something that is motivated by an unacceptable reason. Fear of failure, for example, in carrying out some project will make a child refuse to do it, but he cannot admit this as the reason for his refusal. Instead, he excuses himself on the basis of having to do something else more urgent or important. The avoidance of many uncomfortable situations is rationalized, but if carried to an extreme degree, rationalization can have a very stultifying effect.

Probably the most satisfactory mechanism of defense is *sublimation*, because it allows the discharge of instinctual impulses in an acceptable form. Sublimation primarily involves those drives observed prior to the genital phase: childish curiosity, sadism, exhibitionism, destructive curiosity, etc. The exhibitionist becomes an actor and the sadist a butcher. The adolescent sublimates his sexual drives in athletic pursuits. All other mechanisms of defense either distort reality or are considered to be energy-wasting.

Adolescence is the last phase in personality development to be discussed. It has been described as the time when infantile sexual drives assume their final shape. The subordination of other erotogenic zones to the genital area, the establishment of new sexual aims differing in boys and girls and the finding of new love objects outside the home have been considered the main events of this period. Temporarily the ego is inadequate to meet the demands of defense in the reopening of its battle with the id. The physiologic changes occurring at this time and all of the associated social and psychologic consequences are the causes of this reawakening of the struggle. The inadequacy of the ego reveals itself in many ways, but perhaps Anna Freud[33] has stated it as well as any when she points out that the atmosphere in which the adolescent lives is characterized by ". . . anxieties, the height of elation or depth of despair, quickly rising enthusiasm, the utter hopelessness, the burning—or at other times sterile—intellectual and philosophical preoccupations, the yearning for freedom, the sense of loneliness, the feeling of oppression by the parents, the impotent rages or active hates directed against the adult world, the erotic crushes, and the suicidal fantasies." The hectic intellectual activity is closely related to the defense mechanism of intellectualization (similar to rationalization), which is an attempt to master the danger of instinctual drives by means of thought. These thoughts may be abstract, useless, and at variance with actual behavior, in great contrast to the concreteness of the latency phase. The adolescent may cover up and minimize his anxieties in the sexual sphere by concentrating on problems that are often beyond him in the area of social issues. This is the time of utopias and remaking the world.

Devaluation of parents accompanies the detachment from them. Friendships, often homosexual in the early part of this phase but becoming more heterosexual later, are a striking phenomenon of adolescence and an aspect of the struggle to attain a firm sense of self. The ideals of the leader of the group are accepted wholeheartedly and without criticism. All of these characteristics often lead to conflicts with parents or other adults, adding further to the child's anxieties.

Even the best-informed girl will experience menstruation to some degree as trauma to her body. Some feelings formerly attached to the shame and disgust of elimination may reappear at menarche. Disappointment occurs also when she realizes that she is not going to be accepted as an adult equal despite the onset of this long anticipated physiologic change. Hypochondriacal tendencies are not unusual and are more common in girls than boys.

Masturbation is practiced by most adolescents, but to a greater degree by boys, as a release of sexual tensions. The boy, being more aggressive, may be able to sublimate these tensions in sports or social activities. The dominance of passivity in the feminine personality favors the development and utilization of fantasy in the release of sexual tensions. The earliest love objects of the girl seem by necessity to be unattainable, e.g., a movie star, and are frequently changed, which in itself is a disturbing thing and plagues her with feelings of self-doubt and guilt.

Occasionally the sexual drives are strongly repressed with asceticism. Such boys or girls renounce all interest in sex and often in social intercourse as well. In the extreme they become cold and analytical and develop a contemptuous attitude toward their peers and most adults. Only in a pathologic condition does this persist into adult life.

Although the turmoil of adolescence is inevitable, according to the psychoanalytic theory, resolution of the conflicts takes place with continuing maturity. The censorship of the superego becomes one that is acceptable to the individual and to the society in which he lives. The feud between id and ego never ends but becomes less tumultuous through the use of defense mechanisms, most of which can be guided into useful channels.

Piaget's Theories of Personality Development

Piaget[52, 53] has introduced some concepts of personality development that differ in many points from those of Freud. The self and personality have different stages or levels of development. In infancy and early childhood the individual is entirely egocentric and self-centered, but this changes with age so that she can share another's point of view. The true or final personality is not formed until her thoughts are integrated and her feelings about herself take into account her total life perspective, including all of her environment. Only a brief survey of some of the more important ideas offered by Piaget will be presented. Along with his concepts of cognitive development, outlined earlier, these theories are considered by many to be the most significant since those of Freud.

In essence, the mental development of the child passes through four stages. No external or internal act is executed except as a reaction to motive or a need (an elementary need, an interest, a question, etc.). Human action consists of a continuous readjustment or equilibration. The infant is entirely egocentric. All of her sensorimotor activity is self-related, and there is no conceptualization that is beyond self. Dissociation of the external environment from self is not present. As she begins to grasp and manipulate and develop language, her potentiality for entering the next stage begins.

With the appearance of language the possibility of socialization enters the behavior pattern. More importantly, the development of internalization of words or thought begins. Piaget emphasizes that thought and language are different in their origins, but if symbolism is included as a kind of language, it is this development that marks the next stage and profoundly modifies behavior effectively and intellectually. This stage lasts from approximately ages 2 to 7 years. Egocentricity prevails. When speaking, the conversation is rudimentary and is almost as though the child were speaking to herself. The child still cannot project herself into the thoughts of another. Her environment, the world, was made for her, and things are often conceived of as living and having intent.

The first moral precept of the child is obedience. Parents are loved and considered always correct. In play with others the "rules" are inviolate, though they may be poorly understood. "Truth" is a "must," but if lies must be told, the child will accept punishment. All of her moral values are those of her adults, especially her parents.

The next stage, from 7 to 12, sees the child capable of cooperation because she distinguishes her own point of view from that of another. True discussion is now possible. She searches for logical explanations and justifications, and the animism of early childhood disappears. She can now completely dissociate herself from another person, and her language reflects this. "The child of seven or eight thinks before acting and thus begins to conquer the difficult process of reflection."[52]

These changes lead to important moral concepts that characterize this period. As a function of cooperation among children the feeling of mutual respect arises. Honesty and obeying the "rules" are now based on agreement and esteem among peers. The relationship with parents also changes as the child differentiates between submission and justice.

The adolescent stage is characterized in Piaget's conceptions by still further maturation of thought processes that are only modified to a degree by the physiologic changes of this period, including sexual changes. In this Piaget differs considerably from Freud. What is particularly striking is the development of the elaboration of abstract theories. This is a continuation of the relatively concrete thinking of middle childhood, which now progresses to reflection no longer attached to external reality. Thinking becomes both hypothetic and deductive. Perception of problems involving spatial relationships, size, and quantitation is possible on a level not previously attainable.

Personality achieves its final form in adolescence. It begins, according to Piaget, in late childhood with the autonomous organization of rules and values. Personality is said to exist as soon as a "life plan," which is both a source of discipline for the will and an instrument of cooperation, is formed. This presupposes the intervention of thought and reflection and therefore is not possible before the stage of adolescence. The adolescent sees herself as equal to her elders but different. She desires to correct society's errors and is filled with generous and altruistic projects. Her megalomania leads to visions of great accomplishments on her part. The adolescent therefore contacts adult society by means of ideas of social reform, theoretical systems, and "life plans." Social interaction of younger children occurs largely through the team game, while for the adolescent it is more often through discussion. True adaptation to society results when the adolescent reformer attempts to put her ideas to practical use.

The conception that abstract operational thought of older children and adults has its beginnings in the earliest sensorimotor reactions of the infant has led some psychologists to use Piaget's observations to support their view that there are critical or sensitive periods in human cognitive development. Mental development is construed as the creation of an ever-growing and necessarily more complex copy of the external world through the addition of more and more information. In this view, each of the stages of development must be attained (learned?) at a critical period or time. If this opportunity is missed, the child may fail to realize his or her full intellectual potential. Further support was implied from the "imprinting" phenomenon observed in some lower animals in which a single opportunity must be experienced during a narrow time span. If this does not happen, the "learning" (imprinting) either never occurs or is poorly established. The importance of these concepts as related to child development is especially pertinent in considering the neglected or underprivileged. Are learning disabilities and intellectual retardation due to missed learning opportunities?

Piaget never stated that there were "critical periods," though he implied the sequence of developmental stages was important. Available evidence does not support the view that there are such critical periods during which children must be exposed to a given learning procedure or forever after suffer some intellectual deficit.[60]

Language Development

Speech is a function that is unique to humans and sets them apart from the lower animal forms. The attainment of speech is one of the most important achievements of childhood. The coming of language occurs at approximately the same age in every healthy child throughout the world, strongly supporting the concept that genetically determined processes of maturation rather than environmental factors are the foundation for speech and verbal comprehension.[21] Early aspects of language development are now considered as a biologic phenomenon similar to the development of walking and other predominantly innate varieties of neuromotor coordination. There are morphologic studies to support this concept. The phenomenon of cerebral dominance occurs in no mammal other than the human. The dominance of the left side of the brain for speech (Broca's area) is a most striking example. There is a definite anatomical asymmetry between the temporal speech region on the left and the corresponding region of the right hemisphere.[62]

In the newborn infant evoked auditory responses, as measured by the EEG, are most marked to frequencies found in the human voice. The voice thus qualifies as a potent stimulus with resulting favorable influence in the formation of human bonds of affection.[23] Speech and behavior between mother and child, as long as two years later, are modified by the degree of intimacy permitted in the immediate postnatal period.[20] An analysis of mother-infant communication patterns at 12 weeks indicated they were predictive of later language competence.[86]

It is important to consider the functions of speech and its relationship to the total development of the child.[25, 54] The functions can be divided into two categories, which are interrelated and not mutually exclusive: personal and social. The personal functions of speech include emotional expression, self-communication (note Piaget's reference to this earlier in the chapter), dramatic expression, and vocal play. Primitive forms of speech are evident in the early vocalizations of infants. They coo and gurgle by the sixth week. Syllable-like babbling begins to replace cooing by the fifth to sixth month. These sounds are apparently made for sheer enjoyment and have little communicative value. The cries of displeasure or pain are obvious, as are the sounds of pleasure and contentment. With increasing age the verbalization of emotion serves to neutralize some of the intense feelings and permits symbolization so that social living becomes possible. In the absence of language, humans would command a very meager catalog (recall and classification) of experiences for subsequent reference and comparison. Children learn language in the first two years for coding what they know of the world of objects, events, and relations. They apparently know a great deal more than they are able to talk about.[5]

The social functions of speech are more evident, but not necessarily more important, than the personal ones. These include communication with others on a purely social level, the exchange of ideas or information, and the modifying influences of language on behavior and attitudes of others. It is impossible to think of any culture or civilization without language.

Verbal communication requires the coordination of neuromotor and neurosensory systems with higher centers involving perceptual and conceptual abilities as well as appropriate social and emotional responses. Within two to three years a high degree of specificity has been attained that is largely automatic. By the time the average child has completed his or her 5th year, the basic elements of verbal behavior have become established.[21, 63] Syntax, semantics, and phonology are important parts of language that are continuing to improve throughout the school years. During this time the child increases his or her ability to use the linguistic code, both to speak and understand messages, independently of the states or conditions or circumstances in which speech occurs.[5]

An interesting observation related to these facts is the learning of a foreign language. At age 3 or 4 practically every child entering a foreign community learns to speak the new language rapidly and without accent. This facility declines slowly with age until the early teens when nearly every child loses the ability to speak a new language without an accent and does not learn as rapidly as when younger.[21] Aphasia due to damage to Broca's area in a child can usually be reversed without residual evidence of speech problems. Such a lesion occurring after puberty results in incomplete recovery.

Early levels of development are fairly easily differentiated. Localization of sound stimuli is present in the first few weeks of life, and differentiation of sounds is demonstrated by the second or third month. Vocalization of pleasure-related sounds is apparent by the second or third month in association with vegetative activities. At this level there is a response to appropriate stimuli that is almost at a reflex level.

The ability to integrate sensory stimuli into patterns occurs by age 4 or 5 months. This is manifested by increases in variety and quality of emitted sounds, including babbling and echolalia. Some rudimentary imitation of sounds occurs from the third to tenth month. The development of memory for auditory stimuli is demonstrated by the child's imitation of bisyllabic and trisyllabic sounds near the end of the first year. Between 12 and 18 months the child responds to auditory stimuli as symbols, and he or she learns to make sound patterns as symbols. The child comprehends and creates language. At first the symbolization is attached to easily identifiable objects or actions, while less concrete objects and activities (articles, prepositions, etc.) are learned by repeated exposures and associations. Among the highly complex mechanics of speech is the automatic control of respiration necessary to accomplish it. While talking one inhales slightly faster but exhales much more slowly, resulting in a greatly reduced respiratory rate. The appropriate positioning of lips, tongue, and teeth is further evidence of the intricate neuromuscular coordination necessary for normal language behavior.

Nearly all observers agree that comprehension of spoken language precedes its use by a considerable span of time. There is probably comprehension of gestures and actions before that of language. Nevertheless, there is certainly definite response to the human voice by the second or third month. Truly differential response to different words is present in the normal 9- and 10-month infant. At this time also one notes imitation of syllables and words. Adequate response to simple commands may appear at this time. McCarthy[22] states that symbolic gesture is used long before language proper, but that these overt movements may be accompanied by vocalizations. In the usual process of maturation the child's use of gesture gradually recedes, and its place is taken by real language. Language retardation in some cases is quite correctly attributed to the fact that the child may develop an elaborate system of gesture language (sometimes associated with a "sound language all his own") that is so well understood by parents and siblings that his or her wants are well satisfied. This tends to occur a little more frequently in families with several children. As a matter of fact, studies indicate that only children are often considerably more advanced in their language development than are children with siblings at home.

The first words are usually made up of monosyllables or reduplicated monosyllables such as *dada, mama,* and *bye-bye.* They often are strongly affective, expressing wishes, needs, and feelings. There are marked individual variations in the sizes of vocabularies at any age. Very cautiously we offer a vocabulary development table (Table 6–3), recognizing the limitations and vagaries in its interpretation, but still feeling that it has usefulness in evaluating this phase of development.

Articulation of speech develops slowly at first. So-called baby talk is used by most children during the early years. At 2 years of age about one third of the number of sounds is given correctly, at 4 years, about 75%, and by 6 years, 89%. The observation of the length (number of words) of sentences has some value as a measure of speech maturation. In general a child of 18

TABLE 6–3.—VOCABULARY
DEVELOPMENT OF CHILDREN
TO AGE 6

AGE		
YR	MO	NUMBER OF WORDS
1	0	3
1	3	19
1	6	22
2	0	272
2	6	446
3	0	896
3	6	1,222
4	0	1,540
5	0	2,072
6	0	2,562

months is at the one-word sentence stage. By 2.5 years an average sentence contains three words and in another year four words. By 6.5 years the mean length of sentences becomes five words and at 9.5 years has increased to six or seven words. Grammatically complete sentences are usual by 4 or 5 years, but seldom before this age (Table 6–4).[17]

By 2 years all vowel sounds are used and many of the consonants including *b, p, k, g, w, m, h, n, t,* and *d.* The final consonant in a word is often omitted. By 4 years the consonant sounds *b, t, d, k,* and *g* are mastered but combinations such as *tr, pr, bl,* and *gr* are apt to be faulty. Between 5 and 6 years the former combinations are pronounced well but some trouble with blending *thr, shr, sk, sh, ch, s,* and *z* may persist until 7 to 8 years.

By the age of 4 recognition of plurals, sex differences, and pronouns is comprehended. A year later the child uses plurals and pronouns in his or her everyday speech as well as many adjectives and some adverbs, conjunctions, and prepositions. The child correctly uses "I" instead of "me" or his or her name, i.e., "I want a cookie" instead of "me want a cookie."

Stuttering, a repetition of syllables and words, is normal in young children. The commonest form is that in which the whole word is involved, e.g., "Mother-mother may I go out-out." Ordinarily this occurs late in the second or early in the third year and may last from a few weeks to a year or two. Bloomer[25] points out that stuttering normally is seen when the child first puts words together in phrases or simple sentences and that this characteristic of speech has a tendency to disappear and reappear until the fifth year. Persistence into the sixth year can usually be considered outside the realm of normal. At first the child seldom is concerned with his or her stuttering and at this early age it simply represents a lack of maturation of speech centers. Often it may indicate that thought processes are ahead of the child's vocabulary or ability to express himself or herself clearly.

TABLE 6–4.—PATTERN OF NORMAL LANGUAGE DEVELOPMENT

AGE	VOCALIZATION AND SPEECH	RESPONSE AND COMPREHENSION
1 mo	Much crying and whimpering; produces some vowel and few consonant sounds.	Smiles; decreases activity; startles at loud sounds.
3 mo	Different cries for pain, hunger, and discomfort; decreased crying time; some repetitive sounds ("ga, ga, ga"); coos and sighs.	Vocal gurgle in response to soothing voice; some imitative response to speech.
5 mo	Babbles; vocal play; many repetitive sounds; all vowels, m, k, g, b, and p; laughs out loud.	Imitative response to speech decreased; turns and looks to sound; recognizes familiar voice; vocalizes displeasure.
7 mo	Considerable variety in babbling, loudness and rhythm of all vocalizations; adds d, t, n, and w to repertory of sounds; talks to toys.	Gestures increase as part of vocal responses to stimuli; response to sound is increasingly influenced by visual factors.
9 mo	Cries to get attention; increasing variations in pitch; "mama," "dada," and "baba" part of vocal play but not associated with a person or object.	Retreats from strangers, often accompanied by crying; may imitate hand clapping.
11 mo	May use one word correctly; imitates sounds and correct number of syllables; little crying.	Comprehends "no no"; responds to "bye-bye" or "patty-cake" with appropriate gestures.
1–2 yr	Much unintelligible jargon; all vowels present; improves articulation so that 25% of words intelligible; names many objects by 24 mo.; much echolalia.	Recognizes 150–300 words by 24 mo.; responds correctly to several commands, e.g., "sit down," "give me that," "stand up," "come here," etc.
2–3 yr	Tries new sounds but articulation lags behind vocabulary; 50%–75% of words intelligible; often omits final consonants; jargon nearly absent.	Comprehends 800–1,000 words by 3 yr; responds to many commands using "on," "under," "up," etc.
3–4 yr	Speech nears 100% intelligibility; faulty articulations of l and r frequent; uses 3–4 words in sentences; uses a few plurals by 4 yr.	Recognizes plurals, sex differences, adjectives, and adverbs; comprehends complex sentences.
4–6 yr	Syntax correct by 6 yr; forms 5- or 6-word sentences that are compound or complex (with some dependent clauses); fluent; articulation good except for sh, z, ch, and j; can express temporal relations; voice well modulated in conversation.	Understands 2,500–3,000 words; carries out commands involving 3–4 actions; comprehends "if," "because," and "why."

Some other characteristics of speech at different ages have been recorded, by Metraux.[26] At 24 months, speech is repetitive and is almost compulsive in quality. Screaming and squealing are common as a method of expression. At 3 years the inflection of the voice is unstable and poorly controlled, and gross motor movement often accompanies speech in situations where there is strong emotional feeling. The pronoun "I" is very prominent. By 3.5 years a high, full-volumed yell is often assumed as the normal speaking voice. Stuttering is common and probably reflects the general increase in rate or speed of talking in contrast to earlier months. By 4.5 years the voice is quite well modulated. Often a sentence is preceded with the sound "m" much as the adult uses "ah" when hesitating or searching for words. At this age the child also shows a real interest in words, repeating new ones and asking that they be repeated so he or she gets them right.

Children who come from lower class homes generally acquire language more slowly, retain immature pronunciations longer, have a smaller vocabulary, and speak in shorter sentences than middle class children. In a comparison of mothers giving instructions to their children to perform a simple task, those from a professional or skilled blue-collar family were much more successful in accomplishing their goals than those from unskilled or public assistance families. The differences were related to the efficiency and clarity of the explanation given.[95]

From the time the child enters school, his or her reading skill will be the predominant factor determining success or failure.[17] Unfortunately our knowledge concerning the development of reading skills is very meager. It is closely related to the development of speech and depends upon the maturation of perceptual and cognitive abilities. Many educators use the term "reading readiness" to indicate the stage or age level when reading skills begin to form. The chronologic age will vary significantly, but for most starts between 5 and 6 years and reaches considerable proficiency by age 8. Some very normal children can read by 4 years while a few do not develop the skill until 10 or 11. The reason for the wide variation is unknown. There is some relationship with intelligence. Seldom does a child with an IQ of 70 or below become an adequate reader. It is rare to find reading disabilities in children with superior intelligence.

The early stages of reading are primarily the development of discrimination. It is a process of translation or decoding signs and symbols into meanings and incorporating the new meanings into existing cognitive and affective systems. A crucial conceptualization occurs when the child realizes that the written symbols stand for speech units. Reading is not a skill that comes as a result of maturation. The extent and precision of a child's speaking vocabulary determines his or her effectiveness in reading comprehension even though the process of speech is not involved. It is a fact that many children or adults with reading difficulties have had some deviations from normal speech development.[77]

The Child During the Early School Years

In the period from age 6 to about 11 years the child learns about the outside world and becomes increasingly independent of his parents. He develops a conscience or a sense of responsibility about matters that to him seem important. These are the years when closely knit groups are formed, such as clubs and gangs. During this period the child is introduced to the culture of his society through the public or private school. These are important years for learning how to get along with other people and to abide by the rules of society.

The child's independence of his parents is manifested by his gaining a feeling of individuality and by his desire to be treated as a person rather than as a possession. He is apt to show some impatience toward his parents, who keep telling him the right things to do. Although he loves them as much as ever, he dislikes emotional display about himself. Joining a club is simply another means of showing his ability to accomplish things independently of adults.

His sense of responsibility is manifested in competitive types of games or ones that require some skill. He becomes a small businessman by setting up a lemonade stand or by starting a garden. He may not carry many of these enterprises through to completion, but the urge to do them is present.

Toward the end of this period he thinks in terms of cause and effect and acquires an insight into the actions of machines and some of the fundamentals of human relationships. The desire to accomplish great things occupies his mind when he is not doing schoolwork or homework. He dreams of bold adventures, and one of his favorite heroes may well be a character in a comic strip or story where right always wins. Besides the comics, books, radio, television, and motion pictures furnish him with his ideals.

Because of his desire for independence he may be irritating to his parents and present a problem in discipline. The adult must try to overlook some of his less serious bad habits and, when giving orders, try to be matter-of-fact and friendly. Most obnoxious to the child is "bossiness" or a nagging voice, which one should strive to avoid. School problems are best taken up with the teacher or school authorities. Poor work in school may be due to many causes such as physical defects, poor eyesight or hearing, and poor attention. The highly intelligent child may be bored with his schoolwork, while the child with a low intelligence cannot comprehend his studies. Finally, the school system may be at fault. One should carefully examine and eliminate any or all possible causes instead of punishing the child.

In the following paragraphs are given guides to expected behavior in children to each of the ages listed. It must be stressed that each child has an individual pattern of growth that is unique to him or her. The traits listed, therefore, are not to be taken too rigidly or as absolute models that all children will follow. They illustrate the behavior trends for each age. Such an outline may aid a physician or other interested person in judging very roughly the maturity level of a particular child. Under each age heading are two brief paragraphs. The first describes various factors of behavior such as play, eating, habits, and relations to society. The second lists a few of the more readily tested accomplishments that can be used to appraise normality of development.

Five Years Old

Appetite is usually good, except perhaps for breakfast. The child is slow but persistent in eating and many other activities. He has considerable motor ability and skill. He is poised and controlled. He loves his home and persons and objects associated with it. The stage of the 4-year-old runaway is passed. The outstanding fear of the 5-year-old is loss of his mother. Fears of ghosts or bogeymen and unreal objects have greatly diminished in the past year. The child is serious about himself and concerned with his own ability. He wants to assume responsibilities. He usually gets along with adults very well, although shy at the initial meeting. His memory for past events is surprisingly accurate. Play is apt to follow domestic patterns in both sexes. Both like to "play house," and dolls are favorite objects. The child makes a good adjustment to school and enjoys the routine of planned programs.

He can name four or more colors, repeat a sentence of ten or more syllables, tell which is the heavier of two weights or objects, reconstruct a rectangular card that has been cut diagonally into two pieces, draw a recognizable picture of a man with a body, head, etc., and can identify a penny, nickel, and dime.

Six Years Old

This is a period of physical and psychologic change. It is apt to be a difficult period for the parent who does not understand this transition. The child is restless and has difficulty in making decisions. Activity is almost constant. Appetite continues to be good. A characteristic in eating and nearly all other activity is that he is good at starting things but poor at finishing them. Accidents—spilling of milk, stuffing the mouth too full of food, etc.—are common at the table. Enuresis is rare now. The growing vocabulary includes slang and swearing. "Emotional storms" such as temper tantrums reach a peak at this age and may be difficult to control. Rudeness is another common and difficult problem. Behavior patterns are often explosive and seemingly unpredictable. Jealousy toward siblings is the rule, and sibling play should be supervised. All play is more vigorous than in the 5-year-old, and imagination is a big factor. Several favorite radio or TV programs are followed religiously by many children. The majority like school and want to "learn." Parental love and praise are extremely important throughout this difficult period of growing up.

A vocabulary of about 2,500 words has been acquired. The child can define simple objects in terms of what they are used for, can count correctly to 20 or 30, knows right and left parts of body, knows number combinations making up to 10, draws a man with hitherto unadded features, e.g., neck, clothing, and hands, and differentiates A.M. and P.M.

Seven Years Old

Play is approached more cautiously than when the child was 6. In all respects he is less of a "problem child" than one year before. Although he has definite likes and dislikes, he is less vehement in expressing them; this is true of food, clothing, friends, play, and the like. The child needs only slight help in dressing and undressing and preparing for bed. Bowel and bladder training are complete, and little conversation is directed toward these functions. He or she is aware of and sensitive about sex and in front of the opposite sex avoids self-exposure. Seven becomes a cooperative member of the family group. Neatness and alacrity in dressing or carrying out parental commands are frequently wanting. He is not entirely self-contained, but he is very introspective and desires the approbation of his group and of his parents. One might call the seventh year a pensive one.

He can count by 2s and 5s and grasps the basic idea of addition and subtraction, can tell time, often knows what month it is, can copy a diamond accurately, repeats five numbers in series, e.g., 4, 7, 9, 3, 2, and repeats three of them backward.

Eight Years Old

The 8-year-old's movements increase in "smoothness" and "poise." These words in a large measure describe this age. Yet unsupervised play of a large group may become extremely rowdy, with reversion to "animal spirits." He dislikes being alone and wants his companions to take an interest in his activities, either actively or as interested observers. Segregation of the sexes for the first time becomes important in the choice of playmates and groups. He is becoming more resentful of parental authority. His best behavior is often away from home or when strangers are in the home. Television may occupy much of the child's spare time, but reading interests are expanding and are often related to special interests or hobbies. The child enjoys school and dislikes staying at home. Individual differences are great, but in general this is an age of broadening experiences and exploration intellectually.

The 8-year-old knows the days of the week; he can count backward from

20 to 1; he can make correct change for small amounts of money; comprehension of time and place has begun; he appreciates the difference between a real or historic character versus a fictitious one in cinema and television; and he can describe differences and similarities between two things from memory, e.g., bird and butterfly, dog and cat, or wood and stone.

Nine Years Old

This is an intermediate age—between childhood and the beginnings of adolescence. The child has better control of himself and is seeking and acquiring new forms of independence. He has a growing capacity to complete tasks that he sets for himself or that are expected from him. Even short interruptions will not interfere, for he will return to his work or play. He looks to the future and plans ahead for work and play. He is mature enough to accept blame, and alibiing of the infantile type is less indulged in than formerly. He is essentially truthful and honest. Eating is much neater than formerly, and manners are usually well observed. Dressing is completed without aid. He obeys well and can assume many responsibilities. He will show disgust at both siblings and parents if they do not act as he feels they should. Hero worship has become prominent. The 9-year-old is self-sufficient, self-critical, but not severely so, and he is anxious to please. The sexes remain well separated at parties and other social gatherings. It is usually not difficult to discipline him. His reading material is more realistic than before, although he may still enjoy comic books. His literary interests reflect his general character, a fluctuation between childhood and youth in his thoughts and actions.

He describes objects in detail and does not just tell what they are used for; he knows the day of the month and year, tells time well, arranges weights in the order of heaviness, and can do simple multiplication and division.

Ten Years Old

A very fundamental change that occurs at this age is the beginning of differences in attitudes toward sexuality. The girl is usually more mature socially and more poised than the boy. Sexual maturation has often started in girls, seldom in boys. Both are beginning to think about social problems and are eager to discuss them. There is a strong tendency to categorize civic and school leaders as well as events as either "good" or "bad," though they are apt to select other words. The concept of individuality and singularity of self and of others is becoming well developed. Teamwork and willing submission to fixed rules in play is now possible. Formation of lasting friendships is evident and moving to a new and distant home is often quite traumatic.

Ten-year-olds can use numbers beyond 100 with understanding; they can use simple fractions, repeat 6 digits forward, know how many minutes are in a fraction of an hour, and repeat a 20-syllable sentence.

Eleven Years Old

By this age the girls are falling behind boys somewhat in physical strength and endurance. Girls are apt to be taller than boys at this age and for the next two to three years, owing to the earlier adolescent growth spurt in the female. Membership in groups and clubs is increasing in importance. Children of this age group enjoy taking part in school and community "drives," e.g., paper collection, Red Cross collection, etc. Team games are very popular. If present, shyness may increase and be a difficult problem for some parents to understand. The child is more critical of the products of his labors than ever before. There is an increasing urge for some financial independence from the parents, with the result that he or she will readily take on small jobs after school and during vacations.

He can define some abstract terms, e.g., "justice," "honesty," and "revenge"; he can point out the meaning or moral in fables and can explain the necessity of hygienic measures such as covering the mouth when coughing. It must be realized that by this age the variability of individual interests and the diversity of intellectual pursuits render standardization by simple tests very difficult and of questionable value for the average child.

The Adolescent Child

Since nearly every person who writes about adolescence has his own definition of the word, the reader is requested to refer to chapter 9, section on adolescence and puberty, for this author's definition and the description of the physical and physiologic changes that occur at this time.

In the last three decades there has been a decided change in the psychologic and social pattern of adolescents in the United States, and to some extent, similar developments have taken place in other developed countries of the western hemisphere. There are many reasons for these changes. Some of the major issues can be briefly outlined.[87, 88]

The multigenerational and stable family unit is quickly disappearing, and an increasing number of children are living in single-parent homes.

There have been monumental changes in the school systems. The great increase in teenagers beginning in the 1950s placed considerable pressure on the secondary schools. This combined with the relatively long compulsory education period forced more and more children into a narrower and narrower age group with increasing isolation.

World and regional armed conflicts, social and racial inequalities, and dishonesty in government have led to disillusionment and then rejection of ideas and opinions from parents and other adults.

Improved means of communication, and especially television, have permitted a greater dissemination of information, both good and bad, giving a false sense of knowledge and sophistication.

Other factors that have played a lesser part are the failure of religion to assume any kind of leadership for youth, the atmosphere of permissiveness in rearing children that prevailed from 1940 to 1970, and the rapid technologic progress following World War II that seemed to promise solutions to many social, economic, and educational problems.

The isolation and the disillusionment have led to an adolescent peer society as a semiautonomous social world, with its own set of values and activities. Peers are looked to as the model for dress, music, entertainment, and life style. Peer group relationship is prized over all other associations. Increasing numbers of youngsters continue to leave the mainstream of life, at least temporarily.

It is impossible to say how many teenagers represent the extreme of the mood described above. Both the numbers and the degree of withdrawal depend upon attitudes in the family and in the community. Most individuals manage to pass through adolescence without overt problems, but it is a time of stress.

All adolescents at some time, and in various ways, resolve their own identity crises in order to enter and adjust to the adult world.[15, 30] It is important to understand that "adjust" does not imply acquiescence. Even the most conforming of children seek a measure of independence from parents, which they feel is a necessary step toward the attainment of adulthood.

The process of sexual maturation not only involves structural and physiologic changes but brings with it a series of perplexing and sometimes highly disturbing emotional and social problems. Personal appearance of the individual becomes in many children a source of great conflict. There is apt to be a greater emphasis on "good looks" and on a "normal" physique and anatomy than at any other period in life. Perhaps unfortunately, society in general has so impressed the child with normality that he or she becomes overanxious about his or her own body and its functions and yet is most reticent to converse about it.

Some vital statistics concerning the American adolescent are very disturbing. Although the most frequent cause of death is that of accidents, homicides account for 5,000 teenage deaths annually and suicides for 2,000 to 4,000 each year, making them the second and the third most common causes of death in this age group. Especially in large cities, there is a serious problem of chronic absenteeism in the schools, and approximately 40% of New York City high school students become dropouts.

National estimates for 1980 reveal that among 12- to 17-year-olds, 54% used cigarettes, 70% have used alcohol and 37% continue its use, and 30% have used marijuana and 17% continue to use it. More than 11 million families have had members killed or seriously injured by a drunk driver in the past ten years. More than 40% of all night-time alcohol-related fatalities are caused by teenagers, although they represent only 20% of the licensed drivers.[88]

The end of childhood is recognized by many different rituals or physiologic changes as well as by legal and chronologic indices. In primitive societies it is prescribed on the basis of age by an elaborate ceremonial event. In some religious organizations, it is determined by dogma of the church, e.g., bar mitzvah. Menarche is often used as a point determining prepuberty and postpuberty even though conception may not be possible for another one or two years. Social indications of the end of childhood may be the act of sexual intercourse. Relative to this is the fact that in the United States one fifth of all pregnancies occur in women under 19 years of age, approximately one half of these in adolescents 17 years or younger. More than 66% of these pregnancies are conceived out of wedlock. An opinion held by many adolescents is that improved methods of contraception and treatment for venereal diseases have removed many of the hazards of acting out sexual impulses.

The adolescent is easily hurt when criticized. She feels that she is "grown up," but lacks the experience and knowledge of the adult. She will fluctuate between resentment of parental advice and her desire to fall back on her family when she has some problem. She may develop rather romantic ideas about people or become somewhat obsessed with certain ideals. The adolescent girl is apt to have "crushes" on her teachers. There may be certain social difficulties in the schoolroom owing to the fact that at this time the girls usually are two or three years ahead of the boys in stature and emotional development.

Many of the individual difficulties that appear at this age are the result of conflict between the child and other members of society. Pressure is put on him to assume various adult responsibilities, and his own desires about his future form still another, and perhaps more important, "inner" pressure. The outer pressure may come from parents, friends, or society in general. Limitations to the accomplishments of the individual are the results of these two pressures plus his socioeconomic status, his level of intelligence, and what he is able to achieve throughout this period. It is this relationship between his own aims in life, the aims that others force upon him, his current or past performances, and his sense of satisfaction or frustration pertaining to these performances that will greatly influence his emotional development. The tendency of the adolescent, continually faced with failure owing to the conventions of society or parental misunderstanding, is to react with aggressive rebellion. This leads to further difficulties, and a vicious circle results. Maladjustments are much greater among boys and girls who do not have close, harmonious relationships with their parents and among those whose parents are in discord with each other.

For the normally developing adolescent, acceptance by the social group in which he lives is a very dominant and personal drive. When he is deprived of this acceptance and has not found some measure of success in his group, he often withdraws into himself. Such a child needs help in improving social techniques, or perhaps it would be best to transfer him to a more congenial or otherwise more suitable group. The method of "buying" him into the social group by furnishing him with the biggest and best bicycles, automobiles, etc., a method sometimes used by parents, usually ends in failure for the child. If the boy or girl, with the aid of understanding parents, can objectively see his or her own successes and failures throughout childhood, he or she can nearly always take minor failures in stride in the more sensitive period of adolescence. Children should be taught to make a sensible evaluation of their liabilities and assets progressively throughout childhood. They should be acquainted with the fact that there are both "good" and "bad" in the world, that there are privilege and underprivilege, honesty and dishonesty, charity and wicked selfishness. A realistic philosophy of life is needed, but also one that furnishes them with a motivation to accomplish the best of which they are capable.

Erikson[15] points out that the prime problem and potential danger of adolescence is identity confusion, which can express itself in an excessively long moratorium or in an impulsive attempt to end that moratorium. Erikson sees the identity crisis as a normative stage in the human life cycle. The end of childhood is characterized by marked physical growth, genital maturation, and increased social awareness. Youth is faced with the decision of choices to follow in his or her sexual, social, and occupational roles as an adult. Some adolescents will not make a decision for themselves and become members of activist groups in religion, enter radical politics, or become anarchists or drifters and "dropouts." The appeal of totalitarianisms is another solution in which decisions are made for one.

Early acting out of sexual activities may be an attempt to prove identity in a search for self, but often becomes "genital combat" void of any intimacy. Erikson contends that honest intimacy is possible only when identity is well established in terms of both friendship and love in sexual relationship. The adolescent is perplexed with the physiologic and genital maturation that indicate adulthood and the uncertainty of the part he or she will play in the adult roles ahead. "It is the inability to settle on an occupational identity which most disturbs young people."[15]

Development of the ego normally accomplishes five major steps during adolescence. Separation from the family need not be physical, though it often is, but refers to confidence in his or her own decision making and an ability to perform socially on an equal basis with peers. There is a mastery over instinctual drives, an ability to delay gratification and not act impulsively. There is a beginning orientation toward the future or gaining a sense of oneself as an adult. The development of ego identity is the result of a continual process of personal reflection and observation involving much self-evaluation throughout childhood. In the adolescent, if successful, it brings about a feeling of autonomy and commitment to definite goals and ideologies. The area of ego identity is probably the most vulnerable because it involves self-esteem, which is easily injured due to variations in physical growth, appearance, physical handicaps, poor school performance, and especially noncaring parents. The fifth, and final step, is the establishment of a moral philosophy wherein are formed definitions of values of his or her own and decisions are made accordingly.

Sex is not a problem limited to the adolescent period, yet it is often felt to be of prime importance at this time. The sexual education of the child has proceeded some considerable degree before adolescence is reached, whether or not this is accomplished by the parents. The first questions, particularly when a new baby arrives, are most likely to come at about 3 or 4 years. Until the preadolescent years it is probably wisest to give information only when it is sought. The answer should be straightforward and in terms simple enough for the child to understand. Detailed explanations are not needed, for the child requires only a simple statement and is not yet interested about details. If the parents feel incompetent to answer such questions because of emotional or idealistic conflict or because of inability to give a concise forthright answer, the physician should be consulted. Ideally, before adolescence is reached the child should be well oriented as to the anatomical and functional differences of the sexes. Such information may best be given as a part of the general instruction in anatomy and physiology, which naturally must be kept on an easily understood level. A clear conception should be given of ovulation, fertilization, pregnancy, and birth. Menstruation should be explained before, not after, it occurs in the girl. Nocturnal emission may better be explained to the boy as he approaches puberty. However, one must not overstimulate latent interests unduly, and good judgment concerning each individual must be used. For instance, in dealing with masturbation, no good is served unless anxiety is alleviated, but too permissive an attitude tends to break down the normal defense against such activity.

The traditional idea that marriage must be delayed until economic independence is obtained is one of the difficulties that modern society has placed in the path of the adolescent. Further, any sexual activity before marriage is socially and religiously forbidden in many groups. Early in the adolescent period each boy or girl often experiences a homosexual period of development. During this time romantic and emotional attachments are formed with a person of the same sex and usually of the same age. Hero worship of an older person may also occur. Overt sexual experiences among boys are not uncommon, and a smaller number of girls may have similar participation. When there is an adequate association with the opposite sex, the homosexual phase is rapidly passed through and the heterosexual phase is entered. It is unfortunate that at this time many questions arise regarding the sex role but adequate and good information is not readily available. Too often misinformation is supplied by peers and is accepted. Even though the phenomena of sexuality are more openly discussed by today's youth, sources of information, including many parents and physicians, are often inadequate or judgmental. Caution is necessary in order not to disgust or frighten these future parents by unwarranted lectures on the sins of sex and the horrors of venereal disease. Parents are frequently in need of education to an equal degree with their children. It has been repeatedly stressed that the background experienced by the child, as reflected in parents' attitudes and behavior, is an extremely important element in his or her sexual adjustment.

Of the 10 million teenaged females in the United States, approximately 1 million become pregnant each year. Half of these will give birth and half will have abortions. Two thirds of these girls are unmarried. Approximately 20% of the babies will weigh less than 2,500 gm, mostly to the mothers under 15 years of age. Nine out of ten of the mothers will drop out of school. Sixty percent of the mothers will be on welfare for at least some time.

The cinema, television, and advertising all indicate that sex is an important negotiable commodity. Half of 19-year-olds have had sex and 10% of 13-year-olds. An important reason for sexual intercourse is to hold onto a relationship with a person of the opposite sex. Some girls become pregnant to gain an object of affection, which they lack in their homes. A common theme expressed by many girls concerning parental attitudes toward sexuality runs as follows: "Don't have intercourse. If you do, don't let me know about it. If you do, don't get pregnant." With the easy accessibility of birth control methods, the reasons given for not using them are important to consider. In order of frequency in one study they were the following:

1. The opportunity to use a contraceptive was not available in that situation.
2. Pregnancy unlikely because of infrequent intercourse.
3. Embarrassment to approach a doctor or consult a planned-parenthood clinic.
4. The use of contraceptives indicates promiscuity; being prepared for sex is bad.
5. Use of a condom or diaphragm interferes with total sexual pleasure.
6. Each partner depends upon the other to take precautions.
7. Refusal to associate "a meaningful relationship" with biologic facts.
8. Under the influence of alcohol or drugs.
9. Fear of being "found out" if contraceptive was purchased.
10. Desire to become pregnant.

The results of teenage pregnancies have been discussed in chapter 2. Many of the mothers come from a single parent home. It is not unusual for the parent or parents of the mother to accept the infant but reject the mother, leading to marked depression.[101]

In comparison with older mothers with secure and well-developed identities, the teenage mother is tentative and insecure in her approach to her infant very often. Individual differences do exist and are influenced by age and ego development.[103] The teenage mother becomes less involved with her child and is more likely to leave much of the care to others. Seldom are these babies placed for adoption.

The most important obligation of the physician during this period of life is to realize the conflict that is going on in the child. As Thom[18] has so well stated, it is the physician who must attempt to help the child over this difficult hurdle. He or she must help the child grasp the idea that freedom carries with it obligations and responsibilities; he or she must in turn help parents to understand that the ultimate goal is to train their child to live happily and efficiently in a world that will grant no special concessions.

Parents must recognize and accept changing relationships between themselves and their children. This amounts to a steadily growing equality. In addition parents and educators must realize that social, economic, and moral values change with each new generation and that these are dynamic, not static. One psychologist points out that many of the rules for adolescents are set up by adults who have never satisfactorily established a set of rules for themselves. The adult must serve as an experienced guide who has the advantage of mature ability and greater information in most spheres, and there must at the same time be an equality of human dignity and personal integrity between the adult and the child.

In conclusion, a word of caution should be offered to the reader. It might appear from what has been said that the adolescent period is one of great storm and stress. Although this may be true in isolated cases, it should be emphasized that the majority of children go through this time of life with comparative ease and with few serious scars carried over into adult life. Overemphasis to parents or children as to the possible difficulties that may be encountered has frequently done more harm than good. A common-sense attitude must be taken and individual problems appropriately dealt with as they arise.[12, 18]

Sleep

Periods of sleep and wakefulness in the newborn infant are disorganized and alternate at brief intervals. By the fourth week a definite pattern emerges with sleep predominating at certain times in a 24-hour period. At this same time the intervals of both sleep and wakefulness lengthen. During the third month a constant periodicity begins to develop with the greatest amount of sleep occurring at night. A term baby will sleep from 15 to 18 hours a day with individual intervals lasting 3 to 5 hours and awake periods a maximum of 2 hours.[36]

Recent polygraphic studies have increased our knowledge of sleep and its related physiologic phenomena.[23, 37, 55–57, 59] Sleep can be divided into several stages but these fall into two generally recognized categories. *Active* sleep is characterized by rapid eye movements (REM), irregular heart rate and breathing, facial and body movements, and inhibition of tendon and some other reflexes. Rapid awakening after a period of active sleep is associated with good dream recall in adults. Cerebral blood flow and brain temperature increase during active sleep. In both the premature as well as the term neonate, apnea is more commonly associated with active sleep. *Quiet* sleep has no rapid eye movements, no facial or body movements except an occasional startle; regular respiration and heart rate and normal muscular tonus is present.

With active sleep there is a low-voltage, fast-frequency pattern in the EEG, while during quiet sleep there is high voltage and a slow frequency. In chapter 9 the relationship between sleep patterns and rate of secretion of the pituitary hormones is described, e.g., during quiet sleep there is an increased secretion of growth hormone. Drugs that alter the sleep pattern will also alter hormone production.

It has been hypothesized that active sleep is accompanied by increased protein synthesis in the brain. This is supported by the increased cerebral circulation and temperature. It may also help to explain why active sleep is relatively increased in early infancy.

From 50% to 60% of sleep in the newborn is of the active type. With increasing age the amount of quiet sleep increases and averages 80% in the young adult. This is accomplished by a reduction of the number of intervals of active sleep from seven in children to four in adults per night and some shortening of each interval.[8]

In preterm infants of less than 30 weeks' gestation there are long periods in which it is not possible to identify which type of sleep is present from polygraph tracings. Active sleep is the first pattern to clearly emerge. Not until near the end of normal gestation does the fetus manifest quiet sleep. In certain pathologic states there is a retention of the immature pattern well into the neonatal period. Such patterns may be found in babies of diabetic mothers, small-for-date infants, and following birth trauma.

At approximately three months after birth the infant EEG for the first time shows the presence of "sleep spindles" (low amplitude and increased frequency). In older children and adults these spindles are a constant finding during quiet sleep. Along with the decrease in the amount of active sleep there is a decrease in muscular activity during sleep, from 60% at birth to 25% by six months.

At age 1 and 2 years most of the required sleep can be obtained at night, but one or two daytime naps lasting from one to three hours are still necessary. The requirement of a nap may be waived for a few children as early as 3.5 years, but more often it is not omitted until the child approaches 5 years. By the time nursery school age has been reached (4 to 5 years), the child may be napping only three to five times a week. The amount of sleep necessary then gradually declines so that the average is nine to ten hours at 12 years and eight to nine hours at 17 years. Any given child may vary in his or her requirements from day to day.

It is impossible to answer the question, "How long should my child sleep?" Perhaps the best plan, and certainly the one that reduces the number of so-called behavior problems related to it, is that of self-regulation. This takes into account the individual requirements and allows for normal maturation. To promote sound sleep it is always wise to avoid overstimulation before the child goes to bed. Nor should being put to bed be used as a form of punishment, as this immediately sets up a highly undesirable association that may last for a long time. Dreams and nightmares or night terrors are not uncommon in mild form, beginning about the second or third year and often subsiding to a great extent by the fifth or sixth year. The child may be restless or even awaken crying due to such episodes. Unless they occur frequently and are persistent, such behavior need not be considered alarming. Awakening due to wetting of the bed is not uncommon during late infancy and early childhood. By 3 or 4 years the child usually sleeps through the night without having to get up to urinate. By 5 years and thereafter sleep through the night is usually deep, quiet and peaceful.

Polygraph studies have revealed that some of these sleep disturbances have a definite relation to various stages of sleep. Both nocturnal enuresis (except in the extremely rare instances of organic etiology) and night terrors, pavor nocturnus, are associated with emergent or arousal sleep stage transmissions from deep to light. This pattern often precedes entrance into a REM cycle. Often there is a family history of similar disturbances. Total amnesia of the episode is characteristic of both, and they tend to occur in the first few hours after falling asleep.

In contrast to the above, nightmares occur during REM sleep and there is usually total or partial recall of the events of the dream. They often follow some stressful situation during the day. Because the young child cannot easily distinguish between dreams and reality, he or she may be so frightened that he or she resists returning to sleep. Normally increasing ego development and distinction between fantasy and reality, as the child grows older, reduces the problem.[89]

At 18 months sleep may be resisted for some time after the child is put to bed. The child often delays sleep by crying for his or her mother or, a little later, by demanding a drink of water and the like. Taking a favorite toy or some other object to bed with him or her is common from about 1.5 through 3 or 4 years. Certainly no harm can arise from such a practice, and it often serves to quiet the child and better prepare the child for sleep. Various methods are resorted to by the young child to resist sleep in addition to those enumerated. These may include head rolling, head banging, singing, talking, and thumbsucking. They are so common and occur in so many well-adjusted children that they hardly deserve more attention than mere mention of the fact that they do occur and eventually are given up. The use of restraints or punishment to abolish such behavior always leads to further management difficulties. If let alone the child will "outgrow" these mannerisms by 3 or 4 years of age, although an occasional brief lapse into such action may again appear at times of emotional tension, such as the arrival of another sibling.

Basic Needs of Every Child

Nearly every child psychologist and pediatrician has at one time or another attempted to formulate what he or she considers to be the basic needs or emotional requirements of the child. The author does not pretend that the following list is complete or the final answer to the problem but feels that recognition of these factors is an important step in the attainment of a happy and well-adjusted child.

1. Security and a feeling of belonging to the family and social group. Each child needs not only love but also firm, kindly guidance. Letting the child do whatever he wants to do whenever he wants to do it must eventually lead to a feeling that his adults are unconcerned, and he develops a sense of insecurity.

2. Adaptability or learning to live with the world as it is. In part this means conforming with the group. In part it means facing reality. It does not mean complete and unquestioned acquiescence to the forces of environment.

3. Self-expression and freedom to show one's individuality. Each child should be allowed to "daydream" and use his imagination. Perhaps one of the greatest faults of modern educational methods is the rigidity of planned activity which allows little time for the child's own self-directed activity. Guidance does not mean planning or constant direction and advice. Experience is still a good teacher, though sometimes a hard one.

4. Achievement of success in both large and small matters. Allowing the child some self-expression often leads to his finding his own best capabilities. Praise on the part of the parents and teachers should be real and always commensurate with the task achieved. False praise seldom fools a child.

REFERENCES

1. Prechtl H.F.R.: Patterns of reflex behavior related to sleep in the human infant, in Clemente C.D., Purpura D.P., Mayer F.E. (eds.): *Sleep and the Maturing Nervous System.* New York, Academic Press, 1972.
2. Thomas A., Chesni Y., St. Anne Dargassies A.: *Examen Neurologique du Nourrison.* Paris, La Vie Medicale, 1955.
3. Aldrich, C.A., Hewitt E.S.: Outlines for well baby clinics: Development for the first twelve months. *Am. J. Dis. Child.* 71:131, 1946.
4. Aldrich C.A., Norval M.A.: Developmental graphs in the first year of life. *J. Pediatr.* 29:304, 1946.
5. Bloom L.: Language development. *Rev. Child Devel. Res.* 4:245, 1975.
6. Gesell A., Amatruda C.S.: *Developmental Diagnosis*, Knobloch H., Pasamanick B. (eds.), 3d ed. New York, Harper & Row, 1975.
7. Touwin B.C.L.: The neurological development of the infant, in Davis J.A., Dobbing J. (eds.): *Scientific Foundations of Paediatrics.* Philadelphia, W.B. Saunders Co., 1974.
8. Karacan I., Anch M., Thornby J.I., et al.: Longitudinal sleep patterns during pubertal growth: Four year follow-up. *Pediatr. Res.* 9:842, 1975.
9. Ainsworth M.D.S.: The development of infant-mother attachment. *Rev. Child Devel. Res.* 3:1, 1973.
10. Hogan G.R., Milligan J.E.: The plantar reflex of the newborn. *N. Engl. J. Med.* 285:502, 1971.

11. Thomas A., Chess S.: *Temperament and Development.* New York, Brunner-Mazel, 1977.
12. Daniel W.A.: *The Adolescent Patient.* St. Louis, C.V. Mosby Co., 1970.
13. Brazelton T.B.: *Neonatal Behavioral Assessment Scale.* London, William Heinemann Medical Books Ltd., 1973.
14. Dunan J., Kendrick C.: Studying temperament and parent-child interaction: Comparison of interview and direct observation. *Develop. Med. Child Neurol.* 22:484, 1980.
15. Erikson E.H.: *Identity, Youth and Crisis.* New York, W.W. Norton and Co., Inc., 1968.
16. Klaus M.H., Kennell J.H.: *Maternal-Infant Bonding.* St. Louis, C.V. Mosby Co., 1976.
17. Lillywhite H.S., Young N.B., Olmstead R.W.: *Pediatrician's Handbook of Communication Disorders.* Philadelphia, Lea & Febiger, 1970.
18. Thom D.A.: Psychologic aspects of adolescence. *J. Pediatr.* 19:392, 1941.
19. Martin B.: Parent-child relations. *Rev. Child Devel. Res.* 4:463, 1975.
20. Ringler N.M., Kennell J.H., Jarvella R., et al.: Mother-to-child speech at 2 years, effects of early postnatal contact. *J. Pediatr.* 86:141, 1975.
21. Lenneberg E.H.: *Biological Foundations of Language.* New York, John Wiley & Sons, 1967.
22. McCarthy D.: Language development in children, in Carmichael L. (ed.): *Manual of Child Psychology,* ed. 2. New York, John Wiley & Sons, 1954.
23. Schulte F.J.: The neurological development of the neonate, in Davis J.A., and Dobbing J. (eds.): *Scientific Foundations of Paediatrics.* Philadelphia, W.B. Saunders Co., 1974.
24. Schulte F.J.: Neonatal brain mechanisms and the development of motor behavior, in Stave V. (ed.): *Physiology of the Neonatal Period,* vol. 2. New York, Appleton-Century Crofts, 1970.
25. Bloomer H. H.: The child with speech and language disorders, in Michal-Smith H. (ed.): *Management of the Handicapped Child.* New York, Grune & Stratton, 1957.
26. Metraux R.W.: Speech profiles of the pre-school child 18 to 54 months. *J. Speech Hear. Disord.* 15:37, 1950.
27. Sameroff, A.J., Chandler M.J.: Reproductive risk and the continuum of caretaking casualty. *Rev. Child Devel. Res.* 4:187, 1975.
28. Kagan J.: Emergent themes in human development. *Am. Sci.* 64:187, 1976.
29. Senn M.J.E., et al.: *Psychologic Aspects in the Care of Infants and Children,* a report of the 21st Ross Pediatric Research Conference. Columbus, Ohio, Ross Laboratories, 1956.
30. Erikson E.H.: *Childhood and Society.* New York, W.W. Norton & Co., 1950.
31. Finch S.M.: *Fundamentals of Child Psychiatry.* New York, W.W. Norton & Co., 1960.
32. Freud A.: *The Ego and the Mechanisms of Defense.* New York, International Universities Press, 1946.
33. Freud A.: Adolescence, in *The Psychoanalytic Study of the Child,* vol. 13. New York, International Universities Press, 1958, p. 255.
34. Freud S.: in Brill A.A. (ed.): *The Basic Writings of Sigmund Freud.* New York, Random House, 1938.
35. Spiegel L.A.: Comments on the psychoanalytic psychology of adolescence, in *The Psychoanalytic Study of the Child,* vol. 13. New York, International Universities Press, 1958.

36. Parmelee A.H., Schulz H.R., Disbrow M.A.: Sleep patterns of the newborn, *J. Pediatr.* 58:241, 1961.
37. Debré R., Doumic A.: *Le sommeil de l'enfant.* Paris, Presse Universitaire de France, 1959.
38. Knobloch, H., Pasamanick B.: The distribution of intellectual potential in an infant population, in *The Epidemiology of Mental Disorder: A Symposium in Celebration of the Centennial of Emil Kraepelin.* Washington, American Association for the Advancement of Science, 1959, pp. 249–272.
39. Pasamanick B., Knobloch H., Lilienfeld A.M.: Socioeconomic status and some precursors of neuropsychiatric disorder. *Am. J. Orthopsychiatry* 26:594–601, July, 1956.
40. Knobloch H., Pasamanick B.: Predicting intellectual potential in infancy: Some variables affecting the validity of developmental diagnosis. *Am. J. Dis. Child.* 106:43, 1963.
41. Goodenough F., Harris D.: *Goodenough-Harris Drawing Test.* New York, Psychological Corporation, 1964.
42. Thorndike R.L. (ed.): *Research Problems and Techniques.* AAF Aviation Psychological Program, Res. Rep. no. 3. U.S. Government Printing Office, 1947.
43. Wechsler D.: *Wechsler Intelligence Scale for Children—Revised.* New York, Psychological Corporation, 1974.
44. Kagan J.: Canalization of early psychological development. *Pediatrics* 70:474, 1982.
45. Bender L.: A visual motor Gestalt test and its clinical use. *Res. Monogr. Am. Orthopsychiatry A.*, no. 3, 1938.
46. Graham F.K., Kendall B.S.: Memory-for-designs test: Revised general manual. *Percept. Mot. Skills*, Monogr. suppl. 2, 7:147, 1960.
47. Gibson R., Sullivan D., Dickinson D.: Intelligence in hydrocephalus with and without meningocele (unpublished).
48. Gibson, R.: A comparison of the Leiter and the Binet Intelligence Scales in children with central nervous system dysfunctioning (unpublished).
49. Terman L., Merrill M.: *Stanford-Binet Intelligence Scale: Manual for the Third Revision, Form L-M.* Boston, Houghton Mifflin Co., 1960.
50. Knobloch H., Pasamanick B.: Prediction from assessment of neuromotor and intellectual status in infancy, in Zubin J. (ed.): *Psychology of Mental Development.* New York, Grune & Stratton, 1967.
51. Knobloch H., Pasamanick B., Sharard E.S.: A developmental screening inventory for infants. *Pediatrics* 38:1095, 1966.
52. Piaget J.: *Six Psychological Studies.* New York, Random House, 1967.
53. Piaget J.: *The Psychology of the Child.* New York, Basic Books, 1969.
54. Cameron J., Livson, N., Bayley N.: Infant vocalization and their relationship to mature intelligence. *Science* 153:331, 1967.
55. Kohler W.C., Coddington R.D., Agnew H.W.: Sleep patterns in 2-year-old children. *J. Pediatr.* 72:228, 1968.
56. Coons S., Guilleminault C.: Development of sleep-wake patterns and nonrapid eye movement sleep stages during the first six months of life in normal infants. *Pediatrics* 69:793, 1982.
57. Ross J.L., Agnew H.W., Williams R.L., et al.: Sleep patterns in preadolescent children: An EEG-EOG study. *Pediatrics* 42:324, 1968.
58. Birch H.G., Gussow J.D.: *Disadvantaged Children: Health, Nutrition and School Failure.* New York, Harcourt, Brace & World, 1970.

59. Gould J.B., Lee A.F.S., James O., et al.: The sleep characteristics of apnea during infancy. *Pediatrics* 59:182, 1977.
60. Wolf P.H.: Critical periods in human cognitive development. *Hosp. Pract.* 5:77, 1970.
61. Rabin A. I.: Infants and children under conditions of "intermittent" mothering in the kibbutz. *Am. J. Orthopsychiatry* 28:577, 1958.
62. Geschwind N.: The organization of language and the brain. *Science* 170:940, 1970.
63. Bloomer H.H., Prins T.D.: Speech and language disorders in children, in Brennemann-Kelly (ed.): *Practice of Pediatrics.* New York, Harper & Row, 1967.
64. Neligan G.A., Prudham D.: Family factors affecting child development. *Arch. Dis. Child.* 51:853, 1976.
65. Howell M.C.: Effects of maternal employment on the child. *Pediatrics* 52:327, 1973.
66. Johnston C.M., Deisher R.W.: Contemporary communal child rearing. *Pediatrics* 52:319, 1973.
67. Doyle A.B.: Infant development in day care. *Dev. Psychol.* 11:655, 1975.
68. Deutsch C.P.: Social class and child development. *Rev. Child Devel. Res.* 3:233, 1973.
69. Weinberg W.A., Dietz S.F., Penick E.C., et al.: Intelligence, reading achievement, physical size and social class. *J. Pediatr.* 85:482, 1974.
70. Werner E.E., Bierman J.M., French F. E.: *The Children of Kauai.* Honolulu, University of Hawaii, 1971.
71. *Intellectual Development of Children by Demographic and Socioeconomic Factors.* U.S. Dept. of Health, Education and Welfare, Public Health Service, 1971.
72. Belmont, L., Marolla F.A.: Birth order, family size and intelligence. *Science* 182:1096, 1973.
73. Werner E.E.: Infants around the world: Cross-cultural studies of psychomotor development from birth to two years. *J. Cross-Cultural Psych.* 3:111, 1972.
74. Money J., Ehrhardt A.: *Man and Woman, Boy and Girl: The Differentiation and Dimorphism of Gender Identity from Conception to Maturity.* Baltimore, Johns Hopkins University Press, 1972.
75. Herzog E., Sudia C.E.: Children in fatherless families. *Rev. Child Devel. Res.* 3:141, 1973.
76. Hintzman D.L.: *The Psychology of Learning and Memory.* San Francisco, W.H. Freeman and Co., 1978.
77. Robeck M.C., Wilson J.A.R.: *Psychology of Reading.* New York, John Wiley & Sons, 1974.
78. Piaget J.: Development and learning. *J. Res. Sci. Teaching* 3:176, 1964.
79. Thorpe H.S.: *Developmental Appraisal of the Preschool Child: Ages Three to Six.* Davis, Calif., University of California, Davis, 1973.
80. Frankenburg W.K., Dobbs J.B.: The Denver developmental screening test. *J. Pediatr.* 71:181, 1967.
81. Bayley N.: *Bayley Scales of Infant Development: Birth to Two Years.* New York, Psychological Corporation, 1969.
82. Illingworth R.S.: *The Development of the Infant and Young Child, Normal and Abnormal,* ed. 5. Baltimore, Williams & Wilkins Co., 1972.
83. Boothman R., White E.M., Sweenie S.: Predictive value of early developmental examination. *Arch. Dis. Child.* 51:430, 1975.

84. Lewis M., McGurk H.: Evaluation of infant intelligence. *Science* 178:1174, 1972.
85. *Intellectual Maturity of Children as Measured by the Goodenough-Harris Drawing Test.* U.S. Dept. of Health, Education and Welfare, Public Health Service, 1970.
86. Scribner S., Cole M.: *The Psychology of Literacy.* Cambridge, Harvard University Press, 1981.
87. Clausen J.A.: The young as outsiders. *Science* 187:637, 1975.
88. Cohen M.I.: A new portal in a rapidly moving boundary. *Pediatrics* 73:791, 1984.
89. Anders T.F., Weinstein P.: Sleep and its disorders in infants and children: A review. *Pediatrics* 50:312, 1972.
90. Schwartz E.M., Elonen A.S.: I.Q. and the myth of stability: A 16-year longitudinal study of variations in intelligence test performance. *J. Clin. Psychol.* 31:687 1975.
91. McKay H., Sinisterra L., McKay A., et al.: Improving cognitive ability in chronically deprived children. *Science* 200:270, 1978.
92. Royce J., Murray H., Darlington P.: Pooled analyses: Findings across studies, in *As The Twig Is Bent: Lasting Effects of Preschool Programs,* Consortium for Longitudinal Studies. Hillsdale, N.J., Erlbaum, 1983.
93. Lamb M.: Early contact and maternal-infant bonding: One decade later. *Pediatrics* 70:763, 1982.
94. Thomson M.E., Kramer M.S.: Methodologic standards for controlled clinical trials of early contact and maternal-infant behavior. *Pediatrics* 73:294, 1984.
95. Rutter M.: Early sources of security and competence, in Bruner J.S., Garton A. (eds.): *Human Growth and Development.* Oxford, Clarendon Press, 1978.
96. Kagan J., Klein R.E., Finley G.E., et al.: A cross-cultural study of cognitive development. Monograph of Society for Research in Child Development, 1979.
97. Papalia D.E., Wendkos S.: *A Child's World: Infancy Through Adolescence.* New York, McGraw-Hill Book Co., 1982.
98. Thornton A., Freedman D.: *The Changing American Family, Population Bulletin,* vol. 38. Washington, D.C., Population Reference Bureau, 1983.
99. Rutter M.: Separation experiences: A new look at an old topic. *J. Pediatr.* 95:147, 1979.
100. Jellinek M.S., Slovik L.S.: Divorce: Impact on children. *N. Engl. J. Med.* 305:557, 1981.
101. Lawrence R.A., Merrit T.A.: Infants of adolescent mothers: Perinatal, neonatal and infancy outcome. *Semi. Perinatol.* 5:19, 1981.
102. Wallerstein J.S., Kelly J.B.: *Surviving The Breakup: How Children and Parents Cope with Divorce.* New York, Basic Books, 1980.
103. Levine L., Garcia Coll C.T., Oh W.: Determination of mother-infant interaction in adolescent mothers. *Pediatrics* 75:23, 1985.

7 / Organ Development

> It is the eternal changefulness of life
> that makes it so beautiful.
> —Sigmund Freud

Development implies an increase in complexity, in differentiation, and in function. The term is used in opposition to growth, which means an increase in size. It is possible to have considerable development with very little growth in size, as, for example, during the first days following fertilization of the ovum before implantation has occurred and in instances when the growth of a child is checked by a pathologic condition such as rickets. Each individual is endowed by heredity with certain potentialities for growth and development, which may be more or less than average.

The Embryo

During the fourth week of development, when the ovum is about as large as a grape, the main organ systems become established.[45] The neural folds come together and, by fusing, form the neural tube from which the central nervous system is derived. The remaining parts of the germ disk become the skin (ectoderm) that covers the body of the embryo, portions of it contributing to the special sense organs and to the buccal cavity. The dorsal portion of the yolk sac provides the gut (entoderm), later forming pharyngeal structures, lungs, and hepatic tissue. The mesoblast cells between entoderm and ectoderm, by proliferation and differentiation, form the somites, body cavities, circulatory system, and supporting tissues.

The processes of differentiation are wavelike, in a craniocaudal direction. When the embryo is 9 mm long (6 weeks), its primary anatomy is established and the arm buds are just appearing. During the second month occur those changes in form and differentiation that convert the 3- to 4-mm embryo to the 30-mm fetus.

221

Development of Enzyme Systems

All of the body's metabolic processes, including those responsible for growth and development, are mediated through enzyme systems. At present we do not know all of the enzymes that can exist, and the development of these systems is still under study. The importance of these is so great in an understanding of living organisms that some discussion of them is necessary. A few examples will be given, with no attempt at completeness.

Enzymes are organic (protein) catalysts produced by living cells. They act by varying the rate of chemical reactions without themselves being changed or finally altered by the reaction. A normal living organism is an orderly integrated succession of enzyme reactions. Although the rate of a reaction may be influenced by the amount of an enzyme present, the concentration of the substrate and the substance resulting from its action have a more direct relationship. One therefore usually speaks in terms of activity rather than in measured amounts of enzymes. Some enzymes require for their function the presence of certain organic, usually not protein, compounds, small in molecular size and thermostable. These are called *coenzymes;* the group of B complex vitamins, necessary in many oxidation reactions, are examples.

There is evidence that enzymes appear in response to the presence of their normal substrates, provided the appropriate gene is present, the raw materials are present for enzyme synthesis, and a suitable source of energy is available. It is presumed that this induction of one enzyme may lead to the induction of another, leading to sequential induction. The metabolism of embryonic tissue is characterized mainly by the activity of enzymes concerned in synthesizing proteins and lipoproteins.[124] These systems are much more active in the embryo than in the adult, where growth has ceased and only repair is present. It is sometimes difficult to distinguish between proteins with enzymic activity and those with a structural role, and it is possible that such a line of division is not always there. Some enzyme precursors may be activated by hormones, and the intensity or rate of activity is influenced by them under certain circumstances. Induction or change in activity can occur at any stage in development or with age. The lack of sufficient concentration of a substrate may result in decrease in amount or even disappearance. Conversely, as with the removal of the placenta at birth and a resulting accumulation of a substance, a new enzyme may be formed.

Glucose-6-phosphatase is necessary for the conversion of glucose to glycogen. Glycogen first appears in the fetal liver at about 12 weeks. No glycogen is stored in that organ until after that time, the placenta producing the enzymes and regulating the concentration of glucose in fetal blood until the liver is able to do so.[125]

In the prematurely born infant, tyrosine is present in the urine in fairly large amounts but is absent in the term infant. The liver of the immature infant does not contain a number of the enzymes necessary for complete metabolism of tyrosine, especially the oxidizing system and transaminase. If large amounts of vitamin C are given, the deficient enzymes are activated and the tyrosinuria disappears.[126] Some enzymes, such as intestinal glycosidase, are activated at the time of birth regardless of the degree of maturity. Erythrocyte and plasma lactate dehydrogenase and plasma glutamic oxalacetic transaminase are examples of enzymes that have a higher rate of activity in the newborn infant than later in life.[127, 128] When bone growth is essentially complete, by late adolescence, there is a corresponding fall in circulating alkaline phosphatase.

Cystathionase activity is not present in the liver of prematurely born infants, and may not appear for several weeks, depending upon the degree of immaturity. This enzyme is important in the synthesis of the essential amino acid cystine. This information raises the question of whether it is the amount of cystine rather than the total amount of protein in a diet that is the limiting factor for protein synthesis and growth.

The cerebral cortex has been studied in a number of animals, including humans. Enzyme activities of oxidative metabolism were shown to follow a very interesting pattern. The activity appeared earlier in those animals with earlier maturity. In the guinea pig, who is independent a few days after birth, activity increased by the 41st day of gestation, while in the rat, who is very dependent for the first few weeks after birth, enzyme activity increased during the second week of extrauterine life. Furthermore, the caudal and phylogenetically older areas of the cortex showed the increased activity first. Concomitant with the change in enzyme development there was a decrease in the resistance to injury from anoxia.[127]

Of considerable importance from a practical standpoint is the rate of development of enzymes used by the body to metabolize and detoxify various drugs. The interference of synthetic vitamin K with the conjugation of bilirubin in the newborn is such an example. The greater toxicity of salicylates and morphine in young infants as compared with older infants is a further example showing the significantly reduced enzymatic activity in the immature subject. The slower rate of inactivation and possibly of renal excretion of a long list of drugs is well established.[129]

Musculature

The development of muscle fibers takes place in premuscular mesodermic tissue. The early growth of voluntary muscle is both hyperplastic and hypertrophic, for the fibers increase both in number and in size. From the middle of prenatal life to early maturity the growth of skeletal muscle forms the largest part of the increment of the body. In the middle of pre-natal life skeletal musculature forms about one sixth of the body weight; at birth, one fifth to one fourth; in early adolescence, one third; and in early maturity, two fifths. The gain in musculature in childhood and adolescence is about equal to the growth of all other organs, systems, and tissues combined.[57]

It can be seen that the maximal growth in muscle mass occurs relatively late and follows chronologically the maximal growth in height. It has been found that strength virtually doubles between 12 and 16 years, but the peak increase tends to follow the major increments of height and weight. Tests of motor ability and coordination do not confirm the widely held view that a loss of motor control and awkwardness are associated with the adolescent growth spurt. On the contrary, there is a constant and steady improvement during this period.

Cutaneous Structures

The epidermis (skin) of the 1-month-old fetus consists of a single layer of ectodermal cells. Within another 2 weeks a second layer, termed the stratum germinativum, is added. By 4 months the fetal skin has three distinct regions: a periderm, an intermediate layer, and the stratum germinativum. At this time there is considerable accumulation of glycogen that persists until late fetal life, but is never present in postnatal skin unless injury occurs. The anaerobic glycolytic pathway is apparently the major energy source for rapid epidermal growth. By 9 months' gestation, the characteristic five layers typical of the adult are present. These consist of the stratum germinativum (or basal layer), stratum spinosum (or prickle layer), stratum granulosum, and the stratum corneum. Palmar and plantar surfaces are considerably thicker by virtue of an extra layer, stratum lucidum, beneath the corneum. The red transparent appearance of the prematurely born infant is largely attributable to the thin and poorly developed stratum granulosum. At this time it contains very little keratohyalin granules characteristic of the older child and adult. In the neonate the stratum corneum is thin and virtually fused with the vernix caseosa, which is an excellent reason to avoid too vigorous an attempt to wash away the vernix. Later the corneum will become the effective barrier of the cornified epidermis. With increasing age there is increasing content of fibers rich in collagen in the dermis, which lies beneath the epidermis. It is the increasing thickness and collagen content that characterize the skin changes associated with advancing age.[10, 15, 176]

The secretory or coiled portion of the sweat glands is in the dermis. The eccrine glands are present over most of the body surface and are not associated with hair follicles. These glands are fully developed by the seventh month of gestation, but do not function effectively for many weeks after birth. Adult level of function is not reached until about 2 years. Since the glands are anatomically mature and since they respond mainly to neurogenic stimulus, it may be a functional immaturity of the central nervous system that is responsible for this inefficiency. Because no new sweat glands are added after birth, with the increase in surface area caused by growth there is a corresponding decrease in their density per unit of surface area. The glands on the palms and soles respond to psychogenic stimuli, those on the forehead and axilla to psychic and thermal stimuli, while all other parts of the body respond only to thermal influence.

Apocrine sweat glands are larger, are associated with hair follicles, and are limited to special areas. The largest concentration is in the axilla. Other sites are the anogenital area, the auditory canal (ceruminal glands), and the areolae of the breasts. Both structural and functional maturity occur during adolescence. Like the sebaceous glands, they respond to hormonal stimulus and epinephrine. The ceruminal glands are an exception to this.

Eccrine sweat is largely water, about 99%, and urea. The amount of sodium chloride present increases with age, being two to three times more concentrated in the adult as compared to a year-old child. The concentration also increases in proportion to the salt content of the diet. Eccrine sweat is clear and has little odor. Apocrine sweat is cloudy, contains both lipids and proteins and is odoriferous.

Sebaceous glands are appendices of hair follicles and are distributed over all of the body except the palmar and plantar surfaces. They are acinous glands embedded in the dermis, and their secretion is holocrine in type, consisting of lipids and cellular debris. The lipids are unique in comparison to any other synthesized in the body. This uniqueness and complexity may serve in some protective manner to limit the types of microorganisms that can survive in the skin. This uniqueness may also have served some function in sexual attractiveness and may serve to identify an individual to a pet by a distinctive odor. The glands over the head and upper chest are larger than elsewhere. As previously noted, following birth the amount of secretion remains minimal until androgen production increases just prior to puberty. The problem of acne will be discussed in chapter 9.

The pH of the skin surface drops from a neutral 7.4 at birth to around 5.5 in a period of three to five days. Little further change occurs until puberty when the pH, most notably in the axilla, rises again to a near neutral value. The significance of these changes is not clear.[15]

The fingernails and toenails of the premature infant are very soft and thin. In contrast, the full-term baby has well-formed nails which are firm. In a number of chromosomal abnormalities there are conspicuous changes in the nails, e.g., narrow and hyperconvex in Turner's syndrome and marked hypoplasia in the 18 trisomy syndrome.

Hair follicles are apparent by the third to fourth fetal month. Maturation progresses on a parallel with the sebaceous glands, and just prior to birth there is an abundant amount of very fine silky hair over most of the body called lanugo hair. During the ninth month of gestation this is lost and most of the follicles over the body regress into a resting phase. On the scalp, in contrast, at birth about 80% of the hair follicles are in an actively growing phase. With increasing age, and especially during adolescence, hair growth is accelerated and it becomes coarser. The first appearance of significant quantities of hair in the pubic area and axillae in both sexes, and over the face and chest in males, is influenced by sexual development. (See also chapter 9.) Increase in the amount and coarseness of hair over the shoulders, back, and thighs continues well into adult life. Since normal growth and development of hair is dependent upon adequate nutrition, attempts have been made to use morphologic changes in hair as a means to measure dietary adequacy. Newborn babies who are small for their gestational age, presumably due to fetal undernutrition, have scalp hair shafts of narrower diameter than their normal controls and the hair follicle is more often in a resting phase.[21]

The cheeselike material vernix caseosa covers the normal-term infant in varying amounts. It represents a product resulting from sebaceous gland secretion by the skin and amniotic fluid. The sebaceous glands are not only well developed but are functioning at this time. A short time following birth these glands become relatively dormant until stimulated by the increased amount of circulating sex hormones associated with adolescence. Greenish staining of the vernix, the nails and the umbilical cord are strongly indicative of severe fetal distress. The premature infant may be covered with fine lanugo hair that has been lost by term infants. Small areas of capillary hemangiomas are present in more than half of newborn infants. Typically they appear as small red areas with rather indistinct margins most commonly on the upper eyelids, bridge of the nose, and nape of the neck. "Angel's kiss" was an old-fashioned term applied to them and indicates their importance, for they either completely involute or disappear by reason of thickening of the skin during the first two years of life. They can be easily distinguished from the more severe port wine nevus, which is more intense in color, has sharp margins, and does not blanch with pressure.

Toxic erythema is a skin condition limited to the neonatal period that appears in 30% to 50% of full-term infants between 24 to 48 hours after birth. It is rarely seen in babies with a gestational age under 32 weeks. The lesions are firm, slightly raised, irregular, erythematous patches occurring singly or in groups and varying in size, but averaging about 1.5 cm in diameter. The lesion has an appearance resembling urticaria and may or may not have a central white papule. They last from several hours to a few days. The etiology is unknown but the tissue is heavily infiltrated with eosinophils. Any body surface may be involved. It is completely benign.

Since the neonate has been subjected to hormonal influences prior to birth there is often some sebaceous gland hyperplasia and secretion of sebum. This is manifested by multiple white-to-yellow 1-mm papules over the nose, cheeks, and forehead. It is observed in about half of newborns and is self-limited. The term *milia* is sometimes applied to it. *Miliaria* is a lesion associated with an excessively warm environment and results from obstruction of the sweat glands, which become inflamed, forming small erythematous papules over the trunk and face.

In the normal full-term infant, desquamation is not present at birth and does not begin until a few days later. Desquamation in the premature infant is often delayed for some weeks after birth. Desquamation in the postmature syndrome is often obvious at birth.

Mongolian spots are dark areas, often with a bluish cast, having poorly defined borders and found over the lumbar and sacral areas. They may be single or multiple and are macular in character. They are present in 90% of black, oriental, and American Indian infants at birth. They are less common in other ethnic groups. The pigmentation results from an increased number of melanocytes in the dermis. The pigment in these areas usually becomes inconspicuous within one to two years. Pigmentary changes of the skin associated with sexual development are discussed in chapter 9.

Spider nevi, small red areas with thin capillary "legs" spreading distally, begin to appear at the end of the first year in about 10% to 20% of the population. The number in any individual may increase until puberty. They have no clinical significance and no genetic factors are apparent.[131]

The prepuce is usually adherent to the glans and remains so for some time after birth. The skin of the external genitalia, axillae, and areolae becomes pigmented with the development of secondary sexual characteristics associated with the beginning of adolescence. Adhesions between the labia minora are seldom seen at birth but are not uncommon between 2 and 6 years.[2] They may represent the result of irritation and mild infection, also the lack of estrogenic influence, since the condition is not seen in adolescence.

We have seen that one of the prominent changes in the last trimester of gestation is the addition of subcutaneous fat. Along with a poorly developed sweating mechanism, the failure to accumulate a full quota of subcutaneous fat is a real liability to the premature in maintaining an even body temperature. Such tissue is an important means of insulation against environment.

The thickness of the subcutaneous fat increases throughout the first year. It is this accumulation plus the prominent abdomen that gives the infant his rotund appearance. During the second year there is a definite decrease in this tissue. It is important for both the physician and the parents to realize that this change takes place and that it often coincides with the period when the infant begins to display lack of interest in his food. There is a more gradual loss of adipose tissue during the next few years. At the beginning of adolescence and throughout this period there is a reaccumulation of subcutaneous fat, which is more pronounced in girls than in boys. In estimating total body fat in adolescent boys, it was found that between 12 and 18 years a 50% loss of body fat's contribution to body weight occurs.[130] From this one can presume a change in the total content of fat in the body as well as its distribution in comparison to an earlier age. Skin calipers and roentgenograms have been used to evaluate the amount of subcutaneous tissue present, and an effort has been made to equate these findings with levels of nutrition, including obesity (Table 7–1).

Dermatoglyphics, the study of the pattern and number of dermal ridges on the palms and fingers or soles and toes, has been used as a diagnostic device in detecting or supporting the diagnosis of a number of dysmorphic syndromes.[24, 25] At least 30 entities have been described, but many of these are not sufficiently unique to be very useful. Some examples may be helpful to acquaint the reader with the technique. Multiple low arches formed by the ridges on the fingertips are seen in trisomy 18. A decreased number of ridges on the fingers is a finding in some patients with Turner's syndrome. Trisomy 21 (Down's syndrome) has a number of characteristics including the convergence of three sets of ridges near the middle of the palm

TABLE 7–1.—SKIN FOLD (SUBCUTANEOUS FAT) MEASUREMENTS*†

| | TRICEPS | | | | SUBSCAPULAR | | | |
| | FEMALE | | MALE | | FEMALE | | MALE | |
AGE	MEAN	SD	MEAN	SD	MEAN	SD	MEAN	SD
1 mo.	176	11	175	13	173	12	172	15
3 mo.	190	10	193	12	183	13	182	15
6 mo.	196	12	201	12	186	14	185	15
1 yr	199	14	201	13	182	14	182	16
3 yr	197	14	191	10	169	16	162	15
6 yr	191	15	181	15	162	19	153	17
9 yr	195	19	181	19	168	25	156	19
12 yr	200	20	186	23	184	26	166	26
15 yr	209	18	178	23	199	20	188	21
18 yr	216	16	185	22	203	19	190	18
20 yr	216	16	189	21	203	19	192	18

*Modified from Smith.[6]
†All measurements are in millimeters.

to form a triradius of unusual position, finger loops opening to the radial side of the fourth and fifth finger, and the absence of either a loop or a whorl in the hallucal area of the sole. Seldom have these patterns proven to be pathognomonic for a particular condition. In addition to the dermal ridges, the palmar creases may be helpful, such as the so-called simian line or crease in trisomy 21.

Central Nervous System

The structure and function of the nervous system are more readily understood if we review some of its phylogenetic and embryonic development. In more primitive forms of life, such as the jellyfish, only a diffuse network of neurons exists. Stimulation of such an animal produces a diffuse and often inefficient response. In the earthworm a chain of ganglions has developed, and in the early chordate forms a simple neural tube associated with segmental nerves is present. Response to irritation in both of these forms increases in complexity and in the latter is segmental and more purposeful than the diffuse response displayed by lower forms of organisms. All vertebrates have an enlargement of the cephalic end of the neural tube, i.e., a brain, and in progress upward in the evolutionary scale the brain becomes relatively larger. In higher vertebrates the forebrain, especially the cerebral cortex, assumes a dominant role, reaching its greatest degree of complexity in humans. With development of the brain there is superimposed on the segmental system a controlling influence. A repetition of this phylogenetic development can be seen in humans.[26, 37]

The initial steps in the formation of the nervous system take place very early. An infolding of the thickened dorsal plate of the embryo forms the neural groove and then the neural tube with coincident separation from the parent ectoderm. Certain cells lying near the margin remain independent and assume a position on either side of the tube and just dorsal to it. They are the primordia of the sensory ganglions of the spinal and cranial nerves and indirectly of the sympathetic ganglions. The neural tube rapidly dilates anteriorly as the primordia of the brain; posteriorly it remains relatively uniform in size as the forerunner of the spinal cord.

Initially there are three regional divisions of the brain: forebrain, or prosencephalon; midbrain, or mesencephalon; and hindbrain, or rhombencephalon (Fig 7–1). By six weeks further division of the forebrain and hindbrain results in a five-vesicle stage, the components being the telencephalon, diencephalon, mesencephalon, metencephalon, and myelencephalon, which remain as the major regions of the adult brain.[45]

The myelencephalon becomes the medulla oblongata of the adult, and its central dilatation, with that of the metencephalon, forms the fourth ven-

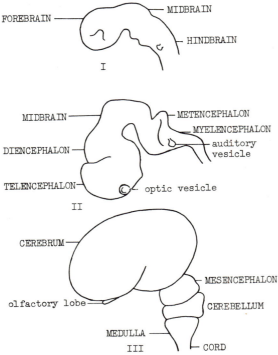

FOREBRAIN — MIDBRAIN

HINDBRAIN

I

MIDBRAIN — METENCEPHALON

MYELENCEPHALON

DIENCEPHALON — auditory vesicle

TELENCEPHALON — optic vesicle

II

CEREBRUM

MESENCEPHALON

olfactory lobe — CEREBELLUM

MEDULLA — CORD

III

Fig 7-1.—Development of the fetal brain. I, at 3 weeks, three regions of the cephalic prominence can be made out. II, at 7 weeks, further division has taken place and the five major areas of the human brain are present. III, by 11 weeks of gestation, the brain has taken on more definitive form. (Modified from Patten.[45])

tricle. Within the substance of the myelencephalon are the nuclei of the sixth to twelfth cranial nerves.

In the metencephalon are found the nuclei of the fifth cranial nerves. It is interesting that the first of the suprasegmental structures to assume recognizable form is the vestibular apparatus of the hindbrain, the flocculonodular lobe of the cerebellum. The pons, which is composed largely of fibers leading to the cerebellar hemispheres, appears late in phylogeny and reaches its height of development only in primates. Such fiber paths appear relatively late in the embryo.

Phylogenetically the mesencephalon is farther advanced than the metencephalon. Three major regions develop in this portion of the brain. In the roof are found the corpora quadrigemina, which are the correlation centers for visual and somatic impulses and visual and auditory impulses. Connections with the cerebral cortex are also present. The middle portion of the mesencephalon gives rise to the third and fourth cranial nerves and the red nucleus. This last structure serves as a relay station for impulses from the cerebellum to both upper (cortical) and lower neuron centers. Late in development in phylogeny is the substantia nigra, which is related to descending tracts from the cerebral cortex. Neither medullation of the tracts nor pigmentation is completed until after birth, the melanin deposits not being complete until about puberty.[45]

In the walls of the diencephalon are found important aggregations of cell bodies known collectively as the thalamus. Proprioceptive impulses—deep pressure, temperature, and pain—are projected to the thalamus. Auditory and visual pathways enter the thalamus also, and all are in turn relayed to the cerebral cortex. In addition important centers of visceral control (body temperature, heart rate, etc.) are found in this area and are mediated through the autonomic nervous system.

The vesicles of the telencephalon become the lateral ventricles with the connecting foramina of Monro and the small third ventricle. Phylogenetically and ontogenetically the cerebral cortex is the last to appear and the last to mature. In the ventrolateral walls of the telencephalon the corpus striatum forms, which contains the basal ganglions. Its connections are most complex, and it is primarily concerned in the coordination of fine and intricate muscular activities. Superimposed on neuron chains in the more stereotyped reactions are mechanisms affording a wide choice of behavior in response to stimuli entering over the various afferent pathways. The centers for these most plastic and highest responses are found in the cortex. It is not until the seventh fetal month that the six cell layers of the cerebral cortex are completely differentiated. At birth the cortex is approximately one half as thick as it is in the adult brain.[17, 45]

Externally certain typical landmarks begin to make their appearance by the third or fourth fetal month. At this time the sylvian fissure is recognizable. During the fifth and sixth months the central, parietooccipital, and calcarine fissures become apparent. All of the primary fissures, or sulci, are present by the eighth intrauterine month, but secondary folds continue to appear for several months after birth.[26, 45]

More important than these gross changes that take place during embryonic and fetal development are the complex cellular changes resulting in the ultimate structure of the brain following the initial formation of the neural plate and groove from the ectoderm. The sequence followed involves localized proliferation in different regions, migration of cells from areas where they were generated to areas where they will reside, aggregation of cells to form definitive parts of the brain, differentiation of immature neurons, formation of connections between neurons, selective death of some cells (in various areas it has been estimated that from 15% to 85% of the original neuronal population is lost), and finally, the elimination of some connections that were initially formed.[60]

Assuming that the fully developed brain contains on the order of 100 billion neurons and multiplication ceases before birth, it can be calculated that neurons are generated in the developing brain at an average rate of over 25,000 per minute.[60] Most of this cell proliferation occurs in the first three months following conception. Only when the neurons stop DNA synthesis and cease mitosis do they migrate to their final destination. The timing of these events is very precise and the position reached is apparently determined by that timing as well as the pattern of dendritic connections. Cells occupying similar positions are generated at the same time. With the exception of the cerebellar cortex, mitosis does not occur in cells following migration. Following migration the neurons generate processes, usually several dendrites that function as receptors and a single axon that serves as a major effector process.

How the axons are directionally guided is not clear but may be a chemotropical phenomenon in some instances involving nerve growth factor. As the neurons mature the number of dendrites and axon connections is considerably reduced. In every region of the developing brain there is a highly programmed phase of cell death that occupies a predictable period for each region. The proliferation and myelinization in the brain do not occur until the last trimester of pregnancy and continue throughout childhood.[26, 60, 175, 186] Biochemically, myelin is a relatively inactive tissue; its primary function is to increase conductive velocity of the axon.

Postnatal growth of the brain is characterized by its rapidity during infancy and early childhood, a much more gradual increment during the middle and late years of the first decade, and a very small terminal increase throughout adolescence. It is not unusual to find the average brain weight in children of 10 years of age as great as that of adults. Nearly half the postnatal growth of the brain has been accomplished by the end of the first year, three fourths by 3 years, and nine tenths by the seventh year[57] (see Fig 7–7 and Table 7–13). The postnatal growth of the cerebral hemispheres is due mainly to an increase in white matter.

The cerebrum shows a gain in weight until the later part of intrauterine existence and a slight decline in rate of growth thereafter through the first decade. The human cerebellum begins its growth spurt relatively late, at about 30 gestational weeks, and ends it much earlier, around the first birthday, than that of the rest of the brain. This high growth velocity may increase its vulnerability to nutritional or other insults at the time. The brain stem is relatively large in the young fetus, declines in proportionate size until the end of the first year, then shows a small relative gain. There are no marked changes in the relative proportions of these parts after the tenth year. The relative weight of the entire central nervous system is high in early life, being one fourth the total body weight in the second fetal month and one tenth at birth. At about age 5 it comprises one twentieth the total weight and at full maturity averages one fiftieth.[50, 174]

The primary function of neurons is intercellular electrochemical communication and information processing through the release of one (or more) of some 30 or more different neuroactive substances termed neurotransmitters. The electrical response of the postsynaptic cell is determined by its own receptors and by the specific neurotransmitter, which may be either excitatory or inhibitory. Among the transmitter chemicals are monamines and amino acids. Neurons with the same transmitter tend to cluster in the brain, e.g., norepinephrine-producing cells were found in the locus ceruleus in the brain stem while dopamine-producing neurons are concentrated in the substantia nigra of the midbrain. The transmitters, through their effect on a cell membrane, initiate enzyme activity in the cell thus producing a physiologic response characteristic of that cell. Inactivation of the transmitter must occur immediately to maintain effective function of the nerve, which can conduct several hundred impulses per second. Enzymatic destruction of the transmitter at the synapse or its rapid reabsorption by the axon has been demonstrated.[132]

Myelinization within the spinal cord begins by the fourth fetal month and appears first in the tracts that are oldest phylogenetically, the ventral and dorsal spinal roots. Corticospinal and tectospinal tracts do not acquire myelin until after birth. Last to receive this investment are the correlation fibers of higher centers, e.g., cerebral cortex and thalamus.

As the vertebral column is formed, the neural arches grow and enclose the spinal cord in the neural canal. Up to about the third fetal month the neural canal and the spinal cord are coextensive, and the segmentally arranged nerves pass outward through the intervertebral spaces directly opposite their point of origin. After this period, differential growth is such that neither the vertebral column nor the neural tube keeps pace with the expansion of the posterior part of the body, and the spinal cord lags farther behind than does the vertebral column. Since the cephalic portion of the nervous system is fixed in the developing cranial vault, the effect of this differential growth is to pull the cord cephalad within the canal. The spinal nerves appear to be dragged caudally from the cord and pass backward through the neural canal until they enter the intervertebral space, which was originally opposite their point of origin. The extent of this displacement is progressively greater in the more caudal regions. In the newborn infant the spinal cord, except for the vestigial filum terminale, ends at the upper border of the third lumbar vertebra, or about one or two vertebral levels below that found in the adult. It is therefore apparent that the differential growth continues until maturity. The cord doubles its weight in the first six months after birth, quadruples in weight in five years, and has increased eightfold by the time adult life is reached.[45, 57]

The choroid plexuses are well formed early in embryonic life, and cerebrospinal fluid is present. From chemical studies of the blood and cerebrospinal fluid in animals and humans it has been postulated that during the first half of intrauterine life the fluid is an ultrafiltrate of the blood and thereafter assumes gradually the character of a secretion. It is probable that the blood-brain barrier is more permeable during the first few months of life than later.[62] The amount of cerebrospinal fluid in the newborn infant has been estimated to range from 30 to 60 ml; in the child of 10 years the upper limit has been estimated at 200 ml. The cerebrospinal fluid protein and the number of cells present are considerably increased in the neonatal period as compared with later life. Findings in the newborn period for normal spontaneous delivery and the absence of abnormal physical findings in one study were as follows[167]:

	DAY 1		DAY 7	
	RANGE	MEAN	RANGE	MEAN
Red blood cells (per cu mm)	0–620	23	0–48	3
Polymorphs (per cu mm)	0–26	7	0–5	2
Lymphs (per cu mm)	0–16	5	0–4	1
Protein (mg)	40–148	73	27–65	47
Sugar (mg)	38–64	48	48–62	55
Chloride (mg)	680–760	720	720–760	720

Values for protein content in the premature and small-for-date infant are higher on the first day (60 to 180 mg) and elevated levels persist for a longer time than in the term newborn.[44] Normal adult values are recorded by age 3 months. Some xanthochromia is present in the fluid after birth and parallels in intensity the serum bilirubin level.

In about 10% of children, beyond the tenth year the pineal body contains enough calcium to be visualized by roentgenologic examination. Since this structure occupies the midline, it is valuable as a point of reference. In adults of advanced age the pineal body is calcified in 80% of the examinations.

In terms of general energy metabolism the brain is the most active of all body organs, a fact reflected in its blood supply and oxygen uptake. The brain is only 2% of the total body weight but requires 20% of the resting utilization of oxygen. The adult brain receives 30% of the heart's output of blood when at rest. By contrast, the normal newborn infant requires 40%

of the utilization of oxygen due to the rapid growth at that time. The brain depends upon glucose as its primary source of energy but in fasting conditions it can metabolize ketones and use them as a source of energy. The rate of brain metabolism is relatively constant day and night.[132]

Both animal and human studies indicate that there may be critical periods of brain growth when an insult or injury may result in irreversible damage. It is important to emphasize that the times of rapid growth in total mass are not necessarily related to the period of rapid proliferation of neural tissue. It is also important to understand that periods of rapid growth and differentiation relative to the time of birth differ greatly in different species. The effect of undernutrition upon the neonatal rat's brain growth will be much more profound than upon a newborn pig or human because this is a period of major proliferation of neurons in the rat but not for the other two animals. Maternal malnutrition would have its major effect in the human in the final trimester when fetal growth begins to approach the limits of function of the placenta. Malnutrition during infancy may reduce brain weight and this may be reflected in a less-than-normal rate of increase in head circumference. Reduced head circumference may be due to a decreased number of cells in the brain (as measured by DNA content).[168] As pointed out in chapter 4, a small head is often associated with reduced intelligence. All of these facts taken together would appear to make a very open and shut case that late fetal and infant malnutrition can be held responsible for mental retardation. However, brain growth that is taking place in late fetal and early infancy periods occurs after all of the neurons are present and, therefore, the brain should be less vulnerable. Irradiation and rubella, for instance, have little influence on fetal development after the first trimester. The reduction in DNA means primarily a reduction in glial cells, which are not considered to be very vital to intellectual functions. Nor can one ignore the impact of a poor socioeconomic environment that so often accompanies poor nutrition.

Dobbing[174] has proposed that there may indeed be two critical periods in human brain development. One is in the embryonic or early fetal period when neural cell proliferation is most rapid and when such accidents as intrauterine infections are most devastating. The second, and a much longer period, is during late fetal life and infancy. Brain growth in total mass during this time is great, though decelerating within a few weeks after birth. The loss of cell numbers at this time may result in a lag in myelinization and, due to a decreased width of the cortical mantle, an increased density of neurons. Some interference with important aspects of cell migration might occur. Perhaps most important of all is evidence that there is risk to dendritic arborization and the establishment of synaptic conductivity.[175] (See also chapter 11.)

The EEG has provided some additional information on the maturation of the brain.[135-137] Prior to 26 weeks following conception the EEG tracing is very irregular and shows no obvious periodicity. Slow waves alternate with periods of no electrical activity. Following this there appear regular bursts of 4 to 7 seconds' activity with amplitudes of 50 to 150 μV. By six to seven months the bursts assume some regularity, and this is associated with an increase in enzymatic activity in the brain. By eight months, 16 to 18 cps impulses predominate with a low amplitude. These changes are very typical of the premature infant regardless of birth weight, and there is little or no difference between the periods of being awake and asleep. One of the major differences between the immature and mature baby is the definite change in the EEG between periods of wakefulness and sleep. The changes that occur in the early years of life are the gradual disappearance of a predominantly slow rhythm of 2 to 4 cps and its replacement by one of 4 to 7 cps. At age 5 years the faster activity of the occipital regions begins to dominate, with impulses of 8 to 12 cps, and the alpha rhythm of the mature brain emerges.

Sensory Development

Motor function precedes sensibility, as shown by the response of the embryo to direct muscle stimulation. Conel[17] states that there is evidence that the motor cortex matures earlier than the special sensory areas.

Tactile Sensation.—With growth more receptors are found in the skin over a wider area and in closer proximity. In early prenatal life the first response to touch is elicited in the region of the face, more particularly the lips. Later responses may follow tactile stimulation of the limbs and finally of the trunk in a cephalocaudal progression. However, even at full term touch and pain are not well differentiated.

The response to painful stimuli (pinprick) follows a fairly definite pattern of development. During the newborn period the stimulus must be strong to cause any response. This hypesthesia lasts about a week. The most characteristic response is immediate, diffuse, with general body movements and crying, and possibly reflex withdrawal of the stimulated member. At age 1 or 2 months the response is more delayed, there is a diminution of the diffuse body movements and reflex withdrawal is less common. When the child reaches 7 to 9 months there results a generalized localization of the point of irritation. Deliberate withdrawal movements occur which are directed away from the stimulus. Gradually the infant's ability to localize the point of irritation becomes more specific. By 12 to 16 months the response is one of carrying the hand directly to the point, rubbing the area, or pushing the stimulus away, and the eyes will fix on the area if this is possible. This last development shows the beginning of cortical participation in behavior of this type.[37]

Proprioceptive receptors are fairly well developed by midfetal life. Stretching, tapping, and causing a change in amniotic fluid pressure will elicit a response in the fetus.[62] These responses carry through into postnatal life and gradually come under the influence of higher centers.

VISUAL SENSATION.—The three primary functions of vision are light perception, color discrimination, and the determination of the size and shape of images. The latter, form vision, is especially concerned with the retinal fovea, which has a more complex relationship with the visual cortex than does the peripheral retina. The visual cortex of the occipital lobe has begun differentiation before birth and is complete by 3 months. The EEG reveals some photic response at birth in the visual cortex but by 6 months these responses are very frequent and the pattern fairly regular to flashing stimuli. By 16 weeks the macula and fovea have completed their structural differentiation and myelinization of the visual fibers is well advanced. Final maturation of the macula is not reached until 6 years.[40] During the first weeks of life there is preferential fixation upon some specific patterned stimuli and similarly preference for specific shapes. These findings strongly imply that the visual perception system functions in a fairly complex manner at the time of birth and is capable of processing information.

As early as 36 hours after birth many infants can both discriminate a number of facial expression and imitate them, indicating the capacity of the neonate to integrate visual and proprioceptive information. It has been recognized for a long time that the human face was the most preferred object of fixation in early infancy.[134]

The light sense is one of the most primitive of all visual functions and is a mechanism of the rods and visual purple. The portion of the retina with the greatest number of rods is fully developed by the seventh fetal month. The pupillary response is present in late fetal life. Even the smallest prematures apparently have some ability to differentiate light and dark.

Color perception is a function of the cones, which are in greatest number in the macula lutea. By means of grasp-and-reward methods of testing, it is believed that color perception for red, yellow, green and blue are present at 3 to 5 months. It is difficult to rule out the factor of brightness in all such tests.

The eye is a compound optical system that refracts (bends) rays of light to focus on the retina. The refractory condition of the eye depends upon three factors: the anteroposterior length of the eye (axial length), the corneal curvature, and the power of the lens. A refractive error (ametropia) results when light is focused anterior to the retina (myopia) or behind the retina (hyperopia). The mean axial length of a full-term infant is about 16.5 mm. Growth of the eye is most rapid during the first 18 months with an average increase in axial length of 3.75 mm and more slowly approaching adult mean of 24.5 mm by 15 to 18 years. The small size of the globe is partly compensated by the greater convexity of the cornea and lens in early life in terms of refraction. Although the lens is very soft and pliable, the accommodation-convergence reflex is not consistently present until approximately 6 months of age. The mean refractory error of term neonates is plus 2 diopters (mildly hyperopic) in 75% and myopic in 25%. Hyperopia tends to increase until age 7 years after which it declines. With advancing age the lens tends to flatten and reaches a steady state after puberty. The anterior and posterior cortical layers of the lens increase at a rate of 0.007 mm per year throughout life, making it possible to "date" the occurrence of insults resulting in permanent lesions.[16, 172]

Recent developments in the assessment of visual acuity in infants have resulted in considerable modification of previously held concepts. Four important techniques in these evaluations are the visually evoked potentials, preferential looking, optokinetic nystagmus, and electroretinography.* It now appears that emmetropia (no refractive errors) is reached near the end of the first year in normal neonates with 20/20 visual acuity. Myopic refractive errors are more common among premature infants, the lower the birth weight the more severe the condition. However, most infants will be emmetropic by the end of the first year unless retrolental fibroplasia develops when myopia can persist.

At birth there is a moderate photophobia and the eyes are usually kept closed. The pupils are miotic but within weeks begin to enlarge and continue to do so for a few years. Psychosensory pupillary reflexes, absent at birth, become apparent at a few weeks. The lacrimal glands are not fully developed at birth but some tearing does occur though the crying reflex is absent for one or two months. Psychic weeping does not develop until the middle of the first year. Temporary obstruction of the lacrimal duct may cause overflow of tears associated with mild inflammation of surrounding skin and conjunctivitis. Spontaneous canalization nearly always occurs by 6 to 8 months.

Depth sense (visual stereognosis) requires the coordinated use of the two eyes and the fusion faculty of the brain. Fusion is not present at birth and does not appear until central vision is established. Depth sense is developed as the visual acuity grows sharper, as the ocular muscles become coordinated, and as the brain learns to fuse images. Binocularity is clearly

---

*These techniques are described and illustrated by Nelson et al.[172]

established by 6 months of age with generally synchronous movements of the eyes. At about the same time early evidence of depth perception becomes manifest but is still poorly developed. Not until 6 or 7 years is depth perception very accurate and improvement continues until the early teens. Commonly at about 2 years, esotropia (convergence) makes its first appearance. If this is monocular, medical attention may be indicated to prevent amblyopia.[12]

Most normal newborn infants will respond to an adequate visual stimulus, such as a bright object (5-cm diameter ball at less than 100-cm distance), by brief fixation of eyes, decreased motor activity, and changes in respiration. Some pursuit of moving objects with appropriate eye and head movements is found in a large number of newborn infants.[138] Very deliberate coordinated following of a moving object is always present by 16 weeks. By 4 to 5 months a visual-motor stage is reached, and the infant makes approaching movements with the upper extremities. Such development proves the establishment of connections between the visual and the neuromuscular mechanism. Not until the sixth to seventh month is a deliberate reaching, prehensile stage reached. It is not until 3 years that the child can look away from the object before completion of the neuromuscular activity and that the digits begin to extend just before they reach the object to be grasped. The child now is able to appraise the location and size of the object without undue effort. Such behavior displays the advancing maturation of cortical areas and their influence on the visual mechanism.

Further evidence of associations between sight and higher centers is shown by the baby at about 3 months when he or she recognizes familiar objects such as his or her bottle. By this time also the movements of the eyes are fairly well coordinated. At 5 or 6 months visual impulses are retained (memory) so that there is an increasing recognition of familiar objects and faces and the response of fear to an unfamiliar face appears.[37]

AUDITORY SENSATION.—The development of the membranous labyrinth occurs early. Its essential gross parts are well defined by the second month of fetal life. Ossification of the periotic capsule begins in the fifth month. At birth the bony investment is complete and there is little if any change in the internal ear thereafter; but later additions increase the size of the petrous bone, tending to bury the labyrinth more deeply. In general, defects of bone or sense organs are more common in the cochlea than in the labyrinth.

The internal ear takes up sensations and passes them to the brain for elaboration and appreciation. The middle ear, concerned with the collecting and transmitting of sound waves to the internal ear, is practically of adult size at birth, although the drum membrane may be smaller and more oblique. The external canal is wholly cartilaginous at birth and much shorter than in the adult. The eustachian tube is shorter and more horizontal at birth. Its shortness, like that of the external auditory canal, is due to the slight development of its bony portion as compared with the cartilaginous.[50]

As with the visually evoked response, several recent studies have been made with auditory evoked response using electroencephalographic methods. Following auditory stimulus seven distinct waves can be identified and are associated with specific areas in the ear or brain, i.e., I, eighth nerve; II, cochlear nucleus; III, superior olivary nucleus; IV, lateral lemniscus; and V, inferior colliculus. Components of waves VI and VII remain to be defined. Differential diagnosis of hearing loss and brain stem lesions can be elucidated by interpretation of response, i.e., amplitude and latency to stimuli of different intensities.[37, 133] The technique has particular value in the premature or low birth weight infant where the risk of deafness is considerable.[183]

Hearing response can be elicited from the fetus as early as 24 weeks and is present consistently after 28 weeks.[3] Grimacing, crying, blinking, and changes in respiratory patterns or heart rate are typical early responses to sounds of 80-decibel loudness. Localization attempts by eye movement or head turning may be evident shortly after birth and are well-established reactions by 3 months. Less intense sounds, e.g., soothing voice, rattle, or small bell may cause changes in activity or stop crying. After 4 months most new sounds (as opposed to ambient sounds) will call forth searching activities. Speech stimulation from parents, siblings, and self become obvious. The infant's sounds become more complex and between 4 and 6 months babbling is a prominent part of vocal play. This is followed by imitative vocalization and finally by words toward the end of the first year.

The period that follows the end of the first year is characterized by the refinement of listening skills. This includes language development through imitating sounds and perfecting control over speech musculature and increasing ability to discriminate the subtleties of sounds in language. Very important is the gradual increase in attention span and the selective listening abilities. (The last is often an aspect causing consternation and dismay to parents of the 3- and 4-year-old.) The basic auditory skills are completely mastered by the 3-year-old and further development, as it applies to communication competence, involves integration, association, and manipulation of those skills.

CHEMICAL SENSATIONS.—Olfactory discrimination of premature infants less than 26 weeks of gestation seems very weak or absent. Beyond 29 weeks, responses to ammonia, peppermint extract, and similar odors appear to indicate definite responses of a discriminatory nature. Taste is present at birth and infants demonstrate a definite preference for sweetness over saltiness or plain water. The fact that newborn babies have ingested large amounts of formula wherein by mistake salt instead of sugar was used in the formula indicates taste is not very accurate at that time. Nevertheless, some studies through observation of facial expression or heart rate have demonstrated distinct reactions to sour and bitter stimuli. Many observers, i.e., parents, nurses, and physicians caring for infants, frequently record their objection to changes in formula of fairly subtle degrees.[48]

DISTURBANCES OF THE SPECIAL SENSES.—These are usually reflected in the total behavior pattern (see chapter 6). The two senses most commonly affected are sight and hearing. Absence of protective blinking to a strong light, absence of the pupillary reflex and failure to follow moving objects with appropriate eye and head movements constitute sufficient evidence of partial or complete blindness. Strabismus of the nonparalytic type may develop from a deficiency in the ability to fuse the image or may arise from reduced visual acuity in the deviating eye.

The deaf infant may show few signs of the defect for several months. A decrease in vocalization is one of the first changes noted, and accompanying this may be diminished laughter and smiling. What vocalization is present is often monotonal and unmodulated. Extreme visual attentiveness may be a suggestive symptom. Loss of contact with the environment affects the entire behavioral development of the deaf child and threatens personality more than intellect. As a result, behavior problems arise that may have been present for some time before the true cause is realized.

Circulatory System

Growth of the heart in weight is characterized by a very slow increment in the first four months of gestation and a steady, more rapid increment thereafter. Then for four to six weeks after birth there is little change in heart size. After this period the heart grows steadily. During the first year its weight is doubled; by 5 years it is increased fourfold and by 9 years, sixfold. From 9 to 16 years there is a second period of rapid growth concomitant with the increased general growth of this period.

In the full-term infant the heart lies midway between the crown of the head and the buttocks, and the axis is more nearly transverse than in later life. As in the adult, the greater part of the anterior surface of the heart is formed by the right auricle and ventricle. Except for the transverse axis and the absence of the shadow of the aortic knob, the roentgenologic picture of the heart does not differ greatly from the outline of the adult's.[54] By the end of the second or third year practically no differences exist between adult and childhood cardiac shadows (Fig 7–2).

All of the components found in the adult ECG are also present from the fetal age of about 5 weeks.[62] By 11 to 12 weeks of gestation the fetal ECG can be accurately recorded through the abdominal wall of the mother, which is about six weeks earlier than auscultatory perception is possible.[139] Fetal viability can be diagnosed by this technic in the face of marked obesity, and it decreases the danger of radiation exposure by avoiding the use of x-ray. For several months after birth there is a right ventricular preponderance (right axis deviation). In the premature infant the general configuration of the ECG resembles that observed in full-term infants of comparable age.[140, 141] A lower voltage is present in all of the major complexes. The smaller the heart and the more rapid the rate, the shorter will be the PR interval. In infants this may be as brief as 0.08 second. At 6 years the range is from 0.12 to 0.17 second, and at 14 years, from 0.13 to 0.19 second. The amplitude of the various segments or waves increases only slightly beyond that found in early infancy. In the precordial leads, V_1 and V_2, the T wave is usually inverted and often diphasic throughout childhood.[20, 31, 51]

The *size of the heart* is best determined by use of the cardiothoracic index[14] (Fig 7–3). This is obtained from a teleroentgenogram made by placing the patient upright in a full frontal plane with the anterior chest wall against the x-ray film cassette. The exposure is made midway between inspiration and expiration. Tube-film distance is 72 in. The cardiothoracic index equals the total diameter of the heart *(MRD + MLD)* divided by the internal diameter of the chest at the level of the dome of the diaphragm *(ID)*. During the first 3 years of life the index may be above 0.5 (0.62 to 0.40), but after this the index of a normal child will be less than 0.5[5] When cardiac size is measured by this method, care must be taken in interpreting

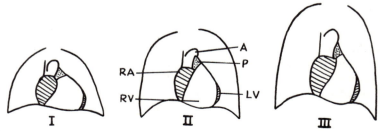

Fig 7–2.—The cardiac shadow at different ages as seen by roentgenography in the anteroposterior position. **I,** early infancy; **II,** 4-year-old child; **III,** adult. *RA,* right auricle; *RV,* right ventricle; *A,* aorta; *P,* pulmonary conus; *LV,* left ventricle.

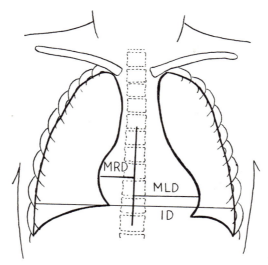

Fig 7–3.—Cardiac roentgenology: method for obtaining measurements of the cardiothoracic index from a teleroentgenogram. See text for details. (From Caffey.[14])

the result, for different phases of respiration from the peak of inspiration to the peak of expiration may change the index by a value exceeding 0.2. Position of the patient may also influence the result. Therefore a standard technique must be rigidly adhered to.[14]

In the evaluation of cardiac function and measurements of chamber size, valve positions, etc., there are presently available several very sophisticated techniques. These include cardiac catheterization, vectocardiography, and phonocardiography. Although the results of studies using such methods are recorded here as part of normal values, indications for their use and interpretation of results is beyond the scope of this book.

The growth in caliber of *arteries* seems related to the volumes or weights of the regions they supply. In the fetus the vessels springing from the main trunk grow in direct proportion to the parts of the body they supply, and those to the placenta grow in proportion to the vascular bed. After birth the trunks to the placenta become fibrotic and close completely in two to five days. These changes in fetal circulation also affect the arch of the aorta. Before birth blood passes to the arch of the aorta from the heart and through the ascending aorta and the ductus arteriosus. Secondary to the closure of the ductus, the ascending aorta grows rapidly, and this growth during early infancy is one of the most striking changes in chest structure in this period (Fig 7–4).

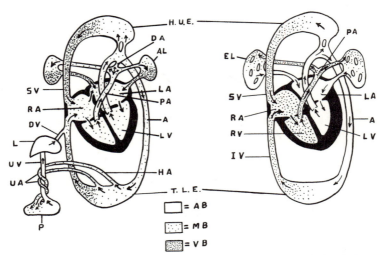

Fig 7–4.—The circulation before and after birth. **Left,** fetal circulation; **right,** normal postpartum circulation. A, aorta; AL, atelectatic fetal lung; DA, ductus arteriosus; DV, ductus venosus; EL, expanded lung; HA, hypogastric artery; HUE, head and upper extremities; IV, inferior vena cava; L, liver; LA, left auricle; LV, left ventricle; P, placenta; PA, pulmonary artery; RA, right auricle; RV, right ventricle; SV, superior vena cava; TLE, trunk and lower extremities; UA, umbilical arteries; UV, umbilical vein. The foramen ovale between the auricles in the fetal circulation is not labeled. Arrows indicate direction of blood flow. The degree of oxygen saturation of the blood is indicated according to the key: AB, arterial; MB, mixed; VB, venous blood.

At term 15% to 25% of the circulating fetal blood volume is in the placenta. Under usual circumstances the ductus venosus, which carries blood from the placenta to the vena cava, closes immediately after birth. Functional closure of the foramen ovale occurs very shortly after birth.[99] With the onset of respiration the pressure in the left atrium (auricle) rises because of the great increase in pulmonary flow. A fall in pressure in the right atrium results from diminished venous return with the interruption of the placental circulation. Anatomical closure does not take place for several weeks, and increased pressure in the right atrium, as from crying, may cause a temporary shunt from right to left. Most infants show a left-to-right shunt during the first 24 hours, which gradually decreases to a small percentage by eight days.[142]

The time of closure of the ductus arteriosus is still a subject of some controversy. Its patency is responsible for a sizeable portion of the shunting of blood during the first day of life. The actual closing process consists of an initial functional closure in response to increased oxygen saturation of the blood passing through it in the first 24 to 48 hours after birth. Anatomical closure ranges from six days to three months in full-term infants. Patency is prolonged in some premature infants. Patency of the ductus in the fetus appears to be maintained by high levels of prostaglandins (PGE_2), a potent muscle relaxer, found in fetal blood and persisting in the premature infant, especially in those with respiratory distress syndrome (discussed later).[20, 99] There is an average reduction of 25% in heart volume during the first 48 hours as a result of fluid shift from the vascular compartment, a reduction in volume upon cessation of the placental circulation, and a decrease in the shunt across the ductus.[100] There is a gradual decrease in size and muscle mass of the right ventricle and a corresponding growth of the left. The right ventricle outweighs the left by 13% at birth; they become equal by the fifth month; and by age 7 years the adult relationship has become established, with the left wall twice as thick as the right.

Because of the frequency with which it is encountered and the resultant morbidity and mortality, the hemodynamics of the respiratory distress syndrome will be given brief consideration. Early in the condition, pulmonary vascular obstruction predominates and a right-to-left shunt occurs at the foramen ovale. In most, if not all, of these infants there is a persistent left-to-right shunt in the ductus with the volume of flow increasing with increasing respiratory difficulty. Thus, until the respiratory problem abates and the pulmonary vascular obstruction subsides, there is virtually a persistence of the circulatory pattern found in the fetus.[55]

Early or late clamping of the cord will cause a number of differences in the circulatory dynamics of the newborn. With so-called placental transfusion from late clamping, there is an expansion of blood volume, increase in heart size, higher systolic blood pressure, and an increased respiratory rate, as compared with the controls with no transfusion. These changes persist for about 48 hours. Pulmonary rales and transient cyanosis are encountered more frequently in the group with late clamping.[143, 144] The increase in blood volume by using this technic may average 166 ml, or an increase of close to 60%. The value to the infant, if any, of one method over the other has yet to be determined.

The volume of fetal pulmonary circulation is greater than was formerly thought. About 12% of the total cardiac output is in the pulmonary flow. Until the third week of life pressure in the pulmonary artery is higher than the average value for older children. Growth of the small fetal pulmonary arterioles is accomplished after birth by an increase in the lumen and a relative decrease in media.

The thickness of the walls of the great veins is doubled between birth and puberty, and their lumens increase two and a half times by early maturity. The growth of the venous trunks, like that of the arterial trunks, tends to follow the increment of the parts they supply.[50]

The fetal *heart rate* is usually between 130 and 160 in health. The heart rate is quite variable throughout life, with a wider variation between the extremes in younger persons. Rates differ only slightly between the sexes, with a slightly higher one predominating in girls at all ages (the increase averages about five beats a minute). It should be obvious that valid figures can be obtained only when the child is fully cooperative, quiet and not emotionally stimulated. Table 7–2 lists average heart rates obtained from several sources for children at rest but not sleeping.[20, 101, 102]

Heart rates during infancy are more variable, the younger the more so, than in later life. Part of this is due to the uncertainty of determining differences between the waking and sleeping status of babies. Both rates and variability are least in deep sleep. Mean rates at 1 week are 128 asleep, 163 awake; at 1 month, 138 asleep, 167 awake; at 6 months, 114 asleep, 149 awake.

Sinus arrhythmia is to be considered a physiologic phenomenon in infancy and childhood.[23] The degree of arrhythmia is somewhat less in the infant, however, than in the older child. This finding is so constant that its absence should be looked upon as suggestive of abnormality. Investigations have shown that the presence and degree of arrhythmia are considerably less in children with rheumatic or congenital heart disease than in healthy ones. Extrasystoles appear frequently in clinically healthy subjects below age 14, but they are relatively more frequent in those with myocardial damage or heart disease. "Escaped heart beats" and mild degrees of sinoauricular block are not common but may be observed in otherwise healthy children. It may be concluded that sinus arrhythmia indicates good heart function, whereas in heart disease the responsible reflex mechanism is for some reason impeded, a condition expressed by regular pulse.[23, 101]

TABLE 7–2.—Average Heart Rate for Infants and Children at Rest

AGE	AVERAGE RATE	2 SD
Birth	140	50
1st mo.	130	45
1–6 mo.	130	45
6–12 mo.	115	40
1–2 yr	110	40
2–4 yr	105	35
6–10 yr	95	30
10–14 yr	85	30
14–18 yr	82	25

Blood pressure in infants may vary from day to day, and the standard deviation from the mean is relatively greater than in children and adults. There is a general trend to increase both systolic and diastolic pressures with age (Tables 7–3 and 7–4). The pressures in premature infants are less than for term infants, an average of 10 mm Hg lower for both systolic and diastolic values for a weight of 2,000 gm as compared to a normal-weight baby.[145] A drop in blood pressure the first hour after delivery is usual and averages about 15 mm Hg. This may be a reflection of the readjustment of blood volume with the increase in pulmonary circulation.[146] Males continue to have a rising blood pressure with increasing age until about 20 years. Girls reach a plateau between 15 and 17 years.[28] To obtain accurate blood pressures, the cuff width should cover at least two thirds of the up-

TABLE 7–3.—NORMAL
BLOOD PRESSURE (MM HG)
IN INFANTS OBTAINED BY
THE FLUSH METHOD

AGE	PRESSURE	2 SD
1st day	50	16
10th day	65	10
1 mo.	65	10
6 mo.	73	10
9 mo.	76	12
12 mo.	78	12

TABLE 7–4.—NORMAL BLOOD
PRESSURE (MM HG) FOR VARIOUS AGES*

AGE	SYSTOLIC	2 SD	DIASTOLIC	2 SD
1 day	78	14	42	14
1 mo.	86	20	54	18
6 mo.	90	26	60	20
1 yr.	96	30	65	25
2 yr.	99	25	65	25
4 yr.	99	20	65	20
6 yr.	100	15	60	10
8 yr.	105	15	60	10
10 yr.	110	17	60	10
12 yr.	115	19	60	10
14 yr.	118	20	60	10
16 yr.	120	16	65	10

*The figures under 1 year were obtained by the Doppler method. From 1 year on, the figures were obtained by auscultation, using the first change in sound to indicate diastolic pressure.

per arm. A small cuff will give an erroneously elevated reading, while a wide cuff's main disadvantage is one of inconvenience. Within fairly wide limits, height and weight do not affect blood pressure.[22] Values found by the auscultatory method in children agree very well with intravascular arterial measurements.[169]

Because of poor cooperation, the obtaining of an accurate blood pressure by the usual technique of auscultation is often difficult during infancy. At least two alternate methods have been devised to remedy this situation. One is called the flush method and is carried out as follows: the hand or foot is compressed by the examiner's hand, or a pressure dressing is used to compress most of the blood from the part. The cuff is inflated to a pressure just beyond the expected reading. Compression of the hand or foot is removed, and the pressure in the cuff is slowly reduced. The abrupt return of normal color, flush, to the anatomical part indicates the blood pressure reading. The method gives a single value that lies midway between systolic and diastolic values and is quite accurate.[67, 68] A second technique is known as the Doppler method and utilizes a transducer in the cuff to transmit ultrasound waves to a recording device. It detects movements of the arterial wall, thus providing very accurate systolic and diastolic pressures.[58] Values in the neonatal period, but several hours postdelivery, are systolic 78, and diastolic 42, 2 standard deviations being 14 mm Hg. Throughout infancy and childhood there are no differences in mean blood pressures between blacks and whites.[51]

Such factors as emotional problems, crying, and moving will modify the blood pressure, especially the systolic. Patience on the part of the examiner is important and, when indicated, sedation may be used to obtain a more reliable reading. Short of anesthesia, blood pressure is relatively little changed by sedatives.

Heart sounds during infancy and childhood are of a higher pitch, shorter duration, and greater intensity than during later life. The first sound is typically the louder over the entire precordium and has a muscular quality or dull characteristic in distinction to the second sound, which is sharp in quality. Until adolescence the pulmonary second sound is regularly louder than the aortic. Innocent or functional murmurs are quite common during childhood. However, there is little agreement as to the actual frequency and considerably more agreement concerning their significance. In the neonatal period the shorter the period of gestation the more often murmurs are present. A single examination during the newborn period revealed an incidence of 1.7%.[70] Examinations repeated as often as hourly, indicated a frequency of greater than 50% during the first 48 hours of life.[66] Many of these probably represent a transient condition such as an incompletely closed ductus arteriosus or a patent ventricular septal defect.[101] Repeated examinations at 6 to 12 months indicate a frequency of murmurs at around 10%. After this time there is a rapid rise and at some time approximately 50% of children will have murmurs with the peak incidence between 6 and 9 years.[23, 69] Some children will retain their murmurs well into adolescence. Richards et al.[70] followed a large group of children for several years and found that a murmur present at birth had a probability of being a congenital lesion in a ratio of 1:12. However, if the murmur persisted to 6 months, the chance for association became 1:3. When a murmur was first heard at 12 months, the probability was 1:50. More than half of the murmurs heard at birth were gone by 6 months, and the same was true at 1 year for those noted initially at 6 months.

Innocent systolic murmurs are commonly designated as vibratory, pulmonic ejection, and venous hum. The first two are most important because they may more easily be confused with murmurs indicating cardiac disease. The exact means by which the vibratory murmur is produced is not known. It occurs early in systole and is maximal in the third and fourth intercostal spaces from the sternum to the apex of the heart. It is low-pitched and is usually loudest in a reclining position. It does not obscure the other heart sounds. The pulmonic ejection murmur is due to turbulence in the outflow tract of the right ventricle. It is loudest in the left second and third intercostal spaces parasternally and early systolic in time. Both murmurs do not exceed grade III in intensity and are not transmitted to other areas. It is not always possible from auscultation alone to distinguish innocent from pathologic murmurs, especially if the murmur is of an intensity of grade III.

A "venous hum" is a common phenomenon found in children and is continuous in character. It is present parasternally, may be either subclavicular or supraclavicular in location and is usually accentuated in the upright position.

In the clinical examination of children there is perhaps nothing more subject to variable interpretation than heart sounds, including murmurs. Failure to recognize organic heart disease is indeed a serious error. However, just as serious is the error of alarming parents solely on the basis of a "heart murmur." Proper evaluation must be made in all cases in which disease is suspected, and this should include the past and present history, other aspects of the physical examination and laboratory data, including electrocardiography and roentgenologic studies.

Circulation at Different Ages

The ventricles in early life fill more slowly and are assisted more materially by a relatively more powerful auricular contraction than in later life.

As long as the heart rate remains above 100 there is no interval of diastasis, the ventricles being in the act of either filling or discharging during the entire cardiac cycle. The figures for cardiac output of the neonate are two to three times greater than for the adult over a given period of time. With growth there is relatively greater development of the left compared to the right ventricle and continued descent of the diaphragm. These changes result in a more vertical position of the heart. Slowing of the heart with age follows increasing vagal control.

Several important physiologic and anatomical features characterize the transitional circulatory pattern in the change from fetal to adult pathways. Some of these have already been mentioned. There is continued patency of the foramen ovale with possible right-to-left shunting. Continued patency of the ductus arteriosus makes possible shunts in either direction. There is the unusual characteristic of the pulmonary vessels, which constrict in response to hypoxia or metabolic acidosis. A lowered systemic arterial blood pressure persists for several hours after birth. Finally, the right ventricular muscle is as thick as the left. The essential elements of the change are the reduction in tone of the pulmonary vascular bed during the first several hours following delivery and an increase in tone of the ductus arteriosus. Within 24 hours the healthy term infant has a functionally closed ductus arteriosus and a mean pulmonary arterial pressure considerably below the systemic arterial value.[99, 101]

Except in the neonatal period the blood volume, relative to weight, does not fluctuate greatly throughout life. Recent studies on newborn infants are not in complete agreement with regard to average blood volumes and the direction in which the volume shifts during very early life.[100, 103, 104] At least a part of this disagreement may relate to the time at which the cord was clamped. If large amounts of blood come from the placenta (often more than 160 ml), redistribution may follow a course much different than would be true if the placental transfusion had not taken place.[147] The size of the infant may also influence the dynamics to some extent.[148] Most investigations support the theory that very soon after birth there is a shift of a large quantity of plasma, as much as 25% of the total, from the vascular compartment. This results in an increased concentration of red cells, with a rise in hematocrit. These changes are believed to occur within a matter of hours, and the mechanism of the shift is not known. Obviously the degree and rapidity of these changes will affect any studies carried out on the blood. The change in plasma volume may be one explanation for the variable results obtained in studies on hemoglobin concentrations or extracellular volumes done in the past. With these facts in mind, it can be said that in the newborn infant the total blood volume ranges from 80 to 110 ml/kg during the first several days. In the premature infant an average figure would be 100 ml/kg, and this falls steadily during the first several weeks.[52] In the older infant and child there is a further decrease to between 75 and 90 ml/kg,[71] and in the adult the average value lies within the range of 70 to 85 ml/kg (approximately 20 to 40 ml/lb). Using a dye method for their determinations, Brines and coworkers[11] found that total blood volume averaged 200 ml at birth and doubled by the end of the first year. There was little difference between the sexes until puberty, when the volume in the male increased rapidly. Average value for an adult male was 5,500 ml and for an adult female 4,200 ml. There was no direct relationship between volume and body length or surface area.

Lymphatic System

The number of lymph nodes and the amount of lymphoid tissue are considerable at birth and increase steadily during childhood but undergo a relative reduction after puberty.[50] Comparable figures hold for most of the lymphatic tissues throughout the body. An interesting German study cited by Scammon[50] revealed that by age 12 cervical and inguinal nodes were palpable in 100% of a series of children. The number of nodes varied but averaged from seven to nine in each area mentioned. Scammon's curves of organ growth (see Fig 7–7) portray the marked hypertrophy that occurs during childhood and the involution or atrophy that takes place during adult life. Tonsils and adenoids, being a part of the lymphogenous ring of Waldeyer, undergo similar changes, and one should realize that hypertrophy of these structures is a normal physiologic process.[33] The maximal development of these tissues during the time when acute infections of the respiratory and alimentary tracts are most common, and during the period of greatest increase in weight and height, has led to the conclusion that they are a part of a natural defense mechanism. They may have an important part in the total pattern of immune body formation (see "Development of Immunity"). Statistical studies have been equivocal regarding the defensive value of the tonsils and adenoids, and it is admitted that little is known of their function in infancy, when they may be most active as a protective mechanism.

The spleen and thymus are phylogenetically the earliest elements of the lymphoreticular system. By the fourth fetal month the spleen has assumed the general structural characteristics it will maintain. At birth it is larger in relationship to body size than at any other time, but it continues to grow, increasing its weight 12-fold by adult life. At the time of birth very few primitive lymphoid follicles are present, and no germinal centers. By 1 year many follicles are apparent and the germinal centers are well developed. Unlike other organs of the lymphatic system, the spleen does not undergo atrophy during adult life.[50, 149] The function of the spleen is the production of immunoglobulins, and it has a special phagocytic role in that it is the primary organ of bacterial sequestration. These protective abilities appear to play an especially important role in the first few years after birth.

The average weight of the thymus at birth is between 12 and 15 gm, but there are wide limits of normal.[8, 50] The birth weight is doubled at 6 months, tripled at 7 years, then remains constant until puberty. The observations of Boyd[8] and others[50] have proved that the lower weights mentioned in the early literature were probably based mainly on specimens that had undergone involution secondary to infection or malnutrition. Such involution may take place rapidly, and a large part of the thymus weight may be lost before the body weight is seriously affected. The thymic tissue, like the lymphatic structures in general, is most abundant when the general nutrition of the individual is at its best. As a general rule, underweight and malnourished children have small thymic shadows on roentgenologic study, and overweight subjects have relatively large thymic shadows.[14] It should be emphasized that there are pronounced variations in the size of the thymic shadow in normal children. Widening of the superior mediastinum on expiration is a normal finding during infancy, and such evidence should not be misinterpreted as an "enlarged thymus." Even in later childhood the organ may have assumed a flat and wide pattern, rather than the more usual narrowing and thickening, giving the impression of a large thymus on roentgenologic examination. Figure 7–5 shows examples of normal thoraxes in which apparent supracardiac widening had no clinical significance.

The function of the lymphoid tissue is primarily to protect against noxious agents, especially the microorganisms. The formation of antibodies is largely accomplished by various parts of the lymphoid system. In addition, structures such as the spleen and peripheral nodes have a filtering action to remove foreign substances from the circulation. During infancy and childhood this tissue characteristically responds to infection by hyperplasia that may outlast the infection for relatively long periods. With advancing age these changes become less pronounced.

Hemopoietic System

The first blood cells to appear in the embryonic circulation arise from the blood islands of the yolk sac. All of the first-formed corpuscles are nucleated, but with continued maturation they assume more and more the character of cells found after birth, and by the tenth fetal week about 90% of the cells in the circulating blood are non-nucleated. In succession, the

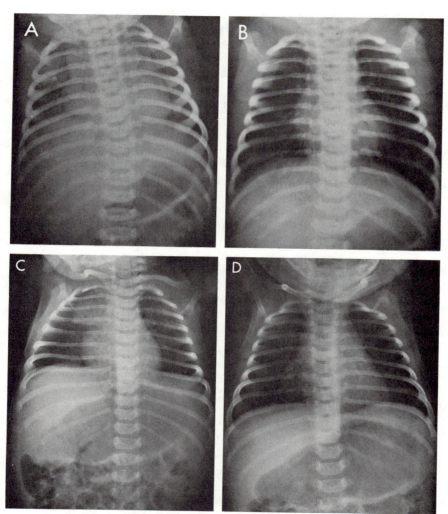

Fig 7–5.—Roentgenography of the infant mediastinum. **A,** pronounced widening of mediastinal and cardiac shadows on nearly complete expiration with the diaphragms high. **B,** same infant a few seconds later, showing change in mediastinal and cardiac shadows produced by inspiration with the diaphragms low. **C,** an apparently abnormal right upper mediastinal shadow caused by improper rotation of the patient. **D,** same infant in normal anteroposterior position.

blood-forming organs are the yolk sac for the first 2 fetal months, the liver throughout the remainder of the fetal period, and the bone marrow, which starts hematopoiesis about halfway through gestation and continues throughout the rest of life. At birth only the lymphocytes are found outside the marrow. However, the liver and spleen, and possibly other organs, retain the ability to make blood cells for some time after birth and in hemopoietic crises may again manufacture cells until early childhood is reached.[45] During the first few days of life the number of normoblasts found in the bone marrow is reduced considerably. At birth they make up about 36% of the cells, but by the end of the first week the number approaches 17% as an average and then remains at this level throughout childhood. There is a relatively slight change in the number or maturity of the granulocytic series; however, there is a general trend for an increase in the number of lymphocytes found in the marrow, from 6% to 8% in the newborn to 35% to 45% at one year and then dropping back to 10% to 15% at 11 years.[72] In the marrow of the long bones there is an increasing replacement of blood tissue with adipose tissue as age advances. Microscopically this fat appears by age 3 or 4 and grossly by age 7. In the adult very small amounts of red marrow remain in the long bones. Red marrow is present in the ribs, vertebrae, sternum, skull, and innominate bones throughout life.

To maintain the normal cellular equilibrium in the circulating blood, the blood-forming organs are furnished with effective reserves sufficient for all demands. At birth there is a very small reserve of cells at or near the stage of definitive maturation, all bone marrow showing hyperplasia of maturing cells at every stage of development. In early fetal life the concentration of red cells and hemoglobin is low, with the red cells larger than normal and often nucleated. As the fetus grows, there is a gradual rise in hemoglobin content and number of red cells, with reduction in red cell diameter and the number of nucleated forms. At birth the values for red cells and hemoglobin exceed those characteristic of adult life. Shortly after birth the number of red cells and the hemoglobin content fall and reach the lowest point at the eight to tenth week of life. In the next two years there is a gradual rise in hemoglobin level, which then normally remains stationary[5, 46, 63] Tables 7–5 to 7–7).

The cellularity of the marrow normally decreases during the first week after birth and attains normal adult levels by the third to fourth month. The greatest change is in the reduction of the erythroid elements, as already noted. Simultaneous with this change is the disappearance of erythropoietin from the plasma. A rise in erythropoietin during the third week coincides with the resumption of marrow activity noted at that time. This glycoprotein, produced in the kidney, is an important hormonal factor influencing red cell production. It is synthesized in increased amounts in

TABLE 7–5.—AVERAGE NORMAL BLOOD VALUES AT VARIOUS AGES†

AGE	RBC (MILLION/ CU MM)	HGB (GM)	WBC/ CU MM	POLY. (%)	LYMP. (%)	MONO. (%)	RETIC. (%)	PLATE/ CU MM
1 day	5.5	21	20,000	70	20	10	3.0	350,000
6 days	5.3	20	15,000	62	31	7	0.7	325,000
2 wk	5.0	18	12,000	31	63	6	1.0	300,000
1 mo.	4.7	16					0.5	
2 mo.	4.0	12					1.0	
3 mo.	4.0	11					2.0	
6 mo.	4.5	11.5	10,000	32	60	6	0.8	300,000
1 yr	4.6	12.5	10,000	38	55	6	1.0	300,000
2 yr	4.7	13.0	10,000	45	49	6	1.0	300,000
5 yr	4.7	13.0	8,000	54	40	6	1.0	300,000
10 yr	4.7	13.0	8,000	60	34	6	1.0	300,000

	MCV (μ^3)	MCH ($\mu\mu_G$)	MCHC (%)	MCD (μ)	HCT
1 day	106	38	36	8.6	53
6 days	103	36	35		49
2 wk	96	33	34		46
1 mo.	90	30	33	8.1	43
6 mo.	77	26	33	7.4	37
1 yr	78	25	32	7.3	37
2 yr	77	25	32		38
5 yr	80	27	34	7.4	40
10 yr	80	27	34	7.4	42
Adult	87	29	34	7.5	45

*From Wintrobe.[63] Used by permission. Note that there may be a wide range within normal limits.

†MCV = mean corpuscular volume; MCH = mean corpuscular hemoglobin; MCHC = mean corpuscular hemoglobin concentration; MCD = mean corpuscular diameter; HCT = hematocrit.

TABLE 7–6.—RANGES OF SOME BLOOD VALUES FROM NORMAL SUBJECTS

AGE	RBC (MILLION/CU MM)	HGB	WBC/CU MM	HCT
1 day	4.8–7.0	14–24	9,000–30,000	44–64
6 days	4.5–6.8	14–22	7,500–22,000	42–60
2 wk	4.1–6.4	12–20	6,500–20,000	38–50
3 mo.	3.7–5.0	9–14	6,000–19,000	28–38
6 mo.	3.8–5.2	10–15	6,000–18,000	30–42
1 yr	3.9–5.4	11–16	6,000–16,000	31–43
10 yr	4.0–5.6	11–16	5,000–10,000	33–45

response to hypoxia, whether this is due to ischemia, anemia, or decreased oxygenation.[5]

The type of hemoglobin present in the late fetus and newborn differs considerably from that found later in life. This early type is called "fetal" hemoglobin in contrast to "adult" hemoglobin. Several chemical differences

TABLE 7-7.—Average Values for Red Cells,
Hemoglobin, and Volume of Packed Red Cells
in Males and Females*

AGE	RBC (MILLION/CU MM)	HGB (GM)	VOL. PACKED RBC (%)
10 yr			
Male	4.7	13.0	38
Female	4.7	13.0	38
14 yr			
Male	5.0	14.0	41
Female	4.7	13.0	39
17 yr			
Male	5.3	15.5	45
Female	4.7	13.5	40
Adult			
Male	5.3	16.0	47
Female	4.7	14.0	42

*From Wintrobe.[63] Used by permission. Note differences between male and female values after menarche.

are known and make possible fairly precise quantitative analysis of the two types. Physiologically the main difference is that fetal hemoglobin has a greater affinity for oxygen than does adult hemoglobin. In the hemoglobin dissociation curve the fetal type is considerably to the left of the adult, i.e., the degree of saturation with oxygen is greater in fetal hemoglobin for the same partial pressure of oxygen as compared with adult hemoglobin. Cord blood contains an average of about 80% of fetal hemoglobin. Adult hemoglobin is first detected in the fetus at about the 13th week of gestation and gradually increases until birth. If anoxia in the fetus exists, a compensatory increase in hemoglobin occurs, and this is mainly of the fetal type.[76] There is evidence that this type is found mainly in the larger red blood cells.[73] Two weeks following birth the average amount of fetal hemoglobin is about 75% of the total, at 5 weeks 55% and by 20 weeks 5%. These are average figures, as there is considerable variation.[74, 75] The life span of the red cells formed during the late fetal and the early neonatal period and containing large amounts of fetal hemoglobin is between 65 and 100 days, compared with 120 days for adult cells.[150] (Using different methods, investigators in the field of cell survival have arrived at different figures, but the shorter life of the cell containing fetal hemoglobin seems well established.)

The blood values found during the first few days to weeks of life may be influenced by several factors.[19, 30] In babies whose cords have been clamped early after delivery the values for hemoglobin, red cells and hematocrit are significantly lower on the first and third days of life than those of babies whose cords were clamped after placental separation. For hemoglobin the average difference between the groups is 3 gm; for red cell count the difference amounts to 1 million cells/cu mm and for hematocrit 7%. The reticulocyte count is higher after early cord ligation than after delayed clamping, the average being 5.9 in the former and 2.7 in the latter. In infants allowed full benefit of the placental blood the icteric index is higher on the third day than in those whose cord was clamped early. It has also been demonstrated that blood values differ in the newborn with the source of the sample.[19] In general capillary blood will give higher values for hemoglobin, red cells, and hematocrit than will venous blood. A third factor to be considered is the time after birth when the blood specimen is obtained. There may be a slight rise in the red blood cell count for a day or two, but this is followed by a rather substantial drop (see Table 7–6). All or some of these factors may account for the differences in values reported for the neonatal period. Nucleated red blood cells, not in excess of 5% of the total number of nucleated cells, may be present normally for several days after birth. Macrocytosis and hyperchromia are characteristic of this period.

Values for hemoglobin in the cord vary from 12 to 22 gm in apparently normal babies. In one series studied there was no relationship between the maturity of the infant and the level found. When these subjects were reexamined at age 2 months, the average hemoglobin level was 11 gm, and this level existed regardless of the value found in the cord at birth.[77] It may be important to point out that the possible benefit from increased stores of iron with the higher initial values would not be evident by 2 months. The reticulocyte count at birth ranges from 3% to 7% in full-term infants but is higher in the premature, sometimes reaching values of 16%.[78] These high counts drop rapidly during the first week but rise slightly again about the end of the second month in response to the physiologic anemia of infancy.

At about 6 years the peripheral blood picture resembles that of the adult. From Table 7–5 it can be seen that the early high leukocyte count of the newborn declines rapidly and that a similar phenomenon occurs with the granulocytes. From age 2 weeks to about 4 years there is a preponderance of mononuclear cells in the peripheral circulation, and for another three to four years the number of these cells remains higher than in the adult.

Cells in the circulating blood reflect accurately the marrow activity with regard to both leukocytes and erythrocytes (see Table 7–5). A relative leukopenia has been found in black children and adults. This difference between the white and black is apparent by one year of age and is unrelated to geographic or other environmental influences. The mean total is 1,000 per cu mm less in blacks at all ages after the first year. The lower count is primarily due to a decreased number of neutrophils.[177]

Platelets are derived from megakaryocytes, which are present in the yolk sac during early embryonic development, in the liver during the hepatic phase of hematopoiesis and lastly in the marrow. Platelets are present in the circulation as early as the 11th week of gestation and at birth the mega-karyocytic activity in the bone marrow and the platelet count in peripheral blood is similar to that of older children and adults. Although one study[151] indicated that the platelet count was considerably decreased in the smallest of premature babies, most other studies have failed to confirm this.[5, 114] A decreased or impaired platelet aggregation has been found in some term and an even higher percentage of premature newborns. Initially platelets adhere to the collagen exposed by injury to a blood vessel. Adenosine di-phosphate (ADP) is released by these platelets, which leads to further ag-gregation. It now appears that poor platelet aggregation is present only in infants born to mothers who received acetylsalicylic acid (aspirin) or chlor-promazine, both of which interfere with release of ADP.[5]

There is no qualitative difference between blood clotting in adults and newborns, but there are very significant quantitative differences. There is no transplacental passage of the soluble clotting factors from mother to the fetus. All of the factors present in cord blood in the neonate have been synthesized by the fetus. Fetal production of the vitamin K–dependent factors (II prothrombin, VII thromboplastin, IX, and X) is relatively poor resulting in deficiency of these factors in the newborn, 30% to 70% of adult values and even lower in premature infants. The administration of vitamin K in term infants prevents further decline and initiates synthesis of the factors. Immaturity of liver function in the premature may prevent optimal response. Those factors not dependent on vitamin K are at normal or near normal levels in the neonate. In spite of low levels of some of the clotting factors, bleeding tendencies in the newborn are quite rare. The complication of vitamin K deficiency almost never occurs in breast-fed in-fants.[81]

The isoagglutinogens determining blood grouping are present in the red blood cells in early fetal life, although they increase in strength during both intrauterine and extrauterine existence.[52] The isoagglutinins also follow a rising curve, but are of relatively less importance from a clinical standpoint. The serums of some infants also have agglutinins passively acquired from the mother, and these may be of such type that they would render trans-fusion of blood from the mother very unwise. Finally, there is evidence that the red cells of the fetus may pass across the placenta and induce specific responses in the maternal serum. In erythroblastosis fetalis (he-molytic disease of the newborn), hemolysins induced in the mother's serum by this means may cross the placental barrier and produce severe blood destruction in the fetus. The Rh factor is the best known of the specific agglutinogens of the fetus responsible for such a train of events.

Development of Immunity

Resistance to infection includes a large number of protective devices that are common to all infants and children and are nonspecific. These include the skin, which acts as a physical barrier, plus its secretions, which have antibacterial properties. The lining mucosa of the intestinal, respiratory and genitourinary tracts also act as barriers by the nature of their physical structure, enzymes and other materials secreted and, in some areas, by ciliary action. Intestinal motility is one of the most important factors in controlling the excessive multiplication of bacteria within the small intestine. Normal indigenous intestinal flora are valuable deterrents to the overgrowth of pathogens.[154] Various cells in the body can function as phagocytes to bacteria, viruses, and their products. For the cells circulating in the blood stream, this action is greatly aided or perhaps completely dependent upon the presence of either *complement* or *opsonins* or both. As the infant's passive immunity conferred by the mother wanes and before the infant has manufactured his or her own catalog of immune globulins, all of these mechanisms assume major proportions.

Interferon is another of the relatively nonspecific products of the organism useful against viral infections.[155] This is a protein substance made in living cells following their exposure to a virus, not necessarily a living virus. It can be produced by all types of living tissue beginning in fetal life, and the proficiency of its synthesis does not appear to be influenced by age. It is of interest to note that the environmental changes that enhance in vitro production of interferon are found in inflamed tissue—a decreased pH, lowered oxygen tension, and elevated temperature. The mechanism of action in inhibiting virus reproduction is through its effect upon the host cell, preventing the formation of RNA, necessary for virus replication. Although interferon is species-specific, only one type is produced by each of the species of animals so far examined that inhibits growth of all homologous and heterologous viruses.

The immunologic system has two functions that are under the control of two different but interacting lymphoid systems. One protects the body against invading microorganisms by the synthesis of specific antibodies released into the serum or occasionally other cellular secretions. The other functions through a cell-mediated mechanism of immunity that is responsible for resistance to some specific bacterial, mycotic, and viral infections and for the surveillance of aberrant cell differentiation in the individual.[82]

The origin of these two systems arises from the stem cell of the yolk sac, which differentiates into a thymic-influenced group, or T cells, and another group that subsequently is derived from the bone marrow and is designated as B cells. The thymus develops from the third branchial cleft and is actively producing cells as early as the second month of gestation. It is the lymphoid cells under the influence of the thymus that will be responsible for the cell-mediated immunities. Animals, including humans, without a thymus or a T cell lymphoid system cannot survive in the usual pathogen-laden environment. Cells of the two systems can now be identified and in healthy persons the B lymphocytes account for 20% to 25% of the circulating lymphocytes and T cells for 75% to 80%. During the first year of life the percentage of B cells is slightly higher.[34] There is some evidence that T cells produce a product that assists the B cells in responding effectively in antibody synthesis.

The thymus-derived lymphocytes tend to be distributed selectively in certain regions of the lymphoid tissue. In nodes they occupy the deep cortical areas and the white matter of the spleen. In the circulation they are the small lymphocytes. Of the B cells, those that produce IgA and IgE will be located in subepithelial regions. The circulating B lymphocytes are larger than the T cells. In the lymph nodes they are in the cortical areas and along the medullary cords. Upon antigenic stimulation, they transform to plasma cells with marked cytoplasmic development including endoplasmic granular production and an accentuated Golgi apparatus. These changes appear to be the morphologic changes necessary for the production of antibody synthesis.

In a germ-free environment neither plasma cells nor germinal centers in the spleen or nodes appear. The thymus is vital for the maturation and function of the lymphoid system during a considerable period after birth. In animals, if thymectomy is done at birth, there is marked impairment of antibody production, in the development of delayed hypersensitivity and in the rejection of homografted tissue.

T cells are not a homogeneous population. At least five different types have been identified each with a different and sometimes conflicting function. These cells can be differentiated in vitro by various techniques including the identity of cell surface antigenic characteristics.[82] Some T cells, termed *memory cells*, are smaller and live much longer than other lymphocytes. They are capable of initiating an effective response upon rechallenge with antigens. *Killer T cells* recognize antigenically foreign cells, e.g., following infection by a virus, and destroy them by direct action through cytotoxicity. *Helper cells* assist B cells in synthesizing antibodies and induce or activate other cells to participate in inflammatory responses or to fulfill their respective genetic programs. Of considerable importance are the so-called *suppressor cells*, which inhibit immune function in other cells. This suppressor activity is a necessary homeostatic control mechanism that keeps the immune system under control and prevents untoward autoimmune reaction. The phenomenon of delayed hypersensitivity, homograft rejection, and some forms of allergy are primarily the result of T-cell function.[38]

Specific immune defense depends upon the integrity of the lymphoid tissues and their ability to respond to a specific stimulus (antigen) with the combined action of B and T cells. A distinguishing feature of this response, especially of the B cells and their synthesis of specific antibodies, is memory. Once an individual has interacted with an antigen, what was learned by the cells concerning the synthesis of an antibody is recalled upon exposure to the same antigen.

The first stage in the specific response to an infecting organism is ingestion by a phagocyte, either fixed (macrophage) or motile (leukocytes), with subsequent lysis and release of an antigen that passes to lymphoid tissue. These repeated infections over the years result in hyperplasia and hypertrophy with formation of follicles in nodes, spleen, and tonsils. With the initial exposure there is the first appearance of plasma cells. These cells make five immunoglobulins. The nature of three of the best understood are indicated in Table 7–8.

IgG contains most of the antibacterial immunoglobulins, and since these are genetically specific, they can stimulate the formation of isoantibodies. Passage across the placenta is by active transport, with an increased rate toward the end of gestation. It is for this reason that the premature infant may have a lower level of IgG than that present in the term infant, which equals that of the mother. The passive immunity acquired by the newborn subject will reflect the mother's past experiences with clinical or subclinical infections and active immunizations. This acquired immunity will protect for six to nine months following birth.

The low frequency of plasma cells in normal human fetuses during the last trimester and the fall in the level of IgG globulin, reaching a nadir at three to four months, is the result of absence of stimulation, rather than an inefficient antibody response. In fact, in appropriate conditions the fetus and neonate can respond to antigenic stimulation by the proliferation of plasma cells and antibody production. (It is significant that patients with agammaglobulinemia have no plasma cells.) Exposure to an increasing ar-

TABLE 7–8.—THE IMMUNOGLOBULINS

	IGG	IGA	IGM
Molecular weight	165,000	150,000–400,000	900,000
Sedimentation rate	7S	7–11S	19S
Half-life (days)	28	5	5
Adult percentage of immunoglobulins	70–80	15–25	3–10
Placental passage	Yes	No	No

ray of antigens, as time progresses, results in an increase in the number and quantity of specific antibodies found in the serum. Normal adult levels are usually reached by the second year (Fig 7–6). This immunoglobulin is the major one produced in combating infections.

IgA is present in the serum in lower concentrations in the child than in the adult and may be absent in the newborn. This immunoglobulin may represent a first line of defense against many infections. It has antibody properties similar to those of IgG but is present in the serum only incidentally. It is synthesized by plasma cells adjacent to epithelial surfaces. There is some evidence that antigens applied locally, e.g., oral poliovirus and influenza virus, may invoke an increased production of specific antibody. This immunoglobulin is found in the intestinal mucosa, in nasal secretions, in colostrum and milk, in bronchial secretions, and in tears.[154, 165]

IgD has not been identified with a specific action. *IgE* is found in the serum in very small amounts. Much higher levels, possibly of diagnostic value, are found in association with severe allergic diseases and parasitic infestation.[18] *IgE* is almost exclusively responsible for the heat-labile reaginic skin-fixing activity associated with atopy by virtue of the attachment of a portion to receptors on basophils and mast cells.

IgM is found in low concentrations in uninfected fetuses as early as the 20th week of gestation. The source of antigens responsible for its production at this time is not known. In normal newborns, synthesis of this im-

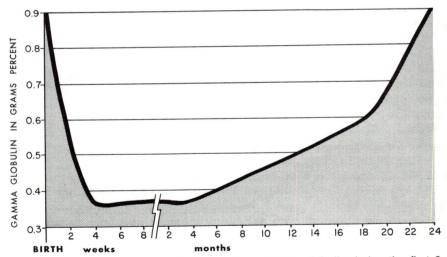

Fig 7–6.—The average level of circulating gamma globulin during the first 2 years of life. Note the rapid fall in the first months of life and the slow rise back to adult levels by the second birthday. (From Orlandini et al.[79])

munoglobulin continues at a rapid rate for the next month and then at a slower rate to reach adult levels by the end of the first year. This information plus other observations indicates that both the fetus and neonate have an increased ability to make IgM, in comparison with IgG and IgA. In fact, the response of IgM to antigenic stimulation remains more rapid than IgG throughout most of the first year. Since IgM is the only antibody found in large amounts in the neonate, regardless of gestational age, who has suffered from an intrauterine infection, it has become an important indicator of that fact. The mean level at birth in the absence of infection is 10 to 11 mg/100 ml of serum. A level above 20 mg/100 ml is strongly indicative of present or past infection. In congenital rubella, toxoplasmosis, and cytomegalic infections, levels in excess of 100 mg/100 ml are not uncommon.[80, 82] Antibodies in IgM also include those responsible for the Wasserman and heterophile tests, the rheumatoid factor, and the somatic antigens of some gram-negative organisms. A very high level of IgM following congenital rubella, as an example, may reduce the ability to synthesize IgG and thus increase the infant's susceptibility to other infections. The high concentration of passively acquired IgG from the maternal organism also serves to depress fetal and neonatal production of that immunoglobulin. Delay of active immunization of infants until after the first year is advisable for rubella due to interference of maternal antibodies prior to that time.

The detailed analysis of antibody structure has provided a basis for studying the molecular genetics of the immune response and an understanding of both the diversity and the commitment of each cell to the synthesis of only one kind of antibody. Immunoglobulins consist of a basic unit comprising two pairs of polypeptide chains, named, according to their molecular weight, light and heavy chains. The unit of the globulin is formed by two identical heavy and two identical light chains. The heavy chains give the molecule its class distinction, i.e., IgA, IgG, or IgM. At the terminal portion of each chain is a variable region in which the sequential arrangement of amino acids changes, a different pattern for each specific antibody. The possible combinations are as infinite as the number of antibodies that will be triggered by each antigen (Table 7–9).[115]

Opsonins, factors in serum that facilitate phagocytosis, appear to be functional during fetal life and are adequately present at birth in full-term infants. In low birth weight infants the activity is decreased, proportionate to the gestational age, toward the following bacteria: *Serratia marcescens, Escherichia coli, Pseudomonas aeruginosa,* and *Staphylococcus aureus.*[149]

The *complement system* is a complex of at least nine different serum proteins closely associated with the humoral antibody system. They usually function in a kind of chain reaction or cascade to facilitate phagocytosis in a manner that would classify some as opsonins. Most important, the reac-

TABLE 7–9.—Immunoglobulins: Range
of Serum Levels at Different Ages
(mg/100 ml)

AGE	IGG	IGM	IGA
Newborn	650–1,200	5–20	0–10
1 mo.	300–500	20–45	10–35
6 mo.	400–800	20–60	15–50
1 yr	500–1,000	30–80	30–90
10 yr	500–1,300	40–120	75–150
Adult	500–1,300	70–120	150–250

tion sequence is set off by the binding of a specific IgG or IgM antibody to its antigen (cell), which results in the complement C1 binding to the antibody. The end result is cell lysis that cannot be accomplished by the antibody alone nor by the complement system alone.[149] Prematurely born babies have lower levels of measurable complement than term infants who have levels about half that of adults. Adult levels are usually reached at around 6 months.[38]

Macrophages arise from bone marrow via the stem cells, circulate briefly as monocytes, migrate to various tissues, e.g., lung, liver, spleen, and brain as well as the reticuloendothelial system, and there mature functionally. Their role is to participate as a major part of the host defense by destruction of viruses, intracellular bacteria, and parasites and as the initial step in stimulating the production of antibodies. They also play an important function in removing the tissue debris of wound healing, senile cells, and tumor cells. The macrophage is both a scavenger and a secretory cell. In both of these functions it facilitates immune responses by presenting antigen to lymphocytes in a form that augments immunogenicity by stimulating lymphocyte differentiation and proliferation and by providing a means for interaction between B and T cells. Macrophages act under T-cell influence to destroy target bacterial cells. Phagocytic activity may be enhanced by the specific action of antibodies, complement, and opsonins.[152]

While T- and B-lymphocyte immune systems may deal directly with injurious agents, their major contribution probably consists in their augmentation of the phagocytic system. Operating in concert, all of the mediators bring about localization, alterations toward destruction within the environment, and finally restoration of the tissue to its normal function.

Clinically it is recognized that both the neonate and premature infant are particularly subject to infection and their resistance is poor as compared with older children. This has led to intensive study of the development of the immune system in these infants. Although some progress has resulted from these studies, it must be admitted that they have yielded very inconsistent data. By the end of the first trimester of human pregnancy, most of the components of defense are present in the fetus. Immunologic competence in the normal infant improves with age. The qualitative and quantitative deficiencies in both the nonspecific and specific defense mechanisms of the newborn as compared with the adult appear to reflect regulatory interactions between T cells, B cells, and macrophages. As one author put it, "Rather than being immunologically null, the neonate may more accurately be described as inexperienced."[165] Since most comparative studies are carried out by in vitro methods, this increases interpretative difficulties.

Maternal milk contains immunoglobulins of the secretory IgA category, complements C3 and C4, interferon, and living leukocytes. In addition to these immunologic components there are additional host-protective factors including lactoferrin, an iron-binding protein, other proteins that bind B_{12} and folic acid, a fatty acid that inhibits growth of staphylococci, and complex sugars that promote growth of *Lactobacillus bifidus*. The levels of these substances are particularly high in colostrum. Infections with enteropathic *E. coli* are reported to be much reduced in breast-fed infants compared with those ingesting cow's milk. In vitro studies have shown that lactoferrin removes the iron necessary for growth of a number of organisms including staphylococci. Infants breast-fed by mothers with high serum antibody titers for coxsackie and poliomyelitis viruses are relatively resistant to oral infections by these organisms. For these reasons many European investigators have advocated the use of breast milk for the vulnerable premature infant.[181, 182]

Maturation of tissue may influence immunity and reaction to antigenic stimuli. In spite of heavy exposure, infection with *Brucella abortus* in young children is as uncommon as that infection is in calves. Apparently immature tissue will not harbor the infectious agent. Allergic reactions in infants usually are manifested by changes in the skin (eczema), which seldom last longer than two years. The more common response in the older child is in a different tissue, the respiratory tract.

During the newborn period, septicemia is far more common than at any other age. There is little tendency to localization of the infection or striking elevation of the temperature. Such symptoms as anorexia, vomiting, diarrhea, and subnormal or erratic temperatures are much more reliable signs of infection in this age group. Some viral infections are noted at this time almost to the exclusion of all other ages, e.g., cytomegalic inclusion disease and the generalized forms of coxsackie and herpes simplex viruses. All are serious, with a high mortality rate. Infections later in life by the latter two viruses are, by contrast, mild and localized. Only in early infancy does one encounter an enteritis from certain strains of *E. coli*. Other pathogens encountered almost exclusively in the neonate or in early infancy include group B streptococci, *Proteus, Klebsiella,* and *Listeria monocytogenes.* Staphylococcal infections may be responsible for severe disease at all ages. Later in infancy and early childhood infections of the upper respiratory tract, including otitis media, are most common. The number of such infections increases each year for the average child until the age of 5 to 6 years. The total incidence for any one child will vary depending upon such factors as home conditions and opportunity of sibling exposure. These infections are often characterized by high fever and not infrequently lead to convulsions. Evidence of growing immunity is exemplified by the rarity of serious infections with *Hemophilus influenzae* in children past 3 or 4 years of age. During the school years the various exanthems make their appearance. The hyperpyrexia with convulsions seen earlier is now uncommon. Possibly because of previous sensitization of tissue by past infections, acute hemorrhagic nephritis and rheumatic fever come into prominence at this time. Rarely do these complications of infection by the hemolytic streptococcus occur before 4 years or after 20 years.

Digestive System

Some aspects of the embryologic development of the gastrointestinal tract are important to an understanding of various congenital anomalies.[45] During the fifth and subsequent fetal weeks there is a conspicuous elongation of the gut, which results in a long loop extending ventrally into the belly stalk (the future umbilicus). At the end of this loop is found the yolk sac, which forms a valuable reference point for orientation in following the rotations of the lower intestinal tract. When the gut tract is viewed in ventral aspect, a counterclockwise twisting of the loop is seen. This initial rotation is the primary factor in establishing the positional relations of the large and small intestine. Referring to the yolk sac, that portion of the gut caudal to its attachment becomes the large intestine and a small portion of the distal ileum, while that portion cephalically located becomes the duodenum, jejunum, and the remainder of the ileum. By the tenth fetal week the abdominal cavity becomes large enough to accommodate the intestines, and at this time the cecum is found in the left upper quadrant. Rotation continues so that the cecum normally passes over the duodenum first to the right upper quadrant and finally descends to its usual position in the right lower quadrant. Descent is not completed until some time after birth. With this rotation is carried the mesentery and the distal portion of the ileum.

If growth of the abdominal cavity is disturbed to the point that it cannot hold all of the mass of the intestines, they may remain protruding into the belly stalk as an umbilical hernia or, if protruded to a severe degree, as an omphalocele. With persistence of the yolk stalk the anomaly of Meckel's diverticulum occurs. This may take several forms. It may remain attached to the abdominal wall as a fibrous cord or may remain patent so that the contents of the ileum have a fistulous opening at the umbilicus. Finally, it may be a simple sacculation of the ileum. Not infrequently the lining of these diverticula contains mucosa typical of gastric mucosa, leading to ulcer formation.

Small pearl-white round areas are rather commonly found in the oral cavity of the newborn infant over the posterior portion of the hard palate. From one to more than half a dozen may be present. They probably represent retention cysts and usually disappear by the tenth day of life. They are sometimes called Epstein's pearls after the Prague physician who first described them. Occasionally petechiae are found over the soft and hard palate; these are rapidly resorbed. They are more commonly found in babies who have had their mouths and pharynges wiped by the gauze-covered finger of the obstetrician following birth.

Although sufficient salivation takes place in the newborn to maintain adequate moisture, many of the cells of the salivary glands do not mature until the third month or later. Drooling, resulting from lack of frequent swallowing, becomes prominent in some infants at about the third month and may increase with the eruption of the first teeth. A protruding tongue, normal in a small percentage of infants during the first several months of life, may accentuate this condition. A short lingual frenum restricting the protrusion of the tongue seldom causes symptoms at any age and rarely, if ever, interferes with nursing or speech development. To the best of our knowledge, we have not seen a true "tongue-tie."

The position of the esophagus in the newborn is the same as in the adult except for its relation to the vertebral column, being one vertebral level higher, with the superior limit at the fourth or fifth cervical vertebra and inferior limit at the ninth thoracic vertebra. At birth it is lined with stratified squamous epithelium five to six cell layers thick. Ciliated cells appear between 12 and 16 weeks of fetal life as a transient condition. Esophageal glands are present at birth but become more complex during later life.[50]

Embryologically, the stomach has the subdivisions and form found in the adult. In the infant the stomach lies with its long axis in the transverse plane of the body. In the second to third year the "cow's horn" form is most frequent. By the seventh to ninth year the "fish hook" type is seen, and from 10 to 12 years onward the stomach is similar to that of an adult.[57] Growth of the stomach is most rapid between birth and the third month of life. At other times the increase in mucosal area is slow and even. Most of the figures in the literature on the capacity of the stomach at various ages are based on postmortem studies and are therefore fallacious. The capacity is fixed only by the maximal limits of distention and varies widely with the size of the infant, the amount of ingested material, and the amount of swallowed air. Very rough approximations are 30 to 90 ml at birth, 90 to 150 ml at 1 month, and 210 to 360 ml at 1 year. By age 2 capacity is 500 ml, and in later childhood the average capacity is between 750 and 900 ml.

The length of the small intestine in the newborn varies from 300 to 350 cm, increases about 50% in the first postnatal year, and is doubled by puberty. The annular type of duodenum is the form most commonly found in the newborn and young infant.[57] The cecum of the infant is much smaller than that of the adult. The appendix is relatively the same length at birth as later, but it grows rapidly during the first year. The ascending colon is relatively shorter in the newborn than in the adult; the transverse colon is relatively long and may be thrown into folds. The sigmoid colon is usually filled with meconium and is thrown far upward in the abdominal cavity, but it regains its usual position a year after birth.

The salivary glands are said to increase threefold in weight during the first 6 months of life and fivefold in the first 2 years and by this time to have acquired all the histologic characteristics of the adult.[57]

At birth the pancreas is at the level of the second or third lumbar vertebra. It assumes adult histologic appearance by the end of the first year though it is functionally capable of secretion from midpregnancy on. By this time granules appear in pancreatic cells and enzyme activity is present in the form of insulin, α-amylase, lipase, trypsin, chymotrypsin, carboxypeptidase, ribonuclease, desoxyribonuclease, phospholipase, elastase, collagenase, and leucine aminopeptidase. Trypsin and lipase activity are lower in premature than in full-term infants and lower at birth than in later life. The levels of most of these enzymes gradually increase to reach adult levels at 3 to 4 years.[32, 65]

In the newborn infant the liver occupies nearly two fifths of the abdominal cavity. The lobulated structure is poorly developed at birth, and lobulation does not become complete until after early childhood. The liver at birth forms 4% of the body weight and by puberty weighs ten times as much. A palpable liver edge is very common throughout infancy and early childhood. The gallbladder of the infant increases in size rapidly during the first 2 years of life.

Sucking in the neonate occurs initially in short bursts of only three or four at a time in response to touching the lips. Very quickly, longer and more efficient attempts result. In the mature newborn this maturation may take only a few hours, but in the premature baby it may require several days. With sucking there are contractions of the esophagus and peristaltic waves; but unless there is actual ingestion of material these shortly disappear. It is normal for small boluses of air to proceed down the pharynx and esophagus to the stomach ahead of material swallowed. The coordinated breathing-sucking pattern gradually disappears by 6 to 8 months when the infant, like the adult, must interrupt sucking and swallowing to breathe. Until about 3 to 4 months the infant will treat solids (food) the same as the nipple, pressing either against the palate with the tongue to express fluid. Between 3 to 4 months the infant distinguishes the difference between the nipple and solid food and propulsion of the solid material to the back of the mouth and pharynx as does the adult. The tone of the inferior esophageal sphincter is poor throughout infancy, resulting in some regurgitation of gastric contents into the esophagus. This gradually diminishes in frequency and quantity so that it rarely persists past the first birthday.[157]

Roentgenologic studies of the intestinal tract of the normal newborn infant reveal that a gas bubble is visualized in the stomach with the first cry. This gas passes rapidly down the tract, entering the ileum within 2 hours and reaching the rectum by three or four hours on the average.[84] If none is present in the sigmoid by 24 hours, it is reasonable to assume that some obstructive lesion is present.[14] The esophagus of the infant may be sinuously curved, and after a few swallows of barium there may be a rather pronounced retention of the material in the lower end for several minutes. Gas bubbles passing upward from the stomach frequently push the barium back, causing regurgitation.[1] In the stomach of an infant less than 3 months old there is seldom evidence of a true peristaltic wave, the stomach appearing to contract as a whole. The gastric emptying time during infancy may vary greatly, normally occurring in two to six hours with barium mixtures. Longer periods are found following milk feedings in comparison with water or glucose-water feedings. In premature infants the emptying time is slightly, but significantly, faster than in term babies fed in a similar fashion. In the premature, on a milk formula, the median time is five to six hours.[105] Examination of the small and large intestines reveals little difference from those of the adult except for the relatively high position of the cecum throughout early infancy and the redundant sigmoid, previously mentioned. However, until age 4 or 5 the colon appears disproportionately large, and megacolon has been mistakenly diagnosed in many normal children as a result of failure to recognize this characteristic. Muscular spasm in the colon is rather frequently observed and has no significance in the absence of other findings.[1]

In the normal full-term infant, saliva has been found in the mouth before food has been taken. Gastric juice is secreted by the mucous membrane of the stomach, and hydrochloric acid is present before birth. There is great variation in the amount of free acid in the infant's gastric secretions, but achlorhydria is rare, except possibly in premature infants, of whom as many as one third have no measurable gastric acidity for at least several days after birth.[112] Secretion of acid by the stomach is under hormonal control of gastrin which is produced by cells of the antrum glands. Stimulation for gastrin involves that by the vagus nerve, triggered by food intake, and the physical stretching of the stomach. Immediately after birth, gastrin in the blood of neonates is significantly higher than in the maternal circulation. This level is further increased with the first feeding. As a result there is a high output of hydrochloric acid right after birth with pH values of gastric juice averaging around 5. Possibly lower values might be found in the absence of swallowed amniotic fluid. After the first feeding, pH values drop as low as 2.2. There follows a gradual fall in output of acid during the next 2 weeks, followed by a rise to adult levels by the end of the fourth month.[27, 85] Because sick infants often develop a relative achlorhydria, vomiting does not result in a decrease in the plasma chloride. With pyloric stenosis, where the obstruction is a purely mechanical one, vomiting can result in a marked reduction in chloride and an electrolyte shift characteristic of metabolic alkalosis.

Both pepsin and renin are present in the fetal stomach and reach adult levels a few months after birth.

Concentrations of duodenal bile acids increase with advancing age throughout infancy. Taurine conjugated bile acids predominate at birth but in the older infant they are mainly conjugated with glycine.[64] Bile acids are essential for the optimal absorption of dietary fat by the small intestine. The low concentration of bile acids and the decreased duodenal concentration of lipase may account for the relatively poor tolerance of fat by some infants.

Numerous functions controlled by the maternal liver in utero must suddenly be assumed by the infant's liver at birth. These include glucose homeostasis, bilirubin metabolism, synthesis of plasma proteins, detoxification of drugs, and development of mechanisms to protect against absorbed endotoxins, microorganisms, and proteolytic enzymes.

There are several indications that there is some degree of physiologic immaturity at birth and for some time thereafter.[49]

1. The physiologic hyperbilirubinemia of the newborn is due to several factors, including the normal hemolysis of the excess of red blood cells, but most importantly to liver immaturity. Adequate excretion of bilirubin is possible only after conjugation of the free form (indirect) with glucuronide to form the soluble direct form. The ability to perform this conjugation depends on an enzyme, transferase, which is quantitatively at a very low level in the newborn and remains so for several days or weeks. This finding is even more marked in the premature infant, who is usually more intensely jaundiced than the full-term infant. Approximately 50% of normal

term infants will have visible jaundice in the first week of life, and 80% of the prematurely born. Chemicals or drugs that compete with the transferase as a conjugating agent will often augment the hyperbilirubinemia. Pregnanediol, a steroid found in the breast milk of a small number of women, is one of the naturally occurring substances that may interfere with conjugation of bilirubin and increase the icterus or prolong it.[110] The relationship of severe forms of hyperbilirubinemia to kernicterus and resulting brain damage is well established. Kernicterus is primarily caused by the unbound bilirubin, which can penetrate the blood-brain barrier. This barrier, however, may be compromised in the face of severe illness and/or marked prematurity. The highest incidence of the condition is found in prematurely born infants with the respiratory distress syndrome and resulting acidosis.[109] It has been postulated that the acidosis and other unidentified factors cause the release of bilirubin loosely bound to albumin and thus permit its accumulation in the brain with resulting nerve damage.[163]

2. During infancy the bile excreted is of low concentration compared with that excreted in later life.

3. The prothrombin level at birth is 20% to 40% of the normal adult level. It slowly rises to the adult level at the end of the first year. The prothrombin time by Quick's method, which measures the time necessary for the formation of thrombin from prothrombin, is about normal at birth and falls by the second or third day, to return to normal by the sixth day. Prothrombin is formed in the liver.* Recent studies indicate that such a simple explanation for the coagulation defect seen in some newborn infants is no longer adequate. A complex series of factors is involved in the conversion of prothrombin into thrombin. In many newborns several of the so-called vitamin K factors may be low, especially factor VII, in addition to a low concentration of prothrombin.[123] (See "Hemopoietic System.")

4. The blood protein values, especially albumin and globulin, are low throughout early infancy. The amino acid levels are essentially the same throughout infancy as in the adult, so one can assume that there is some lag in synthesis.

5. The low blood sugar levels found during the first few days of life may in part be due to lowered gluconeogenesis from protein. It has also been demonstrated that conversion of other sugars (i.e., galactose and fructose) to glucose is slower in the newborn infant.[106]

6. Cholesterol esters are formed chiefly in the liver. The low serum con-

---

*Another factor to be considered is the reduced synthesis of vitamin K in the gut owing to decreased bacterial flora in the neonatal period.

tent of these substances during the first year or more may reflect hepatic immaturity.

7. Excretion of sulfobromophthalein sodium (Bromsulphalein) depends upon two factors of liver metabolism: (1) direct excretion of the free substance and (2) conjugation followed by excretion into bile. Throughout the first week of life from 20% to 30% retention in the 45-minute test is experienced. In the premature infant even higher values are found.[111] By the end of six weeks normal values of less than 10% retention are present.

8. A number of liver function tests that depend upon changes in circulating blood protein, usually associated with disease in older subjects, will give positive reactions for varying periods of time in the newborn. The response to the cephalin cholesterol flocculation test is often positive in the neonate for several days. It is interesting to note that during the first few months of life the response to this test will remain negative, even though liver damage is present to such an extent that it would cause a positive reaction in an older subject. The thymol turbidity test may show a positive reaction for a brief period. The significance of these findings is presently obscure and they do not necessarily imply functional immaturity.

At birth the lower intestine is filled with meconium, a viscid material greenish brown to black and giving a positive result to tests for occult blood. The normal infant passes some fecal material by 24 hours. In one recent study,[87] 69% of the infants had a stool by 12 hours and 94% before 24 hours. The number of stools varies considerably during the first week; they are most numerous between the third and sixth days, when a mean average of five in 24 hours is reached. At this time little difference is noted between breast-fed and bottle-fed infants.[88] From the fourth to the seventh day the infant passes transitional stools that are thin, sour, slimy, brown-to-green, and may contain remnants of meconium. The stools of the breast-fed infant are homogeneous, sour, pasty, and yellow. The number of stools during early infancy varies considerably, usually numbering two to four a day for the breast-fed infant and one to three for the bottle-fed baby. As the diet becomes more varied and the relative amount of milk is diminished, the fecal material becomes more formed and darker and by 2 years does not differ greatly from the adult stool.

The first meconium passed is sterile, but within a few hours all material passed through the intestinal tract contains bacteria. Within a few days a profuse flora is established in the mouth and the large intestine. The small bowel remains relatively sterile throughout life. The intestinal flora of the breast-fed infant is fairly simple with a high preponderance of L. *bifidus* and small numbers of enterococci and coliform bacilli. Breast-milk feedings produce this type of intestinal flora, in contrast to modified cow's milk feedings, because of its high lactose content, low protein, and therefore low buffering action on intestinal contents, and possibly because colostrum and human milk contain some immunoglobulins that influence bacterial growth. Bottle-fed and postweaning stools predominate in anaerobic *Bacteroides* species and aerobic organisms such as *E. coli, Klebsiella,* and *Streptococcus faecalis.* In the older child and adult, staphylococci, streptococci, and yeasts are found in the lower intestinal tract.[178]

Shortly after birth the microorganisms in the infant mouth correspond in type to those in the maternal vagina. By 2 to 5 days the oral and nasal flora consist of *Streptococcus viridans,* coliform bacteria, diphtheroids, and nonpathogenic diplococci, e.g., *Neisseria catarrhalis.*[178]

Respiratory System

By the sixth week of fetal life the trachea, bronchi, and lung buds can be clearly differentiated and their migration toward the thoracic area has begun. This migration is almost completed by the third fetal month, and thereafter the lungs descend very slowly. From its first appearance the right primary bronchus is somewhat larger than the left and is situated at a more acute angle. Although these differences become less marked with growth, they remain sufficient postnatally to account for the fact that foreign bodies more often enter the right bronchus than the left.[45]

The absolute dimensions of the larynx at birth are approximately one third those of the adult, but relative to the rest of the body it is as large as or larger than at maturity. The cavity of the larynx is short and funnel-shaped throughout infancy. Until age 2 or 3 years the growth of these structures is rapid; then there is a slower increment until puberty. At this time, particularly in males, there is again a rapid increase in all dimensions. From about the third year on, the larynx is longer and wider in boys than in girls. In the newborn the upper end of the epiglottis lies at the level of the first cervical vertebra and is easily seen during physical examination. It gradually descends so that at puberty it is opposite the lower half of the third cervical vertebra.[50]

The trachea in the newborn infant is about 4 cm long, roughly one third the adult length. Both diameters, anteroposterior and lateral, increase nearly 300% from birth to puberty. The small lumen explains the respiratory difficulty associated with the inflammations of this organ in the young child. At birth the bifurcation of the trachea lies at the level of the third or fourth thoracic vertebra, at 4 years at the level of the fifth thoracic vertebra, and at 12 years between the fifth and sixth thoracic vertebrae.[50]

The weight of the lungs of a newborn infant in whom respiration has been established is not significantly greater than that in a stillborn infant.[50, 52] This would seem to show that there is no great or sudden influx of blood into the pulmonary bed with the beginning of respiration. However, with the opening of the alveoli there is a vast increase in the pulmonary capillary bed, and the lungs soon accept the entire output of the right heart that was previously shunted through the ductus arteriosus into the aorta. Besides preparing the way for a greater blood volume, the expansion of the lungs and associated unfolding of the coiled capillaries have the effect of lowering the pulmonary vascular resistance. The pulmonary arterial pressure immediately after birth rises abruptly and exceeds the systemic arterial pressure by a considerable degree. During the first several hours, this favors the shunting of blood from left to right across the ductus arteriosus. By the end of the first day the pulmonary pressure has fallen to approximately half of the mean systemic pressure, and it continues to fall but reaches stable levels before the end of the first week.[13, 99] The weight of the lungs is doubled in the first 6 months, tripled by age 1 year, and increased 20 times by adult life. There is little change in topography of the lungs, fissures, or pleura from infancy to maturity. Anteriorly there is slow descent of the lung margin from the fifth to the sixth rib during growth.

In the premature infant several important anatomical features of the respiratory system differ from those of the mature newborn.[35, 61] There may be a conspicuously impoverished pulmonary vascular bed in the immature infant, and this may explain the impediment to gaseous diffusion and the tendency to cyanosis. There may also be a sparsity of pulmonary elastic tissue, contributing to the persistent atelectasis in the premature infant. And finally, the feeble musculature and the soft bony thoracic cage augment the respiratory difficulties.*

The ability of the newborn to breathe appears to be the consequence of weeks of intrauterine practice, a continuation of what went on before. By the use of modern techniques, including ultrasound imaging, it can be demonstrated that movement of the fetal chest, at a frequency of 30 to 70 per minute, is present about 70% of the time during the last half of gestation. Such movements have been detected sporadically as early as the 13th week of gestation. These respiratory movements can be used as a valuable aid in determining fetal well-being. Their presence or absence, amplitude, and duration supply important information since hypoxia, hypoglycemia, and infection may diminish the movements.[59, 61]

Both the fetus and the newborn have an excessive amount of hemoglobin that differs qualitatively from that found after a few weeks of extrauterine life. Both the quantitative and the qualitative characteristics allow more

---

*A relatively decreased (immature) vascularity in the respiratory center of the brain may also be responsible for a reduced sensitivity to stimuli in the smaller premature infants.[35]

oxygen to be carried per unit of blood and a greater uptake of oxygen from the lungs. (See also the characteristics of fetal hemoglobin previously discussed.) However, there may be a resultant lessened efficiency in the release of oxygen to the tissues. A third characteristic of neonatal blood is the relatively small amount of carbonic anhydrase. This tends to retard liberation of carbon dioxide and acquisition of oxygen in the lungs.[52, 59] The clinical importance of a low anhydrase level has yet to be completely evaluated.

The transfer of the respiratory function from the placenta to the lungs is related to umbilical cord occlusion. The stimulus for breathing is mediated through blood gas changes and possibly an added factor of tactile stimulation. In actual measurements these are arterial Po_2 falls from 80 to 15 mm Hg, arterial Pco_2 rises from 40 to 70 mm Hg, and arterial pH falls below 7.35; the tactile stimulation of pressure in the vaginal passage and cooling by exposure are also factors. The rapidity of these changes may be equally as important as the absolute levels. Failure to respond is nearly always secondary to central nervous system depression (as by drugs) or injury.

At the time of birth, most of the alveoli are not expanded fully and are filled with fluid. In addition there is a definite cohesive force of the moist surfaces of the alveoli and smaller bronchi. For these reasons the first breath taken after birth may be the most difficult. Some degree of primary atelectasis may be present roentgenologically for more than a week in a term infant and longer in the prematurely born.[59] The volume of air taken in the first breath varies considerably but averages about half of the estimated vital capacity of the 2- or 3-day-old infant, which ranges from 130 to 160 ml. The pressure exerted by the initial inspiration ranges from 10 to 70 cm H_2O. Much of the fluid in the lungs is extruded through the mouth and nostrils after delivery of the head when the baby is subjected to the thoracic squeeze by the birth canal. Babies born by cesarean section do not experience the squeeze and have delayed clearing of lung liquid often resulting in transient tachypnea. The alveolar CO_2 tension in the normal newborn is below that found after two to three weeks and may reflect the effect of a patent ductus arteriosis recirculating blood through tissues without picking up additional CO_2.[117, 159]

Anatomical growth of the lung is characterized by an individual pattern for the airways, alveoli, and blood vessels. The airways (bronchi, bronchioli, and alveolar ducts) grow predominantly antenatally. The bronchial tree is developed by the 16th week of intrauterine life. The alveoli develop after birth, increasing in number until approximately eight years and in size until the chest wall ceases growing as an adult. The diameter in fixed specimens increases by three to four times from early infancy to puberty. During the first 3 years of life the increase in lung size is mainly due to alveolar multiplication. During the last three months of gestation, in addition to the development of distal (respiratory) bronchioli, terminal saccules with flattened epithelium are formed. Respiratory exchange or function is possible at this time. Just prior to birth, primitive alveoli can be detected in the walls of the saccules which will become the alveolar ducts. Until 11 to 12 years of age there is very sparse elastic tissue present, then a fairly rapid increase to adult proportions occurs.[185]

Vessels associated with the airways and with the alveoli have their independent growth patterns and follow the development of the related structures. Cell types and cell numbers of the respiratory epithelium are established by 6 months' gestation and little change ensues with advancing age.[158, 185] From birth to adult the number of alveoli increases ten times.

Before birth the bronchi and alveoli contain liquid, which is predominantly produced by the lungs themselves. The liquid is different from amniotic fluid in several respects, including a lower urea nitrogen content and the presence of a lipoprotein surfactant, which lowers surface tension and thus maintains the small air spaces and increases the space for available gas exchange once expansion has occurred. After the initial large inspiration, successive breaths have intermediate-sized pressure swings and volume changes. The ratio of the volume expired to that inspired rises, and the rhythm is irregular. Within ten minutes after the first inspiration the normal infant has acquired some 50% to 70% of his or her normal residual capacity. After 30 minutes the lungs are essentially free of excess fluid and the lungs are well expanded. After the first day a continuing regular pattern ensues with some episodic variations related to crying, sleeping, feeding, etc.[158, 164]

Respiration in infants is largely diaphragmatic in character and continues so during early childhood. By the fifth year the costal element becomes more prominent and remains so into adult life. The rate and depth of breathing are quite variable in infancy, and the younger the subject the greater the variation. As shown in Table 7–10, there is a trend of decreasing rate with advancing age. Pauses in breathing (apnea) during sleep of short duration are common throughout early infancy. They may occur as often as several in one minute and appear to be unrelated to the sleep pattern. Apnea in excess of 10 seconds is common during the first week, especially during active (REM) sleep, but becomes infrequent later. Periodic breathing, brief recurring periods of apnea in a sequence of breaths, is characteristic of most premature babies of under 36 weeks of gestation. Usually the periods of apnea last five to ten seconds and the periods of ventilation 10 to 15 seconds. It is rare during the first four to five days after birth. It is more common and lasts longer in smaller infants and occurs mainly during active sleep.[158, 159] With increasing age the frequency and duration of regular breathing episodes become more prominent. The rate and depth of breathing are extremely variable in infancy, and the younger the subject the greater the variations. Table 7–10 shows variations in respiration with changes in age. One of the most common respiratory patterns in the premature infant is periodic breathing. This is characterized by periods of apnea in a sequence of ventilatory movements. The pattern of duration and frequency of apnea from infant to infant or in the same infant at different times undergoes great variation.[158] With increasing maturity more regular respiration occurs.

Recent work involving the study of apnea in the preterm infant has lead to a number of discoveries concerning respiratory regulation. The specific neurons in the brain stem that act to fire rhythmically and generate the efferent impulses to the musculature controlling involuntary respiration are highly dependent upon afferent impulses incident to those neurons. The type of breathing—regular, periodic, or apneic—depends upon both the inherent activity of the medullary centers and the nature of messages received by those centers. Producing hypoventilation through influence on the centers are hyperthermia, hyperinflation of lungs, vigorous nipple-feeding, and catheter suction of the pharynx. Decreasing input to the centers may also decrease their efferent outflow resulting in periodic breathing, hypoventilation, and apnea. This may result from hypoxia over an extended period, anemia, hypoglycemia, central nervous system depressants, sepsis, and other factors. Immaturity of the centers has already been mentioned as an important element in this respect. In summary, apnea and periodic breathing are characteristically present in early infancy, decrease in frequency and duration with age, occur predominantly in periods of active (REM) sleep, and in the neonatal period are observed more often in

TABLE 7–10.—VARIATIONS IN RESPIRATION WITH AGE

AGE	RATE/MIN	TIDAL AIR (CC)	VITAL CAPACITY (L)*
Premature	40–90	12	0.15
Newborn	30–80	19	. . .
1 yr	20–40	48	. . .
2 yr	20–30	90	. . .
3 yr	20–30	125	. . .
5 yr	20–25	175	1.00
10 yr	17–22	320	2.00
15 yr	15–20	400	3.70
20 yr	15–20	500	3.80

*These represent mean figures from several sources for both sexes. Vital capacity for boys averages about 6% greater than for girls.

premature than in term infants. Apnea in excess of 15 seconds at any level of development may be a harbinger of cardiopulmonary or central nervous system pathology.[41, 184]

Both term and preterm infants are obligatory nose breathers. The normal response to nasal obstruction, whatever its cause, is to open the mouth to retain the airway. This reflex is absent for a period of several weeks following birth, even to the point of producing cyanosis and eventual asphyxia.

The change in the relative measurements of the chest with age has been discussed. The conical shape of the adult chest is not attained until near puberty. Functional tests of lung growth during childhood have been compiled.[160]

Auscultation over the chest of the infant reveals that the breath sounds are loud, harsh and seem near to the ear. These characteristics are due to the fact that the tracheal and bronchial sounds are more distinct and are transmitted through less tissue than in the adult. For the same reasons, the percussion note over the lung fields of the infant and young child is more resonant, even tympanitic, than in the older child or adult.

Bronchovascular shadows in roentgenograms of infants and children are often difficult to read properly. They are relatively more prominent than in the adult, and studies have shown that there is no very exact correlation between the size and density of the hilar shadows and the incidence of upper respiratory infections. There is considerable variation among children, so that simple comparison has little value. Evaluation of these markings by the inexperienced has no doubt frequently led to the erroneous diagnosis of bronchitis and even bronchiectasis. It should be remembered also that shadows extending from the hilus are normally more dense in the inferior segments than above. Owing to the heart shadow, they are relatively more prominent on the right side. As in roentgenographic study of the mediastinum, the phase of respiration influences lung markings, and both phases should be observed when examination is made to find pathologic conditions, especially atelectasis, emphysema and nonopaque foreign bodies.[14]

Urinary System and Water Balance

It is the function of the kidneys to help in regulation of the internal environment of the body. They accomplish this in the following manner:

1. Excretion of nitrogenous waste products, mainly in the form of urea.

2. Stabilization of osmotic pressure by selective excretion and reabsorption of electrolytes, sugar, etc.

3. Stabilization of chemical composition by the mechanism of "renal threshold" and selective excretion and reabsorption.

4. Regulation of extracellular fluid volume, which is partly dependent on (2), also through the action of the posterior lobe of the pituitary body in regulating total fluid output.

5. Maintenance of acid-base balance by electrolyte and osmotic regulation, excretion of excessive accumulation of either acid or alkali and the formation of ammonia in the kidneys to neutralize acid and conserve base.

These actions of the kidneys are supplemented and influenced by other organs or systems, especially the following: lungs, through loss of fluid and excretion of bicarbonate; posterior lobe of the pituitary body, by regulation of water and electrolyte excretion from the kidney; and, finally, the adrenal cortex, through control of sodium, potassium and chloride metabolism.

In the discussion on fetal growth we have seen that after birth there is no pronounced change in the proportion of total body water to body weight. However, there is considerable change in the location of that fluid from birth until maturity. The extracellular fluid volume of the newborn infant is nearly double that of the adult, about 40% of the body weight being extracellular fluid in the newborn and 20% in the adult. (These figures are based on methods measuring the sodium space of the body, which is not strictly extracellular.) Evidence so far obtained reveals that the decrease in extracellular volume of fluid occurs mainly at two different periods of rapid growth. There is a great decrease during early infancy and a less pronounced decrease during adolescence. The intervening period is relatively constant (Table 7–11).

Not only does the infant have a greater content of extracellular fluid than the adult, but the rate at which fluids are exchanged is much greater. The average adult takes in and excretes about 2,000 ml of water daily, representing about 5% of total body fluid, or 14% of extracellular fluid. The infant's daily exchange of 600 to 700 ml of water, in contrast, represents about 20% of the total, or nearly 50% of the extracellular volume. Of the water lost, some is by surface evaporation and some through the lungs. In preterm low birth weight infants, insensible water loss is inversely proportional to gestational age. The higher loss in small infants is due to increased

TABLE 7–11.—DISTRIBUTION OF WATER IN THE BODY
AT DIFFERENT AGES*

AGE	TOTAL BODY WATER	EXTRACELLULAR WATER	INTRACELLULAR WATER
Birth	72	40	32
1 mo.	68	32	36
1 yr	64	24	40
Adult	60	20	40

*Each figure is the percentage of body weight.

heat expenditure. Term infants in the first 3 days will have an insensible water loss approximating 1 ml/kg/hr, while an infant of 28 weeks' gestation may lose twice as much. (An average adult at rest will have a loss of about 0.4 ml/kg/hr.) The daily excretion of water by the gastrointestinal tract will average 200 to 500 ml for an infant and 100 to 300 ml for an adult. It should come as no surprise to learn that control of this rapid water exchange by the infant is less precise than that achieved by the older child or adult, and consequently one sees more severe dehydration or overhydration, in the face of illness, in the less mature organism. An additional risk, in sick infants and young children, is the occasional inappropriate secretion of the antidiuretic hormone (ADH) leading to excessive water retention and hyponatremia. It is not always easy to differentiate this entity from mismanagement of fluid and electrolyte balance by the medical crew. Table 7–12 gives daily water requirements for different ages. It is offered not as a therapeutic index but as a means of illustrating the progressive changes that occur in normal subjects.

The composition of the body fluids also has some tendency to differ with age.[36, 42] The total electrolyte concentration in extracellular fluid tends to be slightly greater in the newborn subject than in the adult (as judged from blood analyses). There is a greater concentration of sodium, chloride, phosphates, and organic acids. These differences are even more striking in the premature baby. On the other hand, the concentration of bicarbonate ions is lower in the newborn infant than in the older child, and there is mild acidosis, manifested by a slightly lowered pH. These variations, plus a lowered plasma protein level, cause a reduced colloidal osmotic pressure of the vascular compartment and favor an accumulation of fluid in the tissue spaces and an increased filtration rate of the kidneys. In health these differences between the infant and the adult do not maintain themselves beyond a few weeks or months. The premature and normal newborn infants are usually in a state of well-compensated acidosis and in a state of potential

TABLE 7–12.—Daily Water
Requirements

AGE	BODY WEIGHT (KG)	WATER REQUIREMENT (ML/KG)
3 days	3.0	80–100
10 days	3.2	100–150
3 mo.	5.5	140–160
1 yr	9.5	120–140
6 yr	20.0	90–100
12 yr	38.0	60–80
Adult	70.0	20–40

or, in prematures especially, manifest edema. A study of the growth of the urinary system will aid in a better understanding of these facts.

The growth of the kidneys is slow in the early part of prenatal life and rapid in the later part. Kidney weight is doubled in the first 6 months after birth, trebled by age 1 year, and increased five times by 5 years. By puberty the increase is ten times that of the birth weight of these organs. Formation of the last renal tubules has been estimated to take place from the eighth month of gestation to the end of the first month of life. It is probable that no new glomeruli are formed after the ninth month of gestation, but throughout fetal and neonatal life the glomerular tuft is covered by a much thicker layer of cells than at any later time. This anatomical feature may explain the lowered glomerular filtration rate found during the first nine months of life, in spite of the lowered osmotic pressure of the plasma. The lower blood pressure of the infant may also play a part. All of the glomeruli increase in size after birth, but the peripheral ones grow more rapidly.[94]

At birth the kidneys occupy a large portion of the posterior abdominal wall owing to their relatively large size. Fetal lobulation persists throughout the first year. The ureters in the infant are relatively and absolutely shorter than in the adult. In the newborn the bladder lies close to the abdominal wall, and the lower level is behind the middle of the symphysis pubis. During childhood the bladder descends into the pelvis.[50]

In the fetus glomerular filtration apparently precedes tubular function, and large volumes of urine are passed into the amniotic sac from an early state of development. As tubular activity begins, an initially hypotonic and later a hypertonic urine is produced. The maximal osmolarity of the urine is low by adult standards, due to low solute excretion. Ability to form acid urine is limited, in part due to an inability to utilize phosphate buffers. This limitation continues into early postnatal life.[120] The water exchange between mother and fetus and between amniotic fluid and mother are approximately the same in early pregnancy. As pregnancy progresses, more of the fluid transfer from the amniotic sac is accomplished through the fetus.

In comparison with adult levels of renal function, neonate physiologic immaturity is evident as indicated by the following observations.[36, 53, 56, 98, 180]

1. Glomerular filtration rate is only about 30% to 50% of that of the adult and does not reach normal adult levels until late in the first year. This function is important in removing nitrogenous and other waste products from the blood. The decreased filtration is due to some or all of the following reasons: a low arterial blood pressure in the glomerulus, the smaller volume and surface area of the glomerulus available for filtration for months

after birth and the fact that many of the glomeruli are not yet morphologically well developed and are not available for physiologic function. Fortunately, much of the infant's ingested protein is totally metabolized for growth and the amount of urea presented to the kidney for removal is small.[122] Urea and inulin clearance are conventional tests in the laboratory used to measure this function.

2. A decreased ability to excrete an excessive sodium load resulting in a hypotonic urine compared with plasma. This persists throughout the neonatal and early infancy period. This may lead to an abnormal increase in weight, generalized edema and a rise in serum sodium levels. In the mature child such a load stimulates the kidney to increase glomerular filtration and decrease tubular reabsorption of sodium with consequent increase in excretion of sodium in the urine. The high concentration of aldosterone in the plasma in early infancy may play a part in this apparent lack of response of the immature kidney.

3. A decreased ability to excrete a water load, which is reflected in the urine as an inability to increase urinary volume. This ability improves rapidly over the first few weeks and reaches adult capabilities by one month. A poor response to ADH is present in early infancy, and there is some evidence that the ability to produce ADH in response to its usual stimuli is decreased for a few months after birth.[170]

4. An inability to concentrate urine even when the infant is given little or no fluids. This is thought to be due to the anatomic immaturity of the loop of Henle resulting in a decreased degree of solute gradient between it and the medullary portion of the kidney. The great variability between the degree of maturity of glomeruli and tubules in the immature kidney may account for this as well as other physiologic findings.

5. The plasma threshold for glucose is lower in newborn infants than in adults and is probably accounted for by the greater nephron heterogenity.

6. Sodium-potassium activated adenosine triphosphatase activity is lower in the immature kidney than in the mature kidney. This enzyme is an important link in the energy required for sodium reabsorption by the tubules.[92] At the moment, less is known about the maturation of other enzyme systems necessary for tubular transport.

7. The distribution of blood within the kidney varies with age and this may have functional implications. In infants up to a few months of age, a greater proportion of blood flow goes to the medullary nephrons. In adults subjected to a saline load there is a shift of blood to the cortex, which apparently facilitates sodium excretion. This temporary unique distribution of blood to the medullary area may improve the infant's ability to conserve sodium, but also interferes with the excretion of it.[36]

The finding of a relatively high hydrogen ion concentration, the limitations of the kidneys' capacity to regulate internal environment, and the lowered plasma osmotic pressure suggest that young infants have a very slight chemical margin of safety. Consequently, any disturbance such as diarrhea, infection, or improper feeding can lead rapidly to severe acidosis and abnormal fluid balance manifested by dehydration at one extreme or edema at the other. Proper recognition of these factors is vitally important from a therapeutic point of view.[121]

Although small amounts of urine are usually found in the bladder at birth, the newborn may not void for 12 to 24 hours or longer (Table 7–13). Excretion after this period is frequent. The specific gravity of the urine during the first few days is higher than during the remainder of infancy, when the average values for healthy subjects range from 1.002 to 1.008. By age 5 or 6 this value differs little from that for adults. Fluid intake and other factors obviously influence the results. The reaction of the initial urine of the newborn is acid but later approaches neutrality. Throughout the first year of life the urea content is relatively low. However, on the basis of body weight, the amount of urea excreted in 24 hours is greater in childhood than in adult life. As might be anticipated from the foregoing discussion, the concentration of phosphates, chlorides and sulfates is low early in life but gradually increases with age, especially as more solid food is added to the diet. The percentage of uric acid found in the urine in the neonatal period is much higher than it is subsequently.[3, 52] The cause of this is not known. The excretory rate of uric acid remains relatively high throughout early childhood. The relation of urinary uric acid to urea is 1:14 in the newborn and 1:70 in the adult. Creatine is excreted in variable but large amounts by the infant and to a lesser degree by children to the time of puberty, when it ceases in males and is markedly decreased in females. Creatinine output, conversely, increases throughout the growing period, the quantity being directly related to the amount of body musculature.[52] The quantity excreted by the newborn is about 1 to 3 mg/kg of body weight daily, 10 to 20 mg at age 2 years, and 20 to 40 mg at maturity.

TABLE 7–13.—AVERAGE
DAILY SECRETION OF URINE

AGE	ML/24 hr
1 and 2 days	15–50
3–10 days	50–300
10 days–2 mo.	250–400
2 mo–1 yr	400–500
1–3 yr	500–600
3–5 yr	600–750
5–8 yr	700–1,000
8–14 yr	700–1,500

The Genital Organs*

The relative weight of the testes compared with total body weight is the same in newborn and adult. Periods of active growth are in early infancy and adolescence. There is a fourfold increase in all dimensions from birth to adult life. There is a significant rise in both follicle-stimulating and luteinizing hormones associated with a rise in the plasma testosterone concentration from birth to 3 months and then a decrease by 6 months. Mean testicular volume increases during this period, nearly doubling at 3 months and then decreasing to a relatively stable size by 7 months and lasting to beginning of puberty. Some histologic changes parallel the increase in size. Leydig's cells reach a peak of development after birth and rapidly degenerate after two to three months. Gonocytes, the predominant germ cell in the neonate, disappear after the third month and Sertoli's cells undergo mitosis only during early infancy until the initiation of puberty. The seminiferous tubules at birth are solid but during childhood acquire lumens. Although spermatogonia increase in size and number during childhood, not until puberty do they mature.[187]

The testes lie at the site of the future abdominal (internal inguinal) ring from the fourth to the seventh fetal month. During the latter month they become enclosed in the tunica vaginalis, pass through the inguinal canal, and by the middle of the eighth month are usually attached to the fundus of the scrotum. In over 90% of newborns the testes are found in their final position in the scrotum. The canal is obliterated in part or in toto in more than 80% of infants over 2 months of age.[50] In a recent study by Scorer,[162] it was found that while 96% of testes were in the scrotum at birth in fully mature male infants, only 70% were descended in the prematurely born. However, in both groups, 50% of the undescended gonads did come down into the scrotum by the end of the first month of life. At the end of 1 year the incidence of undescended testicles was less than 1%, and subsequent examinations revealed no further changes.[162]

The ovaries grow rapidly during early postnatal life and have doubled their weight by age 6 months. Between the ages of 12 and 15 years their weight is again doubled (see Table 9–7). The cortex of the ovary, consisting mainly of primordial follicles, forms a thicker portion in the newborn than in later life. It has been estimated that there is a decrease of 90% in the number of ova from birth to maturity. Undeveloped and atretic graafian follicles are common in childhood.

---

*Further discussion of these organs, particularly endocrine relationships, will be found in chapter 9.

During the first weeks of life the uterus undergoes involution, and its weight is decreased by one half from that at birth. The hypertrophy originally present is due to hormone stimulus from the mother. The birth weight of the organ is not regained for about 10 or 11 years. Until adolescence the length of the cervix is twice that of the body of the uterus. Normal relationship is brought about by growth of the corpus uteri while the cervix remains relatively stationary.[50] In adults the lengths of the lumens of the cervix and uterus are about equal. The uterine and cervical glands are simple and tubular until adolescence, when they become longer and branched and undergo the changes characteristic of menstruation.

Increments of Growth

The measurement of the body at regular intervals during its period of growth reveals certain trends in the rate of change common to all normal children. Fetal curves show a phase of slow growth in the early period, a rather marked change in rate about the middle of fetal life and a rapid

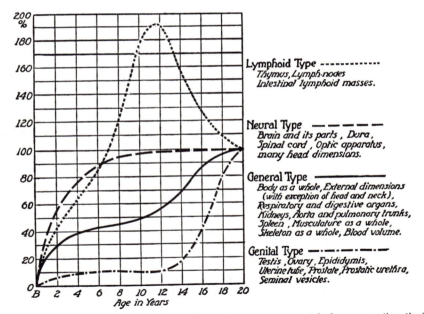

Fig 7-7.—Organ growth curves, drawn to a common scale by computing their values at successive ages in terms of their total (average) postnatal increments. (From Harris J.A., et al.: *The Measurement of Man.* Minneapolis, University of Minnesota Press, 1930.)

TABLE 7–14.—AVERAGE WEIGHTS (GM) OF ORGANS
AT DIFFERENT AGES

	NEWBORN	1 YR	6 YR	PUBERTY	ADULT
Brain	350	910	1,200	1,300	1,350
Heart	24	45	95	220	300
Thymus	12	20	24	30	0–15
Kidneys (both)	25	70	120	170	300
Liver	150	300	550	1,500	1,600
Lungs (both)	60	130	260	410	1,200
Pancreas	3	9	20	40	90
Spleen	10	30	55	95	155
Stomach	8	30	50	80	135

growth thereafter to birth (see Fig 3–1). Growth curves of children from birth to adult life have been presented in chapter 4.

Certain organ systems also undergo fairly definite patterns of growth. The organs of respiration, circulation, digestion, and excretion follow the pattern set by the body as a whole, as exemplified by height or weight curves of a child. Rapid postnatal growth, which slows in later infancy and ceases before puberty, is characteristic of the central nervous system, the eye and much of the auditory apparatus; this is known as the *neural type* of growth. The *genital type* of growth, typical of the sex organs, shows little increase during early life but a rapid development just before and coincident with puberty. The *lymphoid type* of growth is characterized by rapid growth throughout infancy and childhood, ceasing at about the time of puberty and followed by involution. This last type is typical of the tonsils and adenoids, thymus, splenic follicles, lymph nodes, and the lymphatic tissue of the intestines. The four types of growth curves are illustrated in Figure 7–7.

Table 7–14 shows the weights of various organs at different ages. (Similar figures for the endocrine organs are given in Table 9–2.)

Summary of Organ Development

Musculature   Throughout the span of growth there is an increase in muscle mass, with greatest increase during adolescence. Increase in skill, which involves musculature, is more intimately related to maturation of the nervous system.

Skin   At birth the appearance of the skin is an accurate indicator of the length of gestation. Although sweat and sebaceous glands are present at birth, the former do not function efficiently for several months and sebaceous gland function reaches maturity only with the advent of puberty.

Nervous system   Growth and maturation of the central nervous system are most rapid during infancy and early childhood, reflected in part by rapid growth of the head during this time. Increased permeability of the blood-brain barrier shortly after birth is reflected in the physical and chemical differences of the cerebrospinal fluid during early infancy and later life.

Special senses	Most of the special senses are well developed at birth, although their association with higher centers comes about gradually during early life. Vision, owing to continued growth and development of the eyes, does not assume adult level until after the middle of childhood.
Circulatory system	With birth there is considerable change in the paths and relative volumes of blood flow, reflected in the loss of certain fetal structures, and changes in the heart and major vessels. Variations in pulse rate, blood pressure, heart sounds (including functional murmurs), and rhythm characterize development of the circulatory system. There is a steady increase in blood volume throughout the growing period, but this is not directly related to size.
Lymphatic system	The entire lymphatic system is characterized by considerable growth throughout childhood, followed by involution as maturity is approached. Hyperplasia and hypertrophy may be pronounced during early life in response to infection.
Blood	Not until midchildhood does the peripheral blood picture become the same as that of the adult. The differences are apparent in the numbers and types of cells as well as response to infection and noxious agents. Chemical components of the blood fluctuate during the neonatal period, but stabilization and homeostasis are slowly achieved during the first year of life and are relatively well maintained thereafter in health.
Immunity	At birth the infant has received the most important immune globulins across the placenta at levels that are qualitatively and quantitatively equal to those of its mother. For a period of several months after delivery, although there is some ability to synthesize antibodies, the infant is immunologically less competent than in later life. For this and other reasons, there is a changing pattern of infectious disease with increasing age.
Digestive system	Although there is considerable evidence that the digestive system is immature at birth, in usual circumstances there is no impairment of absorption or utilization of the main foods except fat. Liver function, based on adult standards, is definitely immature. Roentgenographic studies of the intestinal tract reveal some changes in position of parts with growth, and some mechanical differences appear with advancing age.
Respiratory system	Initiation of respiration and the associated changes are among the most important events occurring at birth. The newborn infant possesses some immunity to anoxia; nevertheless, beyond a certain point, function of the central nervous system is jeopardized by anoxia. Breathing at first is irregular, in both rate and depth; this persists beyond the neonatal period. Until about the sixth year respiration is largely maintained by the diaphragm; subsequently the thorax plays an equally important role. Anatomical differences between child and adult are of considerable clinical importance relative to symptomatology and physical examination.
Urinary system	The kidneys are physiologically immature at birth and for nearly a year thereafter. This accounts for the ease with which fluid and electrolyte imbalances may occur during infancy with illness. Both the premature and the full-term newborn infant are in a state of well-compensated acidosis due to borderline renal function.

REFERENCES

1. Singleton E.B., Wagner M.L., Dutton R.V.: *Radiology of the Alimentary Tract in Infants and Children.* Philadelphia, W.B. Saunders Co., 1977.
2. Huffman J.W.: Disorders of the external genitalia and vagina. *Pediatr. Clin. N. Am.* 5:35, 1958.
3. Birnholz J.C., Benacerraf B.R.: The development of human fetal hearing. *Science* 222:516, 1983.
4. Sturman J., Gaull G., Räshä N.C.R.: Absence of cystathionase in human fetal liver. *Science* 169:74, 1970.

5. Oski F.A., Naiman J.L.: *Hematologic Problems in the Newborn*, ed. 2. Philadelphia, W.B. Saunders Co., 1972.
6. Smith D.W.: *Growth and Its Disorders*. Philadelphia, W.B. Saunders Co., 1977.
7. Nicolaides N.: Skin lipids: Their biochemical uniqueness. *Science* 186:19, 1974.
8. Boyd E.: Weight of the thymus gland in health and in disease. *Am. J. Dis. Child.* 43:1162, 1932.
9. McDonagh A.F., Lightner D.A.: 'Like a shrivelled blood orange': Bilirubin, jaundice, and phototherapy. *Pediatrics* 75:443, 1985.
10. Solomon L.M., Esterly N.B.: *Neonatal Dermatology*. Philadelphia, W.B. Saunders Co., 1973.
11. Brines J.K., Gibson J.G. Jr., Kunkel P.: The blood volume in normal infants and children *J. Pediatr.* 18:447, 1941.
12. Petrig B., Kropfl W., Julesz B., et al.: Development of stereopsis and cortical binocularity in human infants: Electrophysiological evidence. *Science* 213:1402, 1981.
13. Emmanouilides G., Moss A.J., Duffie E.R., et al.: Pulmonary arterial pressure in human newborn infants from birth to 3 days of age. *J. Pediatr.* 65:327, 1964.
14. Caffey J.: *Pediatric X-Ray Diagnosis*, ed. 6. Chicago, Year Book Medical Publishers, 1972.
15. Behrendt H., Green M.: *Patterns of Skin pH from Birth through Adolescence*. Springfield, Ill., Charles C Thomas, Publisher, 1971.
16. Greenwald M.J.: Visual development in infancy and childhood. *Ped. Clin. N. Am.* 30:977, 1983.
17. Conel J.L.: *The Postnatal Development of the Cerebral Cortex: Vol. I. The Cortex of the Newborn.* Cambridge, Mass., Harvard University Press, 1939.
18. Hamberger R.N.: Allergy and the immune system. *Am. Sci.* 64:157, 1976.
19. McCue C.M., Garner F.B., Hurt W.G., et al.: Placental transfusion. *J. Pediatr.* 72:15, 1968.
20. Rowe R.D., Freedman R.M., Mehrizi A., et al.: *The Neonate with Congenital Heart Disease.* Philadelphia, W.B. Saunders Co., 1981.
21. Bradfield R.B.: Hair tissue as a medium for the differential diagnosis of protein-calorie malnutrition. *J. Pediatr.* 84:294, 1974.
22. Downing M.E.: Blood pressure of normal girls from three to sixteen years of age. *Am. J. Dis. Child.* 73:293, 1947.
23. Epstein N.: The heart in normal infants and children: Incidence of precordial systolic murmurs and fluoroscopic and electrocardiographic studies. *J. Pediatr.* 32:39, 1948.
24. Mulvhill J.J., Smith D.W.: The genesis of dermatoglyphics. *J. Pediatr.* 75:579, 1969.
25. Stough T. R., Seely J.R.: Dermatoglyphics in medicine. *Clin. Pediatr.* 8:32, 1969.
26. Lemire R.J., Loesser J.D., Leech R.W., et al.: *Normal and Abnormal Development of The Human Nervous System.* New York, Harper & Row, 1975.
27. Berger L., Henrichs I., Raptis S., et al.: Gastrin concentration in plasma of the neonate at birth and after the first feeding. *Pediatrics* 58:264, 1976.
28. Moss A.J., Adams F.H.: *Problems of Blood Pressure in Childhood.* Springfield, Ill., Charles C Thomas, Publisher, 1962.

29. Harper R.M., Hoppenbrouwers T., Sterman M.B., et al.: Polygraphic studies of normal infants during the first six months of life: I. Heart rate and variability as a function of state. *Pediatr. Res.* 10:945, 1976.
30. Moss A.J., Monset-Couchard M.: Placental transfusion: Early versus late clamping of the umbilical cord. *Pediatrics* 40:109, 1967.
31. Vaughan V.C., McKay R.J.: *Nelson Textbook of Pediatrics*, ed. 10. Philadelphia, W.B. Saunders Co., 1975.
32. Gryboski J.: *Gastrointestinal Problems in the Infant*. Philadelphia, W.B. Saunders Co., 1975.
33. Kaiser A.D.: The tonsil and adenoid problem, in Brennemann J. (ed.): *Practice of Pediatrics*, vol. II. Hagerstown, Md., W.F. Prior Co., 1947.
34. Fleisher T.A., Luckasen J.R., Sabad A., et al.: T and B lymphocyte subpopulations in children. *Pediatrics* 55:162, 1975.
35. Levine S.Z., Gordon H.H.: Physiologic handicaps of the premature infant. *Am. J. Dis. Child.* 62:274, 1942.
36. Loggie J.M.H., Kleinman L.I., Van Maanen E.F.: Renal function and diuretic therapy in infants and children. *J. Pediatr.* 86:485, 1975.
37. Volpe J.J.: *Neurology of the Newborn*. Philadelphia, W.B. Saunders Co., 1981.
38. Cantor H.: Regulation of the immune system by lymphocyte sets, in Bach F.H., Good R.A. (eds.): *Clinical Immunology*, vol. IV. New York, Academia Press, 1980.
39. McMurray L., Roe J.H., Sweet L.K.: Plasma protein studies on normal newborn and premature infants. *Am. J. Dis. Child.* 75:265, 1948.
40. Mann I.C.: *Development of the Human Eye*. New York, The Macmillan Co., 1928.
41. Schulte F.J., Busse C., Eichhorn W.: Rapid eye movement sleep, motoneurone inhibition, and apneic spells in preterm infants. *Pediatr. Res.* 11:709, 1977.
42. Edelmann C.M., Spitzer A.: The maturing kidney. *J. Pediatr.* 75:509, 1969.
43. Wilson G.S., Miles A.A. (eds.): *Topley and Wilson's Principles of Bacteriology and Immunity*, ed. 4. Baltimore, Williams & Wilkins Co., 1955.
44. Otila E.: Studies on cerebrospinal fluid in premature infants. *Acta Paediatr.* (suppl. 8) 35:3, 1948.
45. Patten B.M.: *Human Embryology*, ed. 3. New York, McGraw-Hill Book Co., 1968.
46. Smith C.H.: *Blood Diseases of Infancy and Childhood*. St Louis, C.V. Mosby Co., 1960.
47. Pratt E.L., Bienvenu B., Whyte M.M.: Concentration of urine by young infants. *Pediatrics* 1:181, 1948.
48. Crook C.: Functional aspects of the chemical senses in the newborn period. *Develop. Med. Child Neurol.* 23:247, 1981.
49. Dawkins M.J.: Biochemical aspects of developing liver function. *B. Med. Bull.* 22:27, 1966.
50. Scammon R.E.: A summary of the anatomy of the infant and child, in Abt, I.A. (ed.): *Pediatrics*, vol. I. Philadelphia, W.B. Saunders Co., 1923.
51. Schachter J., Lachin J.M., Kerr J.L., et al.: Heart rate and blood pressure in black newborns and in white newborns. *Pediatrics* 58:283, 1976.
52. Smith C.A., Nelson N.M.: *The Physiology of the Newborn Infant*, ed. 4. Springfield, Ill., Charles C Thomas, Publisher, 1976.

53. Guingnard J.P.: Renal function in the newborn infant. *Ped. Clin. N. Am.* 29:777, 1982.
54. Walsh S.Z., Meyer W.W., Lind J.: *The Human Fetal and Neonatal Circulation.* Springfield, Ill., Charles C Thomas, Publisher, 1974.
55. Brown R., Pickering K.: Persistent transitional circulation. *Arch. Dis. Child.* 49:883, 1974.
56. West J.R., Smith H.W., Chasis H.: Glomerular filtration rate, effective renal blood flow and maximal tubular excretory capacity in infancy. *J. Pediatr.* 32:10, 1948.
57. White House Conference on Child Health and Protection: *Growth and Development of the Child:* Pt. II. Anatomy and physiology. New York, Century Co., 1933.
58. Hernandez A., Goldring D., Hartman A.F.: Measurement of blood pressure in infants and children by the Doppler ultrasonic technique. *Pediatrics* 48:788, 1971.
59. Milner A.D., Vyas H.: Lung expansion at birth. *J. Pediatr.* 101:879, 1982.
60. Cowan W.M.: The development of the brain. *Sci. Am.* 241:113, 1979.
61. Cousin A.J.: Advanced methods for measurement of fetal breathing movements in the human fetus. *Sem. Perinatol.* 4:261, 1980.
62. Windle W.F.: *Physiology of the Fetus.* Philadelphia, W.B. Saunders Co., 1940.
63. Wintrobe M.M.: *Clinical Hematology,* ed. 6. Philadelphia, Lea & Febiger, 1967.
64. Challacombe D.N., Edkins, S., Brown G.A.: Duodenal bile acids in infancy. *Arch. Dis. Child.* 50:837, 1975.
65. Wara D.W., Barret D.J.: Cell-mediated immunity in the newborn: Clinical aspects. *Pediatrics* 64:822, 1979.
66. Burnard E.D.: The cardiac murmur in relation to symptoms in the newborn. *Br. Med. J.* 1:134, 1959.
67. Forfar J.O., Kibel M.A.: Blood pressure in the newborn estimated by the flush method *Arch. Dis. Child.* 31:126, 1956.
68. Moss A.J., Liebling W., Austin W.O., et al.: An evaluation of the flush method for determining blood pressure in infants. *Pediatrics* 20:53, 1957.
69. Fogel D.H.: The innocent (functional) cardiac murmur in children. *Pediatrics* 19:793, 1957.
70. Richards M.R., Merritt K.K., Samuels M.H., et al.: Frequency and significance of cardiac murmurs in the first year of life. *Pediatrics* 16:169, 1955.
71. Russell S.J.M.: Blood volume studies in healthy children. *Arch. Dis. Child.* 24:88, 1949.
72. Sturgeon P.: Volumetric and microscopic patterns of bone marrow in normal infants and children: I. Volumetric pattern. II. Cytologic pattern. *Pediatrics* 7:577, 642, 1951.
73. Walker J., Turnbull E.P.N.: Hemoglobin and red cells in the human fetus: III. Foetal and adult hemoglobin. *Arch. Dis. Child.* 30:111, 1955.
74. Cook, C.D., Brodie H.R., Allen D.W.: Measurement of fetal hemoglobin in newborn infants. Correlation with gestation age and intrauterine hypoxia. *Pediatrics* 20:272, 1957.
75. Janix J.H.P., Visser H.K.A.: Determination of low percentages of fetal hemoglobin in blood of normal children. *Am. J. Dis. Child.* 92:588, 1956.

76. Karlberg P., Lind J.: Studies of the total amount of hemoglobin and the blood volume in children. *Acta Paediatr.* 44:17, 1955.
77. Marks J., Gairdner D., Roscoe J.D.: Blood formation in infancy: III. Cord blood. *Arch. Dis. Child.* 30:117, 1955.
78. Seip M.: The reticulocyte level and the erythrocyte production judged from reticulocyte studies in newborn infants during the first week of life. *Acta Paediatr.* 44:355, 1955.
79. Orlandini O., Sass-Kortsak T.A., Ebbs J.H.: Serum gamma globulin levels in normal infants. *Pediatrics* 16:575, 1955.
80. Henley W.: The immunoglobulins. *Pediatr. Ann.* 5:372, 1976.
81. Platt O.S.: Newborn bleeding disorders. *Pediatr. Ann.* 8:55, 1979.
82. Bach F.H., Good R.A.: *Clinical Immunobiology,* vol. I. New York, Academic Press, 1972.
83. Gell P.G.H., Coombs R.R.A.: *Clinical Aspects of Immunology.* Philadelphia, F.A. Davis Co., 1968.
84. Frimann-Dahl J., Lind J., Wigelius C.: Roentgen investigations of neonatal gaseous content of the intestinal tract. *Acta Radiol.* 41:256, 1954.
85. Thompson J.: The volume and acidity of the gastric contents in the unfed newborn infant. *Arch. Dis. Child.* 26:558, 1951.
86. Hallbrecht I., Brzoza H.: Evaluation of hepatic function in newborn infants by means of chemical study of cord blood. *Am. J. Dis. Child.* 79:988, 1950.
87. Sherry S.N., Kramer I.: The time of passage of the first stool and first urine by the newborn infant. *J. Pediatr.* 46:158, 1955.
88. Nyhan W.L.: Stool frequency of normal infants in the first week of life. *Pediatrics* 10:414, 1952.
89. Graham B.D., Wilson J.L.: Chemical control of respiration in newborn infants. *Am. J. Dis. Child.* 87:287, 1954.
90. Jones H.E.: The vital capacity of children. *Arch. Dis. Child.* 30:445, 1955.
91. Ferris B.G. Jr., Smith C.W.: Maximum breathing capacity and vital capacity in female children and adolescents. *Pediatrics* 12:341, 1953.
92. Yoshida T.: Substrate metabolism and renal function. *Pediatr. Clin. N. Am.* 23:627, 1976.
93. McCance R.A., Widdowson E.M.: Protein catabolism and renal function in the first two days of life in premature infants and multiple births. *Arch. Dis. Child.* 30:405, 1955.
94. McCrory W.W.: *Developmental Nephrology.* Cambridge, Mass., Harvard University Press, 1972.
95. Prindull G.: Maturation of cellular and humoral immunity during human embryonic development. *Acta Paediatr. Scand.* 63:607, 1974.
96. Fellers F.X., Barnett H.T., Hare K., et al.: Change in thiocyanate and sodium[24] spaces during growth. *Pediatrics* 3:622, 1949.
97. Slater R.J., Sass-Kortsak A.: The turnover and circulation of the plasma proteins in the body. *Am. J. Med. Sci.* 231:669, 1956.
98. Howell R.R.: Diagnostic enzymology, in Cook R.E. (ed.): *The Biological Basis of Pediatric Practice.* New York, McGraw-Hill Book Co., 1968.
99. Lind J., Stern L., Wegelius C.: *Human Foetal and Neonatal Circulation.* Springfield, Ill., Charles C Thomas, Publisher, 1964.
100. Gairdner D., Marks J., Roscoe J.D., et al.: The fluid shift from the vascular compartment immediately after birth. *Arch. Dis. Child.* 33:489, 1958.

101. Nadas A.S., Fyler D.C.: *Pediatric Cardiology*, ed. 3. Philadelphia, W.B. Saunders Co., 1972.
102. Reeve R., DeBoer K.: Sinus arrhythmia: Data and patterns from groups of individuals followed from 1 month to 23 years of age. *Pediatrics* 26:402, 1960.
103. Sisson T.R.C., Whalen L.E.: The blood volume of infants, alterations in the first hours after birth. *J. Pediatr.* 56:43, 1960.
104. Clark A.C.L., Gairdner D.: Postnatal plasma shift in premature infants. *Arch. Dis. Child.* 35:352, 1960.
105. Schell N.B., Karelitz S., Epstein B.S.: Radiographic study of gastric emptying in premature infants. *J. Pediatr.* 62:342, 1963.
106. Cornblath M., Schwartz R.: *Disorders of Carbohydrate Metabolism in Infancy*. Philadelphia, W.B. Saunders Co., 1966.
107. Hemmings W.A.: Protein transfer across the fetal membranes. *Br. Med. Bull.* 17:96, 1961.
108. Valadian I., Stuart H.C., Reed R.B.: Patterns of illness experiences. *Pediatrics* 24:941, 1959.
109. Lin S., Schoenbaum S.C., Monson R.R., et al.: Epidemiology of neonatal hyperbilirubinemia. *Pediatrics* 75:770, 1985.
110. Cashore W.J., Stern L.: Neonatal hyperbilirubinemia. *Ped. Clin. N. Am.* 29:1191, 1982.
111. Oppe T.E., Gibbs I.E.: Sulphobromophthalein excretion in premature infants. *Arch. Dis. Child.* 34:125, 1959.
112. Ames M.D.: Gastric acidity in the first ten days of life of the prematurely born baby. *Am. J. Dis. Child.* 100:252, 1960.
113. Borgstrom B., Lindquist B., Lundh G.: Enzyme concentration and absorption of protein and glucose in duodenum of premature infants. *Am. J. Dis. Child.* 99:338, 1960.
114. Sell E.J., Corrigan J.J.: Platelet counts, fibrinogen concentrations, and factor V and factor VII levels in healthy infants according to gestational age. *J. Pediatr.* 82:1028, 1973.
115. Edelman G.M.: Antibody structure and molecular immunology. *Science* 180:830, 1973.
116. Karlberg P.: The adaptive changes in the immediate postnatal period, with particular reference to respiration. *J. Pediatr.* 56:585, 1960.
117. Vyas H., Milner A.D., Hopkin, I.E.: Intrathoracic pressure and volume changes during the spontaneous onset of respiration in babies born by cesarean section and by vaginal delivery. *J. Pediatr.* 99:787, 1981.
118. Lyons H.A., Tanner R.W., Picco T.: Pulmonary function studies in children. *Am. J. Dis. Child.* 100:196, 1960.
119. Bernstein I.L., Fragge R.G., Gueron M., et al.: Pulmonary function in children: I. Determination of norms. *J. Allergy Clin. Immunol.* 30:514, 1959.
120. Alexander D.P., Nixon D.A.: The foetal kidney. *Br. Med. Bull.* 17:112, 1961.
121. Edelmann C.M., Barnett H.L.: Role of the kidney in water metabolism in young infants. *J. Pediatr.* 56:154, 1960.
122. McCance R.A.: The maintenance of stability in the newly born. *Arch. Dis. Child.* 34:361, 1959.
123. Van Creveld S.: Coagulation disorders in the newborn period. *J. Pediatr.* 97:633, 1959.
124. Richter D.: Enzymic activity during early development. *Br. Med. Bull.* 17:118, 1961.

125. Driscoll S.G., Hsia D.Y.-Y.: The development of enzyme systems during early infancy. *Pediatrics* 22:785, 1958.
126. Kretchmer N.: Enzymatic patterns during development. *Pediatrics* 25:606, 1959.
127. Sereni F., Principi N.: The development of enzyme systems. *Pediatr. Clin. N. Am.* 12:515, 1965.
128. Pojerova A., Tovarek J.: On enzymatic activity in the neonatal period. *Acta Paediatr.* 48:213, 1959.
129. Done A.K.: Developmental pharmacology. *Clin. Pharmacol. Ther.* 5:432, 1964.
130. Heald F.P., Hunt E.E., Schwartz R., et al.: Measures of body fat and hydration in adolescent boys. *Pediatrics* 31:226, 1963.
131. Wenzel J.E., Burgert E.O.: The spider nevus in infancy and childhood. *Pediatrics* 33:227, 1964.
132. Iverson L.L.: The chemistry of the brain. *Sci. Am.* 241:134, 1979.
133. Despland P.-A., Galambos R.: The auditory brain stem response is a useful diagnostic tool in the intensive care nursery. *Pediatr. Res.* 14:154, 1980.
134. Field T.M., Woodson R., Greenberg R., et al.: Discrimination and imitation of facial expressions by neonates. *Science* 218:179, 1982.
135. Fois A.: *The Electroencephalogram of the Normal Child.* Springfield, Ill., Charles C Thomas, Publisher, 1961.
136. Engel R.: Maturational changes and abnormalities in the newborn electroencephalogram. *Dev. Med. Child Neurol.* 7:498, 1965.
137. Rosen M.G., Satran R.: The neonatal electroencephalogram. *Am. J. Dis. Child.* 111:133, 1966.
138. Brazelton T.B., Scholl M.L., Robey J.S.: Visual response in the newborn. *Pediatrics* 37:284, 1966.
139. Mattingly R.F., Larks S.D.: The fetal electrocardiogram. *J.A.M.A.* 183:245, 1963.
140. Vanoni R.P.: Rilievi electrocardiografici del neonato immaturo. *Minerva Pediatr.* 10:1041, 1958.
141. Levine O.R., Griffiths S.P., Levine, A.: Electrocardiographic findings in healthy premature infants. *Pediatrics* 30:361, 1962.
142. Jegier W., Blankenship W., Lind J., et al.: The changing circulatory pattern of the newborn infant studied by the indicator dilution technique. *Acta Paediatr.* 53:541, 1964.
143. Buckels L.J., Usher R.: Cardiopulmonary effects of placental transfusion. *J. Pediatr.* 67:239, 1965.
144. Oh W., Lind J., Gessuer I.H.: The circulatory and respiratory adaptation to early and late cord clamping in newborn infants. *Acta Paediatr. Scand.* 55:17, 1966.
145. Moss A.J., Duffie E.R., Emmanouilides G.: Blood pressure and vasomotor reflexes in the newborn infant. *Pediatrics* 32:175, 1963.
146. Young M.: Blood pressure in the newborn baby. *Br. Med. Bull.* 17:154, 1961.
147. Steele M.W.: Plasma volume changes in the neonate. *Am. J. Dis. Child.* 103:42, 1962.
148. Usher R., Lind J.: Blood volume of the newborn premature infant. *Acta Paediatr. Scand.* 54:419, 1965.
149. Winkelstein J.A.: Opsonins: Their function, identity and clinical significance. *J. Pediatr.* 82:747, 1973.

150. Garby L., Sjolin S., Vuille J.-E.: Studies on erythro-kinetics in infancy: V. Estimation of the life span of red blood cells in the newborn. *Acta Paediatr.* 53:165, 1964.
151. Medoff H.S.: Platelet counts in premature infants. *J. Pediatr.* 64:287, 1964.
152. Albrecht R.M., Hong R.: Basic and clinical considerations of the monocyte-macrophage system in man. *J. Pediatr.* 88:751, 1976.
153. Haworth J.C., Norris M., Dilling L.: A study of the immunoglobulin in premature infants. *Arch. Dis. Child.* 40:243, 1965.
154. Walker W.A.: Host defense mechanisms in the gastrointestinal tract. *Pediatrics* 57:901, 1976.
155. Glasgow L.A.: Interferon: A review. *J. Pediatr.* 67:104, 1965.
156. Miller J.F.A.P.: The thymus and the development of immunologic responsiveness. *Science* 144:1544, 1964.
157. Gryboski J.D.: The swallowing mechanism in the neonate: Esophageal and gastric motility. *Pediatrics* 35:445, 1965.
158. Avery M.E., Fletcher B.D., Williams R.G.: *The Lung and Its Disorders in The Newborn Infant.* Philadelphia, W.B. Saunders Co., 1982.
159. Richards J.M., Alexander J.R., Shinebourne E.A., et al.: Sequential 22-hour profiles of breathing patterns and heart rate in 110 full-term infants during their first 6 months of life. *Pediatrics* 74:763, 1984.
160. De Muth G.R., Howatt W.F., Hill B.M.: The growth of lung function. *Pediatrics* 35:161, 1965.
161. Lawson J.S., Hewstone A.S.: Microscopic appearance of urine in the neonatal period. *Arch. Dis. Child.* 39:287, 1964.
162. Scorer C.G.: The descent of the testes. *Arch. Dis. Child.* 39:609, 1964.
163. McDonagh A.F., Lightner D.A.: 'Like a shrivelled blood orange': Bilirubin, jaundice and phototherapy. *Pediatrics* 75:443, 1985.
164. Phelan P.D., Williams H.E.: Ventilatory studies in healthy infants. *Pediatr. Res.* 3:425, 1969.
165. Lawton A.R., Cooper M.D.: B cell ontogeny: Immunoglobulin genes and their expression. *Pediatrics* 64:750, 1979.
166. Editorial comment: Measurement of skinfold thickness in childhood. *Pediatrics* 42:538, 1968.
167. Naidoo B.T.: Cerebrospinal fluid in healthy newborn infants. *S. Afr. Med. J.* 42:933, 1968.
168. Winick M.: Malnutrition and brain development. *J. Pediatr.* 74:667, 1969.
169. Park M.K., Guntheroth W.G.: Direct blood pressure measurements in brachial and femoral arteries in children. *Circulation* 41:231, 1970.
170. Janovsky M., Martinek J., Stanincova V.: Antidiuretic activity in the plasma of human infants after a load of sodium chloride. *Acta Paediatr. Scand.* 54:543, 1965.
171. Dayton G.O., Jones M.H., Rawson R.A., et al.: Developmental study of coordinated eye movements in the human infant. *Arch. Ophthalmol.* 71:865, 1964.
172. Nelson L.B., Rubin S.E., Wagner R.S., et al.: Developmental aspects in the assessment of visual function in young children. *Pediatrics* 73:375, 1984.
173. Ross E.D., Velez-Borras J., Rosman N.P.: The significance of the Babinski sign in the newborn—a reappraisal. *Pediatrics* 57:13, 1976.
174. Dobbing J.: The later development of the brain and its vulnerability, in Davis J.A., Dobbing J. (eds.): *Scientific Foundations of Paediatrics.* Philadelphia, W.B. Saunders Co., 1974.

175. Purpura D.P., Shofer R.J.: Principles of synaptogenesis and their application to ontogenetic studies of mammalian cerebral cortex, in Clemente C.D., Purpura D.P., Mayer F.E. (eds.): *Sleep and the Maturing Nervous System.* New York, Academic Press, 1972.

176. Moynahan E.J.: The developmental biology of the skin, in Davis J.A., Dobbing J. (eds.): *Scientific Foundations of Paediatrics.* Philadelphia, W.B. Saunders Co., 1974.

177. Caramihai E., Karayalcin G., Aballi A.J., et al.: Leukocyte count differences in healthy white and black children 1 to 5 years of age. *J. Pediatr.* 86:252, 1975.

178. Williams R.F.: Colonization of the developing body by bacteria, in Davis J.A., Dobbing J. (eds.): *Scientific Foundation of Paediatrics.* Philadelphia, W.B. Saunders Co., 1974.

179. Dawes G.S.: Breathing before birth in animals and man. *N. Engl. J. Med.* 290:557, 1974.

180. Kenney R.A.: Renal function. *Pediatr. Clin. N. Am.* 24:651, 1976.

181. Ford J.E., Law B.A., Marshall V.M.E., et al.: Influence of the heat treatment of human milk on some of its protective constituents. *J. Pediatr.* 90:29, 1977.

182. Goldman A.S., Smith C.W.: Host resistance factors in human milk. *J. Pediatr.* 82:1082, 1973.

183. Shannon D.A., Felix J.K., Krumholz A., et al.: Hearing screening of high-risk newborns with brainstem auditory evoked potentials: A follow-up study. *Pediatrics* 73:22, 1984.

184. Kattwinkel J.: Neonatal apnea: Pathogenesis and therapy. *J. Pediatr.* 90:342, 1977.

185. Reid L.: Influence of the pattern of structural growth of lung on susceptibility to specific infections in infants and children. *Pediatr. Res.* 11:210, 1977.

186. Cowan W.M., Fawcett J.W., O'Leary D.D.M., et al.: Regressive events in neurogenesis. *Science* 225:1258, 1984.

187. Cassoria F.G., Golden S.M., Johnsonbaugh R.E., et al.: Testicular volume during early infancy. *J. Pediatr.* 99:742, 1981.

8 / Osseous Development

> Perhaps there is nothing more remarkable
> than the order to which Providence has
> subjected the growth of our bodies.
> —Jacques Quetelet

BONE ALWAYS DEVELOPS by the transformation of preexisting connective tissue. One of these tissues is mesenchyme and the other is cartilage. Bone formation in mesenchyme is referred to as intramembranous ossification and forms the skull, face, ribs, and vertebral bodies. Bone formation in cartilage is known as endochondral ossification and is best exemplified in the bones of the extremities. The models, primordial mesenchyme or cartilage, of the pectoral girdle and upper limb bones appear slightly before those of the pelvic girdle and lower limbs, thus following the cephalocaudal pattern of development. Calcification begins at 8 to 9 weeks and this event is used in establishing the end of the embryonic period and the beginning of the fetus.[13]

The human skeleton passes through the successive stages of connective tissue, cartilage, and bone, and only articular cartilage in the joints persists into adult life as a remnant of the original primordial tissue. Initial ossification appears near the center of the shaft of long bones. In the middle of the bone endochondral tissue produces the matrix, which subsequently undergoes ossification. Simultaneously, on the surface, the periosteum is producing its matrix for eventual bone formation. Both processes are important in remodeling that continues throughout the life span. As growth proceeds, cartilaginous concentrations appear at the ends of each bone to become the epiphyses. At birth, ossification has taken place along the shafts, diaphyses, of all of the long bones and thus they are radiologically visible. With only a few exceptions, most epiphyses become calcified after birth and in a largely predictable order. Linear growth continues as long as there is proliferation of cartilage cells in the epiphyseal plate. These cells, as with other endochondral tissues, lay down the matrix for future osseous formation. Growth ceases when the epiphyseal plate becomes calcified and the diaphysis and epiphysis become fused. These changes are very useful as indicators of maturation of the growing organism.[5-7, 15]

From birth to 4 years the cut surface of a long bone shows a pink texture of trabeculae interspersed with rich red marrow. From 4 to 7 years fat gradually accumulates in droplets, and by 7 years the bony trabeculae have given place to a real marrow cavity. Between 12 and 14 years there is a patch of fat in the midlength of the bone, extending toward both extremities. Changes in the epiphyses of the long bones are comparable to those in the shaft, but the bone trabeculae do not become absorbed and fatty changes are completed by 19 or 20 years. These changes closely parallel the dates of fusion of the epiphyses except in the upper part of the femur. Tibia, sternum, pelvic bones, and vertebrae contain red marrow throughout life, and adult distribution is attained at about 25 years, which roughly corresponds to the date of fusion of their epiphyses.

The skeleton is not only a supporting organ but is also a reservoir of calcium, phosphate, and magnesium ions that can function to stabilize the concentration of these ions in extracellular fluid. The control of concentration of these ions depends upon (1) net entrance of the ion in extracellular fluid from the intestine, (2) balance between flow of ions into bone mineral and their reentrance into the extracellular fluid through solubilization of bone mineral, (3) the balance between uptake and discharge of intracellular ions, and (4) urinary excretion of the ions. Reactions 1 and 2 are the major factors in calcium homeostasis while 2, 3, and 4 are of importance in phosphate homeostasis. Three major hormones largely control concentrations in body fluids and their flow into or out of bone mineral. They are vitamin D hormone, parathyroid hormone, and calcitonin. (See also the material in chapter 9 concerning these hormones.) In very simple terms, at this point, the main action of vitamin D hormone is to increase calcium absoption from the gut, parathyroid hormones increases phosphate excretion through the kidneys, and calcitonin inhibits bone resorption and solubilization of bone minerals.[10, 17, 39]

Collagen and mucopolysacchride form the organic matrix of bone and cartilage. Bone cells make up only a very small fraction of the total mass of bone but they are the controlling units responding to physical and mechanical stress with remodeling (the removal of old bone and formation of new) and to metabolic demands by uptake or release of calcium, phosphate, magnesium, and other ions that might enter the extracellular fluids such as heavy metals, fluoride, or radium. The osteoblast, which some consider to be one form of bone cell that can also assume other forms and functions, produces collagen and plays an important part in matrix mineralization through alkaline phosphate synthesis. Osteocytes are present in the lacunae in mineralized bone and maintain the integrity of the matrix. Osteoclasts are the largest cells and are principally responsible for the dissolution of bone, both mineral as well as organic matrix.[10]

Bone formation and bone growth are not strictly different phenomenon in considering bone metabolism. Bone-derived growth factors produced by osteoprogenitor cells stimulate DNA synthesis and new bone formation. Another bone morphogenic protein induces mesenchymal-type cells to become bone cells. Both are peptides and their precise role in total bone growth is still uncertain.[37] Among the systemic hormones, growth hormone appears to be essential for linear growth possibly through endochondral cell proliferation. This hormone action is mediated by the somatomedins and insulin. Thyroxine is also essential for bone growth, though its action may be more permissive than direct through its profound influence on general metabolism. The sex hormones probably have some effect on growth but far more on maturational changes.[10, 17, 37]

Since bone has the principal function of mechanical support, local factors such as pull of gravity and forces associated with other tissues, e.g., tendons, muscles, and teeth, will influence growth, shape, and density of skeletal tissue. Dissuse atrophy of bones in paralyzed limbs or the mandible of an edentulous individual are further examples. An interesting cause of stimuli to bone growth is venous stasis or fistula and severe pulmonary or cardiac malfunction with poor oxygen arterial saturation and elevated venous CO_2 levels. Such changes are responsible for pulmonary osteoarthropathy (clubbing of the distal phalanges) and increased length and circumference of long bones in affected extremities.[38]

For bone to maintain its proper form while it lengthens and thickens, the growth process involves progressive remodeling, with formation and resorption of all parts of the bone as its dimensions alter. This remodeling begins during the fetal period but is greatly accelerated after birth. The mechanical stresses on the skeleton as the infant becomes increasingly more active and mobile stimulate bone growth and especially remodeling. The annual rate of bone renewal during the first two years after birth is 50% compared with a rate of 5% in the adult. Although remodeling is most active during the growth period it continues throughout life in response to stresses brought about by an individual's changing physical activity.

Measuring Skeletal Maturation

Roentgenologic study of the bones may be of great aid to the pediatrician in evaluating physical development from birth through adulthood. Essentially the record of osseous development depends on two features: growth of the area undergoing ossification, and deposition of calcium in that area. The two do not necessarily keep pace with each other, nor are they always present together. In this chapter will be discussed various methods that have been successfully used in the study of osseous development and their application to measurements of normal growth and development of the child.

The appearance and union of the various centers of ossification follow a fairly definite pattern and time schedule from birth to maturity. This process provides, through x-ray studies, a valuable criterion for estimating normal and abnormal growth. The skeletal maturity of any individual is known as the *bone age*. It must be realized that in this field, as in others in which measurements of growth are made, there is no simple formula for deriving or evaluating growth trends.

Normal osseous development may be disturbed by a number of abnormalities that are specific as to cause and effect, and by others that are less specific in relation to bone but affect the entire organism. The specific factors may be outlined as follows:

1. Inability to respond to the growth hormone. The most striking example of this is achondroplasia, in which proliferation of cartilage is disturbed and linear growth and maturation are retarded.
2. The formation of normal bone matrix is compromised. Since the matrix is made up of protein, a very low protein intake, as experienced in the underdeveloped countries, may cause deficiencies in formation. Scurvy is a classic example of a condition with poorly formed bone matrix. Excesses of corticosteroids in Cushing's disease or with therapy interfere with normal matrix formation.
3. Abnormal mineralization of bony matrix. Several possibilities must be considered here.
   a. Deficiency of the enzymes that free calcium and phosphorus from their organic combinations and allow them to be deposited. Hypophosphatasia is an inborn error of metabolism resulting in poor mineralization due to nearly complete absence of alkaline phosphatase in all tissues. In both hypothyroidism and scurvy, phosphatase content is markedly decreased, which undoubtedly contributes to the delayed mineralization so characteristic of these diseases.
   b. Acidosis (lowered pH of the blood), as seen in chronic renal failure, interferes with mineralization by increasing the ionization of calcium and its solubility product so that its deposition does not occur in the protein matrix.
   c. Concentrations of various substances in the serum bathing the bony matrix will influence the deposition of calcium and phosphorus. The relation of the parathyroid glands in this respect will be discussed in the following chapter. Renal abnormalities associated with low serum

phosphorus, e.g., resistant rickets ("phosphate diabetes"), or renal failure associated with low serum calcium will decrease mineralization. Howland's rule that the product of serum calcium and phosphorus must exceed 35 for the healing of rickets, though subject to some question, still applies in general to these conditions. Relative excesses of serum protein, by binding the calcium, will also interfere.

d. Lack of absorption of the necessary constituents of bone from the intestinal tract is another factor. Vitamin D deficiency and the various malabsorption syndromes are examples of such conditions.

Bone maturation is particularly influenced by the androgenic and estrogenic hormones. Precocious development associated with adrenal hyperplasia, gonadal or brain tumors and iatrogenic causes invariably will advance skeletal development. Obesity is another condition in which there is slight but definite acceleration of the bone age. Chronic malnutrition, chronic or repeated severe infections and hypogonadism produce some degree of retardation. The most marked delay in skeletal maturation is seen in hypothyroidism (see Figs 8–20 and 8–21). Intrauterine infections, especially rubella, and many of the chromosomal abnormalities are associated with a retarded bone age as well as with other bony anomalies. Most other genetic causes of variations in skeletal development have more subtle effects.[12, 16]

Equally as important as dealing with the more severe forms of pathology, is the study of normal variations if we hope to establish standards that will be useful in the clinical care of children, the anthropologic studies of populations or epidemiologic evaluations of environmental influences. There is little question that certain aspects of the order and rate of maturation are under genetic control. The black, for example, shows a more rapid maturation than the white.[14] Interestingly enough, if one studies individual bones in each race, one finds that all bones are not uniformly ahead or behind, e.g., the phalanges in blacks are slightly behind those of white children.[36] From early childhood girls are ahead of boys for a few months and the difference increases with advancing age (Tables 8–1 and 8–2).[5, 14, 24]

The methods for assessment of skeletal maturation or bone age can be divided into three categories with some additional variations.

1. Roentgen films of the subject being studied are compared to a standard atlas of the same anatomical part.[18, 27, 28] The atlases have been compiled from a large number of children selected at 3- to 6-month age intervals and accounting for sex differences. The advantages of this method are it is well established; it is simple in technique; since only one anatomical area is used, the exposure to radiation is minimal. The

TABLE 8–1.—PRESENCE OF SIX OSSIFICATION CENTERS IN ROENTGENOGRAMS OF NEWBORNS*

OSSIFICATION CENTER	UNDER 2,000	2,000–2,499	2,500–2,999	3,000–3,499	3,500–3,999	4,000 OR MORE
			BIRTH WEIGHT (GM)			
Calcaneus						
White boys	100.0					
girls	100.0					
Black boys	100.0					
girls	100.0					
Astragalus						
White boys	72.7	100.0				
girls	83.3	100.0				
Black boys	90.9	100.0				
girls	100.0	100.0				
Distal femoral epiphysis						
White boys	9.1	75.0	85.3	100.0	100.0	
girls	50.0	91.7	98.0	100.0	100.0	
Black boys	18.2	88.5	90.7	94.0	100.0	
girls	50.2	93.8	99.0	100.0	100.0	
Proximal femoral epiphysis						
White boys	0.0	18.8	52.9	78.8	84.1	97.1
girls	0.0	54.2	75.5	85.7	90.7	90.5
Black boys	0.0	38.5	62.7	76.0	80.0	92.9
girls	14.3	40.6	76.7	88.1	86.4	100.0
Cuboid						
White boys	0.0	6.2	14.7	39.8	44.3	60.0
girls	0.0	37.5	57.1	65.2	70.4	76.2
Black boys	0.0	23.1	43.8	58.0	68.2	100.0
girls	21.4	37.5	68.0	78.2	81.8	75.0
Head of humerus						
White boys	0.0	7.7	13.8	41.9	49.0	59.1
girls	0.0	5.6	25.8	41.9	69.4	86.7
Black boys	0.0	0.0	15.2	27.6	48.4	63.6
girls	0.0	10.7	22.7	52.6	38.9	100.0

*Modified from Christie.[3] Figures in each column are percentage of infants in whom the center was present. With some variations, incidence is higher in black than in white infants and in girls than in boys for a particular weight group.

TABLE 8–2.—Percentage of Children in Whom Specified Carpal Bones Have Appeared*

BONE	SEX	B	1	2	3	4	5	6	7	8	9	10	11	12	13	14	15	16
Capitate	F	8	96	100														
	M	2	98	100														
Hamate	F	8	96	100														
	M	2	98	100														
Triangularis	F	0	20	52	79	100												
	M	0	22	50	57	92	84	93	100									
Lunate	F		8	32	50	80	91	99	100									
	M		8	18	36	64	64	87	98	99	100							
Navicular	F				12	30	61	95	99									
	M					4	17	34	51	75	92	99	100					
Multangulum major	F				4	18	53	74	94	99								
	M					4	14	33	51	72	88	96	97	100				
Multangulum minor	F					15	40	65	95	100								
	M					4	22	29	48	81	95	100						
Pisiform	F										1	19	50	79	96	100		
	M									2	6	22	28	66	95	99	99	100

*From Nelson,[10] after Flory.

disadvantages include the wide chronologic age variation included in the individual atlas standard; the necessity of sometimes using relatively insignificant and unreliable changes in moving from one age standard to the next; a fairly wide variation in each individual's interpretation of the differences between standards and between the standard compared to the film in question (see Figs 8–5 to 8–21).

2. A method that totals the time of appearance of a number of secondary (epiphyseal) centers and attributes a maturity rating or age level to the number present.[11] It was initially thought that using a large number of centers would eliminate some of the problems posed by the use of atlases. This is doubtful. Since all areas must be considered, undue attention can be attributed to the appearance or lack of appearance of calcification, or its size, of centers that have been found to have such normal variations as to be very unreliable as predictors. An additional disadvantage is that multiple areas are exposed to radiation.

3. In this method, a scoring system is based upon such factors as appearance of calcification, degree of radiopacity, size, shape, and fusion of epiphyses and diaphyses.[5, 8, 32] In some instances specified areas were designated as being the most reliable for different age ranges. Most authorities using these techniques found that often the carpals and tarsals, featured prominently in some of the atlases, were quite unsuitable indicators of maturity. Consequently, specific bones and detailed descrip-

tions of stages of development that can be seen on the films are used in the scoring. Although these methods seem highly reliable in the hands of the investigators, in the usual clinical setting they have as many errors of prediction as do the others previously described. The means of interpretation are more complex and, therefore, the method is more difficult to teach to others. It takes a considerably greater amount of time to reach a conclusion.[1, 4]

As a result of the attempts to develop the ideal approach to determining skeletal maturity and interpreting its significance, a number of very important findings have resulted.[2, 3, 5] The variations in sex and race have been pointed out and are apparent in some of the tables in this chapter. The standards established by Greulich and Pyle,[18] undoubtedly the most frequently used method in the United States, have been shown to be slightly in advance of the average child in the present generation. This is a finding of the recent USPHS survey.[35, 36] When assessed against the atlas standards, the skeletal ages of the boys were less than their chronologic ages by 2.5 months at 6 years and 13.8 months at 11 years. The differences in girls were similar but not as great: 1.0 month at 6 years and 9.8 months at 11 years.

The correlation of chronologic age with skeletal age is slightly better for girls than for boys, in part, because there is a narrower range of normal variability in the pattern of bone development. It has also been found that this range of variability is more affected by adverse circumstances, e.g., malnutrition, in boys than in girls. Using Sheldon's terminology of body type (see chapter 4), there is a tendency for the endomorphic girl and the mesomorphic boy to have more advanced bone age than other body types of the same sex.[5] The association of advanced skeletal maturity in long-existing obesity is well recognized.[5]

Less easily defined are some of the genetic influences on growth and skeletal maturation unrelated to sex or race. Some children are normally slower in realizing their growth potential than most of their peers. They remain small, but usually above the lowest percentiles on the standard growth charts. Their bone age is compatible with their height age and this finding can usually be interpreted as a reassuring indication of normal adult stature. See also the discussion of delayed adolescence (constitutional slow growth) in chapter 13. Bayley[15] and her co-workers have supplied us with a useful means of predicting adult height based on present height and present bone age (see Figs 4–10 and 4–11). How much variation can be found in the degree of skeletal maturation in normal children? This will vary depending upon the technique used. The Greulich and Pyle[18] atlas gives a standard deviation of 6 months at 3 years and 16 months by 11 years. Added to this is the variation in interpretation by individual radiologists that may be considerable when evaluating identical films.[20] Figure 8–18 is an excellent example to illustrate two principles. The apparent asymmetry between the right and left side of the body may seem very great and has been used as an argument against using a roentgenograph of a single area, such as the wrist. If, however, one recognizes that the variability of the carpal bones is too great to make them useful in such evaluations, the apparent discrepancy is resolved.[8, 32]

Although the USPHS survey did not reveal any geographic differences in the United States,[36] international studies have indicated the need for separate standards for children of different racial and geographic backgrounds.[25, 26, 34] Especially in anthropomorphic studies and serial evaluations used to study cultural and other environmental influences, one must establish one's own base lines. An interesting observation supporting this concept pertains to a group of black African children. In the early months of life their bone development (hand) was accelerated over that of European children of the same age, but by 18 months this relationship was reversed. The older the African child became in chronologic age, the further he or she fell behind in bone age. Similarly, the statural growth rate was initially faster, but before the end of the first year it had dropped below that of European counterparts.[25]

All of the primary ossification centers for the tubular bones appear during fetal life (Fig 8–1). The secondary centers usually appear after birth, except the distal epiphysis of the femur, where ossification takes place during the last two fetal months. Therefore, absence of this center is good presumptive evidence of prematurity. The center in the proximal epiphysis of the tibia is present in approximately two thirds of full-term infants at birth. In infants with fetal malnutrition (see chapter 3), the distal femoral epiphysis is frequently absent even though the gestational age is full term.[29] The time schedule of appearance of some important secondary centers is shown in Figure 8–2.

Figures 8–3 and 8–4 show the normal maturation of the bones of the hands and feet in both sexes. Rarely, one or more carpals are present at birth. Table 8–2 shows the time of appearance of carpal bones in both sexes, and Figures 8–5 to 8–19 show graphically the sequence of appearance of the carpal centers. The author would again like to point out that the calcification of carpal bones may be easily recognized, but they are rather poor indicators of age-related skeletal maturation. The average time of complete calcific union of epiphyses and diaphyses is given in Table 8–3.

The stage of osseous development correlates better with sexual maturation, including menarche, than chronologic age, height, or weight.[23, 24] Most girls have their first menstrual period when their roentgenographic record of skeletal age is between 13 and 13.5 years.

Any list of conditions with which disturbances of osseous development

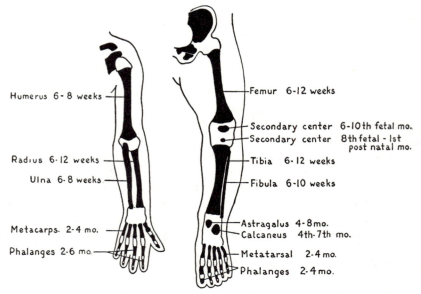

Fig 8–1.—Fetal ossification centers, showing average time of appearance in fetal weeks or months. (From Caffey.[2])

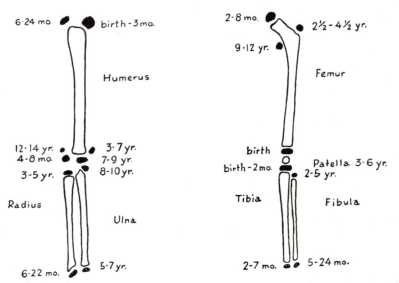

Fig 8–2.—Secondary ossification centers, showing average time of appearance. (From several sources.)

occur should be qualified (Table 8–4). There are individual variations in the reaction to disease so far as skeletal structures are concerned. In general, endocrine abnormalities cause more profound changes than infection or malnutrition. Almost any form of disease that influences height and weight will result in some interference in bone maturation. This interference may be manifest in narrow bands of dense bone in the metaphysis called *lines of arrested growth.* They probably indicate that osteoblastic activity in the region continues, but chondroplasia and linear growth are markedly slowed[2, 30] (Figs 8–20 and 8–21).

Probably the most extreme example of poor nutrition is seen in kwashiorkor and this is associated with pronounced slowing in skeletal matura-

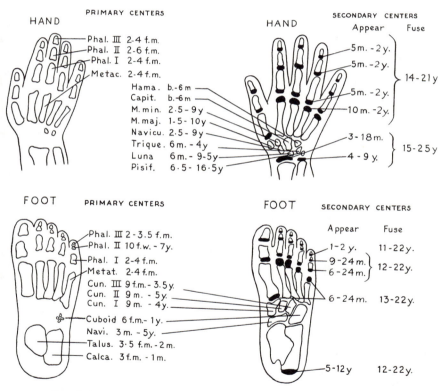

PRIMARY CENTERS
HAND

Phal. III 2-4 f.m.
Phal. II 2-6 f.m.
Phal. I 2-4 f.m.
Metac. 2-4 f.m.

Hama. b.-6 m
Capit. b.-6 m
M. min. 2.5-9 y
M. maj. 1-5-10 y
Navicu. 2.5-9 y
Trique. 6 m.-4 y
Luna 6 m.-9.5 y
Pisif. 6.5-16.5 y

SECONDARY CENTERS
HAND

	Appear	Fuse
	5m. -2y.	
	5m. -2y.	
		14-21y
	5m. -2y.	
	10m. -2y.	
	3-18 m.	
		15-25y
	4-9 y.	

FOOT   PRIMARY CENTERS

Phal. III 2-3.5 f.m.
Phal. II 10 f.w.-7y.
Phal. I 2-4 f.m.
Metat. 2-4 f.m.
Cun. III 9 f.m.-3.5 y.
Cun. II 9 m.-5y.
Cun. I 9 m.-4y.
Cuboid 6 f.m.-1 y.
Navi. 3 m.-5y.
Talus. 3.5 f.m.-2 m.
Calca. 3 f.m.-1 m.

FOOT   SECONDARY CENTERS

	Appear	Fuse
	1-2 y.	11-22 y.
	9-24 m.	12-22 y.
	6-24 m.	
	6-24 m.	13-22 y.
	5-12 y	12-22 y.

f.m. = fetal months; m. = post natal months; y. = year

Fig 8–3.—Ossification centers of the hands and feet, showing time of appearance. Note the wide range of "normal" and compare with Table 8–2. (From Caffey,[2] modified from Scammon R.E., in *Morris' Human Anatomy,* ed. 10. Philadelphia, The Blakiston Co., 1942.)

BOYS

GIRLS

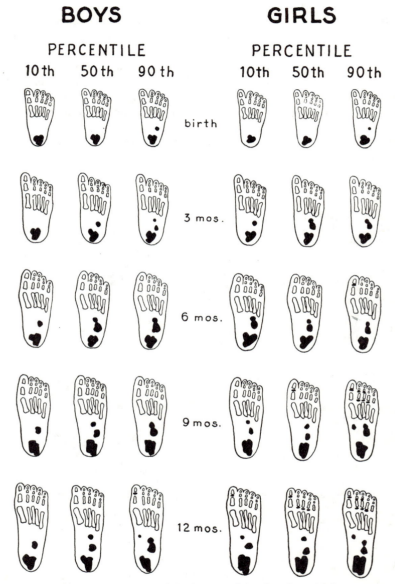

Fig 8–4.—Normal maturation of the bones of the feet from birth to age 1 year expressed as percentiles. (From Caffey,[2] according to Stuart.)

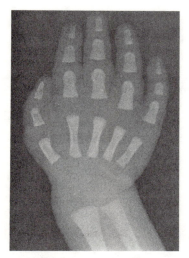

Fig 8–5.—Newborn; no carpal bones are present, and epiphyses are not calcified.

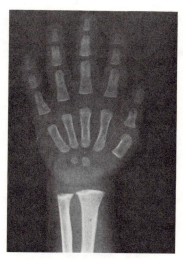

Fig 8–6.—One year; the capitate and hamate are well developed and first appear by age 6 months.

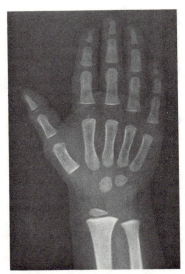

Fig 8–7.—Two years; the distal epiphysis of radius is present in 85% by this age, and one or more epiphyses of the phalanges appear.

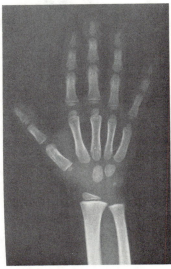

Fig 8–8.—Three years; the third carpal, triangularis, is present, and epiphyses of most of the metacarpals and phalanges are added.

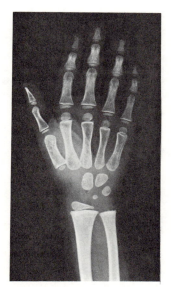

Fig 8–9.—Four years; a fourth carpal appears, and complete appearance of all epiphyses of the phalanges is present.

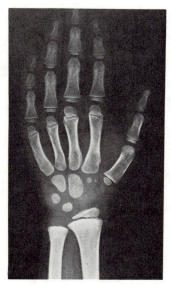

Fig 8–10.—Five years; from five to seven carpals are present (females slightly in advance of males), and the proximal ends of the metacarpals begin to acquire definitive molding.

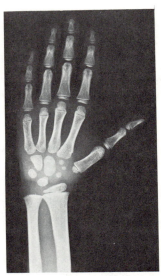

Fig 8–11.—Six years; all carpals except the pisiform are present, and the distal ulnar epiphysis may appear in 60% of girls and 30% of boys.

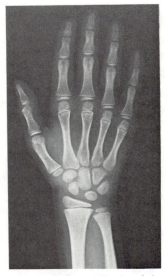

Fig 8–12.—Seven years; the distal epiphysis of the ulna is present in all but 10% of boys. The carpals are undergoing considerable molding with assumption of articulatory surfaces.

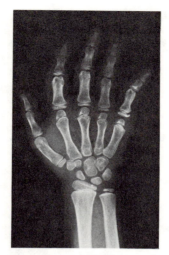

Fig 8–13.—Eight years; no further ossification centers appear, but growth and molding continue. The width of the epiphyses of most phalanges now equals the width of the shafts.

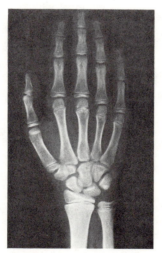

Fig 8–14.—Nine years; the styloid of the ulna becomes prominent. In girls the pisiform may be present.

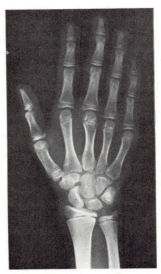

Fig 8–15.—Ten years; the pisiform is present in 50% of girls and rarely in boys. The styloid process of the ulnar epiphysis is well developed, and the epiphyses of the phalanges are wider than their shafts.

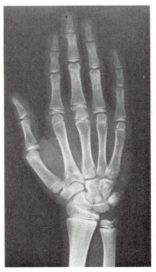

Fig 8–16.—Thirteen years; the pisiform is present (beneath the triquetral), and the carpals have assumed their definitive shapes.

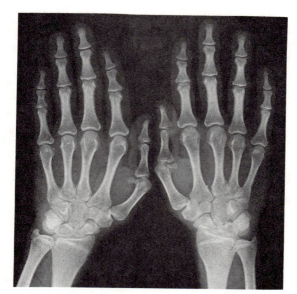

Fig 8–17.—By 17 years the epiphyses of the metacarpals and phalanges have united, and within a year the epiphyses of the radius and ulna unite with their respective diaphyses.

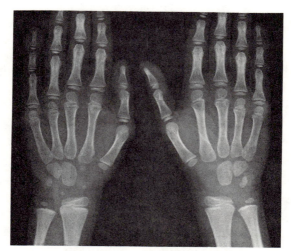

Fig 8–18.—Right and left wrists of a normal boy of 5 years showing a possible variation. There are four carpal centers in the right extremity and six in the left.

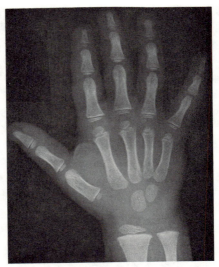

Fig 8–19.—Wrist of a 5½-year-old normal boy (average height, weight, mental development and normal physical examination). A sibling at the same age showed similar apparent retardation of bone development. Both children subsequently developed normally.

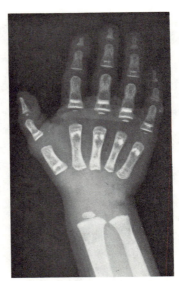

Fig 8–20.—Wrist of a cretin, age 5, who had been treated for several months. Note failure of appearance of carpal centers, the disturbed pattern (distal epiphysis of radius and metacarpal centers appearing before carpal centers) and uneven calcification.

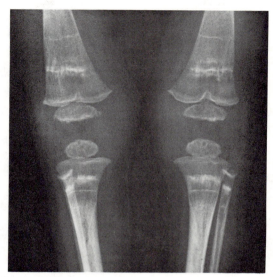

Fig 8–21.—Same patient as in Figure 8–20. Note absence of head of the fibula (normally present by age 5), uneven calcification of the epiphyses (epiphyseal dysgenesis) and so-called lines of arrested growth in shafts of the long bones.

tion. In this condition, as well as in other causes of deviation in bone development, correction of the underlying etiology will result in catch-up bone maturation just as it does in statural growth.

Roentgen films will often reveal other abnormalities associated with specific causes of retarded skeletal maturation. Examples are the short fourth metacarpal in Turner's syndrome, the irregular mineralization known as epiphyseal dysgenesis in hypothyroidism, or longitudinal streaks of poor ossification in the long bones in congenital rubella. Serial films may be useful in evaluating the effectiveness of therapy or as part of a survey to study the results of a disease upon growth.

The rate of linear growth of tubular bones may be of some value when a rapid method of appraisal of bone development is needed, as in the evaluation of response to treatment. Examples are measurement of recovery from malnutrition or progress of therapy in cretinism. Linear growth of the radius is normally 0.25 cm/month for the first year, 0.20 cm/month from 12 to 18 months, and 0.12 cm/month from 18 to 24 months. Table 8–5 gives the average length of several long bones at different ages. The author has not been impressed with the value of using measurements of bone growth as a means of assessing treatment.

TABLE 8–3.—AVERAGE AGE OF UNION OF THE MORE
IMPORTANT EPIPHYSES

BOYS	GIRLS	UNION OF EPIPHYSES
6	6	Head and greater tuberosity of humerus
7	7	Ischium and pubis
12	12	Trochlea and capitellum of humerus
14	13–14	Olecranon and ulna
14	13–14	Epiphysis of calcaneus
15–17	14–16	Proximal epiphysis of radius
15–17	14–16	Trochanter and head of femur
16–18	15–17	Epiphyses of metacarpals and metatarsals
17	16	Coracoid
18–20	17–19	Distal epiphysis of radius
18–20	17–19	Distal epiphysis of ulna
18–20	17–19	Distal epiphysis of tibia and fibula
18–20	17–19	Acromion
18–20	17–19	Head and greater tuberosity of humerus
18–20	17–19	Distal epiphysis of femur
18–20	17–19	Proximal epiphyses of tibia and fibula

AGE (YR) column heads BOYS and GIRLS.

TABLE 8–4.—PATHOLOGIC CONDITIONS ASSOCIATED WITH
ABNORMALITIES OF OSSEOUS DEVELOPMENT

Conditions associated with advanced osseous development
  Hyperthyroidism (acceleration is not a constant finding)
  Adrenogenital syndrome (tumor or hyperplasia of the adrenal cortex)
  Pubertas praecox (Fluhmann)
  Tumors of the ovary (granulosa cell, thecoma, teratoma)
  Interstitial cell tumor of the testes
  Pineal gland tumor (male only)
  Tumors of the third ventricle involving the hypothalamus
  Simple obesity associated with statural overgrowth
  McCune-Albright syndrome (polyostotic fibrous dysplasia)
Conditions associated with delayed osseous development
  Hypothyroidism
  Addison's disease
  Hypopituitarism (dwarfism)
  Pituitary cachexia (Simmonds' disease)
  Prolonged malnutrition
  Chronic illness
  Fröhlich's syndrome (adiposogenital dystrophy)
  Chondrodystrophy (achondroplasia)
  Hurler's syndrome (lipochondrodystrophy)
  Some cases of mental deficiency and Down's syndrome
  Gonadal agenesis (Turner's syndrome)
  Hypogonadism

TABLE 8–5.—MEAN LENGTH (CM) OF LONG BONES (SHAFT)*

	0–2		0–6		1–0		2–0		AGE/YR–MO. 4–0		6–0		8–0		10–0		12–0	
	B	G	B	G	B	G	B	G	B	G	B	G	B	G	B	G	B	G
Humerus	7.3	7.1	8.8	8.7	10.5	10.4	13.0	12.8	16.2	16.2	19.0	19.0	21.6	21.5	23.9	24.0	26.3	26.8
Radius	5.9	5.7	7.0	6.7	8.2	7.9	9.8	9.5	12.3	12.0	14.3	14.0	16.2	15.9	17.9	17.7	19.6	19.8
Ulna	6.7	6.5	7.7	7.6	9.1	8.8	10.9	10.7	13.5	13.3	15.8	15.5	17.7	17.5	19.5	19.4	21.3	21.8
Femur	8.6	8.7	11.2	11.2	13.6	13.4	17.2	16.9	22.4	22.2	26.9	26.9	31.1	31.2	34.9	35.0	38.4	39.3
Tibia	6.9	7.0	8.9	8.9	10.9	10.8	13.9	13.8	18.3	18.2	21.9	21.8	25.2	25.3	28.4	28.6	31.4	32.2
Fibula	6.6	6.6	8.5	8.5	10.6	10.5	13.7	13.5	18.2	18.0	21.7	21.6	24.9	25.0	27.9	28.3	30.7	31.3

*Modified from Maresh.[9] B, boys; G, girls.

Practical Applications

A number of carefully compiled standards are available for determining the existing degree of skeletal maturation in children through radiologic examination. Unfortunately all have their faults or limitations when applied to the evaluation of growth of a specific individual. A large share of the difficulty, one might say disappointment, rests with the clinician who fails to recognize the limits of the information that can be obtained from such an examination, due largely to the inherent variability present in the developing human. Nevertheless, the discriminating use of these standards has been of great value in studying the growth and development of children, both normal and abnormal. Often they can be of considerable aid in the diagnostic appraisal of a particular individual. In this respect they may have some advantage over more complicated procedures because the results are relatively easily and promptly obtained. One must be aware that conclusions drawn from statistically significant differences of large groups are often insignificant when applied to an individual. As in the use of other measurements of growth, the normal genetic variability of bone maturation is considerable and must always be considered when making the final judgment.

REFERENCES

1. Graham C.B.: Assessment of bone maturation: Methods and pitfalls. *Radiol. Clin. N. Am.* 10:185, 1972.
2. Caffey J.: *Pediatric X-Ray Diagnosis*, ed. 6. Chicago, Year Book Medical Publishers, 1972.
3. Christie A.: Prevalence and distribution of ossification centers in the newborn infant. *Am. J. Dis. Child.* 77:355, 1949.
4. Roche A.F., Eyman S.L., Davila G.H.: Skeletal age prediction. *J. Pediatr.* 78:997, 1971.
5. Acheson R.M.: Maturation of the skeleton, in Falkner F. (ed.): *Human Development*. Philadelphia, W.B. Saunders Co., 1966.
6. Rubin P.: *Dynamic Classification of Bone Dysplasias*. Chicago, Year Book Medical Publishers, 1964.
7. Kuhns L.R., Finnstrom Q.: New standards of ossification of the newborn. *Radiology* 119:655, 1976.
8. Garn S.M., Rohmann C.G., Silverman F.N.: Radiographic standards for postnatal ossification and tooth calcification. *Med. Radiogr. Photogr.* 43:45, 1967.
9. Maresh M.M.: Linear growth of long bones of extremities from infancy through adolescence. *Am. J. Dis. Child.* 89:725, 1955.
10. Harrison H.E., Harrison H.C.: *Disorders of Calcium and Phosphate Metabolism in Childhood and Adolescence*. Philadelphia, W.B. Saunders Co., 1979.
11. Wilkins L.: *The Diagnosis and Treatment of Endocrine Disorders in Childhood and Adolescence*, ed. 3. Springfield, Ill., Charles C Thomas, Publisher, 1965.
12. Sontag L.W., Lipford J.: The effect of illness and other factors on the appearance pattern of skeletal epiphyses. *J. Pediatr.* 23:391, 1943.

13. Patten B.M.: *Human Embryology*, ed. 3. New York, McGraw-Hill Book Co., 1968.
14. Garn S.M., Sandusky S.T., Nagy J.M., et al.: Advanced skeletal development in low income Negro children. *J. Pediatr.* 80:965, 1972.
15. Bayer L.M., Bayley N.: *Growth Diagnosis.* Chicago, University of Chicago Press, 1959.
16. White House Conference on Child Health and Protection: *Growth and Development.* Pt. IV. Appraisement of the child. New York: Century Co., 1933.
17. Raisz L.G., Kream B.E.: Regulation of bone formation. *N. Engl. J. Med.* 309:29, 1983.
18. Greulich W.W., Pyle S.I.: *Radiographic Atlas of Skeletal Development of the Hand and Wrist*, ed. 2. Palo Alto, Calif., Stanford University Press, 1959.
19. Krogman W.M.: *The Physical Growth of Children: An Appraisal of Studies 1950–1955*, Child Development Publications. Lafayette, Ind., Purdue University, 1956.
20. House R.: A summary of 49 radiologists' opinions on the skeletal age limits of apparently normal six year old children. *Am. J. Roentgenol.* 64:442, 1950.
21. Dreizen S., Snodgrasse R.M., Webb-Peploe H., et al.: Bilateral symmetry of skeletal maturation in the human hand and wrist. *Am. J. Dis. Child.* 93:122, 1957.
22. Mainland D.: Evaluation of the skeletal age method of estimating children's development: I. Systemic errors in the assessment of roentgenograms. *Pediatrics* 12:114, 1953.
23. Hansman C.F., Maresh M.M.: A longitudinal study of skeletal maturation. *Am. J. Dis. Child.* 101:305, 1961.
24. Pyle S.I., Reed R.B., Stuart H.C.: Patterns of skeletal development in the hand. *Pediatrics* 24:886, 1959.
25. Mackay D.H.: Skeletal maturation in the hand: A study of development in East African children. *Trans. R. Soc. Trop. Med. Hyg.* 46:135, 1952.
26. Falkner F.: Physical growth, in Gairdner D. (ed.): *Recent Advances in Pediatrics.* Boston, Little, Brown & Co., 1958.
27. Pyle S.I., Hoerr N.L.: *Radiographic Atlas of Skeletal Development of the Knee.* Springfield, Ill., Charles C Thomas, Publisher, 1955.
28. Hoerr N.L., Pyle S.I., Francis C.C.: *Radiographic Atlas of Skeletal Development of the Foot and Ankle.* Springfield, Ill., Charles C Thomas, Publisher, 1962.
29. Scott K.E., Usher R.: Epiphyseal development in fetal malnutrition syndrome. *N. Engl. J. Med.* 27:822, 1964.
30. Hernandez R.J., Poznanski A.K., Hopwood N.J., et al.: Incidence of growth lines in psychosocial dwarfs and idiopathic hypopituitarism. *Am. J. Roentgen.* 131:477, 1978.
31. Kopczynska J.: Determination radiologique de la maturation osseuse. *Ann. Radiol.* 7:308, 1964.
32. Tanner J.M., Whitehouse R.H., Healy M.J.R.: *A New System for Estimating Skeletal Maturity from the Hand and Wrist.* Part II. *The Scoring System.* Paris, Centre International de l'Enfance, 1962.
33. van der Werff Ten Bosch J.J.: *Somatic Growth of the Child.* Springfield, Ill., Charles C Thomas, Publisher, 1966.
34. Andersen E.: Skeletal maturation of Danish school children in relation to height, sexual development and social conditions. *Acta Paediatr. Scand.* (suppl.) 185:1, 1968.

35. *Skeletal Maturity of Children 6–11 Years, United States*. U.S. Dept. of Health, Education and Welfare, Public Health Service, 1974.
36. *Skeletal Maturity of Children 6–11 Years: Racial, Geographic Area and Socioeconomic Differentials, United States*. U.S. Dept. of Health, Education and Welfare, Public Health Service, 1975.
37. Vrist M.R., DeLange R.J., Finerman G.A.M.: Bone cell differentiation and growth factors. *Science* 220:680, 1983.
38. Goss R.J.: *The Physiology of Growth*. New York, Academic Press, 1978.
39. Austin L.A., Hunter H.: Calcitonin: Physiology. *N. Engl. J. Med.* 304:269, 1981.

9 / Role of the Endocrine Glands in Normal Growth and Development

Childhood is not from birth to a certain age
   and at a certain age
The child is grown and puts away childish things,
Childhood is the kingdom where nobody dies.
Nobody that matters, that is.
                                    —Edna St. Vincent Millay

It is not the function of this text to give a detailed biochemical review of the mechanism of action of the various hormones involved in growth and development. It does seem necessary to at least acquaint the reader with some of the intricacies involved for a clearer understanding of this very complex field. Perhaps more than any other factor in growth and development, the hormones can effect the most profound changes.

Hormones interact with specific receptors in cellular plasma membranes. In a number of instances, including the trophic hormones of the pituitary, parathyroid hormones, and calcitonin, the hormone-receptor complex influences the membrane enzyme adenylate cyclase that in turn influences the rate of synthesis of cyclic adenosine 3, 5-monophosphate (cyclic AMP) from intracellular adenosine triphosphate. Cyclic AMP regulates a number of intracellular processes; in many situations this involves the activation of protein kinases that phosphorylate cellular constituents. For instance, an increased synthesis of cyclic AMP has been shown to increase ribosomal phosphate content which may be a factor in protein production, both qualitative and quantitative. The effect of the hormones may be either stimulatory or inhibitory.

The steroid and thyroid hormones use a different method of information transfer. They gain access to the intracellular space where they are bound by specific cytoplasmic protein receptors and are then transported to the nucleus. Once in the nucleus the hormone exerts its effect, which has been shown to include alterations in chromatin structure and the template activity of DNA.[33]

323

Growth hormone, somatomedin, prolactin, and insulin have mechanisms of action that presently remain obscure. It might be significant to note that this group, in common with thyroid hormones, influences a very broad spectrum of tissues in contrast to the trophic hormones, which affect only specific target organs.

Hormones may be released in a free active form, e.g., insulin, or bound to a specific protein moiety such as globulin, e.g., cortisol, growth hormone, estrogens, and thyroid. In some cases the binding is very loose (cortisol) and in others firm (thyroid). During pregnancy, maternal thyroid-binding globulin increases, resulting in a considerably elevated total thyroxine level compared to normal. This type of binding may also be partially responsible for the minimal passage of maternal thyroid hormones across the placenta.

With the exception of insulin and somatomedin, which compete for the same receptor sites, each hormone is identified with a highly specific protein receptor in the cell membrane or in the cytoplasm. This accounts for the very high concentrations of some of the hormones in target organs, e.g., estrogen in the uterus and other portions of the genital tract.

The active half-life in the circulation of the different hormones varies considerably and is somewhat related to the duration of its effect upon a particular tissue. Growth hormone has a half-life of only 20 minutes, while thyroid hormones have six to seven days and cortisol has about 48 hours. Therapeutically, giving a single dose of 5 to 10 mg of growth hormone once a week is equally effective as divided doses given daily to hormone-deficient patients. One must conclude, therefore, that the effectiveness in a cell is considerably longer than the measurement of half-life would seem to indicate.

All of the hormones are subject to a negative feedback mechanism that is responsible for the control of the amount of secretion into the circulation. In a normal individual, the level of circulating hormone is the usual stimulus or inhibitor for further secretion. If the amount present temporarily exceeds the physiologic requirements, the feedback is able to decrease the amount released and/or synthesized. If the circulating amount is insufficient, the reverse message is conveyed through this system and increased hormone secretion occurs. The degree of sensitivity of feedback varies with age (maturation) with some hormones. As we shall see later in discussing the gonadotropic hormones, the fetal hypothalamus is very insensitive to gonadotropic levels, during early childhood it is exquisitely sensitive, and then as puberty approaches, the hypothalamus becomes more permissive which allows for the events of sexual maturation. The feedback mechanism for some of the hormones is related entirely or partially to blood levels of chemical substances. Examples are ionizable calcium for the parathyroids and glucose for insulin (Fig 9–1).

ADH - Antidiuretic Hormone
TSH - Thyroid-Stimulating Hormone
GH - Growth Hormone
ACTH- Adrenocorticotropic Hormone
LH - Luteinizing Hormone
FSH - Follicle-Stimulating Hormone

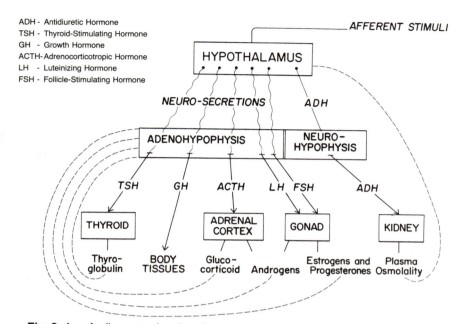

Fig 9–1.—A diagram showing the relationship of the pituitary gland to the hypothalamus and various target organs. Stimulus to production of the pituitary hormones arises from neurosecretions or releasing factors in the hypothalamus; there is a specific one for each hormone. With the possible exception of the growth hormone, all have reciprocal regulatory influences, represented by *broken lines*, back to the pituitary (or hypothalamus) through the hormones secreted by the target organs. In the case of the antidiuretic hormone (vasopressin, ADH), the feedback mechanism is indirect by virtue of changes in plasma osmolality. Since aldosterone production by the adrenal cortex functions largely independently of ACTH, it is omitted. (From Lowrey G.H.: Consideration of pituitary endocrine dysfunction, in Kahn E. (ed.): *Correlative Neurosurgery.* Springfield, Ill., Charles C Thomas, Publisher, 1969.

In addition to hormones mentioned and discussed in this chapter, other growth factors are briefly outlined in chapter 1, which the reader is advised to review at this time. The description of "brain peptides" (which are not limited to the brain) and their function will be strictly limited to their influence, as we now understand them, on somatic growth.

Effects of Maternal and Placental Hormones on the Fetus

There is some doubt at present as to just what hormones can pass across the placenta to the fetus and in what quantities. Most of the protein molecules from the anterior pituitary probably do not pass with any degree of ease from the maternal circulation to the fetal circulation. This is also believed to be true of thyroglobulin, which has a molecular weight of approximately 700,000. Some experimental work has indicated that thyroid hormone may pass, but that it is not in free equilibrium between mother and fetus.[39] Clinical evidence to support this is present in the fact that cretins seldom appear to be hypothyroid until several weeks after birth. However, retardation of osseous development is present at the time of birth, and some of these infants will suffer irreparable neurologic damage even though adequate therapy is begun within the first month or two. It is therefore postulated that the developing fetus must supply his or her own thyroid hormone to have completely normal development. About 75% to 80% of cretins have no demonstrable thyroid gland, thus making them excellent subjects for observation.

As outlined in chapter 3, the placenta is capable of producing estrogen, progesterone, and a gonadotropin, all of which pass to the fetus.[82] In addition, as early as the end of the first trimester the fetal pituitary is synthesizing the gonadotropins FSH (follicle-stimulating hormone) and LH (luteinizing hormone). These trophic hormones do have a definite stimulatory effect upon the developing ovaries and testes with some sex hormone production.[40] As one author[83] has expressed it, "The human fetoplacental unit at midpregnancy may be characterized as a balanced system of physiologic enzyme deficiencies."

The breasts of newborn infants secrete milk in varying amounts decreasing as the infant grows older. With very slight manual expression, 100% of infants less than 3 weeks of age produce milk that upon analysis resembles, but is not identical to, human mother's milk. This so-called "witch's milk" is the result of high levels of estrogens and prolactin in fetal plasma during the last weeks of pregnancy.[41] Further effects of estrogen result in labial hypertrophy and a milky discharge from the vagina. At birth the vaginal mucosa resembles that of the adult in morphology, glycogen content, and surface pH. During a few weeks following delivery, desquamation of the epithelium takes place and the squamous cells are replaced by a single layer of cuboidal cells, the glycogen disappears, and the pH becomes alkaline. In 2% to 3% of female neonates some vaginal bleeding results, probably from the abrupt drop in estrogens and consequent changes in the endometrium.[20, 22] In the male some hypertrophy of the prostatic utricle may be present at birth but rapidly subsides.

The fetal pituitary has the capacity to synthesize growth hormone (GH) by the end of the first trimester.[30] The GH content of the gland steadily increases, as does its size and the number of acidophil cells, until the last ten weeks of gestation. At this time inhibitory influences become operative as the neurophysiologic mechanisms of the hypothalamus mature. At midgestation the amount of GH in the pituitary is nearly equal to that of a 1-year-old child. Serum levels of GH are considerably elevated above childhood normals in the neonate and remain so for several weeks.[58] The functional importance of GH to the fetus or during infancy remains obscure. Evidence from the study of anencephalic fetuses and children with a confirmed diagnosis of growth hormone deficiency indicates it is not essential for physical growth during fetal life or for the first 12 to 18 months following birth. It is possible that the hormone may play a role in neonatal homeostasis in preventing hypoglycemia.[44, 99]

The relatively high levels of prolactin found in the fetal pituitary and in the serum have no clearly understood function at the present time.

Thyroid-stimulating hormone (TSH) in the fetal pituitary follows a pattern similar to the production of GH. The rising levels through midgestation are accompanied by elevated free and globulin-bound thyroxine in the serum. The levels establish a plateau during the last half of pregnancy but they remain elevated for a few days after birth.[58]

Grumbach[40] has hypothesized that early in gestation there is hyperactivity and relatively unrestrained secretion of releasing factors by the hypothalamus. Later, with increasing maturation, inhibitory influences from the central nervous system play a greater role. In part, the fetal secretions of the thyroid and testicle may have some influence in bringing about the change in sensitivity of the releasing centers as a part of the maturational process.

The administration of large doses of testosterone to the mother has caused virilization of the female fetus. Some types of synthetic progesterones have relatively strong androgenic properties and when given to mothers have produced some degree of masculinization.[63] Rarely the administration of synthetic estrogens to pregnant women has resulted in a virilizing effect on the external genitalia of female babies.[64] It is postulated that maternal, placental, or fetal metabolism can alter these steroids to produce a hormone with a greater androgenic effect than the original steroid.

In summary, the infant at birth has already been exposed for some time to potent hormonal substances produced by the mother, the placenta and the fetus. The last two are the more important in influencing development. All of the endocrine glands of the normal neonate have received physiologic stimuli and have synthesized their respective hormones in considerable amounts. Further maturation consists primarily in the further refinement of feedback controls and alterations in sensitivity to stimuli and inhibitors.

The Central Nervous System and Pituitary Gland

Considerable progress has been made in defining the role of the central nervous system in the regulation of pituitary function.[40, 51, 59] Influence upon the anterior pituitary is mediated by neurohumoral substances transported to the gland by the hypophyseal-portal system originating in a capillary network in the median eminence of the hypothalamus. At least four specific releasing factors have been identified as arising in the hypothalamus. All are small polypeptides containing from 8 to possibly 20 amino acids. Not all have been chemically identified as yet. Known stimulators are related to adrenocorticotropic hormone (ACTH), TSH, GH and a single one for both gonadotropins (FSH and LH). Two inhibitors have been identified: one for prolactin and somatostatin for the growth hormone. Somatostatin not only inhibits growth hormone production but also glucogen by the α-cells of the pancreas. This latter finding shows considerable promise in treating juvenile onset diabetes mellitus, since suppression of glucagon decreases insulin requirements and prevents development of ketosis. Figure 9–1 indicates the interrelationship of the releasing factors to the other trophic hormones of the pituitary.

After the first 3 months of life some of the pituitary hormones are secreted in an episodic but rhythmic manner throughout a normal 24-hour day. In the absence of stress, either physiologic or physical, the secretion of ACTH, GH, and the two gonadotropins FSH and LH are largely dominated by the daily sleep-wake pattern. Good correlation exists between the stages of sleep, electroencephalographic tracings, and the plasma levels of these hormones. Throughout childhood the maximum release of GH occurs with deep sleep. In fact, stimulant medications that prevent deep sleep, when used over a long period, can interfere with a child's growth.[32] ACTH and cortisol levels are greatest just prior to awakening some hours after maximal GH level is reached. Prior to puberty the gonadotropins are secreted at a low and nearly steady rate. The onset of the physical changes at puberty are heralded by a dramatic rise in both FSH and LH, which enter the circulation as discrete rhythmic pulses. Experimental studies indicate that this is in response to a similar pulsatile release of the gonadotropin-releasing factor (or hormone) from the hypothalamus. The gonads are thus stimulated to grow and mature as functioning glands.[9, 25]

Less clearly understood are some of the complex interactions involving higher centers of the brain and pituitary. One might use the response to physical or emotional stress as an example. Stress results in an increased production of ACTH with corresponding increase in the corticosteroids from the adrenal cortex. This has been termed an energy-mobilizing action converting proteins into carbohydrates. The release of ACTH is controlled by complex regulatory mechanisms including ACTH-releasing factor from the hypothalamus and vasopressin and catecholamines from the adrenal medulla that act directly on the pituitary. In most primates, and almost certainly in humans, the effect upon the developing brain and subsequent behavior is very definitely related to the kind and amount of sex hormones to which the fetus is exposed.[10]

During growth the histologic appearance of the anterior pituitary changes, reflecting the changes in the products synthesized by the gland. It is probable that all secretory cells are derived from a small chromophobe stem cell. Newer techniques can now differentiate the specific function of cells and make obsolete the old acidophil-basophil-chromophobe nomenclature. At birth, delta cells, which are the producers of gonadotropins, are easily identified. This is followed by their virtual disappearance until about 10 years of age when they increase in number until adulthood. These changes undoubtedly reflect the fetal and then the pubescent exposure to hypothalamic stimulation and its documentation of the high levels of gonadotropins found in the blood. One cell type probably produces both FSH and LH. It is known that a single type is responsible for the synthesis of both prolactin and GH and another for ACTH and the melanocyte-stimulating hormone (MSH). Only TSH is produced individually by one cell type. With the exception of the delta cells, there are no major shifts in the number of cell types with age.[4, 61]

Six hormones are recognized as arising from the anterior pituitary. These are GH, TSH, ACTH, prolactin, and two gonadotropins, FSH and LH (also termed "interstitial cell stimulating hormone"). All have been identified as being polypeptides of relatively high molecular weight (20,000 to 30,000). ACTH and GH are the only hormones that have been synthesized in the laboratory. Growth hormone is unique in that it is very species-specific. Hormone obtained from any species lower than a primate is ineffectual in man. This fact has obvious clinical significance because it means the supply is very limited.

The normal physical growth of an individual depends upon an adequate secretion of the growth hormone and the genetic ability to respond. Growth hormone is present in the blood throughout all of the growing period and well into adult life. Normal levels vary considerably in response to the circadian rhythm and fluctuations in normal stimuli or inhibitors. Levels in very early infancy may be ten or more times higher than later in life. Average fasting early A.M. levels will be 2 to 5 ng/ml. It is estimated that requirements for normal growth will approximate 1 mg per day. Some workers have found slightly higher daytime levels in adolescents, while most have found no fluctuation with age other than that referred to above.[65, 71] The content of GH in the pituitary also remains constant regardless of age. In terms of growth, only the central nervous system, and possibly the adrenals and gonads, are unaffected by the hormone. Normal growth of the fetus occurs in the absence of GH, either from its own pituitary gland, from the mother's or from both. It is highly unlikely that the placental "growth" hormone plays any part (see chapter 3). Although the half-life of pituitary GH is only 20 minutes, its activity after becoming fixed in tissue almost certainly continues.

From clinical and laboratory studies the principal action of this hormone appears to be one of stimulating DNA synthesis and cell multiplication. It is difficult clearly to separate all of the important factors influencing human growth, and perhaps there is considerable overlap in functions.[86] At the risk of oversimplification, the following plan seems to fit our interpretation of the available facts. Embryonic and fetal growth seem largely independent of hormonal influence, though the sex hormones have great impact at this time on ultimate sexual differentiation (see "Gonadal Influences on Growth and Development"). Adequate nutrition, maternal care, and placental development with its intricate vascularity are included; these are most important for both cell multiplication and cell growth in the fetal and early infancy periods. After this critical period nutritional deprivation has its greatest effect on cell size. GH has its major influence on increasing the number of cells of the body (except in those systems already noted) from late infancy until adulthood. Its metabolic functions continue until death. Adequate thyroid hormone is necessary for normal increase in cell size and also for cell multiplication. As with nutrition, it appears that in late fetal and early infant development thyroid hormone plays an important role in cell multiplication and later in life in cell size. At the time of adolescence the sex hormones exert their influence. Androgens—male hormones—primarily cause an increase in cell size, while estrogens may stimulate cell size but also may restrict cell multiplication.

Some of the more important metabolic effects of GH will be outlined. It stimulates the transport of amino acids across cell membranes and the synthesis of protein. Secondary to this action is the decreased excretion of urinary nitrogen. GH promotes the growth of cartilage. Total fatty acid catabolism is increased and free fatty acids are mobilized, causing a delayed increase in their level in serum. Immediately after administration blood glucose levels fall and there is a decreased insulin sensitivity with a prolongation of the disappearance rate of glucose given intravenously. Newborn infants have higher levels of GH than older children or adults. In contrast to the latter, the newborn infant reacts to an increase in blood sugar with an increase in plasma GH. It is postulated that this ability may ensure the mobilization of fat needed to supply energy.[96] Furthermore, the hormone has been used with some measure of success to treat neonatal hypoglycemia. A slight drop in the respiratory quotient probably is a reflection of the effects upon carbohydrate and lipid metabolism. Sodium, potassium, and inorganic phosphate are retained, but there is an increased rate of urinary calcium excretion.

Others factors than sleep are responsible for fluctuations in the secretion of GH. Exercise and physical or emotional stress act as stimulants. Hypoglycemia and prolonged fasting cause an increased production. Very high serum levels are found in most patients with kwashiorkor. Arginine and some other amino acids, by infusion, are strong stimuli as are pyrogens. L-Dopa and norepinephrine through their catecholaminergic effect stimulate production and may represent the fundamental mechanism resulting from pyrogens and hypoglycemia.[65]

Under normal conditions the control of GH secretion is influenced by the following factors. GH-releasing factor stimulates the production of GH, which in turn stimulates the secretion of somatomedin. As a feedback mechanism, elevated levels of GH and of somatomedin stimulate the production of somatostatin, which is a potent inhibitor of GH-releasing factor. Somatostatin is a 14-amino acid polypeptide produced in the hypothalamus and in the pancreas. In addition to its effect on GH, it inhibits the secretion of insulin and glucagon from the pancreas. Moderate to high levels of plasma glucocorticoids will interfere with growth, possibly through inhibition of somatomedin.[29]

Human GH given to dwarfs with pituitary insufficiency will result in accelerated growth and a positive nitrogen balance during the period in which it is administered. Assays of GH in the serum of patients with acromegaly are markedly elevated. For further discussion of abnormal growth and deviations from normal in GH secretion, see chapter 13.

Linear growth is due to growth of the long bones of the extremities. This occurs as a result of proliferation of cartilage in the epiphyseal plates, which is dependent upon GH. The rate of this process may be estimated by measuring the uptake of isotope-labeled sulfur into chondromucoprotein of cartilage. In vitro GH will not produce the proliferation in the absence of normal serum. Originally the ingredient in the serum responsible for the incorporation of sulfur and normal cartilage growth was termed sulfation factor but is now termed somatomedin. There are at least four somatomedins with similar physiologic action and biochemical structure. They are found in many tissues, particularly in the liver, and may be in sufficient concentration in most areas in the body so they do not depend upon blood transportation to accomplish their metabolic role. Nevertheless, in plasma they parallel the level of GH, possess insulin-like activity, and stimulate cellular mitosis. They are peptides with similar, but not identical, amino acid chains to insulin. It has been proposed that they act as mediators to most tissues for the GH. During acute fasting and in chronic states of nutritional deprivation, somatomedin levels fall while GH often rises.[60]

The posterior lobe of the adenohypophysis (pars nervosa) is a part of the neurosecretory system that includes the supraoptic and paraventricular nuclei of the hypothalamus.[45] The hormones vasopressin or antidiuretic hormone (ADH) and oxytocin are produced in these areas and then reach the posterior lobe by the hypothalamo-hypophysial nerve tracts, where they are stored until released into the systemic circulation. Oxytocin is primarily concerned with uterine muscle contracture and has little relevance to growth and development. Vasopressin is discussed in chapter 7 under the subject of water balance.

Insulin

Although the pancreas is well developed by the second trimester, insulin secretion is weak in newborns in response to hypoglycemia for about 72 hours. Insulin's most important function is to increase the transport of glucose and amino acids across the cellular plasma membrane. In contrast to GH, which is lipolytic, insulin enhances the uptake of free fatty acids by the cell. It appears to increase the synthesis of DNA and RNA in target tissues such as muscle and bone. In its absence, cell ribosomes become less efficient in protein synthesis.

Although there is some evidence that the fetal pancreas and beta cells do not respond to hyperglycemia, the newborn infant of a diabetic mother manifests a number of features that indicate maternal hyperglycemia has influenced fetal insulin production. Often there is pancreatic hyperplasia of the beta cells. The infants are large with a surplus of adipose tissue and visceromegaly. They are at considerable risk to develop neonatal hypoglycemia.

The Thyroid Gland

The thyroid gland is probably second only to the pituitary in relative importance in its influence on growth and development.

The thyroid makes its appearance toward the end of the fourth fetal week as a bilobed diverticulum from the floor of the pharynx. Toward the end of the fourth month colloid can be found in the center of the cell mass, and there is evidence that shortly after this time the gland becomes physiologically active. Accessory thyroid tissue may be found along the course of the thyroglossal duct from the base of the tongue to the root of the neck. Occasionally thyroid glands are found substernally.[19]

The thyroid hormones consist of thyroxine (T_4) and triiodothyronine (T_3). It is believed that the latter is the active hormone and that T_4 is converted to T_3 in peripheral tissue. T_3 is about four times more potent than T_4 but it usually constitutes only about 5% to 10% of circulating hormones. Both are transported in blood in strong association with globulin, and small amounts with albumin. Secretion of the hormones is stimulated by pituitary TSH, which functions in the thyroid cell through a cyclic AMP mechanism. Although TSH is under control of a hypothalamic releasing factor, the major negative feedback of thyroid hormones is dependent upon specific receptors in the pituitary. Normal levels of serum T_4 at birth are 7 to 15 μg/100 ml and from midinfancy on are 5 to 10 μg/100 ml. Except for a brief period after birth (see below), T_3 levels range from 90 to 170 ng/100 ml throughout all of childhood.

Early in the second trimester there is an increase of TSH in the fetal serum and a progressive increase in T_4 to a level that exceeds that found in maternal serum at the same time.[84] This differential is maintained until delivery. Immediately following birth there is a marked surge in TSH production by the newborn's pituitary and a response by the capable thyroid. Some workers relate the surge of TSH to neonatal cooling while others feel clamping of the cord in some way is responsible. Mean cord levels of TSH are 10 μU/ml, which rise to a mean of 35 μU/ml by 2 hours and are followed by a drop to the same values found at birth by 72 hours. Mean cord levels of T_4 are 12 μg/100 ml, which rise to a maximum of 25 μg/100 ml by 2 to 5 hours and then slowly fall over the next 6 to 10 days to the same values found at birth. Blood levels of T_3 parallel TSH values: 35 ng/100 ml at birth, 220 ng/100 ml at 2 hours, and 146 ng/100 ml at 72 hours. The neonate is relatively hyperthyroid by virtue of elevations of both T_3 and T_4, though the T_3 elevation is a very brief one. Premature infants follow a similar pattern but the initial surge and response is reduced proportionate to the degree of immaturity.[43, 48, 101] Throughout most of infancy, T_4 levels remain slightly higher than those found later in life. During middle to late adolescence T_4 levels are lower than at any other time throughout childhood.[36]

Thyroid hormones are necessary for the production of all forms of RNA and their presence in the cell stimulates ribosome production and protein synthesis. They also promote oxidative phosphorylation in mitochondria of most cells. The hormones are important for normal maturation of the brain, their absence causing a delay in cell differentiation and at least a transient decrease in cell numbers. They are required for physical growth and development, and, along with the sex hormones, they occupy an essential role in bone development and linear growth. In relationship to pituitary GH they play a permissive role. In their absence GH is relatively ineffective. In the absence of GH, the thyroid hormones may promote some degree of maturation, but no growth.

Since the placenta is essentially impermeable to the thyroid hormones T_3 and T_4 and to TSH, the fetal hypothalamic-pituitary-thyroid system develops free of maternal influence. Does the normal development of the fetus depend upon the presence of a functioning thyroid gland? The answer is not entirely clear. Absence or deficiency of thyroid hormones at birth results in the clinical entity of cretinism. However, at birth such infants appear and behave in a normal manner. Indications that development is not optimum in such babies are retarded bone and tooth maturation by means of x-ray examination and the fact that mental development may be retarded to a degree, even if adequate therapy (thyroid hormones) is begun in the first weeks of life. Congenital hypothyroidism occurs about once in 4,000 births. If unrecognized and untreated, changes in the normal pattern of development take place including progressive lethargy, stunted growth, dry and pale skin, hypothermia, thickened facial features, enlarged tongue, and constipation. Adequate therapy will abolish the physical abnormalities but may not be able to amend the effects upon the brain.[47, 84, 101]

Between 15% to 25% of premature infants have a transient low level of T_4 at birth. It is more common in those neonates who develop the respiratory distress syndrome or are otherwise stressed. Normal values return in 4 to 6 weeks and no ill effects appear to result.[84]

The Adrenal Glands

The adrenal medulla originates from cells of the neural crest that also form the sympathetic ganglions. Very early in embryonic life these cells may be differentiated from the ganglion cells by staining with chromic acid, which they retain; this has led to the term "chromaffin cells." Similar clusters of chromaffin cells found along the aorta persist for many years following birth. The cells of the adrenal cortex arise from the splanchnic mesoderm. Early in fetal life two distinct layers of the cortex can be made out. The inner portion of the cortex, called the reticular zone, becomes mature and well differentiated by the third fetal month, and vacuoles are formed in these cells. The outer portion remains a thin layer and is undifferentiated until after birth. In the neonatal period the adrenal gland is approximately 20 times the relative size found in the adult; this is due to persistence of the fetal reticular layer. By the end of the first month of life the number of these cells has decreased greatly; the final adult character of the adrenal cortex is not attained until about the third year. By the end of the third week after birth the adrenals have lost half of their initial weight. Following this period there is slow increase in weight, and by the third or fourth year the adrenals have regained their original size. The cause of these striking changes, especially the retention of the fetal layer throughout the late fetal development, is not presently known. It has been theorized that some trophic substance from the pituitary or placenta may maintain it until birth.[49] It has also been postulated that this fetal reticular zone is responsible for the relatively large quantities of 17-ketosteroids excreted by the infant in the first few days after birth (Table 9–1).

The adrenal cortex produces three groups of steroid hormones. Accord-

TABLE 9–1.—NORMAL URINE OR PLASMA CONTENT
OF VARIOUS HORMONES OR THEIR METABOLITES

ASSAY	NEONATE	CHILD	ADULT
17-hydroxysteroids urine, mg/24 hr	0.2–3.5	0.5–5.0	1.5–9.0
17-ketosteroids urine, mg/24 hr	1.5–2.5	0.1–1.0	5–12 female 6–22 male
Aldosterone urine, ng/24 hr	1–2	2–10	5–20
Testosterone* plasma, ng/100 ml	230–300	3–10	300–500
Estradiol† plasma, ng/100 ml	100–300	2–4	10–200‡
LH plasma, ng/ml	4–10	0–4	6–20
FSH plasma, ng/ml	0–2	0–4	6–20
Thyroxine plasma, μg/100 ml	7–15	5–10	5–10
GH plasma, ng/ml	20–40	2–5	2–5

*Male only.
†Female only.
‡The wide range of values is a reflection of changing levels throughout the menstrual cycle.

ing to their physiologic functions they are designated as mineralocorticoids (aldosterone), glucocorticoids (cortisol or hydrocortisone), and androgens (testosterone). During the neonatal period corticosterone is the major glucocorticoid secreted, but this is quickly replaced by cortisol. Small and physiologically unimportant amounts of estrogen and progesterone may be produced by the adrenal cortex.

The first group, mineralocorticoids, mainly influence water, sodium, and potassium balance. They control sodium and potassium excretion by the kidneys through the mechanism of reabsorption. With a deficiency of these hormones there is an excessive loss of sodium from the body and an increase in serum potassium content. Secondarily the serum chloride level is lowered due to excessive chloride excretion. The extracellular fluid volume is depleted as a consequence of the electrolyte loss when water is carried off. Dehydration, weakness, microcardia, and circulatory collapse are the end results. Conversely, an excess of aldosterone increases the reabsorption of sodium in the kidney, leading to elevation of the serum sodium level. Serum potassium content falls owing to excessive excretion, and intracellular potassium also is depleted. With the sodium retention there is an increase in the extracellular fluid volume, with resulting edema. Sodium tends to replace the intracellular potassium to maintain osmotic balance. If this exchange reaches any degree of magnitude, degenerative changes appear and weakness, paralysis, and cardiac failure occur. To bring about further extracellular-intracellular ionic balance, the extracellular chloride concentration is decreased. This in turn is compensated for by a rise in serum bicarbonate content. The final result is slight hypernatremia, hypokalemia, hypochloremia, and increased serum bicarbonate content. Eventually hypertension may be present. In a normal individual the hormone output is such that these factors are kept in balance and are related to the sodium and potassium intake and to blood volume. If the volume falls, this causes an increased secretion of aldosterone; conversely, an increased blood volume inhibits hormonal production. It is believed that the juxtaglomerular apparatus of the kidney plays a key role in the rate of secretion of aldosterone. Reduced blood flow in the kidney is followed by an increased release of renin and angiotensin-stimulated aldosterone secretion.

The glucocorticoids are important in control of carbohydrate-protein balances in the body. They promote catabolism and glucogenesis from protein. In large amounts they inhibit carbohydrate utilization by body tissues and increase fat deposition. This results in a hyperglycemia that is resistant to insulin. Increased secretion of these hormones occurs in times of stress, such as infection, burns, trauma, or emotional strain. They are excreted in the urine as 17-hydroxysteroids. They also constitute a group of antiinflammatory agents. It is possible that the excessive secretion of the glucocorticoids during severe and prolonged illness in children is an important factor in the temporary arrest in growth and the increased protein breakdown. In addition to causing these changes, they depress the number of circulating eosinophils, cause involution of lymphatic tissue, and tend to depress immune responses.[4, 22]

Androgens constitute the third and final group. Experimental and clinical evidence indicates that these substances originate in the reticular layer of the cortex. In their physiologic action they resemble androgens from the testes since they promote both masculinization and nitrogen retention. In the female all androgens are derived from the adrenal cortex, whereas in the male a small but relatively potent portion comes from the testes as adolescence progresses.[31] Plasma levels of testosterone remain somewhat elevated for a few months after birth and then decrease to prepubertal values. There appears to be a persistence of fetal levels of LH stimulating the testes. There is no evidence that the adrenals contribute to this.

ACTH from the pituitary controls the quantity of secretions of the glucocorticoids and adrenal androgens. Aldosterone, the mineralocorticoid, is secreted largely independently of ACTH, responding to plasma levels of angiotensin, which, in turn, are responsive to sodium concentration and blood volume changes. ACTH release can respond quickly to stressful situations and may be life-saving in certain circumstances. There is a sensitive feedback or inhibiting action of the glucocorticoids, cortisol, and cortisone (see Fig 9–1), upon the release of ACTH from the pituitary or upon the releasing hormone of the hypothalamus. This permits an excellent balance and regulation of adrenal cortical function. The circadian variations in the plasma levels of the glucocorticoids after the first few months have been described previously. Cortisol circulates in plasma bound to a high affinity binding protein and is released from this bond at specific receptor sites on cell membranes. At birth, plasma levels of cortisol, cortisone, and aldosterone are elevated above subsequent levels found in infancy or prepubertal childhood. It is of interest that plasma levels of the glucocorticoids are not influenced by vaginal or cesarean delivery. Following the neonatal period the levels of most adrenal cortical hormones reach and maintain near adult levels. Transient low plasma levels of glucocorticoids during early infancy are due to reduced corticosteroid binding rather that to reduced production. The elevated aldosterone levels are not easily explained from a physiologic rationale but do reflect the established fact that aldosterone levels throughout childhood vary inversely with age (Table 9–2).[46, 65]

Quantitatively, the important substrates in the second trimester for the adrenal steroids are progesterone and pregnanolone supplied to the fetus by the placenta. The fetal adrenal depends on the hypothalamic-pituitary axis for growth and secretory activity. The anencephalic monsters have very poorly developed adrenals. In both the premature and term infant, large amounts of 17-ketosteroids are present in the blood and urine that fall rapidly to very low levels. These changes undoubtedly reflect the rapid involution of the fetal reticular layer as previously described. Separation of the 17-ketosteriods indicates that those present at birth are considerably different from those present a few weeks later, e.g., dehydroepiandrosterone is present at birth and does not reappear until age 8 or 9 years. Plasma levels in the premature infant remain higher longer than in term neonates,

TABLE 9–2.—Mean Plasma Concentrations of Some Corticosteroids and Progesterone From Infancy to Adulthood*

	NEONATE	1 WEEK	1 YEAR	5 YEAR	12 YEAR	ADULT
Aldosterone	2.51	0.87	0.30	0.30	0.36	0.2
Progesterone	53.0	0.2	0.34	0.36	0.37	0.5
Cortisol	68.0	11.4	75.2	78.3	79.0	89.0
Cortisone	73.7	18.5	10.8	14.0	15.6	15.8
Corticosterone	4.4	0.5	1.0	0.8	0.74	1.1

*Modified after Sippell et al.[46] All values expressed as ng/ml. Specimens obtained in early A.M. Only the means are given to show the trend of values with changing age. The range is quite wide throughout infancy and childhood.

presumably due to slower involution of the fetal layer and slower induction of enzymes necessary for metabolism of the steroid.[85, 91]

The important role of glucocorticoids in lung maturation and production of surfactant has been discussed in chapter 5.

The functional status of the adrenal medulla is measured by the secretion of catecholamines. The release of these substances from sympathetic nerve endings and the adrenal glands is related to the sympathoadrenal system. Adequate levels of catecholamines in blood are important to maintain vegetative functions such as heart rate, vascular tone, body temperature, and blood glucose levels. Epinephrine is produced almost exclusively by the adrenal, while large quantities of norepinephrine are produced by sympathetic ganglion cells as well as the adrenal. Stimulants to catecholamine production from the adrenal are insulin, histamine, and through preganglionic cholinergic nerves. At birth, plasma levels are elevated three to five times above normal adult levels with a ratio of norepinephrine/epinephrine of 6/1 indicating a major source from the nervous system. Within a few hours there is rapid fall and then a leveling off. After the first year, when plasma levels are slightly reduced, the adult level is reached and maintained.[37, 42, 90]

Gonadal Influences on Growth and Development

Sex differentiation from the primordial gonad into testis or ovary is determined by genetics (see chapter 2). The adrenal and gonadal tissues arise from cells of similar origin, the former from the cephalic end of the mesonephric ridge and the latter from the adjacent gonadal ridge located on the ventral border of the mesonephros. Thus the two steroid-producing glands have an intimate genesis. In the future female the earliest and most significant changes occur in the cortex, with greater growth and prominence of these cells, whereas in the future male the medullary areas undergo similar early development at the expense of the cortex.

In the presence of a Y chromosome the predominant phenotype will be male. Even in the rare occurrence of more than one X chromosome, as in XXY Klinefelter's syndrome, the external genitalia are typically male and testes are present. The absence of a Y chromosome results in phenotypic female genital development. The fetal testes produce two important hormones relative to sexual development. One, testosterone, is responsible for the differentiation of the primordial wolffian ducts into the epididymis, vas deferens, seminal vesicles, and prostatic gland. The other hormone is protein in nature and causes regression of the müllerian ducts. In the absence of the fetal testes, the wolffian ducts regress and the müllerian duct system progresses to form the fallopian tubes, uterus, and proximal portion of the vagina. In a sense, female development is a negative procedure since the fetal ovary remains poorly differentiated at the same time that male organogenesis is well underway.[36]

In contrast to the unipotential of the primordia of the gonaducts, the primordia of the external genitalia are bipotential and may differentiate into either male or female type. The direction taken depends upon the predominance of estrogens or androgens. Comparable parts form the following structures: male glans penis/female glans clitoridis, male corpora cavernosa penis/female corpora cavernosa clitoridis, male corpus spongiosum/female bulb of the vestibule, male ventral portion of penis/female labia minora, male scrotum/female labia majorum. Identification of sex from appearance of the external genitalia is usually not possible until about the 10th or 11th week of gestation.[19]

Future reproductive physiology and certain behavioral aspects of maleness and femaleness depend upon the early (fetal and neonatal) exposure of the brain to the sex hormones. One of the major actions of androgens during development is to organize (imprint?) the immature central nervous system into a male direction.[34] The development following duct differentiation includes the appearance of interstitial (Leydig) cells in the testis, which are capable of producing androgenic hormones. It is interesting to note that these cells become dormant and atrophic from four to six weeks following birth and they are not morphologically recognizable again until puberty is approached.

Early in gestation the fetal gonads are capable of stimulation by the abundant amount of chorionic gonadotropin produced by the placenta. As previously described, the fetal pituitary begins synthesis of gonadotropins by the end of the first trimester reaching a peak of production at midterm and then decreasing until birth. As a result, serum testosterone levels in the male fetus are high at midgestation, decreasing in amount but not reaching usual prepubescent values until 4 to 6 months after birth. The chorionic gonadotropins are mainly responsible for testicular stimulation early in pregnancy and the pituitary gonadotropin toward the end of gestation. At term, due to the maturation of the negative feedback mechanism during the last half of gestation the secretion of LH and FSH are greatly diminished. After birth, and for a period of 2 to 4 years, gonadotropic plasma levels in girls are slightly higher than in boys, which may indicate the greater influence of testosterone on the maturation of the hypothalamic-pituitary-gonad axis than estrogens since the fetuses of both sexes are exposed to high estrogen levels of placental origin.[40, 68]

In many animals, including primates, if a male animal is castrated in the neonatal period, the pituitary release of gonadotropins (FSH and LH) becomes cyclic in the adult and is indistinguishable from that of the normal female. If an ovary is transplanted into such an adult male, cyclic ovulation occurs. If, however, a single injection of androgen is given following the castration, the ovulation does not take place. Furthermore, if the normal newborn female animal is given a single injection of androgen, she will be acyclic. Passivity and sexual receptivity characterize the male newborn castrate treated with estrogen as he enters adult life. Conversely, the androgen-treated female newborn becomes more aggressive in behavior, resembling the normal male.[67] Such evidence supports the concept that early exposure to these hormones, even if transient, profoundly influences subsequent development of the brain and its influence upon sex-related behavior and gonadal function.

Even in the young child the ovaries vary considerably in size, and this variation is due primarily to the number and size of small follicular "cysts." Gradual changes in the germinal epithelium at the cortex convert it from a tall columnar type to the thin endothelium-like layer more characteristic of the mature organ. Just before and during adolescence ovarian growth occurs at a fairly rapid rate, and follicular formation increases. The follicles go through the cycle of increasing in size, forming the corpus luteum and the eventual atresia that is characteristic of the mature female. It is probable that ovulation does not take place for several months or years after morphologic maturity is attained.

The male gonads undergo little differentiation or growth after the neonatal changes are completed. For the first 6 to 7 years the tubular epithelium is poorly developed. The connective tissue is abundant and resembles mesenchyme. At approximately 10 years of age the Leydig cells reappear, the tubular cells undergo early differentiation, and the tubules increase in size. Sertoli's cells are well developed and spermatids are present. Beyond age 12 the Leydig cells become larger, and the cytoplasm becomes vacuolated and more intensely stained than previously. Basal membranes of the tubules are well formed, and Sertoli's cells become mature. These maturational steps have considerable practical importance, since they are lacking in the undescended testicle. Varying degrees of fibrotic replacement also take place in the undescended testicle. The time chosen for operative procedures for cryptorchism cannot be arbitrary when based on these facts.[66]

The normally functioning gonad is necessary for proper development of the child. The effects of prepubertal castration demonstrate this: the muscles are less well developed, there is a greater deposition of fat in them, and the bones are longer owing to failure of the epiphyses to close.[4] The time of closure of the epiphyses is closely correlated with the advent of puberty, and the average child grows about 7.5 cm after its onset. With this fact in mind, it is interesting to note that the castrate stops growing at the time puberty normally would have occurred. The same picture results whether the ovaries or the testes are removed. Overactivity of the testicular tissue in prepubertal boys, as in interstitial cell tumors, results in early development of secondary sexual characteristics, a shortened growth span and a final stature less than his genetic potential. In girls, similar symptoms result from granulosa cell tumors in the ovary.[20]

The androgens secreted by the interstitial cells of the testes are activated by the gonadotropins from the pituitary. Their physiologic properties are not essentially different from those previously described for the adrenal cortex. In boys the testes certainly are the most important source of androgens.

Like testosterone, the ovarian estrogens normally are not secreted in physiologic amounts until shortly before puberty. Estrogens do not have any anabolic properties. Their major effect is in accomplishing the development of sexual maturity in girls and accelerating maturation that can be measured as bone age. Further discussion of the role of the gonads in growth and development will be found in the section on adolescence and puberty in this chapter.

The Parathyroid Glands, Vitamin D and Calcitonin

The importance of the parathyroid glands to normal growth and development can be appreciated when it is realized that these glands are responsible for normal bone development, which, in turn, is the limiting factor for statural growth. The parathyroid glands to a great degree regulate calcium and phosphorus metabolism in the body. Other important factors are the production of the parathormone antagonist calcitonin by special cells in the thyroid, the dietary intake of calcium and phosphorus, the availability of vitamin D, the status of physical exercise and the ability of the kidneys to respond to existing metabolic requirements.[1, 3, 4, 75] (See also chapter 8.)

The calcium and phosphorus content of body fluids is of vital importance in bone growth. The calcium in serum is composed of three fractions: (1) calcium ions, (2) calcium bound to protein, and (3) a very small un-ionized portion in solution. Under normal conditions of protein content and hydrogen ion concentration, about 50% of the calcium is in an ionized form in the serum. Recent work indicates that the primary action of the parathyroid hormone is to liberate calcium from bone, making it available to the circulation. This may be accomplished through the use of the citric acid, which keeps the calcium in soluble form both through its effect on the pH as an acid and as a chelating agent.[1, 3] In addition to the direct effect on bone, the hormone enhances calcium absorption from the gut in the presence of vitamin D. Finally, it increases the renal tubular reabsorption of calcium and the excretion of phosphate. The net result of the action of parathormone (PTH) is to increase the serum level of calcium and decrease phosphorus. In normal circumstances the adjustment of the serum calcium to the serum phosphorus level is such that the product of the two, expressed as mg/100 ml, is between 40 and 55 in growing children (30 to 40 in adults). This fact, plus clinical experience, is the basis for the law of Howland and Kramer, which states that rickets will be present in children if the product is below 35 and that rickets will heal if the product rises above 40.

Calcitonin is a polypeptide containing 32 amino acids and is formed by parafollicular C cells found in the thyroid, thymus, and parathyroids. It is secreted in response to hypercalcemia resulting in a lowered serum calcium and phosphate. This is accomplished by inhibition of bone resorption. Its onset of action is more rapid than PTH.[17, 38] Its physiologic importance appears to be one of balancing the homeostatic mechanisms for serum calcium.

Vitamin D is now considered to be a hormone. Cholecalciferol or ergocalciferol, taken in the diet or absorbed from the skin following exposure to ultraviolet rays, is not active in controlling calcium metabolism. Hydroxylation at position 25 occurs in the liver to form 25-hydroxyergocalciferol (25-OH). It is then transported in the blood, tightly bound to a protein, to receptors in renal tubule cells where further hydroxylation takes place to form the highly potent 1,25-dihydroxycholecalciferol (1,25-diOH). Plasma levels of 25-OH vitamin vary considerably depending upon oral intake or sun exposure. A considerable amount can be stored in lipid tissue, which is the reason that toxic doses of vitamin D have such a lingering effect. Although 25-OH vitamin D does have some biologic activity it is much less than the 1,25-diOH form. Vitamin D's major action is to increase calcium absorption from the intestine. Lesser effects are mobilization of calcium from bone and renal tubular reabsorption of calcium and phosphorous.[2, 17, 38]

Bone growth, then, depends on the local condition of the tissues and the serum or body fluids that act as a substrate for the tissues. If some disturbance occurs to diminish the elaboration of the enzymes (phosphatase, phosphorylase), the concentration of phosphate ions will not be sufficient to exceed the solubility product of the complex calcium-phosphate-carbonate salt, and deposition will not take place. However, even though the enzymes may be present in sufficient quantity, if the concentration of calcium or phosphate in the serum is low, the solubility product of the salt cannot be exceeded. Therefore, bone growth may be disturbed in two ways in the process of mineralization. Other factors, too, may interfere, such as poor matrix formation due to abnormality of protein metabolism. Finally, it is known that a lowered pH of the serum, as in chronic acidosis, favors decalcification by its effect on the ionization of the calcium.

The clinical picture of hyperparathyroidism is characterized by decalcification of bone with resultant softening and malformation. Cysts may form in the bone and fractures occur. All of these may contribute to statural abnormality and relative dwarfism.

At birth the parathyroid glands appear to be morphologically similar to those of the adult. Some authors state that hypertrophy is occasionally present late in the first week of life and believe this is caused by the high phosphate content of cow's milk and its effect on serum levels. The relatively low calcium and elevated phosphate levels in the serum of the newborn infant have been attributed, in part, to cow's-milk feedings.

The classic description of the functionally depressed or immature parathyroids being responsible for the low calcium-high phosphorus ratios found in the neonatal period is open to question. Although some work indicates that small-for-gestational-age and premature neonates have depressed parathyroid function leading to hypocalcemia,[54, 55] others have found that serum calcitonin levels were markedly elevated in infants with low calcium levels.[100] The high values of calcitonin in the newborn are consistent with the increased number of C cells found in the thyroid at that time. There is no evidence of impaired renal function being at fault for the associated hyperphosphatemia. Serum concentrations of PTH indicate a slightly reduced level for the first few days of life when compared to older infants, but essentially no change with age thereafter.[3]

Adolescence and Puberty

Adolescence is that period of life associated with accelerated growth in height and weight, the appearance of sexual characteristics and ability to reproduce, and then a rapid deceleration of growth that is terminated by the final maturation of bone with fusion of epiphyses and metaphyses. It is the period of transition from childhood to adulthood. Shakespeare wrote of it in *Twelfth Night:*

> Not yet old enough for a man
> nor young enough for a boy;
> as a squash is before 'tis a
> peascod, or a codling when
> 'tis almost an apple: 'tis
> with him in standing water,
> between boy and man.

Adolescence, has no readily defineable beginning or end, and it may last, in some individuals, for nearly a decade. There is considerable variability in the chronologic ages at which these events occur (Figs 9–2, 9–3, 9–4 and Tables 9–6 and 9–7).

Puberty (from the Latin *pubertas* refers to age of appearance of sexual hair) is defined by common law and most legal statutes as the time when sexual reproducton is possible. Developmentally, this is usually considered to coincide with the appearance of dark, curly pubic hair. Menarche is often used as the dividing line between prepuberty and postpuberty, though ovulation and the ability to reproduce are often not present for another year or two. On the average, puberty is assumed to take place about two years later in boys than in girls. Most of the changes that occur, including the "adolescent spurt" of growth, are steroid (sex hormone) mediated.

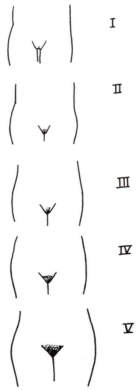

Fig 9–2.—Stages of pubic hair development in the female. Compare with Table 9–4.

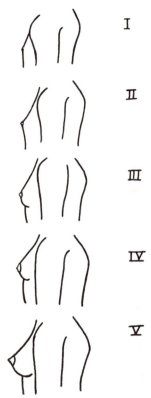

Fig 9–3.—Stages of breast development in the female. Compare with Table 9–4.

This period is accompanied by important psychologic changes that are deeply influenced by the physical alterations. These aspects of adolescence and puberty are discussed in chapter 6.

Generally speaking, the sooner puberty occurs the sooner will the rate of growth decline and finally stop.[27] This can be nicely shown in girls by charting two subjects on the same graph. If the onset of menarche occurs earlier in one, her growth curve levels off sooner than that of the other subject under study. This growth curve may be representative of height, weight, or of body dimensions in general (Fig 9–5). At the same age, the mean height and weight of boys or girls who are more mature sexually are significantly greater than of those who are less mature (Fig 9–6), and the onset of puberty is better correlated with these measurements than with chronologic age.[6] It should be pointed out that growth curves based on

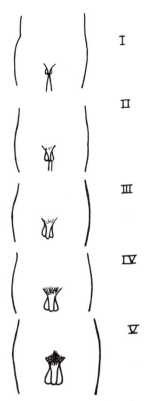

Fig 9-4.—Stages of pubic hair and genital development in the male. Compare with Table 9-5.

cumulative data of large numbers of subjects are misleading or misrepresent the shape of the curve for the individual at the time of adolescence. The curve for the large numbers appears relatively smooth because it covers a number of years for the growth spurt. The curve for the individual is usually relatively abrupt in change at the beginning and end of the growth spurt and covers a time measured in months rather than in years. The maximal yearly increase in height occurs the year before menarche in most girls.

That growth may proceed to some considerable extent after menarche is graphically indicated in Figure 9-7. The average increase after this time was about 3 in. (7.5 cm) in a group of American girls, with a range from under 1 in. to nearly 7 in. Obviously, one must be cautious in giving advice as to how much further increase in stature will occur after the onset of

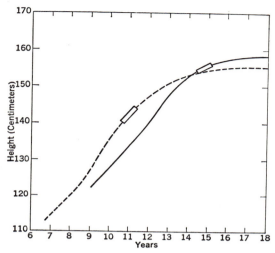

Fig 9–5.—Relation of growth and onset of menarche. The *blocks* in the curves represent the time of menarche in two groups of girls. Girls with early menarche, and presumably reaching maturity early, have a more accelerated growth curve than girls with late menarche, but duration of their growth is shorter. As a result of this growth pattern girls with late maturation are taller, on the average, when final stature is attained. (From Holt L.E. Jr., McIntosh R. (eds.): *Diseases of Infancy and Children,* ed. 11. New York, Appleton-Century Crofts, 1941.)

menstruation. A further interesting observation based on this material is that final height was not predictable from the amount of growth taking place following menarche. There is some trend in the direction of the tallest girls having the greatest amount of postmenarche growth, but many variables are apparent.

Until very recently in the United States, and possibly other developed nations, each succeeding generation of girls experienced an earlier age of the menarche. As with the past history of increasing height in succeeding generations, we may have reached an ultimate limit. For at least two decades, menarche is not occurring earlier and adult height is not increasing. (See also chapter 2.) There do appear to be some genetic factors involved in the normally wide variation found among healthy girls (Table 9–3).[50, 80, 81]

Previous indications that hot climates brought about earlier menarche and other evidences of sexual maturation have been put aside as purely anecdotal.

The pubertal acceleration in height occurs earlier and is of shorter duration and of lesser magnitude in girls than in boys. In girls, on the aver-

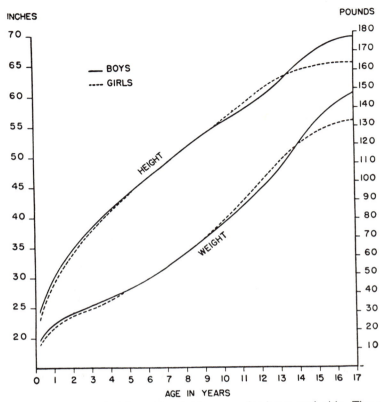

Fig 9–6.—Average height and weight curves for boys and girls. The earlier increase at the time of adolescence for the girls is clearly shown. The fact that most girls are larger than most boys between ages 11 and 13 is probably due to the earlier influence of the sex hormones on physical growth.

age, the peak of the adolescent velocity in growth occurs just prior to or during stage III of her sexual development. In boys this event occurs later during stage IV. All girls will have begun to decelerate their rate of growth before menarche.[88] The age at which each stage of adolescence is reached follows the usual sequence (Tables 9–4 and 9–5) in more than 60% of children; this still permits nearly 40% of normal subjects to deviate from the expected. As an example, breast development in girls reaches stage II or III before the appearance of pubic hair in 75%, but pubic hair reaches stage II or III in 10% before the breasts reach stage II. Menarche occurs most commonly late in stage III. By age 13 more than half of American females have reached stage IV in breast and pubic hair development and

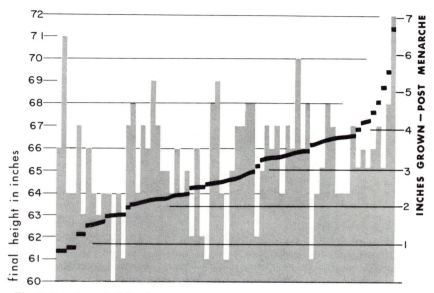

Fig 9–7.—Growth following menarche in 68 normal American girls. The *dark line* indicates the final height and the *shaded areas* the inches grown after menarche. The point at which the dark line crosses a shaded column represents that specific girl's postmenarchial growth and final height. It can be seen that the shortest girls *(far left of chart)* did not show the least amount of growth after menarche, and the same absence of correlation is generally true of the tallest girls *(right)*, who did not necessarily have the greatest postmenarchial growth.

have begun menstruation. Precocious development is considered if sexual development begins before 8 years and delayed development if no signs of sexual changes have begun by 14 years. By age 14.5 approximately half of American boys will have reached stage IV. Precocious development would be considered if sexual development began before 10 years and delayed if no sexual development appeared by 14.25 years. It is interesting to note that sex maturity ratings in the United States do not differ between whites and blacks in terms of sequence and that there is very close agreement in staging the several aspects of sexual development, e.g., pubic hair, breast development, size of testes, in contrast to the English studies of Tanner who found considerable disparity of two or more ordinal ranks.[56]

Not only is there much variation in the ages at which the various sequences of puberty begin, there are also considerable differences among children in the rapidity with which each progresses from one stage to the next. One may remain at one stage for less than six months while another occupies the same stage for two years. The average adolescent will pass

TABLE 9–3.—AGE AT MENARCHE

AGE (YR)	ALL RACES*	WHITE	BLACK
6–9	0.2	0.2	0.2
10	1.2	0.8	4.0
11	12.8	11.6	21.3
12	43.3	41.7	51.2
13	73.2	72.9	74.1
14	91.7	91.4	93.5
15	98.3	98.2	98.7
16–17	99.7	99.6	100.0

*Percentage of girls whose menstrual periods had started, in a survey in the United States by race and age.[12]

through all stages in approximately four years, but normal variations range from 18 months to 8 years. The rate of passage is unrelated to the age of onset of the earliest changes.

The cause or causes for the beginning of puberty remain obscure. Frisch and co-workers have postulated a critical body mass as initiating the onset of puberty and related to the age of menarche.[6] Most authorities have expressed doubt regarding such a relationship.

Hormonal assays have shown the relationship of increased production of hypothalamic gonadotropic-releasing hormone (Gn-RH) and increased release of pituitary LH and FSH as puberty begins.[70] The postulated steps are as follows:

1. At midgestation of the fetal period, maturation of the negative feedback mechanism of the hypothalamic-pituitary-gonad axis takes place. During infancy and childhood the extremely sensitive hypothalamus results in an inhibition of the release of Gn-RH and secondarily LH, FSH, and gonadal hormones.

2. At the onset of puberty, the sensitivity of the hypothalamus declines resulting in an increased release of Gn-RH, FSH, LH, and sex steroids. Initially, this increased release is nocturnal and as early as a bone age of 10 or 11 becomes pulsatile in character with intervals of about 90 minutes. In experiments in primates where the administration of Gn-RH could be controlled in subjects with hypothalamic lesions, continuous administration did not induce pubertal changes while pulsatile administration did, including 28-day ovulatory menstrual cycles.[9] Plasma levels of adrenal androgens increase significantly.[73]

3. In early puberty sleep augmentation of gonadotropin continues, the concentrations of sex steroids increase, and the first physical evidence of sexual maturation appear.

4. By midpuberty (stage III in Tables 9–4 and 9–5) the sleep augmentation of the pulsatile release of gonadotropins increases and daytime plasma concentrations of sex steroids are considerably higher than previously. Just prior to or with the advent of menarche, a positive feedback mechanism appears in the female. Increasing amounts of estrogen exert a stimulating effect upon the hypothalamic gonadotropic-releasing center, triggering an LH and FSH surge at midcycle. This pattern continues into adult life.

5. In the adult physical maturation is complete, sleep augmentation of gonadotropins disappears and statural growth ceases.

TABLE 9–4.—STAGES OF SEXUAL DEVELOPMENT: FEMALE

AGE (YR)	STAGES
0–12	I. Preadolescent. Female pelvic contour evident, breast flat, labia majora smooth and minora are poorly developed, hymenal opening small or absent, mucous membranes dry and red, vaginal cells lack glycogen.
8–13	II. *Breasts:* Elevation of nipple, small mound beneath areola that is enlarging and begins pigmentation. *Labia majora* become thickened, more prominent and wrinkled, *labia minora* easily identified due to increased size along with clitoris, urethral opening more prominent, mucous membranes moist and pink, some glycogen present in vaginal cells. *Hair:* First appears on mons and then on labia major about time of menarche, still scanty, soft and straight. *Skin:* Increased activity of sebaceous and merocrine sweat glands and initial function of apocrine glands in axilla and vulva begin.
9–14	III. Rapid growth peak is passed, menarche most often at this stage and invariably follows the peak of growth acceleration. *Breasts:* Areola and nipple further enlarge and pigmentation more evident, continued increase in glandular size. *Labia minora* well developed and vaginal cells have increased glycogen content, mucous membranes increasingly more pale. *Hair* in pubic region thicker, coarser, often curly (considerable normal variation including a few girls with early stage II at menarche). *Skin:* Further increased activity of sebaceous and sweat glands with beginning of *acne* in some girls, adult body odor.
12–15	IV. *Breasts:* Projection of areola above breast plane and areolar (Montgomery) glands apparent (this development is absent in about 20% of normal girls). Glands easily palpable. *Labia:* Both majora and minora assume adult structure, glycogen content of vaginal cells begins cyclic characteristics. *Hair* in pubic area more abundant, axillary hair present (rarely present at stage II, not uncommonly present at stage III).
12–17	V. *Breasts:* Mature histologic morphology, nipple enlarged and erect, areolar (Montgomery) glands well developed, globular shape. *Hair* in pubic area more abundant and may spread to thighs (in about 10% of women it assumes "male" distribution with extension toward umbilicus). Facial hair increased often in form of slight mustache. *Skin:* Increased sebaceous gland activity and increased severity of acne if present before.

TABLE 9–5.—STAGES OF SEXUAL DEVELOPMENT: MALE

AGE (YR)	STAGES
0–14	I. Preadolescent
10–14	II. *Testes* and *penis:* Increasing size is evident (testicle length reaches 2.0 cm or more). Scrotum integument is thinner and assumes an increased pendulous appearance. *Hair:* First appearance of pubic hair in area at base of penis. *Skin:* Increased activity of sebaceous and apocrine sweat glands and initial function of apocrine glands on axilla and scrotal area begins.
11–15	III. *Testes* and *penis:* Further increase in size and pigmentation apparent. Leydig's cells (interstitial) first appear at stage II, are now prominent in testes. *Hair:* In pubic area more abundant and present on scrotum, still scanty and fine textured, axillary hair begins. *Breasts:* Button-type hypertrophy in 70% of boys at stages II and III. *Larynx:* Changes in voice due to laryngeal growth begin. *Skin:* Increasing activity of sebaceous and sweat glands with beginning of acne, adult body odor.
12–16	IV. *Testes:* Further increase in size, length 4.0 cm or greater, increase in size of *penis* greatest at stages III and IV. *Hair:* Pubic hair thicker and coarser and in most ascends toward umbilicus in typical male pattern, axillary hair increases, facial hair increases over lip and upper cheeks. *Larynx:* Voice deepens. *Skin:* Increasing pigmentation of scrotum and penis, acne often more severe. *Breasts:* Previous hypertrophy decreased or absent.
13–17	V. Rapid growth peak has occurred. *Testes:* Length greater than 4.5 cm. *Hair:* Pubic hair thick, curly, heavily pigmented, extends to thighs and toward umbilicus. Adult distribution and increase in body hair (chest, shoulders, thighs, etc.) continues for more than another 10 years. Baldness, if present, may begin. *Skin:* Acne may persist and increase. *Larynx:* Adult character of voice.

Adrenal androgens stimulate the growth of pubic and axillary hair (adrenarche), increase linear growth rate, and advance bone maturation. Androgens are also important in the development of the labia majora and clitoris. During adolescence, plasma levels of thyroxine decline reaching a nadir at midpuberty. Plasma levels of T_3 remain unchanged. GH potentiates the biologic action of both estrogen and testosterone and therefore plays an important part in the expression of sexual characteristics.

Boys gain consistently more in shoulder width than girls from the time of pubertal onset until its conclusion. At the same time, girls grow more rapidly in hip width than do boys during all phases of the pubertal period. A marked difference in subcutaneous tissue is also present. In girls the amount of subcutaneous tissue increases progressively throughout puberty. In contrast, the average boy experiences a decrease in the amount of subcutaneous tissue during the pubertal period. Pubertal weight gain is not associated with gain in subcutaneous tissue for boys as it is for girls.[72]

Socioeconomic factors are important in the determination of the time of onset of puberty. In nearly every society the more well-to-do girls experience earlier menarche than their peers. The secular changes referred to in chapters 2 and 4 almost certainly have resulted from improvement in nutrition, decreases in severity and frequency of diseases, and the beneficial influence of other amenities that have occurred through the years. Still another factor may be the increased hybridization resulting from greater genetic mixes than was possible previously. Race, age of maternal menarche, and other genetic factors appear to have some, but relatively minor, influences. Malnutrition, chronic disease, and blindness all tend to delay

TABLE 9–6.—Hormones Involved in Adolescent Development

Luteinizing hormone release factor
Activity: Stimulates pituitary to release gonadotropins (LH and FSH)
Source: Hypothalamus
Nature: Decapeptide
Luteinizing hormone
Activity: Preparation and ripening of ovarian follicle, may stimulate release of progesterone, role not clear in prepubertal girl; in male stimulates interstitial (Leydig's) cells of testes to secrete testosterone
Source: Pituitary
Name: LH, a glycoprotein
Follicle-stimulating hormone
Activity: In female, develops ovarian follicle to antrum stage, increases estrogen secretion from follicle; in male, matures sperm and may influence growth of seminiferous tubules
Source: Pituitary
Name: FSH, a glycoprotein
Estrogens
Activity: Feminizing, cause breast development, uterine growth, vaginal maturation, bone maturation, no effect on somatic growth
Source: Mainly ovarian but small and possibly significant amounts from adrenal cortex and testes
Names: Estrone, estradial, estriol
Androgens
Activity: Virilizing, cause penile and prostatic development; promote hair growth of pubic, axillary, facial and general body areas; bone maturation; laryngeal development; sebaceous and sweat gland development; stimulus to somatic growth
Source: Testicles, adrenal cortex, small amounts from ovary
Names: Dehydroepiandrosterone, testosterone, epitestosterone, androstenedione
Progesterones
Activity: Block estrogen effect on endometrium, stimulate endometrial gland secretion, stimulate lobule-alveolar breast formation and growth
Source: Mainly from ovarian corpus luteum, small amounts from testes and adrenal cortex (large amounts from placenta)
Names: Progesterone, pregnenolone

the appearance of puberty.[5, 89] Some of the pathologic conditions associated with abnormalities of sexual development are indicated in Table 9–7.

The occurrence of diffuse nontoxic goiter is sufficiently common among adolescents to warrant some discussion. These goiters do have an increased frequency during the adolescent growth spurt, but the relationship, if any, of one to the other remains obscure. The inclusion of iodine in table salt plus the interregional transportation of foods has not eliminated iodine-deficient goiter though its frequency in this country has been dramatically reduced in comparison to the early 1900s. Recent surveys indicate that about half or more of all adolescent goiters are due to chronic lymphocytic thyroiditis.[46, 79] This is a form of autoimmune disease secondary to an initial low-grade infection in the gland that is responsible for the liberation of the antigenic stimuli. Of the various methods used to identify the significant antibodies, an immunofluorescent technique seems to be the most reliable.[98]

The influence of the endocrine glands on the ultimate stature of human beings depends on several factors. Maturational influences of estrogens and androgens in limiting growth have been mentioned. Very soon after the union of the shafts and the epiphyses of the long bones has taken place, linear growth ceases. The sex hormones have great influence in this category. The fact that eunuchs usually stop growing at the time when puberty would normally occur would suggest that secretion of the pituitary growth hormone diminishes at this time. That this is not true is well established.

TABLE 9–7.—Pathologic Conditions Associated
With Abnormalities of Sexual Development*

Conditions associated with *delayed onset* of puberty
   Pituitary dwarfism
   Hypothyroidism
   Hypogonadism (agenesis, atrophy, surgical or traumatic castration)
   Acromegaly (rare)
   Any severe chronic illness
   Hypothalamic lesions (Frölich's syndrome, Prader-Willi syndrome)
Conditions associated with *precocious* sexual development
   Adrenal cortex tumors or hyperplasia
   Interstitial cell tumors of the testes
   Ovarian tumors (granulosa cell and thecoma)
   Pineal gland tumors (in males only)
   Third ventricle tumors of the brain
   Hydrocephalus (rare)
   Postencephalitis (rare)
   McCune-Albright syndrome (polyostotic fibrous dysplasia)
   Exogenous source of sex hormones

*Besides the endocrine glands, it will be noted that the central nervous system (hypothalamus) may also be involved.

The quantities of this hormone that are present in the pituitary and in the blood are approximately equal in children and adults. Only in the acromegalic and the pituitary dwarf are there variations from this, higher levels being found in the former and the lower levels in the latter. The thyroid hormone and insulin also act synergistically with GH; both are necessary for normal stature, but neither alone promotes growth. We must conclude that some change occurs in the end organs, making them resistant to normal quantities of the growth hormone when full maturity is achieved.

The development of secondary sexual characteristics usually follows a fairly set pattern, although there may be considerable individual variation (see Tables 9–3 and 9–4).[5, 13, 26, 94, 95] Many have observed that the development of sexual characteristics is much more closely correlated with bone maturation than with chronologic age. There is likewise a better correlation between maturation and measurements of height and weight than with age. Enlargement of the breasts and rounding of the contours of the hips are the first discernible changes in girls. Accumulation of subcutaneous fat in girls may be noted in the regions of the thighs, buttocks, chest, lower abdomen, and the mons veneris. By the time of menarche the small budding breasts have progressively enlarged to assume a conical shape. The mature or rounded form gradually develops during the next two to four years. The first appearance of pubic hair precedes menarche by a year or more; it becomes more deeply pigmented and coarser throughout adolescence and into adult life. In approximately 10% of normal girls, pubic hair is present before significant hypertrophy of the breasts occurs. The initial growth of axillary hair may follow menarche or occur shortly before it.[76]

Growth of the breasts is evoked by the increase in amount of circulating estrogens. The initial response is elongation and thickening of the ducts. When progesterone is added, the distal ends of the ducts enlarge to form the lobule-alveoli. The source of the progesterone is the corpus luteum formed following ovulation. In the absence of pituitary growth hormone, however, the effectiveness of these steroids is minimal. With pregnancy there is a marked increase in the steroid hormone that augments the lobule-alveolar development and prepares the breast for lactation. Milk production results from the addition of prolactin by the placenta and the anterior pituitary.

In about 70% of boys, some hypertrophy of the breasts occurs. The peak incidence is between the fourteenth and fifteenth years, after the appearance of pubic hair and the growth of the genitalia has started. As adolescence advances, this *gynecomastia* gradually disappears, but it may persist for as long as two years.[78] Some degree of tenderness, particularly following even minor trauma, is not uncommon. Asymmetric enlargement may be present. Pubic hair first appears with the beginning increase in size of the penis. Axillary and facial hair come shortly thereafter. Puberty is said to be reached in the male when the pubic hair becomes darker, coarser and begins to curl. Other body hair in the male undergoes similar changes, but these are much later and continue well into adult life. The characteristic hairline on the forehead in men is one of the last developments of sex maturation. Deepening of the voice, due to growth of the larynx in the ventrodorsal diameter, occurs at midadolescence (average, 14–16 years) in boys.[21, 24]

Acne vulgaris is so common during adolescence that it has come to be regarded as physiologic rather than pathologic.[11, 97] It is present to some degree in 75% to 90% of children before 18 years of age. It is the result of androgenic stimulation of the sebaceous glands. Circulating testosterone is taken up by the sebaceous gland and converted by enzyme action to dihydrotestosterone, which causes hypertrophy of the gland and increases production of sebum. At the same time there is altered keratinization within the follicular canal resulting in varying degrees of obstruction. The obstructed pilosebaceous unit is called a *comedo*. Two types of comedones are formed: incompletely obstructed ones are termed blackheads and completely obstructed ones are whiteheads. It is the latter that are responsible for the major lesions. These are small elevated papules just beneath the skin surface in early stages. As more sebum is produced the follicle expands and eventually ruptures dispersing its contents into the adjacent dermis. This initiates the inflammatory lesion, which may be severe because of the highly irritating nature of the fatty acids found in sebum. As the disorder increases in intensity, papules, pustules, nodules or cysts develop. Primary sites for acne are the face, chest, back, and shoulders. As fibrous tissue forms to encapsulate the inflamed area, some degree of scarring and cicatrix result in both pitting and keloid scars in the more unfortunate individuals. There does seem to be an indication that the more severe forms follow a dominant inheritance. Acne appears equally in both sexes and all

TABLE 9–8.—Average Weight (gm) of Endocrine Glands and Some Sex Organs at Various Ages*

	NEWBORN	1 YR	6 YR	14 YR	ADULT
Pituitary	0.1	0.2	0.3	0.4	0.5–0.8
Thyroid	2.0	3.0	7	14	18
Adrenals (2)	6–8	4.5	7	10	10–20
Parathyroids	. . .	. . .	. . .	. . .	0.65
Testes (2)	1.5	1.5	1.6	7	35
Ovaries (2)	0.3	0.6	1.9	6	11
Uterus	3.9	1.4	2.8	30	50
Prostate	0.8	0.8	1.3	3.3	17

*From several sources.

races. It tends to start after menarche and increases in intensity with the degree of development of secondary sex characteristics in both boys and girls.

Increased pigmentation of the skin progressively increases with advancing sexual maturation in the axillary, areolar, circumanal, scrotal, penile, and labial areas. Another fairly common change found in the skin of adolescents is "colored" striae. These are most frequently seen over the gluteal areas, thighs and lower abdomen. They are red-purple when first present but fade later to become almost invisible. They are not necessarily associated with obesity, occur in about one third of these children and are more evident in those with the most severe acne.[18]

Muscular development, including strength, progresses rapidly in both sexes, but is more pronounced in the male. Involution of the lymphatic system, reduction in tonsil and lymph node sizes, as well as decreased reaction to most infections, begins at this time and continues for several years. The differences between the sexes at this time in red blood cell counts and hemoglobin values have been noted in chapter 7.

Some descriptions have already been given of the development of the primary sex organs. A few additional statements are necessary. The vaginal mucosa changes from columnar to squamous shortly before menarche. Concurrent with this change there is an increased glycogen content of the mucosa and the pH becomes lowered. As a result, the bacterial flora of the vagina changes. It is probable that during the first one or two years following menarche the menstrual periods of most girls are anovulatory. The first several menses are often irregular and the interval is longer or shorter than is characteristic of later life.[20, 22]

REFERENCES

1. Deftos L.J., Roos B.A., Parthemore J.G.: Calcium and skeletal metabolism. *West. J. Med.* 123:447, 1975.
2. Raisz L.G., Kream B.E.: Regulation of bone formation. *N. Engl. J. Med.* 309:29, 1983.
3. Root A., Gruskin A., Reber R.M., et al.: Serum concentrations of parathyroid hormone in infants, children and adolescents. *J. Pediatr.* 85:329, 1974.
4. Ezrin C., Godden J.O., Volpe R., et al.: *Systematic Endocrinology.* New York, Harper & Row, 1973.
5. Tanner J.M.: *Growth at Adolescence,* ed. 2. Oxford, Blackwell Scientific Publications, 1962.
6. Frisch R.E.: A method of prediction of age of menarche from height and weight at ages 9 through 13 years. *Pediatrics* 53:384, 1974.
7. Raben M.S.: Growth hormone. *N. Engl. J. Med.* 266:31, 82, 1962.
8. Root A.: Growth hormone. *Pediatrics* 36:940, 1965.
9. Knobil E.: Patterns of hormonal signals and hormone action. *N. Engl. J. Med.* 305:1582, 1981.

10. Axelrod J., Reisine T.D.: Stress hormones: Their interaction and regulation. *Science* 224:452, 1984.
11. Hurwitz S.: Acne vulgaris. *Pediatr. Ann.* 5:55, 1976.
12. *Age at Menarche, United States.* U.S. Dept. of Health, Education and Welfare, Public Health Service, 1973.
13. Ehrhardt A.A., Meyer-Bahlburg H.F.L.: Effects of prenatal sex hormones on gender related behavior. *Science* 211:1312, 1981.
14. Williams R.H. (ed.): *Textbook of Endocrinology,* ed. 4. Philadelphia, W.B. Saunders Co., 1968.
15. Ganong W.F., Alpert L.C., Lee T.C.: ACTH and the regulation of adrenocortical secretion. *N. Engl. J. Med.* 290:1006, 1974.
16. Federman. D.D.: *Abnormal Sexual Development.* Philadelphia, W.B. Saunders Co., 1967.
17. Austin L.A., Heath H.: Calcitonin: Physiology and pathophysiology. *N. Engl. J. Med.* 304:269, 1981.
18. Sisson W.R.: Colored striae in adolescent children. *J. Pediatr.* 45:520, 1954.
19. Patten B.M.: *Human Embryology,* ed.3. New York, McGraw-Hill Book Co., 1968.
20. Huffman J.W.: *The Gynecology of Childhood and Adolescence.* Philadelphia, W.B. Saunders Co., 1968.
21. Schonfeld W.A.: Primary and secondary sexual characteristics: Study of their development in males from birth through maturity, with biometric study of penis and testis. *Am. J. Dis. Child.* 65:535, 1943.
22. Villee D.B.: *Human Endocrinology, A Developmental Approach.* Philadelphia, W.B. Saunders Co., 1975.
23. Heald F.P., Masland R.P., Sturgis S.H., et al.: Dysmenorrhea in adolescence. *Pediatrics* 20:121, 1957.
24. Shuttleworth F.K.: *The Adolescent Period: A Graphic and Pictorial Atlas.* Monogram, Society for Research in Child Development, vol. III, no. 3. Washington, D.C., National Research Council, 1938.
25. Weitzman E.D.: Biologic rhythms and hormone secretion patterns. *Hosp. Pract.* 8:79, 1976.
26. Root A.W.: Endocrinology of puberty. *J. Pediatr.,* 83:1, 1973.
27. Stuart H.C.: Physical growth during adolescence. *Am. J. Dis. Child.* 74:495, 1947.
28. Stuart H.C.: Normal growth and development during adolescence. *N. Engl. J. Med.* 234:666, 693 and 732, 1946.
29. Loeb J.N.: Corticosteroids and growth. *N. Engl. J. Med.* 295:547, 1976.
30. Matsuzaki F., Irie M., Shizume K.: Growth hormone in human fetal pituitary glands and cord blood. *J. Clin. Endocrinol.* 33:908, 1971.
31. August G.P., Grumbach M.M., Kaplan S.L.: Hormonal changes in puberty: Correlation of plasma testosterone, LH, FSH, testicular size, and bone age with male pubertal development. *J. Clin. Endocrinol.* 34:319, 1972.
32. Safer D.J., Allen R.P., Barr E.: Growth rebound after termination of stimulant drugs. *J. Pediatr.* 86:113, 1975.
33. Chan L., O'Malley B.W.: Mechanism of action of the sex steroid hormones. *N. Engl. J. Med.* 294:1322, 1976.
36. Gardner L.I.: *Endocrine and Genetic Diseases of Childhood and Adolescence,* ed. 2. Philadelphia, W.B. Saunders Co., 1975.
37. Klein R.: Adrenocortical control of sodium and potassium excretion in newborn period. *J. Clin. Invest.* 30:318–324, March, 1951.

38. Harrison H.E., Harison H.C.: *Disorders of Calcium and Phosphate Metabolism in Childhood and Adolescence.* Philadelphia, W.B. Saunders Co., 1979.
39. Grumbach M.M., Werner S.C.: Transfer of thyroid hormone across the human placenta. *J. Clin. Endocrinol.* 16:1392, 1956.
40. Gluckman P.D., Grumbach M.M., Kaplan S.L.: The human fetal hypothalamus and pituitary gland, in Tulchinsky D., Ryan K.J. (eds.): *Maternal-Fetal Endocrinology.* Philadelphia, W.B. Saunders Co., 1980.
41. Buehring G.E.: Witch's milk: potential for neonatal diagnosis. *Pediatr. Res.* 16:460, 1982.
42. Nakai T., Yamada R.: Urinary catecholamine excretion by various age groups with special reference to catecholamines in newborns. *Ped. Res.* 17:457, 1983.
43. Brien T.G., Fay J.A., Griffin E.A.: Thyroid status in the newborn infant. *Arch. Dis. Child.* 49:225, 1974.
44. Humbert J.R., Gotlin R.W.: Growth hormone levels in normoglycemic and hypoglycemic infants born small for gestational age. *Pediatrics* 48:190, 1971.
45. Hays R.M.: Antidiuretic hormone. *N. Engl. J. Med.* 295:659, 1976.
46. Sippel W.G., Dorr H.G., Bidlingmaier F., et al.: Plasma levels of adolesterone, corticosterone 11-desopycorticosterone, progesterone, 17-hydropyprogesterone, cortisol and cortisone during infancy and childhood. *Pediatr. Res.* 14:39, 1980.
47. Lowrey G.H., Aster R.H., Carr E.A., et al.: Early diagnostic criteria of congenital hypothyroidism: A comprehensive study of forty-nine cretins. *Am. J. Dis. Child.* 96:131, 1958.
48. Fisher D.A., Klein A.H.: The ontogenesis of thyroid function and its relationship to neonatal thermogenesis, in Tulchinsky D., Ryan K.J. (eds.): *Maternal-Fetal Endocrinology.* Philadelphia, W.B. Saunders Co., 1980.
49. Davies I.J.: The fetal adrenal, in Tulchinsky D., Ryan K.J. (eds.): *Maternal-Fetal Endocrinology.* Philadelphia, W.B. Saunders Co., 1980.
50. Provis H.S., Ellis R.W.B.: An anthropometric study of Edinburgh schoolchildren. *Arch. Dis. Child.* 30:328, 432, 1955.
51. Frohman L.A.: Neurotransmitters as regulators in endocrine function. *Hosp. Pract.* 4:55, 1975.
52. Blodgett F.M., Burgin L., Iezzoni D., et al.: Effects of prolonged cortisone therapy on statural growth, skeletal maturation and metabolic status of children. *N. Engl. J. Med.* 254:636, 1956.
53. Fluhman C.F.: Menstrual problems of adolescence. *Pediatr. Clin. N. Am.* 5:51, 1958.
54. Tsang R.C., Chen I.W., Friedman M.A., et al.: Neonatal parathyroid function: Role of gestational age and postnatal age. *J. Pediatr.* 83:728, 1973.
55. Tsang R.C., Light I.J., Sutherland J.M., et al.: Possible pathogenetic factors in neonatal hypocalcemia of prematurity. *J. Pediatr.* 82:423, 1973.
56. Harlan W.T., Grillo G.P., Cornoni-Huntley J., et al.: Secondary sex characteristics of boys 12 to 17 years of age: The U.S. health examination survey. *J. Pediatr.* 95:293, 1979.
57. Ulstrom R.A., Colle E., Burley J., et al.: Adrenocortical steroid metabolism in newborn infants: I. Urinary excretion of free and conjugated 17-hydroxycorticosteroids in normal full-term infants. II. Urinary excretion of 6-beta-hydroxycortical and other polar metabolites. *J. Clin. Endocrinol.* 20:1066, 1080, 1960.
58. Sack J., Fisher D.A., Wang C.C.: Serum thyrotropin, prolactin, and growth

hormone levels during the early neonatal period in the human infant. *J. Pediatr.* 89:298, 1976.

59. McEwen B.S.: The brain as a target organ of endocrine hormones. *Hosp. Pract.* 5:95, 1975.

60. Daughaday W.H.: Regulation of skeletal growth by sulfation factor. *Adv. Intern. Med.* 17:237, 1971.

61. Swanson H.E., Ezrin C.: The natural history of the delta cell of the human adenohypophysis, in childhood, adulthood, and pregnancy. *J. Clin. Endocrinol.* 20:952, 1960.

62. Deanesly R.: Fetal endocrinology. *Br. Med. Bull.* 17:91, 1961.

63. Wilkins L.: Masculinization of female fetus due to use of progestins. *J.A.M.A.* 172:1028, 1960.

64. Bongiovanni A.M., DiGeorge A.M., Grumbach M.M.: Masculinization of the female infant associated with estrogenic therapy alone during gestation. *J. Clin. Endocrinol.* 19:1004, 1959.

65. Onishi S., Miyazawa G., Nishimura Y., et al.: Postnatal development of circadian rhythm in serum cortisol levels in children. *Pediatrics* 72:399, 1983.

66. Shapiro S.R., Bodai B.I.: Current concepts of the undescended testis. *Surg. Gynecol. Obstet.* 147:617, 1978.

67. Mac Lusky N.J., Naflotin F.: Sexual differentiation of the central nervous system. *Science* 211:1294, 1981.

68. Penny R., Olambiwonnu O., Frasier S.D.: Follicle stimulating hormone (FSH) and luteinizing hormone-human chorionic gonadotropin (LH-HCG) concentrations in paired maternal and cord sera. *Pediatrics* 58:41, 1974.

69. Finkelstein J.W.: The endocrinology of adolescence. *Ped. Clin. N. Am.* 27:53, 1980.

70. Corley K.P., Valk T.W., Kelch R.P., et al.: Estimation of GnRH pulse amplitude during pubertal development. *Pediatr. Res.* 15:157, 1981.

71. Lazarus L., Young J.D.: Radioimmunoassay of human growth hormone using ion exchange resin. *J. Clin. Endocrinol.* 26:213, 1966.

72. Faust M.S.: Somatic development of adolescent girls. Monograph, Society for Research in Child Development, Chicago, vol. 42, 1977.

73. Warne G.L., Carter J.N., Faimain C., et al.: The relationship of adrenal androgens to the secretory pattern for cortisol, prolactin and growth hormone during puberty. *Pediatr. Res.* 13:211, 1979.

74. Copp D.H.: Parathyroids, calcitonin and control of plasma calcium. *Recent Prog. Horm. Res.* 20:59, 1964.

75. Avioli L.V., Haddad J.G.: Vitamin D: Current concepts. *Metabolism* 22:507, 1973.

76. Heald F., Daugela M., Brunschuyler P.: Physiology of adolescence. *N. Engl. J. Med.* 268:299, 1963.

77. McNeill D., Livson N.: Maturation rate and body build in women. *Child Dev.* 34:25, 1963.

78. Nydick M., Bustos J., Dale J.H., et al.: Gynecomastia in adolescent boys. *J.A.M.A.* 178:449, 1961.

79. Nilsson L.R.: Adolescent colloid goitre. *Acta Paediatr. Scand.* 55:49, 1966.

80. Young H.B., Zoli A., Gallagher J.R.: Events of puberty in 111 Florentine girls. *Am. J. Dis. Child.* 106:568, 1963.

81. Lee M.M.C., Chong K.S.F., Chan M.M.C.: Sexual maturation of Chinese girls in Hong Kong. *Pediatrics* 32:389, 1963.

82. Conly P.W., Morrison T., Sandberg D.H., et al.: Concentrations of progesterone in the plasma of mothers and infants at time of birth. *Pediatr. Res.* 4:76, 1970.
83. Diczfalusy E.: Steroid synthesis and catabolism in the human fetoplacental unit, in Waisman H.A., Kerr G. (eds.): *Fetal Growth and Development*. New York, McGraw-Hill Book Co., 1970.
84. Erenberg A.: Thyroid function in the preterm infant. *Pediatr. Clin. N. Am.* 29:1205, 1982.
85. Barnhart B.J., Carlson C.V., Reynolds J.W.: Adrenal corticol function in the postmature fetus and newborn infant. *Pediatr. Res.* 14:1367, 1980.
86. Cheek D.B.: *Human Growth: Body Composition, Cell Growth, Energy and Intelligence*. Philadelphia, Lea & Febiger, 1968.
87. van der Werff Ten Bosch J.J.: *Somatic Growth of the Child*. Springfield, Ill., Charles C Thomas, Publisher, 1966.
88. Marshall W.A., Tanner J.M.: Variations in pattern of pubertal changes in girls. *Arch. Dis. Child.* 44:291, 1969.
89. Zacharias L., Wurtman R.J.: Age at menarche. *N. Engl. J. Med.* 280:868, 1969.
90. Voorhess M.L.: Urinary catecholamine excretion by healthy children. *Pediatrics* 39:252, 1967.
91. Sperling M.A.: Newborn adaptation: Adrenocortical hormones and ACTH, in Tulchinsky D., Ryan K.J. (eds.): *Maternal-Fetal Endocrinology*. Philadelphia, W.B. Saunders Co., 1980.
92. Rosenfield R.L., Eberlein W.R.: Plasma 17-ketosteroid levels during adolescence. *J. Pediatr.* 74:932, 1969.
93. Yen S.S.C., Vicic W.J., Kearchner D.V.: Gonadotropin levels in puberty. *J. Clin. Endocrinol.* 29:382, 1969.
94. Sizonenko P.C., Burr I.M., Kaplan S.L., et al.: Hormonal changes in puberty: II. Correlation of serum luteinizing hormone and follicle stimulating hormone with stages of puberty and bone age in normal girls. *Pediatr. Res.* 4:36, 1970.
95. Burr I.M., Sizonenko P.C., Kaplan S.L., et al.: Hormonal changes in puberty: I. Correlation of serum luteinizing hormone and follicle stimulating hormone with stages of puberty, testicular size, and bone age in normal boys. *Pediatr. Res.* 4:25, 1970.
96. Wolf H., Stubbe P., Sabata V.: The influence of glucose infusion on fetal growth hormone levels. *Pediatrics* 45:36, 1970.
97. *Skin Conditions of Youths 12–17 Years, United States*. U.S. Dept. of Health, Education and Welfare, Public Health Service, 1976.
98. Monteleone J.A., Danis R.K., Tung K.S.K., et al.: Differentiation of chronic lymphocytic thyroiditis and simple goiter in pediatrics. *J. Pediatr.* 83:381, 1973.
99. Lovinger R.D., Kaplan S.L., Grumbach M.M.: Congenital hypopituitarism associated with neonatal hypoglycemia and microphallus. *J. Pediatr.* 87:1171, 1975.
100. David L., Salle B.L., Putet G., et al.: Serum immunoreactive calcitonin in low birth weight infants. *Pediatr. Res.* 15:803, 1981.
101. Fisher D.A., Klein A.H.: Thyroid development and disorders of the thyroid function in the newborn. *N. Engl. J. Med.* 304:702, 1981.

10 / Energy Metabolism

I prefer to be called a fool for asking
the question, rather than to remain in
ignorance.

—John Homans

The knowledge of metabolism in infants and children has been used as a practical tool in studies of nutrition such as determining caloric requirements, establishing or ruling out such diagnoses as hypothyroidism, hyperthyroidism, and simple obesity, defining optimal conditions of environment for newborns and prematures, establishing better norms for growth and development, and, finally, improving understanding of the processes of living matter.

Heat is produced in all tissues of the body by oxidative and nonoxidative reactions. In the adult, skeletal muscle produces the greatest portion, even during rest. When external temperature is markedly reduced, the muscle is called upon to produce more heat by shivering. For several months after birth, the infant is unable to shiver or is very inefficient in producing heat by that method. The liver produces more heat than any other internal organ, about 25% of the total body heat at basal levels. The infant is unique in that the brain contributes some 50% to 60% of the total at birth. At approximately 5 years the brain's contribution is 35% and reaches about 24% in the adult.[22] The decline is due principally to an ever-slower growth of the high energy-producing cell mass relative to total body weight. The recognition of the metabolic needs of the brain in early life is an important aspect in planning the optimal nutrition of the neonate.

Temperature Regulation

Temperature regulation is obviously essential to man because wide variations, no matter what the cause, may cause death. This subject is of vital importance in the study of metabolism.

Heat is lost from the body of an adult[3, 12] by the following:

Radiation, conduction, and convection	70%
Evaporation (skin and lungs)	27%
Warming inspired air	2%
Urine and feces	1%
	100%

The same values for heat loss by evaporation have been found in the newborn and premature.[7] These factors are influenced by environment, such as air temperature, humidity, clothing, and metabolism. Body control of these factors is through the following:

1. Redistribution of blood: vasodilatation and constriction influencing skin temperature.

2. Variations in blood volume: rise in temperature causing an increase from tissue fluid dilution of the blood.

3. Secretion of sweat and exhalation of water vapor.

4. Metabolism: the metabolic rate rising when environmental temperature falls much below body temperature. Shivering, already mentioned, is a factor which may cause an increase of 180% in the rate over basal levels.

The regulatory centers for temperature control are located in the hypothalamus and are apparently influenced by skin temperature and by temperature of the blood flowing through them. The thyroid gland and adrenals also play a role in regulating heat production. Removal of either or both causes a lowering of body temperature, whereas administration of thyroid extract or epinephrine increases metabolism and raises body temperature. In cretins and in patients with Addison's disease the body temperature is low.

In the newborn the mechanisms of sweating and shivering are imperfectly developed. Physiologically the sweat glands are immature (see chapter 7). The relatively large surface area compared to body mass, and the meager amount of insulating subcutaneous fat, all contribute to considerable instability of body temperature which is typical of the neonatal period. At the time of birth the infant has a very slightly higher temperature than the mother. Immediately the baby's temperature falls, regardless of the means taken to protect against it. Cold-induced peripheral vasoconstriction is well developed before the time of birth. However, an increased oxygen uptake in response to cold is considerably less pronounced in the first postnatal hour in comparison to what it will be later.[29] Heat loss due to evaporation of amniotic fluid probably contributes to the quick cooling off of the skin. In a nursery with a room temperature between 25 and 28 C, there was a drop of 1.8 C by the third hour as an average for 20 infants.[13] Cooling an infant in a similar fashion in the second postnatal hour results in a smaller decline of rectal temperature and the rate of fall is much slower.[14] Recovery to a "normal" body temperature is relatively prompt, seldom taking more than two to four hours in term neonates. Ambient temperature, humidity, and clothing will obviously have some influence. The rapid recovery would indicate that there is no physiologic immaturity of the hypothalamic center. Crying is a fairly efficient means of increasing the infant's body temperature by increasing the metabolic rate; in some infants this may result in as much as a 180% increase over basal levels. In general, the more mature the baby or the greater the birth weight, the more stable will be the body temperature.

The skin thermoreceptors of the newborn infant are highly sensitive, and a slight decrease in the average skin temperature provokes a prompt peripheral vasoconstriction.[29, 30] Similarly, a change in temperature in the opposite direction causes vasodilatation and some sweating. There does not appear to be a very marked difference between the vascular response in the premature infant, the term infant or the adult. However, the ability to sweat is considerably reduced in the smallest infants and is still quite inefficient in the normal newborn.[31] Sweating, as a response to intradermal nicotine or epinephrine, is considerably less in the low birth weight infant as compared with the full-term infant.[41] These observations suggest that small and premature infants have failed to develop axon reflex sweating. Shivering is an efficient mechanism for increasing metabolism and raising body temperature in the adult and child. Either this mechanism is not well developed in the neonate or other means are more reliable. Many observers have commented upon the rarity of shivering in premature infants. If the environmental temperature is lowered below the neutral temperature range,* restlessness and increased movements do occur. The neutral temperature for infants is higher and has a narrower range than for adults.[32] Studies of heat production in adults subjected to continuous moderate cooling show only a very slight increase in basal metabolic rate. In term newborn infants, similar studies show a decided increase in oxygen consumption, which returns to normal only when the environment is readjusted to the neutral temperature. This is true even though there may be a lag in the body temperature returning to normal. The oxygen consumed may be treble the basal level. This response to chilling has been referred to as chemical or nonshivering thermogenesis and is a phenomenon unique to early infancy. If the infant's body temperature is further depressed, a point may be reached where the response of increasing metabolism is no longer

---

*Neutral temperature range is defined as that set of thermal conditions in the environment in which the oxygen consumption (metabolism) is at a minimum and body temperature is in the normal range of 37 C ±0.5.

possible. Very premature babies, during the first week, do not show an increase in oxygen consumption as a response to subneutral temperatures, but instead show a decrease in central and skin temperature. Factors that may interfere with thermogenesis are the respiratory distress syndrome, extreme prematurity, intracranial hemorrhage, hypoglycemia, and certain drugs.[11, 34, 35, 36]

The nature of the mediator of nonshivering (chemical) thermogenesis appears to be unique to the time of early infancy. Recent studies indicate that norepinephrine secretion is a major mechanism for this adaptation. On exposure to cold there is a consistent increase in urinary norepinephrine and plasma nonesterified fatty acids. The response in premature infants is quantitatively less than in full-term babies. The infusion of norepinephrine in newborn infants does cause an increased oxygen consumption and rise in rectal temperature.[39, 42]

A site of chemical thermogenesis in the infant is brown adipose tissue.[14, 32, 37] Although present in very small amounts in the adult, it makes up a considerable quantity of the total fat present in the full-term as well as in the premature baby. The largest depots are found in the intrascapular area, but some is present in the thorax and in the perirenal areas. In contrast to white adipose tissue, it has a rich nerve and blood supply and a higher content of mitochondrial cytochromes; it contains multilocular lipid cytoplasmic inclusions instead of the single lipid inclusions. Morphologically it can be differentiated by 26 weeks. Although intrauterine malnutrition is usually associated with a marked depletion of white fat, brown fat is spared. Studies in animals and humans indicate that it is metabolically very active under cold stress. Under such environmental conditions, for the first 4 to 6 months of life in human infants, the intrascapular area has the highest skin temperature.[14] It has been suggested that brown adipose tissue serves as a thermogenic source under cold stress, and in response to norepinephrine, by warming the blood as it comes from peripheral structures. The norepinephrine increase is the initial chemical step to the activation of a lipase that hydrolyzes the brown fat. The resulting fatty acids are then oxidized in a highly exothermic reaction. Plasma levels of glycerol, resulting from lipase activity, are elevated as a result of cold exposure in the neonatal period.[5]

The neonatal increments in thyroxine (T_4) and triiodothyronine (T_3) concentration coinciding with an abrupt change in the fetal thermal environment suggest that the relative neonatal hyperthyroidism serves an important role in neonatal thermogenesis. At midgestation (20 weeks) thyroxine monodeiodination is primarily of the α-phenyl ring resulting in a predominate production of "reverse T_3" and increase in both T_3 and T_4. Since reverse T_3 is biologically inactive, it has no influence on metabolic activity but in the premature infant it may be the dominant plasma thyroid product. In the immediate neonatal period there is a remarkable surge of thyroid-stimulating hormone, within minutes of birth, and a very definite but slower response in elevated plasma levels of T_3 and T_4 reaching a peak at 24 hours and then gradually subsiding over the next several days. In healthy premature infants at birth the response at delivery is qualitatively similar but quantitatively decreased. In distressed prematures, T_4 is even further obtunded but T_3 assumes "normal" levels. It is assumed that these observations of thyroid function serve an important function in neonatal nonshivering thermogenesis.[44]

In the low birth weight infant the skin and rectal temperature parallel each other rather closely and fluctuate with extremes of environmental temperature. The survival rate of such infants was significantly higher if they were kept in a thermoneutral (30.0 to 32.5 C) environment for the first few days as compared with slightly cooler conditions.[27, 28, 31] In a comparative study of two groups of low birth weight infants treated equally except for a difference of 1.5 C ambient temperature, the babies exposed to the cooler environment for their first two weeks had a much better ability to maintain a deep body temperature upon subsequent exposure to cold than did the controls. However, the rate of increase in body weight and length was significantly faster in the warmer condition, presumably due to decreased energy expenditure.[40] There is evidence that supplementing the diet of the group raised in the cooler environment would overcome the growth differences.[24] Brief periods of exposing the term or premature neonate to a slightly cooler than neutral temperature during the first few days also appears to accelerate the ability to adapt to future thermal changes.[2, 5]

The possibility that a higher ambient temperature than neutral might have some advantages has received some attention.[20, 43] Using an environmental temperature of 37 C it has been demonstrated to reduce the metabolic rate and therefore to decrease the nutritional caloric requirements. Term, premature, and small-for-date infants could adapt to the higher temperature by increasing their evaporative heat loss, with the degree of sweating being related to gestational age. The premature was the least able to reach and maintain a new thermal equilibrium with any further increase in temperature.

The insensible water loss (loss due to expired air and diffusion through the skin) is directly related to body temperature and metabolic rate. It is also dependent upon ambient temperature. This insensible water loss also represents a heat loss through evaporation and becomes an important element in maintaining body temperature of prematures who have very thin skin and subcutaneous tissue. Insensible water loss and, therefore, the evaporative heat loss of very premature infants can be three to five times greater than that of term infants.[11, 45] Methods used to maintain ideal temperatures must take these facts into consideration, e.g., radiant heat may increase insensible water loss through increased evaporation by as much as 150% compared with an incubator with warm air circulation. At thermoneutral environments the insensible water loss at different weights expressed as ml/kg/24 hr are as follows:

1,000 gm = 64
1,500 gm = 38
2,000 gm = 28
3,400 gm = 22

Within fairly wide limits, the humidity of the environment exerts little influence on survival, although low values may contribute to heat loss by increasing evaporation or insensible loss.

Even in the older child temperature regulation is less exact than in the adult. Bayley and Stolz[25] found that relatively high rectal temperatures predominated in young children, with a gradual decrease beginning at age 2 years. This trend continued through puberty, tending to stabilize at 13 to 14 years in girls and some 4 years later in boys.[26] At 18 months the average temperature was 99.8 F (37.7 C), and 50% of the subjects had temperatures of 100 F (37.8 C) or higher. Daily variations were considerable—as much as 3 F (1.8 C) at 6 years. Such variations were not influenced greatly by the time of day. Active play, however, tended to produce a slight rise. When recordings were properly carried out (mainly referring to adequate time), very little difference was noted between oral and rectal temperatures. Except for the changes at puberty, no differences were noted between the sexes. The following table indicates average body temperatures in well children under basal conditions.

Such fluctuations and apparent deviations from "normal" temperature should be recognized by physicians to avoid unnecessary diagnostic procedures and therapy. A few children appear to have consistently high normal body temperatures, and a smaller number have consistently low normal body temperatures. It has been mentioned that the younger child reacts more violently to infection than the older one, exhibiting higher fever and sometimes convulsions—so-called febrile convulsions. Dehydration and disturbed electrolyte balance may result, especially in the infant and young child. Associated findings with fever are tachycardia and hyperpnea; in the very young the latter may be quite pronounced. A mild glycosuria is occasionally seen in infants with fever in whom the carbohydrate metabolism is otherwise normal.

Fever is caused by a number of substances including infections from bacteria, viruses, and fungi. These inducers of fevers stimulate the produc-

AGE	TEMPERATURE		STANDARD DEVIATION	
	F	C	F	C
3 mo.	99.4	37.5	0.8	0.4
6 mo.	99.5	37.5	0.6	0.3
1 yr	99.7	37.7	0.5	0.2
3 yr	99.0	37.2	0.5	0.2
5 yr	98.6	37.0	0.5	0.2
7 yr	98.3	36.8	0.5	0.2
9 yr	98.1	36.7	0.5	0.2
11 yr	98.0	36.7	0.5	0.2
13 yr	97.8	36.6	0.5	0.2

tion of a heat-labile protein pyrogen by phagocytes. It appears that fever is beneficial to the infected host, recalling Thomas Sydenhom's statement of some 300 years ago, "Fever is Nature's engine which she brings into the field to remove her enemy." Among the defense responses enhanced by fever are increased leukocyte mobility and bactericidal activity, enhancement of interferon activity, and modification of lysosome stability. In experimental animal research, survival to infections was improved if fever was permitted versus those in which temperature was controlled by drugs.[46]

Respiratory Metabolism

"Metabolism is the term employed to embrace the various chemical processes occurring within the tissues upon which heat production and growth of the body depend and from which the energy for muscular activity and for the maintenance of vital function is derived."[3] Heat produced by an animal is largely the result of oxidation of food, and by measuring the oxygen consumed one can compute the metabolism of the body.

The respiratory quotient (RQ) has an important bearing on many phases of metabolism. It is the ratio of the volume of carbon dioxide produced to the volume of oxygen used: $RQ = CO_2/O_2$. For the complete combustion of carbohydrates the respiratory quotient is 1.0. For fat the value 0.71, and for protein, 0.80. Thus the respiratory quotient can be taken as an indication of the type of food being metabolized by the organism. In a human, on a mixed diet, the quotient is around 0.85. A diet high in carbohydrates will raise it, and a diet high in fat will lower it.*

---

*The RQ for a premature or newborn may not truly reflect the source of energy being used, for in both anaerobic metabolism may form some considerable part of the heat production mechanism.

Careful studies of the RQ in the newborn have, in general, revealed high values for the first day. For three or four days after birth there is a drop to rather low levels, followed by a rise to near the adult quotient. These figures give good evidence that during the first day of life carbohydrate is used almost exclusively as the source of energy. The stores of glycogen are soon exhausted, and until breast milk or a formula is taken well, by the fifth or sixth day, fat is utilized for energy needs. This reasoning is substantiated by the observation that the blood sugar content of the newborn is quite low and for a brief period remains low. Table 10–1 shows this rather dramatic change in the respiratory quotient for the first few days of life.[13]

In general, the respiratory quotient for premature infants remains low for a longer period and then rises to a slightly higher level than does that of a more mature infant.[4, 13]

To maintain basal needs of about 1.7 calories/kg (0.8 calories/lb)/hour and, in addition, to provide an allowance for activity, growth, fecal loss, and specific dynamic action, the total food requirement is estimated as 80 calories/kg/day (36 calories/lb/day). However, the spontaneous intake of newborns to the point of satiety by the first day averages 90 calories and by the eleventh day over 100 calories/kg.[13] When a proper caloric intake is being estimated, the baby's activity must be considered. It has already been pointed out that strenuous crying may increase the basal level of metabolism by 180%, so a very active infant will require a higher caloric intake than one who is more lethargic.

The premature infant has a greater requirement, estimated as high as 150 calories/kg. However, Levine and Gordon[7] have shown that 120 calories/kg (55 calories/lb) in a low-fat formula produced excellent results and adequate weight gain when given after the fifth to eighth day of life.

Basal Metabolism in Children

It will be readily realized that in infants and small children many of the criteria cannot be met for obtaining a true basal metabolic rate, e.g., fasting conditions, no muscular activity, and other factors inherent in a true basal condition. However, we can obtain nearly basal levels, and the lacking factors can be considered in the final evaluation. As in an adult, a single reading has little value, but repeated recordings may be a considerable aid. In infants and children under 4 to 5 years the chamber method or direct calorimetry must be used.

Norms of metabolism can be presented only in terms of averages, for the metabolism of the great majority of individuals does not agree exactly with any accepted standard. The following factors, responsible for variations from the normal, must be carefully evaluated.

TABLE 10–1.—CHANGES IN RESPIRATORY
QUOTIENT IN THE NEWBORN

| DAY OF LIFE | RQ | % OF TOTAL ENERGY FROM | |
		CHO	FAT
1st few hours	0.90	66	34
1	0.80	30	70
2	0.74	8	92
3	0.73	5	95
4	0.75	12	88
5	0.79	26	74
6	0.82	38	62
7	0.81	34	66
8	0.81	34	66

PULSE RATE.—Muscular exercise is usually accompanied by an increase in the pulse rate and heat production.

CLIMATE.—Hot weather usually reduces body heat production; the converse is true of cold weather.

GROWTH.—The two stages of rapid growth in childhood, during the first year of life and at puberty, are associated with a greater relative heat production than at any other time. This "growth factor" is most important in comparisons of metabolism of children and adults. The complexities of the relationship of growth and metabolism are not well understood, but we do know that the rate of growth does not necessarily correlate well with the various changes in metabolism. (See also under "Age.")

FOOD INTAKE.—An insufficient diet causes not only a loss of weight but a lowered metabolic rate. In a normal individual the ordinary mixed diet raises the metabolic rate about 6% above the basal level; overfeeding may raise it as much as 40%. This factor, called specific dynamic action, must be considered in the nonfasting child. However, Murlin[11] stated that in children under age 1 year an average feeding increased metabolism very little or not at all over basal levels. In infants fed milk with a very high protein content (40% of the total caloric intake) the metabolic rate may increase as much as 25%. This condition is, of course, rarely to be considered.

AGE.—This is a most important factor for the pediatrician. The younger the individual, the greater will be the tendency to variation from the average. Heat production increases with age so long as growth continues; there follows a period of relative stability corresponding to active maturity, and finally a definite decline which begins about the fifth decade.[1, 3]

Premature Infants.—During the first few weeks of life the heat production of the premature may be very low (between 46 and 92 calories for 24 hours). On the basis of body surface the averages are generally lower than those for a mature newborn. Further, the premature infant may produce less heat on his or her expected birth date than does the full-term infant during any day of the first week of life. Activity, when manifested by a premature, increases the heat production above the basal level by an average of 40%, compared with 65% for the normal newborn. Until height and weight are normal for age, the metabolic rate of the premature remains below that of the normal infant.[7, 13]

Small-for-Date Infants.—The growth-retarded and/or malnourished neonate has a significantly higher metabolic rate than that of preterm infants of similar weight. This finding is in agreement with the concept of the relatively greater susceptibility of such infants to hypoglycemia. The larger and metabolically very active brain is undoubtedly an important factor.

Full-Term Infants.—Depending on the weight of the baby, his or her vitality, and the amount of fat tissue present, the average figures range from 125 to 165 calories produced per 24 hours. It is interesting to note that the smallest baby does not necessarily produce the last amount of heat. For a fairly large series of infants the average figure was 42 calories/kg/24 hours, or about 28 calories/sq m/hour. Judged by weight, the infant at birth is more active metabolically than is the adult but less so than the child of 1 to 3 years.

Older Infants and Children.—Most data indicate that physical development rather than age determines the metabolic rate. Most observers agree that there is an increase in the metabolic rate associated with puberty and that it is related directly to the growth spurt rather than to any identifiable item in sexual maturation.[6, 8, 14] Tables 10–2 and 10–3 give some representative figures of metabolic rates for different ages based upon the more commonly used standards.

SEX.—Until age 8 there is only a slight difference between the sexes. At approximately this time boys have a slightly higher rate than girls. The rise at puberty, when present, occurs about two years sooner in girls than in boys. At the end of the second decade of life there is usually more than 10% difference in favor of the males.

The selection of the most nearly ideal standards for children has been an important part of the studies of metabolism in the pediatric age group. Height, weight, age, surface area, and level of creatinine excretion, either alone or in combination, are the references commonly used in the past.

TABLE 10–2.—Average Basal Metabolic Rates for
Premature and Term Newborns and Adults
According to Different Standards*

	TOTAL BASAL (PER HR)	AV. CALORIES	
		PER SQ M/HR	PER KG/HR
Premature infants	6.48	26.25	2.04
Term infants	6.67	29.16	2.00
Adults	. . .	35–40	1.00

*Data from Smith.[13]

TABLE 10–3.—Results Picked at Random Showing General
Trends of BMR for Normal Subjects*

AGE	WEIGHT (KG)	HEAT/24 HR	HEAT/SQ M/HR	HEAT/KG/HR
2 days	3.45	162	32.1	1.91
5 days	3.34	150	30.5	1.88
6 mo.	5.40	353	40.0	2.75
10 mo.	9.37	479	37.7	2.12
2.5 yr	11.5	585	51.9	2.20
5 yr	15.5	720	52.4	2.01
9 yr	22.0	898	44.9	1.70
10 yr	30.6	1,065	41.3	1.43
14 yr	40.2	1,300	39.2	1.35
18 yr	65.6	1,700	32.8	1.08
Adult	70.0	1,400†	35–40†	1.00†

*Mainly from data of Lewis, Murlin, and Talbot.
†Average figures.

Surface area, based on the Du Bois formula, has become the accepted standard for adults and probably is still the one most used in children. This method, however, has proved to be unsatisfactory. There are several reasons for this. The number of infants and children in whom accurate measurements of surface area have been carried out is less than half a dozen, if normal subjects alone are considered. Widely divergent results have been obtained for children of atypical body build when the basal metabolic rate has been calculated on the basis for surface area.[9, 20, 23] The variability of estimated area must take into consideration the fact that small human beings have greater surface area in comparison with their weight than do larger subjects. For instance, the newborn infant has 16% as much surface area as an adult, but weight is only 5% that of an adult.

Talbot[16] carefully worked out standards based on height and weight and largely ignored age and surface as standards. He stated that evidence better supported the concept that the heat production "regulator" was the active mass of tissue in the infant's and child's body, that is, muscle.[14] This was substantiated by the findings that there was a good correlation between creatinine excretion and total basal caloric output[18] (Tables 10–4 and 10–5). Creatinine as a reference standard is impractical owing to the difficulty of collecting 24-hour urine specimens in the smaller children.

Wetzel[19] has advocated using "developmental level" as the most satisfactory standard for basal heat production. By use of the Wetzel grid the developmental level can be plotted, and the normal heat production is then read from one of the ordinates of the auxodrome. Wetzel and others who have used this method claim considerable accuracy for it. Our own studies have not shown as good a correlation with the Wetzel grid as with height or weight for age based on Talbot's tables, and Eichorn,[21] using the grid, discovered many discrepancies in a group of adolescents.

TABLE 10–4.—Standard Total Calories for Weight*:
Girls and Boys†

WEIGHT (KG)	TOTAL CALORIES PER 24 HR		WEIGHT (KG)	TOTAL CALORIES PER 24 HR	
	GIRLS	BOYS		GIRLS	BOYS
3.0	136	150	36.0	1,173	1,270
4.0	205	210	38.0	1,207	1,305
5.0	274	270	40.0	1,241	1,340
6.0	336	330	42.0	1,274	1,370
7.0	395	390	44.0	1,306	1,400
8.0	448	445	46.0	1,338	1,430
9.0	496	495	48.0	1,369	1,460
10.0	541	545	50.0	1,399	1,485
11.0	582	590	52.0	1,429	1,505
12.0	620	625	54.0	1,458	1,555
13.0	655	665	56.0	1,487	1,580
14.0	687	700	58.0	1,516	1,600
15.0	718	725	60.0	1,544	1,630
16.0	747	750	62.0	1,572	1,660
17.0	775	780	64.0	1,599	1,690
18.0	802	810	66.0	1,626	1,725
19.0	827	840	68.0	1,653	1,765
20.0	852	870	70.0	1,679	1,785
22.0	898	910	72.0	1,705	1,815
24.0	942	980	74.0	1,731	1,845
26.0	984	1,070	76.0	1,756	1,870
28.0	1,025	1,100	78.0	1,781	1,900
30.0	1,063	1,140	80.0	1,805	. . .
32.0	1,101	1,190	82.0	1,830	. . .
34.0	1,137	1,230	84.0	1,855	2,000

*Calories produced under basal conditions compared to weight.
†From Talbot.[16]

TABLE 10–5.—Standard Total Calories for Height* (or Total
Calories For Expected Weight): Girls and Boys†

HEIGHT (CM)	TOTAL CALORIES PER 24 HR		HEIGHT (CM)	TOTAL CALORIES PER 24 HR	
	GIRLS	BOYS		GIRLS	BOYS
48	134	. . .	92	681	725
50	159	. . .	94	695	740
51	. . .	160	96	709	755
52	186	175	98	722	765
54	214	200	100	735	785
56	246	225	105	770	805
58	278	260	110	807	830
60	309	300	115	846	875
62	341	315	120	894	935
64	373	360	125	942	990
66	404	390	130	987	1,045
68	433	420	135	1,057	1,105
70	462	450	140	1,130	1,165
72	489	480	145	1,208	1,220
74	515	510	150	1,294	1,290
76	539	535	155	1,386	1,380
78	560	565	160	1,477	1,480
80	581	590	165	1,544	1,570
82	601	612	170	1,584	1,655
84	619	635	175	1,596	1,720
86	636	660	180	1,600	1,800
88	652	685	190	. . .	1,900
90	666	705			

*Calories produced under basal conditions compared to height. Since the
height standard is based on a normal weight, this can also be called expected
weight.
†From Talbot.[1];16

Figures 10–1 through 10–4 and Tables 10–2 through 10–5 illustrate the
various standards used and the results obtained from some of the more
complete studies.

If physical development is average, the number of calories produced per
kilogram will equal that of normal children of the same age, sex, and physique. If the proportion of inactive body substance (fat, bone, and body
fluids) is small, the caloric output per unit of weight will be greater. Conversely, if there is a greater amount of inactive tissue, as in obese children,
the number of calories produced per unit of weight will be less than the
average. When data obtained from obese but otherwise normal children
were compared with body surface as one standard and height-weight as the
other standard, the difference between the sets of figures amounted to over
25% in many instances. The author made three satisfactory determinations

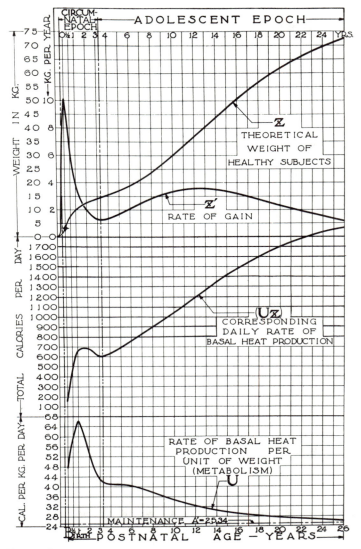

Fig 10–1.—Curves comparing growth and heat production. All curves are plotted against a common abscissa, age. Ordinates for each curve are different, and are properly indicated. For Z the ordinate is weight in kg; for Z′, kg/yr. All curves are based on averages. Note that the curves for theoretical weight and daily rate of basal heat production follow similar patterns, lending support to the selection of weight as the most suitable criterion for the basis of energy (metabolism) studies during growth. The curves also show that heat production and growth are so

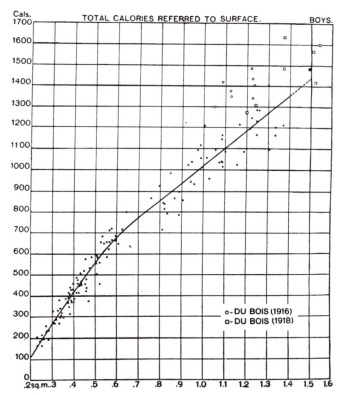

Fig 10–2.—Metabolism curve for boys, based on total calories produced at basal levels referred to surface area (sq m). (From Benedict and Talbot.[1])

closely related as to be part of the same biologic processes. Birth occurs at the peak of the curve for "rate of gain" under normal conditions; the premature must attain this peak in the less favorable conditions of extrauterine existence. Some difficulties of rearing premature infants can thus be attributed to stresses of growth in a relatively adverse environment. Note also that between ages 3 and 4 the average child has reached a low point in rate of gain, a leveling off of theoretical weight and a relative decrease in heat production (whether measured as total calories or based on unit of weight). In this period physiologic anorexia is common. Curve *U* is said to represent true metabolism. The high metabolism of infants is ascribed to "cellular synthesis" and "heat of dissipation" by Wetzel, or to the rapid growth and differentiation that take place during these years. Even during the prepubertal spurt of growth this curve undergoes a steady decline, reaching its lowest level when growth ceases. (From Wetzel.[19])

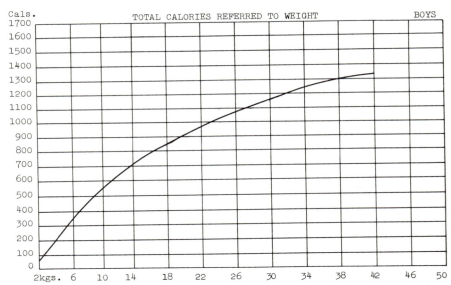

Fig 10–3.—Metabolism curve for boys, based on total calories produced at basal levels referred to weight. (From Benedict and Talbot.[1])

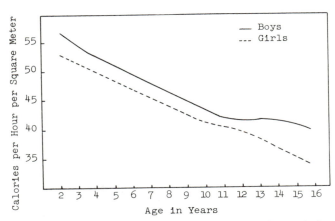

Fig 10–4.—Metabolism curves for boys and girls, based on calories produced per hour per square meter referred to age. Note particularly the tendency to a leveling off in the prepubertal years. (From Lewis et al.[8])

of oxygen consumption on a moderately obese, but otherwise normal, boy. Averaging the three determinations, the basal metabolic rate according to several different standards, was as follows:

STANDARD OF COMPARISON	BASAL METABOLIC RATE
Body surface (Mayo Clinic)	− 19%
Height (Talbot)	+ 10%
Expected weight for age (Talbot)	− 5%
Wetzel grid	− 10%

Formerly basal metabolism determinations were extensively used in evaluating thyroid function. Precise measurements of thyroid and pituitary hormones are more accurate as an indication of thyroid status. Although a low basal metabolic rate may be characteristic of intrauterine dwarfism and indicates a guarded prognosis for complete growth recovery,[9] there are other techniques for making the diagnosis which are both simpler and more reliable. Although still of value in research projects such as determining nutritional needs, metabolic rate per se has little to offer as a diagnostic aid.

Practical Applications

To maintain normal and stable body temperatures in the neonate, the environmental temperature must be higher and in a narrower range than for older subjects. The reasons for this are the greater surface area in relation to mass and the increased thermal conductance of the infant, which results in a greater heat loss. The infant's primary response to a chilling environment is by nonshivering thermogenesis, manifested in an increased oxygen consumption, and later by increased movement. Brown adipose tissue may be an important source of this increase in metabolism. For optimal care of the low birth weight baby continuous monitoring is essential. Skin temperatures are equally valid to rectal temperatures for this purpose. Humidity plays a very secondary role, as compared with temperature, in the survival of the premature infant.

In the older child there is a normal range of fluctuation of the body temperature. This range becomes progressively narrower with increasing age, and the mean value drops approximately one degree from shortly after birth until adolescence.

Determinations of basal metabolism have been of great value in the study of growth and development, but no completely satisfactory standard for children of different ages, shapes, and sizes has been devised. The use of basal metabolism as a diagnostic tool throughout childhood has little merit.

380 / Chapter 10

REFERENCES

1. Benedict F.G., Talbot F.B.: Carnegie Institute of Washington Pub. no. 233, 1915.
2. Evans H.E., Glass L.: *Perinatal Medicine*. New York, Harper & Row, 1976.
3. Kleiber M.: *The Fire of Life: An Introduction to Animal Energetics*. New York, John Wiley & Sons, 1961.
4. Gordon H.H., Levine S.Z.: Respiratory metabolism in infancy and in childhood: Respiratory exchange in premature infants; basal metabolism. *Am. J. Dis. Child.* 52:810, 1936.
5. Perlstein P.H., Hersh C., Glueck C.J., et al.: Adaptation to cold in the first three days of life. *Pediatrics* 54:411, 1974.
6. Johnston J.A.: Factors influencing retention of nitrogen and calcium in period of growth. *Am. J. Dis. Child.* 59:287, 1940.
7. Levine S.Z., Gordon H.H.: Physiologic handicaps of the premature infant: I. Their pathogenesis. *Am. J. Dis. Child.* 64:274, 1942.
8. Lewis R.C., Duval A.M., Iliff A.: Effect of adolescence on basal metabolism of normal children. *Am. J. Dis. Child.* 66:296, 1943.
9. Krieger I., Woolley P.V.: The basal metabolic rate in growth failure of prenatal onset. *Am. J. Dis. Child.* 127:340, 1974.
10. Lewis R.C., Kinsman G.M., Iliff A.: The basal metabolism of normal boys and girls from 2 to 12 years old. *Am. J. Dis. Child.* 53:348, 1937.
11. Sauer P.J.J., Dane H.J., Visser H.K.A.: New standards for the neutral thermal environment of healthy very low birth-weight infants during the first week of life. *Arch. Dis. Child.* 59:18, 1984.
12. Newburgh L.H., Johnston M.W., Newburgh J.D.: *Some Fundamental Principles of Metabolism*. Ann Arbor, Mich., Edwards Bros., 1945.
13. Smith C.A., Nelson N.M.: *The Physiology of the Newborn Infant.*, ed. 4. Springfield, Ill., Charles C Thomas, Publisher, 1976.
14. Rylander E.: Age-dependent reactions of rectal and skin temperatures of infants during exposure to cold. *Acta Paediatr. Scand.* 61:597, 1972.
15. Talbot F.B.: Basal metabolism of girls. *Am. J. Dis. Child.* 52:1, 1936.
16. Talbot F.B.: Basal metabolism standards for children. *Am. J. Dis. Child.* 55:455, 1938.
17. Talbot F.B., Wilson E.B., Worcester J.: Basal metabolism in girls: Physiologic background and application of the standards. *Am. J. Dis. Child.* 53:275, 1937.
18. Talbot F.B., Worcester J., Stewart A.: New creatinine standards for basal metabolism and its clinical application. *Am. J. Dis. Child.* 58:506, 1939.
19. Wetzel N.C.: Growth, in Glasser O. (ed.): *Medical Physics*, vol. I. Chicago, Year Book Medical Publishers, 1944.
20. Sulyok E., Jequier E., Prod'hom L.S.: Respiratory contribution to the thermal balance of the newborn infant under various ambient conditions. *Pediatrics* 51:641, 1973.
21. Eichorn D.H.: A comparison of laboratory determinations and Wetzel grid estimates of basal metabolism among adolescents. *J. Pediatr.* 46:146, 1955.
22. Holliday M.A.: Metabolic rate and organ size during growth from infancy to maturity and during late gestation and early infancy. *Pediatrics* 47:169, 1971.
23. Lamb M.W., Michie J.M.: Basal metabolism of 19 children from two to ten years old. *J. Nutr.* 53:93, 1954.
24. Glass L., Lola R.V., Jaiswal V., et al.: Effect of thermal environment and ca-

loric intake on head growth of low birth weight infants during the late neonatal period. *Arch. Dis. Child.* 50:571, 1975.

25. Bayley N., Stolz H.R.: Maturational changes in rectal temperatures of 61 infants from 1 to 36 months. *Child. Dev.* 8:195, 1937.

26. Iliff A., Lee V.A.: Pulse rate, respiratory rate and body temperature of children between two months and 18 years of age. *Child Dev.* 23:238, 1952.

27. Silverman W.A., Blanc W.A.: The effect of humidity on survival of newly born premature infants. *Pediatrics* 20:477, 1957.

28. Miller H.C., Behrle F.C., Hagar D.L., et al.: The effect of high humidity on body temperature and oxygen consumption of newborn premature infants. *Pediatrics* 27:740, 1961.

29. Brück K.: Temperature regulation in the newborn infant. *Biol. Neonate* 3:65, 1961.

30. Moss A.J.: Duffie E.R., Emmanouilides G.: Blood pressure and vasomotor reflexes in the newborn infant. *Pediatrics* 32:175, 1963.

31. Day R.L., Caliguiri L., Kamenski C., et al.: Body temperature and survival of premature infants. *Pediatrics* 34:171, 1964.

32. Oliver T.K.: Temperature regulation and heat production in the newborn. *Pediatr. Clin. N. Am.* 12:765, 1965.

33. Oliver T.K., Karlberg P.: Gaseous metabolism in newly born human infants. *Am. J. Dis. Child.* 105:427, 1963.

34. Miller H.C., Behrle F.C., Nieman J.L., et al.: Oxygen consumption in newborn premature infants. *Am. J. Dis. Child.* 103:71, 1962.

35. Adamsons K., Gandy G.M., James L.S.: The influence of thermal factors upon oxygen consumption of the newborn human infant. *J. Pediatr.* 66:495, 1965.

36. Scopes J.W.: Metabolic rate and temperature control in the human body. *Br. Med. Bull.* 22:88, 1966.

37. Hull D.: The structure and function of brown adipose tissue. *Br. Med. Bull.* 22:92, 1966.

38. Silverman W.A., Agate F.J., Fertig J.W.: A sequential trial of the nonthermal effect of atmospheric humidity on survival of newborn infants of low birth weight. *Pediatrics* 31:719, 1963.

39. Stern L., Ramos A., Leduc J.: Maturation of chemical thermogenesis in premature infants. *Pediatr. Res.* 2:317, 1968.

40. Glass L., Silverman W.A., Sinclair J.C.: Effect of thermal environment on cold resistance and growth of small infants after the first week of life. *Pediatrics* 41:1033, 1968.

41. Green M., Behrendt H.: Sweating capacity of neonates. *Am. J. Dis. Child.* 118:725, 1969.

42. Schiff D., Stern L., Leduc J.: Chemical thermogenesis in newborn infants: Catecholamine excretion and plasma non-esterified fatty acid response to cold exposure. *Pediatrics* 37:557, 1966.

43. Sulyok E., Jequier E., Prod'hom L.S.: Thermal balances of the newborn infant in a heat-gaining environment. *Pediatr. Res.* 7:888, 1973.

44. Fisher D.A., Klein A.H.: The ontogenesis of thyroid function and its relationship to neonatal thermogenesis, in Tulchinski D., Ryan K.J. (eds.): *Maternal-Fetal Endocrinology.* Philadelphia, W.B. Saunders Co., 1980.

45. Baumgart S.: Partitioning of heat losses and gains in premature newborn infants under radiant warmers. *Pediatrics* 75:89, 1985.

46. Kluger N.J.: Fever. *Pediatrics* 66:720, 1980.

11 / Nutrition in Normal Growth

Pediatricians eat because children don't.
—Meyer Perlstein

The infant, child, and adolescent must have food for growth and for maintenance and repair of body tissues. To supply the caloric requirement alone is not sufficient to promote optimal growth. It is essential to consider quantitatively the basic foodstuffs: proteins, fats, carbohydrates, minerals, and vitamins. In this chapter we will outline our present knowledge of the influence of nutrition on growth and development. Fetal growth and nutrition are considered in chapter 3 and the development of the central nervous system as related to nutrition is discussed in chapter 7. Obesity is presented in chapter 13.

Since there is no adequate definition for "optimal growth" there can be no "optimal diet" for growth. In attempting to designate a near ideal, or even just a satisfactory dietary intake, a number of important variables and unknowns are encountered. These include the individual variations in total energy output from day to day or from year to year. The individual differences in the utilization of food, composition of feces, urine and blood, and changes in body weight. Indeed, day-to-day changes for a single person of any of these items can be considerable. Finally, much of our knowledge in this field has been derived from animal experiments which may not be directly applicable to humans.

In the following pages the definition of *requirement* is that proposed by Foman, "The least amount of that nutrient that will promote an optimal state of health."[10] It is not always possible to arrive at a specific quantity that all experts would agree fulfills the above definition; nevertheless, the variation would not be very great.

Total Caloric Requirements

In this chapter 1 calorie = 1 large calorie = 1 Cal = 1 kcal.
The caloric requirements of children are traditionally divided into (1)

basal metabolism, (2) growth, (3) muscular activity, (4) caloric loss in excreta, and (5) specific dynamic action of foods.

During the first year to 18 months the daily requirement for basal metabolism averages about 55 calories/kg (25 calories/lb) for the healthy infant, or child. After this period the basal requirements gradually decrease to adult levels of 25 to 30 calories/kg. The prematurely born infant's basal requirements will be slightly greater than those of the normal newborn. The small-for-date neonate's requirements will be at least as great as the premature and should be met promptly to avoid hypoglycemia.[3, 14, 17]

The specific dynamic action of food requires from 5 to 7 calories/kg on the average diet. When the diet contains a large proportion of protein, the requirement may be more than doubled.

Approximately 10% of the daily intake is lost in the excreta of the bottle-fed baby and older child and about 8% for the breast-fed child. Most of it is lost in the feces.

The requirements for activity may vary tremendously per individual, at different age levels, and for the two sexes. An average allowance during the first year is 20 calories/kg (9 calories/lb)/day. For the premature or phlegmatic infant this amount may be about halved, whereas for an extremely active infant the requirements may be more than doubled. During adolescence the requirement may also be proportionately high, especially for active boys.

Daily growth requirements are variable since growth is a dynamic process and, for practical purposes, represents calories stored. During the early months of life 20 to 40 calories/kg (10 to 18 calories/lb) may be stored. By the end of the first year this allowance has fallen to 5 to 15 calories/kg. There follows a gradual decline in relation to body weight, with a temporary increase occurring during the spurt of growth that takes place during puberty.[10, 12]

In the low birth weight infant the requirements for growth may be considerably greater than are those for the normal newborn. Especially in the premature infant, where the growth rate can be expected to follow the intrauterine pattern until the time of expected delivery, the caloric demand may be high. Due to marginal renal function in the premature baby, careful monitoring will be required so that fluid and electrolyte balance are normally maintained. Decreased absorption of fat by the premature infant must be taken into account in estimating adequacy of the total caloric intake.

Requirements of the adolescent will vary widely and better correlations exist with physiologic stages of development (see chapter 9) than with chronologic age. The added requirements to meet the demands of the acceleration of physical growth may be relatively short in duration for any one individual but the quantity may be surprisingly large, nearly double those preceding the growth spurt (Table 11–1). An adequate diet may put such a child into a negative nitrogen (protein) balance. For the average American girl the peak increase would be between 11 and 14 years and for boys between 13 and 16 years.[12, 28] It must be recognized that there is as much or more variability in the physiologic demands of the body at this time than at any other, and our knowledge concerning nutrition for the adolescent is extremely meager. The youngster's appetite remains our best index of need.

Table 11–1 shows the distribution of total caloric requirements based on age. In obese and undernourished children one should calculate the total caloric allowance on the expected rather than on the actual weight of the subject, taking care to avoid "nutritional breaks" by any sudden or drastic changes in the diet.

Although the immediate or acute effect of malnutrition in retardation of growth has long been recognized, the fact that permanent impairment may result has been only recently accepted. Particularly disturbing have been the studies showing the effect upon the growth and development of the central nervous system and the potential damage to intellectual and personality development.[39, 40, 42] Work in animals demonstrated that permanent growth retardation could be accomplished as a result of underfeeding early in life. No matter how adequate the nutrition following this critical period, complete recovery was not possible. Additional observations indicated an apparent greater susceptibility to infections and a reduced mental awareness in the deprived animals. If undernutrition was delayed until after the neonatal period, although the growth rate showed a very similar interruption, subsequent adequate nutritional intake permitted complete recovery. Similar findings in humans were suspected but more difficult to prove.[36, 38, 43, 52, 53]

Early restriction of calories, in the late fetal and neonatal periods, slows the rate of cell multiplication. The findings are similar in a gross way for

TABLE 11–1.—TOTAL CALORIC REQUIREMENT PER DAY (CAL/KG)

	LOW BIRTH WEIGHT	8 WK	10 MO.	4 YR	14 YR	ADULT
Basal	60	55	55	40	35	25
Specific dynamic action	7	7	7	6	6	6
Excreta	20	11	10	8	6	6
Activity	15	17	20	25±	20±	10±
Growth	50	20	12	8–10	14	0
	152	110	104	87–89±	81±	47±

animals and human infants.[43, 45, 47, 50] Unfortunately, the type of cell most influenced at these chronologically similar times may be quite different in different species because of the marked maturational variations that are present. For example, at birth the degree of rat brain maturation is much less advanced than that of humans. Probably more significant is the effect that malnutrition may have upon brain cell migrations and synapse formation and function at these crucial times.[43, 46, 50] Additional findings have included deficient and delayed myelination, changes in the EEG, and poor performance on some types of intelligence tests.[47, 52] As pointed out in chapter 3 and chapter 7, malnutrition is often associated with a reduction in brain weight and in head circumference. If severe, both of these physical findings may be an initial indication of mental retardation.

Compounding the problem is the recognition that persons of small size and mental incompetence are productive of offspring with similar findings. In most circumstances, the nutritional deprivation is combined with varying degrees of socioeconomic deprivation and often with infections, especially chronic ones. Where one finds constant hunger, one does not have to look far to discover other undesirable social conditions. A vicious pattern of events can easily be appreciated for the underprivileged child and his or her family: hunger leads to learning apathy, and a constant anxiety about food will certainly dilute and impair any intellectual pursuits.[24, 44]

Suffice it to say that the long-range effects of one isolated episode or of chronic malnutrition can be understood only in the context of the human ecologic conditions including biologic, social, and economic factors that the child and his or her family have experienced. A number of studies suggest that an episode of severe malnutrition in infancy may cause little, or only temporary, intellectual impairment in the context of a lifetime of generally favorable experiences for child development.[11, 13, 53] If, however, severe malnutrition occurs in an ecologic situation that is generally unfavorable for intellectual development, then that early nutritional deprivation will likely have a clear relation to impaired intellectual performance. The prevention will undoubtedly involve considerable political, economic, and social evolution.

The association of an inadequate intake of calories and protein with an increased incidence of acute or chronic infection has long been recognized, but the precise relationship of cause and effect has been difficult to establish. With the increased knowledge of the mechanisms of host defense, it is now possible to quantitate some of the immunologic deficiencies seen in chronic malnutrition.[63, 64] Normal response in antibody production to antigen stimulus is usual for IgG but is frequently reduced for the surface secretory IgA on mucous membranes. All lymphoid organs are grossly reduced in malnutrition, the thymus being most severely affected. The thymus-dependent areas of lymph nodes are depleted. The T lymphocytes are considerably reduced in the peripheral blood and the expected delayed hypersensitivity reactions, an indication of cellular immunity, are absent or markedly reduced. This condition can be rapidly corrected by adequate nutrition. Impaired function of serum complement and opsonic activity has been reported in children with severe deficiencies of calories and protein in their diet. As with most studies of malnutrition, it is difficult to delineate the effect of specific nutrients or the influence of the infections themselves upon the host defense. There does seem to be little doubt, however, that chronic nutritional deficiency reduces a child's resistance to infection and some specific immunologic inadequacies can now be identified.

Protein

Proteins are normal constituents of all animal cells and body fluids except bile and urine. They are important in the regulation of osmotic relations of the intracellular and extracellular fluids and play an important role in the fluid balance of the body. All of the body's enzymes have the properties of proteins, and a considerable number of the hormones are proteins or protein derivatives. Many of the substances associated with immunologic and antigenic phenomena are proteins. In addition to these many functions found in the adult, this foodstuff serves the special function in the child of providing basic building materials for the manufacture of tissues during growth.[17]

Protein needs for growth are both qualitative and quantitative. Our knowledge concerning these needs comes from dietary surveys and measurements of nitrogen balance and creatinine excretion and of the rate and composition of growth at different ages. An adequate protein intake may be defined as one that contains all of the essential amino acids in sufficient amounts to satisfy maintenance needs and to provide the surplus compatible with normal growth. Reliable measures of the adequacy of protein content of the diet are serum levels of albumin and total protein. From a practical standpoint of feeding infants and children, the protein foodstuffs of animal origin in common use in the United States (milk, meat, fish, and eggs) supply all of the essential amino acids, and some foods of vegetable origin supply most of them in reasonably high concentrations.[10, 15]

The amino acid level in the serum during the first few weeks of life is higher than in the older child or adult. The total quantity of amino acids found in the urine is also elevated for a short time after birth, being higher in the low birth weight infant than in the normal newborn. In terms of milligrams excreted per day per kilogram of body weight, the average figures are premature, 8.8; term infant, 7.6; and older child, 2.5. These findings suggest a transient enzyme deficiency.[41]

Studies of all age groups from prematures to adults show that in "normal" amounts proteins are readily digested and assimilated.

For the normal newborn infant a positive nitrogen balance and maintenance of adequate albumin in serum is obtained with a protein intake of 2.2 gm/kg/day. The requirement of the breast-fed baby may be slightly less owing to the high "biologic value" of lactalbumin.[10, 32] Unmodified cow's milk as obtained in most stores or reconstituted evaporated cow's milk contains 3.3% protein and 4.8% lactose. Human milk has considerable variability, especially if feeding continues beyond two to three months, but an average set of values at two to three weeks after birth would indicate 1.2% protein and 7.0% lactose. Both milks contain approximately 67 calories/100 ml. Some of the immunologic properties of human milk are discussed in chapter 7 under "Development of Immunity."

Levine and Gordon[16] were among the first to suggest that a higher protein intake than supplied by human milk could be of real benefit to the premature infant. Their studies indicated a more rapid weight gain and a higher magnitude of nitrogen balance if these babies were supplied with a formula containing 3 to 4 gm/kg/day of protein. They pointed out that to maintain a similar nitrogen balance from human milk, there would be an excessive fluid intake and possibly an amount of dietary fat in excess of the infants' tolerance. An adequate intake of carbohydrate results in a better weight gain and increased nitrogen retention as well as a lowering of the blood urea nitrogen.[29] The addition of carbohydrate offers more expendable body water and spares protein breakdown, with corresponding decrease in nitrogenous waste products that must be handled by already marginally functioning kidneys.

Recently a number of studies have shown that low birth weight babies can be adequately fed with their own mothers' milk. Among the benefits were a shortened interval to regain birth weight and a more rapid rate of growth when compared with pooled human milk from mothers of term infants. Mother's milk from those who delivered low birth weight babies contains higher concentrations of protein, sodium, and chloride than milk from mothers of term neonates. The composition of the weight gain of infants fed their own mother's milk was similar to that of fetuses of similar postconceptional age. The secretory IgA is present in higher concentrations in milk from mothers of preterm infants than in milk from mothers of term infants. The advantages are most obvious during the first month postpartum.[9, 17] Preterm infants fed a commercial formula especially prepared for low birth weight babies resulted in a satisfactory growth rate but a considerably greater accretion of fat.[59]

As the body matures, it becomes richer in protein. At birth the average nitrogen content is about 2% (Fig 11–1). By 4 years the adult proportions are reached, wherein the body contains 3% of nitrogen. Retention of nitrogen decreases rapidly during this period. It is approximately 204 mg/kg/day at age 1 month but only 11.0 mg/kg/day at age 4 years. The marked retention in the early months and years of life that is reflected in these figures is attributed not only to the construction of new tissue but to the maturation of existing tissue.[33] These figures are for average diets, for it has been demonstrated that in young infants simply increasing the protein content of the diet will result in increased nitrogen retention for prolonged periods. In older children such an increased retention is observed for only a brief period. In neither infants nor older children is growth in terms of height or weight greatly influenced by these differences in nitrogen retention.

From the end of the first year until the adolescent growth spurt, protein requirements are fulfilled by an allowance of 1.5 to 2.0 gm/kg/day. It can be demonstrated that children on relatively high caloric diets require less protein to maintain a positive nitrogen balance and growth.

Ingestion of very large portions of protein over a long period may have detrimental results, with diminished growth and diminished nitrogen retention. A very low content of protein in the diet eventually leads to a poor

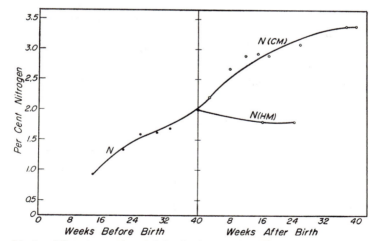

Fig 11–1.—Nitrogen content of the body before and after birth. N(CM), nitrogen content of infants fed cow's milk; N(HM), nitrogen content of infants fed human milk. (From Stearns.[23])

appetite. In children with kwashiorkor, the lack of desire to eat complicates the management. Children who are undernourished but receive adequate protein will continue to have a good appetite.[47]

Table 11–2 shows the average caloric, protein, and water requirements at different ages.

Carbohydrate

Carbohydrates supply the greatest percentage of calories and bulk of the average diet but constitute less than 1% of the total body weight. The relatively small amount stored in the liver and muscles as glycogen is rapidly depleted in periods of starvation. Carbohydrate combined with protein in nucleotides and nucleoproteins may be found in every living cell. It is found combined with fat as cerebrosides and also is present in all connective tissue.

The main function of carbohydrate is to supply readily available energy for heat and muscular work. It spares protein and also exerts an antiketogenic effect by sparing rapid utilization of fat. Carbohydrate not oxidized or stored as glycogen is converted into fat and stored in the various fat depots.

Judging from the respiratory quotients and the blood levels of both term newborn and premature infants, carbohydrate stores are rapidly exhausted in the first few hours of life. However, the infant gastrointestinal tract easily digests and assimilates the disaccharides (milk and cane sugar) and monosaccharides (dextrose) from the time of birth, and once normal feedings have started, the relative hypoglycemia (40 to 80 mg/100 ml) of the first few days of life disappears and the respiratory quotient also rises.[37]

Congenital lactase deficiency is a vary rare inborn error of metabolism. The commonest type of lactase deficiency is that which develops in older children, adolescents or young adults, among some blacks and orientals.

TABLE 11–2.—Average Caloric, Protein, and
Water Requirements per Day

AGE (YR)	CAL/KG	PROTEIN (GM/KG)	WATER (ML/KG)
Premature	120	3.0–4.0	150
Infancy	110	2.0	150
1–3	100	2.0	125
4–6	90	3.0	100
7–9	80	2.5	75
10–12	70	2.0	75
13–15	80	1.5	50
15+	50	1.0	50
Adult	45	0.8	50

Though free of gastrointestinal symptoms in early life they develop diarrhea and cramping after ingesting milk when they are older. Characteristically the stools have a pH less than 6 and sugar is present. Transient lactase deficiency is not uncommonly associated with any gastroenteritis that can damage intestinal epithelium during infancy.[10, 30]

During the first two trimesters of pregnancy, carbohydrate metabolism in the fetus is essentially independent of glucagon and insulin action. In the final trimester, insulin plays a dominant role in directing the disposition of glucose and amino acids for anabolic storage as glycogen, fat, and protein. Glucagon plays little or no role in utero and development of receptors on target tissues is delayed when compared with insulin receptors. At birth there is a surge in glucagon secondary to the surge in catecholamines. Insulin secretion remains at low basal levels for several days. The result is activated glycogenolysis, gluconeogenesis, and ketogenesis, which aid the neonate in adapting to extrauterine life.[37] The newborn infant has a decreased ability to mobilize lipids in a fasting state. This decreases availability of ketones, which can be used by the infant brain as a substitute for glucose, and thus increases the demand for glucose. This situation is further exaggerated in low birth weight neonates.

Carbohydrate metabolism in the neonate is unique in a number of ways and has been the object of considerable study. Especially important is the recognition and prevention of hypoglycemia, which may cause permanent as well as temporary impairment of central nervous system function. Term infants with blood glucose levels below 30 mg/100 ml within the first six to eight hours following delivery have been reported at an incidence of about 10%. The frequency is twice as great in preterm or small-for-date babies. The longer the period of fasting after parturition the higher the incidence. Although many of these infants will exhibit no obvious manifestations of the low blood sugar at the time, this is not a reliable indication that no damage has taken place. The pathogenesis of this potentially dangerous situation is often multiple and may vary in different infants. Glucose is essential for normal brain metabolism. Carbohydrate stores, mostly in the liver, are rapidly depleted by the brain and other glucose-dependent tissues. Glucose-sparing substrates, such as fatty acids and glycerol, are inadequate or poorly utilized. Relative or absolute hyperinsulinism may be present, as in the diabetic mother. An added factor may be poor aerobic oxidation secondary to asphyxia or cold stress. Oral or parenteral administration of glucose is necessary until this usually transient condition is corrected.[37]

The relative requirements of children for carbohydrates do not differ from those of adults and are aimed at supplying a readily available source of energy. In general, it may be stated that not more than about 40% of the total calories in an infant's formula should be in the form of carbohydrates. Later in life the optimal range is believed to be between 40% and 60% of the total caloric intake.[10]

Lipids

The amount of fat present in the body varies with each individual. It is derived from ingested fat and from conversion of carbohydrate and protein in the body. In addition to its most commonly emphasized role as a source of concentrated energy, fat provides structural components for the repair and building of many body tissues, serves as a vehicle for the absorption of the fat-soluble vitamins (A, D, E, and K), spares protein, and is essential in the synthesis of the steroid hormones. There is some evidence that the highly unsaturated fatty acids are essential to life, and these cannot be synthesized by the body.

As a dietary component the lipids impart palatability to food. In addition to the metabolic roles listed above they play a very essential part in maintaining body temperature. Passively they act as an efficient insulator against the environmental temperature. The unique nature and metabolism of brown fat in preserving body temperature have been described in chapter 10.

Few experiments have been carried out on children using low-fat diets, but those few have indicated that fat is essential to normal growth and development. In the rat and dog, diets deficient in linoleic and arachidonic acids caused retarded growth and eczematoid skin lesions. Hansen et al.[8] believe that some infantile eczema is benefited by the addition of the fatty acids to the diet. With the exception of linoleic acid, all fats found in the body can be formed from carbohydrate or protein precursors. Only 1% to 2% of the total calories as linoleic acid satisfy daily requirements that are essential to the synthesis of prostaglandins.

Retention of ingested fat is lower in the newborn than in the older infant or child. With mother's milk the retention is very close to 100%. With cow's milk it is 75% to 85%. The premature infant may lose from 30% to 50% of the ingested fat in the stool, the larger amounts for the most immature. The premature may absorb unsaturated fats or medium-chained triglycerides as well as the more mature infant, but he absorbs saturated fats poorly. By about 2 months of age there is no difference between the infant and adult in fat absorption. A possible reason for this improvement is the increased concentration and the change in composition of the bile salts that are necessary for fat digestion. Formulas for the premature infant are usually recommended to contain minimal amounts of saturated fats.[7, 15, 55, 56]

Once the newborn infant has depleted his or her available glycogen stores (usually within the first day) the infant begins to depend on reserves of fat for energy, as demonstrated by a reduction in the respiratory quotient. During this process there is an increased transport of fat substances in the blood and nearly a twofold increase in the blood lipids between birth and the second week of life, although the total is still lower than in the child or adult.

Although the breast-fed infant obtains nearly 50% of his or her caloric intake from fat, it is the general consensus that after breast feeding is stopped, not over 35% of the total caloric intake should be in the form of fat either for the infant or for the older child. Diets having very low fat contents lead to excessive carbohydrate intake, hunger, and early fatigue.[10, 19] When low-fat diets are prescribed, as in celiac disease or cystic fibrosis of the pancreas, it is customary to supplement them with addition of vitamins, especially A and D.

The value of a diet low in saturated fats in an attempt to reduce the development of atherosclerosis in later life has not been determined. At this time, it seems safe to recommend that the ingestion of saturated fats should be limited but not curtailed to the extent of the "low cholesterol diet" now advised by some nutritionists for all adults. This advice may be especially applicable to children in a family with a known history of myocardial infarction. The tendency to elevated serum cholesterol can be modified to an appreciable extent by a restricted saturated fat diet.[19]

Breast Milk Feeding

Within the past two decades there has been a marked increase in the number of mothers who breast feed their babies for at least a few to several months after birth. Since proprietary formulas are based on cow's milk it is appropriate to compare these sources of infant feeding. It is important to realize that as the duration of breast feeding continues, changes do occur in human milk. For example, the protein content 100 days postpartum is slightly greater than half of what it was at 14 days, while fat and carbohydrate remain relatively stable. Colostrum, which is secreted for the first three to five days, has a much higher protein content than mature breast milk, while its fat and lactose concentration are lower. In general, cow's milk contains three to four times more protein, three times as much calcium, and six times as much phosphorus as mature human milk. Human milk is higher in unsaturated fatty acids and the principal protein is lactoalbumin as opposed to casein, which some authorities believe is more easily digested.[65] The use of whey as a partial replacement for casein in proprietary formulas, especially for premature infants, has given evidence of improved results.[9]

The advantages of breast feeding can be briefly outlined. For the reasons previously given concerning the differences in breast compared with cow's milk, the former has some nutritional superiority. In the low birth weight infant the mother's milk has been shown to be better than pooled milk from mothers who delivered term neonates. The evidence linking breast-feeding in less-developed countries to protection from infectious diseases and other causes of mortality is persuasive. Unanswered is the important problem of whether the protection is due to immune components of breast milk or due to avoiding contact with pathogenic organisms when artificial formulas are prepared in less than ideal circumstances. Studies in the United States seem less certain in attributing protective merits to breast feeding. Conclusions have necessarily been limited by methodologic short-comings that are not easily avoided.[66–69]

There is evidence that obesity is less common in breast-fed than in bottle-fed infants and this may extend into childhood. Causes may be related to feeding techniques, i.e., formula-fed infants are expected to "finish" the bottle while breast infants stop nursing when satiated; the high fat concentration of breast milk at the end of feeding may act as an appetite supressant; and increased serum osmolarity in formula-fed infants leads to excessive thirst and ingestion of more formula than required in terms of nutritional need.[70]

Breast feeding for obvious reasons enhances maternal infant bonding.

Human milk for the human infant is hypoallergenic in comparison with cow's milk. Infants fed breast milk are reported to have a reduced incidence of atopic eczema.

Prolonged breast feeding suppresses ovulation, thereby acting as an important method of population control, particularly in underdeveloped countries where other contraceptive methods are not available or are not used.

Two disadvantages of breast feeding are hyperbilirubinemia and the transmission of drugs and other chemicals. Neonatal jaundice (hyperbilirubinemia) is the most common problem seen in the full-term neonate. Only a small number have levels of serum bilirubin above 13 mg/100 ml, which is assumed to be below the level that may cause brain damage. However, approximately 50% of term newborns have visible jaundice with bilirubin levels above 5 mg/100 ml, and about 10% will require phototherapy. Although the etiology remains obscure, there is little doubt that human milk feeding is associated with more severe and prolonged hyperbilirubinemia than formula feeding.[71, 72] A large number of drugs and chemicals have been identified as passing from the maternal circulation to breast milk. Although the number of substances that are specifically contraindicated during breast feeding is small, they are important to identify.[73]

Minerals

The minerals are essential to normal body structure and function. The child requires at least 12 minerals in proper amounts for formation of new tissues and body fluids. At birth the mineral content of the body is 3% of the total weight. Throughout childhood there is a steady increase, both absolute and relative, so that in the adult 4.35% of the body weight is mineral ash.

The minerals may be divided into three main groups. The important electropositive ions are sodium, potassium, calcium, and magnesium. The electronegative ions are chlorine, phosphorus, and sulfur. Iron and iodine and the trace elements represent a separate group physiologically.

Sodium is found chiefly in the extracellular fluids of the body, with a small amount in muscle, cartilage, and bone cells. With chloride, bicarbonate, protein, and phosphate it regulates the osmotic pressure and ionic equilibrium of body fluids. With calcium, potassium, and magnesium it aids in control of the irritability of the neuromuscular system. The sodium content of the body is regulated by amounts ingested balanced against excretion under control of aldosterone. Except under extreme degrees of dehydration, hydration, or loss from the intestinal tract, the body's control of water and electrolyte balance is very precise. The average daily requirement is met by 1 to 2 gm. This amount is normally found in the content of the food eaten.

Potassium is the most important electropositive intracellular ion. Its functions are almost identical with those of sodium except that the latter is largely extracellular. In addition, it influences the irritability and conductivity of the heart muscle. Potassium metabolism is influenced by the adrenal cortical hormone, possibly by the parathyroid hormone, and by ionic equilibrium of calcium, sodium, and protein.

Since most foods contain an abundant supply of this mineral, a diet low in potassium is difficult to prepare. Between 1 and 2 gm is required daily.

Calcium occurs in the body to a far greater extent than any other positive mineral element. Ninety-nine percent of it is found in combination with phosphates and carbonates as bone. Most of the remainder is found in the plasma, half of this being bound with protein and the other half in ionizable form.

Calcium furnishes important material for structure and growth of bones and teeth, and it supplies ions that function in muscle contraction, in the control of irritability of nerve cells, and in the coagulation of blood and milk. It plays a minor role in electrolyte balance.

Calcium is easily absorbed as a soluble salt from the upper alimentary tract. The degree of absorption is influenced by the amount in the diet, the calcium:phosphorus ratio, the acidity or alkalinity of the intestinal tract, and the presence of vitamin D. The calcium plasma level, which is quite constant at all ages, except in the premature infant at birth when levels are low, is influenced by the parathyroid glands and the acid-base balance. Metabolism, mainly concerned with deposition in bone, is under the control of hormones from the parathyroids, pituitary, adrenal cortex and the sex glands as well as vitamin D.[2, 10, 21] The role of calcitonin in calcium metabolism is discussed in chapter 9.

The amount of calcium retained by the growing child is about 25% of that ingested, under ordinary conditions. During the first year, with an adequate vitamin D intake there is a greater storage in the body, both relative and absolute, when cow's milk is the source of food than when the source is human milk; however, there is no indication that this "supermineralization" is beneficial to the growing child. Levine believes this fact may be of some value in preventing rickets in the premature infant. It should be remembered that when the vitamin D supplement is inadequate, calcium and phosphorus absorption and retention are greater from human milk than from cow's milk. Therefore, in such instances rickets will be less common in the breast-fed infants (Fig 11–2).[10, 23]

The quantity of calcium required by the growing child is estimated at between 50 and 70 mg/kg/day. In general, 1 gm/day with a calcium:phosphorus ratio of 1:1.5 appears satisfactory.

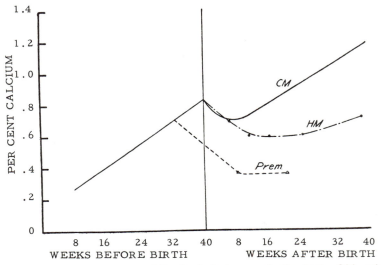

Fig 11–2.—Calcium content of the body before and after birth. *CM,* calcium content of infants fed cow's milk; *HM,* calcium content of infants fed human milk; *Prem,* calcium content of prematures fed human milk. (From Stearns.[23])

Magnesium is found in all body cells, but about 75% is in the skeleton, and a fairly large quantity is in muscle. Knowledge regarding the function of magnesium is meager. It serves as a catalyst in phosphorus and pyruvic acid metabolism and has a role in maintaining the electrolyte balance. It also is concerned with the regulation of nerve impulses and muscle irritability. Magnesium deficiency may occur in severe diarrhea and in malabsorption syndromes. During infancy it may be associated with hypocalcemic tetany. The fact that correcting the low calcium level in the serum does not result in cessation of the tetany is a possible clue to hypomagnesemia. According to Macy,[18] about 15% to 20% of the intake is retained. Requirements are given in Table 11–3. Serum magnesium is maintained normally at 1.5 to 1.8 mEq/L. Parathormone increases renal tubular reabsorption of magnesium. Low serum concentrations increase the release of parathormone.

Phosphorus is distributed in the body as organic compounds and inorganic phosphate. About 70% of the phosphate is found in the skeleton combined with calcium. With potassium, phosphorus forms the most important intracellular mineral constituent of the body. In the organic form it is found in combination with fat, protein, and carbohydrate.

Phosphorus is an important component of bone, muscle, and nerve tissue. It plays a role in the absorption of carbohydrates and their transformation in muscular activity, in the transportation of fatty acids, and as a buffer in the acid-base equilibrium. As cephalin it is essential to the formation of thrombin.

After birth the storage of phosphorus depends on the amount available in the diet, the stimulus to absorption and deposition offered by added vitamin D, and the depression of absorption by large amounts of calcium or fats in the diet.[21]

With adequate vitamin D intake, an infant should have a phosphorus intake of about 0.2 to 0.5 gm daily, children 2 to 10 years about 1.0 gm daily, and adolescents up to 1.5 gm daily. There is no known ill effect from an excess intake of phosphorus.

Chlorine, as the chloride, is a component of all body secretions and excretions. With sodium it constitutes the most important electrolyte in the extracellular fluid, maintaining acid-base and water balances. Chloride excretion is influenced by the antidiuretic factor of the posterior pituitary gland and by the adrenal cortical hormone; however, these influences are probably secondary to water metabolism.

In normal conditions the intake of chloride does not require special consideration because it is abundantly supplied in many foods.

Sulfur is a constituent of all body protein in the form of amino acids. It is also found in combination with lipids and as inorganic sulfur. It occurs

TABLE 11–3.—Recommended D⏐

	AGE (YR)	WEIGHT (KG)	HEIGHT (CM)	ENERGY (KCAL)	PROTEIN (GM)	FAT-SOLUBLE VITAMINS VITAMIN A ACTIVITY (IU)	VITA- MIN D ACTIVITY (IU)	VIT⏐ MIN⏐ ACTI⏐ (I⏐
Infants	0.0–0.5	6	60	kg × 117	kg × 2.2	1400	400	
	0.5–1.0	9	71	kg × 108	kg × 2.0	2000	400	
Children	1–3	13	86	1300	23	2000	400	
	4–6	20	110	1800	30	2500	400	
	7–10	30	135	2400	36	3300	400	1
Males	11–14	44	158	2800	44	5000	400	1
	15–18	61	172	3000	54	5000	400	1
	19–22	67	172	3000	54	5000	400	1
	23–50	70	172	2700	56	5000		1
	51+	70	172	2400	56	5000		1
Females	11–14	44	155	2400	44	4000	400	1
	15–18	54	162	2100	48	4000	400	1
	19–22	58	162	2100	46	4000	400	1
	23–50	58	162	2000	46	4000		1
	51+	58	162	1800	46	4000		1

*See reference 14.

in melanin, vitreous humor, heparin, cartilage, nerve tissue, insulin, thiamine, and enzymes of cellular respiration.

In general, the metabolism of sulfur is linked with protein metabolism since the greater part of the sulfur ingested is in the form of amino acids. Sulfur, as amino acid sulfur, is essential to growth. An adequate protein intake assures a sufficient allowance of sulfur; the ideal intake has not been established.

Iron is found in the body in relatively small amounts—approximately 3 gm in the normal adult. Fifty-eight percent is in hemoglobin, 7% in muscle hemoglobin, 15% as chromatin in the cells and in cytochrome, and the remaining 20% stored in the liver, spleen, bone marrow, and to less extent in other tissues. Almost 75% of the total body iron of the newborn is found in the hemoglobin.[34] It is evident that the chief function of iron is to carry oxygen to the tissues and to aid in oxidation processes carried on by the cells. All cells contain iron as heme proteins. Mitochondrial heme proteins function in utilization of oxygen in production of cellular energy in the form of adenosine triphosphate. Other cytochromes are found in the endoplasmic reticulum of the liver. Some of these are important in oxidative breakdown of drugs and in catabolism of endogenous compounds.[5]

Between the seventh and ninth gestational months, liver iron increases from 5 to 30 mg. Immediately after birth this may rise to 80 to 100 mg,

DIETARY ALLOWANCES REVISED 1974*

	WATER-SOLUBLE VITAMINS						MINERALS					
SCOR-BIC ACID (MG)	FOLA-CIN (μG)	NIA-CIN (MG)	RIBO-FLAVIN (MG)	THIA-MIN (MG)	VITA-MIN B_6 (MG)	VITA-MIN B_{12} (μG)	CAL-CIUM (MG)	PHOS-PHORUS (MG)	IODINE (μG)	IRON (MG)	MAG-NESIUM (MG)	ZINC (MG)
35	50	5	0.4	0.3	0.3	0.3	360	240	35	10	60	3
35	50	8	0.6	0.5	0.4	0.3	540	400	45	15	70	5
40	100	9	0.8	0.7	0.6	1.0	800	800	60	15	150	10
40	200	12	1.1	0.9	0.9	1.5	800	800	80	10	200	10
40	300	16	1.2	1.2	1.2	2.0	800	800	110	10	250	10
45	400	18	1.5	1.4	1.6	3.0	1200	1200	130	18	350	15
45	400	20	1.8	1.5	2.0	3.0	1200	1200	150	18	400	15
45	400	20	1.8	1.5	2.0	3.0	800	800	140	10	350	15
45	400	18	1.6	1.4	2.0	3.0	800	800	130	10	350	15
45	400	16	1.5	1.2	2.0	3.0	800	800	110	10	350	15
45	400	16	1.3	1.2	1.6	3.0	1200	1200	115	18	300	15
45	400	14	1.4	1.1	2.0	3.0	1200	1200	115	18	300	15
45	400	14	1.4	1.1	2.0	3.0	800	800	100	18	300	15
45	400	13	1.2	1.0	2.0	3.0	800	800	100	18	300	15
45	400	12	1.1	1.0	2.0	3.0	800	800	80	10	300	15

reaching a peak at two to three months. At this time there is an increase in erythropoiesis and a steady decrease in liver iron ensues for the next couple of years. In addition there is a paucity of hemosiderin in bone marrow during most of childhood. These observations indicate that iron depots, except for the first two to three months, are marginal. It is not surprising, then, to find that a deficiency of iron in the diet rapidly leads to anemia, and that the two categories of children most susceptible are preschoolers in a low socioeconomic situation and the adolescent girl.[6, 12]

Small amounts of iron are present in the serum bound to a β-globulin *transferrin*. There is an excess of this protein and normally about 66% of serum transferrin is in a free state. When the degree of saturation falls below 15% very little iron will be available for hemoglobin synthesis or for the important cytochrome enzymes. Iron deficiency does not cause a purely hematologic problem but may involve cellular functions resulting in lowered host defense and interfering with optimal neurologic function.[1, 5, 57] The mean values representative of iron and iron-binding capacity during life are shown in the following table.

During periods of rapid growth the need for iron is greater than at other periods of life in order to avoid hypochromic microcytic anemia. The anemia of prematurity, occurring about two to four months after birth, cannot be prevented by giving iron prophylactically, but the severity and duration

AGE	SERUM IRON (μG/100 ML)	IRON-BINDING CAPACITY (μG/100 ML)
Newborn	190	225
1 day	50	50
2 wk	125	230
3 mo	50	250
1 yr	70	250
2 yr	100	250
10 yr	110	280
Adult: Female	110	330
Male	125	300

may be influenced to some extent by early administration of iron. The cause of this anemia is believed to be twofold: (1) the greater portion of storage of iron by the fetus occurs during the last trimester (Fig 11–3), and (2), more important, the premature infant grows relatively rapidly during a short span of time.[5] It has recently been demonstrated that an important percentage of normal infants fed untreated (heat) homogenized whole cow's milk will develop a milk-induced enteric blood loss, often resulting in a reduced iron storage and a mild but definite iron-deficiency anemia. Heating the milk, or substituting a prepared formula, reversed the changes.[49] The American Academy of Pediatrics recommends the use of iron-fortified formulas throughout the first year as a prophylaxis against iron-deficiency anemia.

The iron-accumulated by the fetus is sufficient only for the first few months of life, and the supply may be even less adequate in the case of a maternal iron deficiency, multiple birth, or prematurity. Neither human nor cow's milk contains enough iron to meet the requirements of the infant after the fourth month, so foods supplying this need, such as meat, are a necessary part of the diet by this time. It is of interest to note that 70% of the hemoglobin iron at age 1 year is still derived from fetal stores and 40% at 2 years.[31] These figures emphasize the ability to reuse the available supply. There is evidence that some of the transplacental iron acquired from maternal sources is stored and not utilized until late in the first year.[31] The iron requirements for the growing child vary between 0.5 and 1.0 mg/kg/day during early life and between 0.2 and 0.4 mg for the older child.[18]

The amount of iron in food that can be absorbed depends upon the nature of that food or its combination with other components in the diet. Much of the phosphorus in cereals and legumes is present as phytic acid that forms an insoluble salt with iron and greatly decreases absorption. Similarly, the iron and phosphoproteins in egg yolk form a complex that impedes its availability. Since the iron in meat is primarily present in protein, hemoglobin, or myoglobin, it is less influenced by other ingredients

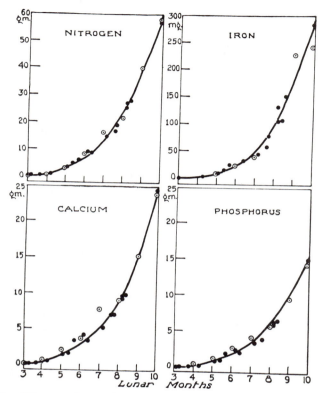

Fig 11–3.—Nitrogen, iron, calcium, and phosphorus content of the human fetus. It is apparent that the fetus retains the greatest proportion of all four of these substances during the final trimester. (From Swanson W.W., lob V.: *Am. J. Obstet. Gynecol.* 38:383, 1939.)

in the diet and is more readily assimilated. These factors are important in explaining the high incidence of iron-deficiency anemia among the poor, especially in the underdeveloped countries.

Iodine is necessary for the formation of the thyroid hormone and thus plays a vital part in body metabolism. It is readily absorbed from the alimentary tract in either organic or inorganic form. After absorption it is rapidly taken up by the thyroid gland. The amount retained by the body depends on the intake and the amount already stored.[21]

The work of Marine has well established the routine use of iodine prophylactically in a "goiter belt" area to prevent simple goiter. Iodized table salt usually supplies adequate iodine in the so-called goiter areas. For infants and children the daily requirements are stated to be 40 to 100 μg and for adolescents 100 to 200 μg.

The following minerals, found in very small amounts in the human body, are essential to normal growth and development.[20, 21, 23] *Fluorine* is apparently necessary for good tooth enamel formatiion. It is also found in bone, but its function here is poorly understood. Nutritional surveys continue to find dental caries to be the most prevalent disease throughout all of childhood, and that the administration of fluoride is a safe and effective means of reducing its incidence.[58] *Copper* is found in larger quantities in the liver of the fetus than in the child after birth, and it is found in larger quantities in the bone marrow after birth than in the liver or bone marrow of the fetus. Since the liver of the fetus and the bone marrow of the infant are the chief sources of red blood cells, these variations lend support to the theory that copper is necessary for hemoglobin synthesis. It is also found in the enzymes tyrosinase and ascorbic oxidase. Since the normal diet contains traces of copper, its deficiency is not to be anticipated in the normal child. *Zinc* is necessary for normal growth and sexual maturation. Although deficiency states are rare, a syndrome found in African and Asian children is associated with marked reduction in the zinc content of plasma, urine, sweat, and tissues. These children are retarded in statural growth, have delayed bone age, and retarded genital development with minimal or absent sexual maturation and a poor response of growth hormone to hypoglycemia. A major factor in the etiology is the diet, which contains large amounts of phytate that binds zinc and makes it unavailable. Phytate is a common ingredient in most grains. Supplementing the diet with zinc for these subjects corrected the growth failure. Since a number of enzymes contain the element, it is probably essential for nucleic acid and protein synthesis.[51]

Vitamins

The vitamins are so well known that they will be considered very briefly and in outline form (see Table 11–3). It is certain that they are essential to normal growth and development. A well-rounded diet usually supplies adequate amounts of them, but during infancy and nutritional disturbances some of them should be given to supplement the diet. Neither human nor cow's milk supplies sufficient amounts of vitamins C and D, so they should be added to the infant's intake.

The major role of vitamins is to act as coenzymes that activate enzymes in basic metabolic processes. Most cannot be synthesized by the body and must be supplied in the diet. Exceptions are vitamin D, conversion of skin sterols by sunlight, and vitamin K, synthesized by intestinal bacteria. Both folacin (formerly known as folic acid) and cobalamin (formerly B_{12}) are important in protein metabolism, folacin playing a major role in the formation of nucleoproteins. Megaloblastic anemia may be caused by a deficiency of either vitamin in early life. Since many babies are being fed goat's milk, it is important to recognize that the content of folacin in goat milk is insufficient to supply the daily requirements and supplements must be given. Pyridoxine (B$_6$) is an essential coenzyme to several enzymes involved in amino acid metabolism. Deficiency causes dermatitis, neuritis, and convulsions in infants and children. Riboflavin and thiamine (B$_1$) are coenzymes for a number of reactions. Deficiency of the former results in photophobia, cheilosis, corneal clouding, and poor growth. Classic beriberi is found in thiamine deficiencies. Niacin is another coenzyme involved in multiple reactions whose deficiency results in pellagra, which is comprised of the "three D's": dementia, diarrhea, and dermatitis.

Vitamin E (α-tocopherol) deficiency is limited to premature infants when hemolytic anemia can occur due to increased fragility of red cells in the absence of this antioxidant.

Vitamin A, D, and K are fat-soluble; therefore, the ability to absorb fat must be present before they can be adequately absorbed. Vitamins A and D may be stored in the liver, so that large quantities given at one time are effective for relatively long periods. Vitamin D is also available in water-soluble form (activated ergosterols).[4, 10]

The body has very poor ability to store any of the water-soluble vitamins; consequently, these vitamins must be ingested frequently in adequate amounts. In general, the factors of the B complex occur together in nature, so that a deficiency of any one is usually associated with a deficiency of the others.

The figures usually given for the requirements of the vitamins have been more or less arbitrarily chosen. Factors such as illness, malnutrition, and increased activity are not considered. Finally, it has recently been demonstrated that some foods have a sparing action on vitamins of the B complex whereas others have an opposite effect. The amounts suggested in Table 11–3 are generally considered to give a wide margin of safety.

Food Habits

As the child grows, he develops food habits. These change with increasing maturation of body and mind and are related to his nutritional requirements, to his personal satisfactions and dissatisfactions, and to the impact of the society around him. The psychologic reaction of the child to the offering of food is receiving much attention at present, and properly so.

The foundations of eating behavior rest on the physiologic mechanisms of hunger and appetite and their gratification. Hunger contractions almost certainly occur in the stomach of the newborn. This is an unpleasant sensation and is relieved by the ingestion of food. The infant, at this time and later on, does not tell when he is hungry by looking at the clock, as do most adults. It seems advisable, therefore, to have a feeding schedule flexible enough to coincide with hunger time. This establishes good feeding behavior at the outset and may avoid trouble later on. It might be well to add at this point that the amount offered should be sufficient to satisfy. Many cases of "colic" in infants are related to underfeeding and poor feeding technique.[25]

The time to add solid food to the infant's diet comes when he is prepared for it and may vary over a wide range from one to perhaps four months. There is no valid indication that immaturity of the gastrointestinal tract precludes the introduction of solid food in the diet even before this, but little is to be gained and the chances of aspiration are certainly increased. The time at which chopped or more coarse food should be added depends on the child's rate of progress and, from a purely nutritional standpoint, makes little difference. An adequate diet may be secured in a variety of ways, and either forcing or overly delaying new food experiences is hardly to be desired. Most "chopped" or "junior" foods need little mastication, so that dentition is not a particularly important consideration until even coarser foods are introduced.

As motor skills increase, the child needs less and less help in eating. Some children are fairly proficient in feeding themselves by 18 months, but in many this skill comes later. The child should be allowed some choice in his diet by this time, and his likes and dislikes should be respected. By age 5 he can handle a knife and fork quite well, although he still needs occasional help. It is important throughout childhood that mealtime be a happy time to ensure good habits.

It is common during the second or third year, sometimes sooner, for the parents to be overly concerned with the child's appetite. This is often a period of psychologic anorexia. It must be realized that by this time the rapid growth that characterized infancy is over. The rate of weight gain reaches its lowest point during this time, and the metabolic rate is at a relatively low level. In addition, this is a period in the child's life when he is becoming aware of himself as an individual and as a part of the family group. His interests are not as concerned with eating as they formerly were. He may like to exert his authority by seeing the effect of his not eating on his parents, especially if they appear worried about it. If these facts are explained to parents and they are assured that no healthy child (physically and mentally) will starve himself if food is available, many disagreeable behavior problems will be avoided. Often asking the child to participate in preparing the food or the table will renew interest. Smaller helpings may also be desirable and make the goal of "cleaning the plate" more easily attained.

During adolescence the appetite is usually increased. Growth in both height and weight is accelerated. Increased fat deposition occurs as a part of sexual maturation in both sexes, though it is more pronounced in females. Unfortunately, adolescence is also a period when food fads are often begun and promoted by false conceptions of nutrition and its relationship to maturational changes. Youth are particularly susceptible to food fads as a means of correcting problems that may include acne, real or imagined ailments, delay in sexual development, or as solace for unfulfilled needs. As we have seen in the psychological development of teenagers, they are strongly influenced in their behavior by their peers, many of whom may follow food cults. They are easy targets for quackery that can result in either excesses of certain nutrients or deficiencies in minerals, calories, or vitamins. Avoidance of animal products may be practiced due to fear of additives, such as hormones and antibiotics, or contamination by radioactive fallout. Although a well-planned vegetarian diet can easily supply all necessary nutrients, many adolescent vegetarians have been found to have inadequate caloric, protein, and iron intakes. Fluid restriction, as found in the Zen macrobiotic diets, has led to serious renal problems. Especially worrisome is the pregnant teenager and the following care of the infant if parents are pursuing a food fad or cult.[60]

Often the adolescent is "too busy" to eat a well-balanced meal and resorts to between-meal snacks, which may constitute more than one fourth of the recommended caloric intake. Often such foods lack both iron and protein content and contribute an important share to dental caries. Parents and other counselors may find it difficult to reform such practices, and mild degrees of dietary deficiencies are not uncommon.[35, 48]

Recent surveys in the United States indicate the overall nutritional status of infants and children is reasonably good.[61, 62] Not surprising was the finding of a direct correlation between the nutritional status and income or socioeconomic level. Both stature and weight were lowest in the poorer population groups. Iron deficiency and iron-deficiency anemia were the most commonly encountered specifically identified problems. In children under 5 years the incidence was as high as 30% in some areas for iron deficiency (transferrin saturation below 20%) and 26% for anemia (hemoglobin below 10 gm). Ethnic and geographic variations in regard to other nutrients were noted but did not constitute major problems.

The effect of illness on appetite is well recognized. The fact that some anorexia may persist beyond the time of obvious signs and symptoms of illness must also be realized to avoid the introduction of poor food habits. Fatigue, excitement, and temporary emotional disturbances occur in every normal child at one time or another, and their interference with appetite should be respected. The small child has a short attention span and often has great difficulty in sitting still during a meal. All of these factors play a part in development related to food intake, and a reasonable attitude toward them is essential.

The environment in which the child eats may also influence him. Some of the more important factors pertain to the economics of the family, the cultural food pattern of the family, the availability of food, and the attitude of the family toward food in general or toward particular preferences or prejudices.

It is apparent that nutrition in children is more than a simple matter of chemistry and physiology based on laboratory studies. The other factors, though only briefly considered, should constantly be kept in mind by the person who must guide parents and children in establishing good habits.

Dietary Requirements

The complexity of the newer and still developing knowledge of the nutrition of children has only been touched upon in this chapter. Nutrition is still an inexact science in many ways, yet great things are expected or hoped for in its use. For the obese, the hypertensive, the hyperactive, the small, the depressed, the athlete, the adolescent with acne, the slow ma-

TABLE 11–4.—Requirements of Some Essential Nutrients

Estimation of total caloric requirements, daily
  Infancy: 100–120 calories/kg expected weight for age.
  Childhood: 1,000 calories basic plus 100 calories for each year, e.g., a boy aged 9 should have 1,000 plus 900, or 1,900 calories daily.
Estimation of protein requirements, daily
  Infancy: 2 gm/kg; an adequate amount is assured if the infant consumes 100 ml whole milk/kg.
  Childhood: 1.5 gm/kg until puberty, when slightly more is desirable.
  If about 20% of the required caloric intake is protein, the requirement will be met.
Minerals, daily
  Calcium, 1.0–1.5 gm
  Phosphorus, 0.5–1.0 gm
  Iron, 16 mg
  Iodine, 100–200 mg (trace)
Vitamins: see Table 11–3
Composition of daily diet to satisfy basic growth needs

Milk	600–800 ml
Meat, poultry, fish	1 serving (5–6 weekly)
Liver	1 serving weekly
Eggs	1 (3–4 weekly)
Vegetables, 1 raw, 1 pigmented	2 servings
Fruit, fresh, 1 citrus	2 or more servings
Butter	2 tsp
Bread (enriched or whole grain) and cereals . .	Enough to meet caloric needs
Salt (iodized).	Seasoning

turer, the constipated, the sterile, the infertile, the sick, the infirm, etc., whatever the problem, somehow a change in diet is going to improve the situation. The numerous food fads and cults in which food plays an important role are examples of the ignorance many people have regarding food. The flourishing businesses of "natural food stores" and "vitamin shops" are further examples of entrepreneurs exploiting the often gullible but hopeful public for their own gains.

No attempt has been made to outline the actual preparation of formulas or diets since this is done in most textbooks of pediatrics or nursing and in dietary manuals. Some basic data are presented in Table 11–4 which may be useful to the reader.

REFERENCES

 1. Buckley R.H.: Iron deficiency anemia: Its relationship to infection susceptibility and host defense. *J. Pediatr.* 86:993, 1975.
 2. Harrison H.E., Harrison H.C.: *Disorders of Calcium and Phosphate Metabolism in Childhood and Adolescence.* Philadelphia, W.B. Saunders Co., 1979.
 3. Reichman B.L., Chessex P., Putet G., et al.: Partition of energy cost of growth in the very low birth-weight infant. *Pediatrics* 69:446, 1982.
 4. Wasserman R.H., Taylor A.N.: Metabolic roles of fat-soluble vitamins D, E and K. *Am. Rev. Biochem.* 41:179, 1972.
 5. Oski F.A., Naiman J.L.: *Hematologic Problems in the Newborn,* ed. 2. Philadelphia, W.B. Saunders Co., 1972.
 6. Owen G.M., Kram K.M., Gary P.J., et al.: A study of nutritional status of preschool children in the U.S., 1968–70. *Pediatrics* 53:597, 1974.
 7. Räihä, N.C.R.: Biochemical basis for nutritional management of preterm infants. *Pediatrics* 53:147, 1974.
 8. Hansen A.E., Knott E.M., Wiese H.F., et al.: Eczema and essential fatty acids. *Am. J. Dis. Child.* 73:1, 1947.
 9. Gross S.J.: Growth and biochemical response of preterm infants fed human milk or modified infant formula. *N. Engl. J. Med.* 308:237, 1983.
10. Foman S.J.: *Infant Nutrition,* ed. 2. Philadelphia, W.B. Saunders Co., 1974.
11. Wharton B.A.: Child health and nutrition, in Apley J. (ed.): *Modern Trends in Paediatrics.* London, Butterworth, 1970.
12. Young C.M.: Adolescents and their nutrition, in Gallagher J.R., Heald F.P., Garell D.C. (eds.): *Medical Care of the Adolescent.* New York, Appleton-Century Crofts, 1976.
13. Lloyd-Still J.D., Hurwitz I., Wolff P.H., et al.: Intellectual development after severe malnutrition in infancy. *Pediatrics* 54:306, 1974.
14. National Research Council Food and Nutrition Board: *Recommended Dietary Allowance,* ed. 8. Washington, D.C., National Academy of Sciences, 1974.
15. Räihä N.C.R.: Nutritional proteins in milk and the protein requirements of normal infants. *Pediatrics* 75:136, 1985.
16. Levine S.Z., Gordon H.H.: Physiologic handicaps of the premature infant. *Am. J. Dis. Child.* 64:297, 1942.
17. American Academy of Pediatrics, Committee on Nutrition: Nutritional needs of low birth-weight infants. *Pediatrics* 75:976, 1985.
18. Macy I.G.: *Nutrition and Chemical Growth in Childhood,* vol. I, Evaluation. Springfield, Ill., Charles C Thomas, Publisher, 1942.

19. Hennekens C.H., Jesse M.J., Klein B.E., et al.: Cholesterol among children of men with myocardial infarction. *Pediatrics* 58:211, 1976.
20. Goodhart R.S., Shils M.E. (eds.): *Modern Nutrition in Health and Disease.* Philadelphia, Lea & Febiger, 1973.
21. Shohl A.T.: *Mineral Metabolism.* Am. Chem. Soc. Monogr. Ser. New York, Reinhold Publishing Corp., 1939.
22. Goldman H.I., Goldman J.S., Kaufman I., et al.: Late effects of early dietary protein intake on low-birthweight infants. *J. Pediatr.* 85:764, 1976.
23. Stearns G.: Mineral metabolism of normal infants. *Physiol. Rev.* 19:415, 1939.
24. Graham G.G.: Environmental factors affecting the growth of children. *Am. J. Clin. Nutr.* 25:1184, 1972.
25. Stevenson S.S.: The adequacy of artificial feeding in infancy. *J. Pediatr.* 31:616, 1947.
26. Sewards J.F., Serdula M.K.: Infant feeding and infant growth. *Pediatrics* 74:728, 1984.
27. Windle W.F.: *Physiology of the Fetus.* Philadelphia, W.B. Saunders Co., 1940.
28. Heald F.P.: *Adolescent Nutrition and Growth.* New York, Appleton-Century Crofts, 1969.
29. Calcagno P.L., Rubin M.I.: Effect of added carbohydrate on growth, nitrogen retention and renal excretion in premature infants. *Pediatrics* 13:193, 1954.
30. Christopher M.L., Bayless T.M.: Role of the small bowel and colon in lactose induced diarrhea. *Gastroenterology* 60:845, 1971.
31. Smith C.A., Cherry R.B., Maletskas C.J., et al.: Persistence and utilization of maternal iron for blood formation during infancy. *J. Clin. Invest* 34:1391, 1955.
32. Lebenthal E., Lee P.C. Heitlinger L.A.: Impact of development of the gastrointestinal tract on infant feeding. *J. Pediatr.* 102:1, 1983.
33. McLaren D.S., Burman D.: *Textbook of Pediatric Nutrition.* Edinburgh, Churchill Livingstone, Inc., 1976.
34. Schulman I.: Iron requirements in infancy. *J.A.M.A.* 175:118, 1961.
35. American Academy of Pediatrics, Committee on Nutrition: Nutritional aspects of vegetarianism, health foods, and fad diets. *Pediatrics* 59:460, 1971.
36. Tanner J.M.: Relationships of different bodily tissues during growth and in the adult, in *Diet and Bodily Constitution.* Ciba Foundation Study Group. Boston, Little, Brown & Co., 1964.
37. Cornblath M., Schwartz R.: *Disorders of Carbohydrate Metabolism in Infancy,* ed. 2. Philadephia, W.B. Saunders Co., 1976.
38. Smith C.A.: Prenatal and neonatal nutrition. *Pediatrics* 30:145, 1962.
39. McCance R.A.: Some effects of undernutrition. *J. Pediatr.* 65:1008, 1964.
40. McCance R.A.: Food, growth and time. *Lancet* 2:261, 671, 1962.
41. Waisman H.A., Kerr G.R.: Amino acid and protein metabolism in the developing fetus and the newborn infant. *Pediatr. Clin. N. Am.* 12:551, 1965.
42. Widdowson E.M.: Early nutrition and later development, in *Diet and Bodily Constitution.* Ciba Foundation Study Group. Boston, Little, Brown & Co., 1964.
43. Dobbing J., Sands J.: Vulnerability of developing brain: IX. The effect of nutritional growth retardation on the timing of the brain growth spurt. *Biol. Neonate* 19:363, 1971.
44. Scrimshaw N.S.: Synergism of malnutrition and infection: Evidence from field studies in Guatemala. *J.A.M.A.* 212:1685, 1970.
45. Winick M.: Malnutrition and brain development. *J. Pediatr.* 76:667, 1969.

46. Chase H.P., Dorsey J., McKhann G.M.: The effect of malnutrition on the synthesis of a myelin lipid. *Pediatrics* 40:551, 1967.
47. Chase H.P., Martin H.P.: Undernutrition and child development. *N. Engl. J. Med.* 282:933, 1970.
48. Hodges R.E., Krehl W.A.: Nutritional status of teenagers in Iowa. *Am. J. Clin. Nutr.* 17:200, 1965.
49. Woodruff C.W., Clark J.L.: The role of fresh cow's milk in iron deficiency. *Am. J. Dis. Child.* 124:18, 1972.
50. Cheek D.B., Graystone J.E., Read M.S.: Cellular growth, nutrition and development. *Pediatrics* 45:315, 1970.
51. Gordon E.F., Gordon R.C., Passal D.B.: Zinc metabolism: Basic, clinical, and behavioral aspects. *J. Pediatr.* 99;341, 1981.
52. Stock M.B., Smythe P.M.: 15-year developmental study on effects of severe undernutrition during infancy on subsequent physical growth and intellectual functioning. *Arch. Dis. Child.* 51:327, 1976.
53. Richardson S.A.: The relation of severe malnutrition in infancy to the intelligence of school children with differing life histories. *Pediatr. Res.* 10:57, 1976.
54. Räihä N.C.R., Heinonen K., Rassin D.K., et al.: Milk protein quantity and quality in low-birth-weight infants: Metabolic responses and effects on growth. *Pediatrics* 57:659, 1976.
55. Katz L., Hamilton J.R.: Fat absorption in infants of birth weight less than 1,300 gm. *J. Pediatr.* 85:608, 1974.
56. Chessex P., Reichman B.L., Verellen G.J.E., et al.: Influence of postnatal age, energy intake and weight gain in the very-low birth-weight infant. *J. Pediatr.* 99:761, 1981.
57. Dallman P.R.: Iron, vitamin E and folate in the preterm infant. *J. Pediatr.* 85:742, 1974.
58. Report of American Academy of Pediatrics Committee on Nutrition: Fluoride as a nutrient. *Pediatrics* 49:456, 1972.
59. Reichman B., Chessex P., Putet G., et al.: Diet, fat accretion, and growth in premature infants, *N. Engl. J. Med.* 305:1495, 1981.
60. Robson J.R.K.: Food faddism. *Pediatr. Clin. N. Am.* 24:189, 1977.
61. Garn S.M., Clark D.C.: Nutrition, growth, development and maturation: Findings from the Ten-State Nutrition Survey of 1968–1970. *Pediatrics* 56:306, 1975.
62. Owen G., Lippman G.: Nutritional status of infants and young children: U.S.A. *Pediatr. Clin. N. Am.* 24:211, 1977.
63. Chandra R.K.: Immuno-competence in undernutrition. *J. Pediatr.* 81:1194, 1972.
64. Katz M., Stiehm E.R.: Host defense in malnutrition. *Pediatrics* 59:490, 1977.
65. Hurley L.S.: *Developmental Nutrition.* Englewood Cliffs, N.J., Prentice-Hall, Inc., 1980.
66. Jason J.M., Nieburg P., Marks J.S.: Mortality and infectious disease associated with infant feeding practices in developing countries. *Pediatrics* 74:702, 1984.
67. Hanson L.A., Ahlstedt S., Anderson B., et al.: Protective factors in milk and the development of the immune system. *Pediatrics* 75:172, 1985.
68. Weinberg R.J., Tipton G., Klish W.J., et al.: Effect of breast-feeding on morbidity in rotavirus gastroenteritis. *Pediatrics* 74:250, 1984.
69. Holmes G.E., Hassanein K.M., Miller H.C.: Factors associated with infections among breast-fed and babies fed proprietary milks. *Pediatrics* 72:300, 1983.

70. Kramer M.S.: Do breast-feeding and delayed introduction of solid foods protect against subsequent obesity? *J. Pediatr.* 98:883, 1981.
71. Osborn L.M., Reiff M.I., Bolus R.: Jaundice in the full term neonate. *Pediatrics* 73:520, 1984.
72. Kivlahan C., James E.J.P.: The natural history of neonatal jaundice. *Pediatrics* 74:364, 1984.
73. American Academy of Pediatrics, Committee on Drugs: The transfer of drugs and other chemicals into human breast milk. *Pediatrics* 72:375, 1983.

12 / Facial Growth and Dentition

Adam and Eve had many advantages, but the
principal one was that they escaped teething.
—Mark Twain

The Craniofacial Skeleton

The embryonic origin of the bones making up the cranium and face are
a mixture of intramembranous ossification and endochondral ossification
(see chapter 8). This mixture permits the marked variations in the rate and
pattern of growth in this area as well as explaining some of the peculiarities
of the malformations, congenital or acquired, that are encountered. The
teeth, in part derived from ectodermal tissue, also have considerable influence on facial growth. For purposes of discussion, we shall divide the skull
into the neurocranium, a protective enclosure for the brain, and the viscerocranium, the main skeleton of the jaws.

The neurocranium consists of an endochondral portion that forms the
base of the cranium as the occipital bone, the sphenoid, the ethmoid, and
the petrous and mastoid portions of the temporal bone. The intramembranous ossification forms the cranial vault. During fetal life and well into childhood, the bones of the vault are separated by dense connective tissue
membranes, the sutures and fontanels (see Figs 4–5 and 4–6). The softness
of the bones and their relatively pliable sutures enable the skull to undergo
considerable molding during birth (Fig 12–1). The same construction also
permits rapid brain growth.[3]

The endochondral portions of the viscerocranium originate in the first
two branchial arches to form the malleus, incus, and stapes of the middle
ear and the styloid process of the temporal bone. Some endochondral ossification also occurs in the condyle of the mandible. Intramembranous
bone formation occurs within the boundaries of the first branchial arch to
form the maxilla and premaxilla, the zygoma, the squamous portion of the
temporal bone, and the mandible.

The primitive buccal cavity is bounded by the frontonasal process and

411

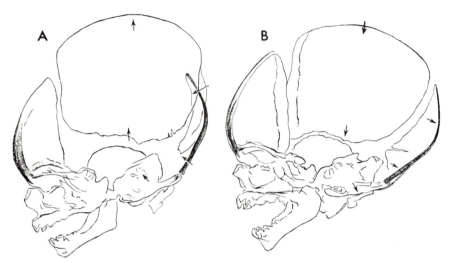

Fig 12–1.—A, tracing of roentgenogram of neonatal skull on first day of life, demonstrating molding of bones of the calvarium with overlapping of their edges and narrowing of sutures caused by compression during passage of head through the birth canal. Parietals are displaced upward, and temporals and occipital are rotated counterclockwise. **B,** tracing of roentgenogram on third day of life, showing re-expansion of cranium and widening of sutures and fontanels, as compared with **A,** after parietal, occipital, and temporal bones have returned to normal positions. (Courtesy of Dr. H. C. Moloy; from Caffey.[4])

the maxillary and mandibular processes of the first branchial arch. The frontonasal process elaborates into paired median and lateral nasal folds that form the nares. The palate develops from two parts, a median process extending from the premaxilla and two lateral processes from the maxilla. Normally development begins at the fifth week of gestation and is completed by fusion of all three processes at 12 weeks. Fusion occurs in an anterior-to-posterior direction. At the same time they also fuse with the nasal septum. The posterior portions of the lateral processes do not become ossified and form the soft palate and uvula.[30]

Failure of fusion results in the condition of cleft palate and the degree of failure can vary considerably. The resulting intercommunication of both nasal and oral cavities leads to serious phonation problems and frequent infections that include the middle ear. Since normal swallowing depends upon juxtaposition of tongue and palate, feeding is a real problem during infancy.

The anlagen of the sinuses are first found during the third fetal month when the face is assuming some definitive characteristics. Although present at birth, major growth and development is postnatal (Fig 12–2). Their pres-

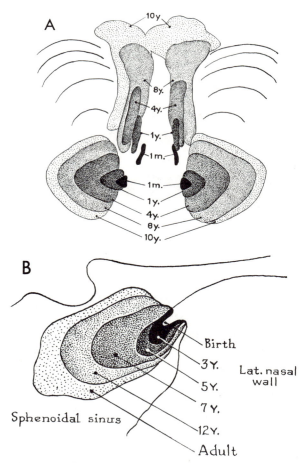

Fig 12–2.—A, composite drawing showing changes in size and shape of maxillary and frontal sinuses during infancy and childhood; *m,* month; *y,* year. **B,** diagram illustrating postnatal growth of sphenoid sinus from birth to maturity. (Redrawn from Scammon in Abt's *Pediatrics;* from Caffey.[4]) *(Continued)*

ence is very influential in facial growth. In the neonate the maxillary sinuses and ethmoid cells are so small that radiologic identification is virtually impossible. The frontal sinuses originate, as do the maxillary sinuses, by the direct extension of nasal mucosa and growth takes place by further evagination and concurrent resorption of bone. On the average, the frontal sinuses are apparent on radiologic examination by age 3 years and extend upward to the orbital roof by 6 or 7 years. Maxillary sinuses can often be visualized by the end of the first year.[20]

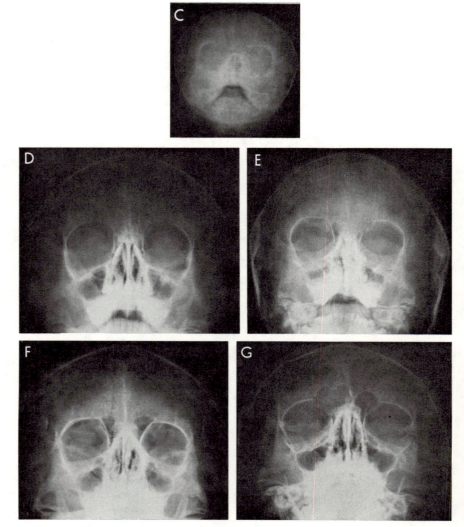

Fig 12–2 (cont.).—C–G, dorsoventral projections; sphenoid sinuses not visualized. **C,** newborn. **D,** 2 years. **E,** 4 years; definite budding upward from the ethmoids, the beginning of the frontal sinuses. **F,** 9 years; frontal sinuses have penetrated to a point above the supraorbital ridges. **G,** 12 years; sinuses are fully defined and pneumatization of zygoma appears as air-containing slits above maxillary antrums.

At birth, pneumatization of the temporal bone has barely begun, and there is but a single cell, the mastoid antrum, in communication with the superior part of the middle ear. Further pneumatization occurs through outgrowth of air cells from the mastoid antrum into the solid bone which reach the tip by about 5 years.[4]

At birth the cranium is large in proportion to the rest of the skeleton and to the face. The small jaws and lack of developments of paranasal sinuses account for these disproportions (Figs 12–3 and 12–4).

Growth of the cranial vault is rapid during infancy and early childhood, though at a constantly decelerating rate. The mechanism that produces normal suture closure and cessation of neurocranial growth is poorly understood. Spreading of the sutures, due to increased intracranial pressure, can occur until late adolescence when final ossification takes place. Premature closure (synostosis) of the sutures may be congenital and leads to some bizarre head shapes. The more common ones include scaphocephaly associated with the sagittal suture, oxycephaly with the coronal suture, and microcephaly with multiple sutures. Often these are found in combination with other anomalies.[34]

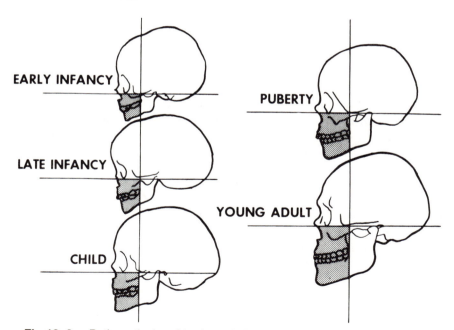

EARLY INFANCY

LATE INFANCY

CHILD

PUBERTY

YOUNG ADULT

Fig 12–3.—Both vertical and horizontal planes go through the same anatomical landmarks in each illustration. Age of the "child" is 5 years. These figures show the increasing growth of the bones of the face (maxilla and mandible) from infancy to maturity.

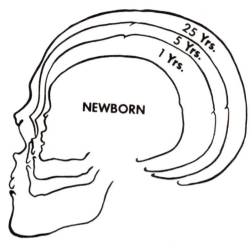

Fig 12–4.—Profiles of the skull at different ages emphasizing the relatively greater increase in size of the facial bones versus the cranium during infancy and childhood.

Skull bones are soft at birth and remain so through early infancy. The asymmetry of the head from molding at delivery will be self-limiting. Congenital torticollis and persistent positioning of an infant may result in some flattening of the cranial vault that usually disappears, or is greatly modified, if normal growth follows.

The inclination of the sutures determines the direction of growth of the maxilla, which is forward and downward (Fig 12–5). Remodeling and appositional bone growth result from enlargement of the maxillary and frontal sinuses and the alveolar ridges and cause the eventual mature facial contour.

In the newborn infant the mandible is poorly developed with small alveolar processes, short rami, and short condyles. The main growth center of the mandible is in the condyles. It is interesting to note that, unique to the human, the deep portion of the condyle has endochondral bone formation while its outer layers are membranous. Growth results in an increase in overall mandibular length as well as increase in height and width of the rami. As with the maxilla, the vector of growth is forward and downward. In both the upper and lower alveolar processes, the teeth develop at a rapid rate and their size has considerable influence on the pattern of growth. With increasing age the mental region of the mandible becomes more prominent resulting in a well-developed chin in the adult.

The varying speeds with which each dimension of the face and cranial vault is accomplished are given in Table 12–1. It can be seen that cranial size is completed much earlier than any portion of the face.[24]

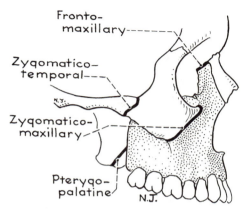

Fig 12–5.—Paired parallel sutures of nasomaxillary complex. The resultant vector of growth at these sutures is downward and forward in a direction similar to the growth vector of the mandible.

Growth of the Teeth

The entire process by which a human being gets teeth constitutes a highly interesting interaction of the ectodermal and mesodermal tissues throughout the early years of life.

Precisely, the basal layer of cells of the stratified squamous epithelium lining the oral cavity begins to proliferate rapidly about the 34th day of embryonic life and develops a ridge along the free margins of the jaws, the dental lamina. About the sixth week of intrauterine life, ten ovoid swellings appear at intervals about this ridge of ectodermal tissue, the tooth buds of the ten primary teeth (Fig 12–6, left). Continuing rapid proliferation of the epithelial cells leads to the development of a budlike "invasion" of the underlying mesodermal connective tissue. A concomitant stimulation of this embryonic connective tissue leads to a rapid proliferation of its cells, which

TABLE 12–1.—PERCENTAGE OF ADULT FACIAL AND CRANIAL DIMENSIONS
ACHIEVED AT DIFFERENT LEVELS

	CRANIUM OF ADULT DIMENSIONS				FACE OF ADULT DIMENSIONS			
AGE (YR)	WIDTH	HEIGHT	LENGTH	BIZYGO-MATIC WIDTH	BIGONIAL WIDTH	HEIGHT	LENGTH	VOLUME RATIO CRANIUM: FACE
0	. . .	. . .	. . .	56	. . .	38	40	8:1
2	86	92	86	80	. . .	68	70	5:1
6	92	96	90	83	83	80	80	3:1
12	98	99	96	90	93	89	87	2.5:1
		max. attained by 15 yr						
18	100	100	100	100	100	100	98	2:1

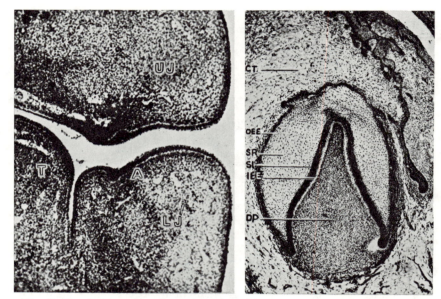

Fig 12–6.—Left, section through mouth of human embryo about 6 weeks old. Opposing collections of cells in upper and lower jaws are the beginnings of primary tooth buds. Invagination has already started. *T,* tongue; *A,* arch of mandible; *UJ,* upper jaw; *LJ,* lower jaw. **Right,** section through developing tooth—advanced "bell stage"—in fetal mandible at about 4 months. By the time of birth the crowns of all 20 primary (deciduous) teeth are in the process of calcification and enough inorganic calcium has been deposited to permit their detection on x-ray films (see Fig 12–10). *CT,* connective tissue of mandible; *OEE,* outer enamel epithelium; *SR,* stellate reticulum; *SI,* stratum intermedium; *IEE,* inner enamel epithelium; *DP,* dental pulp. It should be remembered that both primary (deciduous) and secondary (permanent) teeth are fully formed and their crowns calcified months to years before they erupt.

produces the dental papilla, the organ responsible later for the formation of the dentin and pulp. The continued proliferation of the epithelium produces a caplike enamel organ surrounding the outer end of the dental papilla.

Further proliferation of the epithelial cells at the deep margins of the cap leads to the development of a bell-shaped enamel organ (Fig 12–6, right). The innermost layer of cells (the interior of the bell) later will produce the specialized tall, hexagonal, columnar cells, the ameloblasts, which will lay down the enamel matrix. A large portion of the dental papilla becomes enclosed in this invaginated bell, and the outermost layer of its peripheral cells then undergoes differentiation to the tall, columnar odontoblasts. The basement membrane separating the layer of ameloblasts of the enamel organ from the odontoblasts of the dental papilla later becomes the dentoenamel junction of the calcified crown. The remaining embryonic connective tissue of the interior of the dental papilla becomes the dental pulp. The outer layer of enamel epithelium of the bell-like ectodermal invasion and the stellate cells that separate it from the inner specialized layer of ameloblasts begin to serve as a nutritive mechanism as soon as calcification begins. This occurs between the fourth and the sixth month of uterine life at the dentoenamel junctions of the 20 primary teeth. It then reduces to a thin layer of cells on the completion of the enamel, the reduced enamel epithelium. The remnants of the remaining ameloblasts degenerate to a thin, acellular, chitinous membrane on completion of the enamel, but the layer of odontoblasts remains around the periphery of the pulp as a permanent mechanism for the formation of secondary dentin.

Following the laying down of dentin and enamel, activity of the deepest margins of the invaginated bell (the epithelial root sheath) initiates the formation of the root or roots and molds their shape. Continued extension of the original ridge-like dental lamina lingually and distally leads similarly to a cycle of developmental events which produces the permanent teeth. The tooth germs of the succedaneous permanent teeth appear lingually to those of the primary teeth from the fifth month in utero (central incisors) to ten months after birth (second bicuspids), and the tooth germs of the three permanent molars appear progressively distal to those of the second primary molar from four months of fetal life (first molar) to the fourth or fifth year of life (third molar).[17, 21, 26, 29]

With the development of the roots of the primary teeth the crowns move occlusally until the reduced enamel epithelium fuses with the oral epithelium, the epithelium over the tips of the cusps of the crowns degenerates and the crown gradually erupts into occlusion with its opponent from the opposite arch. The remnant of the inner layer of cells of the bell, now a thin degenerated membrane, the enamel cuticle, gradually wears away, and the sole remaining evidence of the original fetal invasion of ectodermal tissue, now returned to the oral cavity, is the enamel, without cells, without nerve supply, without blood supply, hence without any direct systemic connection. As a child grows the crowns of the permanent teeth develop, the roots of the primary teeth resorb, the permanent teeth, both succedaneous and molars, erupt, occlusion of the permanent teeth in the two arches establishes, and the attrition of the enamel of the crowns begins.

This life cycle of dental histophysiologic events now may be summarized briefly into six periods for diagnostic purposes: (1) growth, (2) calcification and maturation, (3) eruption of primary teeth, (4) resorption of roots of primary teeth, (5) eruption of permanent teeth, and (6) attrition. The period of growth may be divided further into five distinct but overlapping periods of rapid change prior to the second period of the cycle, the period of calcification and maturation. These five periods are (1) initiation, the development of the dental lamina and tooth buds; (2) proliferation, the rapid growth of cells by which the initiated tooth develops through the stages of the bud, cap and bell, along with the concomitant changes of the dental papilla; (3) histodifferentiation, the development of the specialized cells, the ameloblasts and odontoblasts; (4) morphodifferentiation, the stage of development of final characteristic contour and size of the crowns of the various teeth; and (5) apposition, the deposition of the matrix of the enamel progressively outward along the length of the ameloblast from the dento-enamel junction. This activity terminates in the external contour of the crown and the deposition of the matrix of the dentin inward, an activity which reduces the size of the pulp by reducing the size of the pulpal chamber.[27, 28]

Factors Influencing Normal Tooth Growth and Development

Although the preceding description of normal dental histophysiologic events follows a known sequence, it tells nothing of the biologic factors that may influence the rate of development, the dimensions, the morphology, the number, and the eruption sequence of the teeth.

Recent investigations have revised the chronology of the various events which make up the pattern of the development of the individual teeth. It should be of interest to one who would regularly observe the development in the oral cavity to be familiar with these factors and to understand the causes of seeming irregularities which may occur in the dynamic individual known as the "growing child."

There is considerable range of time in tooth development and eruption, as indicated in Tables 12–2 and 12–3. Although there is some correlation of advancement and retardation in both osseous and dental development, it is not a very close one. Calcification and eruption of teeth do occur at a slightly earlier age in girls than in boys but not to the same degree as in bony maturation.[11, 12] There are genetic influences in dental growth as exemplified by a closer correlation of time of calcification and eruption in siblings than in unrelated individuals. Also, within the boundaries of the United States, black children have slightly more advanced permanent tooth eruption than do whites. Although tooth development and eruption may be delayed, as in hypothyroidism, or advanced, as in the adrenogenital syndrome, endocrine influences are less marked and less reliable diagnostically in dental tissue than in osseous tissue.[10, 15]

Genetic factors are the major determinants of tooth size and morphology,

TABLE 12–2.—CHRONOLOGY OF DEVELOPMENT OF THE HUMAN DENTITION*

	PRIMARY DENTITION							
	CALCIFICATION BEGINS		CROWN COMPLETED		ERUPTION		EXFOLIATION	
TOOTH	MAXILLA	MANDIBLE	MANDIBLE (MO.)	MAXILLA (MO.)	MAXILLA (MO.)	MANDIBLE (MO.)	MAXILLA (YR)	MANDIBLE (YR)
Central incisor	14 wk in utero	14½ wk in utero	1½	2½	9⅓	7½	6–7	6–7
Lateral incisor	16 wk in utero	16½ wk in utero	2½	3	11	13¼	7–8	7–8
Cuspid	17 wk in utero	17 wk in utero	9	9	19½	19⅔	10–12	9–12
1st molar	5 wk in utero	15½ wk in utero	6	5½	15⅔	16	9–11	9–11
2d molar	19 wk in utero	18 wk in utero	11	10	28	26½	10–12	10–12

	PERMANENT DENTITION							
	CALCIFICATION BEGINS		CROWN COMPLETED		ERUPTION		ROOT COMPLETED	
TOOTH	MAXILLA	MANDIBLE	MAXILLA (YR)	MANDIBLE (YR)	MAXILLA (YR)	MANDIBLE (YR)	MAXILLA (YR)	MANDIBLE (YR)
Central incisor	3–4 mo.	3–4 mo.	4½	3½	7–7½	6–6½	10–11	8½–10
Lateral incisor	10–12 mo.	3–4 mo.	5½	4–4½	8–8½	7¼–7¾	10–12	9½–10½
Cuspid	4–5 mo.	4–5 mo.	5½–6½	5½–6	11–11⅔	9¾–10¼	12½–15	12–13½
1st premolar	1½–1¾ yr	1¾–2 yr	6½–7½	6½–7	10–10⅓	10—10¾	12½–14½	12½–14
2d premolar	2–2¼ yr	2¼–2½ yr	7–8½	7–8	10¾–11¼	10¾–11½	14–15½	14½–15
1st molar[17]	32 wk in utero	32 wk in utero	4–4½	3½–4	6–6⅓	6–6¼	9½–11½	10–11½
2d molar	2½–3 yr	2½–3 yr	7½–8	7–8	12¼–12¾	11¾–12	15–16½	15½–16½
3d molar	7–9 yr	8–10 yr	12–16	12–16	20½	20–20½	18–25	18–25

*From several sources, see text.

TABLE 12–3.—Eruption Ages (Months) for Primary Teeth*

	EARLY		AVERAGE			LATE	
PERCENTILES	MIN.	10	30	50	70	90	100
Mandibular central incisor	4	5	6	7.8	9	11	17
Maxillary central incisor	5	6	8	9.6	11	12	15
Maxillary lateral incisor	6	7	10	11.5	13	15	21
Mandibular lateral incisor	6	7	11	12.4	14	18	27
Maxillary 1st molar	8	10	13	15.1	16	20	28
Mandibular 1st molar	8	10	14	15.7	17	20	27
Mandibular cuspid	8	11	16	18.2	19	24	29
Maxillary cuspid	8	11	17	18.3	20	24	29
Mandibular 2d molar	8	13	24	26.0	28	31	34
Maxillary 2d molar	8	13	24	26.2	28	31	34

*From Horowitz and Hixon.[14]

which vary distinctly in different population groups. Tooth morphology and size play an important role in the etiology of malocclusions. It has been suggested that in population areas where there is considerable mixture of ethnic and racial groups, the incidence of malocclusions rises.[17, 23] There is also a definite difference in the average size of teeth between the sexes.[9]

Tooth agenesis, except in such conditions as ectodermal dysplasia, is relatively rare. The teeth most frequently missing in the permanent dentition are third molars, mandibular bicuspids, and maxillary incisors.[14]

The biologic event of permanent tooth eruption in the normal individual is probably more related to root age than to any environmental influence. Under unusual circumstances, exceptions to the previous statement have been noted. Prolonged undernutrition may delay eruption of the permanent teeth. Premature loss of primary teeth due to caries may accelerate eruption (Fig 12–7).[13, 18, 25, 32]

Probably more relevant to future prevention of malocclusion problems is a normal sequence of appearance of the permanent dentition. Ordinarily the mandibular teeth erupt ahead of the maxillary except in the cuspid-bicuspid region (Table 12–4).

The Development of Occlusion

Development of Primary Occlusion

Interdentation of the primary teeth occurs before age 3 in most instances. There is less variability in occlusal relations in the primary than in the permanent dentition; however, some of the variations seen are of great clinical significance.

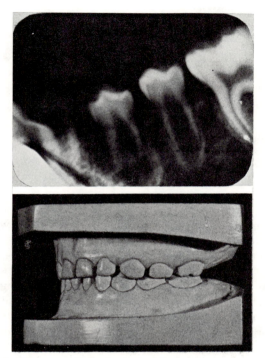

Fig 12–7 (top).—Boy, age 7; periapical radiograph showing early eruption of permanent (bicuspid) teeth following premature loss of the primary molars due to carious abscesses. Note the very incomplete root formation.
Fig 12–8 (bottom).—Age 5 years; normal primary occlusion.

The mandibular denture occludes within the maxillary denture throughout its circumference. Most primary arches are ovoid, and there seems to be less variation in conformation than in permanent arches. Usually there is generalized spacing of all the anterior teeth, although there are somewhat wider spaces mesial to the maxillary cuspids and distal to the mandibular cuspids—termed primate spaces, since they are particularly prominent in the dentitions of certain lower primates.

Contrary to popular opinion, the spacing between the primary teeth is not due to growth in width, for little increase in this dimension is seen. Spacing is either present or absent in primary dentitions; it does not increase with age.

It will be observed (Fig 12–8) that each mandibular tooth occludes one cusp anteriorly to the corresponding tooth in the maxilla. This is normal, and any deviations from this pattern are symptomatic of malocclusion. The most posterior surfaces of the second primary molars usually form a straight

TABLE 12–4.—NORMAL SEQUENCE OF
ERUPTION OF PERMANENT TEETH[19]*

MANDIBLE	MAXILLA
1. First molar	2. First molar
3. Central incisor	5. Central incisor
4. Lateral incisor	6. Lateral incisor
7. Cuspid	8. First bicuspid
9. First bicuspid	10. Second bicuspid
11. Second bicuspid	12. Cuspid
13. Second molar	14. Second molar

*The numbers indicate the usual sequence of eruption.

terminal plane. Interproximal cavities, sucking habits, or a deformity of the facial skeleton may cause development of a terminal plane with a step. This plane largely determines the occlusal relationship of the first permanent molars which erupt just behind the second primary molars.

The primary occlusion is usually very stable, showing fewer anomalies than either the mixed or the permanent dentition. The most typical malocclusion is that caused by a severe sucking habit. Many children engage in sucking habits during the first three years of life with little damage; still, such habits can give rise to severe problems in the development of occlusion. An anterior open bite is typical. An open bite may also lead to a perverted tongue thrust during the swallowing act, which may further compound the malocclusion as well as producing defects of speech. If the anteroposterior relationship remains normal and the habit ceases by age 4, the condition is self-correcting most of the time. If the mandibular teeth are occluding one cusp posteriorly, the problem seldom resolves itself and severe malocclusion may result in the permanent dentition.

Development of the Permanent Occlusion

1. MIXED DENTITION STAGE.—That period when both primary and permanent teeth are in the mouth is known as the *mixed dentition*. Those permanent teeth that follow into a place in the arch once held by a primary tooth are called *successional* or *succedaneous teeth*, e.g., incisors, cuspids, bicuspids. Those permanent teeth that erupt posteriorly to the primary teeth are termed *accessional teeth*.

With the arrival of the first permanent tooth begins the hazardous process of transition from the primary to the permanent dentition. During this period, which normally lasts from age 6 to 12 years, the dentition is highly susceptible to environmental changes.

2. FIRST MOLAR ERUPTION.—In most children the first molars are the first permanent teeth to erupt. Before their eruption the primary arches should display a straight terminal plane (vertical tangent touching the distal surfaces of both second primary molars) or, more favorably, a mesial step (distal surface of the lower second primary molar mesial to the distal surface of the upper second primary molar).

3. INCISOR ERUPTION.—(a) Mandibular incisors. The eruption of the first permanent molars is followed almost immediately by the eruption of the mandibular central incisors. They, in turn, are followed by the mandibular lateral incisors. Some have claimed that the incisors frequently erupt before the molars in the permanent dentition and that this predisposes to malocclusion. Lo and Moyers[19] found this sequence to occur so rarely that it has little significance. The mandibular incisors develop lingually to the resorbing roots of the primary incisors, the latter being moved labially as they are exfoliated. If the roots of the primary teeth are not properly resorbed, the permanent incisors may erupt into the oral cavity behind the primary incisors. Removal of the primary incisors allows the tongue to push the permanent incisors labially to their correct position. When the normal primary spacing is present, the permanent incisors erupt without showing crowding and attain good alignment. Lack of spacing in the primary anterior segment may be the result of a narrow alveolar arch. The permanent incisors, then, are more apt to be crowded on eruption.

(b) Maxillary incisor eruption. The maxillary central incisors erupt just after the mandibular central incisors. They may also follow the lower lateral incisors. There is a marked change in incisal angulation with the eruption of the permanent central incisors, the almost vertical primary tooth being replaced by a permanent one with a decided labial inclination. The central incisors erupt with a slightly distal inclination and some space between them. This is diminished with the eruption of the lateral incisors and completely closed as the cuspids wedge their way into place.

The maxillary lateral incisors may experience more difficulty in assuming their normal position. As they erupt, they are often seen slightly labial to the central incisors. As the cuspid erupts, it releases its pressure against the root of the lateral incisor, permitting the latter to fall into line.

4. CUSPID AND BICUSPID ERUPTION.—The favorable development of occlusion in this region is largely dependent on two factors: proper tooth size–arch length ratio and maintenance of a desirable sequence of eruption.

(a) Mandible. The most favorable eruption sequence in the mandible is cuspid, first bicuspid, second bicuspid. All three should precede the second molar.

If the teeth are too large for the alveolar space, the second bicuspid may have insufficient room and be forced to erupt lingually. A similar malocclusion is seen when the primary molars have been destroyed by caries or when they are exfoliated prematurely. The early loss or destruction of the primary molars permits the permanent molars to tip forward, decreasing the amount of space available for the cuspids and bicuspids.

(b) Maxilla. The eruption sequence, it will be remembered, is different in the maxilla, i.e., first bicuspid, second bicuspid, and cuspid. The maxillary anterior segment is not prone to collapse lingually, since it is supported by the mandibular arch. It is, however, very easily displaced labially, e.g., by thumbsucking or a tongue thrust.

When the maxillary primary molars are lost prematurely, the cuspid is blocked out of position labially. Extreme labial malpositioning of maxillary cuspids and lingual malpositioning of mandibular second bicuspids are often signs of the same problem—insufficient space. The malocclusion varies with the jaw because of the difference in eruption sequence. In each instance the last tooth to erupt in front of the first molar is the tooth forced out of position.

5. Second Molar Eruption.—The second molars should erupt after all teeth anterior to them are in position, the mandibular tooth preceding the maxillary.

6. Third Molar Eruption.—The third molars erupt so late that they are almost solely a problem of the adult. It has been contended that the eruption of the third molars forces the dentition forward, causing crowding of the teeth, but the evidence to support this theory is unconvincing.

The Origin of Malocclusion

Malocclusions are of three general types: skeletal or osseous (genetic), dental and functional, or muscular.

1. The mixing of races seen on this continent has resulted in many genetic combinations not favorable to the production of harmonious facial development. Many malocclusions are due to unfavorable or disharmonious bone growth. The commonest problems are mandibular retrognathism, mandibular hypertrophy, and asymmetry of the face. In addition there may be insufficient bony support for the dentition, i.e., the bones are not big enough for the teeth, or the teeth are too large for their bony base.

2. Improper care of the primary dentition may result in premature loss of deciduous teeth, permitting drifting of the permanent teeth or tooth buds (Fig 12–9). Pernicious pressure habits can also cause malpositioning of teeth. A related condition is the effect of mouth breathing. When the dominant mode of respiration is oral the result is longer faces and narrower maxillae.[5]

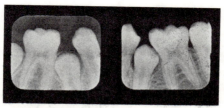

Fig 12–9.—Periapical radiographs, showing premature loss of the primary second molars, which has allowed the permanent molars to shift in a forward direction, causing the permanent second bicuspid to be impacted in their line of eruption.

3. A malrelationship of the mandible causes malocclusion. Most functional malrelationships of the mandible are due to reflexes learned to avoid malpositioned teeth. For example, functional mandibular retraction is frequently seen when the maxillary dental arch is narrowed. The muscles simply retrude the lower jaw to permit occlusion with a wider portion of the maxilla.

It is thus seen that not all malocclusions have a similar etiologic history. Because of the variance in origin, the prognoses are not the same. It is much easier to correct tooth malpositions and functional malrelationships due to muscle reflexes than it is to overcome inherent genetic patterns of bone growth. Early diagnosis is the first step in minimizing the effects of malocclusion.

The Teeth in Clinical Appraisal of a Child's Development

For clinical estimation of dental ages, Table 12–2 can be used in connection with an examination of the child's mouth to ascertain the number of erupted and exfoliated teeth along with a careful examination of the development of the posterior mandibular teeth as exhibited in a size no. 2 posterior bitewing or in a lateral jaw radiograph.

Average dental development of children, beginning with the full-term infant at birth, is shown in Figures 12–10 through 12–15 and summarized in Table 12–5.

Nolla[25] recently completed a serial radiographic study by yearly increments of growth) of 25 boys and 25 girls at the University of Michigan's Elementary School (Tables 12–6, A and B; Fig 12–16). Beginning her study of the 50 children at 4 years (48 months) of age, Nolla computed the percentage of completion for the teeth through 18 years (216 months). A value of 60.0 indicates that development of the crown is complete (see values in boldface). Girls, it will be noted, are about one year ahead of boys in dental development but advance at the same annual rate.

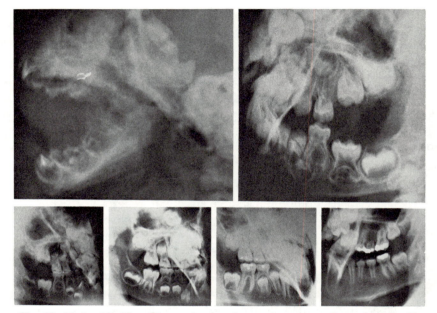

Fig 12–10 to 12–15.—Stages in development and eruption of teeth. To a certain extent a physician, like a veterinarian, can tell the age of his patient by looking at the teeth. X-rays help in this estimation.

Fig 12–10 (top left).—Newborn; lateral radiograph of jaws. Enough inorganic calcium has matured in crowns of all 20 primary teeth so that incisal and occlusal surfaces are outlined.

Fig 12–11 (top right).—Age 16 months; lateral radiograph of jaws. Primary first molars have erupted (12–14 months); primary cuspids are erupting, and crowns of their permanent successors are about one-fifth calcified. Primary second molars will erupt to complete preschool dentition at 20–24 months. Crowns of first and second bicuspids (position indicated by radiolucent follicles between roots of lower primary molars) have not begun to calcify, and crowns of first permanent molars are about one-third calcified.

Fig 12–12 (bottom left).—Girl, age 4 years; lateral jaw radiograph. Primary second molars have erupted to complete preschool dentition (2–2½ years). Crown of permanent first molar has completed calcification; root beginning. Crown of first bicuspid beneath roots of primary first molar is about one-third calcified, and calcification of the crown of the second bicuspid and permanent second molar has begun.

Fig 12–13 (bottom, left center).—Boy, age 6; lateral jaw radiograph. Permanent first molar is erupting into occlusion. Crowns of both bicuspids are nearing completion of calcification. Crown of permanent second molar is two-thirds complete in calcification.

Fig 12–14 (bottom, right center).—Boy, age 10; lateral jaw radiograph. The lower primary cuspid and primary first molar have exfoliated, and the permanent cuspid and permanent first bicuspid are erupting. Normally the permanent cuspid erupts ahead of the first bicuspid in the mandible. Note that the apical ends of the erupting permanent teeth have not completed their full development.

Returning to the chronology of dentition (see Table 12–2), a few examples may be cited to illustrate the use of such a table. Individual children may be expected to vary considerably from any average established for a population, and for this reason considerable advance or retardation should be permitted as a range of normality. The premature infant may be expected to be considerably retarded if development is measured from date of birth, whereas the full-term infant with a family history of early dental development may be born with the two mandibular incisors erupted or erupting. Unless these two prematurely erupted incisors are obviously malformed supernumerary teeth and the diagnosis is confirmed radiographically, they should *not* be extracted.

If one who is studying a radiograph of a child's mandible notes that the crown of the first permanent molar is completed, and the crowns of the second bicuspid and the second permanent molar have just begun to exhibit calcification, he or she concludes that this child has a dental age of 2.5 to 3.0 years. If a mother asks whether a severe illness at age 6 years caused the irregular, hypoplastic incisal edges of her daughter's newly erupted centrals, the answer obviously is "No"; the incisal edges of the mandibular incisors are calcified by 16 to 18 months and the entire crowns by 4 to 5 years.

The Dental Anomalies

Interference during any stage of the growth of teeth, as well as interferences during the periods of calcification, the eruption or the exchange of the two dentitions, will lead to anomalous development that may involve one or more teeth but not necessarily the child's occlusion. For example, a disturbance during initiation may produce too many or too few teeth; during proliferation, extra cusps or roots, twinning, fusion, and dental tumors; during histodifferentiation, odontomas and dentinogenesis imperfecta (opalescent dentin); during morphodifferentiation, peg-shaped teeth, Hutchinson's incisors, and unusually small or unusually large teeth; during apposition, hypoplasia of tetany, rickets, and heredity; during calcification, mottled enamel, vital staining, and amelogenesis imperfecta; and during eruption, impaction, ectopy, and ankylosis. Most of these anomalies gradually are being shown to exhibit a familial pattern of development.

Probably a more useful classification of the dental anomalies can be made on the basis of their characteristic appearance rather than on the basis of

Fig 12–15 (bottom right).—Age 11½ years; lateral jaw radiograph. Both lower bicuspids have erupted, and the permanent second molar has begun to erupt. The apical ends of the permanent first molar have completed their development. Note the congenitally missing maxillary permanent second bicuspid.

TABLE 12–5.—RADIOGRAPHIC DETERMINATION OF SERIAL DEVELOPMENT OF MANDIBULAR POSTERIOR TEETH

AGE LEVEL	CORONAL CALCIFICATION	ERUPTED	COMPLETION OF ROOTS
Birth	*Primary* ⅗, incisors ⅓, cuspids Tips of cusps calcified in united ring, 1st molar Tips of cusps calcified, still isolated in separate centers of calcification, 2d molar *Permanent* Sometimes traces in tips of mesial cusps, 1st molars	None	None
9–10 mo.	*Primary* Enamel completed all teeth *Permanent* Tips of cusps calcified, still isolated, 1st molars Trace of incisal edges, centrals, laterals Tips of cuspids	*Primary* Centrals Laterals	None
1 yr	*Permanent* (balance of table) Cusps united in ring, 1st molars ⅕–¼, centrals, laterals ⅐–⅙, cuspids	Add *primary* 1st molars	None
16–18 mo.	⅓, 1st molars ¼–⅓, centrals, laterals ⅙–⅕, cuspids Tip of cusp, some 1st bicuspids	Add *primary* cuspids	*Primary* Centrals and laterals completed
2 yr	½–⅔, 1st molars ⅖–½, centrals, laterals ¼, cuspids Tips of cusps, all 1st bicuspids Tips of cusps, some 2d bicuspids	Add *primary* 2d molars	None added
2½–3 yr	Completed, 1st molars ⅔, centrals, laterals ⅜, cuspids ½, 1st bicuspids ⅙, 2d bicuspids Trace, tips mesial cusps, 2d molars	Add none	*Primary* 1st and 2d molars completed Some cuspids completed
4½ yr	¾–⅚, 1st bicuspids ⅝–¾, 2d bicuspids ⅝–¾, cuspids ⅓, 2d molars Completed, centrals and laterals	Add none	*Primary* All cuspids completed *Permanent* (balance) ⅓, 1st molars

TABLE 12–5.—*Continued*

6–7 yr	Completed, 1st, 2d bicuspids, cuspids ⅔, 2d molars	*Permanent (balance)* 1st molars Centrals	⅜–½, 1st molars
7–8 yr	Completed, 2d molars Trace tips of cusps, some 3d molars	Add laterals	½–⅔, 1st molars ⁶⁄₇, centrals ¾, laterals Variable amt., 1st, 2d bicuspids, cuspids
9–10 yr	Beginning calcification, most 3d molars	Add most cuspids, many 1st bicuspids	Completed centrals, laterals, 1st molars ½, 1st bicuspid ⅓, 2d bicuspid ¼, 2d molar
12 yr	¼–⅚, 3d molars	Add 2d bicuspids, most 2d molars	Completed, many cuspids, 1st bicuspids ⅔, 2d bicuspids ⅓, 2d molars

the period of initiation. These deviations in development, then, may be grouped as anomalies of number, of shape, of texture and of position. It would be beneficial to the children concerned if most of these anomalies could be detected early and the children referred promptly to a children's dentist or an orthodontist.

ANOMALIES OF NUMBER.—Of the missing teeth, the absence of maxillary lateral incisors (Fig 12–17) and the mandibular second bicuspids most frequently is detected in children. The absence of either creates a problem of occlusion. Supernumerary teeth occur most often in the midline of the maxillary arch, where they interfere with eruption and alignment of the normal incisors (Fig 12–18). Extra teeth may accompany cleidocranial dysostosis.

A few children exhibit the bizarre condition known as ectodermal dysplasia, in which many surface structures may be involved as a syndrome of ectodermal deviations. Along with variations or complete absence of sweat and sebaceous glands, adult hair, eyebrows, eyelashes, and fingernails, the teeth may be totally or partially missing. Those anterior teeth which do erupt are characteristically conoid.

ANOMALIES OF SHAPE.—Not infrequently the maxillary laterals fail to develop as typical incisors but erupt as small, cone-shaped, "peg" teeth. The crowns of the late-maturing bicuspids may not even resemble teeth; Hutchinsonian permanent incisors and molars have been described in many textbooks. A number of anterior permanent teeth may erupt malformed

TABLE 12–6, A.—Age Norms for Mandibular Teeth for Boys*

AGE	CENTRAL INCISOR 1/1	LATERAL INCISOR 2/2	CUSPID 3/3	1ST BICUSPID 4/4	2D BICUSPID 5/5	1ST MOLAR 6/6	2D MOLAR 7/7	3D MOLAR 8/8	ALL TEETH EXCL. 3D MOLAR	ALL TEETH INCL. 3D MOLAR
4	**71.5**	**68.6**	42.7	34.8	20.4	**64.4**	20.8	0	323.2	323.2
5	75.5	71.9	51.5	43.0	33.1	71.5	30.8	0	377.3	377.3
6	79.5	76.1	**57.4**	51.6	42.7	76.9	40.7	0	424.9	424.9
7	88.8	83.2	65.9	**60.8**	53.6	83.3	51.5	8.8	487.1	495.9
8	95.0	90.4	73.5	68.8	**62.4**	89.5	**59.4**	14.2	539.0	553.2
9	95.9	95.4	79.7	75.4	70.3	94.5	66.8	18.1	578.0	596.1
10	98.5	98.5	85.5	81.1	76.5	97.9	73.2	20.9	611.2	632.1
11	100.0	100.0	90.9	87.8	83.4	99.0	78.9	27.6	640.0	667.6
12	100.0	100.0	95.8	94.1	89.5	99.5	84.6	35.2	663.5	698.7
13	100.0	100.0	98.5	96.9	93.7	100.0	89.3	44.9	678.4	723.3
14	100.0	100.0	99.5	98.8	96.5	100.0	93.9	53.9	688.7	742.6
15	100.0	100.0	100.0	100.0	99.0	100.0	96.6	**62.8**	695.6	758.4
16	100.0	100.0	100.0	100.0	100.0	100.0	99.9	71.1	699.9	771.0
17	100.0	100.0	100.0	100.0	100.0	100.0	100.0	76.1	700.0	776.1
18	100.0	100.0	100.0	100.0	100.0	100.0	100.0	79.3	700.0	779.3

*Note: 0–100 = percentages of tooth development; at 60% crown is complete (values in boldface).

TABLE 12–6, B.—AGE NORMS FOR MANDIBULAR TEETH FOR GIRLS*

AGE	CENTRAL INCISOR 1/1	LATERAL INCISOR 2/2	1ST CUSPID 3/3	1ST BICUSPID 4/4	2D BICUSPID 5/5	1ST MOLAR 6/6	2D MOLAR 7/7	3D MOLAR 8/8	ALL TEETH	
									EXCL. 3D MOLAR	INCL. 3D MOLAR
4	69.3	66.9	56.5	39.1	28.6	70.2	26.7	0	357.3	357.3
5	75.5	71.7	61.8	50.5	38.3	74.4	39.4	0	411.6	411.6
6	84.5	79.2	67.1	60.2	47.1	80.3	50.3	23.5	468.7	492.2
7	93.4	86.0	72.4	67.2	57.6	86.1	60.4	18.8	523.1	541.9
8	98.8	94.7	77.9	72.9	65.6	92.7	67.2	21.1	569.8	590.9
9	100.0	99.5	83.4	79.6	73.2	98.2	73.5	23.2	607.4	630.6
10	100.0	100.0	90.4	84.8	79.2	99.7	78.6	32.9	632.7	665.6
11	100.0	100.0	96.4	91.7	85.0	100.0	82.6	37.7	655.7	693.4
12	100.0	100.0	99.7	97.1	91.9	100.0	88.6	47.7	677.3	725.0
13	100.0	100.0	100.0	100.0	93.7	100.0	95.0	**58.5**	688.7	747.2
14	100.0	100.0	100.0	100.0	93.8	100.0	97.4	65.6	691.2	756.8
15	100.0	100.0	100.0	100.0	96.5	100.0	97.8	69.9	694.3	764.2
16	100.0	100.0	100.0	100.0	99.7	100.0	98.7	75.6	698.4	774.0
17	100.0	100.0	100.0	100.0	100.0	100.0	99.0	80.3	699.0	779.3
18	100.0	100.0	100.0	100.0	100.0	100.0	100.0	80.5	700.0	780.5

*Note: 0–100 = percentages of tooth development; at 60% crown is complete (values in boldface).

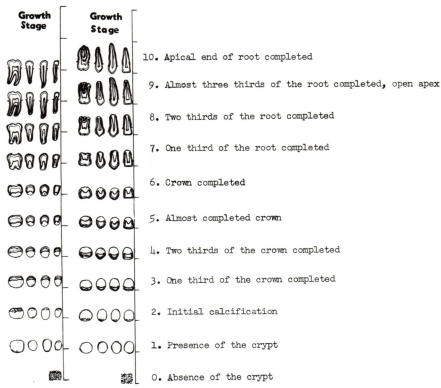

Growth Stage	Growth Stage	
		10. Apical end of root completed
		9. Almost three thirds of the root completed, open apex
		8. Two thirds of the root completed
		7. One third of the root completed
		6. Crown completed
		5. Almost completed crown
		4. Two thirds of the crown completed
		3. One third of the crown completed
		2. Initial calcification
		1. Presence of the crypt
		0. Absence of the crypt

Fig 12–16.—Drawings made from roentgenograms of developing permanent teeth, to be studied in conjunction with Tables 12–6, A and B. Beginning with stage 1 (of Nolla's 10 stages assigned to developing teeth), in which the tooth bud is hardly more than a ring of cells, the tooth develops to stage 10, where it is complete. Note that the crown develops much sooner than the root, as seen in Figure 12–11, where the 6-year molar has a well-developed crown but no roots as yet. A value of 60 (6 in the drawings) indicates that the crown of the particular tooth is complete.

from a traumatic episode that has involved the primary predecessor. Attention already has been called to the conoid teeth that accompany ectodermal dysplasia, and it should be kept in mind that extensive irradiation of the jaws during the period of growth of the teeth halts dental development at the particular level reached.

ANOMALIES OF TEXTURE.—Two hereditary anomalies of development alter the structure of teeth in a unique pattern. One anomaly, involving odontoblasts, produces dentinogenesis imperfecta, or hereditary opalescent

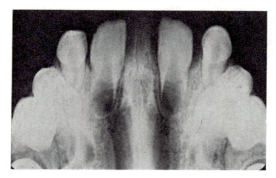

Fig 12–17.—Periapical radiograph showing a maxillary midline supernumerary tooth that remained unerupted.

dentin. Most of the affected teeth exhibit a peculiar amber color, abrade early and extensively and, radiographically, exhibit roots that appear rather small for their crowns but with highly calcified or completely missing pulpal chambers and root canals. Amelogenesis imperfecta, on the other hand, involves maldevelopment by the ameloblasts. Such teeth develop and erupt (infrequently they fail to erupt) with very little, imperfectly formed enamel. The frail enamel stains and abrades or wears until the teeth become quite disfiguring. The only solution usually is extraction of the teeth and preparation of complete dentures early in life, or a full mouth reconstruction. Rarely are either of these conditions accompanied by caries; in fact, most of the involved members of the families studied at the School of

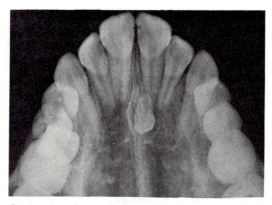

Fig 12–18.—Occlusal radiograph illustrating how congenitally missing maxillary lateral incisors permit a wide diastema to remain between the maxillary central incisors.

Dentistry of the University of Michigan have submitted samples of saliva that provide negative counts of lactobacilli.

Staining and hypoplasia of tooth enamel have long been recognized as hazards of tetracycline therapy in infancy and early childhood. The staining occurs only if the drugs are used during the period of crown calcification and the degree is related to the amount used (frequency and dosage). To spare the more visible anterior teeth, tetracyclines should be avoided, whenever possible, during the first 6 to 7 years.[31]

Enamel hypoplasia is the most common abnormality of development and mineralization of teeth. It is manifested as a quantitative defect of enamel tissue normally laid down by ameloblasts resulting in band-like irregularities or pitting. It occurs in close to 10% in permanent teeth and more commonly in primary teeth and predisposes them to caries. The incidence of this defect is associated with hypocalcemia in vitamin D deficiency, neonatal tetany, hypoparathyroidism, hemolytic conditions, and prematurity. It is more common in developing countries where malnutrition and diarrhea are prevalent.[29]

ANOMALIES OF POSITION.—Radiographic examination frequently detects a first permanent molar erupting ectopically into the distal roots of the second primary molar. Unless the dentist interferes at an early period, pressure of its crown results in resorption of the roots of the primary molar, premature exfoliation of that tooth, and serious loss of space in the arch. In another type of anomalous development a number of children are found with the roots of the primary molars apparently ankylosed while the bony arches increase in their occlusal dimension, due to an elaboration of the alveolar bone which provides support for the developing permanent teeth. Such ankylosed primary molars actually have been found completely submerged (Fig 12–19). A dental anomaly of position also accompanies the

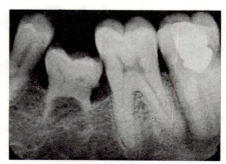

Fig 12–19.—Periapical radiograph showing an ankylosed primary second molar that is no longer at the occlusal level. Note also the congenitally missing permanent second bicuspid.

syndrome of craniocleidodysostosis; the primary teeth are retained into adulthood and the permanent teeth remain unerupted.

Since most of the dental anomalies that have been described have deleterious implications for a child's appearance or the alignment of the teeth, it appears pertinent to re-emphasize their early detection and the referral of the patient for treatment. It is of interest to note, too, that the anomalies of dental development may accompany anomalous development in other areas of a child's body. Amelogenesis imperfecta, for example, has been associated with failure of the permanent teeth to erupt, tremendous overgrowths of the fibrous tissue of the gingivae, degenerative macules of the retina, and the annoying dermal condition, epidermolysis bullosa.

Certain other systemic pathologies may produce uncommon deviations in the growth and development of the dentition, such as overretention of the primary teeth, producing a very delayed eruption of the permanent teeth. This deviation may be seen in the child with Down's syndrome (trisomy 21).

REFERENCES

 1. Ranly D.M.: *A Synopsis of Craniofacial Growth*. New York, Appleton-Century Crofts, 1980.
 2. Broadbent B.H.: The face of the normal child. *Angle Orthod*. 7:209, 1937. (Report of the classic studies done in the growth of the face by the Bolton Foundation at Western Reserve University; a special cephalometric study.)
 3. Brodie A.G.: On the growth pattern of the human head from the third month to the eighth year. *Am. J. Anat*. 68:209, 1941.
 4. Caffey J.: *Pediatric X-Ray Diagnosis*, ed. 6. Chicago, Year Book Medical Publishers, 1972.
 5. Bresolin D., Shapiro G.G., Shapiro P.A., et al.: Facial characteristics of children who breathe through the mouth. *Pediatrics* 73:622, 1984.
 6. Garn S.M., Lewis A.B.: Relationship between sequence of calcification and the sequence of eruption of the mandibular molar and premolar teeth. *J. Dent. Res*. 36:992, 1957.
 7. Garn S.M., Lewis A.B., Polacheck D.L.: Variability of tooth formation. *J. Dent. Res*. 38:135, 1959.
 8. Finn S.B.: *Clinical Pedodontics*, ed. 4. Philadelphia, W.B. Saunders Co. 1973.
 9. Garn S.M., Lewis A.B., Kerewsky R.S.: Sex differences in tooth size. *J. Dent. Res*. 43:306, 1964.
10. Garn S.M., Lewis A.B., Blizzard R.M.: Endocrine factors in dental development. *J. Dent. Res*.(suppl.) 44:243, 1965.
11. Garn S.M., Lewis A.B., Kerewsky R.S.: Genetic, nutritional and maturational correlates of dental development. *J. Dent. Res*.(suppl.) 44:228, 1965.
12. Garn S.M., Lewis A.B., Kerewski R.S., et al.: Sex differences in intra-individual tooth size communalities. *J. Dent. Res*. 44:476, 1965.
13. Grøn A.-M.: Prediction of tooth emergence. *J. Dent. Res*. 41:573, 1962.
14. Horowitz S.L., Hixon E.H.: *The Nature of Orthodontic Diagnosis*. St. Louis, C.V. Mosby Co., 1966, chapters 5 and 9.

15. Hurme V.O.: Ranges of normalcy in the eruption of permanent teeth. *J. Dent. Child.* 16:11, 1949.
16. Korf S.: Eruption of permanent incisors following premature loss of their antecedents. *J. Dent. Child.* 32:39, 1965.
17. Kraus B.S., Jordan R.E.: *The Human Dentition Before Birth.* Philadelphia, Lea & Febiger, 1965, p. 109.
18. Lauterstein A.M.: A cross sectional study in dental development and skeletal age. *J. Am. Dent. Assoc.* 62:161, 1961.
19. Lo R.T., Moyers R.E.: Studies in the etiology and prevention of malocclusion: I. The sequence of eruption of the permanent dentition. *Am. J. Orthod.* 39:460, 1953.
20. Maresh M.M.: Paranasal sinuses from birth to adolescence. *Am. J. Dis. Child.* 60:58, 1940.
21. Meredith H.V.: Order and eruption for the deciduous dentition. *J. Dent. Res.* 25:43, 1946.
22. Meredith H.V.: Relation between the eruption of selected mandibular permanent teeth and the circumpuberal acceleration in stature. *J. Dent. Child.* 26:75, 1959.
23. Moorrees C.F.A.: *The Aleut Dentition.* Cambridge, Mass., Harvard University Press, 1957.
24. Enlow D.H.: *The Human Face, An Account of the Postnatal Development of the Craniofacial Skeleton.* New York, Harper & Row, 1968.
25. Nolla C.M.: *The Development of the Permanent Teeth,* M.S. thesis. University of Michigan, Ann Arbor, 1952.
26. Robinow M., Richards T.W., Anderson M.: The eruption of the deciduous teeth. *Growth* 6:127, 1942.
27. Turner E.P.: The growth and development of the teeth, in Davis J.A., Dobbing J. (eds.): *Scientific Foundation of Paediatrics.* Philadelphia, W.B. Saunders Co., 1974.
28. Schour I., Massler M.: Development and growth of teeth, in Orban B. (ed.): *Oral Histology and Embryology.* St. Louis, C.V. Mosby Co., 1944.
29. Nikiforuk G., Fraser D.: The etiology of enamel hypoplasia: a unifying concept. *J. Pediatr.* 98:888, 1981.
30. Moore K.L.: *The Developing Human.* Philadelphia, W.B. Saunders Co., 1973.
31. Levine R.S., Turner E.P., Dobbing J.: Deciduous teeth contain histories of developmental disturbances. *Early Human Devel.* 3:211, 1979.
32. Garn S.M., Sandusky S.T., Nagy J.M., et al.: Negro-caucasoid differences in permanent tooth emergence at a constant income level. *Arch. Oral Biol.* 18:609, 1973.
33. *An Assessment of the Occlusion of the Teeth of Children, 6–11 Years.* U.S. Dept. Health, Education and Welfare, Public Health Service, 1973.
34. Smith D.W.: *Recognizable Patterns of Human Malformation,* ed. 2. Philadelphia, W.B. Saunders Co., 1976.

13 / An Outline of Abnormal Growth

Know you what it is to be a child? . . . It is to have a spirit yet streaming from the waters of baptism; it is to believe in love, to believe in loveliness, to believe in belief; it is to be so little that the elves can reach to whisper in your ear; it is to turn pumpkins into coaches, and mice into horses, lowness into loftiness, and nothing into everything, for each child has its fairy godmother in its soul.

—Francis Thompson

Strictly speaking, any outline of abnormal growth must include almost all of the many congenital anomalies and dystrophies, for they represent abnormalities of growth. Our outline, however, is limited primarily to the aberrations of statural growth in infancy and childhood. Obesity also is discussed.

In the preceding chapters the major factors that influence normal growth have been considered. Much of our knowledge has resulted from studies of abnormal subjects. This chapter is included mainly to help the reader to a better understanding of the potentialities of growth and how growth may deviate from the usual pattern; it is not meant to be an exhaustive treatise.

Dwarfism

The schema in Figure 13–1 will suggest many possible causes of small stature, most of which are discussed in this chapter. Very often it is difficult if not impossible to designate the primary cause, and combinations of factors often exist, e.g., malnutrition and anemia. Some are difficult to evaluate in terms of degree of effectiveness, e.g., psychologic implications of lack of tender loving care (T.L.C. in the figure). The purpose of this diagram is to point out the multiplicity and diversity of etiologic conditions leading to retarded growth.

Some authors and most laypeople will make a distinction between the terms *dwarf* and *midget,* referring to the former as small but disproportioned and the latter as small and well proportioned in all physical aspects. No distinction will be made in this discussion.

439

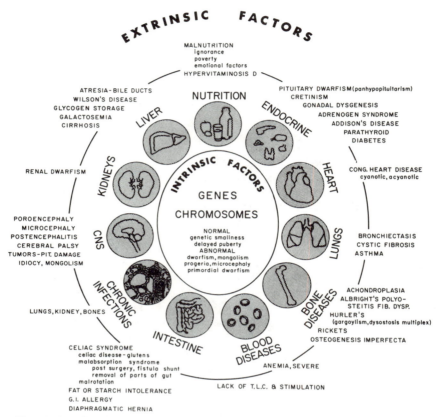

EXTRINSIC FACTORS

MALNUTRITION
Ignorance
poverty
emotional factors
HYPERVITAMINOSIS D

NUTRITION

ATRESIA-BILE DUCTS
WILSON'S DISEASE
GLYCOGEN STORAGE
GALACTOSEMIA
CIRRHOSIS

LIVER

PITUITARY DWARFISM(panhypopituitarism)
CRETINISM
GONADAL DYSGENESIS
ADRENOGEN SYNDROME
ADDISON'S DISEASE
PARATHYROID
DIABETES

ENDOCRINE

INTRINSIC FACTORS

GENES
CHROMOSOMES

NORMAL
genetic smallness
delayed puberty
ABNORMAL
dwarfism, mongolism
progeria, microcephaly
primordial dwarfism

RENAL DWARFISM

KIDNEYS

HEART

CONG. HEART DISEASE
cyanotic, acyanotic

POROENCEPHALY
MICROCEPHALY
POSTENCEPHALITIS
CEREBRAL PALSY
TUMORS-PIT. DAMAGE
IDIOCY, MONGOLISM

CNS

LUNGS

BRONCHIECTASIS
CYSTIC FIBROSIS
ASTHMA

CHRONIC INFECTIONS

LUNGS, KIDNEY, BONES

BONE DISEASES

ACHONDROPLASIA
ALBRIGHT'S POLYO-
STEITIS FIB. DYSP.
HURLER'S
(gargoylism, dysostosis multiplex)
RICKETS
OSTEOGENESIS IMPERFECTA

CELIAC SYNDROME
celiac disease-glutens
malabsorption syndrome
post surgery, fistula shunt
removal of parts of gut
malrotation
FAT OR STARCH INTOLERANCE
G.I. ALLERGY
DIAPHRAGMATIC HERNIA

INTESTINE

BLOOD DISEASES

ANEMIA, SEVERE

LACK OF T.L.C. & STIMULATION

Fig 13–1.—Conditions frequently leading to small stature.

Talbot[12] has used the term "dwarf" to designate any child moderately or conspicuously shorter than 90% of children in the community of the same chronologic age. Retarded growth may be due either to a slow rate or to an unusually short period of growth.[10, 11] The diagnosis of dwarfism will depend on a number of factors, one of the most important being the age of the child. The achondroplastic child would be placed in this category at an early age. An individual with Turner's syndrome would probably not be recognized as being unusually short until late childhood or adolescence. In the person with the adrenogenital syndrome the first impression is of over-growth; but as adolescence is approached short stature becomes promi-nent, unless proper therapy has been instituted earlier. The boy or girl who has a delayed onset of the adolescent growth spurt, often associated with some delay in osseous maturation, may be considered a "dwarf" by family or self until the mechanisms that set off the long-awaited adolescence finally begin to work.

The most common causes of short stature as seen in our clinic are listed below in the order of their frequency.

1. Constitutionally delayed growth
2. Genetic: familial, Turner's and Down's syndromes, trisomies
3. Chronic systemic diseases: central nervous system, cardiovascular, pulmonary, gastrointestinal, renal
4. Endocrine disorders: hypothyroidism, hypopituitarism, adrenal hyperplasia, Cushing's syndrome, diabetes mellitus
5. Skeletal diseases
6. Psychological dwarfism
7. Intrauterine growth retardation
8. Primordial

In attempting to determine the etiology of retarded stature, a number of approaches may be necessary. Even after exhaustive studies, a definite conclusion may be impossible unless the child can be followed through his or her entire growth period.

HISTORY.—History and examination of the growth pattern followed in the past can be very helpful. Many syndromes are associated with small size at birth, including multiple births, many of the chromosomal abnormalities, and intrauterine undernutrition. In congenital hypothyroidism (cretinism) a slow rate of growth may go unnoticed for several months, and is associated with a very placid personality, constipation, and the delayed appearance of developmental milestones. Retardation of statural growth in Turner's syndrome may be so gradual that parents become aware of it only after several years. A past history of medications is important since some medications can have a deleterious influence on growth. The use of large amounts of glucocorticoids in conditions such as asthma or rheumatoid arthritis (Fig 13–2) can cause growth failure. Prolonged and continuous use of central nervous system stimulants, as in the hyperkinetic syndrome, can disturb the important sleep-growth hormone release pattern with resulting slowing of statural growth (see chapter 9). Hurler's syndrome, refractory rickets, and a host of other metabolic diseases associated with short stature are among those with hereditary backgrounds. Investigation of relatives with unusual heights may be rewarding in establishing the origin of these genetic conditions. In the families of most children with delayed onset of puberty, a history of similar growth pattern is found in a sibling, parent, or grandparent. Malnutrition, chronic and recurrent disease, and physical abuse or neglect are diagnoses established more readily through the history than by other parts of the examination.

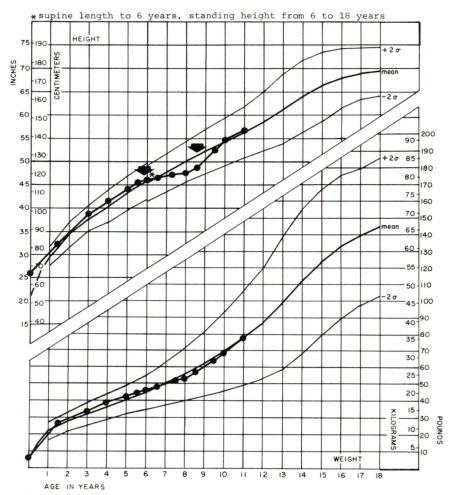

Fig 13–2.—Iatrogenic dwarfism of a temporary nature from corticosteroid treatment for rheumatoid arthritis. Normal development until shortly before his sixth birthday, when he developed low-grade fever and swelling and pain in both knees. Laboratory tests were negative. For approximately 3½ years large doses of corticosteroids (prednisone) were used, which were successful in relieving his symptoms but retarded statural growth and caused a cushingoid appearance. Note the recovery after withdrawal of the drug, with a short period of actual acceleration in growth rate until his former level was obtained. Recently an arthritic patient was seen who had been on corticosteroids from age 2 to 14 and whose height was only 45 in. at the latter age.

PHYSICAL EXAMINATION.—This must be carefully done, with special reference to measurements of dimensions or porportions and attention to details. The determination of body proportions (trunk-extremity length) will aid in the differential diagnosis of hypothyroidism with a high ratio, as compared with primordial dwarfism with a normal ratio. Small head circumference is an outstanding feature of the "bird-headed" dwarf, while a large head is characteristic of many patients with achondroplasia. Children with congenital heart disease or with metabolic abnormalities often appear chronically ill, in contrast to many cases of statural retardation with other causes where the child appears healthy and happy. Some diseases are associated with quite specific findings that help to identify them, e.g., webbing of the neck and lymphedema of hands and feet in Turner's syndrome, short extremities and redundant skin in classic achondroplasia, ectodermal abnormalities (skin, hair, nails, and teeth) in Hutchinson-Gilford syndrome, bowing and other deformities of the long bones in rickets of all types, and the typical facies in cretinism, Hurler's syndrome, Cockayne's syndrome, or the severe form of metaphysial dysostosis. Multiple anomalies are associated with the majority of the chromosomal abnormalities, frequently involving all three germinal layers.

ROENTGENOLOGIC EXAMINATION.—This may be limited or extensive enough to cover the entire skeleton and certain soft-tissue areas. Minimal examination should include hand and wrist films for "bone age." The most severe retardation is found in hypothyroidism, while less marked delay is present in hypopituitary dwarfing and Turner's syndrome. Often films of this area will add other information. Short metacarpals are characteristic of pseudohypoparathyroidism and of Turner's syndrome, while in Hurler's syndrome other changes occur that are pathognomonic. Skull films are useful in eliminating craniopharyngiomas that may cause growth retardation through hypothalamic dysfunction. In about 80% of cases there is abnormal intracranial calcification. In many bone diseases (Table 13–1) a complete skeletal examination may be necessary. Especially early in life, the findings may be subtle and difficult to interpret. When indicated, of course, studies of the heart, lungs, kidneys, or other systems should be obtained.

LABORATORY EXAMINATION.—These will vary and depend upon the findings available from the history and physical examination. Anemia and severe renal disease can be rather promptly investigated without elegant equipment. Other systemic diseases may be more difficult to verify and require elaborate testing. Some of the endocrinopathies can be attacked directly; others, only by indirect means. A buccal smear or chromosome count is indicated in all girls of short stature. It must be remembered that not all patients with Turner's syndrome will have all the typical findings of

TABLE 13–1.—Diseases of Bone Causing Dwarfism

DISEASE	GROWTH RETARDATION	PHYSICAL CHARACTERISTICS	ROENTGEN FINDINGS	CHEMICAL FINDINGS
Achondroplasia	+ + +	Short extremities, large head. Genetic dominant.	Tubular bones short and thick, often metaphysial flaring. All bones involved, including skull and pelvis.	Normal.
Morquio's disease, osteochondrodystrophy	+ +	Often obvious only after second or third year. All joints have increasing loss of mobility with age. Short neck, kyphosis, scoliosis. Genetic recessive.	All the epiphyses show irregularity, fragmentation, but shafts are normal.	Normal (mucopolysaccharides in urine in rare instances; see gargoylism).
Ollier's disease, dyschondroplasia, enchondromatosis	+ to + + +	Dwarfing varies with the bones involved. First evident after infancy. Firm tumor of bone with growth failure in length of involved bone. Rarely genetic.	Radiolucent tumors, especially of hands, feet, long bones of arms and legs. Often asymmetrical.	Normal.
Albers-Schönberg disease, osteopetrosis congenita	+ to + + +	Great variety. In most severe cases, death occurs in early childhood. Small, gracile habitus, delayed puberty. Hepatomegaly and splenomegaly. Intracranial pressure and cranial nerve palsy occasionally. Genetic dominant and recessive types.	Dense and sclerotic bone, narrow marrow space, metaphysial widening. All bones involved.	Normal.

Osteogenesis imperfecta, fragilitas ossium	+ to +++	Considerable variety. Most severe form may have intrauterine fractures. Growth failure dependent upon frequency and severity of fractures. May resemble achondroplasia. Blue scleras. Genetically dominant.	Thin, delicate cortex of all bones. General decreased mineralization. Number of, and deformity from, fractures depends upon severity.	Normal.
Rickets (see text for various types)	0 to ++	The earlier present and longer the duration, the more severe growth retardation. In some of the renal forms, complete correction of growth may not occur. Some deformity, usually bowing, accompanies dwarfing. All bones involved. Sporadic and sex-linked dominant in refractory type.	Bone demineralized, trabeculae prominent, metaphysial end flattened or cupped and frayed appearance, increased distance between epiphyses and metaphysis.	Vitamin D deficient—low phosphorus, elevated alkaline phosphatase (serum). Refractory—low phosphorus, elevated alkaline phosphatase. Renal failure—high phosphorus, low calcium acidosis, high BUN, etc.
Hypophosphatasia	0 to +++	Several types or variations. The earlier manifested, the more severe. Earliest forms have marked deformities of extremities and skull, hypertension, renal failure, mental retardation. Mild forms resemble vitamin D deficient rickets. Genetic recessive.	Nearly complete to slight lack of ossification and calcification, premature closure of sutures in skull, widening of metaphyses.	Alkaline phosphatase very low or absent, high calcium (serum), phosphorylethanolamine (urine).

continued

TABLE 13–1.—*Continued*

DISEASE	GROWTH RETARDATION	PHYSICAL CHARACTERISTICS	ROENTGEN FINDINGS	CHEMICAL FINDINGS
Gargoylism, Hurler's and Hunter's syndromes, dysostosis multiplex	+ to +++	Facial features coarse, progressive flexion deformities of joints (especially in hands), hepatomegaly, splenomegaly, corneal opacity, mental retardation, short life span. Genetic recessive, both autosomal and sex-linked.	Tubular bones shortened, thickened and epiphysial plates irregular. More marked in upper extremities. Phalanges and metacarpals become tapered. Skull is scaphoid and sella "boot"-shaped.	Mucopolysaccharides (urine).
Multiple epiphysial dysplasia, chondrodystrophia calcificans	+ to +++	The earlier manifested, the more severe the dwarfing and joint contractures. Mildest forms resemble mild achondroplasia. Genetic recessive.	Long bones, vertebrae and hands and feet involved. Stippled or punctate epiphyses in severe form, irregular and small epiphyses in mild form. Long bones short and slight thickening.	Normal.
Metaphysial dysostosis	+ to +++	Mild to severe forms. Dwarfing secondary to decreased bone growth plus deformities from bowing and contractures. Micrognathia and hypertelorism often present. Genetics unknown.	Metaphysial portion irregular, cystic, widened and showing varying degrees of deformity. Resembles severe rickets, but epiphyses are normal.	Normal (some reports of abnormalities have appeared but are not consistent).
Hyperparathyroidism	0 to +++	Short stature only in severe forms with long bone deformity, convulsions, mental retardation.	Bone demineralization, cysts, variable deformity of long bones.	Elevated calcium, low phosphorus, progressive renal failure.
Diastrophic dwarfism[40]	++ to ++++	Short extremities, hip dysplasia, equinovarus deformity of feet, short fingers, abducted thumbs, malformed ears.	Flattened epiphyses, short long bones, underdeveloped metacarpals and phalanges.	Normal.

the "textbook case." Tests for thyroid function are mandatory if bone maturation is relatively more delayed than statural growth. An increasing number of centers are now able to determine growth hormone levels. A single determination has little value. Gonadotropic hormone analysis has value after adolescence has begun. If growth hormone deficiency does exist, there is often an associated deficiency of one or more of the other pituitary hormones.

Constitutionally Delayed Growth

The most common type of small stature has been designated either as "delayed onset of adolescence" or "constitutionally delayed growth." It occurs in either sex, although boys are seen in clinics more often than girls. From infancy, most of these children will be smaller than their peers and make up the lower percentiles of the growth curves. Puberty and its associated growth spurt is delayed by two to four years. Bone age studies will indicate that the degree of maturation is compatible with the height but behind the chronologic age (Fig 13–3). In the majority of families a sibling or parent has followed a similar pattern of growth. The patient eventually attains a height that is commensurate with his or her genetic potential.

Bone Diseases

ACHONDROPLASIA (CLASSIC CHONDRODYSTROPHY).—This disorder follows a dominant type of inheritance or may occur sporadically. The primary pathologic changes are limited to parts of the skeleton that develop from cartilage. The cartilage cells appear to mature less rapidly than normal, and the patterns of growth are very irregular. The disturbance of proportion and the retardation of growth begin during intrauterine existence. The major clinical feature is the pronounced shortness of all the long bones of the extremities and consequent dwarfism. The skull is frequently large and indicates a mild degree of hydrocephalus, although seldom resulting in mental retardation. The nose is somewhat flattened. The development of the trunk is essentially normal, but lordosis is often prominent. The skin of the extremities is loose and forms folds. In the hyperplastic type the ends of the long bones widen in mushroom fashion.

There are probably mild or forme fruste variants; but in older individuals, not previously examined by roentgen techniques, these may be indistinguisable from other syndromes, such as multiple epiphysial dysplasia (see Table 13–1).

OLLIER'S DISEASE (DYSCHONDROPLASIA).—There is an excess of hypertrophic cartilage at the growing ends of the long bones involved in this

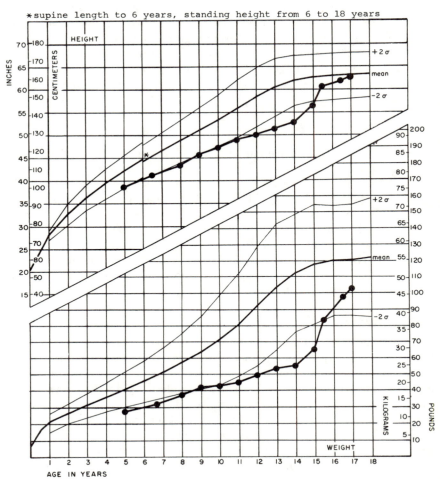

*supine length to 6 years, standing height from 6 to 18 years

Fig 13–3.—Delayed adolescence in a girl. Normal delivery and birth weight of 7 lb 4 oz was followed by a slow but steady growth rate. General health was good. At age 12 a careful evaluation of her growth failure gave no clue to a possible cause. Significantly, at that time her "bone age" was estimated at 9 years, which equaled her "height age." Menses began at 15 years, which also had been true of her mother. (Growth charts used in Figures 13–2 to 13–11 based on Stuart and Meredith's data as described in chapter 4.)

disease. Normal resorption does not take place, and linear growth is decreased. Single or multiple lesions may exist in an asymmetrical or symmetrical pattern. The degree of statural retardation depends entirely upon the severity of the condition, and some degree of asymmetry is usually present. Inspection and palpation, as well as roentgenology, disclose the nature of the tumors.[22]

ALBERS-SCHÖNBERG DISEASE (OSTEOPETROSIS).—In the more severe forms of this disease, death occurs in infancy. Statural growth is not markedly affected in most circumstances and probably is secondary to anemia, lowered resistance to disease, and the influences of central nervous system damage due to some encroachment of the thickened skull. The primary defect is failure of the transformation of spongiosa to cancellous bone, and all bones assume a dense and thickened appearance. Growth failure probably resembles that found in any chronic illness. Splenomegaly and hepatomegaly are commonly found.

OSTEOGENESIS IMPERFECTA (FRAGILITAS OSSIUM).—This condition goes through a wide spectrum of bone changes from very severe, even causing fetal death, to mild, with the first appreciation of its existence only in adolescence. Dwarfism, if present, is the result of numerous fractures of the extremities with impactions, angulations, and overlapping of fragments. Associated findings are large cranial vault of extreme thinness (crane à rebord), poor dentition, and blue scleras. Occasionally the appearance resembles achondroplasia, but x-ray examination corrects this impression. The pathologic change is failure of periosteal intramembranous bone formation due to lack of osteoblasts. The condition is inherited as a dominant trait in the less severe forms.

RICKETS.—The changes in the bone that are recognized by x-ray examination as rickets can be caused by a number of different conditions; but in all instances the essential feature is lack of calcification of the organic matrix of bone. In "ordinary" rickets there is a deficiency of vitamin D intake and a poor absorption of calcium from the gut, with a level of extracellular calcium too low to permit deposition in bone. Vitamin D may also promote reabsorption of phosphorus from the kidney, tending to balance the extracellular rise of calcium. In rickets the blood calcium levels are normal or low, the phosphorus levels are always low until healing is complete and the alkaline phosphatase levels are elevated in active disease. As we have seen (chapter 8), the products of calcium and phosphorus must be above a certain level, at a normal pH, before they are deposited in the bone. Even though osteoblastic activity is increased in rickets, as shown by the high alkaline phosphatase, it will not free enough phosphorus on the bone surface to exceed the solubility product of the calcium-phosphorus salts. The resulting softness of the bone leads to the characteristic deformities and consequent reduction in stature.

In "refractory rickets," tubular function of the kidney is altered so that normal reabsorption of phosphorus is not obtained. For this reason the descriptive term *phosphate diabetes* has been used. The blood level of phosphorus is often very low, often below 2.0 mg/100 ml while the calcium level is normal and the alkaline phosphatase is elevated. In some patients there is an associated aminoaciduria. Doses of vitamin D that cure ordinary rickets are not effective; but when large doses—often exceeding 500,000 units daily—are given, healing takes place.[6, 19] However, one seldom is able to obtain normal levels of phosphorus, and the patient usually has some growth retardation.

Rickets associated with renal acidosis will be described under organic disorders.

HYPOPHOSPHATASIA.—This is an inborn error of metabolism in which the tissues cannot synthesize alkaline phosphatase. Structural changes in the bone occur that roentgenologically resemble severe rickets with resulting dwarfism. Variants of the disease exist which are related to age and severity. If symptoms appear in early infancy, hypercalcemia, hypertension, renal failure, and mental retardation accompany the retarded growth, and life expectancy is low. In the milder forms that are first manifest at an older age, structural as well as biochemical findings are less severe. The presence of phosphorylethanolamine in the urine is unique to this disease. The pattern of inheritance is recessive.

METAPHYSIAL DYSOSTOSIS.—This bone dysplasia is known in two forms, which actually may represent different entities, since the cause is unknown. The more severe form results in extreme deformities of the bones, owing to softness. The other form often seems to appear later in childhood, and the deformities are less marked. X-ray examination gives typical findings, with involvement of the metaphysial areas and sparing of the epiphyses. The findings may resemble mild rickets or progress to severe widening and demineralization with severe bending.

DISEASES OF THE SPINE.—Infection, hemivertebrae, and lytic lesions, such as tumors or Cushing's disease, may result in growth failure or actual collapse of vertebrae with reduction in stature.

Generalized Diseases

Many diseases of infants and children may cause either temporary or permanent retardation of growth. Only a few will be outlined here.

GALACTOSURIA.—This is one of the so-called inborn errors of metabolism. The fault lies in the inability of the body to change galactose and lactose, the milk sugars, into glucose and glycogen. The enzymes necessary for this change are absent, and when these milk sugars reach high levels, they act as toxic agents. This is a relatively rare congenital disease accompanied by retarded growth, mental retardation, and cataracts in the more severe cases. Hepatomegaly is often pronounced, owing to cirrhosis. As a result, glycogen storage is reduced, causing hypoglycemia of such degree that it may represent the most prominent physiologic abnormality and cause the major symptomatology. It is probably this disturbed carbohydrate physiology that accounts for the retarded growth. Galactosuria and galactosemia are universal findings in these cases.

GLYCOGEN STORAGE DISEASE (VON GIERKE'S DISEASE).—There are several types of glycogen storage disease, all of which have certain clinical similarities. All are caused by the deficiency of specific enzymes that are necessary for either the storage of glycogen or for the mobilization of the glycogen stored in the liver, muscle, kidney, and other organs. In one of the more common forms of the disease the error of metabolism is the relative absence of glucose-6-phosphatase, which permits glycogen conversion into glucose. Excessive glycogen storage results. In another type of the disease the debrancher enzyme necessary to break the complex chains of glycogen to simpler forms is absent. In yet another form an abnormal type of glycogen is produced that is resistant to normal glycogenolysis. Retarded growth characterizes all forms of glycogen storage disease, and hepatomegaly, cirrhosis, and hypoglycemic symptoms may occur.

DIABETES MELLITUS.—Children with severe and poorly controlled diabetes may show a reduction in both height and weight.[3] In refractory diabetes dwarfism may be pronounced. With improved methods of control, including close attention to adequacy of diets, one rarely sees pronounced statural abnormalities in diabetic children today. Some authors have stated that the height of the average diabetic child is greater than normal at the time of onset of the disease, but other workers in the field have published contradictory figures.

MUCOPOLYSACCHARIDOSES.—These diseases are genetically determined in which the mucopolysaccharides (primarily dermatan, heparan, and keratan sulfates) are stored in tissues and excreted in large amounts in the urine. The abnormal storage of this material affects a wide variety of tissues resulting in problems of morphogenesis and function. The alteration in a child's appearance has led to appellation of "gargoyle." Pathologic changes include slow and irregular cartilage growth, hepatomegaly, splenomegaly, and changes in the central nervous system leading to lowered mentation and often clouding of the cornea to a degree resulting in blindness. Kyphosis in some of the patients contributes to the reduced stature. Among the syndromes grouped under this classification are Morquio, Hurler, Hunter, and Scheie.[23, 24]

Sphingolipidoses.—There are a number of specific diseases in this group all of which are characterized by systemic disorders of fat metabolism with storage of abnormal lipid products in various organ systems of which the central nervous system is a primary target. The enzymatic defects have been largely identified, and diagnosis through amniocentesis is possible. No treatment is available and early death is characteristic of most of these diseases. Although retarded growth is common, the outstanding symptoms relate to the central nervous system. The conditions include Gaucher's disease, Niemann-Pick's disease, Fabry's disease and Tay-Sachs disease. These inborn errors of metabolism are genetically recessive and often ethnically related. Hypothalamic or pituitary involvement may be responsible for the retarded growth.[14, 24]

Nutritional Privation.—Nutritional deficiency probably contributes to a large number of entities, as well as being a primary cause of stunted growth. As pointed out in previous chapters, the deprivation may occur in utero due to maternal malnutrition or placental malfunction, or it may occur after birth. The earlier it takes place, especially if severe in degree, the more likely it is to cause permanent growth retardation, probably by actual reduction in total cell number. If growth is impaired by an unsatisfactory diet, other poor socioeconomic factors are apt to be present. The result is an adult who is often less healthy than average, and in women there is an inferior obstetric record and the production of small babies who tend to grow to be small adults and perpetuate the trend.[42] Poor nutrition may further complicate other conditions. Fatigue and respiratory distress may interfere with adequate oral intake in congenital heart disease.[38] A number of children have been studied who suffered from psychologic deprivation associated with unusual eating patterns and extremely short stature. Growth hormone levels were abnormally low, even following usual methods of stimulation. Improving the environment resulted in a more normal food intake, resumption of statural growth, and a return to normal of growth hormone levels.[39]

It is quite possible that the small size often observed in the child and adult with mental retardation is associated with mild but chronic undernutrition. There is no evidence that decreased stimulation of the pituitary by the higher central nervous system plays a part.[37]

CHRONIC INFECTIONS.—A large number of diseases could be listed under this classification. A few examples are hookworm infestation, malaria, dysentery, pulmonary disease, syphilis, and osteomyelitis. Gardiner-Hill[7] stated that such diseases may cause a premature "senescence of growing cartilage" with calcification. Growth failure may be either temporary or permanent.

Organic Disorders

CONGENITAL HEART DISEASE.—The greatest extent of retardation of growth occurs in diseases of the cyanotic group, including tetralogy of Fallot, complete transposition of the great vessels, and a condition in which both great vessels arise from the same ventricle. The acyanotic group shows growth retardation most severely in ventricular septal defects with pulmonary hypertension and in complicated atrial septal defects. Even in the less involved abnormalities some degree of growth failure usually is present.[25] In nearly all of these the failure of growth, when present, is believed to be due to anoxia hampering cellular metabolism. In a recent study of growth of children with congenital heart disease corrected by surgery, Adams et al.[15] found that many did not regain normal stature or weight even after relatively long periods of observation. An associated growth defect of a genetic basis was postulated as a possible explanation. It seems more likely that early impairment of growth results in metabolic changes that become irreversible at the cell level.[38]

HEPATIC INSUFFICIENCY.—Prolonged hepatic insufficiency, as in cirrhosis and congenital atresia of the biliary passages, notoriously slows growth and may be associated with rickets due to poor absorption of fat-soluble vitamins.

MALABSORPTION SYNDROMES.—Children who have the celiac syndrome and pancreatic cystic fibrosis may simply remain small without showing rickets, or rickets may be superimposed on the primary disease. In both diseases there is poor absorption of ingested foodstuffs, particularly fats, and to less extent proteins. Consequently, vitamins A and D are poorly absorbed. In pancreatic cystic fibrosis there is the additional factor of the chronic pulmonary infection that retards development. Recently added to the list of causes for malabsorption are the deficiencies of sugar-splitting enzymes, which result in diarrhea with strongly acid stools due to bacterial fermentation of the sugars as they pass into the lower gut. One interesting observation that has been made in many of these severely malnourished children is the small head circumference. This measurement was considerably below 2 standard deviations for either their age or in comparison with their height. Psychometric evaluation following successful treatment did not indicate an appreciable lowering of mentation while still in early childhood. Delay in bone maturation is commonly associated with severe nutritional privation from whatever cause.

Renal Dwarfism.—Several different syndromes may be included under this classification. It is recognized that any chronic renal insufficiency of a severe grade may impair growth. Such impairment may be seen with chronic nephritis and chronic urinary tract infection and as a result of congenital abnormalities. The retention of abnormal metabolites and the usual accompanying acidosis so change the internal environment that optimal cellular function is impossible. The resulting dwarfism usually is accompanied by retarded ossification but may or may not result in the syndrome known as renal rickets.[48, 49]

In a few patients with renal insufficiency of long duration the condition may be associated with generalized bone disease. Roentgenologically these changes are not easily distinguished from vitamin D deficient rickets; hence, the term "renal rickets" has been applied. In these individuals there is always a marked retention of phosphorus, and this is said to be responsible for the hyperplasia of the parathyroid glands that is nearly always present. Because of this finding at autopsy, it has been postulated that renal rickets is secondary to hyperparathyroidism.

The Fanconi syndrome, a type of renal acidosis, may lead to a clinical picture resembling rickets and causing dwarfism. The syndrome as usually described is characterized by a family history (often consanguinity), impaired growth at an early age, "rickets," albuminuria, an increase in urinary glucose, organic acids, ammonia, phosphorus, and calcium, a persistently alkaline urine reaction, hypophosphatemia but normal calcium levels in the blood, and lowered blood bicarbonate content without uremia. Degenerative changes in the renal tubules represent the main morphologic change. The condition has been ascribed to abnormal tubular function with failure of resorption of certain important solutes. It would appear that the bone changes in this condition are due to the acidosis caused by increased urinary excretion of base secondary to increased excretion of organic acids. An added feature is the low serum phosphorus content (Fig 13–4).

Brief mention should be made of another type of renal acidosis sometimes associated with rickets-like bone changes. In this condition there is no glomerular pathology as in renal rickets. The fundamental change is due to damage or anomaly of the tubules. In the presence of damaged kidney tubules, ammonia is not formed to be excreted in combination with acid and, furthermore, an acid urine is not easily formed. In this eventuality, calcium, being a base, is in demand and appears in increased amounts in the urine. The serum calcium level tends to fall, and consequently parathy-

AN OUTLINE OF ABNORMAL GROWTH / 455

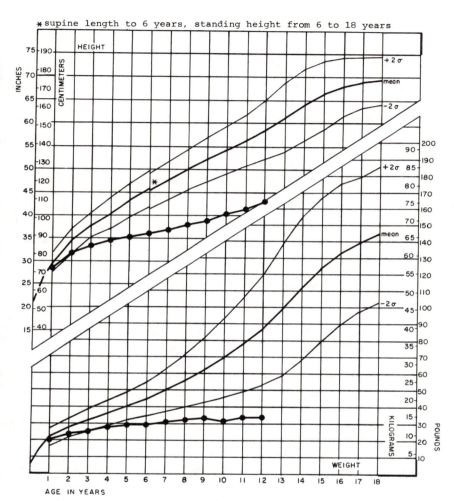

*supine length to 6 years, standing height from 6 to 18 years

Fig 13–4.—Dwarfism secondary to severe renal disease (Fanconi's syndrome with cystinosis). Metabolic abnormalities present in this boy were proteinuria, glucosuria, aminoaciduria, metabolic acidosis, and cystine crystals in the cornea and bone marrow. Clinically the child appeared chronically ill and had a very poor appetite. Just before death occurred after his 12th birthday, his BUN reached 110 mg/100 ml.

roid hyperplasia results. This tends to counteract the low serum calcium level but causes hypophosphatemia. In the presence of a low or normal serum calcium content and a low serum phosphorus level, calcium is not deposited in osteoid tissue. It should be explained that this condition and renal rickets differ not only in their pathologic physiology in relation to the

kidneys but also in the mechanism by which the bone changes are produced. In the simplest terms, renal rickets is caused by bone destruction,
whereas osteomalacia due to renal acidosis is caused by lack of bone formation (or lack of calcification, exactly as in vitamin D deficient rickets).[21]

ENDOCRINE DISORDERS.—The role of the endocrine glands in growth
and development has been reviewed in chapter 9. True endocrine deficiencies are relatively uncommon causes of short stature. Infants with congenital hypothyroidism (cretinism) are often identified by newborn screening
methods on blood specimens. If unrecognized and untreated, in a few
months classic features begin to appear. Growth in length and weight is
retarded. Facial features become grossly thickened, the skin dry, the
tongue thick, and an umbilical hernia is often present. Lethargy and constipation are prominent symptoms. If adequate therapy is delayed for even
a few months, mental development may be permanently retarded. Although children with acquired hypothyroidism may appear mentally alert,
their general activity slows down and so does growth. Roentgenologic studies reveal severe delay in bone maturation.[17]

There are a number of kinds of pituitary dwarfism depending upon
which pituitary hormone or hormones are deficient. It may be that a large
percentage of so-called pituitary deficiencies are really hypothalamic releasing hormone deficiencies. For purposes of discussion, it is useful to
divide them into two categories: isolated growth hormone deficiency and
multiple pituitary hormone deficiencies. Multiple deficiencies are most evident by lack of sexual development as well as short stature. Hypoglycemia
is a frequent association either symptomatic or by laboratory tests. Adrenal
and thyroid insufficiencies are rare. Bone maturation is decreased in varying degrees. The cause in many patients is obscure. Of specific causes, the
most common is craniopharyngioma. Perinatal injury to the hypothalamus
has been implied as a frequent factor. In one study, nearly half of the
children with diagnosed hypopituitarism had a history of a traumatic birth
and over 40% had neurologic abnormalities.[51]

Isolated growth hormone deficiency is characterized by short stature
with normal sexual development. It may have a genetic basis since it can
appear more than once in a family and is probably autosomal recessive.[43]
Bone age is delayed moderately. It is of interest to note, and diagnostically
it is important, that normal growth occurs for the first 18 to 24 months in
most of these children (Fig 13–5). The incidence of isolated growth hormone deficiency is unknown but one survey estimated it at one in 30,000
births and it probably is more common than multiple deficiencies.[6, 9]

A rare type of dwarfism (Laron) is due to depressed levels of somatomedin. Plasma growth hormone levels are elevated well above normal. Chil-

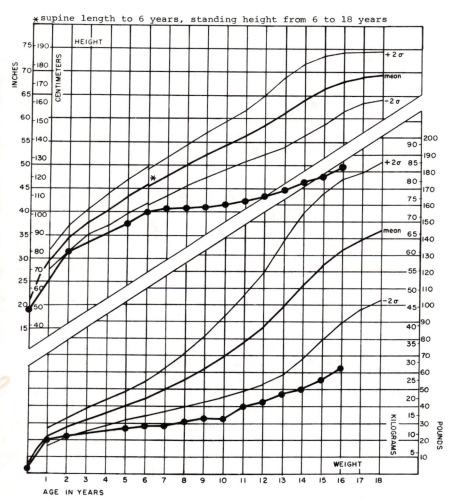

Fig 13–5.—Probable pituitary dwarf. Although growth never ceased, the pattern of a near normal rate during infancy followed by a decided slowing down is typical of many pituitary deficiencies. On several occasions, tests for thyroid and adrenal cortex function and the integrity of the pituitary-adrenal axis were normal. Bone maturation persisted at about 2–3 years behind chronologic age. When this boy was last seen, at age 16, he still appeared very immature and there was no evidence of sexual maturation.

dren with this disorder have short stature, increased subcutaneous fat, acromicria, sparse hair, dental dysplasia, and high pitched voice. (See chapter 9 for the role of somatomedins in normal growth.) This type of dwarfism is more common in consanguineous marriages.[36]

Studies of African pygmies indicate they have a major deficiency in insulin-like growth factor (IGF-1), a potent growth factor closely resembling somatomedin. Pygmies have normal amounts of circulating growth hormone.[50] In the absence of IGF-1, growth hormone is ineffective.

Hyperfunction of the adrenal cortex, as in the adrenogenital syndrome, will result in a temporarily accelerated rate of growth with virilization, due to increased secretion of androgens. However, premature union of the epiphyses and diaphyses eventually precludes further increase in length, so that the final stature falls short of the expected norm. Adrenal tumors, with onset later in life, may produce a similar disturbance* (Fig 13–6).

Gonadal tumors with hormonal function are extremely rare in boys and are uncommon in girls. Precocious sexual development in such instances is associated with accelerated bone maturation; so the pattern of growth that is followed will be similar to that just described for adrenal cortical hyperfunction except that the precocity is isosexual, i.e., masculinizing in boys and feminizing in girls. Tumors of the hypothalamus and other lesions in this area may cause precocious sexual development. Except for the early onset and rapid development of secondary sex characteristics plus the usual signs of an intracranial lesion, the pattern of development is the same as that normally followed by each sex as puberty is approached (Fig 13–7). Pineal tumors in boys produce a similar syndrome.

Polyostotic fibrous dysplasia (McCune-Albright syndrome) is characterized by cystic bone changes that tend to be asymmetrical, brown pigmented areas of the skin and precocious growth and sexual development. Most of the cases so far described with the endocrine changes have been in females. In all instances noted the premature epiphysial union, which is invariably a part of the precocity, results in stature below normal by the time growth ceases.

Hypogonadism of a congenital nature is seen in Turner's syndrome, which is caused by an XO-chromosome distribution. The external genitalia are typically female, but the cells lack the chromatin body associated with a normal genetic female. The internal genital organs are quite rudimentary, often being fibrous bands. Such children are dwarfed, lack sexual development, and frequently have other anomalies, such as webbing of the neck, increased carrying angle of the arms, micrognathia, mild mental retardation, pigmented nevi, and congenital heart defects. As the chronologic

*A few cases have been reported of feminizing adrenal tumors in boys.

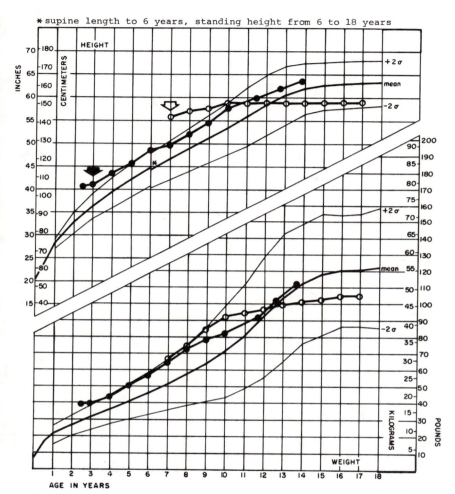

Fig 13–6.—Adrenogenital syndrome in sisters, showing the effectiveness of early therapy as compared to late therapy. Virilization was apparent in both at birth; but until pubic hair, acne, and accelerated growth were noted, the diagnosis was not entertained. At the time suppressive treatment with hydrocortisone was begun *(arrows)*, the older girl's bone maturation was estimated at 15 years and the younger sibling's at 7 years. Before therapy both had elevated urine contents of 17-ketosteroids.

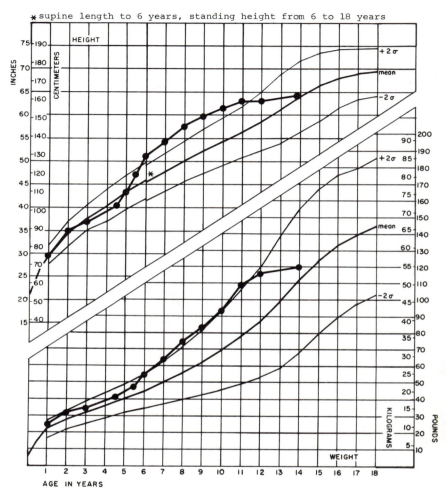

Fig 13–7.—Precocious sexual development and overgrowth secondary to a hypothalamic tumor surgically removed at 10 years of age. From the growth pattern it seems certain that the tumor had been present since age 6 years. Enlargement of genitalia (both phallus and scrotum), pubic hair, acne, and deepening of the voice preceded progressive loss of vision and headaches, which finally brought the boy to the clinic. At age 10 bone maturation was 5 years advanced and the urine content of 17-ketosteroids and gonadotropins was at a late adolescent level.

time of puberty approaches, the levels of urinary gonadotropins are elevated above normal, but estrogen levels remain very low or absent (Fig 13–8). A very similar syndrome in which no chromosomal abnormalities have been identified has been described in boys.[8] The genitalia are underdeveloped with absent (to palpation) or small and often undescended testes.

Hyperparathyroidism may cause dwarfism as a result of the changes in bone—softening with decalcification, cyst formation, and fractures leading to severe malformations. In this condition, lowered serum phosphate and increased calcium and phosphatase contents are typical.

Although it cannot be stated at this time that the condition termed pseudohypoparathyroidism fits into the classification of endocrine dwarfism, it can be stated that an endocrine dysfunction exists in this syndrome, first described by Albright. The blood and physical changes are those of hypoparathyroidism, and in addition there are short stature and other anomalies. The interesting feature that sets these children apart from others with hypoparathyroidism is that they do not respond to parathyroid hormone therapy. It is this inability of the body to respond that has led to the present nomenclature of the disease. Short stature, tendency to obesity, characteristic round face, striking shortening of the metacarpals, and the occasional finding of exostoses are typical of this syndrome.

Hereditary and Primordial Dwarfism

The best examples of hereditary dwarfism are to be found in isolated areas of Africa, India, Melanesia, and the Philippine Islands. It is not certain whether more than one race is involved. All individuals have dark skin and curly hair; but the facial features, such as thickness of the lips, flatness of the nose, and breadth of the face, differ among the African pygmies, the Asian pygmies, and the Negritos.[28] The average adult height of the male is under 5 feet (128 cm). Birth weight is less than normal compared with other races, but seldom would be classified as "premature." It must be admitted that statistics are meager. The pattern of growth is apparently normal, although slow, and with very little prepuberal spurt; however, the appearance of secondary sex characteristics follows the usual course.

As previously noted, very recently (1981) it was found that the African pygmy has a specific growth factor deficiency. This finding may well stimulate more intensive investigation of other hereditary short people.

Most authorities refer to the primordial dwarf as the small individual with normal proportions who undergoes sexual maturity at the expected

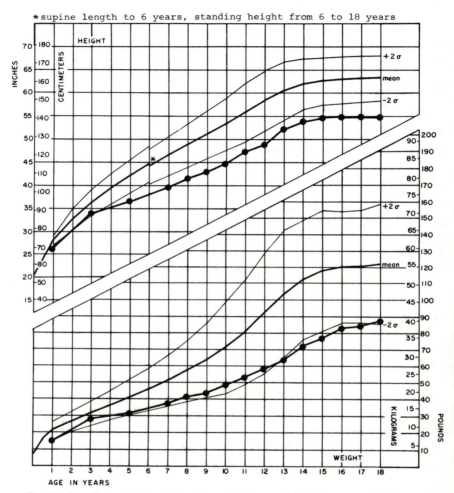

Fig 13–8.—Turner's syndrome (gonadal agenesis). Note especially the gradual deviation below the normal with increasing age. At birth it was observed that this girl had lymphedema of the hands and feet, which slowly disappeared over the period of infancy. Webbing of the neck and micrognathia were also present. Sexual maturation occurred at 15 years, after estrogen therapy was begun. The "bone age" was 3 years behind chronologic age at 15 years. Buccal smears did not contain any chromatin body, and the urinary gonadotropins were considerably elevated.

age and shows no evidence of any endocrine disorder. Essentially the diagnosis is made by exclusion. Although the true incidence of this type of retarded stature is unknown, it would appear to be very small, with the exception of the hereditary dwarfs. Most of the sporadic, as well as familial, types of dwarfism have other abnormalities—some of a serious nature, similar to those described in the following section. However, many cases cannot be classified in our present state of ignorance.

Other Types of Dwarfism

Many different syndromes associated with remarkably short stature have been described—some sporadic, some familial—but often having certain findings that are repeated sufficiently often in different patients to make one think that there could be a common pathogenesis. Many eponyms have resulted, which may be confusing; but it is often difficult to find an adequate scientific label that is both brief and descriptive. A few representative types are indicated here, with only the major features being outlined. [7, 10, 18, 20, 29, 30]

ASSOCIATED RENAL ABNORMALITIES.—Syndromes described by Lowe, Lightwood, and Fanconi now bear their names. Fanconi's syndrome has already been referred to previously (see Fig 13–4). Lowe's syndrome is evident shortly after birth, with mental retardation, cataracts, glaucoma, and rickets. It appears only in males, and metabolic abnormalities include acidosis and aminoaciduria. Lightwood's syndrome also manifests itself in early infancy, with failure to thrive, metabolic acidosis, hyperchloremia, hypokalemia, and inability to form acid urine or urinary ammonia. [21]

ASSOCIATED SKIN MANIFESTATIONS.—The Hutchinson-Gilford syndrome is typical of a class of dwarfism associated with progeria. Ectodermally derived structures are severely affected. The skin is thin and smooth, and alopecia and poorly enameled teeth are present. Arthritic changes occur early in life. The face is small with a prominent nose. Bone maturation is normal. No obvious familial tendency exists. Syndromes associated with pigmentation of the skin and hypersensitivity to light, similar to xeroderma pigmentosum but milder, have been described by Cockayne, Rothmund-Thomson, and Werner. In Cockayne's syndrome, progeria and cataracts are present, and often neurologic findings, such as deafness and low mentality, are noted. Arthritic changes and early graying of the hair are common. Dwarfing becomes apparent in early childhood. The condition described by Rothmund-Thomson resembles that of Werner except for earlier age of onset. Because of this difference, the dwarfism is more pronounced in the former syndrome. Skin becomes pigmented and is light-sensitive. Nails and hair are dysplastic, and teeth have poor enamel formation. Lack of subcutaneous fat and atrophic skin lends to the appearance of senility. Cataracts develop in more than half of the patients.

ASSOCIATED BONE CHANGES.—Cornelia de Lange first described the syndrome that now bears her name.[29] Severe growth and mental retardation with microbrachycephaly, some degree of micromelia or phocomelia, especially of the upper extremities, and hirsutism are typical findings. Genitalia in males are small, but no patient has yet been followed into adolescence to determine development at that time. Facial features include heavy eyebrows growing over the midline, an anteverted nose due to nasal cartilage hypoplasia, and thin lips with the angles of the mouth turning down. Evidence now present supports a recessive type of inheritance. The Ellis-van Creveld syndrome is also called "chondroectodermal dysplasia." There is a symmetrical and progressive distalward shortening of the extremities, and the tubular bones appear short and thick by x-ray examination. Both the nails and the teeth are poorly formed. Polydactylism of the hands is a constant finding. Inconstant features are congenital heart disease and mental retardation. Genetic influences are not known.

INTRAUTERINE DWARFISM.—A large number of dwarfs would probably fit into this category, including some already described in which low birth weight is a common finding (Fig 13–9). At least three types have been differentiated by some authors. All are characterized by very small size at birth but normal duration of pregnancy and continued slow growth thereafter, with normal maturation of osseous tissue and sexual development. Virchow-Seckel[20] syndrome is best described by the synonym "bird-headed dwarf." Microcephaly and some degree of mental defectiveness is usual. Russell described a dwarfism associated with a large cranium and a relatively small and undeveloped face. Silver first brought our attention to a group of dwarfs with asymmetry of the body (similar to hemiatrophy) and precocious sexual development with early elevation of the urinary gonadotropins.[47]

CHROMOSOMAL ABNORMALITIES.—In the past few years many different malformations associated with chromosomal abnormalities have been reported. In most two findings were common: growth retardation and mental retardation. Many other associated anomalies have been described, with some tendency to repeat if the autosomal defect was the same in the different patients. It would serve little purpose to go through the long list.[11, 47]

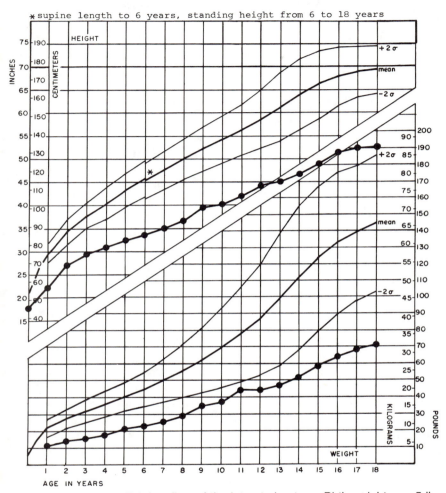

Fig 13–9.—Primordial dwarfism of the intrauterine type. Birth weight was 5 lb, but pregnancy was estimated to be full term. The only abnormalities noted were microcephaly (below 2 standard deviations for both age and height) and mild mental retardation, evidenced by her being placed in a special education class. Sexual maturation was slightly delayed, but menarche occurred at 16 years. Bone maturation at 8, 10, and 16 years matched chronologic age.

Giantism

The pathogenesis of giantism is less complicated than that of dwarfism, owing to the fact that there are fewer causes. The following classification covers the majority of cases seen in any clinic.

Hereditary Giantism

In hereditary giantism there is usually abnormal height in one or both parents or in close relatives. Such individuals are well proportioned, although they may have somewhat longer extremities than the average person. Bone maturation follows a normal course of growth. As with hereditary dwarfs, Africa furnishes the best examples of this type of giantism in the Dinka tribe of the Sudan and the Watutsi of Ruanda-Urundi. In both of these the male often reaches a height of over 7 ft (196 cm).

Pituitary and Hypothalamic Giantism

Hyperfunction of the eosinophilic cells of the anterior pituitary before fusion of the epiphyses will cause excessive growth. In many of the cases recorded abnormal growth started just before or at the time of puberty, and the abnormal height was attained in the next few years. Such giants may grow to a height of 8 ft or more. Usually some degree of acromegaly is superimposed on the giantism. Frequently there are signs of intracranial tumor with expansion of the sella turcica. Pituitary giantism has been described in infancy, but is extremely rare.[9]

A number of patients with giantism and signs of neurologic abnormalities but without evidence of direct involvement of the pituitary have been described by Sotos et al.[31] The author has followed four such patients, two into puberty. These children have mild to moderate degrees of mental retardation, and some, but not all, have abnormal pneumoencephalograms with hydrocephalus. Very early in life it was noted that growth was excessive, and then by about 4 to 6 years of age a normal rate was maintained so that the relative excess in size was not lost. In two of the patients, bone maturation proceeded at a normal pace and adolescence occurred at the expected time. Adult height in each was above the 97th percentile. Mild acromegalic changes were present—large hands and feet and prognathia—that exaggerated the awkwardness associated with the neurologic deficit (Fig 13–10). The etiology of this type of giantism is not presently known but may well reflect an abnormality of the central nervous system, especially the hypothalamus, and its control over the secretion of growth hormone from the pituitary. Fasting blood assays on three patients in our laboratory have been in the normal range.

*supine length to 6 years, standing height from 6 to 18 years

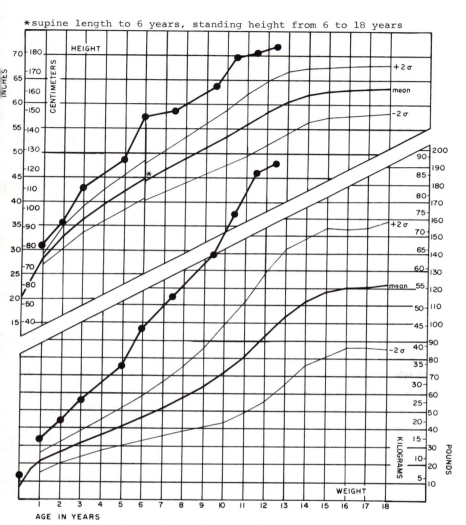

Fig 13–10.—Giantism of the cerebral type. In addition to the large size of this girl, she had some acromegalic features, with large hands and feet and moderate prognathism. Mental retardation was severe, but repeated x-ray examinations of the skull failed to show evidence of abnormality. Bone maturation was compatible with age, and breast development was well advanced and pubic hair present at 12½ years.

Marfan's Syndrome

Most patients with Marfan's syndrome are enough taller than the average for their age so that it is very noticeable. Although sporadic cases exist, the usual mode of inheritance is autosomal dominant. In addition to excessive linear growth, these children are thin and have disproportionately long arms, legs, fingers, and toes (arachnodactyly). The skull may be long and narrow. Associated findings that are less constant than those just described include subluxation of the lens; a number of deformities of the heart and great vessels; scoliosis and kyphosis; and arthrogryposis.

Eunuchoid Giantism

In the experience of the author this is a rare type of giantism, and the medical literature gives little support to its existence. The cases described have invariably been males in which the hypogonadism was primary or secondary. Such boys are tall, with long extremities and delayed or absent sexual maturation. Presumably because of late fusion of the epiphyses growth is prolonged, leading to increased height. The urinary excretion of androgens is low, while gonadotropins are elevated.

Obesity

A universally accepted definition of obesity is probably an impossibility. It would differ in every cultural group and among the different races. The genetic background determining body type would be an important factor. Age would be considered an essential variant by many people. If one uses most of the modern growth tables or curves, obesity may be considered to exist in any child who weighs 20% or more above the mean for his height.

Obesity may be encountered at any age but is most often brought to the attention of the clinician during adolescence. Most of these children are found to have been overweight since infancy or early childhood but have become more sensitive about it as they grow older. Among high school children in the United States its frequency has been estimated at 15% to 20%.

There are still many misconceptions about obesity. The fact that most of these children are referred to an endocrinologist for diagnosis and treatment indicates this. Only a small fraction of the total are actual endocrine problems. Hypothyroidism as a factor in obesity is extremely rare. We have seen only one in which the two conditions coexisted. Wilkins[18] stated that he had seen only two in more than 200 hypothyroid children. As a matter of fact, most children with thyroid deficiency are below normal in weight for their age, and virtually all are below normal for stature. This is certainly true for the congenital group in every instance. This is in direct contrast to the usual obese child, who is taller than the average for his age.

Cushing's syndrome, due to tumor or hyperplasia of the adrenal cortex, is seldom seen in the pediatric age group. These subjects are obese but nearly always shorter than normal, owing to the excessive output of corticoids, osteoporosis, and collapse of vertebral bodies. In addition there are hirsutism, hypertension, glycosuria, and a diabetic type of glucose tolerance curve. None of these findings is present in simple obesity. The skin striae found in Cushing's syndrome are similarly found in many adolescents with no abnormalities. Steroid determination in the urine will confirm the diagnosis if doubt exists.

Another rare type of obesity is Fröhlich's syndrome. Unfortunately, this term has been much abused and often incorrectly used. The condition is a specific entity associated with a lesion of the hypothalamus causing, in addition to obesity, short stature, retarded or absent sexual development, visual failure, headaches, and other signs of intracranial pressure. In the same category, i.e., obesity due to intracranial lesions, we can include the Laurence-Moon-Biedl syndrome. Other findings in this condition are mental retardation, syndactylism, and retinitis pigmentosa. It is extremely rare. Also, one might mention the obesity occasionally seen with other forms of mental retardation, although the psychologic factor may play a part, in that such children may find excessive eating one of the few forms of pleasure.

The Prader-Willi syndrome is another example in this category. In addition to obesity it is characterized by mental retardation, short stature, hypogenitalism, glucose intolerance, and frank diabetes mellitus in some.

When all of these rare types are pooled, they make up less than 1% of the total of overweight children.

Often the child, parents, or physician believes that prepubescent boys have genitalia that are too small, and when this is associated with obesity, it is often concluded that some glandular abnormality is present. If the pubic fat pad is pushed back and the chronologic age rather than the overall body size is taken into consideration, it will be seen that the genital organs are quite normal. It must be remembered that these organs undergo very little growth until adolescence is well along. Furthermore, size of body is not a good index of maturity. Most of these boys will have normal development and often a drop in weight as they approach puberty without any therapy.

It has been stated that obesity occurring early in life is associated with fat cell hyperplasia, while that occurring later in childhood causes fat cell hypertrophy.[46] Some authorities assume obesity that begins in early life is more intractable to treatment due to the differences in the number of lipid cells present. The author would point out that fat is equally mobilizable from big as well as small cells. Weight reduction can be accomplished on the same diet at the same rate in both subjects, all other factors being the same, e.g., age and exercise. The emotional problems associated with the greater degree of habituation in the child with the early onset are not to be denied.

A number of important physical findings are frequently present in obese children when this is due to increased caloric intake alone. They tend to be slightly taller than their peers. Bone maturation and sexual development are more advanced. In girls, menarche occurs earlier than in those of average weight.

Interesting social and psychologic findings have been reported from a number of clinics.[2, 16, 46] Obesity is more prevalent in the lower socioeconomic classes. This is especially true for girls. It is more common in the United States in the children of first and second generation immigrants. It is found more often in the firstborn and among bottle-fed than breast-fed children. It is more apt to occur in infants and children whose mothers had excessive weight gain during the pregnancy. In 70% to 80% of the families at least one other member is obese.

Unfortunately many people still associate some degree of obesity with good health during infancy and early childhood. Mothers become upset when their 2- or 3-year-old is more interested in exploring the world than in eating. It should be recalled that in contrast to early infancy, growth is relatively slow and energy requirements are low. The normal child at this age also assumes a more mature body build and proportions that are much different in appearance than that of the infant.

One of the most disturbing findings of the majority of these studies is the fact that fat infants often become fat children who become fat adolescents who become fat adults.[4, 16, 33, 35, 41]

The psychologic factors in obesity have been well analyzed by a number of workers who have emphasized their importance.[16, 33, 46] Many of the children have feelings of insecurity and are overprotected by their parents. Very frequently other personality problems are evident; these include nocturnal enuresis, severe school difficulties, and social problems with few or no intimate friendships of their own age. The onset of obesity following some surgical procedure is not uncommon, according to parental histories. Most of these children have had the onset of this overweight problem early in childhood, often by 4 or 5 years of age. Perhaps because parents are prone to accept a little "pudginess" at this age as a reflection of good health, they are not concerned until many more years have passed. In fact, many parents deny that their children were overweight at the early ages until proof is obtained by plotting past weights upon a standard growth curve. Such children often eat to excess because it gives them a feeling of pleasure and satisfaction that is difficult to obtain in other ways. It is not unusual to find that the mothers have rejected them but feel that their duty has been well done if the children are fed adequately. This pattern of substituting food for love may go back to infancy, or it may begin at age 3 or 4 in response to the frequent "feeding problems" present at this time.

The consequences of excess adipose tissue are multiple and increase in severity and frequency with advancing age. Hypertension, cerebral vascular accidents, increased surgical risks, and possibly coronary artery disease are among the possible complications. Diabetes mellitus is 50 times more frequent in the obese than the lean population. Equally important as the physical and biochemical abnormalities are the psychologic traumas that obesity causes to the child and his or her family.[16, 45]

In conclusion, a number of important facts need emphasis. Most obesity has its onset early in life, often in the first few years.[32–34] The association of this with psychologic problems is very significant in these children, and the combination often leads to a vicious circle in which each problem augments the other. To many parents, obesity in the preschool child represents an indication of healthfulness. To attain this deceptive goal, poor eating habits are well established by the time the overweight child desires to correct the situation. Finally, it is agreed that those who are obese as juveniles will make up a very large percentage of the grossly obese adults.[34, 35]

REFERENCES

 1. Arnaud C.D.: Parathyroid hormone: Coming of age in clinical medicine. *Am. J. Med.* 55:577, 1973.
 2. Weil W.B.: Current controversies in childhood obesity. *J. Pediatr.* 91:175, 1977.
 3. Boyd J.D., Kantrow A.H.: Retardation of growth in diabetic children. *Am. J. Dis. Child.* 55:460, 1938.
 4. Fisch R.O., Bilek M.K., Ulstrom R.: Obesity and leanness at birth and their relationship to body habitus in later childhood. *Pediatrics* 56:521, 1975.
 5. Caffey J.: *Pediatric X-ray Diagnosis*, ed. 6. Chicago, Year Book Medical Publishers, 1972.
 6. DeLuca H.F.: Vitamin D: A new look at an old vitamin. *Nutr. Rev.* 29:179, 1971.
 7. Gardiner-Hill H.: The abnormalities of growth and development: The clinical and pathological aspects. *Br. Med. J.* 1:1241, 1302, 1934.
 8. Gardner L.I.: *Endocrine and Genetic Diseases of Childhood and Adolescence*, ed. 2. Philadelphia, W.B. Saunders Co., 1975.
 9. Bacon G.E., Spencer M.L., Hopwood N.J., et al.: *A Practical Approach to Pediatric Endocrinology*. Chicago, Year Book Medical Publishers, 1982.
10. Warkany J.: Dwarfs and other little people: An overview. *Semin. Roentgenol.* 8:135, 1973.

11. Felson B. (ed.): Dwarfs and other little people. *Semin. Roentgenol.* 8:133, 1973.
12. Talbot N.B.: Dwarfism in children. *Bull. N. Engl. Med. Ctr.* 7:117, 1945.
13. Dorst J.P., Scott C.I., Hall J.G.: The radiologic assessment of short stature-dwarfism. *Radiol. Clin. N. Am.* 10:393, 1972.
14. Bernsohn J., Grossman H.J. (eds.): *Lipid Storage Diseases: Enzymatic Defects and Clinical Implications.* New York, Academic Press, 1971.
15. Adams F.H., Lund G.W., Disenhouse R.B.: Observations on the physique and growth of children with congenital heart disease. *J. Pediatr.* 44:674, 1954.
16. Lowrey G.H.: Obesity in adolescence. *Am. J. Public Health* 48:1354, 1958.
17. Lowrey G.H., Aster R.H., Carr E.A., et al.: Early diagnostic criteria of congenital hypothyroidism. *Am. J. Dis. Child.* 96:131, 1958.
18. Wilkins L.: *Diagnosis and Treatment of Endocrine Disorders in Childhood and Adolescence,* ed. 3. Springfield, Ill., Charles C Thomas, Publisher, 1965.
19. Fraser D., Salter R.B.: The diagnosis and management of the various types of rickets. *Pediatr. Clin. N. Am.* 4:417, 1958.
20. Seckel H.P.G.: *Bird-Headed Dwarfs.* Springfield, Ill., Charles C Thomas, Publisher, 1960.
21. Jones R.W.A., Rigden S.P., Barratt T.M., et al.: The effects of chronic renal failure on growth, nutritional status and body composition. *Pediatr. Res.* 16:748, 1982.
22. Rubin P.: *Dynamic Classification of Bone Dysplasias.* Chicago, Year Book Medical Publishers, 1964.
23. Schenk E.A., Haggerty J.: Morquio's disease: A radiologic and morphologic study. *Pediatrics* 34:839, 1964.
24. Rosenberg R.N.: Biochemical genetics of neurologic disease. *N. Engl. J. Med.* 305:1181, 1981.
25. Mehrizi A., Drash A.: Growth disturbance in congenital heart disease. *J. Pediatr.* 61:418, 1962.
26. Parkin J.M.: Incidence of growth hormone deficiency. *Arch. Dis. Child.* 50:904, 1975.
27. Kaplan S.A.: *Growth Disorders in Children and Adolescents.* Springfield, Ill., Charles C. Thomas, Publisher, 1964.
28. Coon C.S.: *The Origin of Races.* New York, Alfred A. Knopf, 1963.
29. Ptacek L.J., Opitz J., Smith D.W., et al.: The Cornelia de Lange syndrome. *J. Pediatr.* 63:100, 1963.
30. Husson G.S., Parkman P.: Chondroectodermal dysplasia (Ellis-Van Creveld syndrome) with complex cardiac malformation. *Pediatrics* 28:285, 1961.
31. Sotos J.F., Dodge P.R., Muirhead D., et al.: Cerebral gigantism in childhood: A syndrome of excessively rapid growth with acromegalic features and a non-progressive neurologic disorder. *N. Engl. J. Med.* 271:109, 1964.
32. Robertson A.F., Lowrey G.H.: Overweight children. *Mich. Med.* 63:629, 1964.
33. Börjeson M.: Overweight children. *Acta Paediatr.* (suppl. 132) 51:1, 1962.
34. Heald F.P., Hollander R.J.: The relationship between obesity in adolescence and early growth. *J. Pediatr.* 67:35, 1965.
35. Charney E., Goodman H.C., McBride M., et al.: Childhood antecedents of adult obesity. *N. Engl. J. Med.* 295:6, 1976.
36. Najjar S.S., Khachadurian A.K., Ilbawi M.N., et al.: Dwarfism with elevated levels of growth hormone. *N. Engl. J. Med.* 284:809, 1971.
37. Lowrey G.H., Bacon G.E., Fisher S., et al.: Fasting growth hormone levels in

mentally retarded children of short stature. *Am. J. Ment. Defic.* 73:474, 1968.
38. Levy R.J., Rosenthal A., Miettinen O.S., et al.: Determinants of growth in patients with ventricular septal defects. *Circulation* 57:793, 1978.
39. Silver H.K., Finkelstein M.: Deprivation dwarfism. *J. Pediatr.* 70:317, 1967.
40. Horton W.A., Rimoin D.L., Lachman R.S., et al.: The phenotypic variability of diastrophic dysplasia. *J. Pediatr.* 93:609, 1978.
41. Eid E.: Follow-up study of physical growth of children who had excessive weight gain in first six months of life. *Br. Med. J.* 2:74, 1970.
42. Thomson A.M.: Adult stature, in van der Werff Ten Bosch (ed.): *Somatic Growth of the Child.* Springfield, Ill., Charles C Thomas, Publisher, 1966.
43. Sheikholislam B.M., Stempfel R.S.: Hereditary isolated somatotrophin deficiency: Effects of growth hormone administration. *Pediatrics* 49:362, 1972.
44. Zach P.M., Harlan W.R., Leaverton P.E., et al.: A longitudinal study of body fatness in childhood and adolescence. *J. Pediatr.* 95:126, 1979.
45. Mann G.V.: The influence of obesity on health. *N. Engl. J. Med.* 291:178, 1974.
46. Winick M. (ed.): *Childhood Obesity.* New York, John Wiley & Sons, 1975.
47. Smith D.W.: *Recognizable Patterns of Human Malformation,* ed. 2. Philadelphia, W.B. Saunders Co., 1976.
48. McSherry E.: Disorders of acid-base equilibrium. *Pediatr. Ann.* 10:44, 1981.
49. Broyer M.: Growth in children with renal insufficiency. *Pediatr. Clin. N. Am.* 29:991, 1982.
50. Merimee T.J., Zaph J., Froesch E.R.: Dwarfism in the pygmy: Isolated deficiency of insulin-like growth factor 1. *N. Engl. J. Med.* 305:965, 1981.
51. Craft W.H., Underwood L.C., Van Wyk J.J.: High incidence of perinatal insult in children with idiopathic hypopituitarism. *J. Pediatr.* 96:397, 1980.

Appendix

The following tables give values that are frequently used in the appraisal of infants and children. References for these tables will be found under the appropriate chapter and section in the main text.

Important Values Used in Physical Appraisal of Infants and Children

AVERAGE HEAD CIRCUMFERENCE OF
AMERICAN CHILDREN

AGE	MEAN		STANDARD DEVIATION	
	IN.	CM	IN.	CM
Birth	13.8	35	0.5	1.2
1 mo	14.9	37.6	0.5	1.2
2 mo	15.5	39.7	0.5	1.2
3 mo	15.9	40.4	0.5	1.2
6 mo	17.0	43.4	0.4	1.1
9 mo	17.8	45.0	0.5	1.2
12 mo	18.3	46.5	0.5	1.2
18 mo	19.0	48.4	0.5	1.2
2 yr	19.2	49.0	0.5	1.2
3 yr	19.6	50.0	0.5	1.2
4 yr	19.8	50.5	0.5	1.2
5 yr	20.0	50.8	0.6	1.4
6 yr	20.2	51.2	0.6	1.4
7 yr	20.5	51.6	0.6	1.4
8 yr	20.6	52.0	0.8	1.8
10 yr	20.9	53.0	0.6	1.4
12 yr	21.0	53.2	0.8	1.8
14 yr	21.5	54.0	0.8	1.8
16 yr	21.9	55.0	0.8	1.8
18 yr	22.1	55.4	0.8	1.8
20 yr	22.2	55.6	0.8	1.8

Average Chest Circumference and Intercristal
Width of American Children

AGE	CHEST CIRCUMFERENCE		PELVIC BICRISTAL DIAMETER	
	IN.	CM	IN.	CM
Birth	13.7	35	3.2	8
3 mo	16.2	40	4.3	11
6 mo	17.3	44	4.8	12
1 yr	18.3	47	5.1	13
18 mo	18.9	48	5.5	14
2 yr	19.5	50	6.0	15
3 yr	20.4	52	6.2	16
4 yr	21.1	53	. . .	. . .
5 yr	22.0	55	7.2	18
6 yr	22.5	56	. . .	. . .
7 yr	23.0	57	8.2	20
8 yr	24.0	59	. . .	. . .
9 yr	24.5	60	8.5	21
10 yr	25.1	61	. . .	. . .
12 yr	27.0	66	9.0	22
14 yr	29.0	72	11.0	28
16 yr*	31.0	77	. . .	. . .
18 yr*	33.0	82	12.2	31
20 yr*	34.5	86	12.6	32

*Males only.

WEIGHT AND HEIGHT PERCENTILE TABLE: BOYS (BIRTH TO AGE 18)

WEIGHT IN LB			WEIGHT IN KG				HEIGHT IN IN.			HEIGHT IN CM		
10%	50%	90%	10%	50%	90%	AGE	10%	50%	90%	10%	50%	90%
6.3	7.5	9.1	2.86	3.4	4.13	Birth	18.9	19.9	21.0	48.1	50.6	53.3
8.5	10.0	11.5	3.8	4.6	5.2	1 mo	20.2	21.2	22.2	50.4	53.0	55.5
10.0	11.5	13.2	4.6	5.2	6.0	2 mo	21.5	22.5	23.5	53.7	56.0	60.0
11.1	12.6	14.5	5.03	5.72	6.58	3 mo	22.8	23.8	24.7	57.8	60.4	62.8
12.5	14.0	16.2	5.6	6.3	7.3	4 mo	23.7	24.7	25.7	60.5	62.0	65.2
13.7	15.0	17.7	6.2	7.0	8.0	5 mo	24.5	25.5	26.5	61.8	65.0	67.3
14.8	16.7	19.2	6.71	7.58	8.71	6 mo	25.2	26.1	27.3	63.9	66.4	69.3
17.8	20.0	22.9	8.07	9.07	10.39	9 mo	27.0	28.0	29.2	68.6	71.2	74.2
19.6	22.2	25.4	8.89	10.7	11.52	12 mo	28.5	29.6	30.7	72.4	75.2	78.1
22.3	25.2	29.0	10.12	11.43	13.15	18 mo	31.0	32.2	33.5	78.8	81.8	85.0
24.7	27.7	31.9	11.2	12.56	14.47	2 yr	33.1	34.4	35.9	84.2	87.5	91.1
26.6	30.0	34.5	12.07	13.61	15.65	2½ yr	34.8	36.3	37.9	88.5	92.1	96.2
28.7	32.2	36.8	13.02	14.61	16.69	3 yr	36.3	37.9	39.6	92.3	96.2	100.5
30.4	34.3	39.1	13.79	15.56	17.74	3½ yr	37.8	39.3	41.1	96.0	99.8	104.5
32.1	36.4	41.4	14.56	16.51	18.78	4 yr	39.1	40.7	42.7	99.3	103.4	108.5
33.8	38.4	43.9	15.33	17.42	19.91	4½ yr	40.3	42.0	44.2	102.4	106.7	112.3
35.5	40.5	46.7	16.1	18.37	21.18	5 yr	40.8	42.8	45.2	103.7	108.7	114.7
38.8	45.6	53.1	17.6	20.68	24.09	5½ yr	42.6	45.0	47.3	108.3	114.4	120.1
40.9	48.3	56.4	18.55	21.91	25.58	6 yr	43.8	46.3	48.6	111.2	117.5	123.5
43.4	51.2	60.4	19.69	23.22	27.4	6½ yr	44.9	47.6	50.0	114.1	120.8	127.0
45.8	54.1	64.4	20.77	24.54	29.21	7 yr	46.0	48.9	51.4	116.9	124.1	130.5
48.5	57.1	68.7	22.0	25.9	31.16	7½ yr	47.2	50.0	52.7	120.0	127.1	133.9
51.2	60.1	73.0	23.22	27.26	33.11	8 yr	48.5	51.2	54.0	123.1	130.0	137.3
53.8	63.1	77.0	24.4	28.62	34.93	8½ yr	49.5	52.3	55.1	125.7	132.8	140.0
56.3	66.0	81.0	25.54	29.94	36.74	9 yr	50.5	53.3	56.1	128.3	135.5	142.6
58.7	69.0	85.5	26.63	31.3	38.78	9½ yr	51.4	54.3	57.1	130.6	137.9	145.1
61.1	71.9	89.9	27.71	32.61	40.78	10 yr	52.3	55.2	58.1	132.8	140.3	147.5
63.7	74.8	94.6	28.89	33.93	42.91	10½ yr	53.2	56.0	58.9	135.1	142.3	149.7
66.3	77.6	99.3	30.07	35.2	45.04	11 yr	54.0	56.8	59.8	137.3	144.2	151.8
69.2	81.0	104.5	31.39	36.74	47.4	11½ yr	55.0	57.8	60.9	139.8	146.9	154.8
72.0	84.4	109.6	32.66	38.28	49.71	12 yr	56.1	58.9	62.2	142.4	149.6	157.9
74.6	88.7	116.4	33.84	40.23	52.8	12½ yr	56.9	60.0	63.6	144.5	152.3	161.6
77.1	93.0	123.2	34.97	42.18	55.88	13 yr	57.7	61.0	65.1	146.6	155.0	165.3
82.2	100.3	130.1	37.29	45.5	59.01	13½ yr	58.8	62.6	66.5	149.4	158.9	168.9
87.2	107.6	136.9	39.55	48.81	62.1	14 yr	59.9	64.0	67.9	152.1	162.7	172.4
93.3	113.9	142.4	42.32	51.66	64.59	14½ yr	61.0	65.1	68.7	155.0	165.3	174.6
99.4	120.1	147.8	45.09	54.48	67.04	15 yr	62.1	66.1	69.6	157.8	167.8	176.7
105.2	124.9	152.6	47.72	56.65	69.22	15½ yr	63.1	66.8	70.2	160.3	169.7	178.2
111.0	129.7	157.3	50.35	58.83	71.35	16 yr	64.1	67.8	70.7	162.8	171.6	179.7
114.3	133.0	161.0	51.85	60.33	73.03	16½ yr	64.6	68.0	71.1	164.2	172.7	180.7
117.5	136.2	164.6	53.3	61.78	74.66	17 yr	65.2	68.4	71.5	165.5	173.7	181.6
118.8	137.6	166.8	53.89	62.41	75.66	17½ yr	65.3	68.5	71.6	165.9	174.1	182.0
120.0	139.0	169.0	54.43	63.05	76.66	18 yr	65.5	68.7	71.8	166.3	174.5	182.4

WEIGHT AND HEIGHT PERCENTILE TABLE: GIRLS (BIRTH TO AGE 18)

WEIGHT IN LB			WEIGHT IN KG			AGE	HEIGHT IN IN.			HEIGHT IN CM		
10%	50%	90%	10%	50%	90%		10%	50%	90%	10%	50%	90%
6.2	7.4	8.6	2.81	3.36	3.9	Birth	18.8	19.8	20.4	47.8	50.2	51.0
8.0	9.7	11.0	3.3	4.2	5.0	1 mo	20.2	21.0	22.0	50.4	52.8	55.0
9.5	11.0	12.5	4.1	5.0	5.8	2 mo	21.5	22.2	23.2	53.7	55.5	59.6
10.7	12.4	14.0	4.85	5.62	6.35	3 mo	22.4	23.4	24.3	56.9	59.5	61.7
12.0	13.7	15.5	5.3	6.2	7.2	4 mo	23.2	24.2	25.2	59.6	61.0	64.8
13.0	14.7	17.0	5.9	6.8	7.7	5 mo	24.0	25.0	26.0	60.7	64.2	67.0
14.1	16.0	18.6	6.4	7.26	8.44	6 mo	24.6	25.7	26.7	62.5	65.2	67.8
16.6	19.2	22.4	7.53	8.71	10.16	9 mo	26.4	27.6	28.7	67.0	70.1	72.9
18.4	21.5	24.8	8.35	9.75	11.25	12 mo	27.8	29.2	30.3	70.6	74.2	77.1
21.2	24.5	28.3	9.62	11.11	12.84	18 mo	30.2	31.8	33.3	76.8	80.9	84.5
23.5	27.1	31.7	10.66	12.29	14.38	2 yr	32.3	34.1	35.8	82.0	86.6	91.0
25.5	29.6	34.6	11.57	13.43	15.69	2½ yr	34.0	36.0	37.9	86.3	91.4	96.4
27.6	31.8	37.4	12.52	14.42	16.96	3 yr	35.6	37.7	39.8	90.5	95.7	101.1
29.5	33.9	40.4	13.38	15.38	18.33	3½ yr	37.1	39.2	41.5	94.2	99.5	105.4
31.2	36.2	43.5	14.15	16.42	19.73	4 yr	38.4	40.6	43.1	97.6	103.2	109.6
32.9	38.5	46.7	14.92	17.46	21.18	4½ yr	39.7	42.0	44.7	100.9	106.8	113.5
34.8	40.5	49.2	15.79	18.37	22.32	5 yr	40.5	42.9	45.4	103.0	109.1	115.4
38.0	44.0	51.2	17.24	19.96	23.22	5½ yr	42.4	44.4	46.8	107.8	112.8	118.9
39.6	46.5	54.2	17.96	21.09	24.58	6 yr	43.5	45.6	48.1	110.6	115.9	122.3
42.2	49.4	57.7	19.14	22.41	26.17	6½ yr	44.8	46.9	49.4	113.7	119.1	125.6
44.5	52.2	61.2	20.19	23.68	27.76	7 yr	46.0	48.1	50.7	116.8	122.3	128.9
46.6	55.2	65.6	21.14	25.04	29.76	7½ yr	47.0	49.3	51.9	119.5	125.2	131.8
48.6	58.1	69.9	22.04	26.35	31.71	8 yr	48.1	50.4	53.0	122.1	128.0	134.6
50.6	61.0	74.5	22.95	27.67	33.79	8½ yr	49.0	51.4	54.1	124.6	130.5	137.5
52.6	63.8	79.1	23.86	28.94	35.88	9 yr	50.0	52.3	55.3	127.0	132.9	140.4
54.9	67.1	84.4	24.9	30.44	38.28	9½ yr	50.9	53.5	56.4	129.4	135.8	143.2
57.1	70.3	89.7	25.9	31.89	40.69	10 yr	51.8	54.6	57.5	131.7	138.6	146.0
59.9	74.6	95.1	27.17	33.79	43.14	10½ yr	52.9	55.8	58.9	134.4	141.7	149.7
62.6	78.8	100.4	28.4	35.74	45.54	11 yr	53.9	57.0	60.4	137.0	144.7	153.4
66.1	83.2	106.0	29.98	37.74	48.08	11½ yr	55.0	58.3	61.8	139.8	148.1	157.0
69.5	87.6	111.5	31.52	39.74	50.58	12 yr	56.1	59.8	63.2	142.6	151.9	160.6
74.7	93.4	118.0	33.88	42.37	53.52	12½ yr	57.4	60.7	64.0	145.9	154.3	162.7
79.9	99.1	124.5	36.24	44.95	56.47	13 yr	58.7	61.8	64.9	149.1	157.1	164.8
85.5	103.7	128.9	38.78	47.04	58.47	13½ yr	59.5	62.4	65.3	151.1	158.4	165.9
91.0	108.4	133.3	41.28	49.17	60.46	14 yr	60.2	62.8	65.7	153.0	159.6	167.0
94.2	111.0	135.7	42.73	50.35	61.55	14½ yr	60.7	63.1	66.0	154.1	160.4	167.6
97.4	113.5	138.1	44.18	51.48	62.64	15 yr	61.1	63.4	66.2	155.2	161.1	168.1
99.2	115.3	139.6	45.0	52.3	63.32	15½ yr	61.3	63.7	66.4	155.7	161.7	168.6
100.9	117.0	141.1	45.77	53.07	64.0	16 yr	61.5	63.9	66.5	156.1	162.2	169.0
101.9	118.1	142.2	46.22	53.57	64.5	16½ yr	61.5	63.9	66.6	156.2	162.4	169.2
102.8	119.1	143.3	46.63	54.02	65.0	17 yr	61.5	64.0	66.7	156.3	162.5	169.4
103.2	119.5	143.9	46.81	54.2	65.27	17½ yr	61.5	64.0	66.7	156.3	162.5	169.4
103.5	119.9	144.5	46.95	54.39	65.54	18 yr	61.5	64.0	66.7	156.3	162.5	169.4

AVERAGE HEART RATE FOR
INFANTS AND CHILDREN AT REST

AGE	AVERAGE RATE	2 SD
Birth	140	50
1st mo	130	45
1–6 mo	130	45
6–12 mo	115	40
1–2 yr	110	40
2–4 yr	105	35
6–10 yr	95	30
10–14 yr	85	30
14–18 yr	82	25

Important Laboratory Values Found in Infants and Children

AVERAGE NORMAL BLOOD VALUES AT VARIOUS AGES*

AGE	RBC (MILLION/ CU MM)	HGB (GM)	WBC/ CU MM	POLY. (%)	LYMPH. (%)	MONO. (%)	RETIC. (%)	PLATE/ CU MM
1 day	5.5	21	20,000	70	20	10	3.0	350,000
6 days	5.3	20	15,000	62	31	7	0.7	325,000
2 wk	5.0	18	12,000	31	63	6	1.0	300,000
1 mo	4.7	16					0.5	
2 mo	4.0	12					1.0	
3 mo	4.0	11					2.0	
6 mo	4.5	11.5	10,000	32	60	6	0.8	300,000
1 yr	4.6	12.5	10,000	38	55	6	1.0	300,000
2 yr	4.7	13.0	10,000	45	49	6	1.0	300,000
5 yr	4.7	13.0	8,000	54	40	6	1.0	300,000
10 yr	4.7	13.0	8,000	60	34	6	1.0	300,000

	MCV (μ)	MCH ($\mu\mu_G$)	MCHC (%)	MCD (μ)	HCT
1 day	106	38	36	8.6	53
6 days	103	36	35		49
2 wk	96	33	34		46
1 mo	90	30	33	8.1	43
6 mo	77	26	33	7.4	37
1 yr	78	25	32	7.3	37
2 yr	77	25	32		38
5 yr	80	27	34	7.4	40
10 yr	80	27	34	7.4	42
Adult	87	29	34	7.5	45

*MCV = mean corpuscular volume; MCH = mean corpuscular hemoglobin; MCHC = mean corpuscular hemoglobin concentration; MCD = mean corpuscular diameter; HCT = hematocrit.

AVERAGE VALUES FOR RED CELLS, HEMOGLOBIN,
AND VOLUME OF PACKED RED CELLS IN
MALES AND FEMALES

AGE	RED CELLS (MILLION/CU MM)	HGB (GM)	VOL. PACKED CELLS (%)
10 yr			
Male	4.7	13	38
Female	4.7	13	38
14 yr			
Male	5.0	14	41
Female	4.7	13	39
17 yr			
Male	5.3	15.5	45
Female	4.7	13.5	40
Adult			
Male	5.3	16	47
Female	4.7	14	42

NORMAL URINE OR PLASMA CONTENT OF VARIOUS
HORMONES OR THEIR METABOLITES

ASSAY	NEONATE	CHILD	ADULT
17-hydroxysteroids urine, mg/24 hr	0.2–3.5	0.5–5.0	1.5–9.0
17-ketosteroids urine, mg/24 hr	1.5–2.5	0.1–1.0	5–12 female 6–22 male
Aldosterone urine, ng/24 hr	1–2	2–10	5–20
Testosterone* plasma, ng/100 ml	230–300	3–10	300–500
Estradiol† plasma, ng/100 ml	100–300	2–4	10–200‡
LH plasma, ng/ml	4–10	0–4	6–20
FSH plasma, ng/ml	0–2	0–4	6–20
Thyroxine plasma, μg/100 ml	7–15	5–10	5–10
GH plasma, ng/ml	20–40	2–5	2–5

*Male only.
†Female only.
‡The wide range of values is a reflection of changing levels throughout the menstrual cycle.

NORMAL VALUES FOR CONSTITUENTS OF BLOOD*

SUBSTANCE	PREMATURE	NEONATE	INFANT	5–15 YR
Aldolase, IU	(6.0–18.0)	(7.2–20.0)	(3.6–10.0)	(1.8–4.9)
Ammonia, μg/100 ml	(100–250)	(90–150)	(45–80)	(45–80)
Bilirubin, total				
mg/100 ml	<8.0	<6.0	<1.0	<1.0
Urea N, mg/100 ml	(20–47)	19 (10–30)	(6–20)	(6–15)
NPN, mg/100 ml	(24–63)	45 (25–62)	35 (25–45)	(25–35)
Uric acid, mg/100 ml	3.25	3.5 (2.7–5.1)	3.0	3.0
Amino acid				
Nitrogen, mg/100 ml		(3.0–4.0)	(3.0–4.5)	(3.0–4.5)
Creatinine, mg/100 ml	(0.5–3.0)	(1.0–2.0)	(1.0–2.0)	(1.0–2.0)
Serum protein,				
gm/100 ml	5.6 (4.5–6.0)	6.1 (5.0–6.9)	5.9 (5.0–6.6)	(6.5–8.0)
Albumin	(2.5–3.5)	(3.0–4.5)	(3.8–5.0)	(4.5–6.0)
Globulin	(1.0–2.2)	(1.3–2.4)	(1.4–2.4)	(2.0–3.0)
Gamma globulin	(0.5–0.9)	(0.8–1.0)	(0.3–0.6)	(0.9–1.3)
Fibrinogen	0.4	(0.2–0.4)	(0.2–0.4)	(0.2–0.4)
Glucose				
(fasting), mg/100 ml	(27–90)	(47–102)	(70–120)	(70–120)
Total lipids, mg/100 ml		(100–600)	470	(500–700)
Cholesterol, mg/100 ml	(45–100)	(45–170)	(70–180)	(130–240)
Triglycerides,				
mg/100 ml		(5–40)	(7–100)	(10–200)
Lipoproteins, total				
mg/100 ml		(170–440)	(240–800)	(500–1100)
Electrolytes, mEq/L				
Total base	159 (152–171)	153 (148–160)	152	152
Sodium	(138–159)	144	144	144
Potassium	(4.0–7.0)	(4.0–7.0)	(4.0–5.5)	(4.0–5.5)
Chloride	(104–120)	(102–110)	(100–107)	(100–107)
Bicarbonate	(12.7–25.3)	(18–27)	(23–28)	(23–28)
Serum calcium,				
mg/100 ml	(7.8–9.0)	(8.0–10.0)	(10–12)	(10–12)
Serum phosphorus,				
mg/100 ml	(6.0–8.5)	(6.5–8.5)	6.0	5.0
Alkaline phosphatase,				
IU	. . .	(70–225)	(50–150)	(50–250)
Acid phosphatase,				
IV/L		(10–16)	(9–13)	(0.5–12)
Serum bilirubin, mg/100 ml	(1.5–7.5)	(1.4–6.0)	(0.2–0.8)	(0.2–0.8)
Lactic acid, mg/100 ml	(15–30)	17	10	10
Iron serum, μg/100 ml	. . .	(60–140)	(30–90)	(50–100)
Lactate dehydrogenase, IU	. . .	(308–1500)	(200–800)	(100–180)
Phospholipids, μg/ml	. . .	(1.0–1.8)	(2.0–3.5)	(2.4–4.4)
Transaminase				
SGOT, units	. . .	(10–120)	(5–50)	(5–45)
SGPT, units	. . .	(10–90)	(5–50)	(5–50)

*Average figures are given as a single value; the range is enclosed in parentheses. Data from various sources.

Cerebrospinal Fluid Values at Different Ages

	DAY 1		DAY 7		AFTER FIRST YEAR RANGE
	RANGE	MEAN	RANGE	MEAN	
Red blood cells	0–620	23/cu mm	0–48	3/cu mm	0/cu mm
Polymorphs	0–26	7/cu mm	0–5	2/cu mm	0–1/cu mm
Lymphs	0–16	5/cu mm	0–4	1/cu mm	0–4/cu mm
Protein	40–148	73 mg	27–65	47 mg	15–40 mg
Sugar	38–64	48 mg	48–62	55 mg	50–90 mg
Chloride	680–760	720 mg	720–760	720 mg	650–750 mg

Organ Weights

Average Weights (gm) of Organs at Different Ages

	NEWBORN	1 YR	6 YR	14 YR	ADULT
Brain	350	910	1,200	1,300	1,350
Heart	24	45	95	220	300
Thymus	12	20	24	30	0–15
Kidneys (2)	25	70	120	170	300
Liver	150	300	550	1,500	1,600
Lungs (2)	60	130	260	410	1,200
Pancreas	3	9	20	40	90
Spleen	10	30	55	95	155
Stomach	8	30	50	80	135
Pituitary	0.1	0.2	0.3	0.4	0.5–0.8
Thyroid	2.0	3.0	7	14	18
Adrenals (2)	6–8	4.5	7	10	10–20
Parathyroids	. . .	. . .	. . .	. . .	0.65
Testes (2)	1.5	1.5	1.6	7	35
Ovaries (2)	0.3	0.6	1.9	6	7
Uterus	3.9	1.4	2.8	30	50
Prostate	0.8	0.8	1.3	3.3	17

Index